Mountain Lions are found throughout the Am[ericas]

SIZE Mountain lions can grow to be more than 8 feet long.

Atlantic
Ocean

Pacific
Ocean

Pacific
Ocean

Indian
Ocean

D1294955

YOUNG Kittens stay with their mothers for about 1½ years, learning to hunt and care for themselves.

YOUNG Mountain lion cubs are born with spots, which fade in the first year.

HSP
Science

Harcourt
SCHOOL PUBLISHERS

Visit *The Learning Site!*
www.harcourtschool.com

HSP
Science

Mountain Lion

SCHOOL PUBLISHERS

Copyright © 2009 by Harcourt, Inc.

All rights reserved. No part of this publication may be reproduced or transmitted in any form or by any means, electronic or mechanical, including photocopy, recording, or any information storage and retrieval system, without permission in writing from the publisher.

Requests for permission to make copies of any part of the work should be addressed to School Permissions and Copyrights, Harcourt, Inc., 6277 Sea Harbor Drive, Orlando, Florida 32887-6777. Fax: 407-345-2418.

HARCOURT and the Harcourt Logo are trademarks of Harcourt, Inc., registered in the United States of America and/or other jurisdictions.

Printed in the United States of America

ISBN-13: 978-0-15-360941-1
ISBN-10: 0-15-360941-9

6 7 8 9 0914 14 13 12 11
4500282857

If you have received these materials as examination copies free of charge, Harcourt School Publishers retains title to the materials and they may not be resold. Resale of examination copies is strictly prohibited and is illegal.

Possession of this publication in print format does not entitle users to convert this publication, or any portion of it, into electronic format.

Science on Location Photo Credits

Life: 41 (r) Jeff Vanuga/Corbis; 41 (br) Kevin Schafer/Riser/Getty Images; 40 (bg) Stuart Westmorland/Corbis; 42 (bg) David M. Barron/oxygengroup; 43 (bc) National Zoological Park/oxygengroup; 43 (l) Roberta Olenick/Photolibrary; 44 (br) David Haring/Duke Lemur Center; 44 (bg) David Haring/Duke Lemur Center; 45 (br) David Haring/Duke Lemur Center; 45 (tl) David Haring/Duke Lemur Center.

Earth: 250 (l) Arkansas Department of Parks & Recreation; 251 (c) Arkansas Department of Parks & Tourism; 251 (bg) Arkansas Department of Parks and Recreation; 252 (bg) Don Voelker; 253 (b) Don Voelker; 254 (bg) Vladimir Pcholkin/Photographer's Choice RF/Getty Images; 254 (inset) POLYCOR INC. www.polycor.com; 255 (b) AGE Fotostock/SuperStock.

Physical: 508 (t) Advanced Animations LLC; 508 (c) Advanced Animations LLC; 509 (bg) Advanced Animations LLC; 509 (br) Lester Lefkowitz/Getty Images; 510 (b) Cindy Charles/PhotoEdit, Inc.; 510 (bg) Earl Crabb; 510 (tl) Courtesy of Circus Center, San Francisco. Photo by Peter Varshavsky; 512 (bg) Dave G. Houser/Corbis; 512 (bl) Joe McNally/Getty Images; 513 (r) Ted Thai/Time Life Pictures/Getty Images.

Consulting Authors

Michael J. Bell
*Associate Professor of Early
    Childhood Education*
College of Education
West Chester University of
    Pennsylvania
West Chester, Pennsylvania

Michael A. DiSpezio
Curriculum Architect
JASON Academy
Cape Cod, Massachusetts

Marjorie Frank
*Former Adjunct Professor,
    Science Education*
Hunter College
New York, New York

Gerald H. Krockover
*Professor of Earth and Atmospheric
    Science Education*
Purdue University
West Lafayette, Indiana

Joyce C. McLeod
Adjunct Professor
Rollins College
Winter Park, Florida

Barbara ten Brink
Science Specialist
Austin Independent School District
Austin, Texas

Carol J. Valenta
Senior Vice President
St. Louis Science Center
St. Louis, Missouri

Barry A. Van Deman
President and CEO
Museum of Life and Science
Durham, North Carolina

Senior Editorial Advisors

Napoleon Adebola Bryant, Jr.
Professor Emeritus of Education
Xavier University
Cincinnati, Ohio

Tyrone Howard
Associate Professor
Graduate School of Education and
    Information Studies
University of California, Los Angeles
Los Angeles, California

Robert M. Jones
Professor of Education Foundations
University of Houston–Clear Lake
Houston, Texas

Mozell P. Lang
Former Science Consultant
Michigan Department of Education
Science Consultant, Highland Park
    Schools
Highland Park, Michigan

Jerry D. Valadez
K–12 Science Coordinator
Fresno Unified School District
Fresno, California

Contents

Introductory Chapter

Getting Ready for Science   1

Essential Questions

Lesson 1 What Tools Do Scientists Use?. 2
Lesson 2 What Inquiry Skills Do Scientists Use?. 14
Lesson 3 What Is the Scientific Method?. 24
Chapter Review and Test Preparation. 36
Safety in Science 38

Big Idea
To plan and carry out an experiment, scientists observe and ask questions.

LIFE SCIENCE

Science on Location and Projects for Home or School 39

A   Processes of Living Things   47

Chapter 1 Cells to Body Systems 48
Essential Questions

Lesson 1 What Are Cells?. 50
Lesson 2 How Do Cells Work Together?. 60
Lesson 3 How Do Body Systems Work Together?. 70
Science Spin Weekly Reader **Technology**
Saving Stephanie. 84
Chapter Review and Test Preparation 86

Big Idea
All living things are made of cells. Cells work together to make up tissues, organs, and organ systems.

Chapter 2 Classifying Living Things. 88
Essential Questions

Lesson 1 How Are Living Things Grouped? 90
Lesson 2 What Are Vertebrates and Invertebrates? 100
People in Science
Marjory Stoneman Douglas 110
Karl Ammann 111
Chapter Review and Test Preparation 112

Big Idea
Living things are classified in different ways. Some animals have a backbone, while others do not.

Chapter 3 Plant Growth and Reproduction **114**

[Essential Questions]

Lesson 1 How Do Plants Grow? 116

Lesson 2 How Do Plants Reproduce? 126

(Science Spin Weekly Reader) **Technology**
Farms of the Future 138

Chapter Review and Test Preparation 140

Big Idea
Plants have a variety of structures to help them carry out life processes.

Chapter 4 Animal Growth and Heredity **142**

[Essential Questions]

Lesson 1 How Does Cell Division Affect Growth? 144

Lesson 2 How Are Characteristics Inherited? 154

Lesson 3 What Other Factors Affect Characteristics? 168

People in Science
Wei Shi 178
Gregor Mendel 179

Chapter Review and Test Preparation 180

Unit A Visual Summary 182

Big Idea
Animal characteristics are passed from parents to their children. Characteristics are either learned or inherited.

UNIT B Interactions Among Living Things 183

Chapter 5 Energy and Ecosystems **184**

[Essential Questions]

Lesson 1 How Do Plants Produce Food? 186

Lesson 2 How Is Energy Passed Through an Ecosystem? 196

(Science Spin Weekly Reader) **Technology**
Trash Man 208

Chapter Review and Test Preparation 210

Big Idea
Living things interact with one another in the environment. Energy flows from the sun to plants to animals.

Chapter 6 Ecosystems and Change **212**

[Essential Questions]

Lesson 1 How Do Organisms Compete and Survive
in an Ecosystem? 214

Lesson 2 How Do Ecosystems Change Over Time? 224

Lesson 3 How Do People Affect Ecosystems? 234

People in Science
Shirley Mah Kooyman 244
Alissa J. Arp 245

Chapter Review and Test Preparation 246

Unit B Visual Summary 248

Big Idea
Ecosystems change over time, both naturally and as a result of human activities.

EARTH SCIENCE

Science on Location and Projects for Home or School 249

 Processes That Change Earth 257

Chapter 7 The Rock Cycle 258
Essential Questions

Lesson 1 What Are Minerals?. 260
Lesson 2 How Do Rocks Form? 270
Lesson 3 How Are Rocks Changed?. 282
People in Science
    Mack Gipson, Jr. 292
    Florence Bascom 293
Chapter Review and Test Preparation 294

> **Big Idea**
> Rocks and minerals are formed and changed through different Earth processes.

Chapter 8 Fossils 296
Essential Questions

Lesson 1 What Do Fossils Show About Earth's History? 298
Lesson 2 How Are Fossils Like Today's Living Things?. 310
Science Spin Weekly Reader **Technology**
Attack of Guinea-Zilla!. 320
Chapter Review and Test Preparation. 322

> **Big Idea**
> Fossils of animal and plant remains help us understand Earth's history.

Chapter 9 Changes to Earth's Surface 324
Essential Questions

Lesson 1 What Are Some of Earth's Landforms?. 326
Lesson 2 What Causes Changes to Earth's Landforms? 336
Lesson 3 How Do Movements of the Crust Change Earth? 348
Science Spin Weekly Reader **Technology**
Meltdown! 360
Chapter Review and Test Preparation 362

> **Big Idea**
> Earth's surface is constantly changing.

Chapter 10 Using Resources 364

Essential Questions

Lesson 1 How Do People Use Soil and Water Resources? 366

Lesson 2 How Can People Conserve Resources? 376

People in Science

    William Rathje 386

    Dorothy McClendon 387

Chapter Review and Test Preparation 388

Unit C Visual Summary 390

Big Idea
People use resources in many ways, sometimes causing pollution.

UNIT D Cycles on Earth and in Space   391

Chapter 11 Weather and the Water Cycle 392

Essential Questions

Lesson 1 What Causes Weather? 394

Lesson 2 What Conditions Affect the Water Cycle? 404

Lesson 3 How Can Patterns in Weather Be Observed? 414

Science Spin Weekly Reader **Technology**
On the Lookout 426

Chapter Review and Test Preparation 428

Big Idea
Weather is a measurable and predictable part of the water cycle.

Chapter 12 Earth's Oceans 430

Essential Questions

Lesson 1 What Are the Oceans Like? 432

Lesson 2 How Does Ocean Water Move? 442

Lesson 3 What Forces Shape Shorelines? 452

People in Science

    Wen-lu Zhu 462

    Hugo Loaiciga 463

Chapter Review and Test Preparation 464

Big Idea
Oceans are complex systems that interact with Earth's land, air, and living organisms.

Chapter 13 Earth, Moon, and Beyond 466

Essential Questions

Lesson 1 How Does Earth's Orbit Affect the Seasons? 468

Lesson 2 How Do Earth and the Moon Compare? 478

Lesson 3 What Makes Up Our Solar System? 488

Science Spin Weekly Reader **Technology**
Beyond the Shuttle 502

Chapter Review and Test Preparation 504

Unit D Visual Summary 506

Big Idea
Earth is part of a solar system, which is made up of many different objects orbiting a sun.

PHYSICAL SCIENCE

Science on Location and Projects for Home or School 507

UNIT E Matter and Energy   515

Chapter 14 Properties of Matter 516
Essential Questions
Lesson 1 What Is the Structure of Matter? 518
Lesson 2 What Are Physical Properties and Changes? 530
Lesson 3 What Are Chemical Properties and Changes? 542
People in Science
    Claudia Benitez-Nelson. 550
    Yuan Tseh Lee 551
Chapter Review and Test Preparation 552

Big Idea
All matter has properties that can be observed, described, and measured.

Chapter 15 Energy 554
Essential Questions
Lesson 1 What Are Kinetic and Potential Energy?. 556
Lesson 2 What Are Some Forms of Energy? 566
Lesson 3 How Is Heat Transferred? 578
Lesson 4 How Do People Use Energy Resources? 588
Science Spin Weekly Reader **Technology**
    Dream Machines 598
Chapter Review and Test Preparation 600

Big Idea
Energy exists in many forms and can be changed from one form to another.

Chapter 16 Electricity 602
Essential Questions
Lesson 1 How Are Electricity and Magnetism Related? 604
Lesson 2 What Are Static and Current Electricity? 614
Lesson 3 What Are Electric Circuits? 624
People in Science
    Hertha Marks Ayrton 634
    Meredith Gourdine. 635
Chapter Review and Test Preparation 636

Big Idea
Electricity is a form of energy that plays an important role in our lives.

Chapter 17 Sound and Light **638**

Essential Questions

Lesson 1 What Is Sound? 640

Lesson 2 What Is Light? 652

Science Spin Weekly Reader **Technology**
A Sound Idea 664

Chapter Review and Test Preparation 666

Unit E Visual Summary 668

Big Idea
Sound and light travel as waves of energy.

UNIT F Forces and Motion 669

Chapter 18 Forces **670**

Essential Questions

Lesson 1 What Forces Affect Objects on Earth Every Day? 672

Lesson 2 What Are Balanced and Unbalanced Forces? 682

Lesson 3 What Is Work, and How Is It Measured? 692

People in Science
Ephraim Fischbach 702
Patricia Cowings 703

Chapter Review and Test Preparation 704

Big Idea
Forces, such as magnetism and gravitation, interact with objects, such as you and Earth, to produce motion.

Chapter 19 Motion **706**

Essential Questions

Lesson 1 What Factors Affect Motion? 708

Lesson 2 What Are the Laws of Motion? 720

Science Spin Weekly Reader **Technology**
Building a Safer Race Car 732

Chapter Review and Test Preparation 734

Unit F Visual Summary 736

Big Idea
Motion can be observed, measured, and described.

REFERENCES

Picture Glossary R1

Index R32

Getting Ready for Science

What's the Big Idea?

To plan and carry out an experiment, scientists observe and ask questions.

Essential Questions

Lesson 1

What Tools Do Scientists Use?

Lesson 2

What Inquiry Skills Do Scientists Use?

Lesson 3

What Is the Scientific Method?

Student eBook
www.hspscience.com

Safety is important when conducting experiments.

What do yOU wonder?

This rocket won't travel into space, but it works just like rockets that carried people to the moon. How do rocket scientists try out their designs? What variables can they test to make a rocket fly farther and faster? What questions do this father and daughter need to ask before they launch their rocket? How does this relate to the **Big Idea?**

Investigate how to measure a specific item in the right way.

Read and learn about different science tools and how they help us make better observations.

Essential Question

What Tools Do Scientists Use?

Fast Fact

That's a BIG Kite!
One of the largest kites ever flown is the Megabite. It is 64 m (210 ft) long (including tails) and 22 m (72 ft) wide. That's only about 6 m (20 ft) shorter than a 747 jet airliner! Kite fliers around the world are always trying to set new records. How high can a kite go? How big or small can a kite be? Setting a record depends on accurate measurements. In the Investigate, you'll practice several different ways of measuring objects.

Flying kites uses science.

microscope [MY•kruh•skohp]
A tool that makes small objects
appear larger (p. 8)

balance [BAL•uhns] A tool
that measures the amount
of matter in an object (the
object's mass) (p. 11)

3

Measuring Up!

Guided Inquiry

Start with Questions

You use measurements every day. Your clothes and shoes have been measured to fit you. You eat foods that are packaged in measured amounts.

- What is a measurement?

- What are some ways you could measure this blimp?

Investigate to find out. Then read and learn to find out more.

Prepare to Investigate

Inquiry Skill Tip

Variables are factors that can change or be kept the same during an experiment or investigation. A good experiment changes only one variable at a time.

Materials

- tape measure
- balloon
- hand lens
- ruler
- string
- spring scale

Make an Observation Chart

	Balloon	Balloon with Air
Hand lens		
Length		
Circumference		
Weight		

Follow This Procedure

1. **Observe** an empty balloon with a hand lens. Copy the chart, and **record** your observations.

2. **Measure** the length and circumference of the balloon. **Record** your measurements.

3. Use the spring scale to **measure** the weight of the balloon. **Record** its weight.

4. Now, blow up the balloon.

5. Match a length of string to the length of the balloon. **Measure** that string length with a ruler or tape measure. **Record** the length.

6. **Measure** the circumference of the balloon as in Step 5. **Record** your measurement.

7. **Measure** the weight of the balloon with the spring scale. **Record** your measurement.

Step 2

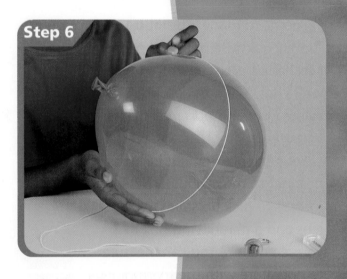

Step 6

Draw Conclusions

1. How did the measurements change when you blew up the balloon? Why?

2. Do you think that your measurement of the length of the empty balloon or the blown-up balloon was more accurate? Why?

3. **Inquiry Skill** Work with another group to identify variables in your measurements. What variables caused different groups to get different measurements?

Independent Inquiry

How can you find the volume of a blown-up balloon? Plan and conduct a simple investigation **to find out.**

VOCABULARY
microscope p. 8
balance p. 11

SCIENCE CONCEPTS
▶ how tools are used to make better observations
▶ why a balance and a scale measure different things

⭐ **Focus Skill** **MAIN IDEA AND DETAILS**
Look for details about how and when each tool is used.

Main Idea
detail   detail   detail

Using Science Inquiry Tools

People in many jobs must use tools. Cooks use pots and pans. Mechanics use screwdrivers and wrenches. Scientists use tools to measure and observe objects in nature.

Your Science Tool Kit includes a dropper to move liquids, as well as forceps to pick up solids. A hand lens and a magnifying box help you see details. You can measure temperature with the thermometer, length with the ruler or tape measure, and volume with the measuring cup. The spring scale measures weight.

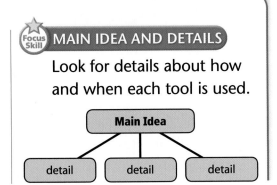

◀ A thermometer measures the temperature of liquids and the air. It measures in degrees Celsius (°C).

⭐ **Focus Skill** **MAIN IDEA AND DETAILS**

What are four tools you can use to measure objects?

A tape measure helps you measure the length of curved or irregular surfaces. ▶

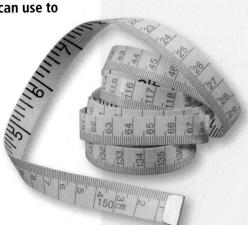

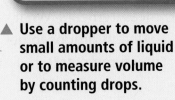

▲ Use a dropper to move small amounts of liquid or to measure volume by counting drops.

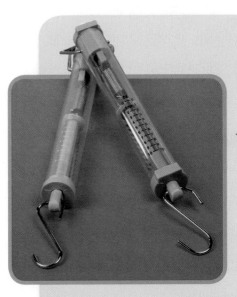

◀ A spring scale measures forces, such as weight or friction. It measures in units called newtons (N).

▲ A ruler measures the length and width of objects in centimeters (cm) and millimeters (mm).

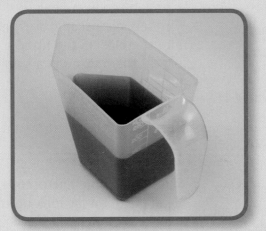

▲ You can place an insect, pebble, or other small object in the magnifying box. Looking through the lid helps you see the object clearly.

▲ A measuring cup is used to measure the volume of liquids. It measures in liters (L) and milliliters (mL).

◀ Forceps help you pick up or hold small objects. They are handy for holding small objects under the hand lens.

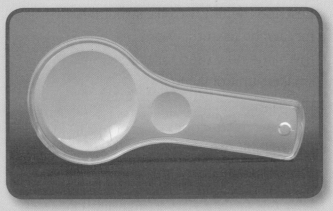

▲ A hand lens makes objects look larger and helps you see more detail.

Microscopes

Without a telescope, you can't identify what look like tiny objects in the sky. In the same way, you can't see tiny parts of an insect, colored particles in a rock, or cells in a leaf without a microscope. A **microscope** is a tool that makes small objects appear larger. It lets you see details you couldn't see with your eyes alone.

People have known for a long time that curved glass can *magnify*, or make things look larger. An early Roman scholar read books through a glass ball filled with water. People started making eyeglasses a thousand years ago. They called the curved glass a *lens* because it looked like a lentil—a bean!

An early scientist named Anton van Leeuwenhoek (LAY•vuhn•hook) used a lens to see creatures in a drop of pond water. He called them animalcules.

In the late 1500s, a Dutch eyeglass maker put a lens in each end of a hollow tube. Changing the length of the tube made tiny objects look three to nine times their actual size. This was probably the first "modern" microscope.

In the 1600s, Robert Hooke used a microscope to study thin slices of cork. To describe the tiny, boxlike structures he saw, he used the word *cell*, the name now used for the smallest unit of living things.

Today, microscopes can magnify objects thousands of times. So a tiny "animalcule" might look as large as a whale!

▲ Van Leeuwenhoek was the first person to see microscopic organisms. He placed tiny samples on the tip of a needle and looked at them through a single lens.

Using a simple microscope, you can make things look up to 400 times their actual size! ▼

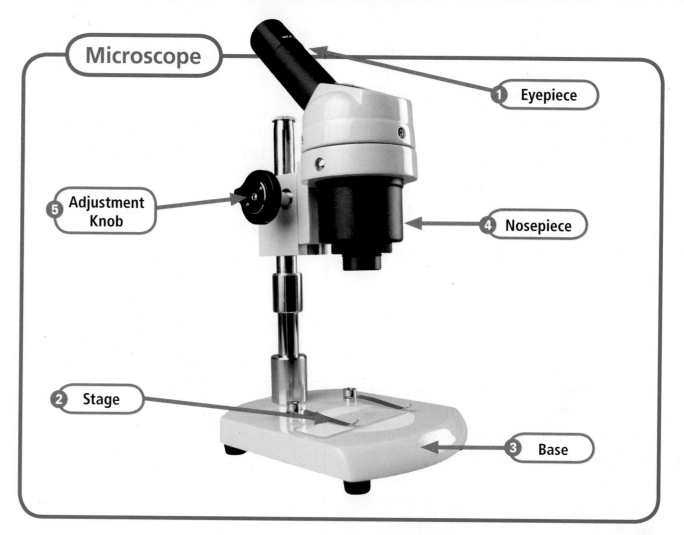

Microscope

1. **Eyepiece**
5. **Adjustment Knob**
4. **Nosepiece**
2. **Stage**
3. **Base**

Most classroom microscopes have several main parts:

1. The eyepiece contains one lens and is mounted at the end of a tube.

2. The stage holds the slide or object you are looking at.

3. The base supports the microscope. It usually holds a lamp or mirror that shines light through the object.

4. A nosepiece holds one or more lenses that can magnify an object up to 400 times.

5. Adjustment knobs help you focus the lenses.

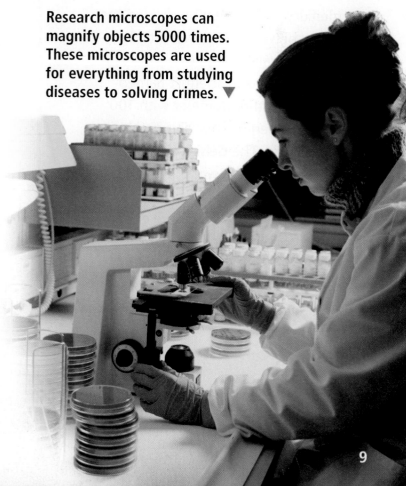

Research microscopes can magnify objects 5000 times. These microscopes are used for everything from studying diseases to solving crimes. ▼

MAIN IDEA AND DETAILS What are the main parts of a microscope?

9

Measuring Temperature

"Boy, it's hot today! It feels much hotter than yesterday." Without a thermometer, temperature isn't much more than how a person feels.

In 1592, an Italian scientist named Galileo found that a change in temperature made water rise and fall in a sealed tube. This device, a simple thermometer, helped Galileo study nature in a more precise way.

In the early 1700s, a German scientist named Fahrenheit sealed mercury in a thin glass tube. As it got warmer, the liquid metal took up more space. The mercury rose in the tube. As it cooled, the mercury took up less space. So the level of liquid in the tube fell. But how was this thermometer to be marked? What units were to be used?

Fahrenheit put the tube into freezing water and into boiling water and marked the mercury levels. Then he divided the difference between the levels into 180 equal units—called degrees.

In 1742, a Swedish scientist named Celsius made a thermometer with 100 degrees between the freezing and boiling points of water. The Celsius scale is used in most countries of the world. It is also the scale used by all scientists.

Thermometers can't measure extreme temperatures. For example, many metals get to several thousand degrees before they melt. Scientists have other temperature-sensing tools to measure very hot and very cold objects.

 MAIN IDEA AND DETAILS

How does a thermometer work?

Measured on a Celsius thermometer, water boils at 100 degrees and freezes at 0 degrees. On a Fahrenheit thermometer, water boils at 212 degrees and freezes at 32 degrees.

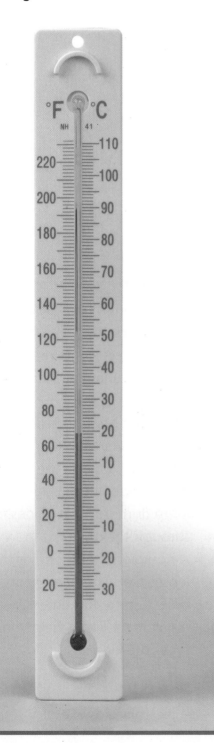

Balance or Spring Scale?

Suppose you're a merchant in Alaska in the early 1900s. A man wants food in exchange for some gold he got from the bottom of a river. But how much is the gold worth?

To find out, you use a tool that looks like a small seesaw. You place the gold at one end of a beam. Then you add objects of known mass at the other end until the beam is level. The objects balance! A **balance** is a tool that measures the amount of matter in an object—the object's *mass*.

The balance in your classroom measures mass by balancing an unknown object with one or more objects of known mass. Mass is measured in grams (g) or kilograms (kg).

When you want to measure an object's weight, you use a spring scale. You hang an object from a hook on the scale and let gravity pull it down. Gravity is a force that pulls on all objects on or near Earth. Weight is a measure of the force of gravity's pull. The unit for this measurement is the newton (N).

People often confuse mass and weight. But think what happens to the mass of an astronaut as he or she goes from Earth to the International Space Station. Nothing! The astronaut's mass stays the same, even though his or her weight goes down. The pull of gravity from Earth is countered by the space station's great speed in orbit.

 **MAIN IDEA AND DETAILS**

> **What does a balance measure? What does a spring scale measure?**

▲ Find an object's mass, or amount of matter, by first placing the object on one pan. Then add a known mass to the other pan until the pointer stays in the middle.

▲ When you hang an object on the hook of the spring scale, you measure the force of gravity pulling on the object. This is the object's weight.

Do They Balance?

Place a blown-up balloon on one pan of a balance and an empty balloon on the other pan. Do they have the same mass? Why or why not?

Safety in the Lab

Working in the lab is fun. But you need to be careful to stay safe. Here are some general rules to follow:

- Study all the steps of an investigation so you know what to expect. If you have any questions, ask your teacher.
- Be sure you watch for safety icons and obey all caution statements.

Scientists in the lab wear safety goggles to protect their eyes. Smart students do the same thing! When you work with chemicals or water, a lab apron protects your clothes.

Be careful with sharp objects!

- Scissors, forceps, and even a sharp pencil should be handled with care.
- If you break something made of glass, tell your teacher.
- If you cut yourself, tell your teacher right away.

Be careful with electricity!

- Be especially careful with electrical appliances.
- Keep cords out of the way.
- Never pull a plug out of an outlet by the cord.
- Dry your hands before unplugging a cord.
- If you have long hair, pull it back out of the way. Roll or push up long sleeves to keep them away from your work.
- Never eat or drink anything during a science activity.
- Don't use lab equipment to drink from.
- Never work in the lab by yourself.
- Wash your hands with soap and water after cleaning up your work area.

Focus Skill **MAIN IDEA AND DETAILS**

What are four ways to keep safe in the lab?

Essential Question

What Tools Do Scientists Use?

In this lesson, you learned about several tools scientists use to make measurements and to observe.

1. **MAIN IDEA AND DETAILS** Draw and complete a graphic organizer to show the supporting details for this main idea: Tools are used to make observations in science.

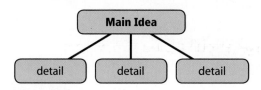

2. **SUMMARIZE** Write three sentences that explain the difference between a balance and a spring scale.

3. **DRAW CONCLUSIONS** Why are different tools used to measure mass and weight?

4. **VOCABULARY** Write one sentence describing each vocabulary term.

Test Prep

5. **Critical Thinking** You are doing an investigation and accidentally spill water on the floor. How could this be a safety problem?

6. Why is using a thermometer or measuring cup more scientific than estimating temperature or volume?
   A. It is easier.
   B. It is more accurate.
   C. It looks more scientific.
   D. It uses up more class time.

Make Connections

 Writing

Narrative Writing
Use reference materials to learn about the life of Anton van Leeuwenhoek. Write a **story** that includes what he is famous for and what kinds of things he observed using his microscope.

 Math

Choose Measuring Devices
A bottle is half full of water. Describe three things you could measure about the water, and name the tools to use for the measurements.

 Health

Measuring for Health
Which science tools are also used by doctors, nurses, lab workers in hospitals, or others involved in health care? Describe how they are used.

Investigate how well different paper airplanes fly.

Read and learn about the many different inquiry skills used by scientists to help gather information.

Essential Question

What Inquiry Skills Do Scientists Use?

Fast Fact
Taking to the Air

In December 1903, bicycle makers Orville and Wilbur Wright successfully completed the first powered airplane flight. The flight lasted only 12 seconds and covered only about 37 m (120 ft). In 2003, people celebrated the 100-year anniversary of powered flight by building a plane exactly like the Wrights' *Flyer*. Like the Wright brothers' plane, it failed several times before finally flying about 30 m (100 ft)! In the Investigate, you'll make and test a "flyer" of your own.

A replica of the Wright brothers' plane

Smithsonian
National Air and Space Museum
Steven F. Udvar-Hazy Center

investigation
[in•ves•tuh•GAY•shuhn] A procedure carried out to gather data about an object or event (p. 18)

inquiry [IN•kwer•ee] An organized way to gather information and answer questions (p. 18)

experiment
[ek•SPEHR•uh•muhnt] A procedure carried out under controlled conditions to test a hypothesis (p. 21)

15

Design an Airplane

Start with Questions

Before scientists carry out investigations, they often ask questions about what might happen and why. Then they make an explanation they can test.

- What makes a paper airplane fly?

- How can you test a hypothesis about paper airplanes?

Investigate to find out. Then read and learn to find out more.

Prepare to Investigate

Inquiry Skill Tip

A good hypothesis explains as many facts, measurements, and observations as possible. Before you write a hypothesis, summarize the information you know. After you write the hypothesis, check that it explains all of the facts in the summary.

Materials

- thick paper
- tape
- ruler or tape measure
- stopwatch

Make an Observation Chart

Data Table			
Trial		Airplane 1	Airplane 2
1	time		
	distance		
2	time		
	distance		
3	time		
	distance		

Follow This Procedure

1. Design a paper airplane. Then fold a sheet of thick paper to make the plane.

2. **Measure** a distance of 10 m in an open area. Mark one end of the distance as a starting line, and place a stick or stone every half meter from the starting line.

3. Test-fly your plane. Have a partner start the stopwatch as you're releasing the plane and stop it when the plane lands. **Record** the flight time in a table like the one shown.

4. **Measure** the distance the plane flew. **Record** the distance in the table.

5. Repeat Steps 3 and 4 for a second and a third trial.

6. Make a second airplane, with wings half as wide as on your first plane.

7. Test-fly your second plane three times. **Record** all your measurements in the table.

Draw Conclusions

1. How did changing the width of the wings affect the way your plane flew?

2. **Inquiry Skill** Why did some students' planes fly farther or longer than those of others? Write a **hypothesis** to explain your thinking.

Step 1

Step 3

Independent Inquiry

On one of your planes, add a paper-clip weight. Then fly the plane. What happens to the distance and time it flies? **Infer** the weight's effect on the plane.

VOCABULARY
investigation p 18
inquiry p 18
experiment p 21

SCIENCE CONCEPTS
▶ how inquiry skills help you gather information
▶ how an investigation differs from an experiment

Focus Skill **MAIN IDEA AND DETAILS**
Look for information on when to use inquiry skills.

Main Idea

detail   detail   detail

What Is Inquiry?

Suppose you wanted to learn about the way parachutes work. How would you begin? You might read a book about parachutes. Or you might investigate the subject on your own. An **investigation** is a procedure that is carried out to gather data about an object or event. An investigation can be as simple as measuring an object or observing a response to a stimulus. In this lesson, you investigated the way in which wing size affected flight.

So how can you begin your investigation about parachutes? Scientists usually begin an investigation by asking questions. Then they use inquiry skills to answer their questions. **Inquiry** is an organized way to gather information and answer questions. What questions do you have about parachutes?

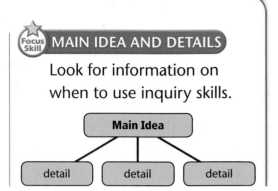

Inquiry Skills

Observe—Use your senses to gather information about objects and events.

Measure—Compare the length, mass, volume, or some other property of an object to a standard unit, such as a meter, gram, or liter.

Gather, Record, and Display Data—Gather data by making observations and measurements. Record your observations and measurements in an organized way. Display your data so that others can understand and interpret it.

Use Numbers—Collect, display, and interpret data as numbers.

How does a parachute enable a person to jump from an airplane without getting hurt? ▶

How can you get answers to your questions? First, you might observe how parachutes are made. Look for diagrams in books or on the Internet. Go to a local airport, and ask to see some parachutes. Then gather, record, and display the data you collected. Measure and use numbers to express the data if possible.

You might wonder how a round parachute compares to a parachute like the one pictured on the previous page. What do they have in common? How are they different? What other shapes can a parachute have?

Once you compare different shapes, you can classify them. Some parachutes are used for doing tricks. Others are used to gently land heavy objects, such as space capsules. Some help sky divers land on a small target.

Now you've gathered a lot of data. The next step is to interpret the data. For example, how does the size or shape of the parachute relate to its use? Is there any pattern in the data? What shape of parachute appears easiest to control?

Data and observations can be used in many ways. It all depends on what questions you want to answer. You can use the data and logical reasoning to draw conclusions about things you haven't directly observed. For example, you might notice that narrow parachutes are used for tricks. From that, you can infer that this shape is easier to control. Or you might predict which parachute might win a sky-diving contest.

Focus Skill **MAIN IDEA AND DETAILS**

What are inquiry skills used for?

Inquiry Skills

Compare—Identify ways in which things or events are alike or different.

Classify—Group or organize objects or events into categories based on specific characteristics.

Interpret Data—Use data to look for patterns, to predict what will happen, or to suggest an answer to a question.

Infer—Use logical reasoning to come to a conclusion based on data and observations.

Predict—Use observations and data to form an idea of what will happen under certain conditions.

How does the size or shape of a parachute affect the way it works? ▶

19

Using Inquiry Skills

Suppose you were in a contest to find a way to drop a raw egg from a balcony without breaking the egg. What kind of parachute would you use?

First, you might plan and conduct a simple investigation. You might make parachutes of different shapes and sizes. You could tie weights on them, drop them, and see how they behave. How long do they stay in the air? How gently do they land? You could make observations and take measurements.

Inquiry Skills

Plan and Conduct a Simple Investigation—Use inquiry skills to gather data and answer questions.

Hypothesize—Suggest an outcome or explanation that can be tested in an experiment.

Experiment—Design a procedure to test a hypothesis under controlled conditions.

This experiment tested hypotheses about the type of parachute that would prevent a dropped egg from breaking! What variables were involved? ▼

Control Variables—Identify and control the factors that can affect the outcome of an experiment.

Draw Conclusions—Use data and experimental results to decide if your hypothesis is supported.

Communicate—Share results and information visually, orally, or electronically.

With that information, you could hypothesize. What design has the best chance to protect the egg? You may think that a large, round parachute is the best design. You could experiment to test your hypothesis. An **experiment** is a procedure you carry out under controlled conditions to test a hypothesis.

An experiment has more steps than a simple investigation. You have to decide what you will test. Then you have to be sure you control variables.

What are variables, and how can they be controlled? A variable is a factor, such as size, that can have more than one condition, such as large and small. You wouldn't test both the size and shape of parachutes at the same time. Why not? You wouldn't know whether the size or the shape caused the results. Suppose you compared a small, square parachute and a large, round one. How would you know if the size or the shape made a difference?

To test your hypothesis that large, round parachutes are best, you could first test round parachutes of different sizes. Everything except parachute size would be the same. You'd use the same egg size for each drop. You'd drop the eggs from the same height. And you'd drop each one several times to check the results. Then you'd do the whole thing again, using parachutes with different shapes instead of sizes! As before, you'd control all other variables.

During the experiment, you'd be careful to write down exactly what you did and how you did it. You'd record all observations and measurements.

The final step in an experiment is to draw conclusions. Did your experiment support your hypothesis? Was a large, round parachute the best way to protect the egg? What did the experiment show?

Finally, you'd write up your experiment to communicate your results to others. You might include tables for your data or draw diagrams of your parachute design.

 **MAIN IDEA AND DETAILS** Why do you have to control variables in an experiment?

What Causes Lift?

Cut a strip of newspaper or notebook paper about 2–3 cm wide and 10 cm long. Hold the end of the strip in your hand, and blow gently over the top of it. What happens? How might the result relate to airplane wings?

Models, Time, and Space

Have you ever watched a leaf fall from a tree? You might think of a falling leaf as a model for a parachute. It could give you ideas for a parachute design. Or you might make a model and test it before making an actual parachute. That can be very practical. Companies that build rockets, for example, save a lot of time and money by making and testing models before building the real things.

How will your parachute interact with what is attached to it? Thinking about time and space relationships is an important inquiry skill. For example, how do you make sure the parachute in a model rocket pops out at the right time? There's a lot to think about! Inquiry skills are ways to make sure your thinking and tests really work.

★ **MAIN IDEA AND DETAILS**

How do models help an investigation?

Inquiry Skills

Make a Model—Make a mental or physical representation of a process or object. Use a model that someone else has built or something from nature that is similar to what you are investigating.

Use Time/Space Relationships—Think about ways in which moving and nonmoving objects relate to one another. Figure out the order in which things happen.

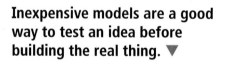

Inexpensive models are a good way to test an idea before building the real thing. ▼

What Inquiry Skills Do Scientists Use?

In this lesson, you learned about inquiry, investigations, and experiments. You also learned about several inquiry skills scientists use to guide the way they answer questions.

1. 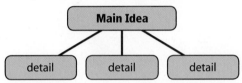 **MAIN IDEA AND DETAILS** Draw and complete a graphic organizer to show the supporting details of this main idea: Scientists use inquiry skills to help them answer questions.

```
        Main Idea

detail     detail     detail
```

2. **SUMMARIZE** Write a three-sentence summary of the difference between an investigation and an experiment.

3. **DRAW CONCLUSIONS** If you wanted to learn more about birds, would you be more likely to make observations first or to experiment first?

4. **VOCABULARY** Use the vocabulary terms in a paragraph describing how scientists study the natural world.

Test Prep

5. **CRITICAL THINKING** Alberto shines red light on one group of plants and blue light on another. He measures the height of the plants each day. What hypothesis is he testing?

6. A factor that can affect the outcome of an experiment is called a
   A. hypothesis.   **C.** variable.
   B. prediction.   **D.** model.

Make Connections

 Writing

Narrative Writing
What inquiry skills do you use in everyday life? Write a screenplay about a day in your life. **Describe** how you use inquiry skills.

 Math

Displaying Data
Make three different charts, tables, or graphs that show how many of your classmates were born in each month of the year.

 Social Studies

Making Inferences
Use reference materials to find out how archaeologists make inferences. What information do they use to infer what life was like hundreds of years ago?

Investigate the factors that affect the distance a balloon rocket travels.

Read and learn about the steps in the scientific method and how scientists apply them.

What Is the Scientific Method?

Fast Fact

Reaching for the Stars

SpaceShipOne was the first successfully launched private spaceship! It traveled nearly 112 km (70 mi) above the surface of Earth. The ship reached a speed of Mach 3— three times the speed of sound. However, *SpaceShipOne* wasn't built or launched by a government or a major aerospace company. It was built by a private company. In the Investigate, you too will build your own rocket.

SpaceShipOne

scientific method
[sy•uhn•TIF•ik METH•uhd] A series of steps that scientists use when performing an experiment (p. 28)

hypothesis [hy•PAHTH•uh•sis] A statement that provides a testable possible answer to a scientific question (p. 29)

evidence [EV•uh•duhns] Information, collected during an investigation, to support a hypothesis (p. 32)

25

Build a Rocket!

Start with Questions

When scientists carry out investigations, they often make predictions about what will happen. In this investigation, you'll build a balloon rocket.

- How do you think your balloon rocket will travel?

- What do you think you can do to affect the way a rocket travels?

Investigate to find out. Then read and learn to find out more.

Prepare to Investigate

Inquiry Skill Tip

Predict means to use information, data, measurements, and observations from the past to make an educated guess about the future. When you make a prediction, you say what you think will happen.

Materials

- goggles
- string, 5 m
- drinking straw
- 2 chairs
- balloon
- tape
- timer/stopwatch
- tape measure

Make an Observation Chart

Trial	Time (sec)	Distance (cm)
1		
2 (more air)		
3 (less air)		

Follow This Procedure

CAUTION: Wear safety goggles during this investigation.

1. Thread one end of a string through a straw.

2. Place two chairs about 4 m apart, and tie one end of the string to each chair.

3. Blow up a balloon, and pinch it closed.

4. Have a partner tape the balloon to the straw, with the balloon's opening near one chair.

5. Release the balloon. Use a stopwatch to time how long the balloon keeps going.

6. **Measure** and **record** the distance the balloon traveled. Also record its travel time.

7. Repeat Steps 3–6 with more air in the balloon. Then repeat Steps 3–6 with less air in the balloon than on the first trial.

Step 2

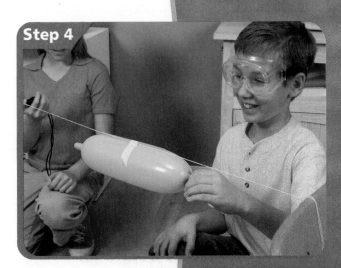
Step 4

Draw Conclusions

1. Why did the balloon move when you released it?

2. How did the amount of air in the balloon affect the travel time and distance?

3. **Inquiry Skill** Would changing the shape of the balloon affect the distance it travels? **Predict** what would happen if you used a large, round balloon and a long, skinny balloon with the same amount of air.

Independent Inquiry

Plan an investigation to find out how the angle of the string affects the travel time and distance. How do you think the results will change when the angle is varied?

...

VOCABULARY
scientific method p. 28
hypothesis p. 29
evidence p. 32

SCIENCE CONCEPTS
▶ what steps are in the scientific method
▶ how scientists use the scientific method

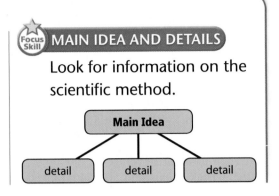

Focus Skill MAIN IDEA AND DETAILS
Look for information on the scientific method.

```
        Main Idea
       /    |     \
  detail  detail  detail
```

Observe / Ask Questions to Form a Hypothesis

In the Investigate, you predicted what would happen if you changed the shape of the balloon in your rocket. How can you tell if your prediction is right? As a scientist, you would follow a series of steps called the **scientific method**.

Scientists use the scientific method to plan and carry out investigations. Some of the steps are the same as inquiry skills. Some other inquiry skills are also used in planning experiments.

There are five steps in the scientific method:

1 Observe, and ask questions.

2 Form a hypothesis.

3 Plan an investigation.

4 Conduct the investigation.

5 Draw conclusions and communicate results.

All investigations start with a testable question. In the Investigate, you were asked how changing the shape of a balloon would affect the way a rocket flies. This is a logical question that came from the Investigate. It can be tested in another investigation.

1 Use your senses to make observations. Then write *one* question you would like to answer.

② A possible answer to your question is a *hypothesis*. A hypothesis is an explanation that can be tested.

After you've formed your question, the next step in the scientific method is to form a hypothesis. A **hypothesis** is a possible answer to your question. It is an explanation and must be testable. In the Investigate, you might have hypothesized that a rocket with a round balloon would not travel as far as one with a long balloon. When you make a hypothesis, you don't have to worry about whether it is right or wrong. The results of an investigation will either support the hypothesis or fail to support it.

MAIN IDEA AND DETAILS

What is a hypothesis?

Flying Objects

Write a hypothesis about which will travel farther: a rocket with a long balloon or one with a round balloon. Use the scientific method to test your hypothesis.

3 Planning an investigation takes several steps. Careful planning can help ensure the success of your investigation.

Plan and Conduct an Investigation

Suppose you've decided to test your hypothesis that a rocket with a round balloon will travel a shorter distance than a rocket with a long balloon. How can you test this hypothesis?

You can plan an investigation by first deciding what variables you will control. Remember that many variables can affect the outcome of your investigation. In your investigation, the balloon shape will change. All of the other variables must stay the same, so that you know that your results are due to the shape.

After deciding what variables you will control, plan your procedure. Write down the steps you will follow to do your test. Note the materials you will need, and decide how you will gather and record your data.

By the time you reach the step where you're ready to conduct an investigation, you've already asked a question and given a likely answer. You've decided how to test your hypothesis, written instructions for the procedure, chosen materials, and planned how you will measure and record your data.

Now the fun begins! As you follow your planned procedure, observe and measure carefully. Record everything that happens. Write down what you observe and what you measure. Finally, record your data in a way that is easy to understand and interpret.

MAIN IDEA AND DETAILS What steps go into planning an investigation?

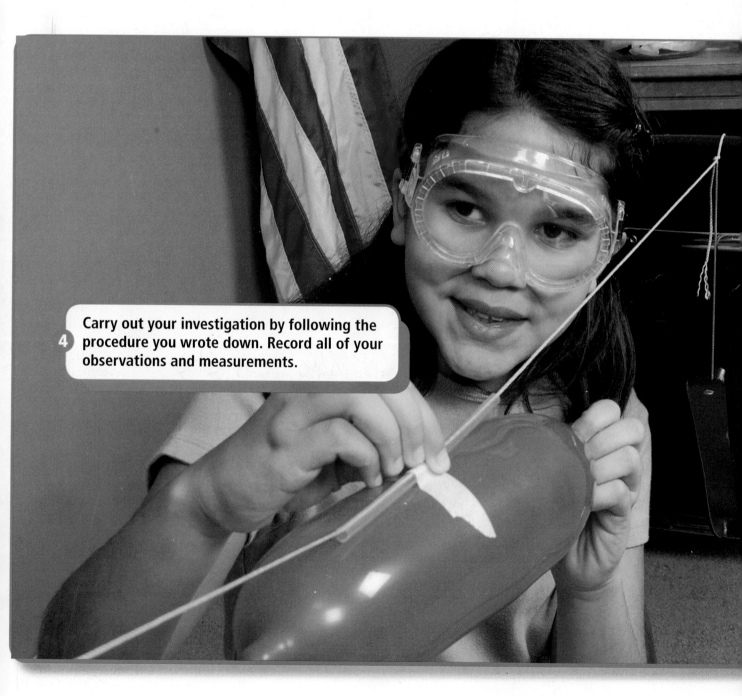

4 Carry out your investigation by following the procedure you wrote down. Record all of your observations and measurements.

Draw Conclusions and Communicate Results

After you collect your data, organize it by using appropriate graphic representations. Use charts, tables, or graphs to display your findings.

For your balloon investigation, you might make a table and then a bar graph. They would help you analyze your observations and the data you collected. Try to identify patterns in the data. These can help you determine whether the **evidence**—the information you gathered during the investigation—supports your hypothesis.

If your data does not support your hypothesis, that's OK! Remember, your investigation was designed to answer a question. Your hypothesis was just one possible answer to that question. Even if the data does not support the hypothesis, you have still gathered important information.

> **Draw Conclusions—**
> **5** Organize and analyze your observations and data. Does the evidence support your hypothesis?

Communicate Results—Your report should be detailed enough to enable others to repeat your investigation.

The final part of the scientific method is writing a report of your findings. In your report, describe your test—what you did and how you did it. Use your charts, tables, and graphs to display your data. Describe the evidence you used to draw conclusions about whether the investigation supported your hypothesis. Communicate clearly, and finish with a statement about whether your hypothesis was supported.

A good report will allow others to carry out the same investigation so that they can see if they get the same results. This is how scientists check each other's investigations to make sure that conclusions are correct.

 **MAIN IDEA AND DETAILS**

Why is it important to communicate results?

Before and After

People don't always start with the scientific method. Suppose you have questions about something scientists have already studied. All you need to do is read about it. But when studying the natural world, you often find new problems that puzzle you. You think, "I wonder what would happen if. . . " That's when inquiry skills, investigations, and experiments come in handy.

What happens after you've done an experiment? Even if an experiment supports your hypothesis, you might have other questions—about the same topic—that can be tested. And if your hypothesis wasn't supported, you might want to form another hypothesis and test that.

Scientists never run out of questions. The natural world is filled with things that make people wonder. By asking questions and using the scientific method, scientists have learned a lot. They've learned how to send people to the moon. They've learned to cure many diseases. But there are still many things to be learned. Who knows? Maybe you're the one to make the next big discovery!

Focus Skill **MAIN IDEA AND DETAILS**

What do scientists do when experiments show their hypotheses to be incorrect?

▲ Computers can be used to research a problem, display data, and share the results of experiments with scientists all over the world.

Tables and charts make it easy for other people to understand and interpret your data. ▼

Make a Helicopter

Cut a piece of paper 3 cm wide and 13 cm long. Following the drawing above, make a cut down the middle of half the paper. Fold one flap forward and one flap to the back. Fold the base up to add weight at the bottom. Drop your helicopter, and watch it fly. How does adding a paper clip to the bottom change the way the helicopter flies?

What Is the Scientific Method?

In this lesson, you learned that the scientific method is a series of steps used to plan and conduct an investigation.

1. **MAIN IDEA AND DETAILS** Draw and complete a graphic organizer to show the supporting details of this main idea: The scientific method has five steps.

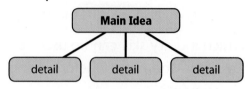

2. **SUMMARIZE** Use your graphic organizer to summarize and explain the steps of the scientific method.

3. **DRAW CONCLUSIONS** During which step of the scientific method would you identify variables and figure out how to control them?

4. **VOCABULARY** For each letter in *method*, write a science-related word starting with the same letter.

Test Prep

5. **CRITICAL THINKING** Karla heard that for making ice cubes, hot water is better than cold water because it freezes faster. How could she test that idea as a hypothesis?

6. What does an experiment test?
   A. a fact
   B. a hypothesis
   C. a theory
   D. a variable

Make Connections

 Writing

Expository Writing
Write a letter to a friend, **explaining** how he or she could use the scientific method to test a balloon rocket.

 Math

Display Data
Make a table to display how long the balloon rockets flew in the Investigate. Then make a graph of the results.

 Social Studies

Scientific Method
Use reference materials to compare how the Greeks studied science and what Francesco Redi added to their method. Write a story about what he showed.

Vocabulary Review

Use the terms below to complete the sentences. The page numbers tell you where to look in the chapter if you need help.

microscope p. 8   **inquiry** p. 18

balance p. 11   **experiment** p. 21

investigation p. 18   **scientific method** p. 28

1. An organized way to gather information is called _____.

2. A tool used to measure the mass of an object is a _____.

3. To test a hypothesis, you plan and conduct an _____.

4. A tool that makes objects appear larger is a _____.

5. A series of steps used by scientists to study the physical world is the _____.

6. When you gather information about an object or event, you carry out an _____.

Check Understanding

Write the letter of the best choice.

7. Which tool is used to measure volume in the metric system?
   - **A.** balance
   - **B.** measuring cup
   - **C.** spring scale
   - **D.** thermometer

8. **MAIN IDEA AND DETAILS** Which of the following steps to solve a problem is done first?
   - **F.** test a hypothesis
   - **G.** interpret data
   - **H.** form a hypothesis
   - **J.** observe, and ask questions

9. Which inquiry skill can be used to save time and money before doing an experiment?
   - **A.** form a hypothesis
   - **B.** make and use models
   - **C.** classify objects
   - **D.** draw conclusions

The diagram shows four tools. Use the diagram to answer questions 10 and 11.

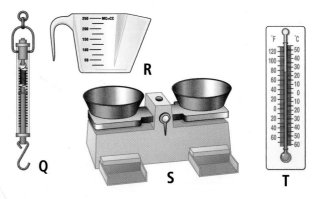

10. Which tool is used to measure the weight of an object?
   - **F.** Tool Q
   - **G.** Tool R
   - **H.** Tool S
   - **J.** Tool T

11. Which tool measures in grams?
   - **A.** Tool Q
   - **B.** Tool R
   - **C.** Tool S
   - **D.** Tool T

12. MAIN IDEA AND DETAILS Comparing, measuring, and predicting are examples of what process?

- **F.** communicating
- **H.** inquiry
- **G.** hypothesizing
- **J.** investigating

13. When conducting an experiment, which is the best way to record data?

- **A.** Make a bar graph while taking the measurements.
- **B.** Write everything down after you are finished.
- **C.** Make a table to record your data as you collect it.
- **D.** Write things down on a sheet of paper and organize it later.

14. Juan is making and flying airplanes with different shaped wings. What is he doing?

- **F.** experimenting
- **H.** investigating
- **G.** hypothesizing
- **J.** communicating

15. Why do scientists do each part of their investigation several times?

- **A.** to be sure their data is accurate
- **B.** to make their experiment look more impressive
- **C.** to use up all of their materials
- **D.** because it's fun

16. If you wanted to see more detail on the surface of a rock, what tool would you use?

- **F.** dropper
- **H.** microscope
- **G.** forceps
- **J.** thermometer

Inquiry Skills

17. Andrea is testing balloon rockets by using balloons with different amounts of air. **Identify** three **variables** Andrea needs to control.

18. Which boat do you **predict** will finish second in the race? Why?

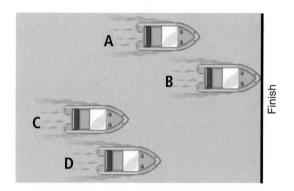

Critical Thinking

19. Why are safety goggles important when students are doing an investigation with scissors or glass?

20. Different amounts of water were placed in 4 beakers. The beakers were heated at the same rate. The data shows how long it took each beaker to boil.

The Big Idea

| 2.0 min | 4.0 min | 6.0 min | 7.9 min |

What conclusion is supported by the experiment? Explain.

Doing investigations in science can be fun, but you need to be sure you do them safely. Here are some rules to follow.

1. **Think ahead.** Study the steps of the investigation so you know what to expect. If you have any questions, ask your teacher. Be sure you understand any caution statements or safety reminders.

2. **Be neat.** Keep your work area clean. If you have long hair, pull it back so it doesn't get in the way. Roll or push up long sleeves to keep them away from your activity.

3. **Oops!** If you spill or break something, or get cut, tell your teacher right away.

4. **Watch your eyes.** Wear safety goggles anytime you are directed to do so. If you get anything in your eyes, tell your teacher right away.

5. **Yuck!** Never eat or drink anything during a science activity.

6. **Don't get shocked.** Be especially careful if an electric appliance is used. Be sure that electric cords are in a safe place where you can't trip over them. Don't ever pull a plug out of an outlet by pulling on the cord.

7. **Keep it clean.** Always clean up when you have finished. Put everything away and wipe your work area. Wash your hands.

LIFE SCIENCE

Science on Location and Projects for Home or School

Humpback Whale National
Marine Sanctuary 40
The Hidden Zoo 42
Leaping Lemurs! 44
Survey of Plants and Animals . . . 46

UNIT A

Processes of Living Things 47

CHAPTER 1
Cells to Body Systems 48
CHAPTER 2
Classifying Living Things 88
CHAPTER 3
Plant Growth and
Reproduction 114
CHAPTER 4
Animal Growth and
Heredity. 142

UNIT B

Interactions Among Living Things 183

CHAPTER 5
Energy and Ecosystems 184
CHAPTER 6
Ecosystems and Change 212

HAWAIIAN ISLANDS HUMPBACK WHALE NATIONAL MARINE SANCTUARY

Each November, around 5,000 visitors head to the Hawaiian Islands Humpback Whale National Marine Sanctuary. It is located along the coasts of six Hawaiian islands. These visitors aren't normal tourists. Each weighs a little more than an eighteen-wheel truck and is about half as long as a football field. As you have probably guessed, these visitors don't carry cameras or walk on two legs. They are humpback whales, some of the largest mammals in the world.

Protecting the Humpbacks

Most of the humpback whales in the northern Pacific Ocean spend the winter around Hawai'i. There they breed and nurse their newborns. Scientists estimate that about 15,000 humpbacks once lived in the North Pacific. Today, there are only about 7,000. Many of the whales were hunted for their bones and blubber. The water around the Hawaiian Islands is a very important habitat for humpback whales. The U.S. government made the area a sanctuary for the whales. The sanctuary is a safe place for the whales to breed every winter. Scientists hope it will help the humpback whale population recover.

Think and Write

1. **Scientific Thinking** What might happen to an organism if it lost the habitat it uses for breeding?

2. **Scientific Thinking** What benefits do people get by keeping the humpback whale from becoming extinct?

Scientists aren't sure why humpback whales leap out of the water.

THE HIDDEN ZOO

If you visit the National Zoo in Washington, D.C., you will see many amazing animals. But what you won't see is the most amazing part of the National Zoo. Behind the scenes, the National Zoo runs the Conservation and Research Center in Front Royal, Virginia. The center's main facility houses 30 to 40 endangered species at a time. Scientists at the center study the behavior, genetics, and reproduction needs of these species.

Bringing Back the Black-Footed Ferret

The scientists at the center use what they learn about a species to help the species breed. If a species comes too close to extinction in the wild, the animals that have been successfully bred at the center may be released. One species that the center is working to save is the black-footed ferret. This ferret is the most endangered mammal in North America. It is so rare that scientists once thought it was extinct. Then, a small population was found in Wyoming in 1981. After much hard work, the center's scientists have been able to increase the number of black-footed ferrets from 18 to more than 550. The black-footed ferret is still endangered, but with the help of the scientists from the Conservation and Research Center, it is on its way back from the edge of extinction.

Think and Write

1 **Scientific Inquiry** The natural prey of the black-footed ferret is the prairie dog. How will loss of prairie dog habitats affect the black-footed ferret?

2 **Scientific Inquiry** By what percent has the black-footed ferret population increased since 1981?

Black-footed ferret

Prairie dog

LEAPING LEMURS!

Millions of years ago, ancient primates spread out over Africa, Asia, and South America. Most of these ancient primates developed into the monkeys and apes we are familiar with today. A small group developed into lemurs, aye-ayes, and other primates called *prosimians* (proh•sim•ee•uhnz). Most prosimians are found on the island of Madagascar, a country off the coast of southeastern Africa. They have lived there for thousands of years. However, when humans moved to the island about 2,000 years ago, the lemurs and aye-ayes began to die off. As Madagascar's forests have been turned into farmland, both lemurs and aye-ayes have become endangered.

Scientists at the Duke Lemur Center study lemurs in a natural environment.

An aye-aye's long fingers help it hold food and climb trees. They also help an aye-aye remove insects from inside trees.

The Duke Lemur Center

The Duke Lemur Center is the world's largest prosimian sanctuary. It houses more than 230 lemurs, as well as other prosimian species, including aye-ayes, lorises, and bush babies. Scientists at the center study everything about prosimians. Among other things, they study how prosimians move, eat, see, sound, and reproduce.

The scientists also breed prosimians. One of the center's recent successes was breeding two aye-ayes that had both been born in captivity. That had never been done before. Male aye-ayes usually learn how to mate from other male aye-ayes in the wild. Scientists at the center hope that their breakthrough in aye-aye breeding will help preserve the species.

Think And Write

1. **Scientific Inquiry** What is the relationship between the human population on Madagascar and the endangerment of prosimians?

2. **Scientific Thinking** Why do you think it is important for scientists to breed aye-ayes that were born in captivity?

Project | Survey of Plants and Animals

Materials

- blank paper
- pencil
- ruler

Plants	Animals

Procedure

1. Various animals and plants are mentioned in Unit A. Research some of your state's plants and animals. List each species you researched that is mentioned in the book and that also lives in your state.

2. Draw a chart like the one below. List each of the organisms you read about under the correct heading.

Draw Conclusions

1. Do you think this list is a good representation of the plants and animals of your state? Why or why not?

2. Describe how you would do a complete survey of the plants and animals of your state.

Design Your Own Investigation

What Lives Near Your School?

With the help of your teacher, design and carry out a survey of the plants and animals around your school. As well as you can, describe or draw each one you find. If you don't know the name of a plant or an animal, use your written description or drawing to try to identify it in a nature book. Prepare a poster to display your results and your drawings.

Processes of Living Things

UNIT
A
LIFE SCIENCE

CHAPTER 1
Cells to Body Systems 48

CHAPTER 2
Classifying Living Things 88

CHAPTER 3
Plant Growth and Reproduction . . . 114

CHAPTER 4
Animal Growth and Heredity 142

Unit Inquiry

Plant Growth

Living things respond to factors in their environments. A plant's roots grow toward the ground because they respond to gravity. Another environmental factor that plants respond to is light. How do plants respond to light? For example, will plants grow toward a light source? Plan and conduct an experiment to find out.

Cells to Body Systems

All living things are made of cells. Cells work together to make up tissues, organs, and organ systems.

Essential Questions

Lesson 1

What Are Cells?

Lesson 2

How Do Cells Work Together?

Lesson 3

How Do Body Systems Work Together?

Go online
Student eBook
www.hspscience.com

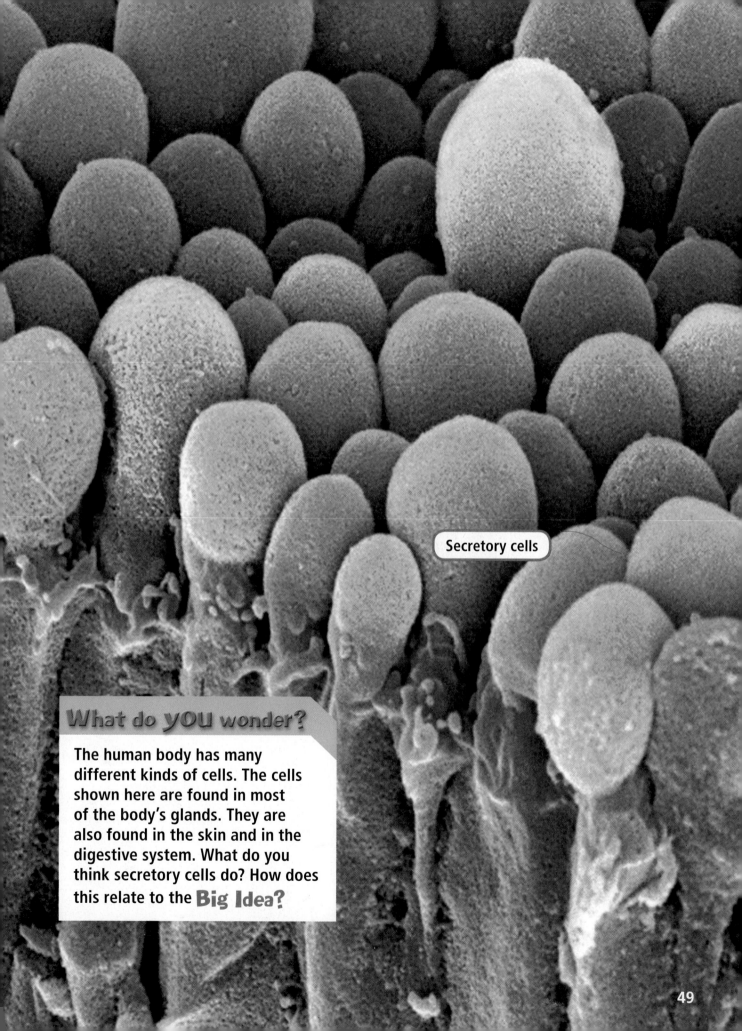

Secretory cells

What do YOU wonder?

The human body has many different kinds of cells. The cells shown here are found in most of the body's glands. They are also found in the skin and in the digestive system. What do you think secretory cells do? How does this relate to the **Big Idea?**

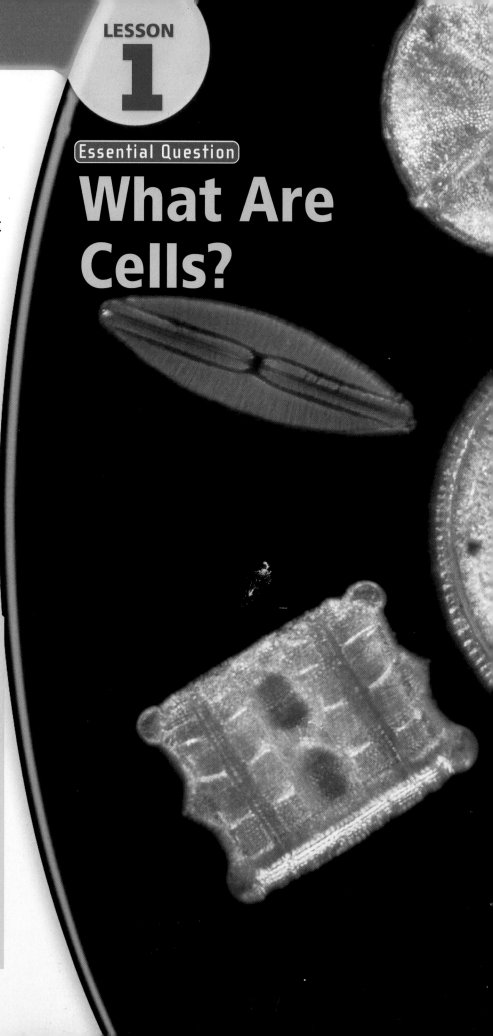

Investigate the structure of a cell.

Read and learn about how every living thing is made of cells.

Essential Question

What Are Cells?

Fast Fact

Nature's Kaleidoscope

The beautiful designs on this page may look like those in a kaleidoscope, but these designs occur in nature. This photograph of tiny single-celled organisms called diatoms was taken through a microscope. In the Investigate, you'll observe other cells through a microscope.

Diatoms

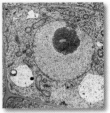

cell [SEL] The basic unit of structure and function of living things (p. 54)

microscopic [my•kruh•SKAHP•ik] Too small to be seen without using a microscope (p. 54)

organism [AWR•guhn•izm] Any living thing that maintains vital life processes (p. 54)

cell membrane [SEL MEM•brayn] The thin covering that surrounds every cell (p. 56)

nucleus [NOO•klee•uhs] The part of a cell that directs all of the cell's activities (p. 56)

cytoplasm [SYT•oh•plaz•uhm] The jellylike material inside a cell between the cell membrane and the nucleus (p. 56)

protist [PROHT•ist] A simple, single-celled or multi-celled organism with a nucleus and organelles (p. 58)

Observing Cells

Start with Questions

Cells are the basic unit of life. Cells help an organism carry out its life functions.

- How are the building blocks of all organisms alike and different?

- Do you think this onion had cells that helped it grow and live?

Investigate to find out. Then read and learn to find out more.

Prepare to Investigate

Inquiry Skill Tip

When scientists observe, they watch something very closely, gathering information by using their senses and scientific instruments.

Materials

- dropper
- red food coloring
- microscope slide
- slice of onion
- coverslip
- paper towels
- microscope
- colored pencils
- prepared slide of animal skin cells

Make an Observation Chart

Observing Cells	
Plant Cell	Animal Cell

Follow This Procedure

CAUTION: **Food coloring stains. Avoid getting it on your clothing.**

1 Use the dropper to place one drop of food coloring in the center of the slide. Break the onion slice, and pull off a piece of onion skin. Put the onion skin in the drop of food coloring. Gently lower the coverslip at an angle so that it spreads the food coloring. Use a paper towel to remove any excess food coloring.

2 **Observe** the onion skin cells under the microscope. Use the colored pencils to **record** your observations in a drawing.

3 **Observe** the prepared slide of the animal skin cells. Use colored pencils to **record** your observations in another drawing.

Draw Conclusions

1. **Compare** the onion skin cells and the animal skin cells.

2. **Inquiry Skill** When scientists **observe**, they use their senses to learn about objects and events. In the center of most cells are structures that direct how the cells function. Look for these structures. Based on what you **observe**, how many directing structures do you think each cell has?

Step 1

Step 2

Independent Inquiry

In what ways do you think all plant cells are alike? Design and conduct a simple experiment **to test your ideas.**

VOCABULARY
cell p. 54
microscopic p. 54
organism p. 54
cell membrane p. 56
nucleus p. 56
cytoplasm p. 56
protist p. 58

SCIENCE CONCEPTS
▶ how living things are made of cells
▶ why different cells have different jobs

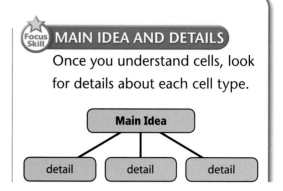

MAIN IDEA AND DETAILS
Once you understand cells, look for details about each cell type.

```
          Main Idea
    ┌─────────┼─────────┐
 detail    detail    detail
```

Cells

You've probably seen cork stoppers in jars and cork bulletin boards. But did you know that cork comes from the bark of an oak tree? In 1665, Robert Hooke, an English scientist, observed a layer of cork through a microscope. He saw the same kind of structures you observed in the onion skin. Because the structures he saw looked like tiny rooms, Hooke named them cells.

The microscope you used in the Investigate enabled you to observe and compare cells from an animal and a plant. A **cell** is the basic unit of structure and function in living things. Most cells are **microscopic**—they can be seen only with a microscope. Hooke's description of cells encouraged other scientists to learn more about them. Using microscopes, they found that all cells share some characteristics. They found that different cells do different jobs. Scientists also learned that all organisms are made up of cells. An **organism** is any living thing that maintains vital life processes.

You may see hundreds of different organisms each day. Each of these is made up of cells. Some simple organisms are just a single cell. But most plants and animals are made up of huge numbers of cells.

The single cell of this amoeba carries out all the functions the organism needs to stay alive.

▲ The outer cells of this plant's leaf help keep the plant from losing too much water. Inner cells of the leaf make food for the plant. Each plant cell also carries out life functions for itself.

▲ A salamander's skin cells don't look like a plant's outer cells, but they also help keep the organism from drying out. As in the plant, each cell carries out life functions for itself.

Plants and animals have different types of cells, each with its own job. For example, your body has digestive cells, which help you break down food, and nerve cells, which help you sense and respond to your surroundings. Different types of cells work together to carry out functions that keep an organism alive. To carry out its own functions, each cell has structures called *organelles*, which help keep the cell alive.

(Focus Skill) MAIN IDEA AND DETAILS How do cells keep organisms alive and healthy?

Insta-Lab

A Cell Model
Carefully use a plastic knife to cut a peeled hard-boiled egg in half. Compare it to the animal skin cells you observed in the Investigate. Why is an egg a good model for animal cells?

Plant and Animal Cells

All cells have similar structures and organelles. Every cell is surrounded by a thin covering called the **cell membrane**. This structure protects the cell, holds its contents together, and controls what goes in and out of the cell. Most organelles are also surrounded by membranes. Each type of organelle has a specific function that helps the cell.

Most cells have a nucleus. The **nucleus** directs all of a cell's activities, including reproduction. Inside the nucleus are *chromosomes* (KROH•muh•sohmz), threadlike structures that contain information about the characteristics of the cell. When a cell reproduces, the nucleus divides and each new cell gets identical chromosomes.

Between the cell membrane and the nucleus is a jellylike material called **cytoplasm** (SYT•oh•plaz•uhm). Cytoplasm contains chemicals that help keep a cell healthy.

Several kinds of organelles are suspended in the cytoplasm. *Mitochondria* are the "powerhouses" of a cell. They release energy from nutrients. *Vacuoles* store nutrients, water, or waste materials until the cell uses or releases these substances.

Plant cells have structures not found in animal cells. A thick *cell wall* helps support a plant cell. The cell wall lies outside the cell membrane. In the cytoplasm of many plant cells are *chloroplasts*. Chloroplasts make food for plant cells.

 **MAIN IDEA AND DETAILS** What purposes does the cell membrane serve?

Science Up Close

Comparing Plant and Animal Cells

Plant and animal cells have certain structures in common. They have a nucleus, a cell membrane, cytoplasm, and organelles. Study the differences between plant and animal cells.

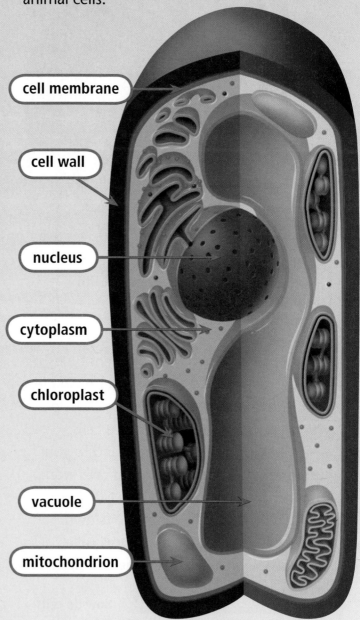

cell membrane

cell wall

nucleus

cytoplasm

chloroplast

vacuole

mitochondrion

Plant cells have different sizes, shapes, and functions, but most have the same organelles.

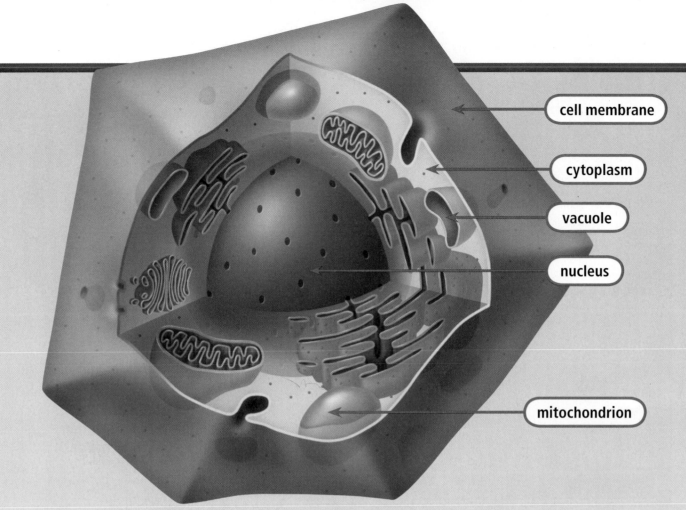

cell membrane

cytoplasm

vacuole

nucleus

mitochondrion

Like plant cells, animal cells have different sizes, shapes, and functions. They also have most of the same organelles. How is an animal cell different from a plant cell?

Cell Structures

Structure	Function	Kind of Cell
Nucleus	directs a cell's activities	plant and animal
Chromosome	inside nucleus; contains information about cell	plant and animal
Cell membrane	holds a cell together and separates it from its surroundings	plant and animal
Cell wall	supports and protects a plant cell	plant
Cytoplasm	a jellylike substance containing chemicals that help the cell stay healthy	plant and animal
Chloroplast	makes food for the cell	plant
Vacuole	stores food, water, or wastes	plant and animal
Mitochondrion	releases energy from nutrients	plant and animal

 For more links and animations, go to **www.hspscience.com**

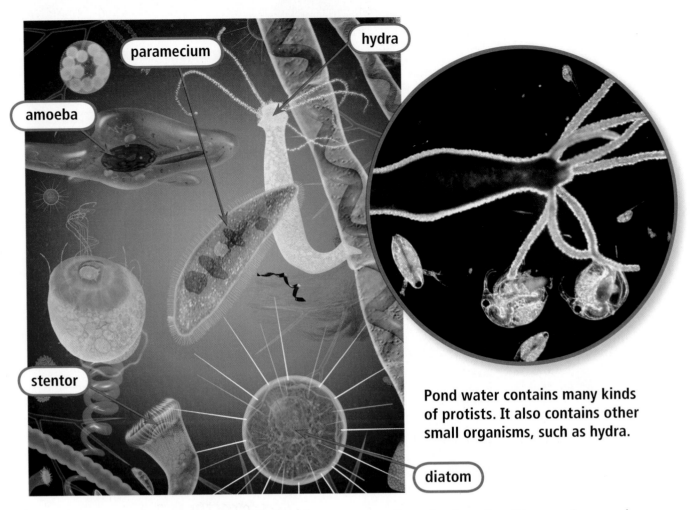

paramecium

hydra

amoeba

stentor

diatom

Pond water contains many kinds of protists. It also contains other small organisms, such as hydra.

Single-Celled Organisms

What do you think of when you hear the word *bacteria*? Many people think of germs. But not all bacteria are harmful. Many of these single-celled organisms are helpful. Some enrich the soil by breaking down dead plants and animals. Others help animals digest food. Still others help make food. Cheese and yogurt are foods that form when certain bacteria mix with milk.

Bacterial cells are different from plant and animal cells. Like plant cells, bacterial cells are surrounded by cell walls. But bacteria do not have a nucleus or membrane-bound organelles. Instead, their chromosomes and other materials float in the cytoplasm.

Another kind of single-celled organism makes up most of the group called protists. A **protist** (PROHT•ist) is a simple organism,

usually a single cell, with a nucleus and organelles. Some protists have cell walls and chloroplasts. These protists are plantlike. Other protists have no cell walls or chloroplasts and are animal-like.

The diatoms (DY•uh•tahmz) shown at the beginning of this lesson are plantlike—they have chloroplasts and make their own food. They are part of a group of protists called *algae* (AL•jee). Algae produce a lot of Earth's oxygen. They also produce a lot of food for ocean life.

Animal-like protists are called *protozoa*. They get food by "eating" other small organisms, such as algae and bacteria.

Focus Skill **MAIN IDEA AND DETAILS**

How do bacterial cells differ from plant and animal cells?

What Are Cells?

In this lesson, you learned that all living things are made up of cells and that plant and animal cells have different structures. You also learned about single-celled organisms.

1. (Focus Skill) **MAIN IDEA AND DETAILS** Draw and complete a graphic organizer to show the supporting details of this main idea: Cells.

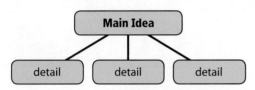

Main Idea

detail — detail — detail

2. **SUMMARIZE** Write a one-paragraph summary about the similarities and differences between plant and animal cells.

3. **DRAW CONCLUSIONS** You're looking at a slide through a microscope, and you see cells with cell walls but without chloroplasts. What kind of cells are you looking at? How do you know?

4. **VOCABULARY** Use lesson vocabulary and other lesson terms to make a crossword puzzle.

Test Prep

5. **Critical Thinking** Suppose you observe cells through a microscope. How might you infer whether the cells are animal cells?

6. What is the function of a cell's nucleus?
   A. to make food
   B. to direct the cell's activities
   C. to protect the cell
   D. to keep the cell healthy

Make Connections

 Writing

Expository Writing
Imagine a cell as being a city. Write a **description** of how each part of the cell helps carry out a task that is important for the maintaining of the city.

 Math

Solve a Problem
Imagine that a single cell divides into 2 every 15 minutes. If each of these cells also divides in 2, and so on, how long will it take for a single cell to produce 500 cells?

 Language Arts

Word Parts
The word *cytoplasm* contains the word parts *cyto-* and *-plasm*. Use a dictionary to find the meanings of the parts. How do those meanings relate to the meaning of the word?

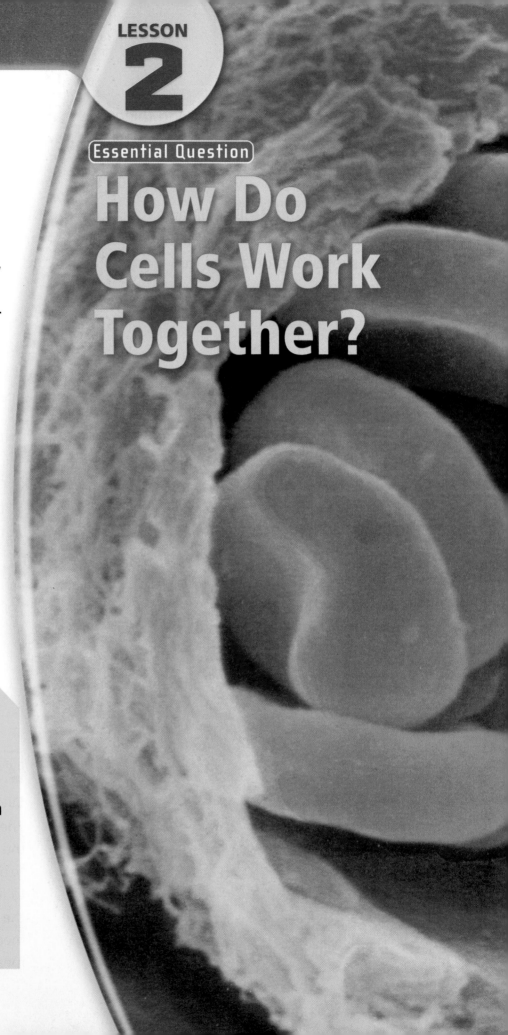

Investigate the differences between a plant's different structures.

Read and learn how cells, tissues, and organs work together in body systems to help our bodies function properly.

Essential Question

How Do Cells Work Together?

Fast Fact

Liquid Tissue

In the blood vessel shown here, red blood cells are carrying oxygen to other parts of the body. In the Investigate, you'll see different types of cells that work together to keep organisms functioning.

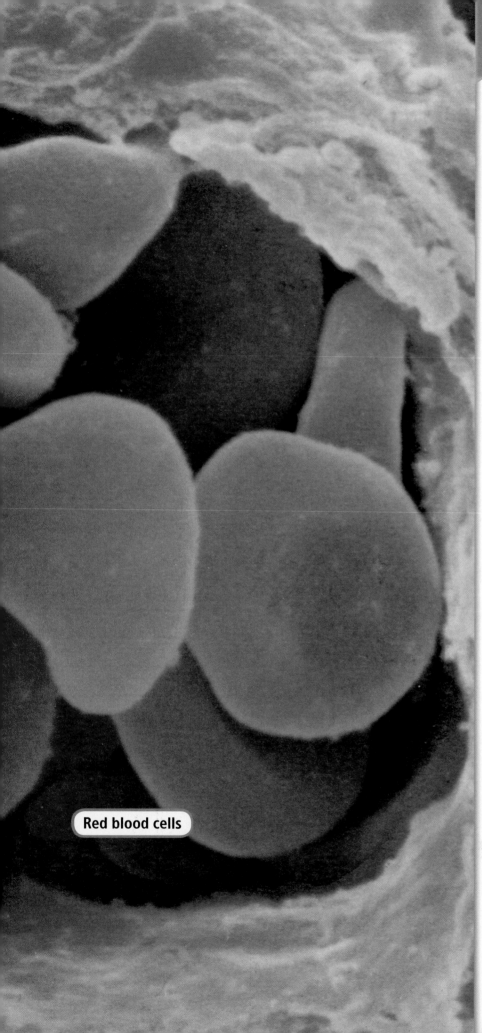

Red blood cells

tissue [TISH•oo] A group of cells that work together to perform a certain function (p. 64)

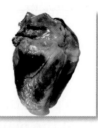

organ [AWR•guhn] A group of tissues that work together to perform a certain function (p. 65)

organ system [AWR•guhn SIS•tuhm] A group of organs that work together to do a job for the body (p. 66)

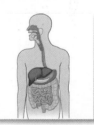

digestive system [dih•JES•tiv SIS•tuhm] The organ system that turns food into nutrients that body cells need for energy, growth, and repair (p. 66)

Cells and Tissues

Guided Inquiry

Start with Questions

Each part of an organism works with all the other parts to help the organism carry out its life functions.

- How do the cells in your body work together?

- Are the cells of a plant the same in different parts of the plant?

Investigate to find out. Then read and learn to find out more.

Prepare to Investigate

Inquiry Skill Tip

Recording your observations of objects enables you to compare them and infer reasons for the differences. When you infer, you use what you observe to explain those differences.

Materials

- prepared slides of a plant root, a plant leaf, and a plant stem
- microscope
- colored pencils

Make an Observation Chart

Plant Part	Observation
Plant root	
Plant leaf	
Plant stem	

Follow This Procedure

1. Place the slide of the plant root on the stage of the microscope. Turn the focus knob until you can see the cells clearly. **Observe** the root cells. Use the colored pencils to **record** your observations in a drawing.

2. Repeat Step 1, using the slide of the plant leaf. Again, use the colored pencils to **record** what you **observe**.

3. Repeat Step 1, using the slide of the plant stem. **Record** your observations.

4. **Compare** the cells from the different parts of a plant. What similarities did you **observe**? What differences?

Draw Conclusions

1. You **observed** cells from three different parts of a plant. Based on your observations, what conclusion can you draw about cells that look similar in all three parts?

2. **Inquiry Skill** When scientists **compare** objects, they often infer reasons for any differences. What can you infer about why leaf cells contain more green structures than do stem cells?

Step 1

Step 2

Independent Inquiry

Form a **hypothesis** about similarities and differences among animal cells. Using prepared slides of animal cells, test your hypothesis.

VOCABULARY
tissue p. 64
organ p. 65
organ system p. 66
digestive system p. 66

SCIENCE CONCEPTS
▶ how tissues are formed of similar cells
▶ how tissues work together in organs
▶ how body systems are groups of organs that work together

COMPARE AND CONTRAST
(Focus Skill)
Look for ways that tissues, organs, and organ systems are alike and different.

alike	different

Cell, Tissue, Organ

Your body is made up of trillions of cells. Each cell is able to carry out its own life functions. But your body's cells—like those in other organisms made up of many cells—also work together. Cells that work together to perform a certain function form a **tissue**. There are four kinds of tissue in your body.

Your body is covered and lined with *epithelial* (ep•ih•THEE•lee•uhl) *tissue*. Epithelial tissue is in your skin. It also lines your internal organs.

Most of your body mass is *muscle tissue*. Whenever you move, muscle tissue contracts and relaxes to move your skeleton. The bones and cartilage of your skeleton are made of *connective tissue*. Tendons and ligaments are connective tissue, too. Tendons connect bones to muscles. Ligaments connect bones to bones.

Signals from another kind of tissue, *nervous tissue*, "tell" muscles when to contract. Nervous tissue is found in the brain, spinal cord, and nerves.

Muscle tissue is made up of cells that contract when they receive signals from the brain. The contraction and relaxation of muscle tissue moves the skeleton.

The heart is an organ made up of muscle tissue, epithelial tissue, nervous tissue, and connective tissue. These tissues work together to pump blood to all parts of your body.

Just as cells work together to form tissues, tissues work together to form organs. An **organ** is several kinds of tissue working together for the same function. Your skin is an organ. It is made up of many layers of epithelial tissue. It also has muscle tissue, nervous tissue, and a layer of connective tissue. These tissues work together to protect your body.

Your heart is an organ that pumps blood to all parts of your body. It contains each of the different kinds of tissue. The heart is mostly muscle tissue, but it also has connective tissue. It is lined and covered with epithelial tissue. Nervous tissue in the heart receives signals from the brain to make it beat faster or slower.

The lungs are organs that take in oxygen from the air. They are made up of epithelial tissue and connective tissue.

The lungs, the heart, and all other organs rely on a very special kind of connective tissue—blood. The red cells in blood deliver oxygen to all other cells of the body. The liquid part of blood, called *plasma*, delivers nutrients and helps remove wastes from body cells. White blood cells help your body fight diseases. And platelets help blood clot if you get cut.

The lungs are made up of epithelial tissue and connective tissue. These tissues work together to take in oxygen from the air and move it into the blood.

Focus Skill COMPARE AND CONTRAST

How are muscle tissue and connective tissue alike? How are they different?

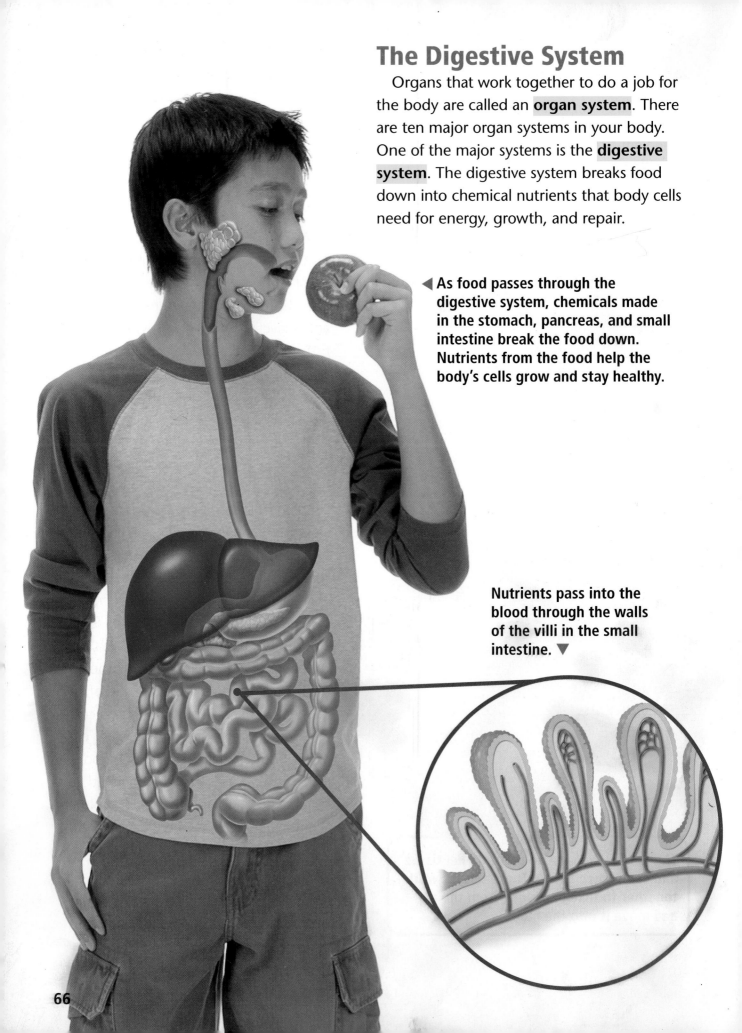

The Digestive System

Organs that work together to do a job for the body are called an **organ system**. There are ten major organ systems in your body. One of the major systems is the **digestive system**. The digestive system breaks food down into chemical nutrients that body cells need for energy, growth, and repair.

◀ As food passes through the digestive system, chemicals made in the stomach, pancreas, and small intestine break the food down. Nutrients from the food help the body's cells grow and stay healthy.

Nutrients pass into the blood through the walls of the villi in the small intestine. ▼

The digestive system helps the body get the nutrients it needs from food. First, chemicals break food down into nutrients. Then, nutrients are moved into the blood. Blood moves the nutrients to each of the body's cells.

Most people think the stomach is the first body organ involved in digestion. But digestion of certain foods starts as soon as you take a bite! As you chew, food is broken into smaller pieces. Glands in your mouth produce saliva. Saliva contains chemicals that begin breaking down some carbohydrates. Together, chewing and saliva begin digesting starchy foods. Starchy foods, like breads and pasta, begin to break down into sugars. You can investigate this yourself. Try chewing an unsalted cracker for a minute or two. You'll notice that its starchy taste soon becomes sweet.

From the mouth, food travels down the *esophagus*, a long tube that leads to the stomach. In the stomach, strong muscles churn the food with acid and other chemicals that break down proteins.

From the stomach, partly digested food moves into the small intestine. There, chemicals from the pancreas and gallbladder complete digestion.

Once digestion is complete, the *circulatory system* moves nutrients throughout the body. The small intestine is lined with fingerlike bumps called *villi* (VIL•eye). Villi have many blood vessels. Nutrients move from the small intestine into the blood vessels of the villi. Then they are carried by the blood throughout the body.

Focus Skill COMPARE AND CONTRAST

How are villi like the roots of a plant?

How are they different?

◀ **Peristalsis (pair•uh•STAL•sis) is the wavelike contraction of muscles in the organs of the digestive system. It helps move food through the system.**

Insta-Lab

Make a Model
You can make a model of food moving through the digestive system. Cut the foot off one leg of a pair of pantyhose. Put an inflated balloon into the other end. Then use both hands to squeeze the balloon along the length of hose. How does this model peristalsis?

1. This is a specialized cell of the digestive system. It produces acid to help break down food.

2. Digestive cells form a type of epithelial tissue that helps in digestion.

3. Layers of different kinds of tissue form a digestive organ—the stomach.

4. The stomach is part of the digestive system—an organ system that breaks food down into nutrients and moves the nutrients into the blood.

Eating a sandwich may seem simple, but it takes cells, tissues, organs, and an organ system to get nutrients from food. ▶

Body Organization

Suppose you join a local sports team. The team might be part of a regional league that is part of a state or national organization. From the smallest unit— you—to the national organization, all parts of the group work together to do the same thing—help you learn, play, and enjoy a sport.

Your body is also organized for one function—to keep you alive and healthy. Each of your cells works to keep itself healthy. But cells also work with other cells to form tissues. Tissues work together in organs, organs work together in systems, and systems work together to keep your body functioning.

Focus Skill **COMPARE AND CONTRAST** How are cells like systems? How are they different?

68

Essential Question

How Do Cells Work Together?

In this lesson, you learned that multicellular organisms have specialized tissues, organs, and systems. You also learned how the organs of the digestive system work together in the digestion of food and the absorption of nutrients.

1.  **COMPARE AND CONTRAST** Draw and complete a graphic organizer that compares and contrasts cells, tissues, organs, and organ systems.

   alike ——— different

2. **SUMMARIZE** Write a one-paragraph summary detailing how food moves through the digestive system.

3. **DRAW CONCLUSIONS** What part of the digestive system isn't working properly in people who cannot absorb nutrients? Explain.

4. **VOCABULARY** Use the lesson vocabulary and other lesson terms to write a paragraph about the digestive system.

Test Prep

5. **Critical Thinking** What is the relationship between the digestive system and the circulatory system?

6. Which is an example of a tissue?
   A. the heart
   B. a nucleus
   C. a muscle
   D. a vacuole

Make Connections

 Writing

Narrative Writing

Write a **creative story** describing an adventure through the digestive tract. Tell about the "stops" you make along the way, including the various organs.

 Math

Calculate

Count how many times your heart beats in 15 seconds. Multiply by 4 to find how many times your heart beats in a minute. Run in place for two minutes and repeat. How much faster is your heart rate now?

 Health

Lifeblood

Blood is a vital tissue. When a person loses a lot of blood due to an injury, a transfusion can save his or her life. Contact your local blood bank to learn about blood transfusions.

Investigate your reaction time.

Read and learn about some of the different organ systems of the body and how they work together and interact.

Essential Question

How Do Body Systems Work Together?

Fast Fact

Miles and Miles

The average adult's brain has about 100 *billion* nerve cells like those shown here. If laid end to end, these cells would extend about 3.2 million km (2 million mi)! Nerve cells help your brain react to your environment. In the Investigate, you'll test your own reaction time.

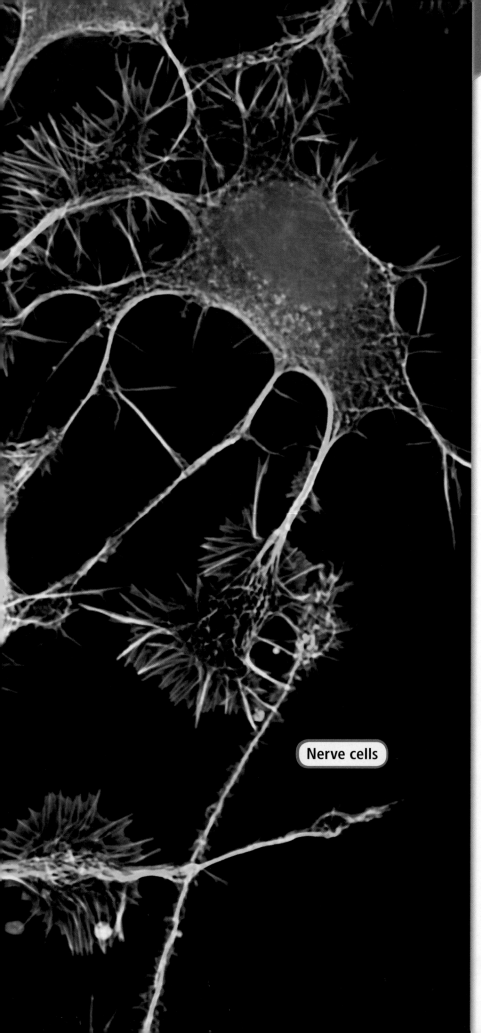

Nerve cells

circulatory system
[SER•kyoo•luh•tawr•ee
SIS•tuhm] The organ system—
made up of the heart,
blood vessels, and blood—
that transports materials
throughout the body (p. 74)

respiratory system
[RES•per•uh•tawr•ee SIS•tuhm]
The organ system, including
the lungs, that exchanges
oxygen and carbon dioxide
between the body and the
environment (p. 77)

skeletal system [SKEL•uh•tuhl
SIS•tuhm] The organ system,
including the bones, that
protects the body and gives it
structure (p. 78)

muscular system [MUHS•kyoo•
ler SIS•tuhm] The organ system
that includes the muscles and
allows the body to move (p. 78)

nervous system [NER•vuhs
SIS•tuhm] The organ system—
including the brain, spinal
cord, and nerves—that senses
your surroundings and controls
other organs (p. 80)

excretory system [EKS•kruh•
tawr•ee SIS•tuhm] The organ
system, including the kidneys
and bladder, that removes waste
materials from the blood (p. 82)

71

Testing Reaction Time

Guided Inquiry

Start With Questions

Have you ever tripped and caught yourself before you hit the ground?

- How quickly do your body and brain react?

- Do you think a tennis player reacts more quickly than other people?

Investigate to find out. Then read and learn to find out more.

Prepare to Investigate

Inquiry Skill Tip

You can infer based on what you observe and record or on other information you have on a subject.

Materials

- metric ruler
- reaction time chart

Make a Data Table

Trial	Reaction Time (sec)
1	
2	
3	

Follow This Procedure

❶ Sit with your arm resting on a table and your wrist hanging over the edge. Hold your hand sideways, ready to catch the ruler with your fingers.

❷ Have your partner hold the ruler above and perpendicular to your hand, as in the picture, so you'll be able to catch it.

❸ Have your partner let go of the ruler. Try to catch it as quickly as possible.

❹ Note the measurement on the ruler at the place where you caught it. Compare this number to the reaction time chart to find out how long it took you to catch the ruler. Record your results.

❺ Repeat Step 4 three times, and then trade places with your partner. Make graphs to compare your results.

Draw Conclusions

1. How did your reaction time change with each trial? Why?

2. **Inquiry Skill** What can you infer about the messages your brain receives and sends to enable you to catch the ruler?

Reaction Time Chart	
Distance on Ruler (cm)	Reaction Time (sec)
5	0.10
10	0.14
15	0.18
20	0.20
25	0.23
30	0.25

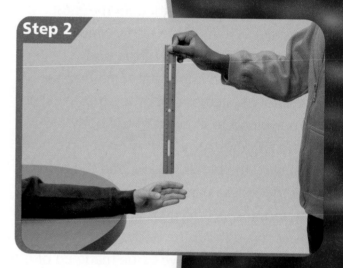
Step 2

Independent Inquiry

Now you know how to measure reaction time. Hypothesize how you might improve yours. Plan and conduct an experiment that would test your hypothesis.

VOCABULARY
circulatory system p. 74
respiratory system p. 77
skeletal system p. 78
muscular system p. 78
nervous system p. 80
excretory system p. 82

SCIENCE CONCEPTS
▶ that the body has different systems with different roles
▶ how body systems interact

SEQUENCE

Look for ways to organize in steps each of the processes described in this lesson.

Circulatory System

If you were asked to identify the most important system in the body, which would you choose? Though all of the body's systems perform important functions, the circulatory system is one of the most vital. It pumps blood to all parts of the body.

The **circulatory system** is made up of the heart, the blood vessels, and the blood. Together, these parts of the circulatory system transport oxygen, nutrients, and wastes throughout the body.

Blood is a connective tissue made up of several parts. The liquid part, called plasma, is mostly water. Nutrients from food and waste products from cells dissolve in plasma. Nutrients and other chemicals are carried to the body's cells. Waste products, which result from cell functions, are carried away from the cells so they can be removed from the body.

The solid part of blood includes red blood cells, white blood cells, and platelets. Red blood cells carry oxygen to all body cells. White blood cells help fight infection. Platelets help the blood clot, and they stop bleeding from wounds.

Blood leaves the heart through blood vessels called *arteries*. Arteries lead to small blood vessels called *capillaries* (KAP•uh•lair•eez). Capillaries are so tiny that blood cells move through them in single file. Capillaries lead to larger blood vessels called *veins*. Veins return blood to the heart.

Blood is a kind of connective tissue that is part of the circulatory system. It travels through blood vessels, carrying oxygen and nutrients to body cells and carrying wastes away from body cells. Blood vessels are one kind of organ of the circulatory system. ▼

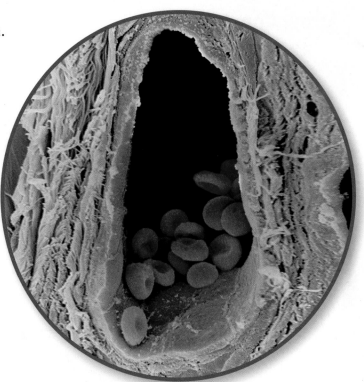

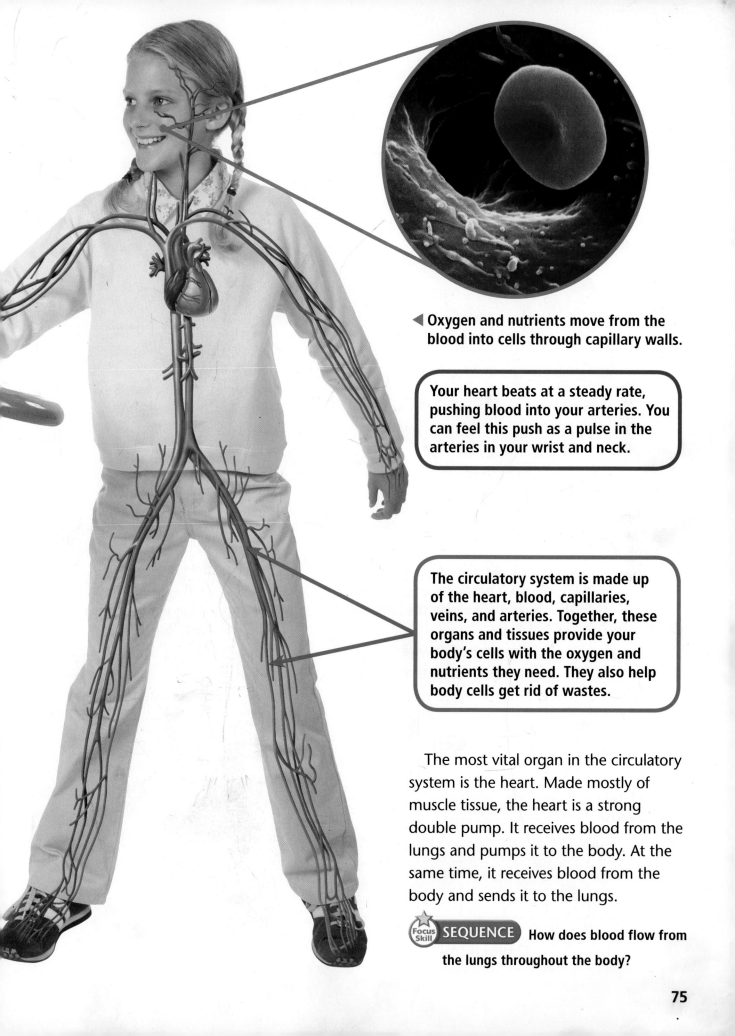

◀ Oxygen and nutrients move from the blood into cells through capillary walls.

Your heart beats at a steady rate, pushing blood into your arteries. You can feel this push as a pulse in the arteries in your wrist and neck.

The circulatory system is made up of the heart, blood, capillaries, veins, and arteries. Together, these organs and tissues provide your body's cells with the oxygen and nutrients they need. They also help body cells get rid of wastes.

The most vital organ in the circulatory system is the heart. Made mostly of muscle tissue, the heart is a strong double pump. It receives blood from the lungs and pumps it to the body. At the same time, it receives blood from the body and sends it to the lungs.

Focus Skill SEQUENCE How does blood flow from the lungs throughout the body?

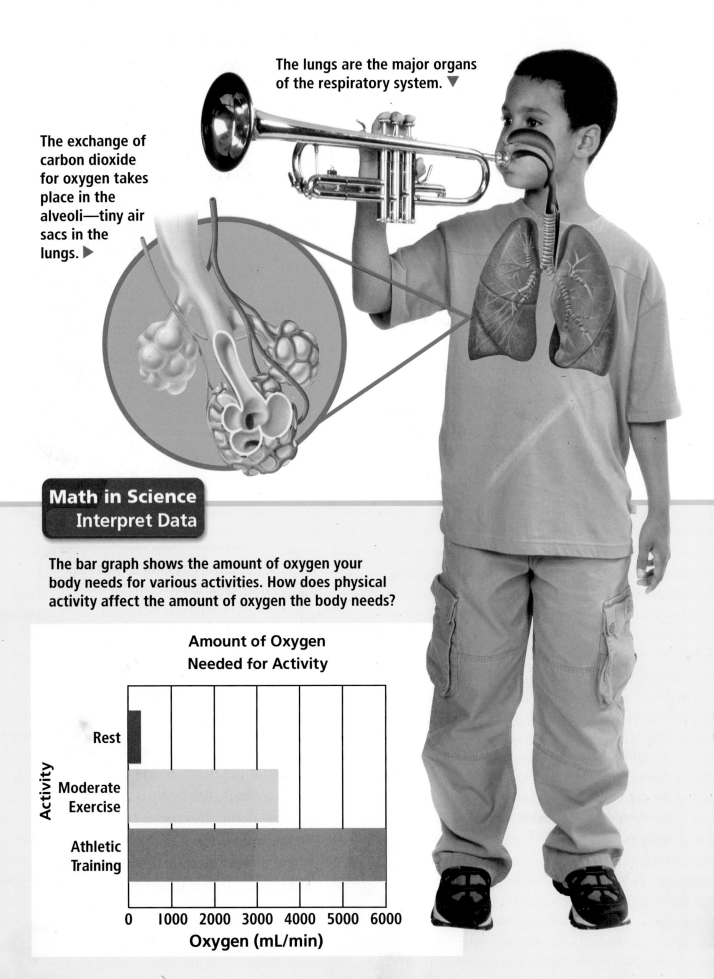

The lungs are the major organs of the respiratory system. ▼

The exchange of carbon dioxide for oxygen takes place in the alveoli—tiny air sacs in the lungs. ▶

Math in Science
Interpret Data

The bar graph shows the amount of oxygen your body needs for various activities. How does physical activity affect the amount of oxygen the body needs?

Amount of Oxygen Needed for Activity

Activity:
- Rest
- Moderate Exercise
- Athletic Training

Oxygen (mL/min): 0 1000 2000 3000 4000 5000 6000

Respiratory System

Think of all the things you do each day. You go to school, you might play on a sports team, you participate in clubs, you play outdoors, and you do homework. You need a lot of energy! So your cells need a lot of oxygen. The **respiratory system** is a group of organs and tissues that exchange oxygen and carbon dioxide between your body and the environment.

When you breathe, your body gets the oxygen it needs. Tiny hairs in your nose filter the air you inhale. Next, capillaries in your nasal passages warm the air. Warm, clean air then travels down your *trachea*, or windpipe. In your chest, the trachea branches into two large tubes called *bronchi* (BRAHNG•ky). Each bronchus leads to a lung.

The lungs are the main organs of your respiratory system. In the lungs, the bronchi branch into smaller and smaller tubes. At the end of the smallest tubes are tiny air sacs called *alveoli* (al•VEE•uh•ly). The walls of the alveoli are only one cell thick and are surrounded by capillaries. Gases are exchanged between the air in the alveoli and blood in the capillaries.

The capillaries of the alveoli receive oxygen-poor blood from the heart. This blood contains a lot of carbon dioxide (CO_2). Your body produces CO_2 as a waste product of cell functions. CO_2 passes from the blood plasma into the alveoli. Your body gets rid of the CO_2 when you exhale. Oxygen from the air you inhale passes into the blood, and red blood cells pick up the oxygen. Oxygen-rich blood travels back to the heart. From the heart, it is pumped throughout the body, to every body cell.

Focus Skill **SEQUENCE** How does oxygen get from the air into your blood?

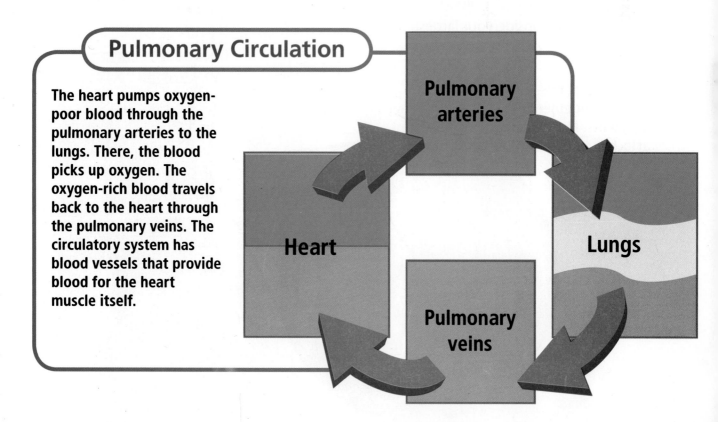

Pulmonary Circulation

The heart pumps oxygen-poor blood through the pulmonary arteries to the lungs. There, the blood picks up oxygen. The oxygen-rich blood travels back to the heart through the pulmonary veins. The circulatory system has blood vessels that provide blood for the heart muscle itself.

Pulmonary arteries

Lungs

Pulmonary veins

Heart

Skeletal and Muscular Systems

Imagine a mammal with no skeleton. Do you picture a shapeless blob on the ground? That's probably what the mammal would look like!

Your **skeletal system** includes bones, cartilage, and ligaments. Made up mainly of bones, it gives your body its form and protects many of your organs. The skeletal system works with the muscular system. The **muscular system** includes muscles and tendons that move bones.

An adult's skeleton is made up of 206 bones. *Cartilage* is spongy connective tissue that cushions the ends of many bones. Bands of connective tissue called *ligaments* hold bones together.

Without your skeleton's well-organized bony structure, you would not be able to sit, stand, or move. Your brain, heart, and lungs would be at risk of injury, and your circulatory system would lack blood cells. That's because blood cells are produced inside your largest bones.

The skeletal system supports your body. It also protects many of your internal organs. ▼

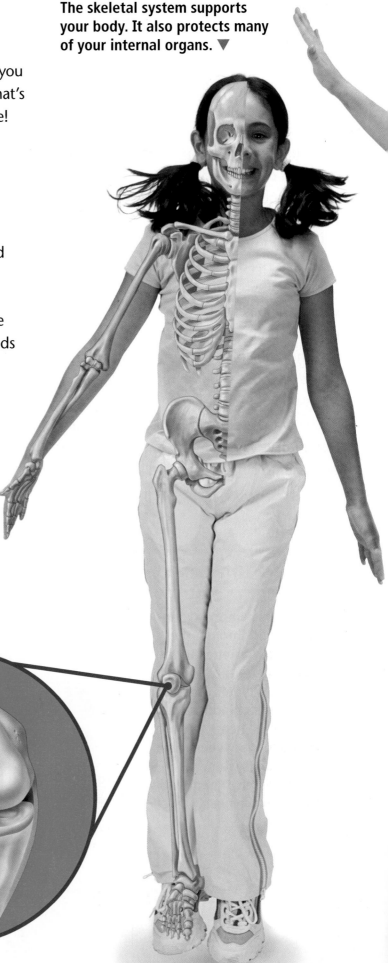

The bones at this joint are held together by ligaments. Muscles are attached to bones by tendons. ▶

Skeletal muscles work with the skeletal system to help you move your body. ▼

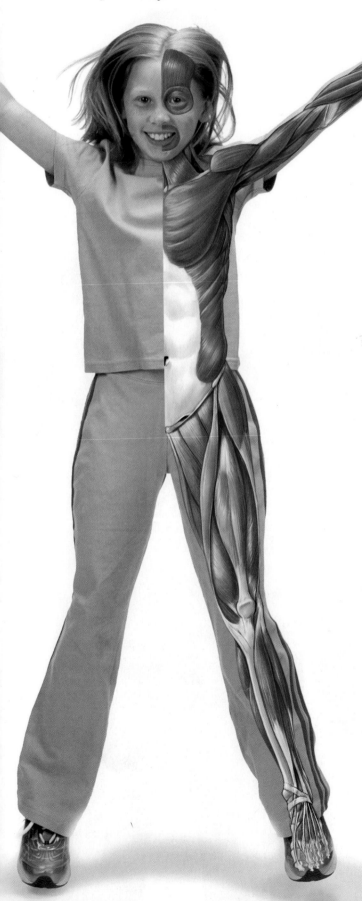

You're probably aware of the muscles that support and move your body. These muscles are *skeletal muscles*. They are made of groups of muscle tissue held together by connective tissue. Skeletal muscles usually are attached to bones, either directly or by bands of connective tissue called tendons.

Skeletal muscles often work in pairs. This means that one muscle contracts to bend a joint and another muscle contracts to straighten it. Skeletal muscles are *voluntary muscles*, because you can control them.

There are two other kinds of muscle. *Smooth muscle* makes up most of the walls of the body's organs, including blood vessels and digestive organs. There, contractions help move blood or food through tubes. *Cardiac muscle* makes up the walls of the heart. It contracts strongly to pump blood to all parts of the body. These two types of muscles are sometimes called *involuntary muscles*—you can't control their movements.

(Focus Skill) **SEQUENCE** How do opposing muscles cause movement at a joint?

Insta-Lab

Muscle Contraction
Measure around your upper arm when your elbow is straight and when it's bent. Record and compare the measurements. Describe the muscle that you infer controls the bending of your arm. Explain your reasoning.

Nervous System

Your **nervous system** enables you to sense your environment and to react to it. The nervous system directs other systems' activities, and it connects all the tissues and organs in your body to your brain. This amazing system is the least-understood part of your body.

The nervous system has two parts. The *central nervous system* is made up of the brain and spinal cord. The spinal cord is a bundle of nerves, about as thick as a pencil, that extends from the brain all the way to the hips. The central nervous system receives and interprets signals from the nerves throughout the body. The central nervous system sends signals up and down the spinal cord and determines responses that are needed. The brain sends signals through nerves that direct all of the body's voluntary muscles. It also controls the body's automatic functions, like contraction of cardiac muscle, respiration, digestion, and circulation.

The *peripheral* (puh•RIF•uh•ruhl) *nervous system* is made up of sensory organs, such as your eyes and ears, and touch sensors in your skin.

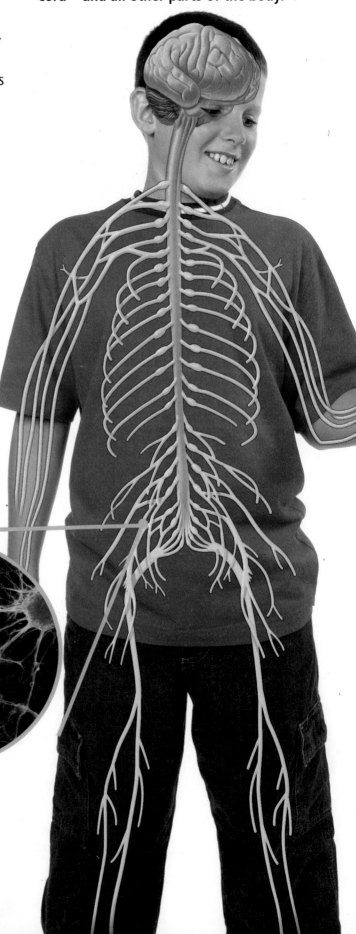

Nerve signals travel between the central nervous system—the brain and spinal cord—and all other parts of the body. ▼

A synapse (SIN•aps) is a gap between nerve cells. Chemical signals travel across synapses, helping deliver messages to and from the brain. ▶

80

▲ If you accidentally prick your finger on a thorn, your hand pulls back in a reflex action. This happens even before the information travels to your brain. The nerve signal triggered by the thorn takes a "shortcut," signaling the spinal cord to "tell" the muscles in your arm to pull your hand out of danger.

Sensory organs have special nerves called *sensory receptors*. The receptors detect changes in your surroundings and send signals along nerves to the central nervous system. Sensory receptors in your ears, for example, detect vibrations. They "tell" your brain about the vibrations, and the brain interprets them as sounds.

Has your doctor ever struck your knee with a small rubber mallet? If so, you likely experienced a reflex response. *Reflexes* are automatic responses to certain stimuli. When the doctor struck your knee, a nerve signal traveled to your spinal cord, where it took a "shortcut." Before traveling on to your brain, the signal in your spinal cord triggered a nerve in your muscles to jerk your leg. You kicked *before* your brain was even aware there was a tap!

Reflexes often occur in response to stimuli that cause pain. The brain is bypassed at first. Your body part is quickly pulled away from the source of the pain. Eventually, your brain senses the pain—but not until after your body has responded. However, not all reflexes, like when your eyes close as you sneeze, are in response to pain.

 SEQUENCE

What is the sequence of events in a reflex?

Excretory System

You know that body systems work together to carry out life functions. They digest food and release nutrients. They carry oxygen and nutrients to body cells, and they remove wastes from body cells. Carbon dioxide is eliminated when you exhale. Other wastes, such as ammonia, are removed from the body by the **excretory system**.

Ammonia, a waste product of certain cell functions, enters the blood. It is carried by blood plasma to the liver. The liver converts ammonia into *urea*, which travels through the blood to the kidneys. As blood flows through the *kidneys*, which are the main organs of the excretory system, urea and other wastes are filtered from the blood. The result is urine. Urine flows through tubes called *ureters* to a muscular organ called the *bladder*. When the bladder is full, urine is then eliminated from the body.

Focus Skill SEQUENCE How is ammonia removed from the body?

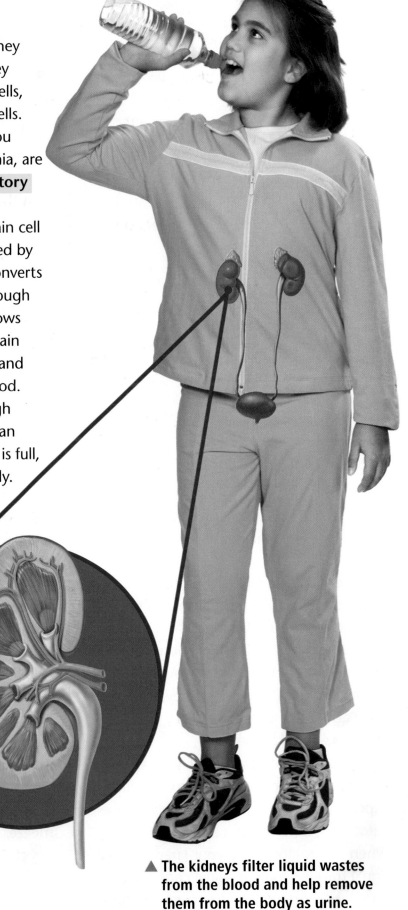

Liquid wastes are removed from the blood through capillaries in the kidneys. Materials the body needs, mostly water and salts, are returned to the blood. ▶

▲ The kidneys filter liquid wastes from the blood and help remove them from the body as urine.

Essential Question

How Do Body Systems Work Together?

In this lesson, you learned about many different organ systems in the body, including the circulatory, respiratory, skeletal, muscular, nervous, and excretory systems. You learned how the organs in these systems work together to perform many different functions in the body.

1.  **SEQUENCE** Draw and complete a graphic organizer that shows the sequence of oxygen as it enters the body through the lungs.

2. **SUMMARIZE** Write a one-paragraph summary explaining the flow of blood through the circulatory system.

3. **DRAW CONCLUSIONS** Between the trachea and the esophagus is a flap of tissue that closes when you swallow. What is its function?

4. **VOCABULARY** Use the information in the lesson to write a clue for each vocabulary term. Then hide each term in a grid of letters to make a word-search puzzle.

Test Prep

5. **Critical Thinking** In what ways do the digestive and circulatory systems work together?

6. Tendons are connective tissues that
   A. make blood cells.
   B. carry signals from nerves.
   C. connect bones to bones.
   D. connect muscles to bones.

Make Connections

 Writing

Narrative Writing
Write a **narrative** about the "travels" of a nerve signal. Explain how the signal causes movement in an arm or a leg.

 Art

Pointillism
In the nineteenth-century style of painting called pointillism, pictures are painted with small dots of color. The brain interprets the many dots as smooth forms. Make a picture of your classroom using the pointillist style.

 Physical Education

Circulatory System
You can improve the health of your circulatory system by lowering your resting heartbeat rate. Measure your heartbeat rate at rest. Then exercise for 30 minutes a day for a month. How much does your resting heartbeat rate drop?

Science Spin

From Weekly Reader

TECHNOLOGY

Saving Stephanie

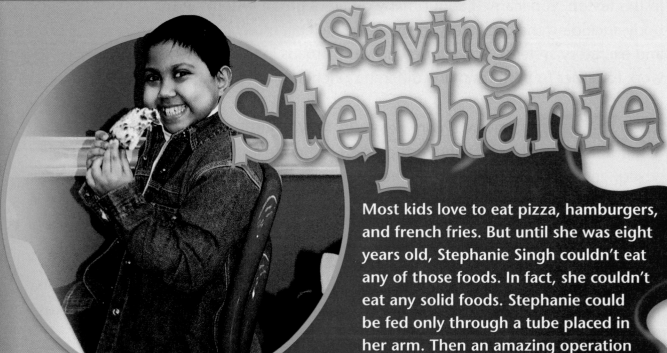

Most kids love to eat pizza, hamburgers, and french fries. But until she was eight years old, Stephanie Singh couldn't eat any of those foods. In fact, she couldn't eat any solid foods. Stephanie could be fed only through a tube placed in her arm. Then an amazing operation changed Stephanie's life.

Stephanie's Favorite Foods

macaroni and cheese
homemade soups

Eating Through a Tube

Stephanie was born with visceral myopathy, a rare condition that doesn't allow the intestine to develop properly. The intestine is a long tube made up of two main parts. The first part, the small intestine, is connected to the stomach at one end. Partially digested food flows from the stomach into the small intestine. The small intestine absorbs nutrients from the food. Food that cannot be digested further flows into the large intestine. The large intestine then eliminates the undigested food waste from the body.

Because of her condition, Stephanie's small intestine couldn't break down food into nutrients. Stephanie would have starved, even if she had eaten plenty of food. To keep her alive, Stephanie's doctors connected a tube into her arm. The tube delivered nutrient-rich fluids directly into her bloodstream.

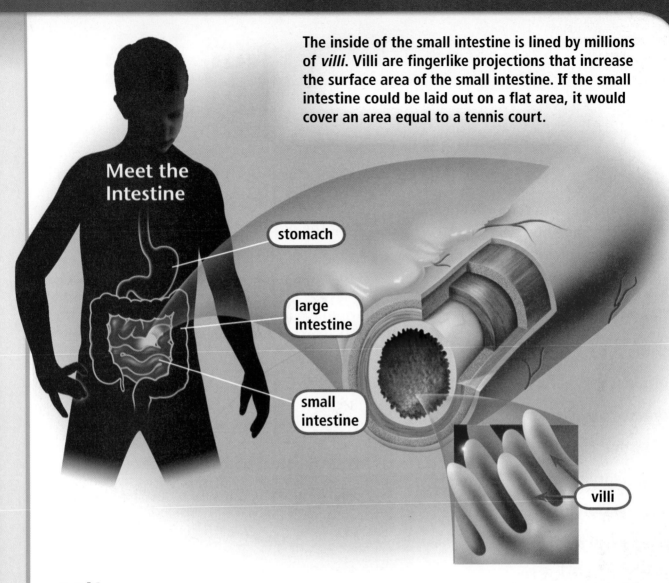

The inside of the small intestine is lined by millions of *villi*. Villi are fingerlike projections that increase the surface area of the small intestine. If the small intestine could be laid out on a flat area, it would cover an area equal to a tennis court.

Meet the Intestine

stomach

large intestine

small intestine

villi

A Lifesaver

To help Stephanie, doctors performed an intestine transplant. Doctors perform many different types of transplant operations, including heart, liver, and kidney transplants. However, an intestine transplant is a risky and dangerous operation.

The intestine has special cells that protect a person's body from bacteria in food. When a healthy intestine is put into a patient's body, the patient's immune system attacks the transplanted organ. But those special bacteria-fighting cells in the intestine fight the body's immune system. The cells fight one another, often causing the patient's body to reject the transplanted organ.

After performing the operation, doctors gave Stephanie medicine to keep her immune system from attacking the transplanted intestine. Since the operation, Stephanie can eat anything she wants.

Think and Write

❶ How else is your immune system at work in your body?

❷ Why would the human body fight to reject a transplanted organ?

Find out more. Log on to
www.hspscience.com

Vocabulary Review

Use the terms below to complete the sentences. The page numbers tell you where to look in the chapter if you need help.

cell p. 54

nucleus p. 56

tissue p. 64

organ p. 65

organ system p. 66

digestive system p. 66

respiratory system p. 77

skeletal system p. 78

muscular system p. 78

nervous system p. 80

1. Cells that work together to carry out a function make up a _____.

2. The group of organs and tissues that exchanges oxygen and carbon dioxide in the lungs is the _____.

3. A group of organs that work together to carry out life processes is an _____.

4. Tissues that work with your skeleton to help you move make up the _____.

5. A group of tissues working together to perform a function is an _____.

6. Structures that support and protect your body are in the _____.

7. The basic unit of structure and function of living things is the _____.

8. The organelle that directs a cell's activities is the _____.

9. The mouth, esophagus, stomach, and intestines are parts of the _____.

10. Organs and tissues that work together to help you sense your environment make up the _____.

Check Understanding

Write the letter of the best choice.

11. What is the purpose of a cell membrane?

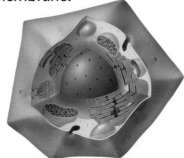

A. to keep the cell dry
B. to keep the cell warm
C. to hold the contents of the cell together
D. to provide a sticky surface for the cell

12. SEQUENCE How does oxygen-rich blood travel from the heart to capillaries around the body?

    F. through arteries

    G. through cardiac muscle

    H. through pulmonary veins

    J. through veins

13. MAIN IDEA AND DETAILS Which is **not** a kind of connective tissue?

    A. nerve   **C.** cartilage

    B. bone   **D.** muscle

14. Which term describes both a diatom and an amoeba?

    F. animal   **H.** plant

    G. bacteria   **J.** protist

15. How are plant cells different from animal cells?

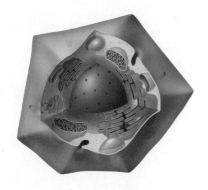

    A. Plant cells have membranes and a nucleus, but animal cells do not.

    B. Plant cells have cell walls and chloroplasts, but animal cells do not.

    C. Plant cells have cell walls and organelles, but animal cells do not.

    D. Plant cells have no nucleus or organelles, but animal cells do.

16. Which systems work together to provide the body's cells with oxygen?

    F. circulatory and digestive

    G. respiratory and digestive

    H. respiratory and circulatory

    J. respiratory and excretory

Inquiry Skills

17. Compare bacteria cells to plant cells.

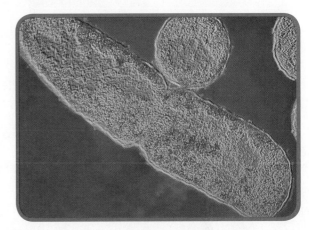

18. Describe the **sequence** of events that takes place to remove ammonia from the body.

Critical Thinking

19. The large bones work with the circulatory system to produce blood cells. Why is this important?

The Big Idea

20. Jamie is helping his mother cook. As he adds pepper to the food, he sneezes. What kind of action is his sneezing? Why? Which two systems act together to cause Jamie's sneeze? Explain.

CHAPTER 2

Classifying Living Things

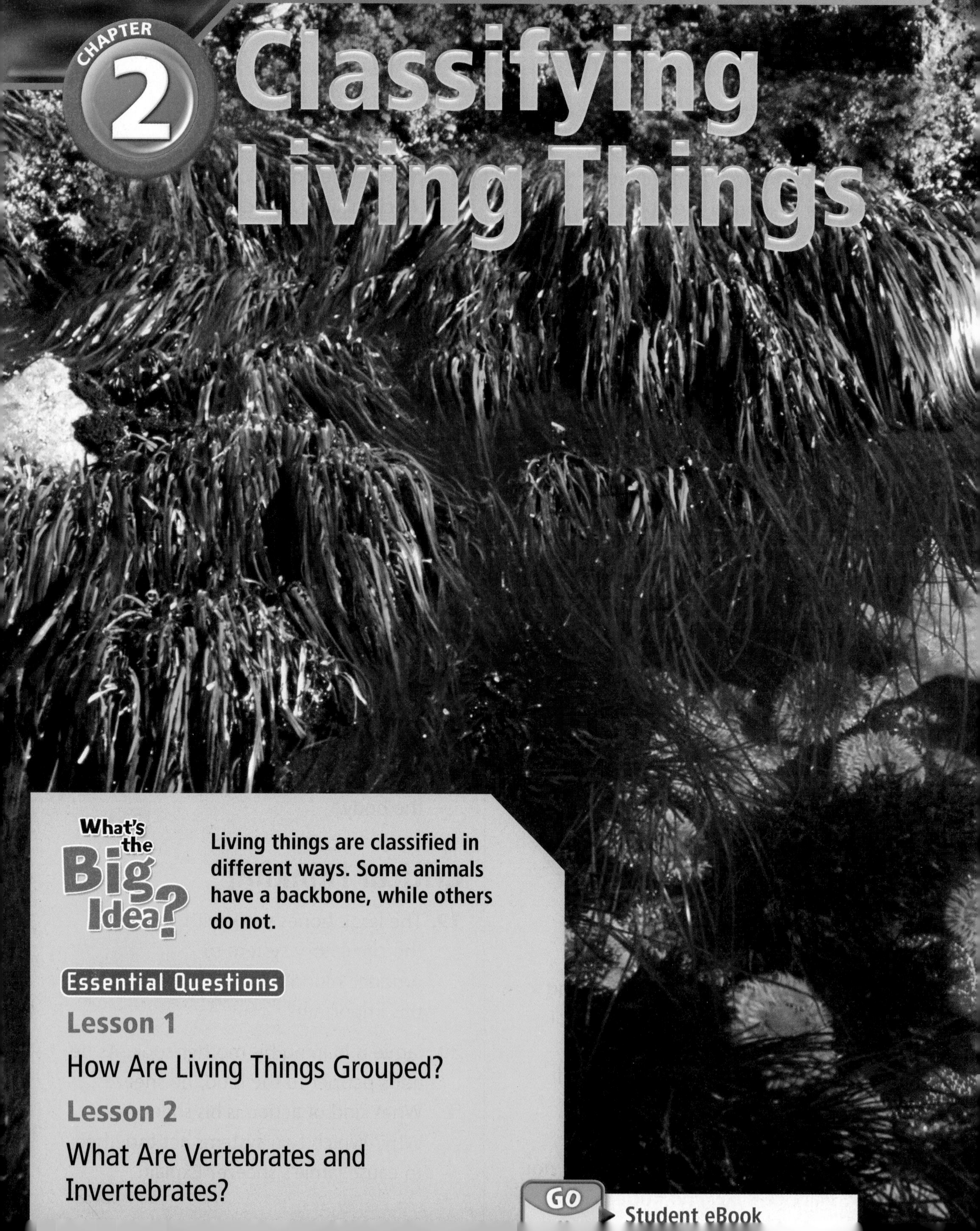

What's the Big Idea?

Living things are classified in different ways. Some animals have a backbone, while others do not.

Essential Questions

Lesson 1

How Are Living Things Grouped?

Lesson 2

What Are Vertebrates and Invertebrates?

GO ▶ Student eBook

Tide pool

What do **yOU** wonder?

Hardy life forms inhabit tide pools
on rocky shores. How many kinds
of organisms can you identify
in this tide pool? Can tide-pool
organisms be classified in similar
ways? How does this relate to the
Big Idea?

Investigate ways scientists classify.

Read and learn about how scientists classify living things.

Essential Question

How Are Living Things Grouped?

Fast Fact

A Sea Full of Fishes

There are plenty of kinds of fish in the sea! How does the number of different fishes compare with the numbers of other kinds of animals? In the Investigate, you will compare and classify different objects— shoes!

Pacific kelp "forest"

classification [klas•uh•fih•KAY•shuhn] The process of grouping similar things together (p. 94)

kingdom [KING•duhm] A major, large group of similar organisms (p. 95)

species [SPEE•sheez] A unique kind of organism (p. 96)

Classify Shoes

Guided Inquiry

Start with Questions

Grouping similar things together makes it easier to identify them and easier for scientists to share information about them.

- How would you classify all the shoes that the students in your class are wearing?

- Do you think dogs are grouped and classified in the same way as shoes?

Investigate to find out. Then read and learn to find out more.

Prepare to Investigate

Inquiry Skill Tip

Objects can be classified in many ways, based on their characteristics. Often you will classify objects based on their physical characteristics. You can also classify objects based on how they are used, the materials from which they are made, or how they react in certain situations.

Materials

- newspaper
- shoes

Make an Observation Chart

Shoe Characteristics	
1. has laces	6.
2.	7.
3.	8.
4.	9.
5.	10.

Follow This Procedure

1. Work on the floor, or cover a table with newspaper. Take off one of your shoes. Put it in a pile with your classmates' shoes.

2. Make a list of all the characteristics of the shoes that you can observe. An example is whether a shoe has laces.

3. Think of a way to divide the shoes into two groups, based on a characteristic you can observe. For example, you might make one group of shoes with laces and another group of shoes without laces.

4. Use another characteristic to divide both groups into even smaller groups.

5. Continue to classify the shoes, based on their characteristics, until each shoe is in a division of its own.

Draw Conclusions

1. What characteristics did you use to make your groups?

2. In what other ways might you classify shoes?

3. **Inquiry Skill** Scientists classify organisms to find similarities and differences. Why must you compare and contrast things when you classify them?

Step 1

Step 3

Independent Inquiry

Gather ten or more small objects from home or from your classroom. Then develop a way to classify them.

VOCABULARY
classification p. 94
kingdom p. 95
species p. 96

SCIENCE CONCEPTS
▶ how scientists classify living things
▶ what the major groups of living things are

Focus Skill **MAIN IDEA AND DETAILS**

Look for characteristics that separate groups of living things.

Main Idea
detail   detail   detail

Classification

When you walk into your kitchen at home, you probably know where to find most things. The forks are in a drawer with the spoons and knives. Milk and meat are in the refrigerator. Canned soups and vegetables are on a pantry shelf or in a cupboard. Pots, pans, and dishes have their places, too.

Putting similar items together in a kitchen makes cooking and cleaning up easier. The process of **classification**, or grouping similar things together, makes sense for anyone who uses a kitchen. It also makes sense for scientists who study living things.

No one can know everything about the 10 million or more different kinds of organisms that may live on Earth. By identifying characteristics that living things share, scientists can group similar organisms together. To do this, scientists look for similarities in the way organisms look, live, eat, move, grow, change, and reproduce.

Focus Skill **MAIN IDEA AND DETAILS** What is classification? How is it useful to scientists?

What characteristics do these two animals share? Do you think scientists classify the hawk and the bat in the same group? Why or why not? ▶

The Five Kingdoms

One classification system divides all organisms into five *kingdoms*: Animals, Plants, Fungi, Protists, and Bacteria. What characteristics does each kingdom have?

Animals

Bacteria

Plants

Protists

Fungi

Grouping Living Things

Scientists classify for many reasons. Classifying living organisms makes finding and sharing information easier. When scientists discover an organism that's new to them, they can learn some things about it by learning about similar organisms that have already been classified and studied.

Scientists classify living organisms into major, large groups called **kingdoms**. All members of each kingdom have certain characteristics. Different methods of classification have different numbers of kingdoms—either five or six.

Scientists classify animals together because animals are made of many cells and because they feed on other living or once-living things. Plants also have many cells, but they make their own food.

Most fungi also are many-celled organisms. However, they don't make or eat food. They absorb it, usually from the remains of other organisms. Protists are mostly one-celled organisms. Some make food, as plants do. Others take in food, as animals and fungi do.

Bacteria are all one-celled. Their cells have no nucleus. Most feed the way fungi do, but some make their own food. Some scientists group all bacteria in one kingdom. Others separate them into two kingdoms.

Focus Skill **MAIN IDEA AND DETAILS**

What is a kingdom? How do the kingdoms of living organisms differ?

Smaller Groups

Kingdoms are convenient groups, but they are very large. Each kingdom includes thousands of different organisms. Just as you did with shoes in the Investigate, scientists classify organisms into smaller and smaller groups. The members of each group share more and more characteristics. The smallest group contains only one kind of organism.

The first step is to divide each kingdom into smaller groups. A *phylum* (FY•luhm) is a major group within a kingdom. Organisms in a phylum have more characteristics in common than do organisms in different phyla (plural). Phyla are divided into *classes*, classes are divided into *orders*, and orders are divided into *families*. Just as in your family, members of the same family share many characteristics. Like human families, they have individual differences. A *genus* (JEE•nuhs) is a subdivision of a family. Finally, each genus can contain one or more *species* (SPEE•sheez). A **species** is a unique kind of organism.

Every different kind of living thing has its own scientific name. This name includes the names of the smallest two groups—genus and species. For example, the scientific name for the house cat is *Felis domesticus*. *Felis* is the name of its genus. The name of its species is *domesticus*. House cats—and only house cats—have this name. When scientists use this name, they know they're talking about a house cat, not some other kind of cat.

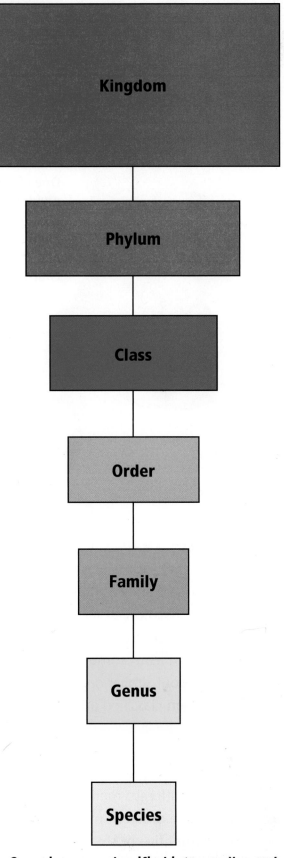

▲ Organisms are classified into smaller and smaller groups—from kingdom to species.

To divide large groups into smaller groups, scientists look for characteristics that some members of one group have but others don't. In the example shown here, the butterfly is the only animal in the top group that doesn't have a backbone. Therefore, the butterfly doesn't belong to the same phylum as the other animals. At the next level, all the animals except the fish are mammals, so the fish doesn't belong to the same class as the others.

As the groups get smaller, each group includes organisms that are more alike and more closely related. For example, the genus *Felis* includes both the house cat and the ocelot. They are more closely related to each other than they are to the tiger. But they are both closer relatives of tigers than they are of bears, whales, fish, or butterflies.

Focus Skill **MAIN IDEA AND DETAILS**

What is one detail about the species level of classification?

▲ A classification system identifies related groups. The house cat (*Felis domesticus*) and the ocelot (*Felis pardalis*) share a genus, so they are very close relatives.

Classify Buttons
Pile a dozen or more buttons of different sizes, shapes, and colors on the table. Call this a "kingdom" of buttons. Based on the buttons' characteristics, find ways to divide them into smaller groups, until each button is its own "species." What scientific name will one particular button have?

This tree can grow large because transport tubes carry food and water to all its parts.

Plants without transport tubes are usually small.

Groups of Plants

Like animals, plants are classified according to similar characteristics. One of these characteristics is *vascular tissue*, or transport tubes. Some plants have vascular tissue in their roots, stems, and leaves. These transport tubes carry water and food.

The tree shown here has vascular tissue. Some of the tubes carry food made in the leaves to cells in the trunk and roots. Other tubes carry water from roots in the soil to cells in the trunk and leaves. There are nine divisions, or phyla, of vascular plants.

Some plants, such as mosses, don't have vascular tissue. They absorb water directly through the surfaces of their cells. There are three divisions, or phyla, of nonvascular plants, or plants without transport tubes.

Scientists divide each of these phyla into smaller groups. For example, three phyla of vascular plants don't make seeds to reproduce. Instead, new plants grow from structures called spores. Ferns are an example of these kinds of plants.

Other phyla of vascular plants make seeds, but they don't all make seeds in the same way. Flowering plants make seeds inside a fruit. Most of the plants we grow in gardens are flowering plants. Nonflowering plants make seeds in cones. These *coniferous*, or cone-bearing, plants include pine, spruce, and fir trees. You will learn more about plants in the next chapter.

(Focus Skill) **MAIN IDEA AND DETAILS**

What characteristics are used to divide plants into major groups?

Lesson Review

How Are Living Things Grouped?

In this lesson, you learned how living things are classified by kingdom, phylum, class, order, family, genus, and species.

1. **MAIN IDEA AND DETAILS** Draw and complete a graphic organizer to show how classification groups are divided into smaller groups.

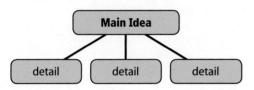

```
        Main Idea
    /       |       \
 detail   detail   detail
```

2. **SUMMARIZE** Write a three- or four-sentence summary of how scientists classify animals into smaller and smaller groups.

3. **DRAW CONCLUSIONS** Explain how classification groups show how closely related organisms are.

4. **VOCABULARY** Write one or two sentences to explain what an organism's scientific name includes.

Test Prep

5. **Critical Thinking** Explain how living things' characteristics are used to classify them.

6. Which of the following organisms are the most closely related?
   A. *Ursus arctos* and *Ursus maritimus*
   B. *Felis ursus* and *Ursus arctos*
   C. *Felis arctos* and *Ursus felis*
   D. *Ursus ursus* and *Felis felis*

Make Connections

 Writing

Expository Writing
Write a **paragraph** explaining how a grasshopper, a turtle, an elephant, a dog, and a polar bear could be classified into one, two, three, four, or five groups.

 Math

Read a Circle Graph
What does this circle graph tell you about where most species of animals live?

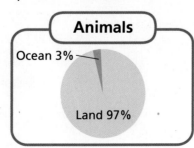

Animals

Ocean 3%

Land 97%

Music

The Orchestra
Find out how and why musical instruments in an orchestra are classified into groups such as woodwinds, strings, and percussion.

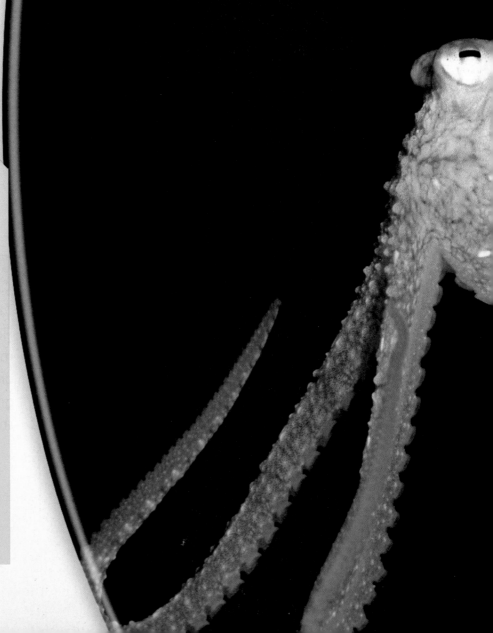

Investigate the characteristics of a backbone.

Read and learn about the differences between vertebrates and invertebrates and about how different structures can have similar functions.

[Essential Question]

What Are Vertebrates and Invertebrates?

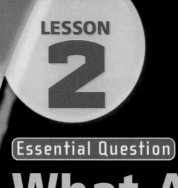

Fast Fact

Awesome Octopus

Scientists classify octopods in the animal phylum Mollusca. Octopods are related to snails and clams. The largest octopus can weigh more than 45 kg (100 lb) and grow longer than 9 m (30 ft). Like all mollusks, an octopus has no backbone. In the Investigate, you will build a model of a backbone.

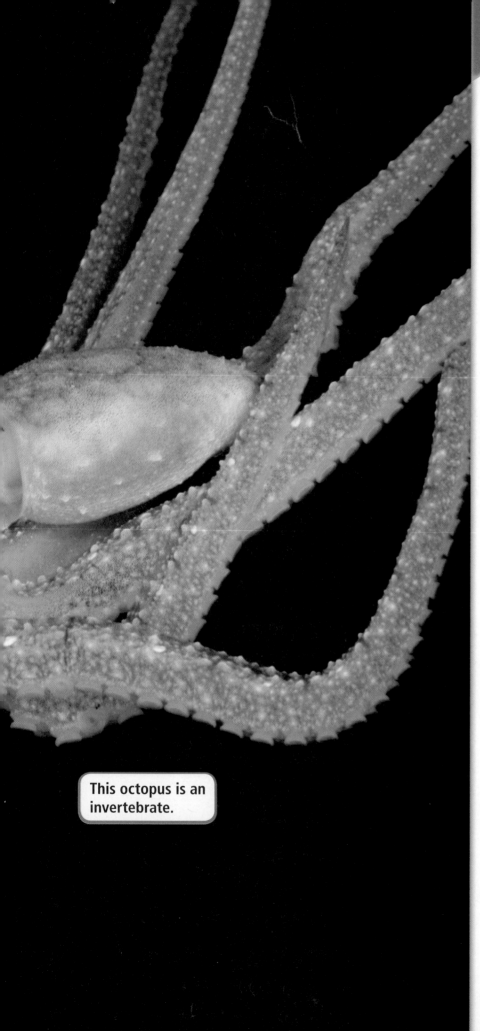

This octopus is an invertebrate.

vertebrate [VER•tuh•brit] An animal with a backbone (p. 104)

invertebrate [in•VER•tuh•brit] An animal without a backbone (p. 106)

Build a Model Backbone

Start with Questions

You have a backbone. It allows you to sit up straight and to turn your head.

- What do you think you'd be like without a backbone?

- Do all animals, such as this chicken, have a backbone?

Investigate to find out. Then read and learn to find out more.

Prepare to Investigate

Inquiry Skill Tip

Models are useful for helping you communicate your observations during an investigation. The model should be chosen carefully so that it has the main characteristics of the real object. You can use the model to show others how the real object would react in certain situations.

Materials

- chenille stick
- wagon-wheel-shaped pasta pieces
- soft candy rings

Make an Observation Chart

Object	Observations
Pasta	
Pasta and Candy	

Follow This Procedure

CAUTION: Never put any materials you use in an Investigate in your mouth.

1. Bend one end of the chenille stick. Thread a piece of pasta onto the other end, and push it down to the end.

2. Thread more pieces of pasta onto the stick. Push them together. When the stick is full, bend the end.

3. Gently bend the chenille stick with its pasta pieces. What do you observe?

4. Straighten one end, and remove all but one piece of pasta. Repeat Step 2, but add candy rings between the pieces of pasta. Gently bend the chenille stick again. Now what do you observe?

Draw Conclusions

1. A real backbone has a spinal cord, bones called *vertebrae* (VER•tuh•bray), and soft discs between the vertebrae. What does each part of your model represent?

2. **Inquiry Skill** Scientists need to communicate their results to other scientists. Use your model to communicate how a real backbone works.

Step 1

Step 4

Independent Inquiry

Think about how a chicken's neck supports the chicken's head while letting it move. Then plan and conduct a simple investigation to test your ideas.

VOCABULARY
vertebrate p. 104
invertebrate p. 106

SCIENCE CONCEPTS
▶ how vertebrates and invertebrates differ
▶ how different structures can have similar functions

COMPARE AND CONTRAST
Look for ways in which animal groups are alike and different.

| alike | different |

Animals with a Backbone

What do a giraffe and a snake have in common? At first, you might think, "Not much." Giraffes grow very tall, while most snakes are small. Giraffes are warm-blooded. They have fur, and they give birth to live young. Snakes are cold-blooded. They have scales, and most lay eggs. But as the pictures show, these two animals have one important thing in common—each has a backbone.

Scientists divide the animal kingdom into two large groups, based on the backbone. An animal with a backbone is a **vertebrate** (VER•tuh•brit). This term comes from *vertebrae*—bones that make up a backbone.

Scientists classify vertebrates into at least five phyla. *Mammals* have hair and produce milk for their young. *Birds* have feathers, which keep them warm and help most of them fly. *Reptiles* have dry, scaly skin, and most lay their eggs on land. *Amphibians* begin life in water, but when they are adults, most live on land. *Fish* have scales and live their entire lives in water.

COMPARE AND CONTRAST How are vertebrates alike? How are they different?

◀ A giraffe has seven vertebrae in its neck. That's as many as a human has. A giraffe's neck is long because each of the vertebrae is large.

Some snakes have as many as 300 vertebrae. ▶

Fish have gills that absorb oxygen dissolved in water.

Most adult amphibians live on land but return to water to lay eggs. Salamanders are amphibians.

Reptiles have dry, scaly skin. Amphibians don't.

All birds have feathers, but not all birds can fly. This cardinal fluffs up its feathers to help keep it warm.

Like most mammals, this agouti has hair.

Insta-Lab

Strong and Flexible

Roll and tape a sheet of construction paper into a tube. Stand the tube on end. See how many books it will hold. Cut slits about 2 cm apart along both sides of the tube. Test again with books. What conclusion can you draw about backbones made of many vertebrae instead of just one?

Animals Without a Backbone

Vertebrates are the animals most familiar to us, but they are actually the smallest part of the animal kingdom. Most species of animals are invertebrates. An **invertebrate** (in•VER•tuh•brit) is an animal without a backbone.

The simplest phyla of invertebrates include the sponges—the living kind, not the kind many people use for cleaning—jellyfish, anemones, and coral. They live mostly in the oceans.

Some simple invertebrates, including several phyla of worms, live on land, too. Roundworms are plentiful in the soil.

You can't tell their heads from their tails. Earthworms are different. They have a head end and a tail end. Their bodies are divided into segments that look like rings. Giant earthworms can grow to be several meters (yards) long.

A more complex invertebrate phylum is the *mollusks*. Mollusks include soft-bodied animals such as the octopus and the squid. Octopods are smart. They can solve problems and remember things, and their vision is thought to be as good as a human's. Some mollusks have shells. Examples include snails, clams, and oysters. The largest invertebrate—the giant squid—is a mollusk.

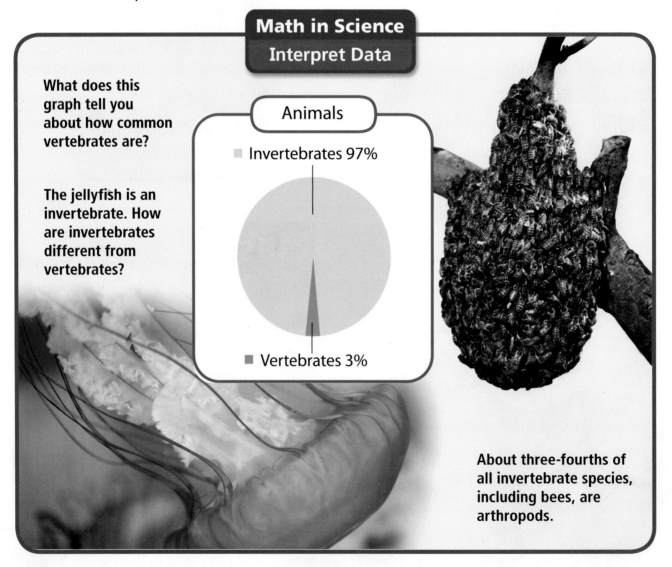

Math in Science
Interpret Data

What does this graph tell you about how common vertebrates are?

The jellyfish is an invertebrate. How are invertebrates different from vertebrates?

Animals

■ Invertebrates 97%

■ Vertebrates 3%

About three-fourths of all invertebrate species, including bees, are arthropods.

Sea stars, sand dollars, and sea urchins belong to a phylum of invertebrates called *echinoderms* (ee•KY•noh•dermz). They have different shapes, and most have body parts in multiples of five. Many echinoderms have hard spines.

The largest phylum of invertebrates is the *arthropods*. Arthropods have jointed legs and two or more body segments. The joints and segments let them move freely.

All arthropods have skeletons, but unlike a vertebrate skeleton, an arthropod's skeleton is on the outside of its body. The skeleton isn't made of bone. It's a hard material made by the skin. To grow, an arthropod must shed its skeleton. Then its skin produces a new, slightly larger skeleton.

Scientists classify arthropods into several classes. If you eat seafood, you probably know about one class—*crustaceans*. Many crustaceans have claws, and some have antennae on their heads. Examples include crabs, lobsters, and shrimp.

The largest class of arthropods is the *insects*. Adult insects—such as beetles, mosquitoes, butterflies, roaches, and bees—have six legs. They also have three body segments: head, thorax, and abdomen. The legs and wings are in pairs on the thorax.

Spiders are arthropods, but they aren't insects. They are *arachnids*. Most arachnids have eight legs. The class also includes mites, ticks, and scorpions.

Focus Skill COMPARE AND CONTRAST

How are invertebrates alike? How are they different?

This queen conch is a mollusk. It lives in the Caribbean in sand, grass beds, and coral reefs. ▼

This cuttlefish isn't really a fish. It's actually a mollusk. It's a close relative of the octopus and the squid. ▼

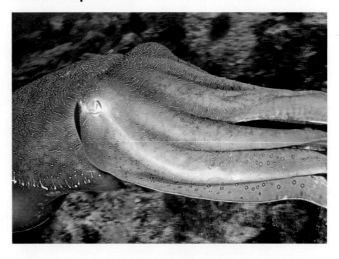

The most common arthropods are insects, such as the praying mantis and the butterfly. Many insects have wings and can fly. ▼

Form and Function

The function of wings is flight, but the structure of wings varies.

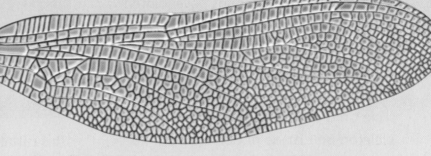

▲ The wing of a dragonfly is a flat piece of the same material that makes up the insect's external skeleton.

▲ The wing of the hummingbird has hollow bones inside. On the outside, it is covered with feathers.

Structure and Function

When classifying living organisms, scientists look at both structure and function. *Structure* is the form of a body part. *Function* is what a structure does. A wing, for example, is a structure. Its function is flight.

Living organisms that aren't closely related sometimes have body parts that perform the same function. However, the structures are usually different.

For example, grasshoppers and frogs both jump by using powerful hind legs. Scientists who study the skeletons, joints, and muscles of grasshoppers and frogs observe that their legs are not constructed the same way at all. Because function can be misleading, scientists rely mostly on structure when classifying.

 COMPARE AND CONTRAST

How are structure and function different? How are they related?

108

What Are Vertebrates and Invertebrates?

In this lesson, you learned that some animals have a backbone but others do not. You learned about the differences between vertebrates and invertebrates.

1. **COMPARE AND CONTRAST** Draw and complete a graphic organizer that compares and contrasts vertebrates and invertebrates.

2. **SUMMARIZE** Write a two- or three-sentence summary of the different types of invertebrates.

3. **DRAW CONCLUSIONS** Why are few large invertebrates found living on land?

4. **VOCABULARY** Write a sentence that explains the difference between vertebrates and invertebrates.

Test Prep

5. **Critical Thinking** Which do you think is the more successful group of animals—the vertebrates or the invertebrates? Explain.

6. From what characteristic do vertebrates get their name?
   A. the number of legs they have
   B. the size of their brains
   C. the bones in their backs
   D. the way their muscles work

Make Connections

 Writing

Persuasive Writing
Write a **paragraph** to convince your reader that it's better to have a skeleton on the outside, as an arthropod does, than a backbone, as a vertebrate does.

 Math

Make a Bar Graph
Find out the total numbers of bones in the bodies of several different vertebrates. Make a bar graph to compare them.

 Literature

Two-Line Rhyme
How many words can you think of that rhyme with *ant*? Write a short rhyme about an invertebrate.

Marjory Stoneman Douglas

While others saw in the Everglades nothing but a marshy wasteland, Marjory Stoneman Douglas saw "the simplicity, the diversity, the related harmony of the forms of life they enclose." Ms. Douglas began observing the Everglades as a reporter in 1919. At the time most people believed that the Everglades were a problem to be overcome in the path of development. Ms. Douglas, however, discovered a thriving ecosystem in the Everglades.

▶ **MARJORY STONEMAN DOUGLAS**

▶ Nature conservationist and writer

Ms. Douglas became a leader among those working to save the Everglades. She wanted the government to establish an Everglades National Park. That dream was realized in 1947, the same year Ms. Douglas's book *The Everglades: River of Grass* was published. In 1970, Ms. Douglas founded an organization called Friends of the Everglades, which includes research scientists, engineers, and other citizens. This group was able to prevent the construction of an airport in the Everglades.

Think and Write

❶ Why do you think people considered the Everglades a problem to be overcome?

❷ Why was action to save the Everglades necessary?

Karl Ammann

▶ **KARL AMMANN**

▶ Wildlife photographer and conservation activist
▶ Advisor to The World Society for the Protection of Animals

Karl Ammann photographs wild animals all over the world. In 1988, Ammann was photographing wildlife along the Zaire River in Africa. He was shocked to find that each year, thousands of gorillas and chimpanzees were hunted and killed. The meat from those animals, many of whom are endangered, was then sold in nearby towns.

It was then that Ammann decided to write books and articles about what was going on and to make other people aware of this problem. His work has helped increase the local government's efforts in protecting the animals.

Today, Ammann lives in Africa, where he and his wife have adopted a pair of chimpanzees who were orphaned when their parents were killed.

Think and Write

1. Why do these animals need to be protected?
2. What are the results of people hunting and killing gorillas and chimpanzees?

Career Entomologist

To be an entomologist, you have to love bugs. These scientists study all aspects of insects—how they live, eat, and reproduce. Some entomologists constantly search for new species of insects. Others do research to develop ways to control insects that are pests to people.

Vocabulary Review

Use the terms below to complete the sentences. The page numbers tell you where to look in the chapter if you need help.

classification p. 94

kingdom p. 95

species p. 96

vertebrate p. 104

invertebrate p. 106

1. The largest group used to classify living things is a _____.

2. An animal that has no backbone is an _____.

3. An animal that has a backbone is a _____.

4. The process of grouping things that are similar is _____.

5. A single kind of living thing is a _____.

Check Understanding

Write the letter of the best choice.

6. Which of these is a major group of living things within a kingdom?
   - **A.** class
   - **B.** genus
   - **C.** order
   - **D.** phylum

7. **MAIN IDEA AND DETAILS** Which of the following is a characteristic used to classify living things into kingdoms?
   - **F.** one-celled or many-celled
   - **G.** whether they can fly
   - **H.** the number of legs they have
   - **J.** whether they live in the ocean or on land

8. **COMPARE AND CONTRAST** The beetle is an arthropod. The snail is a mollusk. How are these two animals alike?

   - **A.** Neither can fly.
   - **B.** Both live in the ocean.
   - **C.** They have six legs.
   - **D.** Neither has a backbone.

9. To which group does a clam belong?
   - **F.** arthropod
   - **G.** mammal
   - **H.** mollusk
   - **J.** vertebrate

10. What's wrong with classifying in the same phylum all animals that swim?

A. Swimming has a different function for each one.

B. They use different structures to swim.

C. They can't survive in the same environment.

D. There are too many of them for one group.

11. Which of these animals is **not** a vertebrate?

F.

G.

H.

J.

12. Which organism is an arthropod with six legs?

A. arachnid   C. insect

B. echinoderm   D. mollusk

13. Which is the first characteristic that divides plants into two big groups?

F. flowers   H. seeds

G. leaves   J. transport tubes

14. One major group of seed plants makes fruits. What does the other group usually make?

A. cones   C. leaves

B. flowers   D. tubes

15. Which kingdom is sometimes separated into two kingdoms?

F. bacteria   H. plants

G. fungi   J. protists

16. Which structure does a pine tree use to reproduce?

A. cone   C. fruit

B. flower   D. spore

Inquiry Skills

17. Explain why living things **classified** in the same genus are more alike than those that are only in the same class.

18. Explain what **making a model** of a backbone shows about how strong and flexible it is.

Critical Thinking

19. Two plants are named *Vinca minor* and *Vinca rosea*. Are they close relatives? Explain.

20. Two organisms belong to the same kingdom and the same phylum but not to the same class. Can they be in the same family or order? Are they close relatives? Explain.

The **Big** Idea

Plant Growth and Reproduction

What's the Big Idea?

Plants have a variety of structures to help them carry out life processes.

Essential Questions

Lesson 1

How Do Plants Grow?

Lesson 2

How Do Plants Reproduce?

GO online

Student eBook
www.hspscience.com

What do YOU wonder?

The azaleas you see in this photo are flowering plants that grow naturally in woodlands. How do you think these azaleas meet their basic needs? How does this relate to the **Big Idea?**

Azaleas

Investigate the parts of a vascular plant.

Read and learn about the differences between vascular and nonvascular plants and about how plants make their own food.

Essential Question

How Do Plants Grow?

Fast Fact

Mangroves

This red mangrove is not like most trees, whose roots are only underground. Mangroves have "prop roots," which spread out above the ground, giving the trees additional support in the shallow water where they grow. In the Investigate, you'll study roots and other parts of plants.

Red mangrove

vascular tissue [VAS•kyuh•ler TISH•oo] Tissue that supports plants and carries water and food (p. 121)

xylem [ZY•luhm] Vascular tissue that carries water and nutrients from roots to every part of a plant (p. 121)

phloem [FLOH•em] Vascular tissue that carries food from leaves to all plant cells (p. 121)

photosynthesis [foht•oh•SIHN•thuh•sis] The process in which plants make food by using water from the soil, carbon dioxide from the air, and energy from sunlight (p. 124)

117

Vascular Plant Parts

Guided Inquiry

Start with Questions

You probably saw many different types of plants on the way to school today.

• How would you classify the plants you saw?

• Do you think this cycad plant has roots? Why or why not?

Investigate to find out. Then read and learn to find out more.

Prepare to Investigate

Inquiry Skill Tip

When you infer, you draw conclusions based on your observations. You should also use information you already know.

Materials

● potted plant
● newspaper
● ruler
● hand lens

Make an Observation Chart

Plant Part	Details	Observations
Leaf	Length: Width:	
Stem	Bend: yes / no (circle one) Branches: yes / no (circle one)	
Roots	Shape: Length:	

Follow This Procedure

1. Hold the potted plant upside down over the newspaper. Tap the pot gently until the plant comes out. Shake the soil from the roots so you can see them clearly.

2. Observe the leaves of the plant. Measure and calculate their average length and width. Use the hand lens to observe the leaves more closely. Record your observations.

3. Observe the stem. Use the hand lens to see it in more detail. Does it bend? Does it have branches? Record your observations.

4. Observe the roots. Notice their shape. Measure and calculate their average length. Use the hand lens to observe them more closely. Record your observations.

5. Make a drawing of the plant. Label all the parts.

6. Put the soil and the plant back into the pot, and water the plant lightly.

Draw Conclusions

1. What did you observe about each part of the plant?

2. **Inquiry Skill** What can you infer about the functions of roots, stems, and leaves?

Step 2

Step 4

Independent Inquiry

Look at a carrot that has its leaves attached. Compare it to the potted plant. Draw a picture of a carrot growing in soil.

VOCABULARY
vascular tissue p. 121
xylem p. 121
phloem p. 121
photosynthesis p. 124

SCIENCE CONCEPTS
▶ how nonvascular plants get water and nutrients
▶ how the parts of vascular plants function

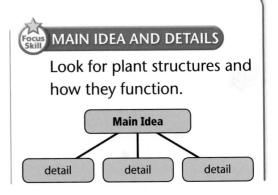

MAIN IDEA AND DETAILS
Look for plant structures and how they function.

Nonvascular and Vascular Plants

Have you ever seen a rock or log covered with a moist, velvety green plant? What you've seen isn't really one plant, but many tiny moss plants.

Mosses are *nonvascular plants*. Nonvascular plants don't have true roots, but they are anchored in the ground by small, rootlike structures. They have parts that look like stems, but these aren't true stems. And they have small, leaflike structures that make food. But they aren't true leaves because they don't have veins. Nonvascular plants don't have any tissue for carrying materials throughout the plant.

Nonvascular plants absorb water and nutrients from their surroundings. Water in the plants carries food and nutrients directly from cell to cell. Because of this, the plants cannot grow very tall. Their small size allows them to absorb enough water to carry materials throughout the plants. When there is not enough water, a nonvascular plant such as moss quickly dries out and turns brown. When it rains, many mosses turn green again.

If you look at moss with a hand lens, you can see individual moss plants. The plants grow close to a surface, allowing all their cells to receive water and nutrients. ▶

Mosses grow on rocks, on trees, and in other places where they can absorb nutrients and moisture.

Trees, like the one shown here, are more complex than mosses. Trees belong to a group called *vascular plants*, which contain vascular tissue. **Vascular tissue** supports plants and carries water and food. Roots, stems, and leaves all contain vascular tissue.

There are two types of vascular tissue. **Xylem** (ZY•luhm) carries water and nutrients from roots to other parts of a plant. **Phloem** (FLOH•em) carries food from leaves to the rest of the plant. With these tissues, vascular plants are not dependent on water moving only from cell to cell, as in mosses.

Vascular plants vary more than nonvascular plants. They include tiny duckweed (a fraction of an inch long) and giant redwood trees. They also include cacti that grow in deserts, which have little water, and orchids that grow in damp rain forests.

MAIN IDEA AND DETAILS

What does each type of vascular tissue do?

Xylem cells in the trunk of a tree transport water. Phloem cells, just under the bark, transport food. Each year, new layers of xylem and phloem cells grow. You can tell the age of a tree by counting the rings of xylem.

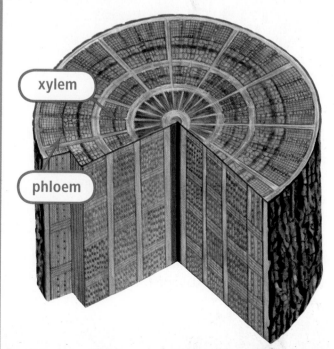

xylem

phloem

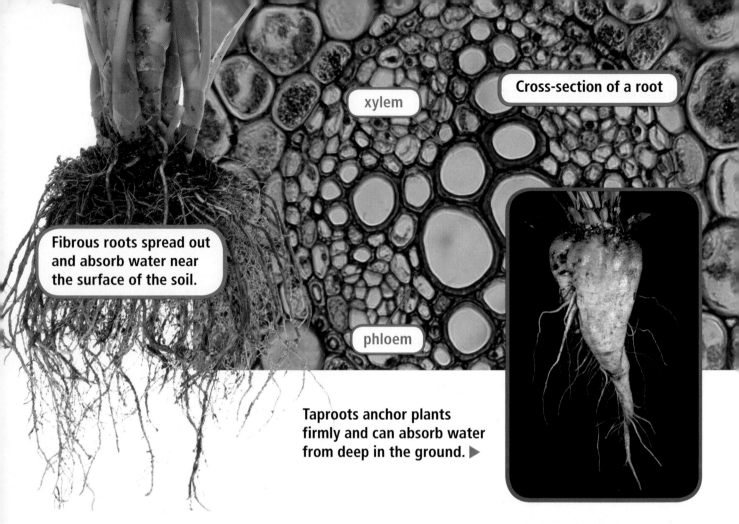

xylem

Cross-section of a root

phloem

Fibrous roots spread out and absorb water near the surface of the soil.

Taproots anchor plants firmly and can absorb water from deep in the ground. ▶

Roots and Stems

Roots absorb water and nutrients from the soil. In the Investigate, when you looked at the roots of the potted plant, you may have noticed the tiny hairs covering them. Root hairs absorb water and nutrients. Xylem cells take the water and nutrients from the root hairs and move them to the stem.

Roots are a plant's anchor and are adapted to the environment and the needs of the plant. A taproot is one large, strong root that pushes deep into the soil. It anchors the plant firmly. Some taproots also store food. The plants use the stored food when they make flowers and fruits. Some taproots store so much food that people use them for food, too. Carrots and beets are examples of plants with large taproots.

Other plants have fibrous roots. Fibrous roots are thin and branching, and they form a mat below the surface of the ground. They spread out and absorb water from a large area, taking in as much as possible.

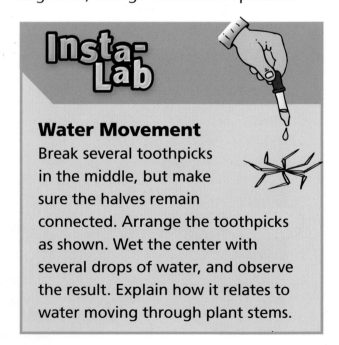

Insta-Lab

Water Movement

Break several toothpicks in the middle, but make sure the halves remain connected. Arrange the toothpicks as shown. Wet the center with several drops of water, and observe the result. Explain how it relates to water moving through plant stems.

The mat of roots holds the plant in the soil and keeps the soil from washing away. Grasses are often used to hold the soil because they have many fibrous roots.

Some roots grow above the ground and help hold a plant upright. The mangrove tree you saw on pages 116 and 117 is one such plant. Corn is another. Roots that grow above the ground are known as prop roots.

Like roots, stems carry water and nutrients. Stems act as pipelines for transporting water and nutrients between roots and leaves. In a stem, as in larger roots, vascular tissue is gathered into bundles. In some plants, the bundles are scattered all through the stem. In trees and many other flowering plants, the bundles are arranged in a ring. You can see these rings in the enlarged view at the right.

Stems also provide support. They usually grow from the ground and hold the leaves up to the sunlight. Trees and other tall plants have woody cells in their stems, making the stems stronger. In plants without woody stems, water pressure holds the stems upright. A droopy stem is a clue that a plant might need water. Some plants, such as cacti, store water and food in fleshy stems.

New plants can grow from some stems. For example, strawberry plants have stems called runners, which grow sideways. New plants grow from the runners.

 **MAIN IDEA AND DETAILS**

What functions do roots perform?

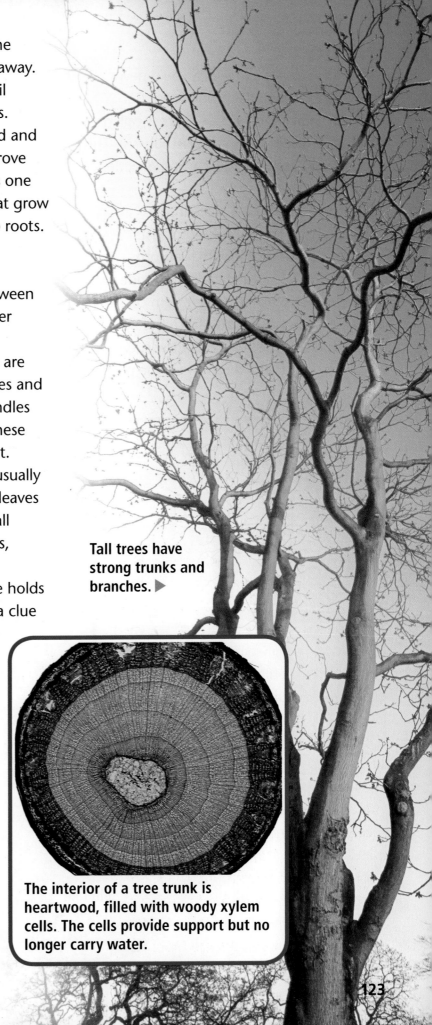

Tall trees have strong trunks and branches. ▶

The interior of a tree trunk is heartwood, filled with woody xylem cells. The cells provide support but no longer carry water.

Leaves

Just from looking at a leaf, you'd never know that it's manufacturing food. But leaves do make food—by a process called **photosynthesis** (foht•oh•SIHN•thuh•sis). This process uses light energy, carbon dioxide, and water to make sugar.

Photosynthesis takes place inside chloroplasts in leaf cells. Chloroplasts contain a green pigment that absorbs sunlight. Leaves get the carbon dioxide for photosynthesis from the air. Xylem cells in leaf veins bring in water from the soil. Phloem cells in the veins carry the sugar from photosynthesis throughout the plant.

Oxygen, a waste product, goes into the air. You will learn more about photosynthesis in another chapter.

The outer layer of cells in a leaf is the *epidermis*. It protects the leaf from damage. Many leaves have a waxy coating on the epidermis. The coating helps keep moisture inside the leaf. Some water does escape through tiny holes, called *stomata*, on the underside of the leaf. Stomata open and close, letting carbon dioxide in and oxygen out. Stomata can also close when water is in short supply.

Focus Skill **MAIN IDEA AND DETAILS** What process takes place in the chloroplasts of leaf cells?

◀ Most leaves are flat, which helps them easily absorb sunlight. Without sunlight, leaves cannot make food.

The green color of a leaf comes from chlorophyll, a green pigment found in chloroplasts. Stomata let carbon dioxide into leaves and let oxygen escape. Xylem in leaf veins brings in water, and phloem carries food throughout the plant. ▼

xylem

phloem

stomata

How Do Plants Grow?

In this lesson, you learned that vascular plants have transport tubes that move water and nutrients through the plant. You also learned that nonvascular plants absorb water and nutrients from their surroundings.

1. 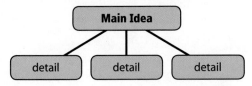 **MAIN IDEA AND DETAILS** Draw and complete a graphic organizer about the details of photosynthesis.

```
        Main Idea

detail     detail     detail
```

2. **SUMMARIZE** Write a one-paragraph summary explaining photosynthesis.

3. **DRAW CONCLUSIONS** You get energy from cereal that you eat. What other sources does food energy come from?

4. **VOCABULARY** Describe two kinds of vascular tissue.

5. **CRITICAL THINKING** Why is it hard to pull all of a plant out of the ground?

6. Which part of a plant lets oxygen exit the leaf?
   A. root hairs
   B. stem
   C. stomata
   D. xylem

Make Connections

 Writing

Narrative Writing
Write a **story** about the travels of a water drop from the soil to a leaf. You might also tell what happens to the water after it gets to the leaf.

 Math

Solve a Problem
Two mature trees can produce enough oxygen for a family of four. A mature tree produces about 118 kg (260 lb) of oxygen a year. About how much oxygen does a person use in a year?

 Art

Draw a Picture
Draw a picture of a tree that you would like to sit under. Label the parts of the tree that are used for photosynthesis.

Investigate two different ways that plants reproduce.

Read and learn about the differences between spores and seeds and about the kinds of plants that have each of these.

Essential Question

How Do Plants Reproduce?

Fast Fact

Yoo-hoo!

The color, smell, and shape of flowers attract pollinators such as insects. Some flowers even look like insects, which lures real insects to land on them! Pollinators help with plant reproduction by transferring sticky pollen between flowers, starting the development of seeds. In the Investigate, you'll observe seeds and other plant parts that help plants reproduce.

Flowers attract pollinators.

spore [SPAWR] A single reproductive cell that can grow into a new plant (p. 130)

gymnosperm [JIM•noh•sperm] A plant that produces naked seeds (p. 132)

angiosperm [AN•jee•oh•sperm] A flowering plant that has seeds protected by fruits (p. 133)

germinate [JER•muh•nayt] To sprout (p. 136)

127

Spores and Seeds

Start with Questions

Plants reproduce by using different parts. Some have seeds. Some have spores. Some have cones. Some have flowers.

- Do you think one way is better for plant reproduction than another? Why or why not?

- How do you think apple trees reproduce?

Investigate to find out. Then read and learn to find out more.

Prepare to Investigate

Inquiry Skill Tip

Don't confuse a hypothesis with an inference or a conclusion. A hypothesis is a testable, possible explanation for observations.

Materials

- fern frond
- hand lens
- white paper
- apple
- plastic knife

Make an Observation Chart

Plant	Observations	Number of Seeds or Spores
Fern		
Apple		

Follow This Procedure

CAUTION: Be careful when handling sharp objects such as knives.

1. **Observe** the fern frond, or leaf. Look at both sides of the frond, using the hand lens.

2. Hold the frond over a sheet of white paper. Rub the underside of the frond so that the contents of the spots on the frond fall onto the paper.

3. **Observe** the paper with the hand lens. There should be one or more clusters of small objects on the paper. Notice if there are dustlike particles on the paper. These particles are spores.

4. **Observe** the apple closely. Use the knife to cut the apple through the middle, vertically. Look at the inside of the apple with the hand lens.

5. Take the seeds out of the apple. **Observe** them with the hand lens. How many seeds are there? **Record** all your observations.

Draw Conclusions

1. How do the seeds of an apple compare to the spores of a fern?

2. **Inquiry Skill** Based on your observations, hypothesize about the function of an apple.

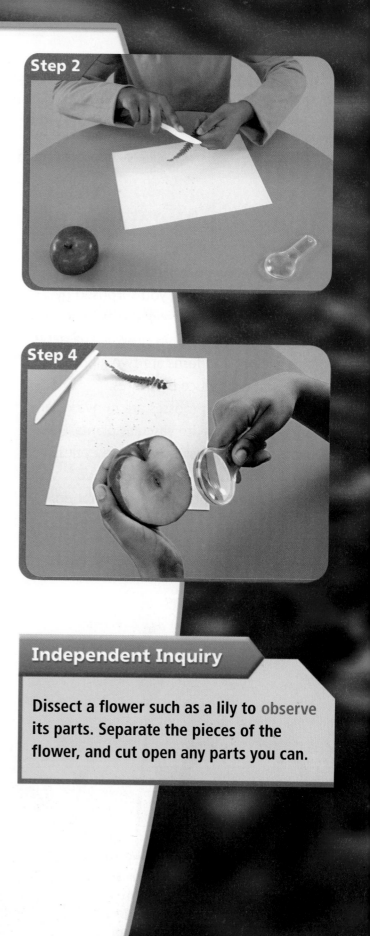

Step 2

Step 4

Independent Inquiry

Dissect a flower such as a lily to observe its parts. Separate the pieces of the flower, and cut open any parts you can.

VOCABULARY

spore p. 130
gymnosperm p. 132
angiosperm p. 133
germinate p. 136

SCIENCE CONCEPTS

▶ how simple plants
and vascular plants
reproduce

▶ how seeds germinate

Focus Skill **COMPARE AND CONTRAST**

Look for differences in
reproductive structures.

[alike]━━━[different]

Simple Plants Reproduce

Most plants reproduce by means of spores
or seeds. When you looked at the spores
in the Investigate, were you surprised by
how tiny they were? A **spore** is a single
reproductive cell that can grow into a new
plant. Mosses and ferns are two kinds of
plants that reproduce by spores.

Remember that mosses are nonvascular
plants, while ferns are vascular plants.
Mosses and ferns have similar life cycles,
though. They both reproduce in two
different generations. In one generation,

called the *sporophyte generation*, the
plants reproduce by spores. In the other
generation, called the *gametophype
generation*, the plants reproduce by gametes,
which are male and female cells.

Although spores can be carried by the
wind, the gametophyte generation needs
a moist environment to reproduce. Male
reproductive cells (gametes), called *sperm*,
swim to the female gametes, called *eggs*.

This close-up of moss shows spore
stalks growing on the parent plants.
The stalks are the sporophytes. The
green plants are the gametophytes.

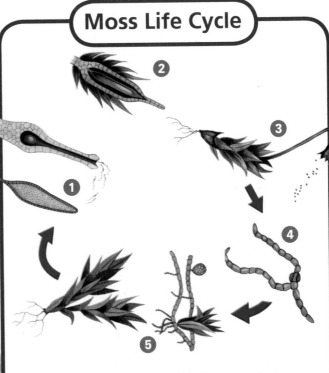

Moss Life Cycle

(1) Spores are released. (2) Gametophytes
grow from spores. (3) Structures on female
gametophytes produce eggs. Structures on
male gametophytes produce sperm. (4) Egg
and sperm join. (5) New sporophyte grows.

Gametes join to form a cell called a *zygote*. This process is known as *fertilization*. A fertilized egg grows into a sporophyte, a plant that reproduces by spores.

You've probably seen moss growing on rocks or logs. The green plants are the moss gametophytes. Moss sporophytes are tall, thin stalks that grow from the gametophytes. The stalks have capsules on top, where the spores are produced. When mature, the capsules pop open, and wind carries away the moss spores.

In ferns, the sporophytes are more visible than the gametophytes. You've probably never even seen a fern gametophyte. They are tiny and grow flat on the ground. After fertilization, a fern sporophyte grows from the gametophyte. Eventually, the sporophyte will outgrow the gametophyte and live on its own.

In the Investigate, you observed the underside of a fern frond. You saw spore cases in clusters. The clusters are called *sori* (SAWR•eye). Sori have springlike devices that toss spores several meters from the frond. Once in the air, the spores can be blown even farther by a light breeze.

Focus Skill COMPARE AND CONTRAST How are fern sporophytes and moss sporophytes different? How are they alike?

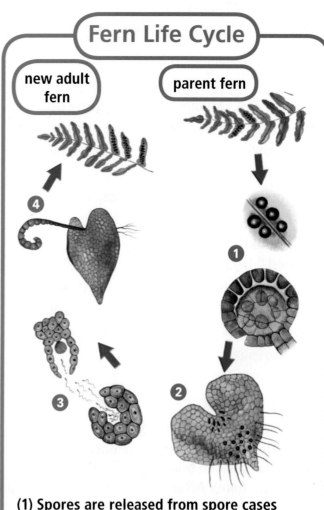

Fern Life Cycle

new adult fern

parent fern

(1) Spores are released from spore cases in sori and grow into tiny, heart-shaped gametophytes. (2) Each gametophyte has both male and female structures. (3) Sperm swim to other gametophytes to fertilize eggs. (4) A fertilized egg develops into a leafy fern plant—the sporophyte. Note: The sporophyte is not drawn to scale. The fern sporophyte is many times larger than the gametophyte.

Notice the clusters of sori on the underside of the frond. Each one is filled with hundreds of spores. ▶

Fern leaves are called fronds. Fronds are usually divided into several leaflets. ▼

131

Seed-Bearing Plants

Have you ever seen a pine tree with cones hanging from its branches? If so, you were looking at a vascular plant that grew from a seed. The cones that you saw probably contained more seeds. Seeds enable plants to grow in many environments. Unlike plants that reproduce by spores, seed plants don't need water for fertilization.

The seeds of pines are considered "naked," because they are protected only by a seed coat. This is in contrast to seeds that are protected inside a fruit. A plant that produces naked seeds is classified as a **gymnosperm** (JIM•noh•sperm).

You might have seen male pinecones covered with yellow *pollen.* Pollen contains sperm. Female cones are larger and grow high on trees, above the male cones. *Ovules* grow on the scales of female cones. Ovules contain eggs.

Mature male cones release millions of pollen grains. They look like a golden dust cloud as they're blown by the wind. Some pollen settles on ovules. Sperm from the pollen fertilize the eggs, and then seeds develop.

When the seeds are mature, the cone scales separate and the seeds, which have wings, travel on the wind. If a seed lands in a suitable habitat, a new tree begins to grow. Then a new life cycle begins.

Pollen is produced in male cones. Ovules are produced at the bases of the scales in female cones (shown here). After fertilization, seeds develop on the scales. ▼

▲ **Seeds stay attached to the scales of a female cone. When the cone is mature, the scales open and the seeds are released.**

▲ When a fruit tree is in bloom, insects go to it and pollinate the flowers. Sperm in the pollen of one flower can fertilize the eggs in other flowers. The eggs become seeds, and the flowers grow fruit around them.

Gymnosperms are very different from flowering plants, such as apple trees. Apple trees have flowers instead of cones. Flowers produce seeds inside fruit. A flowering plant, which has seeds protected by a fruit, is classified as an **angiosperm** (AN•jee•oh•sperm).

Seed development is more complex in angiosperms. Their protected seeds have made it possible for angiosperms to live in nearly all parts of the world.

 COMPARE AND CONTRAST

How are gymnosperm seeds and angiosperm seeds different? How are they alike?

Math in Science
Interpret Data

Numbers of Plant Species

This circle graph shows the number of species of flowering plants compared to the number of all other plant species. What might you infer from the data about the success of flowering plants compared to other types of plants?

Comparing Types of Plants

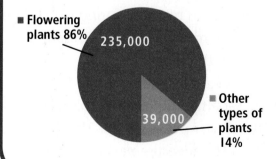

- Flowering plants 86% 235,000
- Other types of plants 14% 39,000

For more links and animations, go to **www.hspscience.com**

Inside a Flower

Look inside a flower to see the parts that work together to make seeds.

Stigma—collects pollen

Anther—makes pollen

Ovary—contains ovules. After fertilization, the ovary develops into a fruit.

Ovules—produce eggs. Eggs are fertilized by sperm from pollen and develop into seeds.

Petals—attract insects for pollination.

Pollen tube—grows from pollen grain. The tube enables sperm to travel into ovules to fertilize eggs.

Flowers to Seeds

On pine trees, male and female cones are separate. But in many flowering plants, the male and female reproductive organs are together in the same flower.

Flowers start as buds protected by leaflike sepals. In time, the sepals drop back and the flower petals unfold. The petals are often like advertisements for flowers.

They lure animals to the flowers with their colors, making it more likely that the animals will transfer pollen. Many flowers also have attractive scents. Sometimes the scents attract certain animals even though people might think the scents are pretty bad. Flowers also make sugary nectar that attracts and feeds insects and birds. If you stand in a field of wildflowers, you'll probably see bees flying between flowers.

Bees feed on flowers' sugary nectar. As a bee crawls into a flower to get nectar, pollen sticks to the bee's hairy legs. The pollen is from some of the flower's male parts called *anthers*. In the center of a flower is a female part called the *stigma*. When a bee goes into another flower, some of the pollen on its legs clings to the sticky top of the stigma.

After fertilization, a tiny plant called an *embryo* develops in the ovule. An embryo has a root and one or two leaves. The ovule wall develops into a protective seed coat, and the ovary becomes the fruit.

Insta-Lab

Cool Beans
Your teacher will give you a bean that has been soaking in water. The bean is a seed. Take it out of the water and break it open. Observe it with a hand lens. Hypothesize how the parts of the seed help it grow.

Fruits that attract seed-eating birds are small enough to fit in a beak. Birds can carry seeds far away from the plants that produced them. ▼

Different fruits are specialized in ways that help with seed dispersal, or the spread of seeds. Have you ever had a burr stuck to you? Burrs are fruits that are adapted to stick. The large fruit of a coconut is adapted to float on water. Many fruits can be eaten by animals. The animals then deposit the seeds on the soil.

Focus Skill COMPARE AND CONTRAST What are the differences between pollen transfer in a pine tree and in many flowering plants?

Fruits of some seeds are carried by wind. Some have wings. Others, like this dandelion, have structures like little parachutes. ▼

Seed Germination

Seeds are adapted so that they **germinate**, or sprout, when conditions are right for growth of the embryo. A thick, hard seed coat protects the embryo until the seed germinates. Sometimes seeds stay in the ground for several years before conditions are right for growth.

The timing of seed germination depends on the needs of the plant. Some seeds germinate when there are enough hours of light. Most need to have warm soil, a condition that happens in the spring. Seeds also need water.

When the time is right, a seed absorbs water and expands. This breaks the seed coat, and the embryo begins growing. First, the root emerges from the seed and begins to anchor the embryo and take up water. Then, a shoot pushes up.

The leaves of an embryo can't make food as the leaves of a mature plant do. But the embryo needs energy to grow. Where does the energy come from? When you opened a lima-bean seed, you saw structures around the embryo. These structures, called *cotyledons* (kaht•uh•LEE•duhnz), contain food that provides energy until the plant can make its own food.

When the first leaves emerge from the ground, they turn green, as chlorophyll for photosynthesis is produced. Rapid growth begins, and the embryo becomes a plant seedling.

Focus Skill **COMPARE AND CONTRAST**

How do the leaves of an embryo differ from the leaves of a mature plant?

A seed with a tiny embryo inside remains in the ground until conditions are right for the seed to germinate.

After the seed coat splits, the embryo root begins to grow down into the soil. Now the embryo can get water.

Food in the seed feeds the embryo as the shoot grows up toward the light.

The stem grows, leaves develop, and roots spread in the soil. Now the seedling can make its own food.

Essential Question

How Do Plants Reproduce?

In this lesson, you learned that most plants reproduce by using either spores or seeds. You also learned some of the characteristics of seed-bearing plants and how flowers help some plants reproduce.

1.  **COMPARE AND CONTRAST**
Draw and complete a graphic organizer comparing and contrasting mosses, ferns, gymnosperms, and angiosperms.

```
  alike  ----  different
```

2. **SUMMARIZE** Write a one-paragraph summary of the process of seed germination.

3. **DRAW CONCLUSIONS** Why do ferns produce so many spores? Why don't flowering plants produce as many seeds?

4. **VOCABULARY** Provide the terms that complete this sentence: *Gymnosperm is to _____ as _____ is to flower.* Think of similar sentences to use in a game.

Test Prep

5. **CRITICAL THINKING** What time of year would be best for planting bean seeds? Why?

6. In which structure do seeds develop?
   A. anther   **C.** pollen grain
   B. ovary   **D.** spore

Make Connections

 Writing

 Math

 Language Arts

Expository Writing
Write a paragraph that **explains** how you use plants every day. Write about both gymnosperms and angiosperms.

Display Data
Read the directions on several seed packets to find out how long it takes for the seeds to germinate. Make a bar graph comparing the germination times of the seeds.

Word Origins
Research the origins of the words for the two seed-plant groups—*gymnosperms* and *angiosperms*. Share your findings with the class.

Farms of the Future

Could you grow a garden in your bathroom? Is it possible to have a farm without soil? It might sound like something from the future, but that kind of growing is happening today with *hydroponics*. Hydroponics is the growing of plants in nutrient-rich solutions.

Growing in Water

Hydroponic farming has been around for many years. Researchers are now using hydroponics to develop new techniques to grow food quickly, in an environmentally safe way.

With hydroponics, plant roots grow directly in water and are supported by materials such as peat moss, sand, or gravel. Nutrients are added to the water to imitate the nutrients plants would normally get out of soil. Soil is not needed. And hydroponic plants grow about twice as fast as plants grown in soil.

New Techniques

Today, researchers are finding new ways to use hydroponics. Scientists in New Mexico, for example, are showing that hydroponics can work in a desert environment by growing alfalfa plants. They have shown that less water is needed to grow hydroponic food than to grow the same amount of food in soil. That is important.

Hydroponic flowers

Growing and packing hydroponic lettuce

Hydroponic lettuce

Many parts of the world, where water is hard to find, could benefit from hydroponics.

Hydroponic farming is also helping Florida's beaches. When hurricanes hit Florida, they erode the sand on the beaches. Researchers grow plants called sea oats hydroponically and then transplant the sea oats to beaches. The sea oats trap sand and help restore beaches. Because hydroponic plants grow very quickly, researchers can grow and replant the sea oats as a way to preserve beaches.

More Healthful Food?

Many researchers and hydroponic farmers believe that hydroponics is the farming method of the future. In addition to saving water, hydroponically farmed fruits and vegetables are more healthful to eat because the plants receive a well-balanced diet in their water.

The nutrient-filled water helps give the fruits and vegetables vitamins and minerals, which are passed on to people who eat them. Fruits and vegetables grown in soil get their nutrients from the land, but pollution and chemicals in the soil can limit the amount of nutrients the plants receive.

Think and Write

1 How are hydroponic plants and plants grown in soil different?

2 Do you think hydroponic plants might taste different from plants grown in soil? Why or why not?

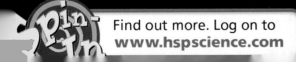

Find out more. Log on to
www.hspscience.com

Vocabulary Review

Use the terms below to complete the sentences. The page numbers tell you where to look in the chapter if you need help.

vascular tissue p. 121

xylem p. 121

phloem p. 121

photosynthesis p. 124

spore p. 130

gymnosperm p. 132

angiosperm p. 133

germinate p. 136

1. A single reproductive cell that can grow into a new plant is a _____.

2. A plant with naked seeds is a _____.

3. Water is transported in vascular tissue called _____.

4. When the ground is warm and wet, a seed can sprout, or _____.

5. A plant with flowers and protected seeds is an _____.

6. Plants produce food by _____.

7. Food is transported in vascular tissue called _____.

8. Conducting tubes are made of _____.

Check Understanding

Write the letter of the best choice.

9. Which one of these plants is a nonvascular plant?
   A. cactus   **C.** moss
   B. fern   **D.** pine

10. Which type of tissue is the arrow pointing to?

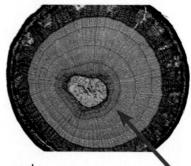

   F. cork
   G. dogwood
   H. phloem
   J. xylem

11. Which is a product of photosynthesis?

   A. carbon dioxide
   B. nitrogen
   C. sugar
   D. water

12. MAIN IDEA Which part of a flower makes the fruit?

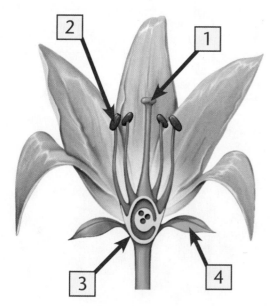

F. 1　　　H. 3
G. 2　　　J. 4

13. COMPARE AND CONTRAST Kris is allergic to pollen. Which of these plants should she avoid?

A. fern　　　C. moss
B. frond　　　D. pine

14. Which kind of plant would you choose to attract butterflies to your garden?

F. angiosperm
G. fern
H. gymnosperm
J. moss

15. Where does a seed develop in a pine tree?

A. in an ovule
B. on a scale
C. in an ovary
D. on a leaf

16. On a trip through the desert, Tim saw many plants like the one shown below.

Which kind of roots would you expect to find on this plant?

F. aerial　　　H. prop
G. fibrous　　　J. tap

Inquiry Skills

17. Hypothesize what would happen to a nonvascular plant if it grew too tall.

18. Angiosperms from one continent can be found growing on other continents. **Infer** how this can happen.

Critical Thinking

19. A hill behind your house is washing away. What kind of plant might help keep the soil in place? Tell why.

20. Trees and shrubs benefit people in many ways. How can trees reduce the amount of carbon dioxide in the atmosphere?

Animal Growth and Heredity

What's the Big Idea?

Animal characteristics are passed from parents to their children. Characteristics are either learned or inherited.

Essential Questions

Lesson 1

How Does Cell Division Affect Growth?

Lesson 2

How Are Characteristics Inherited?

Lesson 3

What Other Factors Affect Characteristics?

GO online

Student eBook
www.hspscience.com

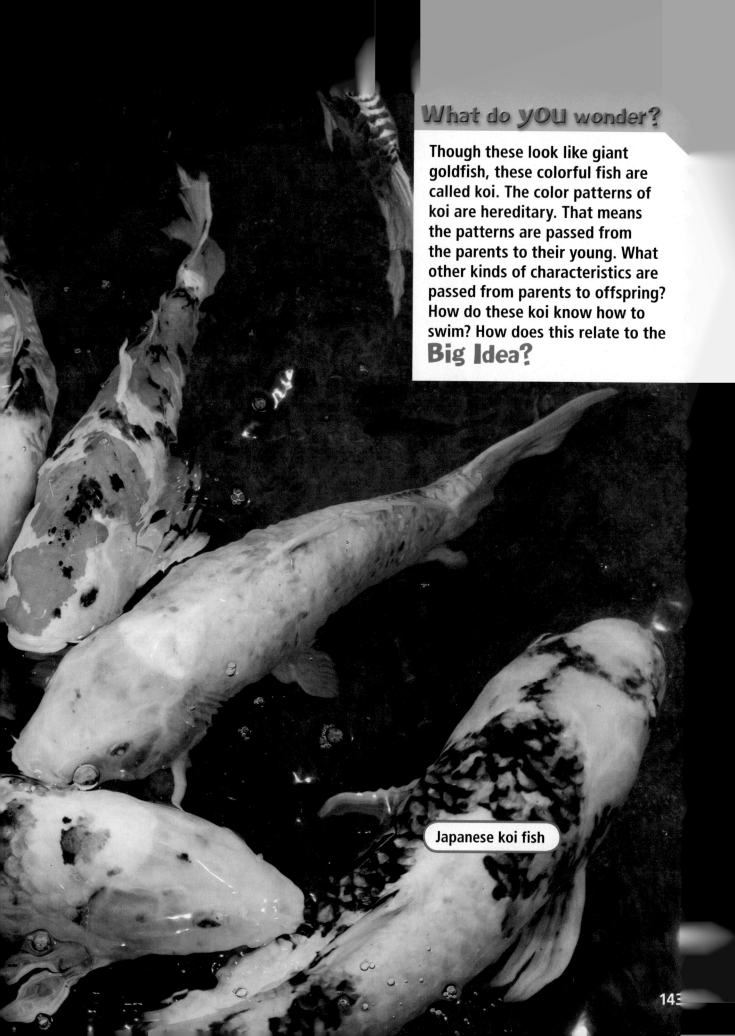

What do YOU wonder?

Though these look like giant goldfish, these colorful fish are called koi. The color patterns of koi are hereditary. That means the patterns are passed from the parents to their young. What other kinds of characteristics are passed from parents to offspring? How do these koi know how to swim? How does this relate to the

Big Idea?

Japanese koi fish

Essential Question

How Does Cell Division Affect Growth?

Investigate cell division and reproduction.

Read and learn how organisms grow and develop, and about the process of mitosis.

Fast Fact

Doubling Up

When a cell divides, the two new cells are identical to the original cell. Some single-celled organisms, such as certain bacteria, can divide as often as every 30 minutes. In 5 hours, a bacterial cell can become 1024 cells! In the Investigate, you'll see how different types of cells divide.

life cycle [LYF SY•kuhl] The stages that a living thing passes through as it grows and changes (p. 149)

mitosis [my•TOH•sis] The process by which most cells divide (p. 150)

chromosome [KROH•muh•sohm] A threadlike structure in the nucleus, made up of DNA (p. 150)

Animal-cell division

Cell Reproduction

Guided Inquiry

Start with Questions

You know that cells are the basis for all life.

- How do cells reproduce and grow into animals and plants?

- Did this boy and this puppy develop in a similar way?

Investigate to find out. Then read and learn to find out more.

Prepare to Investigate

Inquiry Skill Tip

When you observe details during an investigation, you should think and act as a detective would. Notice how properties have changed and what caused these changes.

Materials

- prepared slide of plant mitosis
- prepared slide of animal mitosis
- microscope

Make an Observation Chart

Plant Mitosis   Animal Mitosis

Follow This Procedure

1. Put the plant mitosis slide on the microscope stage. Focus until you see cells clearly. Observe the cells that show division.

2. Make drawings to record what you see in different cells.

3. Replace the plant mitosis slide with the animal mitosis slide. Observe the cells that show division.

4. Make drawings to record what you see in different cells.

5. Compare your drawings of plant cell division with your drawings of animal cell division. How are they alike? How are they different? Record your comparisons.

Draw Conclusions

1. What part of a cell changes as the cell divides? What changes take place?

2. How many new cells does each cell division produce?

3. **Inquiry Skill** Scientists observe and ask questions, based on their observations. What questions do you have about cell division, based on your own observations?

Step 1

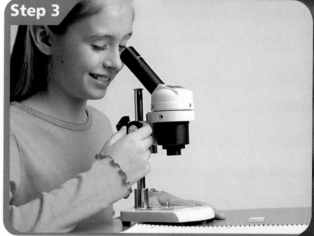

Step 3

Independent Inquiry

Now that you've observed cells dividing, make models showing the stages of cell division.

VOCABULARY
life cycle p. 149
mitosis p. 150
chromosome p. 150

SCIENCE CONCEPTS
▶ how cells that already exist make new cells
▶ how cell division helps organisms grow

Focus Skill MAIN IDEA AND DETAILS
Look for details about how cell division helps organisms grow.

Main Idea

detail   detail   detail

Growth and Development

All organisms start life as a single cell. In plants and animals, the cell then begins dividing. The one cell divides into two cells. The two cells divide into four cells, and so on. By the time a plant or an animal is complete, its body is made up of trillions of cells.

Even in a complete organism, like you, cells continue to divide. Your bone cells divide, building more bone tissue. Your skin cells divide, producing new skin tissue. You grow and change.

Sometimes the changes are obvious. For example, you get taller and outgrow your clothes. But sometimes you can't see the changes, especially when they happen to tissues inside the body. By the time you're an adult, your body will be made up of about 100 trillion cells!

As you know, each type of cell has a special function. During cell division, most body cells make exact copies of themselves. When bone cells divide, they make new bone cells. When muscle cells divide, they make new muscle cells. The new cells have the same functions as the old cells. This enables body organs and systems to function properly as you grow.

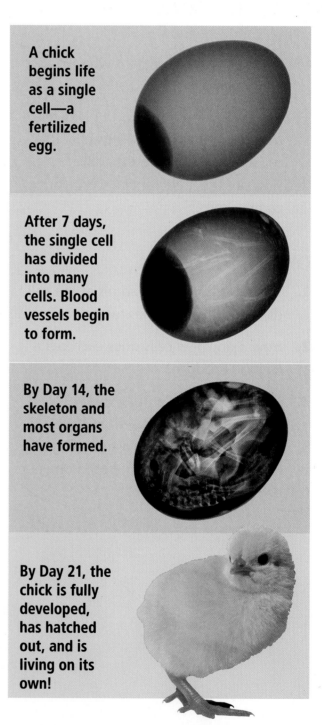

A chick begins life as a single cell—a fertilized egg.

After 7 days, the single cell has divided into many cells. Blood vessels begin to form.

By Day 14, the skeleton and most organs have formed.

By Day 21, the chick is fully developed, has hatched out, and is living on its own!

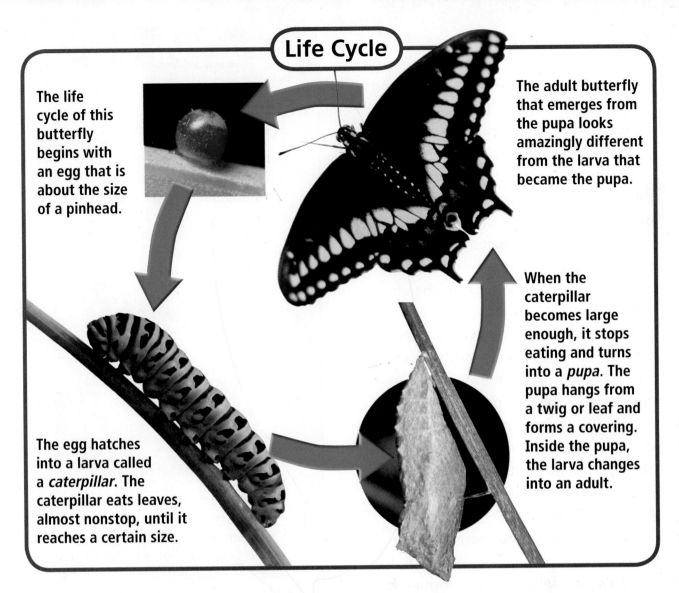

Life Cycle

The life cycle of this butterfly begins with an egg that is about the size of a pinhead.

The adult butterfly that emerges from the pupa looks amazingly different from the larva that became the pupa.

When the caterpillar becomes large enough, it stops eating and turns into a *pupa*. The pupa hangs from a twig or leaf and forms a covering. Inside the pupa, the larva changes into an adult.

The egg hatches into a larva called a *caterpillar*. The caterpillar eats leaves, almost nonstop, until it reaches a certain size.

As living things grow and develop, most pass through several stages. These stages make up an organism's **life cycle**. A life cycle begins with a fertilized egg. Some animals develop inside their mothers' bodies. Then they are born. Others develop inside a protective egg, and then hatch out.

Some organisms, like bacteria and protists, are mature as soon as they are formed. They can reproduce immediately. Others, such as mammals, spend months or years growing and developing before reaching maturity.

Some animals change a great deal as they mature. Animals such as butterflies and frogs actually have one kind of body when they're young and a very different kind of body when they're mature. The changes they undergo as they grow and mature are called *metamorphosis*.

Other animals do not change much during their lives. The young are smaller than the adults, but otherwise look pretty much like the adults. Mammals, birds, reptiles, and most fish have this kind of development.

A life cycle starts with a fertilized egg. The organism grows and matures. Eventually it reproduces, and a new life cycle starts.

 MAIN IDEA AND DETAILS

How does cell division help organisms grow?

Cell Division

The process by which most cells divide is called **mitosis** (my•TOH•sis). What makes it happen? Scientists aren't completely sure what triggers it. But they know that the process is directed by the nucleus.

The nucleus contains threadlike structures called **chromosomes**, which are made up of a complex chemical called *DNA*. DNA carries a code in its structure. The DNA code has all the information that directs how a cell functions, including when to divide.

Before mitosis begins, an exact copy of each chromosome is made, producing a pair. During mitosis, the identical chromosomes of each pair separate, resulting in two sets that are identical to the original chromosomes. The sets pull apart. Then the cell membrane pinches in the middle, forming two new cells. Each cell is just like its parent cell.

Have you ever skinned your elbow or knee? Almost immediately, cells in the area started mitosis. New skin cells formed to replace the lost tissue. Soon the scrape disappeared, and your skin was smooth and complete again. This process of replacing tissue is called *regeneration*.

In humans, regeneration is limited to healing wounds. But in some animals, regeneration can replace entire body parts. For example, if a sea star loses an arm, nearby cells undergo rapid mitosis. Soon the sea star has a new arm.

Mitosis

In mitosis, each new cell gets a copy of the parent cell's chromosomes. This passes along the DNA code. The new cells look and function just like the parent cell.

▲ Before a cell starts mitosis, its chromosomes make copies of themselves. Each original and its copy are joined. The cell now has enough DNA for *two* cells.

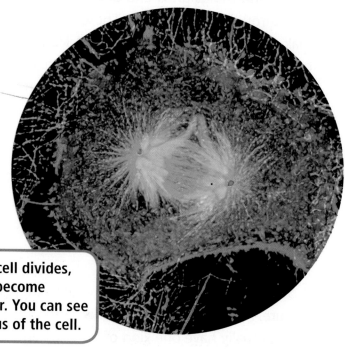

Before an animal cell divides, its chromosomes become shorter and thicker. You can see them in the nucleus of the cell.

150

▼ As cell division starts, the membrane around the nucleus disappears. The chromosomes become shorter and thicker. Centrioles form at the cell's poles.

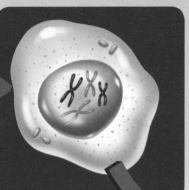

◄ The members of the chromosome pairs separate. One member of each pair moves to one side of the cell, and the other member moves to the opposite side of the cell.

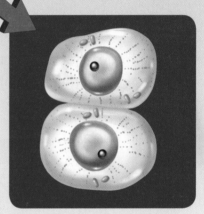

A *spindle* made of thin tubes forms across the cell. The chromosome pairs—with the members of each pair still joined— line up along the center of the spindle. ▶

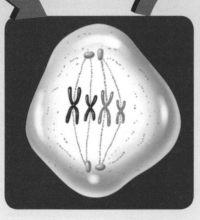

After the chromosomes separate, the spindle breaks down. Each set of chromosomes becomes enclosed by a new nuclear membrane. Finally, the cell membrane pinches in two. ▶

You know that many organisms have only one cell. When the cell divides, the whole organism reproduces. This process is called *asexual reproduction* because there is no joining of cells from different parents. For example, yeast is a single-celled fungus that reproduces when a tiny bud forms on a parent cell. Mitosis takes place in the cell, and a copy of its chromosomes is passed into the growing bud. When the bud is fully grown, it breaks off and begins living on its own.

MAIN IDEA AND DETAILS

Why do members of chromosome pairs separate during mitosis?

Insta-Lab

Separating Chromosomes

Use two 10-cm pieces of thread to represent chromosomes. Starting at one end, pull apart one of the threads into two threads. Now pull apart the other original thread, but start at the middle. How do you think chromosomes separate during cell division?

Reproduction

Most multicellular organisms reproduce by the joining of cells from two different individuals. This is called *sexual reproduction*. Cells from each parent join, forming a fertilized egg, or *zygote* (ZY•goht). A zygote receives chromosomes from each parent.

It's important for a zygote to contain the right number of chromosomes. The cells of every organism have a specific number of chromosomes. If they have too many or too few, the cells don't work properly.

Organisms that reproduce sexually have two types of cells—body cells and reproductive cells, or *gametes* (GAM•eets). Gametes contain only half the number of chromosomes of body cells. When two gametes join, the zygote has the same number of chromosomes as body cells.

Gametes are formed during a process called *meiosis* (my•OH•sis). During meiosis, the number of chromosomes in a cell is divided in half. For example, human body cells have 46 chromosomes. Each human gamete has 23 chromosomes.

Meiosis occurs in two stages. During the first stage, the chromosomes are copied and the cell divides. In the second stage, the two new cells divide again, *without* copying their chromosomes. So, each of the four new cells—the gametes—has only half the number of chromosomes that body cells have.

Focus Skill **MAIN IDEA AND DETAILS**

Why must gametes contain half the number of chromosomes that body cells have?

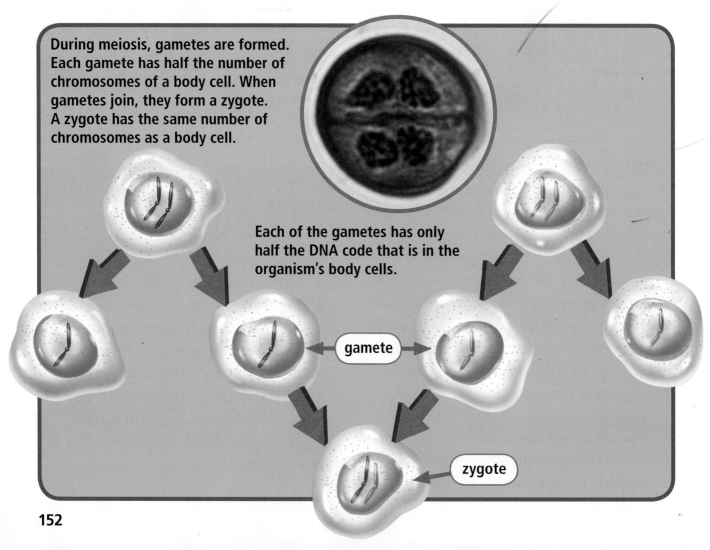

During meiosis, gametes are formed. Each gamete has half the number of chromosomes of a body cell. When gametes join, they form a zygote. A zygote has the same number of chromosomes as a body cell.

Each of the gametes has only half the DNA code that is in the organism's body cells.

gamete

zygote

Essential Question

How Does Cell Division Affect Growth?

In this lesson, you learned that living things grow and develop and go through life cycles. You also learned that cells divide and form new cells that are identical to the parent cells.

1. 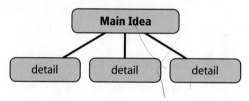 **MAIN IDEA AND DETAILS** Draw and complete a graphic organizer that shows the functions of mitosis.

2. **SUMMARIZE** Write a three- or four-sentence summary describing an animal life cycle.

3. **DRAW CONCLUSIONS** If an organism has 12 chromosomes in its body cells, how many chromosomes do its gametes and zygotes have?

4. **VOCABULARY** Without looking back in this lesson, write a definition for each vocabulary term: *life cycle, mitosis, chromosome.*

Test Prep

5. **CRITICAL THINKING** Why are chromosomes duplicated before mitosis?

6. During mitosis, which part of the cell pinches in to make a new cell?
   A. cell membrane   **C.** cytoplasm
   B. cell wall   **D.** nucleus

Make Connections

 Writing

Expository Writing
Suppose you're a science writer for a newspaper. Write a **descriptive article** detailing the process of mitosis.

 Math

Display Data
Use library or Internet resources to find out the number of chromosomes in the body cells of five different animals. Make a bar graph to compare the numbers. Which animal has the most? The least?

 Health

Mutations
Sometimes, changes occur during the copying of chromosomes. The results are called *genetic mutations.* Use library or Internet resources to identify a genetic mutation. Tell classmates what you learned.

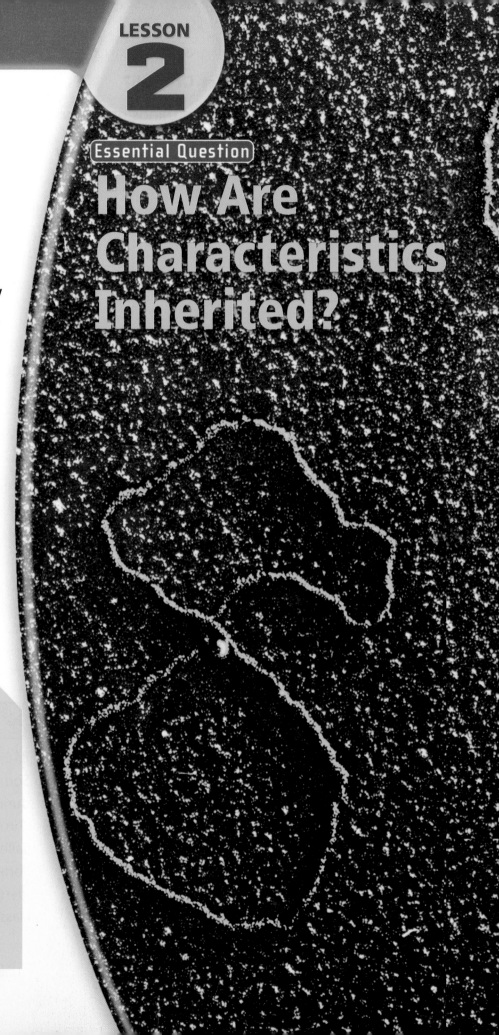

Investigate the inherited characteristics shared by students in your class.

Read and learn how certain characteristics are inherited from parents, and how these characteristics help organisms survive and reproduce.

Essential Question

How Are Characteristics Inherited?

Fast Fact

The Code of Life

These strands of DNA look oddly twisted. But they contain all the information that cells need to carry out life processes and pass on traits. You'll learn about some inherited traits in the Investigate.

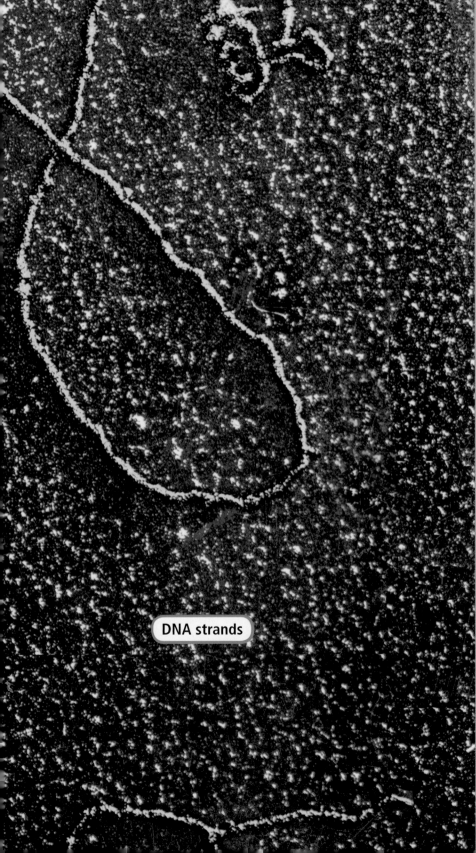

DNA strands

inherited trait [in•HAIR•it•ed TRAYT] A characteristic passed from parents to their offspring (p. 158)

dominant trait [DAHM•uh•nuhnt TRAYT] A trait that appears even if an organism has only one factor for the trait (p. 160)

recessive trait [rih•SES•iv TRAYT] A trait that appears only if an organism has two factors for the trait (p. 160)

gene [JEEN] The part of a chromosome that contains the DNA code for an inherited trait (p. 166)

Inherited Characteristics

Guided Inquiry

Start with Questions

Some people can roll their tongue and some can't.

- Why do you think this is so?

- Does this family share certain traits?

Investigate to find out. Then read and learn to find out more.

Prepare to Investigate

Inquiry Skill Tip

When you think about what you can infer from your investigation, first consider your observations. How can you explain them? Try to interpret them based on your knowledge.

Materials

- mirror

Make an Observation Chart

Characteristic	Result (circle one)		Class Totals
Tongue rolling	yes	no	
Earlobes	attached	free	
Folded hands	left	right	

Follow This Procedure

1. Make a table like the one shown.

2. Stick out your tongue, and try to roll its edges up, toward the middle. Use the mirror to help you make your observation. Record the result in the table.

3. Use the mirror to observe the shape of your earlobes. Are they attached to your face, or do they hang free? Record the result in the table.

4. Fold your hands in front of you. Observe which of your thumbs falls naturally on top. Record the result in the table.

5. Your teacher will now ask all students to report their results. Tally the results in the table as students report them. Then find the number of students who have each trait. Use numbers to calculate the fraction of the class that has each trait. Then make a graph of the class results.

Draw Conclusions

1. Which trait in each pair occurred more often in your class?

2. **Inquiry Skill** Scientists often infer an idea after making observations. Infer whether a person could learn to roll his or her tongue. Explain.

Step 2

Step 4

Independent Inquiry

Predict **whether the results will be the same for another group. Then** gather data **to test your prediction.**

VOCABULARY
inherited trait p. 158
dominant trait p. 160
recessive trait p. 160
gene p. 166

SCIENCE CONCEPTS
▶ how certain characteristics are passed from parents to their young
▶ how genes influence inherited traits

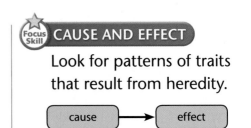

CAUSE AND EFFECT
Look for patterns of traits that result from heredity.

cause ➔ effect

How Characteristics Are Inherited

You may have a friend who looks a lot like her parents. She may share her mother's eye color and dimples or have the same type of hair or skin color as her father. These and many other traits are inherited. An **inherited trait** is a characteristic passed from parents to their offspring.

In humans, hair color, eye color, and skin color are inherited. Freckles, hair texture, and earlobe shape are inherited, too. So are some behaviors. For example, the tendency to be right-handed or left-handed is inherited.

In animals, eye color is inherited. So are fur color and texture. Each of the puppies in the picture on this page inherited some traits from its parents, including facial shape and hair texture. All the puppies have faces that are the same shape, and all have similar hair texture. The puppies are not identical, though. One puppy doesn't look much like its parents. But its fur color was inherited.

For thousands of years, farmers have selected animals through breeding. They've bred animals having some desirable traits with animals having other desirable traits so that the offspring would have these traits, too. Farmers knew that traits were passed from parents to their offspring. But they didn't know how.

The way traits are passed from parents to offspring interested Gregor Mendel.

Most of the puppies in this litter look like the parents. But even the one that looks different inherited many of its parents' traits. ▼

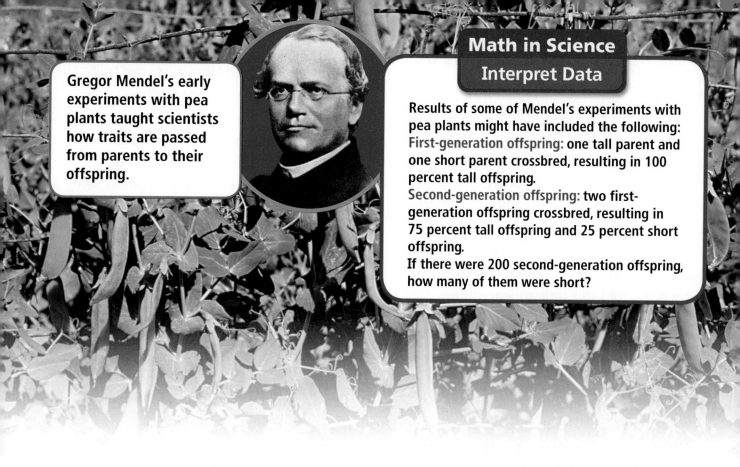

Gregor Mendel's early experiments with pea plants taught scientists how traits are passed from parents to their offspring.

Math in Science
Interpret Data

Results of some of Mendel's experiments with pea plants might have included the following:
First-generation offspring: one tall parent and one short parent crossbred, resulting in 100 percent tall offspring.
Second-generation offspring: two first-generation offspring crossbred, resulting in 75 percent tall offspring and 25 percent short offspring.
If there were 200 second-generation offspring, how many of them were short?

Mendel was a nineteenth-century Austrian monk. His work in a monastery garden made him want to understand how traits are inherited. Mendel noticed that some pea plants were tall and others were short. He thought that these traits were inherited, but he didn't know how. In 1857, he began experimenting.

First, he bred tall pea plants with short pea plants. All the offspring—the first generation—were tall. When these tall plants were allowed to breed, three-fourths of the offspring—the second generation— were tall. But one-fourth were short. These results led Mendel to hypothesize that a characteristic is controlled by a pair of *factors*. Each parent passes one of its pair of factors to an offspring. The way the factors combine in the offspring controls which trait appears in each individual.

Mendel learned that traits can skip a generation. As shown above, when he bred tall plants with short plants, the offspring were all tall. But short plants appeared again in the second generation. Inheritance in all organisms, including people, works this way. You can inherit a trait—blue eyes, for example—that neither of your parents shows, as long as people before them in your family had that trait.

Focus Skill **CAUSE AND EFFECT** Why are some pea plants short, while others are tall?

Thanks to the work of Gregor Mendel, we know that this child inherited her deep-blue eyes from her parents, even though they both have brown eyes! ▶

Dominant and Recessive Traits

Mendel did hundreds of experiments and kept careful records of his results. Again and again, he found that first-generation offspring of tall plants and short plants were tall, but second-generation offspring included about one-fourth short plants. He hypothesized that the first-generation plants must have a hidden factor for shortness. How else could this trait appear in the second generation?

In pea plants, tallness is a strong trait, or a **dominant trait**. If an organism has one factor for a dominant trait, that trait appears. Shortness in pea plants is a weak trait, or a **recessive trait**. A recessive trait appears only if an organism has two factors for the trait. If both a dominant factor and a recessive factor are present, the dominant trait appears. This explains why three-fourths of Mendel's second-generation pea plants were tall. Plants with one or two factors for tallness were tall. Only plants with two factors for shortness were short.

Look at the example about fur color in mice. Three of the offspring are dark brown, and one is light brown. Both parents have dark brown fur, which is dominant. For light brown fur to appear, both parents must have a factor for light brown fur.

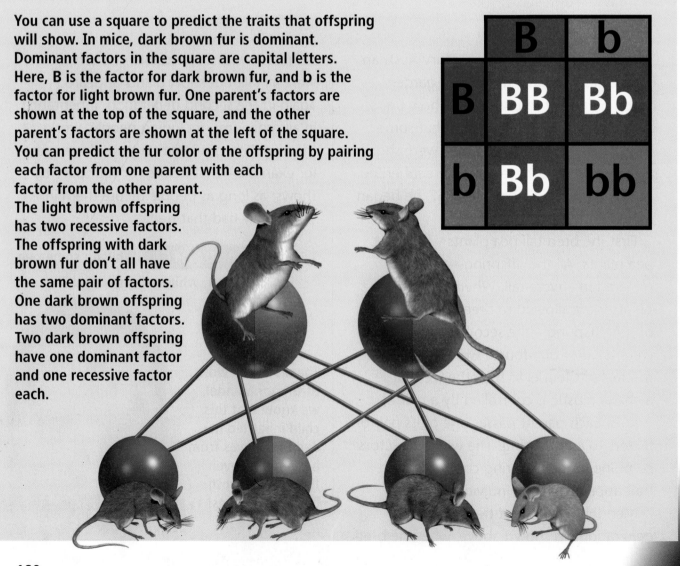

You can use a square to predict the traits that offspring will show. In mice, dark brown fur is dominant. Dominant factors in the square are capital letters. Here, **B** is the factor for dark brown fur, and **b** is the factor for light brown fur. One parent's factors are shown at the top of the square, and the other parent's factors are shown at the left of the square. You can predict the fur color of the offspring by pairing each factor from one parent with each factor from the other parent.

The light brown offspring has two recessive factors. The offspring with dark brown fur don't all have the same pair of factors. One dark brown offspring has two dominant factors. Two dark brown offspring have one dominant factor and one recessive factor each.

	B	b
B	BB	Bb
b	Bb	bb

In humans, having blue eyes is a recessive trait. Can two brown-eyed parents have a child with blue eyes? Yes, but they must both have a hidden factor for blue eyes.

In the Investigate at the beginning of this lesson, you observed several inherited traits. The ability to roll your tongue is a dominant trait. If you can roll your tongue, you inherited either two dominant factors (one from each parent) or one dominant factor and one recessive factor. If you aren't able to roll your tongue, you inherited two recessive factors (one from each parent).

Unattached earlobes are dominant, and attached earlobes are recessive. If your earlobes are unattached, you inherited at least one dominant factor. If you have attached earlobes, you inherited two recessive factors.

Even though right-handedness is dominant, most people rest the left thumb on top when they fold their hands. Resting the left thumb on top is dominant. If you rest your right thumb on top, what factors did you inherit?

(Focus Skill) CAUSE AND EFFECT What are the possible results of breeding a dark brown mouse with a light brown mouse?

◀ Most dogs have fur, but this dog has hardly any! It inherited a recessive factor for hairlessness from each of its parents.

Insta-Lab

Heads or Tails
Toss a pair of coins 32 times, and record how they land. Suppose heads represents a dominant factor and tails represents a recessive factor. Calculate the number of times a dominant trait is expected to appear. Compare this number with your coin tosses.

Adaptations

If you were walking through a tropical rain forest, you might see colorful birds, screeching monkeys, and tiny, green frogs. You would not see an Arctic fox. The Arctic fox lives in cold places. It has adaptations that keep it warm in cold weather and help it hide from predators. *Adaptations* help living things meet basic needs and survive in their environments. Adaptations are inherited traits. They are passed down from parents to offspring.

An adaptation might make it easier to live in a place that is hot, cold, dry, or wet. These traits also help living things find mates, find shelter, reproduce, hunt, and hide. Adaptations are physical features or behaviors that living things develop over a long time, passing from generation to generation. Individuals that have helpful adaptations are more likely to survive and reproduce. Most animals of the species will eventually have these characteristics.

There are three kinds of adaptations. The first kind of adaptation is a physical part of a living thing. The Arctic fox, for example, has a small body with thick fur all over. The fur keeps the fox warm during the coldest winters. Having a short snout and small ears helps conserve heat energy. Also, the fox has white fur in winter and brown fur in summer. These colors help the fox hide in its environment during both seasons.

Arctic foxes have adaptations to help them survive in both winter and summer.

Anteaters have very sharp claws that help them rip open termite and ant nests. Once an anteater has opened a nest, it uses its long, sticky tongue to pick up many termites or ants. The claws and tongue are adaptations that help the anteater meet its basic need for food.

A second kind of adaptation is the way a living thing behaves. For example, deserts are very hot during the day. Animals such as rattlesnakes and Gila monsters move around at sunrise and sunset, when temperatures are cooler. During the hot part of the day, they burrow underground or stay cool under rocks. Some animals move to warmer places in the winter. This movement, called *migration*, is an adaptation. Migration is an inherited trait passed from parents to offspring.

A third kind of adaptation involves important life processes. People sweat, for example, to keep their bodies from becoming too hot. The rattlesnake has adaptations to make venom. Venom is a poison. It helps the snake hunt. It also protects the snake against enemies.

Focus Skill **CAUSE AND EFFECT** **Why do animals become adapted to their environments?**

Two of a giraffe's adaptations are its long legs and neck.

Anteaters have many adaptations.

163

Survival and Reproduction

How do living things become adapted to their environments? Arctic foxes did not originate in the cold regions where they live now. They moved there many, many years ago. Some of those long-ago foxes had fur that turned lighter in winter. They could hide from predators more easily in winter than foxes whose fur stayed brown. They also caught food more easily because they were harder to see in the snow. They could sneak up on prey. The foxes with lighter winter fur bred with other foxes that had the lighter fur. Their offspring also had lighter fur in the winter. This happened again and again. Eventually, the winter fur was white, and all the foxes of that species shared the trait.

All animals have adaptations for survival. Adaptations can help an animal survive attacks from predators. Some snakes make venom that they can inject with their fangs. Porcupines have sharp, thick hairs called quills on their backs. When an animal tries to bite or scratch the porcupine, the painful quills get stuck in that animal's snout, head, or paw.

Most of an armadillo's body is covered by thick skin-like armor. An armadillo will roll up into a ball when it is threatened, making it very hard for a predator to bite it or grab it. An armadillo's armor also protects it if it runs from a predator into a patch of thorns or thick underbrush.

All of these animals have adaptations that help defend against attack from predators.

Black bears only have one or two cubs at a time.

Adaptations help animals survive so that they can reproduce. If a species can't successfully reproduce, it may become extinct. *Extinction* is the death of all organisms of a species.

All living things reproduce, but not every living thing reproduces in the same way. As you have learned, plants and animals reproduce in different ways. Mammals, for the most part, reproduce in the same way, but there are still differences. How often a mammal reproduces, the length of the pregnancy, and how many offspring it has are adaptations. Some animals, such as the black bear, reproduce once a year and have only one or two offspring at a time. The pregnancy lasts about seven months.

Other animals, such as rabbits, reproduce two or three times a year and can have up to 20 offspring at a time. The pregnancy lasts only about a month.

These adaptations related to reproduction are inherited traits. A female bear has only one or two cubs, because they mature very slowly and need a lot of attention. Rabbits mature very quickly and don't need as much care as young bear cubs. Not all of the rabbits will survive into adulthood. However, because there are so many in a litter, enough will survive to keep rabbits from becoming extinct. These animals will pass on these traits to their offspring. Adaptations are very important for living things. Adaptations make sure that a species meets its basic needs, as well as making sure that it will survive and reproduce over and over again.

 CAUSE AND EFFECT How did the Arctic fox get white fur in winter?

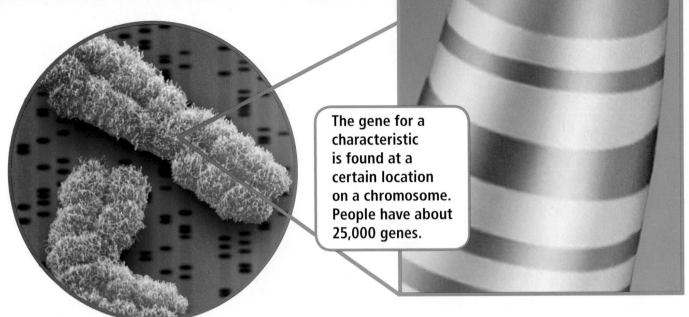

The gene for a characteristic is found at a certain location on a chromosome. People have about 25,000 genes.

Genes

Today, Mendel's factors are known to be different forms of genes. A **gene** is the part of a chromosome that contains the DNA code for an inherited trait. A gene for a particular trait is found at a specific place on a chromosome. All inherited traits—tongue rolling, thumb position, and thousands more—are controlled by genes.

Unless you have an identical twin, you are genetically unique. You share some characteristics with most humans, but there is no one else with exactly the same combination of factors that you have.

What makes you different from everyone else? Remember that during meiosis, each gamete gets only half the chromosomes of a body cell. So half of your chromosomes came from your father and the other half came from your mother. The particular combination of forms of genes you inherited is what makes you unique. You may have eyes like your mother's or hair like your father's—but there's no one else exactly like you.

Focus Skill **CAUSE AND EFFECT** How does meiosis affect inheritance through genes?

Scientists can now study individual genes to figure out how certain diseases are inherited.

Essential Question

How Are Characteristics Inherited?

In this lesson, you learned that physical characteristics are inherited from parents and can be either dominant or recessive. You also learned that organisms develop adaptations over time to cope with change and to ensure the survival of a species through reproduction.

1. **Focus Skill** **CAUSE AND EFFECT** Draw and complete a graphic organizer that shows how an organism's genetic makeup affects its traits.

2. **SUMMARIZE** Write a summary of Gregor Mendel's research and work on inherited traits.

3. **DRAW CONCLUSIONS** A dark brown mouse is bred with a light brown mouse. Out of four offspring, how many are likely to be dark brown?

4. **VOCABULARY** Write clues for the vocabulary terms, and make a word-search puzzle with the terms. Ask a classmate to solve the puzzle.

Test Prep

5. **CRITICAL THINKING** How can two brown-eyed parents have a blue-eyed child?

6. What are Mendel's "factors"?
   A. chromosomes
   B. pieces of DNA
   C. forms of genes
   D. traits

Make Connections

 Writing

Expository Writing
Choose one of the traits you've read about. Then write an **explanation** of the inheritance of this trait in your family.

 Math

Use Fractions
Suppose a mother has two dominant genes for right-handedness, and a father has two recessive genes. Construct a square to predict the probability of right-handedness in their children.

 Health

Genetic Testing
Because some gene combinations cause disease, many states require checking for genetic disorders at birth. Use Internet resources to learn which genetic disorders are checked for in your state.

Essential Question

What Other Factors Affect Characteristics?

Investigate behaviors that are inherited and behaviors that are learned.

Read and learn how organisms are born with instincts, while other behaviors are learned.

Fast Fact

Spiderwebs

A spider can spin a complicated web without learning how to do so. It can spin its first web without experience and without even a model of a finished web. The ability to spin a web is inherited. In the Investigate, you'll classify some of your own behaviors as inherited or learned.

This spider is demonstrating an inherited behavior: spinning a web.

Vocabulary Preview

instinct [IN•stinkt] A behavior that an organism inherits (p. 172)

learned behavior [LERND bee•HAYV•yer] A behavior that an animal acquires through experience (p. 174)

environment [en•VY•ruhn•muhnt] All the living and nonliving things that surround and affect an organism (p. 176)

169

Learned and Inherited Behaviors

Guided Inquiry

Start with Questions

You can do some things because you've learned how to do them. Some things you just know how to do, without learning.

- Why do you think you didn't have to learn how to do some things?

- Does this photo of a sleeping koala show a learned behavior or an inherited behavior?

Investigate to find out. Then read and learn to find out more.

Prepare to Investigate

Inquiry Skill Tip

Your inferences should be based on observations, but you also use your prior knowledge. Be sure that your knowledge is accurate. Ask your teacher if you aren't sure.

Materials

- pen and paper

Make an Observation Chart

Behavior	Learned	Inherited
Waking up		X
Brushing teeth		
Eating		
Walking		
Sleeping		
Reading		
Using a computer		

Follow This Procedure

1. Make a table like the one shown.

2. The left-hand column lists common behaviors. Some of these are skills you learned how to do. Others are behaviors you inherited.

3. Think about each behavior. Then record which behaviors you learned and which you inherited. The first one is classified for you.

4. Think about activities you've done in the past few hours. Then add four behaviors to the table. Record which behaviors you learned and which you inherited.

Draw Conclusions

1. Compare the number of learned behaviors to the number of behaviors you inherited.

2. Choose one behavior you learned. Communicate to a classmate how you learned that behavior.

3. **Inquiry Skill** Scientists often infer the reason for something, based on their observations. Infer whether most human behaviors are learned or inherited. Explain.

Step 3

Step 4

Independent Inquiry

Research hunting behavior in lions. Is it inherited, learned, or both? Compare **this behavior to some of your behaviors, such as eating and walking.**

VOCABULARY
instinct p. 172
learned behavior p. 174
environment p. 176

SCIENCE CONCEPTS
▶ how instinct and the environment affect characteristics
▶ how learning can affect traits

Focus Skill CAUSE AND EFFECT
Look for ways that environment and learning affect traits.

cause → effect

Instincts

Many of the things you do, such as reading, writing, playing games, and acquiring new skills, are learned. But some, such as eating and sleeping, are *instinctive*. An **instinct** is a behavior that an organism inherits. Since instincts are inherited, they are passed from parents to their offspring.

Have you ever observed a bird making a nest or watched a cat grooming itself? If so, you're familiar with some instinctive animal behaviors. These help an animal survive in its surroundings.

Behaviors for building shelters, caring for young, and finding food are usually instinctive. Ospreys, for example, build their nests away from other birds, protect their young, and hunt for fish instinctively.

Canada geese instinctively fly south for the winter and eat grains and water plants.

This osprey chose a particular place for her nest, and she instinctively knows how to build a nest and care for her young. ▶

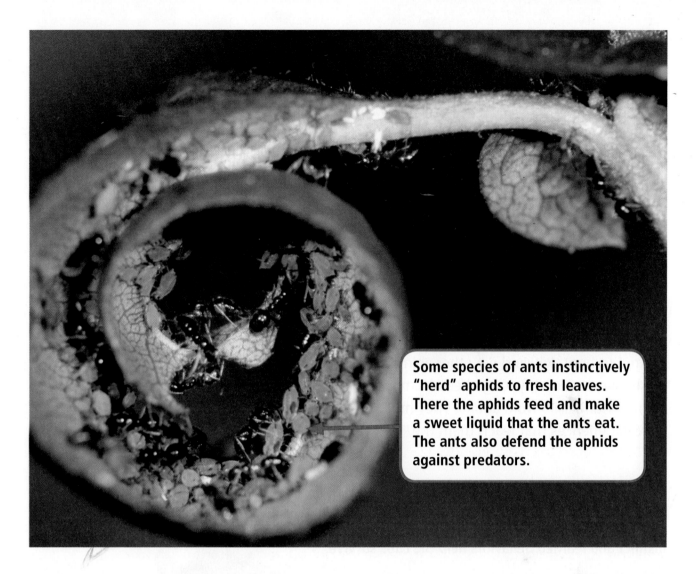

Some species of ants instinctively "herd" aphids to fresh leaves. There the aphids feed and make a sweet liquid that the ants eat. The ants also defend the aphids against predators.

Squirrels instinctively collect and store nuts and other seeds for the winter.

Cats instinctively eat when they're hungry, sleep when they're tired, and cover their wastes. They also instinctively care for their young, feeding them and protecting them from danger.

Instincts are not just behaviors of individual animals. Instincts are usually shared by all members of a species or by all the males or all the females of a species. Certain species of ants, for example, instinctively "herd" and defend aphids, insects that provide the ants with food.

In addition to sharing species instincts, different breeds within a species may have slightly different instincts. Beagles, for example, don't have to be taught to track small animals. But they can't herd sheep. Border collies don't have to be taught to round up sheep, but they can't hunt rabbits, as beagles do. These two dog breeds have specific instincts that guide their behavior. However, neither breed needs to be taught fear—both are born knowing to avoid danger.

What instincts were you born with? You were able to eat and sleep when you needed to. And you were able to communicate with your parents when you needed things—your crying was instinctive.

 **CAUSE AND EFFECT** What effect do instincts have on an animal's survival?

Learned Behaviors

Many behaviors are instinctive. Canada geese, for example, build nests on the ground using grasses and mosses. Geese do not have to learn how to sit on their eggs to keep them warm—that behavior is an instinct, too. However, not all behaviors are instincts. When a young Canada goose hatches, it learns how to hide, find food, and fly by watching its parents and by practicing.

A **learned behavior** is a behavior an animal acquires through experience. Cheetahs, for example, are born with the instinct to hunt, kill, and eat other animals. To survive, however, young cheetahs must learn hunting skills from adults. They must have experiences that teach them the best ways to track, hunt, and kill. A young cheetah needs both the instinct to hunt and experiences that develop hunting skills.

You were born with the instinct to cry, but you learned to vary the pitch and loudness of your crying, depending on your needs. As you grew and developed, you learned many other behaviors. You learned how to walk and talk. You learned how to dress yourself, how to bathe, and how to brush your teeth. Though you had the instinct to eat, you learned table manners and how to use spoons, forks, and knives.

Not all learned animal behaviors are used for survival. Animals may learn some less important behaviors from people. A parrot, for example, may mimic simple human speech. Like many people, you may have taught your dog to "shake hands."

These cheetah cubs were born with the instinct to hunt, but their mother teaches them hunting skills. Together, instinct and learned behaviors help the cubs survive. ▼

174

This service dog has learned behaviors that help its owner.

Have you ever seen dolphins doing tricks or seen a circus act with trained animals? These performances often include behaviors that are similar to instinctive behaviors. But the animals are trained to perform the behaviors at specific times or on command.

Some animals can learn behaviors that are helpful to people. These behaviors aren't necessary for the animals' survival but can be very useful to the animals' human companions.

Service animals are trained to do tasks that help people with disabilities. Guide dogs help owners who can't see, by leading them as the owners walk. Hearing dogs alert their owners to sounds such as ringing phones and doorbells. Mobility-assist dogs help physically disabled people with tasks such as carrying objects or opening doors.

Dogs aren't the only animals that can be trained to help people. Capuchin monkeys, for example, have also been trained to help people do some simple everyday tasks.

CAUSE AND EFFECT

How are most animal behaviors learned?

Model a Beak
Birds have the instinct to eat certain foods, such as seeds. Place a few beans in a graduated cylinder. Try to remove them with a "beak" made up of your thumb and index finger. Then try this with forceps. Why is it important for birds to feed from certain plants?

Environmental Influences

Some characteristics or behaviors are the result of *environmental influences.* An organism's **environment** is everything in its surroundings that affects it, including water, soil, air, weather, landforms, and other living things.

All living things have needs. Animals need food, water, space, and shelter. Plants need nutrients, water, and sunlight. When an environment changes, all the things that live there are affected. Sometimes, animals lose their shelter, or they can't find enough food or water. So they must move to get the things they need.

Sometimes, changes in the environment force animals to change their behavior. In areas where food becomes less plentiful, some animals may learn to eat different foods. Wolves usually eat deer or mountain goats. If there aren't enough of those animals, wolves may learn to eat cattle or sheep.

Sometimes, the environment causes a physical change in a species over time. Pollution kills many plants and animals. But these poisons can also damage the chromosomes of living organisms and can affect their offspring. Look at the frog in the picture. The defects in its body are the result of pollution that changed the frog's DNA. If the DNA change occurs in the frog's gametes, its offspring will inherit the body defects.

Focus Skill **CAUSE AND EFFECT** How can the environment affect future generations?

◀ Poisons in an environment harm the populations living there. This frog has defects because pollutants damaged its DNA. How might this damage affect future generations?

Human activities, such as farming, affect the environment. Here, chemicals used in farming have run off from a field, polluting the water.

Essential Question

What Other Factors Affect Characteristics?

In this lesson, you learned that some behaviors are instincts that organisms inherit and some are acquired through experience. You also learned that the environment can have an influence on an organism's behavior.

1. 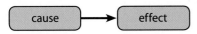 **CAUSE AND EFFECT** Draw and complete a graphic organizer that shows the types of factors that affect characteristics.

cause → effect

2. SUMMARIZE Write a one-paragraph summary of instinctive and learned behaviors. Give one example of how each type of behavior helps organisms survive.

3. DRAW CONCLUSIONS How might the number of oak trees in a park affect the number of squirrels that can live there?

4. VOCABULARY Write a definition of the term *instinct*.

Test Prep

5. CRITICAL THINKING What is the difference between an instinct and a learned behavior?

6. Which of the following is **not** a survival instinct for dogs?

 A. barking
 B. eating
 C. shaking hands
 D. sleeping

Make Connections

 Writing

Persuasive Writing

Choose an animal behavior. Write an essay telling your **opinion** about whether the behavior is instinctive or learned. Give reasons to support your opinion.

 Math

Compare Numbers

Use library resources to learn how the number of people in the world has increased since 1650. Make a graph to show the increase. How do you think the increase has affected other living things?

 Language Arts

Using Tables

Use your library or the Internet to find out how animals survive cold winter months. Make a cause-and-effect table to summarize your findings. Label causes *instinctive* or *learned*.

Wei Shi

All cells carry out the same basic life functions. But in organisms made of many cells, each kind of cell also has a special function. What "tells" a cell to do its job? What makes the cells in the respiratory system carry out their respiratory functions?

▶ **DR. WEI SHI**

▶ Assistant Professor of Research, Developmental Biology Program, Saban Research Institute of Children's Hospital Los Angeles and University of Southern California

Dr. Wei Shi, a molecular scientist who started his education in China, may have asked himself these questions. Dr. Shi wondered why breathing problems are so common in babies under a year of age. He wanted to learn whether certain substances affect the ability of respiratory cells to carry out their jobs. He became interested in learning which of the molecules called growth factors cause normal respiratory structures to form and function in a baby.

Dr. Shi's research showed how two substances help the lungs form. His discoveries gave doctors a better understanding of respiratory illnesses in newborns.

 Think and Write

1 How can learning about molecules help solve medical mysteries?

2 Why is it important to understand the breathing problems that affect babies?

Gregor Mendel

▶ **GREGOR MENDEL**

▶ "The Father of Modern Genetics"

Gregor Mendel, a monk who lived more than 130 years ago, noticed differences among the pea plants in his garden. Some were tall, while others were short; some had smooth peas and some had wrinkled peas. Mendel *cross-pollinated* the plants. He took the pollen from one plant and placed it in the flower of another plant.

Mendel planted the seeds made by the cross-pollinated plant. Based on the traits of the parent plants, he predicted certain traits of the offspring. Mendel had discovered *genetic heredity*, the passing along of traits from parents to offspring through *genes*.

 Think and Write

1 Why do you think Mendel's discovery was important?

2 How does Mendel's discovery relate to you?

Career Medical Scientist

Medical scientists research human diseases and their cures. They do most of their work in laboratories. Medical scientists have helped develop vaccines, medicines, and treatments for many diseases.

Vocabulary Review

Use the terms below to complete the sentences. The page numbers tell you where to look in the chapter if you need help.

life cycle p. 149   **dominant trait** p. 160

mitosis p. 150   **gene** p. 166

chromosome p. 150   **environment** p. 176

1. Part of a chromosome that contains the DNA code for a trait is a _____.

2. The stages an organism passes through make up its _____.

3. A strong characteristic that always appears when there is a gene for it is a _____.

4. Body cells divide during _____.

5. A threadlike structure found in the nucleus of the cell is a _____.

6. All the living and nonliving things that affect an organism make up its _____.

Check Understanding

Write the letter of the best choice.

7. In what part of the cell do changes first take place during mitosis?
   - **A.** cell membrane
   - **B.** cell wall
   - **C.** chloroplasts
   - **D.** nucleus

8. **CAUSE AND EFFECT** 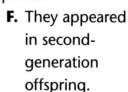 How did Mendel learn about traits caused by hidden factors in pea plants?
   - **F.** They appeared in second-generation offspring.
   - **G.** They appeared in first- and second-generation offspring.
   - **H.** They never appeared in offspring.
   - **J.** They appeared in first-generation offspring.

9. **MAIN IDEA AND DETAILS** During mitosis, what does a new cell get an exact copy of?
   - **A.** cell wall
   - **B.** chromosomes
   - **C.** dominant traits
   - **D.** gametes

10. Which is **not** an inherited behavior?
    - **F.** eating
    - **G.** reading
    - **H.** seeking shelter
    - **J.** sleeping

11. If an organism has 46 chromosomes in each body cell, how many are in a zygote?
    - **A.** 18
    - **B.** 23
    - **C.** 46
    - **D.** 92

12. What are Mendel's *factors* now called?
    - **F.** chromosomes
    - **G.** strands of DNA
    - **H.** forms of genes
    - **J.** nucleus

13. What are inherited behaviors called?

   A. environments   **C.** old behaviors

   B. instincts   **D.** recessive traits

14. Which sequence describes mitosis?

   F. Chromosomes are copied, chromosomes separate, cell membrane pinches.

   G. Cell membrane pinches, chromosomes are copied, chromosomes separate.

   H. Chromosomes separate, chromosomes are copied, cell membrane pinches.

   J. Cell membrane pinches, chromosomes separate, chromosomes are copied.

15. How is hunting both learned and instinctive in animals?

   A. Animals learn to hunt.

   B. Animals have the instinct to hunt.

   C. Animals have the instinct to hunt but must learn hunting skills.

   D. Animals have the instinct to teach their young how to hunt.

16. Which is an example of a learned behavior?

   F. a snow hare turning white in the winter

   G. a deer standing still in headlight beams

   H. a coyote eating new kinds of prey

   J. a person rolling his tongue

Inquiry Skills

17. Describe the expected results of a cross between two brown-eyed parents. **Predict** the likelihood that their children will have blue eyes.

18. **Compare** meiosis and mitosis. What is the outcome of each?

Critical Thinking

19. Does a person learn an inherited behavior? Explain.

20. An instinct is a behavior that is passed from parents to their offspring. Explain how instincts can help an animal survive. Give an example of learning that improves on an instinct. Explain how the resulting behavior helps an animal.

The **Big Idea**

Visual Summary

Tell how each picture shows the **Big Idea** for its chapter.

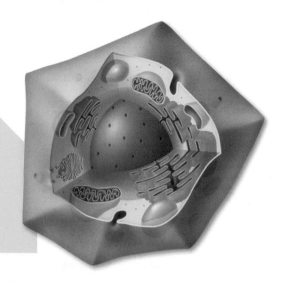

Big Idea

All living things are made of cells. Cells work together to make up tissues, organs, and organ systems.

Big Idea

Living things are classified in different ways. Some animals have a backbone, while others do not.

Big Idea

Plants have a variety of structures to help them carry out life processes.

Big Idea

Animal characteristics are passed from parents to their children. Characteristics are either learned or inherited.

Interactions Among Living Things

UNIT
B
LIFE SCIENCE

CHAPTER 5
Energy and Ecosystems 184

CHAPTER 6
Ecosystems and Change 212

Unit Inquiry

Removing Pollution from Water

Living things interact with each other and with the physical environment. Human activity can sometimes pollute the physical environment. Living things in the ocean can suffer greatly from pollution. How can visible pollution be removed from water? For example, can certain materials be used to filter polluted water? Plan and conduct an experiment to find out.

Energy and Ecosystems

Living things interact with one another in the environment. Energy flows from the sun to plants to animals.

Essential Questions

Lesson 1

How Do Plants Produce Food?

Lesson 2

How Is Energy Passed Through an Ecosystem?

Student eBook
www.hspscience.com

Whale shark

What do YOU wonder?

What does a huge shark like this eat? Where does it get the energy it needs? How does this relate to the **Big Idea?**

Investigate the use of carbon dioxide by plants.

Read and learn about different plant structures that help the plant make food.

Essential Question

How Do Plants Produce Food?

Fast Fact

Working Plants

These flowers and trees produce some of the oxygen you breathe. They also take carbon dioxide out of the air. In the Investigate, you will observe that a plant takes in carbon dioxide.

Many plants make their own food.

transpiration (tran•spuh•RAY•shuhn) The loss of water from a leaf through the stomata (p. 191)

photosynthesis (foht•oh•SIHN•thuh•sis) The process in which plants make food by using water from the soil, carbon dioxide from the air, and energy from sunlight (p. 192)

chlorophyll (KLAWR•uh•fihl) A green pigment that allows a plant to absorb the sun's light energy (p. 192)

producer (pruh•DOOS•er) A living thing, such as a plant, that makes its own food (p. 194)

consumer (kuhn•SOOM•er) An animal that eats plants, other animals, or both (p. 194)

Using Carbon Dioxide

Guided Inquiry

Start with Questions

Plants make their own food. They use carbon dioxide in this process.

- What is one source of carbon dioxide?

- What else are these plants using to make food?

Investigate to find out. Then read and learn to find out more.

Prepare to Investigate

Inquiry Skill Tip

Your predictions during an investigation should be based on your observations and on the scientific knowledge you already have.

Materials

- safety goggles
- 2 plastic cups
- water
- dropper
- bromothymol blue (BTB)
- 2 test tubes with caps
- *Elodea*
- funnel
- plastic straw

Make an Observation Chart

Solution	Observations
With Elodea	
Without Elodea	

Follow This Procedure

CAUTION: Wear safety goggles during this investigation.

① Fill one cup about two-thirds full of water. Use a dropper to add BTB until the water is blue.

② Put a straw into the cup, and blow into it.

CAUTION: DO NOT suck on the straw. If the solution gets in your mouth, spit it out and rinse your mouth with water.

③ Observe and record changes in the water.

④ Put *Elodea* in one test tube. Use a funnel to fill both test tubes with BTB solution. Cap both tubes.

⑤ Turn the tubes upside down, and put them in an empty cup. Place the cup on a sunny windowsill. Predict what changes will occur in the test tubes.

⑥ After 1 hour, observe both tubes and record your observations.

Draw Conclusions

1. What changes did you observe in the BTB solution during the activity?

2. **Inquiry Skill** Scientists use what they know to predict what will happen. After you blew into the water, how did your observations help you predict what would happen next?

Step 2

Step 5

Independent Inquiry

Plan and conduct an experiment to test the effect of sunlight on the changes in the BTB solution. Predict what will happen. Then carry out your experiment.

VOCABULARY
transpiration p. 191
photosynthesis p. 192
chlorophyll p. 192
producer p. 194
consumer p. 194

SCIENCE CONCEPTS
▶ how leaves use carbon dioxide and give off oxygen
▶ how the parts of plants make food by means of photosynthesis

Focus Skill **MAIN IDEA AND DETAILS**

Look for details about how plants make and store food.

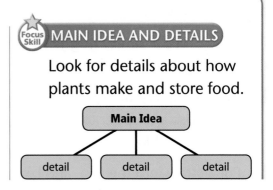

Plant Structures

You are probably familiar with the basic parts of plants. These parts include roots, stems, and leaves. Some of those parts produce food for the plant.

Roots Roots have two main jobs. They anchor plants, and they take in water and nutrients. Tubes in the roots carry water to the stems. The roots of some plants, such as carrots, also store food.

Different plants have different types of roots. For example, the roots of desert plants spread out just below the surface to catch any rain that falls. Some plants, like the dandelion, have one main root to reach water deep underground.

Stems Stems support a plant and enable its leaves to reach the sunlight. Stems also contain tubes that carry water and nutrients to the leaves. Other tubes carry food to all parts of the plant. The stems of some plants, such as sugar cane, store food.

Just as plants have different roots, they also have different stems. Small plants tend to have flexible, green stems. Most of these plants live for just one year.

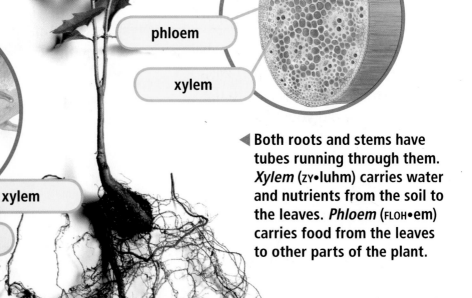

phloem

xylem

xylem

phloem

◀ Both roots and stems have tubes running through them. *Xylem* (ZY•luhm) carries water and nutrients from the soil to the leaves. *Phloem* (FLOH•em) carries food from the leaves to other parts of the plant.

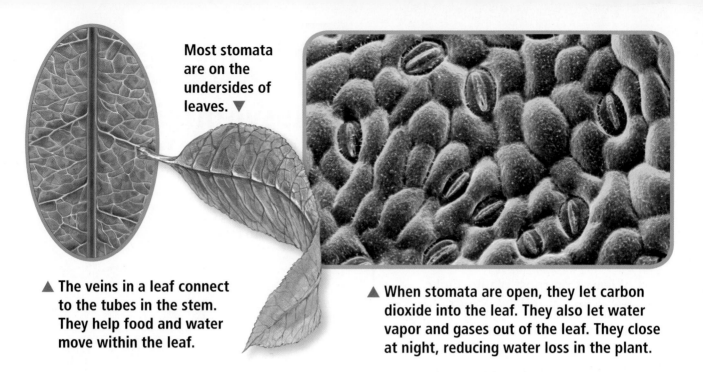

Most stomata are on the undersides of leaves. ▼

▲ The veins in a leaf connect to the tubes in the stem. They help food and water move within the leaf.

▲ When stomata are open, they let carbon dioxide into the leaf. They also let water vapor and gases out of the leaf. They close at night, reducing water loss in the plant.

Larger plants and trees need more support. They usually have stiff, woody stems, and live for many years.

Leaves Leaves have one main job—to make food for the plant. A leaf can be as small as the head of a pin, or it can be wide enough to support a frog on the surface of a pond. Some leaves are very specialized. The leaves of the Venus' flytrap are able to catch food for the plant. They snap shut when an insect lands on them. Then the leaves help digest the insect.

Most leaves are thin and have several layers of cells. The outer layer, called the *epidermis* (ep•uh•DER•mis), keeps the leaf from drying out. The upper epidermis is often covered with a layer of wax. This helps keep water in. The lower epidermis has many small openings called *stomata*.

Stomata usually open during the day so the leaf can take in carbon dioxide to make food. Stomata close at night to keep the plant from drying out. The loss of water through leaves is called **transpiration**.

Just below the upper epidermis is a closely packed layer of cells in which most

of the food is made. Just above the lower epidermis is a spongy layer of cells. Air spaces among these cells contain carbon dioxide, oxygen, and water vapor.

Veins, which connect to the tubes in the stems, are found in the center of most leaves. In broad leaves, the veins have many branches. They carry the water needed to make food to cells throughout the leaf.

Focus Skill MAIN IDEA AND DETAILS

What is the main job of each plant part?

What's in a Leaf?
Get a filter from your teacher, and tape one of the short edges to a pencil. In a bowl, grind green leaves with rubbing alcohol. Pour the mixture into a jar. Set the pencil across the top of the jar so the filter hangs down and touches the mixture. Watch what happens.

191

Photosynthesis

Plants make food in a process that uses water from the soil, carbon dioxide from the air, and energy from sunlight. This process, called **photosynthesis**, produces food for the plant and releases oxygen into the air.

Recall that plant cells contain organelles called chloroplasts. Cells with chloroplasts are found in the inner layers of leaves on most plants. Only cells with chloroplasts can make food.

Chloroplasts contain a green pigment, or coloring matter, called chlorophyll (KLAWR•uh•fil). **Chlorophyll** enables a plant to absorb light energy so that it can produce food. It also makes plants green. Plants contain small amounts of other pigments as well. In autumn, many plants stop producing chlorophyll, so you can see the other pigments. This is what makes some leaves change color in autumn.

Photosynthesis begins when sunlight hits the chloroplasts. The energy absorbed by the chlorophyll causes water and carbon dioxide to combine to form sugar—the food that plants need to live and grow.

Oxygen is produced as a byproduct of photosynthesis. It is released into the air through the stomata. About 90 percent of the oxygen you breathe is produced during photosynthesis by plants and plantlike protists. Plants also help you by taking carbon dioxide, which your body does not need, out of the air.

 **MAIN IDEA AND DETAILS** What does a plant need for photosynthesis?

Science Up Close

Photosynthesis

Sunlight provides energy for plants to make food.

Plants take in carbon dioxide from the air.

After making food, the leaves release oxygen through their stomata.

Chlorophyll absorbs energy from sunlight. The plant needs this energy, along with carbon dioxide and water, to make food.

The food made by the plant is stored in the plant's leaves, stems, seeds, and—in some plants—roots.

Plant roots take in water, which is necessary for photosynthesis.

For more links and animations, go to www.hspscience.com

It All Starts with Plants

All organisms need energy to live and grow. That energy comes from food. Plants are called **producers** because they produce, or make, their own food. Animals can't make their own food, but they need energy from food to survive. When animals eat plants, the animals receive the energy that's stored in those plants. The word *consume* means "to eat," so we call animals that eat plants or other animals **consumers**.

You are a consumer. For example, when you eat a salad, you take in the energy stored in the lettuce leaves and carrot roots. When you eat strawberries, you get the energy that was stored in the fruit and seeds of the strawberry plants.

In fact, you and every animal on Earth depend on plants. Even animals that eat only other animals depend on plants. Without plants, animals such as deer and rabbits, which eat only plants, would starve. Then animals such as wolves, which eat deer and rabbits, would have nothing to eat. They, too, would starve.

The energy from sunlight moves from plants to animals that eat plants to animals that eat other animals. Without sunlight, every living thing on Earth would die.

MAIN IDEA AND DETAILS

Define the terms *producer* and *consumer*.

These bison get the energy they need by eating grasses. Without plants, the bison couldn't survive.

Essential Question

How Do Plants Produce Food?

In this lesson, you learned that plants make their own food and have structures that aid in this process. You also learned that every animal on Earth depends on plants, whether it eats plants or not.

1. (Focus Skill) **MAIN IDEA AND DETAILS** Draw and complete a graphic organizer to show the supporting details of this main idea: Several parts of a plant help in photosynthesis.

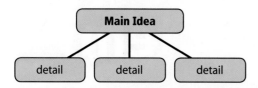

2. SUMMARIZE Write one paragraph summarizing how the roots, stems, and leaves of a plant help it survive.

3. DRAW CONCLUSIONS What would happen if all plants had the same kind of roots?

4. VOCABULARY Make a crossword puzzle, including clues, using this lesson's vocabulary terms. Then exchange puzzles with a partner, and solve his or her puzzle.

Test Prep

5. CRITICAL THINKING How would Earth's atmosphere change if plants stopped carrying out photosynthesis?

6. Which gas do plants need for photosynthesis?

  A. carbon dioxide

  B. carbon monoxide

  C. nitrogen

  D. oxygen

Make Connections

 Writing

Narrative Writing
Write a **myth** that "explains" a concept in this lesson, such as why plants have roots, why some leaves change color in the fall, or why animals depend on plants. Illustrate your story.

 Math

Make a Table
Suppose you want to conduct a two-week experiment to see how different amounts of sunlight affect five sunflower seedlings. Make a table that you could use to record your results.

 Language Arts

Word Meanings
Identify the parts of the word *photosynthesis*. Explain how the parts' meanings relate to the fact that plants make their own food. Then list at least three other words that have one of the word parts found in *photosynthesis*.

Ordering What Eats What

Guided Inquiry

Start with Questions

Each animal in a food chain has a particular role, even you. Are you a producer or a consumer? Herbivore or carnivore?

- Are there more producers or more consumers in a food chain?

- What role does this bird have in the food chain?

Investigate to find out. Then read and learn to find out more.

Prepare to Investigate

Inquiry Skill Tip

When you classify organisms, it may help to make a table with a column for each organism. Make a row for each different characteristic, and describe how the organisms are alike and different.

Materials

- index cards
- markers
- pushpins
- bulletin board
- yarn

Make an Observation Chart

Food Chain			
	Organism:	Organism:	Organism:
Characteristic:			
Characteristic:			
Characteristic:			
Characteristic:			

Follow This Procedure

❶ You will be assigned an organism. On an index card, draw it, write its name, or both.

❷ Research to **classify** your organism. Is it a producer, a plant-eating consumer, or a meat-eating consumer? Is it a consumer that eats both plants and meat? Or is it an organism that gets its energy from the remains of dead organisms?

❸ Work with members of your group to put your cards in an **order** that shows what eats what.

❹ Pin your team's cards in **order** on the bulletin board. Connect your cards with yarn to show what eats what. Then use yarn to show which of your team's organisms eat organisms from other teams.

Draw Conclusions

1. **Classify** each organism on your group's cards. In which group does each belong?

2. **Inquiry Skill** When scientists **classify** things, they better understand relationships between them. Could you put your team's cards in another order? Why or why not? Which card must always be first? Which card must always be last?

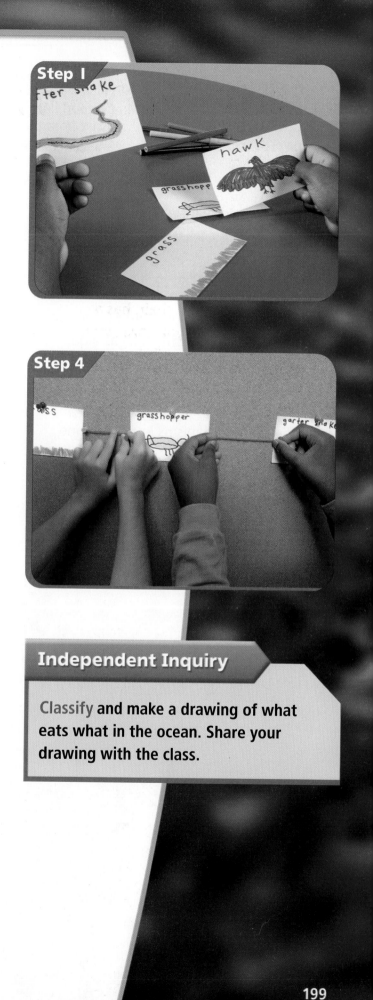

Step I

Step 4

Independent Inquiry

Classify and make a drawing of what eats what in the ocean. Share your drawing with the class.

VOCABULARY
ecosystem p. 200
herbivore p. 200
carnivore p. 200
food chain p. 201
decomposer p. 201
food web p. 202
energy pyramid p. 205

SCIENCE CONCEPTS
▶ how food energy is passed from plant to animal to animal in an ecosystem
▶ how food chains make up food webs

 **SEQUENCE**

Look for the order of events in the transfer of energy.

Energy Transfer

You read that plants make their own food through the process of photosynthesis. So do a few other organisms, such as algae and lichens (LY•kuhnz). Plants are the main producers in most land ecosystems.

An **ecosystem** (EE•koh•sis•tuhm) includes all the organisms in an area and the environment in which they live. This is a tundra ecosystem. All the organisms shown here are part of a tundra ecosystem. An ecosystem includes many kinds of organisms.

Some tundra animals, like caribou, eat plants and other producers. The food energy stored in the reindeer moss is transferred to the caribou. An animal that eats plants or other producers is an **herbivore**. Herbivores are also called first-level consumers.

Other tundra animals, such as wolves, don't eat plants. They get their energy by eating other animals, like caribou. Food energy stored in the caribou is transferred to the wolf. An animal that eats mainly other animals is a **carnivore**. Carnivores are also called second-level consumers.

Reindeer moss, a lichen, makes food by photosynthesis. The food energy is stored in the organism.

The caribou gets its energy by eating reindeer moss.

Some animals, called *omnivores*, eat both plants and other animals. Omnivores can be first-level or second-level consumers. The bear shown on the first page of the lesson is an omnivore. So are most people.

In another ecosystem, a large carnivore, such as a hawk, might eat a smaller carnivore, such as a snake. That makes the hawk a third-level consumer. Each time something eats something else, food energy is transferred from one organism to the next. The transfer of food energy between organisms is called a **food chain**.

When plants and animals die, what happens to the food energy stored in their remains? The remains are broken down and the food energy is used by decomposers. A **decomposer** is a consumer that gets its food energy by breaking down the remains of dead organisms. Decomposers can be animals, such as earthworms. Many decomposers are fungi. Others are single-celled organisms—protists or bacteria.

Decomposers use some of the nutrients as food. The rest become mixed into the soil. Then plant roots can take up these nutrients. In this way, decomposers connect both ends of a food chain.

You know that all the organisms in an ecosystem depend on producers to make food. Then food energy is transferred through the ecosystem from one consumer level to another. All along the way, decomposers get energy from the remains of dead organisms. Any nutrients not used are returned to the soil.

SEQUENCE

After food energy is taken in by a second-level consumer, what can happen next?

The wolf gets the energy it needs by eating caribou.

When the moss, caribou, and wolf die, decomposers break down their remains. Then the reindeer moss and other producers can take up any remaining nutrients.

Food Webs

You know that most animals eat more than one kind of food. For example, a hawk might eat a mouse that ate seeds. The same hawk might also eat a small snake that ate grasshoppers and other insects. The insects, in turn, might have eaten grass. An organism, such as the hawk, can be a part of several food chains. In this way, food chains overlap. A **food web** shows the relationships among different food chains.

Carnivores eat consumers such as herbivores, omnivores, and other carnivores.

Prairie Food Web

The producers in this prairie ecosystem include grasses, clover, and purple coneflowers. First-level consumers, or herbivores, include insects, mice, ground squirrels, and bison. Second-level and third-level consumers—carnivores—include spiders, snakes, and hawks. The decomposers that you can see are mushrooms. What you can't see are the millions of single-celled decomposers. They are in the soil, helping recycle nutrients.

Pond Food Web

In this pond ecosystem, the producers include water plants and algae. Here the first-level consumers, or herbivores, include insects and tadpoles. Second-level and third-level consumers include fish. Some of the birds, such as ducks, are herbivores, while others are carnivores. The turtle is an omnivore, eating insects, tiny fish, and plants. The water is full of decomposers, such as snails, worms, and single-celled protists.

Carnivores also limit the number of animals below them in a food web. For example, without snakes, the number of mice in the prairie ecosystem would keep increasing. In time, the mice would eat all the available food. Then the mice would starve, and so would hawks, which eat mice.

Organisms in an ecosystem depend on one another for survival. A change in the number of one kind of organism can affect the entire ecosystem!

Focus Skill **SEQUENCE** If all the mosquitoes in a pond died, what might happen next?

Energy Pyramid

Not all the food energy of plants is passed on to the herbivores that eat them. Producers use about 90 percent of the food energy they produce for their own life processes. They store the other 10 percent in their leaves, stems, roots, fruits, and seeds.

Animals that eat the producers get only 10 percent of the energy the producers made. These herbivores then use for their life processes 90 percent of the energy they got from the producers. They store the other 10 percent in their bodies.

The owl is a third-level consumer. It takes a lot of grass, locusts, and snakes to provide the owl with the energy it needs.

Owl

The snakes are second-level consumers. They pass on to the owl only 10 percent of the energy they receive from the locusts.

Snakes

Math in Science
Interpret Data

Suppose the grasses at the base of this energy pyramid produce 100,000 kilocalories of energy. How many kilocalories would be passed to each of the other levels?

The locusts are first-level consumers. They pass on to the snakes only 10 percent of the energy they receive from the grasses.

Locusts

The grasses are producers. They pass on to the locusts only 10 percent of the energy they produce.

Grasses

204

An **energy pyramid** shows that each level of a food chain passes on less food energy than the level before it. Most of the energy in each level is used at that level. Only a little energy is passed on to the next level.

Because each level passes so little energy to the next, the first-level consumers need many producers to support them. In the same way, the second-level consumers need many first-level consumers to support them. This pattern continues up to the top of the food chain.

That's why the base of an energy pyramid is so wide. That's also why only one or two animals are at the top of the pyramid.

Most food chains have only three or four levels. If there were more, a huge number of producers would be needed at the base of the pyramid! Sometimes, things in the environment may cause the number of organisms at one level of the pyramid to change. Then the whole food chain is affected. Suppose a drought kills most of the grasses in an area. Then some of the first-level consumers will starve. Many second-level and third-level consumers will go hungry, too.

Suppose people cut down a forest to provide space for houses. The second-level and third-level consumers may not be able to find enough small animals to eat, so they may leave that ecosystem. With fewer carnivores to eat them, the number of small animals will increase over time. If there isn't enough food for their larger numbers, many will starve.

When a change in numbers occurs at any level of a food chain, the entire chain will be affected.

 **SEQUENCE** What can happen to a food chain if the number of second-level consumers increases?

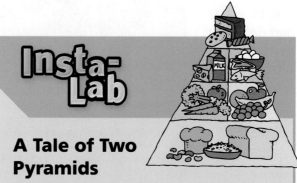

A Tale of Two Pyramids

Compare the energy pyramid with this pyramid, which was once used to classify foods. How are they alike? How are they different? Who are the consumers at each level of the food pyramid?

Natural Cycles

Most ecosystems depend on the water cycle to provide plants with the water they need for photosynthesis. Other cycles affect ecosystems, too.

For example, nitrogen also has a cycle. Nitrogen compounds are important for all living organisms. Nitrogen is a gas that makes up most of Earth's atmosphere. Before nitrogen gas can be used as a nutrient, it must be changed to a form that plants can take up through their roots.

Some nitrogen is changed, or *fixed*, by lightning. Lightning burns air, producing nitrogen-rich compounds that dissolve in rain. Plant roots can absorb these compounds. Bacteria found in some plant roots also change nitrogen gas into compounds that plants can use.

When a plant or animal dies and decays, nitrogen returns to the soil. Animal wastes also contain nitrogen. Decomposers change these wastes and remains of organisms into the nitrogen compounds plants need.

Carbon and oxygen also have a cycle. You learned that plants use carbon dioxide to make food and that they release oxygen as a byproduct. Plants and animals use this oxygen and release more carbon dioxide.

Carbon is stored in organisms, too. Burning wood, coal, and natural gas releases carbon dioxide into the air.

 **SEQUENCE** What part do decomposers play in the nitrogen cycle?

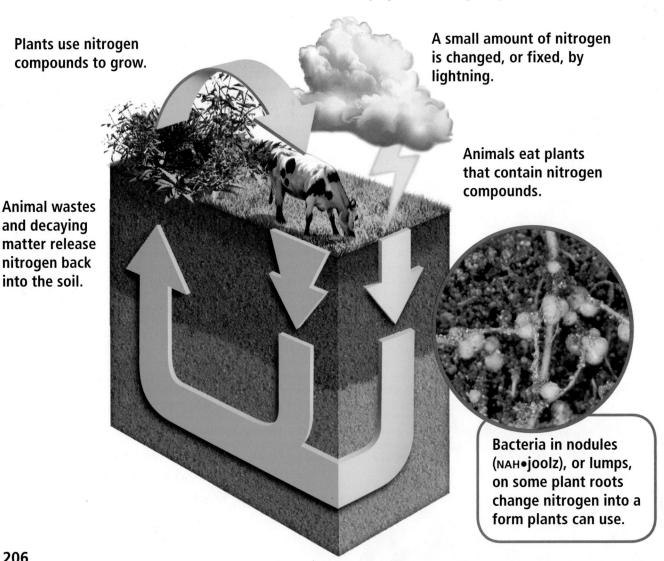

Plants use nitrogen compounds to grow.

A small amount of nitrogen is changed, or fixed, by lightning.

Animals eat plants that contain nitrogen compounds.

Animal wastes and decaying matter release nitrogen back into the soil.

Bacteria in nodules (NAH•joolz), or lumps, on some plant roots change nitrogen into a form plants can use.

Essential Question

How Is Energy Passed Through an Ecosystem?

In this lesson, you learned about some roles animals have in an ecosystem, such as producer, consumer, herbivore, and carnivore. You learned how food chains connect and overlap to form food webs.

1. **SEQUENCE** Draw and complete a graphic organizer showing the sequence of these organisms in a food chain: bear, grasshopper, mushroom, salmon, grass.

2. **SUMMARIZE** Write a one-paragraph summary explaining the nitrogen cycle.

3. **DRAW CONCLUSIONS** What is your role in a food chain or a food web? Explain your answer.

4. **VOCABULARY** Write a sentence for each of this lesson's vocabulary terms. Leave a blank space in each sentence for the term. Have a partner fill in the correct terms.

Test Prep

5. **CRITICAL THINKING** What is your favorite food? What level of consumer are you for that food?

6. Which of these is **not** essential in a food chain?
   A. decomposer
   B. first-level consumer
   C. producer
   D. second-level consumer

Make Connections

 Writing

Expository Writing
Imagine that you have discovered an animal that was thought to be extinct. Write a **paragraph** that describes the animal and explains how it fits into a food web in its ecosystem.

 Math

Solve a Problem
An eagle ate 2 fish and received 20 kilocalories of energy. The fish had eaten many insects. How many kilocalories were produced by the plants that the insects ate?

 Social Studies

Food Choices
In some parts of the world, meat protein is scarce. Find out what kinds of insects some people eat to add protein to their diets. Present a report to share what you learn.

Trash Man

Chad Pregracke grew up on the banks of the Mississippi River. He spent summers fishing, sailing, water-skiing, and canoeing. When Pregracke was 15 years old, he started working with his brother, a commercial shell diver.

Like a modern-day Tom Sawyer and Huck Finn, the brothers spent their nights camping on river islands and their days combing the pitch-black river bottom for clamshells.

During their travels, Pregracke noticed that the riverbanks were lined with trash. "We're talking refrigerators, barrels, tires.

There was this one pile of 50 or 60 barrels that had been there for [more than] 20 years.… I saw there was a problem, basically in my backyard. And I wanted to do something about it," explained Pregracke.

Taking Action

In addition to collecting clamshells, Pregracke started picking up the garbage. He also wrote letters to local companies, requesting donations to launch a cleanup. Pregracke began this cleanup alone in 1997.

pollutants include heavy metals, such as iron, copper, zinc, tin, and lead; oil from spills; and sewage.

Water pollution can cause human health problems and harm aquatic ecosystems. An ecosystem is a community of living things and its environment.

He single-handedly cleaned 160 kilometers (100 miles) of the Mississippi River shoreline with community donations and a grant from a local corporation.

Since then, Pregracke's project has grown. He now has a ten-person crew, a fleet of barges and boats, and thousands of volunteers to help keep the Mississippi and other rivers in the United States clean. "There's been a lot of accomplishments, and I've had a lot of help," said Pregracke. "But I feel like I'm just getting started."

Phantom Garbage

Although Pregracke has hauled tons of garbage from the Mississippi, the river is still polluted by a type of waste that can't be picked up with a forklift: runoff.

Rainwater either soaks into the ground or flows over Earth's surface as runoff. Runoff transports ground pollution to rivers, oceans, lakes, and wetlands. Many of the pollutants in runoff come from oil, antifreeze, and gasoline leaked by automobiles; pesticides sprayed on lawns; and fertilizers spread on fields. Other water

✍️ Think and Write

1 How might runoff pollution affect your drinking water?

2 What can you do to help keep rivers clean?

Did You Know?

- The majority of Americans live within 10 miles of a polluted body of water.

- Water pollution has caused fishing and swimming to be prohibited in 40 percent of the nation's rivers, lakes, and coastal waters.

- Your own daily habits can help reduce water pollution. For more information, visit the U.S. Environmental Protection Agency's water website for kids.

Find out more. Log on to
www.hspscience.com

Vocabulary Review

Use the terms below to complete the sentences. The page numbers tell you where to look in the chapter if you need help.

producers p. 194   **decomposers** p. 201

herbivores p. 200   **food web** p. 202

food chain p. 201   **energy pyramid** p. 205

1. To survive, all consumers rely on
_____.

2. Nutrients are returned to the soil by
_____.

3. Animals that eat producers are
_____.

4. Grass-insect-bird-hawk is an example of
a _____.

5. The fact that each level of a food chain passes on less food energy than the level before it is shown in an _____.

6. The relationship among different food chains in an ecosystem is a _____.

Check Understanding

Write the letter of the best choice.

7. Which of the following is the process in which stomata release water from a leaf?
   A. chlorophyll
   B. photosynthesis
   C. respiration
   D. transpiration

8. Which of the following is the substance that enables a leaf to use sunlight to produce food?
   F. chlorophyll
   G. photosynthesis
   H. respiration
   J. transpiration

9. How much energy is passed from each level of an energy pyramid to the next?
   A. 10 percent
   B. 20 percent
   C. 80 percent
   D. 90 percent

10. **SEQUENCE** To which group do
     herbivores pass their energy?
    F. first-level consumers
    G. plants
    H. producers
    J. second-level consumers

11. **MAIN IDEA AND DETAILS** What is the
    source of all food energy on Earth?
    A. decomposers
    B. herbivores
    C. producers
    D. carnivores

12. Which process produces most of the oxygen in Earth's atmosphere?
    F. burning
    G. photosynthesis
    H. respiration
    J. transpiration

13. Which of these is **not** a consumer?

    A. caribou   **C.** owl

    B. mouse   **D.** reindeer moss

14. The relationships between organisms in an ecosystem can be shown in many ways. Which way is shown here?

    F. energy pyramid

    G. food chain

    H. food pyramid

    J. food web

15. Which gas does photosynthesis produce?

    A. ammonia

    B. carbon dioxide

    C. nitrogen

    D. oxygen

16. Which of the following must plants have for photosynthesis?

    F. soil   **H.** warmth

    G. stems   **J.** water

Inquiry Skills

17. Which three of the organisms below should be **classified** in the same group? Explain your answer.

18. Kendra will perform an experiment in which she cuts the stem of a sunflower and then puts the stem into the soil. **Predict** what will happen, and explain why.

Critical Thinking

19. Not all producers are plants. Some protists are also producers. How can you tell by looking at a protist whether it is a producer?

20. The diagram shows a sequence of four organisms.

The Big Idea

grass ➡ grasshopper ➡ snake ➡ hawk

If this were part of a food web, would more arrows point toward the second-level consumer or away from the second-level consumer? Explain.

Ecosystems and Change

What's the Big Idea?

Ecosystems change over time, both naturally and as a result of human activities.

Essential Questions

Lesson 1

How Do Organisms Compete and Survive in an Ecosystem?

Lesson 2

How Do Ecosystems Change over Time?

Lesson 3

How Do People Affect Ecosystems?

GO online Student eBook
www.hspscience.com

What do YOU wonder?

Many animals share their ecosystems with people. Here an elk is searching for food and water in a neighborhood. How might the neighborhood—a dramatic change in the natural ecosystem of the elk—affect the survival of these animals? How does this relate to the **Big Idea?**

Investigate ways that some animals use color to hide in their environments.

Read and learn how groups of animals depend on and compete with other groups of animals in an ecosystem.

Essential Question

How Do Organisms Compete and Survive in an Ecosystem?

Fast Fact

That's Fast!

This chameleon's tongue shoots out at about 21.6 km/hr (13.4 mi/hr)! This enables the chameleon to catch fast-moving insects. It can even zap insects more than one and a half body lengths away. In the Investigate, you'll find out how some insects avoid being captured, even by chameleons.

population [pahp•yuh•LAY•shuhn] A group of organisms of one kind that live in one location (p. 218)

community [kuh•MYOO•nuh•tee] A group of populations that live together (p. 218)

competition [kahm•puh•TISH•uhn] A kind of contest among populations that need to get a certain amount of food, water, and shelter to survive (p. 219)

adaptation [ad•uhp•TAY•shuhn] A trait or characteristic that helps an organism survive (p. 219)

symbiosis [sim•by•OH•sis] A relationship between different kinds of organisms (p. 220)

predator [PRED•uh•ter] An animal that kills and eats other animals (p. 222)

prey [PRAY] An animal that is eaten by a predator (p. 222)

Chameleon capturing prey

Using Color to Hide

Start with Questions

Organisms must do many different things to survive in an ecosystem. Hiding is one way that some organisms survive.

- What might make it easier for an animal to hide?

- How is the animal in this picture hiding?

Investigate to find out. Then read and learn to find out more.

Prepare to Investigate

Inquiry Skill Tip

After conducting an experiment, compare your predictions with your results. If they are different, try to understand why. Many scientific discoveries have been made through unexpected results.

Materials

- hole punch
- red, blue, green, and yellow sheets of acetate
- large green cloth
- clock or watch with a second hand

Make an Observation Chart

Number of Insects Found				
	Red	Blue	Green	Yellow
Hunt 1				
Hunt 2				
Hunt 3				
Hunt 4				
Total				

Follow This Procedure

1. Make a table like the one shown.

2. Using the hole punch, make 50 small "insects" from each color of acetate.

3. **Predict** which color would be the easiest and which would be the hardest for a bird to find in grass. **Record** your predictions.

4. Spread the green cloth on the floor, and randomly scatter the insects over it.

5. At the edge of the cloth, kneel with your group. In 15 seconds, each of you will pick up as many insects as you can, one at a time.

6. Count the number of each color your group collected. **Record** the data in the table.

7. Repeat Steps 5 and 6 three more times. Then total each column.

Draw Conclusions

1. Which color did you predict would be easiest to find? Which color was collected most often? Least often? Why?

2. **Inquiry Skill** Scientists predict what they expect to happen and then observe what happens. **Predict** what might happen to green insects if the grass turns brown.

Step 2

Step 2

Independent Inquiry

Predict how different body shapes might help insects hide in grass. Then plan an investigation to test your prediction.

VOCABULARY
population p. 218
community p. 218
competition p. 219
adaptation p. 219
symbiosis p. 220
predator p. 222
prey p. 222

SCIENCE CONCEPTS
▶ how populations depend on and compete with one another
▶ how adaptations help plants and animals compete

(Focus Skill) MAIN IDEA AND DETAILS
Look for details about how organisms interact.

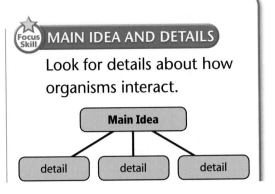

Interactions in Nature

In the last chapter, you learned about different kinds of ecosystems. You also learned that ecosystems include many kinds of plants and animals. All the organisms of one kind in an ecosystem are called a **population**. For example, a pond ecosystem might have populations of frogs, waterlilies, insects, duckweed, and protists.

Populations living and interacting with each other form a **community**. For example, in a pond community, some insects eat plants. Then frogs eat insects.

Another part of an ecosystem is the physical environment, which includes the sun, air, and water. The soil and climate are also part of the environment. Populations interact with the environment. Plants grow in sunlight and take water and nutrients from soil. Fish and frogs live in water that birds and other animals drink.

To survive, each population needs a certain amount of food, water, shelter, and space. They need to meet their basic needs.

Competition can take many forms. These moray eels compete for shelter in a coral reef.

As this water hole dries up, many organisms compete for water.

Counting the Survivors

This graph shows the average number of young produced and the number that survive the first year. What can you say about survival rates compared to the numbers of young produced?

Survivors

Y-axis (Young): 0, 50, 100, 150, 4000

X-axis (Species): Bald Eagle, Green Sea Turtle, Trout

- ■ Number of young produced
- ■ Number of young that survive the first year

After sea horses hatch, they are on their own. Many starve or are eaten by other fish. Sea horses have as many as 1000 young, which helps increase their chances of survival.

Some animals have few young, but take care of them after birth. This care helps the young survive.

The challenge of meeting these needs leads to **competition**, a kind of contest among populations.

Populations often compete for the same sources of food. For example, alligators and snapping turtles both eat fish. When there isn't much food, individuals of the same population compete with each other.

In winter, deer compete with each other for food.

Too little food leads to increased competition. Increased competition limits the number of organisms that can share an ecosystem. For this reason, food is a *limiting factor*. It limits the size of a population.

To survive and compete in an ecosystem, animals have developed many kinds of adaptations. An **adaptation** is a characteristic that helps an organism compete in an ecosystem. A turtle survives the winter by burrowing into the mud. A tiger's coloring enables it to sneak up on prey. Some plants smell so bad that animals won't eat them. All of these characteristics are adaptations.

(Focus Skill) **MAIN IDEA AND DETAILS** What do organisms compete for in an ecosystem?

219

Mistletoe sends its roots into the tree on which it grows. It takes nutrients from the tree. The mistletoe benefits, but the tree is harmed.

▲ The barnacles on this humpback whale eat scraps the whale misses. The barnacles benefit, but the whale is not affected.

Symbiosis

Populations don't always compete with each other. Sometimes a relationship between organisms helps each of them meet basic needs. A relationship between different kinds of organisms is called **symbiosis** (sim•by•OH•SIS).

There are three kinds of symbiosis. In the first kind, both organisms benefit. For example, some ants take care of tiny insects called aphids. The ants guide the aphids to leaves. Then the ants protect the aphids while the aphids eat. When an ant rubs an aphid, the aphid gives off a sweet liquid. The ant drinks this liquid. This relationship, called *mutualism*, helps both the ant and the aphid.

In the second kind of symbiosis, only one organism benefits and the other isn't affected. An example is the relationship between sharks and small fish called remora.

A remora attaches itself to the shark by using a sucker on its head. Being near a shark protects the remora. The remora also eats scraps from the shark's meals. The remora benefits, and the shark isn't affected much. This relationship is called *commensalism*.

Some bacteria in your large intestine have this kind of relationship with you. They feed on the food in your intestine without harming you. Other bacteria help supply you with vitamin K. This relationship is an example of mutualism. You provide food, and the bacteria help keep you well. You both benefit.

In the third kind of symbiosis, called *parasitism*, one organism benefits but the other is harmed. The organism that benefits is called a *parasite*. The organism that is harmed is called a *host*. Parasites steal food.

▲ The birds on this rhino are eating insects that bother the rhino. The birds get dinner, and the rhino gets relief from the insects. Both benefit.

Some harm the hosts in other ways. Some parasites release chemicals into the host. In time, these chemicals may harm or kill the host.

Viruses and many one-celled organisms—such as bacteria, some protists, and some fungi—are parasites. They cause diseases such as polio, measles, and influenza. During the Middle Ages, a parasite caused an illness called the Black Plague, which killed about one-third of the population of Europe.

Bacteria and viruses spread as long as they can find hosts. Vaccinations can stop the spread of some of these parasites. When the parasites can't find new hosts, they die.

Roundworms and tapeworms are parasites that live in their hosts' intestines. They absorb food from their hosts, harming or killing them.

The sea lamprey is also a parasite. This eel attaches itself to a fish. Unlike the remora, the lamprey drills a hole into the fish and sucks its blood. The wound often becomes infected.

 MAIN IDEA AND DETAILS Give one example for each kind of symbiosis.

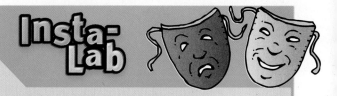

Human Symbiosis
With a partner, think of human activities that are examples of symbiosis. Then act out your examples. Have classmates classify the types of symbiosis being acted out.

Predator-Prey Relationships

To survive, animals must eat. They must also avoid being eaten. An animal that eats other animals is called a **predator**. For example, hawks and wolves are predators. Animals that are eaten, such as mice and rabbits, are called **prey**.

It's easy to see why predators need prey. However, prey need predators, too. Otherwise, prey populations would grow very large. Then the prey would have to compete with each other to meet their basic needs. Many would end up starving.

The number of prey and the number of predators are closely related. Any change in one leads to a change in the other. For example, if a prey animal's food supply increases, it will be easier for more prey to survive long enough to reproduce. More prey means more food for predators, so the number of predators goes up, too.

On the other hand, a drought might kill much of the grass and other plants in an ecosystem. Then the number of prey that eat the plants is likely to drop. Soon the ecosystem will have fewer predators, too.

Predators help keep the number of prey in balance. For example, wolves keep the deer in some ecosystems to a manageable number. If there were too many deer, they might eat all of the available food. Then more deer would die of starvation than from the attacks of wolves.

Focus Skill **MAIN IDEA AND DETAILS**

What symbiotic relationship is most like a predator-prey relationship?

The cheetah's markings keep it hidden until it gets close to its prey—an antelope. Then the predator's speed enables it to chase down its prey. ▼

Essential Question

How Do Organisms Compete and Survive in an Ecosystem?

In this lesson, you learned that one population of animals competes for survival with other populations in an ecosystem, and that sometimes animals must adapt to changing environments. You also learned that sometimes animals work together to survive and meet their basic needs.

1. **MAIN IDEA AND DETAILS** Draw and complete a graphic organizer that shows the supporting details of this main idea: Organisms both depend on and compete with one another.

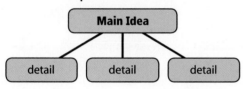

Main Idea

detail   detail   detail

2. **SUMMARIZE** Write a three- or four-sentence summary of the predator-prey relationship.

3. **DRAW CONCLUSIONS** A certain forest is home to a large number of hawks. What does this tell you about the number of mice and other small animals that live there?

4. **VOCABULARY** Use the lesson vocabulary terms to create a quiz that uses matching.

Test Prep

5. **CRITICAL THINKING** What are three of the populations in an ecosystem near you?

6. Which of these is an adaptation that helps a skunk defend itself against predators?
   A. its stripe   C. its odor
   B. its tail   D. its size

Make Connections

 Writing

Expository Writing
You have discovered a new kind of organism in a rain forest. Write a brief **description** explaining how this organism meets its needs. Include any symbiotic relationships it has.

 Math

Solve a Problem
For a certain fish, only 5 of every 100 eggs hatch and survive to adulthood. If this fish lays 5,000 eggs, how many will become adults?

 Health

Parasites
Learn more about the parasites that affect people, such as tapeworms or the viruses that cause smallpox or influenza. Then, in an oral or written report, share what you learned.

Investigate changes in an ecosystem by using a model.

Read and learn how an ecosystem changes and how this change affects organisms living there.

Essential Question

How Do Ecosystems Change over Time?

Fast Fact

Missing Marshes

Many of the world's ecosystems are changing. Salt marshes like this one are quickly disappearing. By 2025, two-thirds of Africa's farmable land will be too dry for growing crops. In the Investigate, you'll model how an ecosystem can change from a pond into dry land.

Salt marsh

succession [suhk•SESH•uhn] A gradual change in the kinds of organisms living in an ecosystem (p. 228)

extinction [ek•STINGK•shuhn] The death of all the organisms of a species (p. 232)

Observing Changes

Start with Questions

Ecosystems change all the time. Sometimes, change is quick, while at other times, it takes hundreds of years.

- What kind of effect does this have on organisms in an ecosystem?

- How do you think this forest has changed over the years?

Investigate to find out. Then read and learn to find out more.

Prepare to Investigate

Inquiry Skill Tip

It is often useful to make a model for an investigation, but think carefully about the changes you see in a model. Sometimes, the changes wouldn't occur in a real-life situation. Other changes might occur in the real situation but not in the model.

Materials

- ruler
- potting soil
- plastic dishpan
- water
- duckweed
- birdseed

Make an Observation Chart

Day	Water Depth (cm)	Observations
1	4cm	
4		
7		

226

Follow This Procedure

1. **Make a model** of a pond by spreading 5 cm of potting soil in the dishpan. Dig out a low space in the center, leaving 1 cm of soil. Pile up soil around the low space to make sides about 10 cm high.

2. Slowly pour water into the low spot until the water is 4 cm deep. Put duckweed in the "pond."

3. Sprinkle birdseed over the soil. Do not water it. Make a drawing or take a photograph to **record** how your pond looks.

4. After three or four days, **measure** and **record** the depth of the water in the pond. **Record** how the pond looks now.

4. Sprinkle more birdseed over the soil, and water it lightly.

5. Wait three or four more days, and observe how your pond has changed. **Measure** and **record** the depth of the water. **Compare** your three observations.

Draw Conclusions

1. What caused the changes you observed?

2. **Inquiry Skill** Scientists often **make models** and observe changes, just as you did. Which of the changes you observed might occur in a real pond? What other changes might occur in a real pond?

Step 1

Step 3

Independent Inquiry

Make a model of another ecosystem, such as a forest floor. If possible, include some insects. Observe and record the changes that take place over time.

227

VOCABULARY
succession p. 228
extinction p. 232

SCIENCE CONCEPTS
▶ how changes in ecosystems affect the organisms there
▶ how these changes can cause the extinction of some organisms

CAUSE AND EFFECT

Look for the causes of changes in ecosystems.

cause ⟶ effect

Primary Succession

Ecosystems change every day, but the changes are usually too slow to notice. Some organisms die out, while others start to thrive. A gradual change in the kinds of organisms living in an ecosystem is called **succession**. Unlike the changes you observed in the Investigate, succession in nature can take thousands of years.

What causes succession? One cause is a change in climate. When a region becomes drier, for example, some of the organisms that live there will no longer be able to meet their needs. If fewer plants survive in the dry climate, herbivores will have to move to find food or they'll die. A loss of herbivores leads to a loss of predators. Meanwhile, plants and animals that can live with less water begin to thrive. They will slowly replace the organisms that cannot live in the drier climate.

Succession can also be caused by the organisms living in an ecosystem. For example, a large herd of deer can kill many trees by eating too many leaves. Then the deer and other animals in the ecosystem can no longer find enough food or shelter. To survive, they must move to new areas.

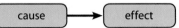

Primary Succession

① At the edge of a pond, plants trap soil in their roots. As the plants die and decay, the soil gains nutrients.

② More plants begin to grow in the rich new soil at the edge of the pond. The pond is starting to get smaller.

With fewer small animals to eat, the predators also leave or die. Because fewer trees shade the forest floor, plants that thrive in the sun begin to grow. Much of the ecosystem has changed.

Adding new plants or animals to an ecosystem is another cause of succession. For example, a vine called *kudzu* has taken over many ecosystems of the southern United States. Kudzu was brought to the United States from Japan in 1876. Farmers were paid to plant it because, they were told, kudzu could control erosion and feed animals.

The climate of the South was perfect for kudzu. It could grow 30 cm (1 ft) a day! Soon this vine was everywhere. It killed whole forests by climbing on trees and preventing sunlight from reaching the trees' leaves. In 1972, kudzu was declared to be a weed. By then, it had affected many ecosystems in the South by changing both the plants and the animals that lived there.

Succession can be primary or secondary. *Primary succession* begins with bare rock. The first plants to grow, such as lichens (LY•kuhnz), are called pioneer plants. Lichens can grow without soil, and they can survive harsh conditions. As they grow, lichens produce chemicals that help weather the rock they grow on. In time, a thin layer of soil forms, allowing mosses to grow.

As mosses grow and die, they add nutrients to the thin soil. Soon grass seeds begin to sprout. Then birds and other animals come to eat the grasses and their seeds. The animals' droppings add more nutrients to the soil and help spread seeds. When the soil is deep enough and rich enough, larger plants, including trees, begin to grow. In time, the ecosystem becomes stable, and changes stop. The result is known as a *climax community*.

Focus Skill CAUSE AND EFFECT

What are three causes of succession?

The pond ecosystem continues to grow smaller, while the land ecosystem grows larger.

Small shrubs now grow where the pond was. In time, they will be replaced by larger trees.

229

Secondary Succession

Rebirth of a Forest

1. **Fire destroys all the organisms living above ground.**

2. **Roots that survive underground and seeds blown in by the wind begin to sprout, forming new plants.**

Secondary Succession

Secondary succession helps rebuild damaged ecosystems. This kind of succession occurs in places that already have soil. It often happens after a forest fire or a volcanic eruption has destroyed the original ecosystem.

Primary succession is a very slow process. Secondary succession is not. It happens quickly because soil is already there and the soil usually contains many seeds. Animals and wind bring in more seeds. Some roots of original plants survive underground, and they start sending up new shoots. In secondary succession, as with primary succession, the first plants are hardy. But they don't have to be as hardy as those growing on bare rock. The soil is deep enough for strong roots, and ashes from burned trees add nutrients to the soil.

You might have heard about eruptions of Mount St. Helens in Washington State. This volcano exploded on May 18, 1980, covering the mountain with a thick layer of ash and mud. Yet by the summer of 1981, the mountainside bloomed with pink fireweed flowers. A few years later, shrubs began to grow there. Many insects, birds, and other animals have already returned. Now you can find young fir trees on the mountain's slopes. Even with more eruptions, a mature forest will one day cover Mount St. Helens again.

3. New growth appears among the blackened tree trunks. Many insects and other small animals return to the forest.

For more links and activities, go to www.hspscience.com

Where secondary succession occurs, there is also some primary succession. Secondary succession cannot occur without primary succession. You can find bare rock after a volcanic eruption. Fire, followed by erosion of the soil, also uncovers bare rock. Lichens would begin growing on the rock. Mosses would grow next, and so on, until the ecosystem of the bare rock would be the same as that restored by secondary succession. But this may take hundreds of years. Remember, primary succession happens very slowly.

 CAUSE AND EFFECT

What is the main result of primary succession and of secondary succession?

Insta-Lab

Regrowth

Make a drawing showing regrowth of a climax community in an area that has had a fire, a flood, a volcano, or other natural disaster. Be sure to include several stages of secondary succession in your drawing.

Extinction

Sometimes changes in an ecosystem cause the extinction of an entire species. **Extinction** is the death of all the organisms of a species.

Many organisms can adapt to slow changes in an ecosystem. But some cannot. When an environment changes, some organisms living in it will die. Plants and some animals can't move to other ecosystems to meet their needs.

A species with just a few small populations in different places is more likely to become extinct than a species with many large populations. A population that lives in a small area, such as on a remote island, is in more danger than a population spread out over a large area. Any change in the island environment could wipe out an entire population.

An environmental change can be so great that it affects many populations of different species. You might know that most dinosaurs became extinct about 65 million years ago. But did you know that more than 70 percent of all the other organisms on Earth were also wiped out? This mass extinction was probably due to a drastic change in the worldwide climate.

Some scientists hypothesize that the cause was an asteroid striking Earth. It may have thrown up a dust cloud so big that it blocked out the sun. Some plants died, followed by many herbivores and most carnivores. Of course, most changes in ecosystems are more gradual.

Many human actions, too, can lead to extinctions. You'll learn more about that in the next lesson.

 **CAUSE AND EFFECT** How can a change in climate cause extinctions?

Beginning 40,000 years ago, thousands of plants and animals became trapped in tar that rose to Earth's surface. Fossils of nearly 200 kinds of organisms, including saber-toothed cats, have been identified in the La Brea tar pits in California. ▼

Saber-toothed cats became extinct about 11,000 years ago. The cause was probably climate change or hunting.

Essential Question

How Do Ecosystems Change Over Time?

In this lesson, you learned how an ecosystem can change over time with primary succession and secondary succession of organisms. You also learned how these successions can lead to the extinction of certain animals that aren't able to adapt to the changes.

1. **CAUSE AND EFFECT** Draw and complete a graphic organizer to show the causes of this effect: Succession occurs.

2. **SUMMARIZE** Write a one-paragraph summary of the process of secondary succession.

3. **DRAW CONCLUSIONS** How are pioneer plants different from plants in a climax community?

4. **VOCABULARY** Write a paragraph using each vocabulary term twice.

Test Prep

5. **CRITICAL THINKING** Describe ways that people affect succession.

6. Which of these is the final result of secondary succession?
   A. adaptation
   B. rebuilt ecosystem
   C. competition
   D. final extinction

Make Connections

 Writing

Narrative Writing
Choose a wild area or park near you. Write a **description** of its present stage of succession. Describe how human activities have influenced its natural succession.

 Math

Make an Estimate
Florida is 65,700 sq mi in area. Texas covers 268,600 sq mi. Florida has 111 species in danger of extinction. Texas has 91. Which state has more endangered species per square mile?

 Art

Succession
Use any kind of media to illustrate the stages of primary or secondary succession. Set the succession in a certain climate, and research the plants that should be shown.

Investigate the effects of pollution on a water ecosystem.

Read and Learn how the actions of people can negatively affect the environment, and then how people can help the environment.

Essential Question

How Do People Affect Ecosystems?

Fast Fact

Too Much Paper!

More than 40 percent of the trash in this landfill is paper! Despite widespread recycling programs, paper is still the most common item tossed in the trash. Unfortunately, paper buried in a landfill is very slow to decay. Newspapers can still be read 40 years after they were buried. In the Investigate, you'll explore how human actions can affect other parts of our ecosystems.

A landfill and seagulls

pollution [puh•LOO•shuhn]
A waste product that harms living things and damages an ecosystem (p. 238)

acid rain [AS•id RAYN] A mixture of rain and acids from air pollution that falls to Earth (p. 238)

habitat [HAB•i•tat] An area where an organism can find everything it needs to survive (p. 239)

conservation [kahn•ser•VAY•shuhn] The use of less of a resource to make the supply last longer (p. 240)

reclamation [rek•luh•MAY•shuhn] The process of cleaning and restoring a damaged ecosystem (p. 242)

Observing Effects of Fertilizer

Guided Inquiry

Start With Questions

Humans can have both positive and negative effects on the environment.

- How do you think pollution forms?

- How might these crops be affected by the nearby construction?

Investigate to find out. Then read and learn to find out more.

Prepare to Investigate

Inquiry Skill Tip

You can obtain meaningful results in an investigation only if you identify and control variables. The variable you choose to change depends on the goal of your investigation. Sometimes you may want to change more than one variable. If so, you should plan a separate investigation for each variable you change.

Materials

- marker
- 4 cups with lids
- pond water
- dropper
- liquid fertilizer

Make an Observation Chart

Day	Observations	Day	Observations
1		7	
2		8	
3		9	
4		10	
5		11	
6		12	

Follow This Procedure

1. Use a marker to number the cups 1–4.

2. Fill each cup with the same amount of pond water.

3. Use a dropper to put 10 drops of liquid fertilizer in cup 1, 20 drops in cup 2, and 40 drops in cup 3. Do not put any fertilizer in cup 4.

4. Put lids on the cups, and place them in a sunny window.

5. **Observe** the cups every day for twelve days, and **record** your observations.

Step 1

Draw Conclusions

1. Which cup had the most plant growth? Which had the least? What **conclusion** can you **draw** about fertilizer and plant growth?

2. As organisms die and decay in water, they use up the oxygen in the water. Which cup do you **infer** will eventually contain the least amount of oxygen? Explain your answer.

3. **Inquiry Skill** Scientists **identify and control variables** in their experiments so they can observe the effect of one variable at a time. Which variables did you control in setting up the four cups? Which variable did you change?

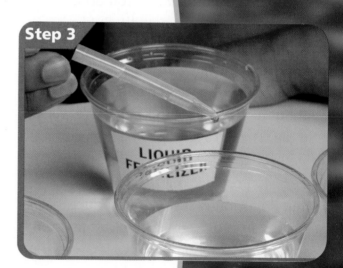
Step 3

Independent Inquiry

Suppose you want to study the effect of sunlight on fertilizer in pond water. **Plan an experiment** that will identify and control the variables. **Then carry out your experiment.**

VOCABULARY
pollution p. 238
acid rain p. 238
habitat p. 239
conservation p. 240
reclamation p. 242

SCIENCE CONCEPTS
▶ how people's actions can change the environment
▶ how the environment can be protected and restored

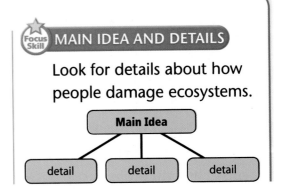

MAIN IDEA AND DETAILS

Look for details about how people damage ecosystems.

Main Idea

detail   detail   detail

Damaging Ecosystems

In the Investigate, you observed how fertilizer affects pond water. You observed that it speeds up plant growth. But isn't plant growth a good thing?

In time, plants in water will die. As they decay, they will use up oxygen in the water. Without oxygen, any fish living there will also die. The decaying fish will use up still more oxygen.

Decaying organic matter can pollute water. **Pollution** is any waste product that damages an ecosystem. Chemicals used on crops and lawns also pollute water. Heavy rain carries them from the fields to streams, rivers, and lakes.

Air can be polluted, too. Burning fossil fuels, such as coal, oil, and gas, is a major cause of air pollution. Certain chemicals in fossil fuels mix with water vapor in the air. The combination produces acids. When these acids fall to Earth with rain, we call it **acid rain**.

Acid rain can damage trees, crops, and other plants. It has made many bodies of clean-looking water acidic. Acidic water affects organisms differently. For example, it might kill all the small fish in a pond but not harm the larger fish. Then that pond's food chain would be affected. The plants eaten by small fish, as well as big fish that eat small fish, would be affected by this.

A strip mine can pollute the groundwater as well as the land. ▼

This bear now has to share its ecosystem with people.

Trash threatens wildlife in many ways. Animals can get cut by broken glass or snared by plastic drink-can holders. Small animals can even get trapped inside containers.

▲ Every year, snowmobiles add tons of pollutants to the air in places such as Yellowstone National Park.

Ecosystems can also be damaged by changing them. For example, most of our prairie ecosystems have been turned into farms. Prairies once had many communities. Now most of the land is used to grow only one crop.

People fence off many ecosystems. This reduces the size of habitats or forces animals to share habitats with people. A **habitat** is an area where an organism can find everything it needs to survive. Fences make it hard for animals to migrate, or move, to different habitats. Fences also cut through hunting grounds of predators such as mountain lions and wolves.

When people cut down forests for timber, they destroy habitats. Habitats are also destroyed when people fill wetlands to make space for houses and shopping malls.

Sometimes people introduce organisms from other regions, such as the kudzu vine

you read about. These organisms crowd out native plants and animals, changing and often damaging the ecosystem.

 **MAIN IDEA AND DETAILS** What are three ways that people damage ecosystems?

Melting a Sculpture
Make a "sculpture" from a piece of chalk. Use a paper clip to carve the chalk. Then stand the chalk upright in a clay base. Drip vinegar or lemon juice onto your sculpture. How does the vinegar, an acid, affect your sculpture? How is this like acid rain affecting a statue?

▲ Beach walkovers help protect the fragile ecosystem of the dunes.

Protecting Ecosystems

Many laws have been passed to protect ecosystems. For example, most wetlands can no longer be filled in. Regulations control how industries can get rid of possible pollutants. New cars must have devices that reduce air pollution. And before developers can build, they must describe how a project might affect the environment.

But laws alone are not enough. Each person can have a role in protecting ecosystems. One way is through the **conservation**, or saving, of resources. Conservation of resources includes three actions: reduce, reuse, and recycle.

Reduce means "use fewer resources." For example, if you walk or ride your bike instead of riding in a car, you save gasoline. Opening windows instead of turning on an air conditioner helps reduce the amount of coal burned to produce electricity. Burning gasoline and coal also causes acid rain.

Reuse means "use resources again, instead of throwing them away." For example, you can give outgrown clothes and toys to a charity. That way, someone else can use them. You can also use glasses and dishes that can be washed and used over and over.

That saves plastic and paper that would be thrown away.

Some items can be reused for a new purpose. For example, a plastic drink bottle can be reused as a planter, a bird feeder, or a funnel. Reusing items saves resources and space in landfills, too.

Recycle means "collect used items so their raw materials can be used again." For example, glass, paper, aluminum, and some plastics can be ground up or melted and made into new products. And recycling often uses less energy than producing the same items from new resources.

Most glass can be recycled. Recycled glass melts at a lower temperature than the resources used to make new glass. Recycling glass requires 30 percent less energy than making new glass.

Nearly all kinds of paper can be recycled. Making new paper from old paper uses 20 percent less energy than making paper from trees. However, paper coated with wax, foil, or plastic is too costly to recycle.

Recycling aluminum helps a lot. Recycling just two cans saves the energy equal to a cup of gasoline. Making a can from recycled aluminum uses only 4 percent of the energy needed to make a can from new resources.

Plastics make up about 10 percent of our waste. Some kinds of plastic are hard to recycle. However, soft-drink bottles are easy. The recycled bottles can be used to make carpeting, boards, new bottles, and many other products.

Reducing, reusing, and recycling save resources and energy. These actions reduce pollution and help protect ecosystems.

MAIN IDEA AND DETAILS List six ways you can help protect ecosystems.

Juice boxes are hard to recycle because most contain paper, plastic, and aluminum. Pouring juice from a large container into a glass means fewer juice boxes end up in landfills.

Discarded batteries can leak pollutants into the soil. In some states, it is illegal to put batteries in the trash. Instead, use rechargeable batteries.

Old newspapers take up about 13 percent of all the space in landfills. Yet they are easy to recycle into new paper.

Restoring Ecosystems

Damaged ecosystems are not always lost. Some can be cleaned and restored. The process is called **reclamation**. But reclamation is costly and takes time.

Removing pollutants is often part of reclamation. We now know that wetlands can help filter pollutants out of water. Yet the United States has lost most of its wetlands. In the 1970s, builders were filling in 500,000 acres of wetlands a year.

Now the rate of wetland loss has slowed. Many programs are helping to protect remaining wetlands or even to restore them.

For example, many wetlands have been restored along Florida's Gulf Coast. The bays of Fort DeSoto Park, near St. Petersburg, Florida, had become clogged with soil. The water quality was poor. The plants and animals were struggling to survive. Now the water moves freely. This change has also improved water quality in wetlands nearby.

Fragile ecosystems are being restored across the nation. Perhaps there is a reclamation project near you.

MAIN IDEA AND DETAILS

Why are wetlands important in reclamation?

This area used to be a strip mine. The first step in reclaiming a strip mine is removing mining wastes. Then soil must be added to provide a base for trees and plants. Reclamation of a large strip mine can take many years and cost millions of dollars.

Essential Question

How Do People Affect Ecosystems?

In this lesson, you learned about some of the damaging effects that humans can have on ecosystems through pollution and change to habitats. You also learned that humans can work to protect ecosystems and to restore habitats.

1. **(Focus Skill) MAIN IDEA AND DETAILS** Draw and complete a graphic organizer with supporting details for this main idea: People's actions can change an ecosystem.

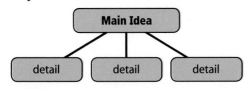

2. **SUMMARIZE** Write a one-paragraph summary about ways that people can help protect an ecosystem.

3. **DRAW CONCLUSIONS** How is conservation different from reclamation?

4. **VOCABULARY** Make up quiz-show answers for the vocabulary terms. See if a partner knows the correct questions for the answers, such as "What is pollution?"

Test Prep

5. **CRITICAL THINKING** What specific things can people do to avoid the cost of restoring an ecosystem?

6. Which of these is a cause of acid rain?
   A. burning forests
   B. burning fuels
   C. runoff from farmers' fields
   D. decaying organisms in the water

Make Connections

 Writing

Persuasive Writing
Some people think recycling is not worth the effort. Write a **letter** for your school or community newspaper, urging readers to recycle. Try to motivate them to help protect ecosystems.

 Math

Make a Pictograph
Make a pictograph showing U.S. recycling rates: cardboard, 70%; newspaper, 60%; aluminum cans, 49%; soft-drink bottles, 36%; glass, 22%.

 Literature

Life Preservers
Read about the life of a well-known naturalist, such as Rachel Carson, Henry David Thoreau, John Burroughs, or John Muir. In a written or oral report, share what you learned.

Shirley Mah Kooyman

▶ **SHIRLEY MAH KOOYMAN**

▶ Botanist
▶ Coordinator for the Minnesota Landscape Arboretum

The health of plants is important to our survival. Shirley Mah Kooyman feels that plants are sometimes taken for granted—that people forget they are living things. Ms. Kooyman is a botanist, or plant scientist, in Chanhassen, Minnesota. An important part of her work is discovering what makes plants grow. The knowledge that she gains is used by scientists who work to find ways to grow healthier plants.

In her work, Ms. Kooyman seeks to better understand some growth processes of plants. She knows that in addition to light energy, water, proper temperature, and rich soil, plants need certain hormones. Hormones are chemical "messengers" that "tell" plants to grow. Plant hormones are produced in stems and roots. From there they travel to other parts of the plant.

Today, scientists are able to make artificial plant hormones. The advantage of artificial hormones is that they can be produced in greater amounts than natural hormones. Farmers can use artificial hormones to speed up plant growth and produce larger crops. Ms. Kooyman also teaches people about plants and the joys of gardening.

 Think and Write

1 Why is it important to understand what makes plants grow?

2 How might artificial hormones help make plant products more affordable?

Alissa J. Arp

▶ **ALISSA J. ARP**

▶ Ecological physiologist
▶ Vice President for Research and Dean of the College of Natural Sciences at Hawai'i Pacific University

How can tube worms live in a zone of crushing pressure 7000 meters (23,000 ft) below sea level? How do clams live in the untreated sewage sent into the ocean by some coastal cities? These are questions that Alissa J. Arp tries to answer.

Dr. Arp is an ecological physiologist. She studies marine animals that live under harsh conditions. She tries to learn how these animals can live in toxic chemicals, extremely cold temperatures, and total darkness. Her research takes her from polluted mud flats along the coast to cracks in the crust of the ocean floor.

Some of Dr. Arp's research may be important for humans. For example, animals who live in toxic chemicals have adaptations to get rid of poisons. Humans may be able to use some of these animals to clean up polluted environments.

Think and Write

1. How are animals that Dr. Arp studies able to survive in toxic chemicals?
2. How might Dr. Arp's research be used to help humans living in industrial areas?

Career Ecologist

Ecologists study the relationships between living things and their environments. People who wish to become ecologists should study subjects such as botany, zoology, and chemistry in college.

Review and Test Preparation

Vocabulary Review

Use the terms below to complete the sentences. The page numbers tell you where to look in the chapter if you need help.

competition p. 219

adaptation p. 219

predators p. 222

prey p. 222

succession p. 228

extinction p. 232

conservation p. 240

reclamation p. 242

1. Grasses replace mosses in a process called _____.

2. Recycling is one kind of _____.

3. The number of organisms in a population is limited by _____.

4. A hummingbird's long beak is an _____.

5. Cleaning up polluted water is an example of _____.

6. Earthworms can be _____.

7. The death of all earthworms would be an _____.

8. Big cats are usually _____.

Check Understanding

Write the letter of the best choice.

9. How can we reduce the amount of acid rain that falls?
   A. by driving less
   B. by restoring wetlands
   C. by planting more trees
   D. by cleaning up polluted water

10. What forms a community?
    F. symbiotic relationships
    G. several populations
    H. an ecosystem
    J. succession

11. Which of these is usually in the last stage of succession?
    A. bushes   C. mosses
    B. lichen   D. trees

12. **CAUSE AND EFFECT** Which of these could possibly lead to an extinction?
    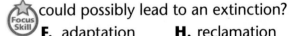
    F. adaptation   H. reclamation
    G. pollution   J. symbiosis

13. **MAIN IDEA AND DETAILS** Which statement is most accurate?
    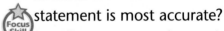
    A. All ecosystems change in a way that is often gradual.
    B. People cause all the changes in ecosystems.
    C. Succession is a cause of change in ecosystems.
    D. Competition is the main cause of change in ecosystems.

14. Which of these is **not** a predator or prey?

   F. corn

   G. alligator

   H. ant

   J. antelope

15. Which of these is **not** a result of human actions?

   A. acid rain

   B. conservation

   C. extinction

   D. symbiosis

16. What is shown in the photo below?

   F. competition

   G. extinction

   H. succession

   J. symbiosis

Inquiry Skills

17. In an experiment, you water one plant with a certain amount of plain water. You water an identical plant with the same amount of a mixture of vinegar and water. You put both plants in a sunny window. Which **variables are you controlling** in this experiment?

18. Suppose the number of organisms in one population in a community suddenly increases. **Predict** what might happen, and explain why.

Critical Thinking

19. Explain how recycling is like mutualism.

20. Study the photograph below, and answer all three questions.

What concept from this chapter does the photograph illustrate? What organisms probably grew here before this photograph was taken? What kinds of organisms will grow here next?

Tell how each picture shows the **Big Idea** for its chapter.

CHAPTER **5**

Big Idea

Living things interact with one another in the environment. Energy flows from the sun to plants to animals.

CHAPTER **6**

Big Idea

Ecosystems change over time, both naturally and as a result of human activities.

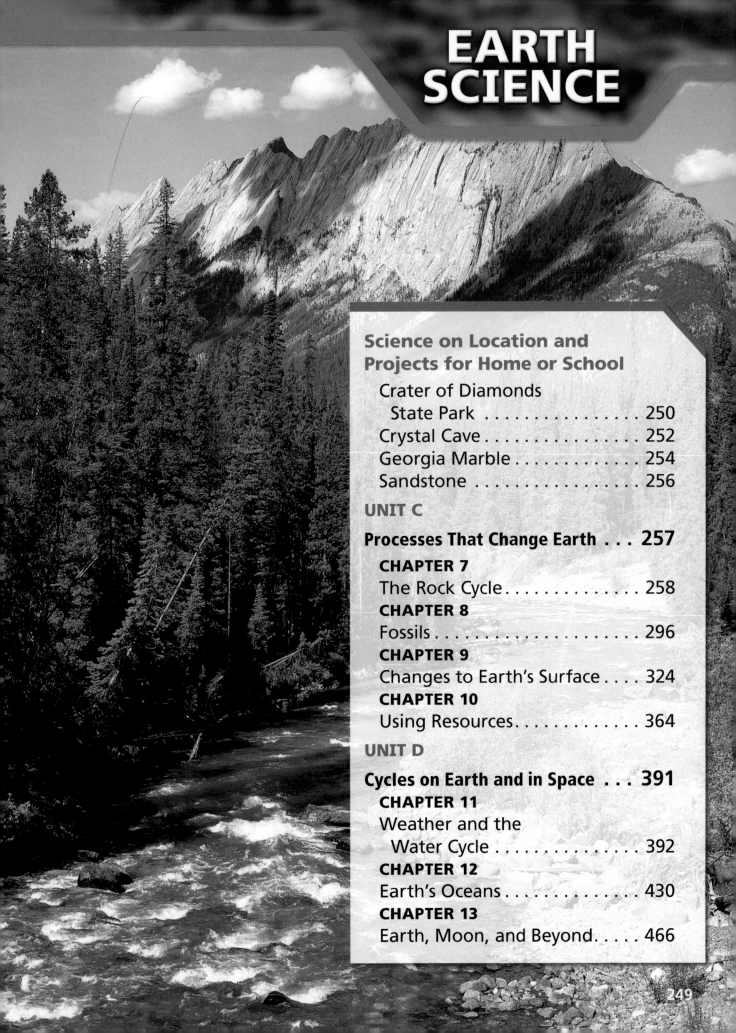

EARTH SCIENCE

Science on Location and Projects for Home or School

Crater of Diamonds
State Park 250
Crystal Cave 252
Georgia Marble 254
Sandstone 256

UNIT C

Processes That Change Earth . . . 257

CHAPTER 7
The Rock Cycle 258
CHAPTER 8
Fossils 296
CHAPTER 9
Changes to Earth's Surface 324
CHAPTER 10
Using Resources 364

UNIT D

Cycles on Earth and in Space . . . 391

CHAPTER 11
Weather and the
Water Cycle 392
CHAPTER 12
Earth's Oceans 430
CHAPTER 13
Earth, Moon, and Beyond 466

CRATER OF DIAMONDS STATE PARK

Would you enjoy looking for buried treasure? If so, you might want to visit Crater of Diamonds State Park near Murfreesboro, Arkansas. Visitors to the park are allowed to search a plowed field for rocks and minerals. They hope to follow in the footsteps of John Huddleston, a local farmer who found diamonds on this land back in 1906. Since the area became a state park in 1972, more than 25,000 diamonds have been discovered. Park officials estimate that an average of two diamonds a day are found.

Though many of the diamonds found in the park are about the size of a match head, some much-larger ones have been unearthed on the site. In 1924, a huge 40-carat white diamond was discovered. Called the Uncle Sam diamond, it is the largest diamond ever found in North America.

Crater of Diamonds

DIAMOND
FIELD PORTAL

Step off the path.

Step onto the Crater.

Your discoveries begin now!

Structure of Diamonds

Like most other minerals, diamonds are crystals. The particles that form these crystals are arranged in a repeating pattern. As a result of its crystal pattern, the diamond is the hardest known natural material on Earth. Diamonds are formed under very high heat and pressure. They form deep underground and were brought to the surface many years ago by volcanic eruptions.

Think And Write

1 **Scientific Thinking** Suppose you take a trip to Crater of Diamonds State Park and discover a gem about the same size as the Uncle Sam diamond. Write an entry in your diary describing your find. Explain how you found your gem, what you plan to call it, and what you will do with it.

2 **Scientific Inquiry** Why do diamonds form only deep underground?

Most diamonds found in the park are white, brown, or yellow.

MINE SHAFT BUILDING

Crater of Diamonds State Park is the world's only diamond-producing site where members of the public can search for diamonds—and keep what they find!

Crystal Cave

Have you ever seen a geode dangling from a key chain or necklace? Geodes are rock formations with crystals on the inside. Many geodes are small enough for you to hold in the palm of your hand. But on South Bass Island in Lake Erie, you can actually walk inside a geode! Crystal Cave is the largest geode in the world. It was discovered in 1897 when workers were digging a well. Located 12 meters (40 ft) below the ground, Crystal Cave is lined with light blue crystals. Some of the crystals are as long as 48 centimeters (18 in.). When the cave was first discovered, it was small. Over the _____ made it bigger by

Inside Crystal Cave

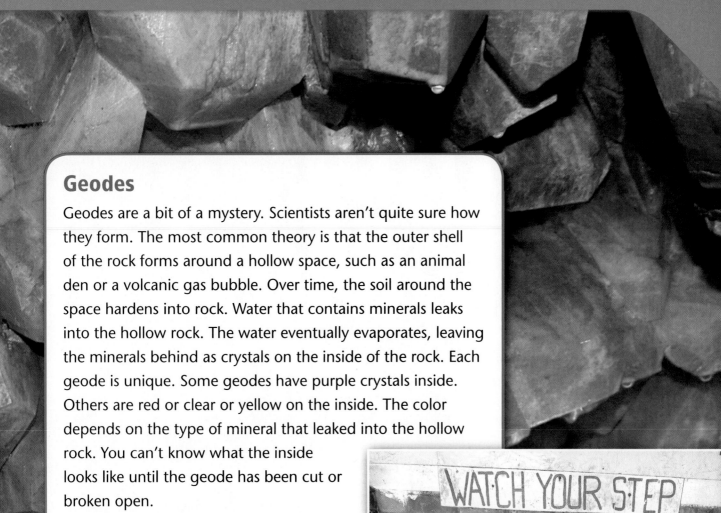

Geodes

Geodes are a bit of a mystery. Scientists aren't quite sure how they form. The most common theory is that the outer shell of the rock forms around a hollow space, such as an animal den or a volcanic gas bubble. Over time, the soil around the space hardens into rock. Water that contains minerals leaks into the hollow rock. The water eventually evaporates, leaving the minerals behind as crystals on the inside of the rock. Each geode is unique. Some geodes have purple crystals inside. Others are red or clear or yellow on the inside. The color depends on the type of mineral that leaked into the hollow rock. You can't know what the inside looks like until the geode has been cut or broken open.

Think And Write

1 **Scientific Thinking** What kinds of tests might you do on the crystals in Crystal Cave to find out what minerals they are made from?

2 **Scientific Inquiry** Are all geodes the same? Why or why not?

The entrance to Crystal Cave

Georgia Marble

Marble quarry

About 5,000 years ago, Native Americans mined white, gray, and pink marble near what is now Tate, Georgia. Today, the Polycor company still mines marble near Tate. In fact, its marble quarries are some of the deepest in the world. And the marble veins, or layers, which stretch about 6 kilometers (4 mi), are some of the longest known.

Workers remove the marble from the ground. Then they cut and polish it for a variety of uses, from floors to roofs to sculptures. Georgia marble is highly prized for its beauty. It has been used to build many famous structures, including the statue of Abraham Lincoln in the Lincoln Memorial in Washington, D.C., and the State House in Providence, Rhode Island.

The Lincoln Memorial is made from Georgia marble.

Qualities of Marble

Marble is a metamorphic rock. It can be many colors, including white, black, green, pink, and brown. Marble's color depends on its mineral makeup. The swirls of color in some marble come from sand or dirt that may have been present as the marble formed. Because marble is a fairly soft rock when it is first taken from the ground, it is popular with sculptors. Sculptors and architects also use marble for its beauty. Marble becomes harder as it ages and can be resistant to many types of erosion. Many ancient buildings made of marble still stand today.

Think and Write

1. **Scientific Thinking** Why do you think some kinds of rock are used more widely than others for buildings and statues? Write a sentence or two about the characteristics that make a rock useful for construction.

2. **Scientific Inquiry** Use reliable Internet sources and other references to find out how marble mining has changed over the years. Write a paragraph describing these changes.

The Rhode Island State House is also made with Georgia marble.

Project | Sandstone

Materials

- 2 paper cups
- scoop
- sand
- white glue
- craft stick
- a sandstone rock

Procedure

1. Half-fill one paper cup with sand. Add a few drops of white glue.

2. Use the craft stick to mix the sand and glue. Add enough glue to make the mixture sticky but not wet.

3. Stack the second cup inside the first. Press down on it to pack the mixture tightly.

4. Remove the second cup, and let the mixture dry overnight.

5. Tear the first paper cup away from the mixture. Compare your "sandstone" with the sandstone rock.

Draw Conclusions

Which of the three rock types did you model? How is your "rock" similar to and different from the sandstone rock? How does the way you made it model one way this type of rock forms in nature?

Design Your Own Investigation

What's Your Soil Like?

Examine a sample of soil from a location near your home. Think about what you have learned about how soil is made, what's in it, and what its properties are. Design some tests to help you learn more about the soil in your sample. Then test the soil, and report the results.

Processes That Change Earth

CHAPTER 7
The Rock Cycle 258

CHAPTER 8
Fossils 296

CHAPTER 9
Changes to Earth's Surface 324

CHAPTER 10
Using Resources 364

Unit Inquiry

Buffering Ability of Soils

Most underground caves are in a type of rock called limestone. Acids dissolve limestone, which can be a problem in some parts of the country where the rain is acidic. Some soils are a good buffer for acid rain, which means that the soil neutralizes the acids as the rain flows through it. Are soils from your town a good buffer for acid rain? Plan and conduct an experiment to find out.

CHAPTER 7

The Rock Cycle

What's the Big Idea?

Rocks and minerals are formed and changed through different Earth processes.

Essential Questions

Lesson 1

What Are Minerals?

Lesson 2

How Do Rocks Form?

Lesson 3

How Are Rocks Changed?

Student eBook
www.hspscience.com

What do YOU wonder?

What could cause rocks to look like those in this photo? How does this relate to the **Big Idea?**

Joshua Tree National Park, in California

259

Investigate some of the properties of minerals.

Read and learn about minerals and some of their properties.

Essential Question

What Are Minerals?

Fast Fact

Giant Gems!

The Crown Jewels of Great Britain are set with thousands of diamonds, rubies, and sapphires. One diamond weighed 621.2 g (21.9 oz) before it was cut! A diamond is the hardest mineral known. That's one property that makes it a valuable gem. What property might make tanzanite, shown here, valuable? You'll learn about other mineral properties in the Investigate.

Cut and polished tanzanite

mineral (MIN•er•uhl) A naturally occurring, nonliving solid that has a specific chemical makeup and a repeating structure (p. 264)

streak (STREEK) The color of the powder left behind when you rub a mineral against a rough white tile or a streak plate (p. 265)

luster (LUS•ter) The way a mineral's surface reflects light (p. 265)

hardness (HARD•nis) A mineral's ability to resist being scratched (p. 266)

261

Mineral Properties

Start with Questions

The diamond in a ring comes from underground. It is the hardest mineral found in nature.

- What other properties does a diamond have?

- Is salt similar to a diamond in any way?

Investigate to find out. Then read and learn to find out more.

Prepare to Investigate

Inquiry Skill Tip

When you classify objects, first observe their properties. Compare and contrast the properties with those of other objects. Group the objects according to the properties that they share.

Materials

- 6 labeled mineral samples
- hand lens
- streak plate
- steel nail
- pre-1983 penny

Make an Observation Chart

Mineral Sample	Color	Streak	Hardness
1			
2			
3			
4			
5			
6			

Follow This Procedure

1. Copy the table.

2. Use the hand lens to **observe** each mineral's color. **Record** your observations in the table.

3. With each mineral, draw a line across the streak plate. What color is each mineral's streak? Record your observations.

CAUTION: Use caution with the nail. It's sharp.

4. Test the hardness of each mineral. Try to scratch each mineral with your fingernail, the penny, and the steel nail. Then try to scratch each mineral with each of the other minerals. Record your observations in the table.

5. **Classify** the minerals by using the properties you tested: color, streak, and hardness. For each mineral, make a label that lists all three properties.

Draw Conclusions

1. How are the mineral samples different from one another?

2. **Inquiry Skill** Scientists **classify** objects to make them easier to study. How do you think scientists classify minerals?

Step 3

Step 4

Independent Inquiry

Obtain five additional mineral samples. **Classify** each sample according to its color, streak, hardness, and one new property.

Read and Learn

VOCABULARY
mineral p. 264
streak p. 265
luster p. 265
hardness p. 266

SCIENCE CONCEPTS
▶ what minerals are
▶ how to identify minerals

Look for details about how minerals are classified.

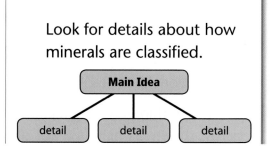

Some Mineral Properties

You probably have heard the word *mineral* before. Beautiful minerals such as diamonds and rubies are used in jewelry. But what exactly is a mineral? A **mineral** is a naturally occurring, nonliving solid that has a specific chemical makeup and a *crystalline*, or repeating, atomic structure.

You may already be familiar with several kinds of minerals. Quartz, diamond, and salt are all minerals. So are the ores of metals such as copper, silver, and iron. There are hundreds of different minerals. So how do scientists identify minerals? Scientists use *mineral properties*, or characteristics, to identify and classify the more than 2000 different minerals that have been found.

One property of minerals that's easy to see is color. Minerals come in a rainbow of colors. Color alone cannot be used for identification. For example, some minerals, such as quartz, are found in many different colors. Scientists need to use additional properties when classifying most minerals.

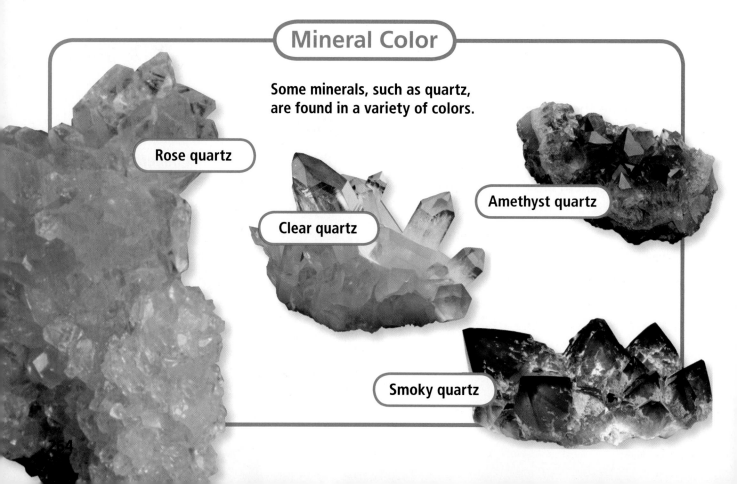

Mineral Color

Some minerals, such as quartz, are found in a variety of colors.

Rose quartz

Clear quartz

Amethyst quartz

Smoky quartz

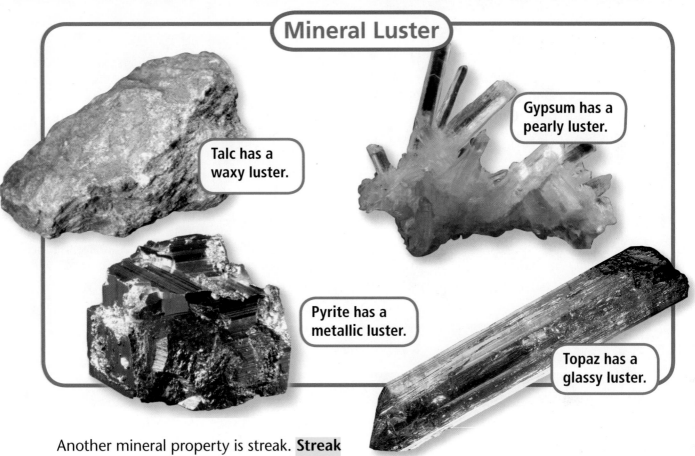

Mineral Luster

Talc has a waxy luster.

Gypsum has a pearly luster.

Pyrite has a metallic luster.

Topaz has a glassy luster.

Another mineral property is streak. **Streak** is the color of the powder left behind when you rub a mineral against a rough white tile, or a streak plate. Many minerals make a streak that is the same color as the mineral. However, some minerals do not. For instance, hematite is silver, black, or dark brown. But its streak is red-brown. Streak is a better property for mineral identification than color, because streak does not vary. All colors of quartz make the same streak.

The way a mineral's surface reflects light is a property called **luster**. Many minerals have a metallic luster. Think of how light reflects off metals such as gold, silver, and copper. Pyrite, or fool's gold, has a metallic luster. Other minerals have a nonmetallic luster. The luster of a nonmetallic mineral can be described as dull, glassy, pearly, waxy, and so on.

 **MAIN IDEA AND DETAILS** What are three visible properties of minerals?

Mineral Streak

The colors of these two pieces of hematite are different, but their streak is the same.

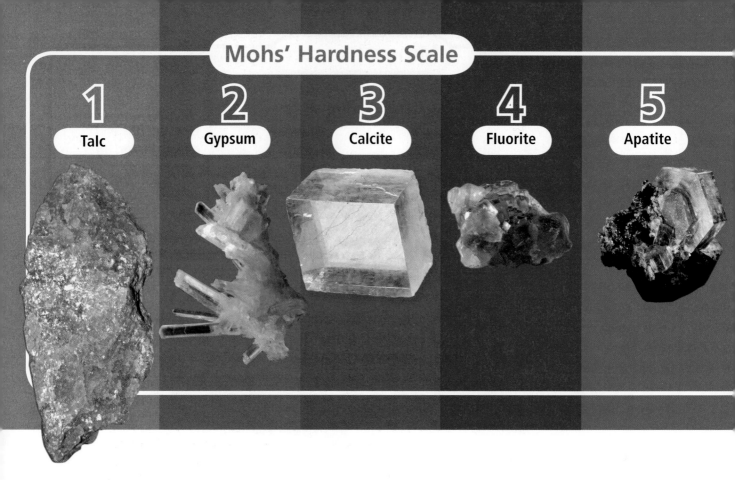

Mohs' Hardness Scale

1	2	3	4	5
Talc	Gypsum	Calcite	Fluorite	Apatite

Insta-Lab

Pass the Salt, Please!

Most minerals are crystalline in structure. Examine some grains of table salt with a hand lens. Note whether individual grains look like tiny crystals. Describe their shape.

Mineral Hardness

Most people would agree that objects such as rocks, nails, and glass are hard. An important property of minerals is hardness. **Hardness** is a mineral's ability to resist being scratched. Some minerals are so hard that they can't be scratched by anything. Others scratch easily. A German scientist, Friedrich Mohs (MOHZ), found that minerals can be classified by how hard they are to scratch. He came up with a scale that ranks minerals from 1 to 10 according to their hardness.

The scale is called the *Mohs' hardness scale.* On this scale, the softest mineral—talc—is classified as a 1. Diamond, the hardest mineral, is classified as a 10. Any mineral higher on the scale can scratch any mineral lower on the scale.

6	7	8	9	10
Orthoclase	Quartz	Topaz	Corundum	Diamond

The Mohs' scale is easy to use. If you have minerals for which you know the hardness, you can use them to determine the hardness of an unknown mineral. You can also use common materials to test a mineral's hardness. For example, your fingernail has a hardness of about 2.5. That means your fingernail should be able to scratch any mineral that has a hardness of 1 or 2. A copper penny has a hardness of 3. (Be sure the penny was made before 1983. Pennies made after that are mostly zinc.) Steel nails have a hardness of about 5.5, and ordinary glass has a hardness of about 6.

Focus Skill MAIN IDEA AND DETAILS How can you determine the hardness of a mineral?

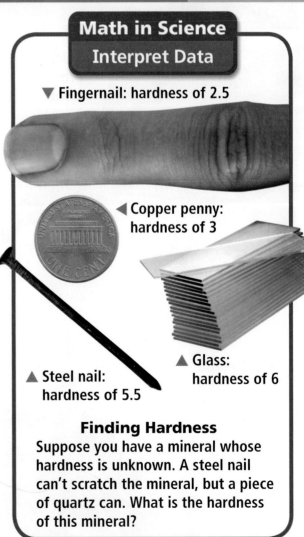

Math in Science

Interpret Data

▼ Fingernail: hardness of 2.5

◀ Copper penny: hardness of 3

▲ Steel nail: hardness of 5.5

▲ Glass: hardness of 6

Finding Hardness
Suppose you have a mineral whose hardness is unknown. A steel nail can't scratch the mineral, but a piece of quartz can. What is the hardness of this mineral?

Unique Properties of Minerals

You have unique characteristics that make you different from everyone else. Some minerals have unique properties that make them different, too. For example, the crystal structure of calcite (KAL•syt) refracts, or bends, light a certain way. If you place a picture behind a piece of calcite, you will see a double image of the picture.

The mineral magnetite (MAG•nuh•tyt) is magnetic. Magnetite is also called lodestone, after the word *lode*, which means "way." Lodestone can be used in a compass to help you find your way.

Some kinds of minerals glow under ultraviolet, or "black" light. Just as quartz can be found in many different colors, certain minerals glow in different colors. For example, corundum can glow red, yellow, green, or blue.

A few minerals—such as quartz—develop an electric potential when pressure is applied to them. This will also happen to quartz when the temperature changes. Because of this property, quartz is often used in computers, cell phones, radios, televisions, and watches.

Focus Skill **MAIN IDEA AND DETAILS**

What are four special properties of minerals?

◄ Calcite produces a double image.

◄ Fluorite glows, or fluoresces, under certain kinds of light.

Magnetite attracts materials containing iron. ▶

Essential Question

What Are Minerals?

In this lesson, you have learned that minerals are nonliving, naturally occurring substances and that they have certain properties that scientists use to identify them.

1. **MAIN IDEA AND DETAILS** Draw and complete a graphic organizer with supporting details for this main idea: Minerals can be identified by their properties.

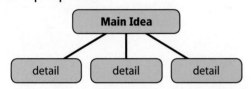

Main Idea

detail   detail   detail

2. **SUMMARIZE** Write a one-paragraph summary of these mineral properties: streak, luster, hardness.

3. **DRAW CONCLUSIONS** Suppose you have two mineral samples with the same hardness. What other mineral properties could you use to decide whether the two samples are the same mineral?

4. **VOCABULARY** Choose a mineral, and write a short paragraph describing its streak, luster, and hardness.

Test Prep

5. **CRITICAL THINKING** What characteristic of a mineral does the term *luster* describe?

6. Which of the following mineral properties can be expressed by a number?

   A. color   **C.** luster

   B. hardness   **D.** streak

Make Connections

 Writing

Expository Writing
Write two paragraphs **comparing and contrasting** different ways minerals can be classified.

9÷3 Math

Use Measuring Devices
Collect several mineral samples that are about the same size. Use a balance to find the mass of each sample. Explain why minerals that are the same size may have very different masses.

 Social Studies

Mineral Collage
Cut out pictures of minerals from old magazines. You may find minerals shown in many things, such as buildings, jewelry, and coins. Use the mineral pictures to make a mineral collage.

Investigate a process for identifying types of rocks.

Read and learn about the three different groups of rocks and how they form.

Essential Question

How Do Rocks Form?

Fast Fact

The Sands of Time

This rock formation in Arizona is part of the famous Vermilion Cliffs. It is a 200-million-year-old sand dune that has turned to rock! In the Investigate, you'll identify some other kinds of rock.

Vermilion Cliffs, Arizona

Vocabulary Preview

rock [RAHK] A natural substance made of one or more minerals (p. 274)

igneous rock [IG•nee•uhs RAHK] Rock that forms when melted rock cools and hardens (p. 274)

deposition [dep•uh•ZISH•uhn] The process in which sediment settles out of water or is dropped by wind (p. 276)

sedimentary rock [sed•uh•MEN•tuh•ree RAHK] Rock formed when sediments are cemented together (p. 276)

metamorphic rock [met•uh•MAWR•fik RAHK] Rock formed when high heat and great pressure change existing rocks into a new form (p. 278)

271

Identifying Rocks

Start with Questions

Rocks are everywhere. They can be found in all kinds of shapes, sizes, and colors.

- Are all rocks formed by the same process?

- How do you think the rocks used in this castle formed?

Investigate to find out. Then read and learn to find out more.

Prepare to Investigate

Inquiry Skill Tip

You can classify the same objects by different properties. Rocks, for example, can be classified by color, by texture, or by how they formed. A certain type of rock may fall into two or more categories, depending on how you classify it.

Materials

- hand lens
- 5 labeled rock samples
- safety goggles
- dropper
- vinegar
- paper plate

Make an Observation Chart

Rock Sample	Color	Texture	Picture	Bubbles When Vinegar Added
1				
2				
3				
4				
5				

Follow This Procedure

1 Copy the table. In the column labeled *Picture*, make a drawing of each rock.

2 Use the hand lens to **observe** each rock. In the table, **record** each rock's color.

3 Look at the grains that make up each rock. Notice their sizes. Are their edges rounded or sharp? How do the grains fit together? Under *Texture* in the table, **record** your observations.

4 **CAUTION: Put on the safety goggles.**

Vinegar makes bubbles form on rocks that contain calcite. Put the rocks on the paper plate. Use the dropper to slowly drop some vinegar onto each rock. **Observe** the results, and **record** your findings.

5 **Classify** the rocks into two groups so that the rocks in each group have similar properties.

Draw Conclusions

1. What properties did you use to **classify** the rocks?

2. **Inquiry Skill** Scientists **classify** objects to make them easier to study. One way scientists classify rocks is by how they form. Choose one of the rocks, and describe how it might have formed.

Step 2

Step 4

Independent Inquiry

Hypothesize about the best property to use to identify rocks. Plan and conduct an investigation to test your hypothesis.

VOCABULARY
rock p. 274
igneous rock p. 274
deposition p. 276
sedimentary rock p. 276
metamorphic rock p. 278

SCIENCE CONCEPTS
▶ how rocks form
▶ how people use rocks

CAUSE AND EFFECT
Look for what causes rocks to form.

cause ⟶ effect

Igneous Rocks

What are mountains, valleys, hills, beaches, and the ocean floor made of? Rocks! Rocks are found almost everywhere on Earth. You've probably seen many different kinds of rocks. But all rocks have one thing in common— minerals. A **rock** is a natural solid made of one or more minerals. In fact, you might think of most rocks as mineral mixtures.

Rocks are classified into one of three groups depending on how they form. Rock that forms when melted rock cools and hardens is called **igneous rock** (IG•nee•uhs). Igneous rocks can form underground, or they can form on Earth's surface.

Igneous rocks that form underground cool much more slowly than those that form on the surface. Below ground, the surrounding rocks hold in the heat much longer than on the surface. On the surface, melted rock cools quickly.

This igneous rock, called *rhyolite*, cooled quickly. It contains the same minerals as granite, but the mineral crystals are smaller.

This igneous rock, called *granite*, cooled slowly. It has large mineral crystals.

Each mineral's crystals have a certain shape. When melted rock cools slowly, the crystals have more time to grow bigger. Because of this, igneous rocks that form underground have large crystals.

When melted rock cools quickly, it hardens before any crystals can grow large. As a result, igneous rocks that form above ground have small or no crystals.

The size of mineral crystals is not the only difference among igneous rocks. Different igneous rocks contain different amounts or different kinds of minerals. That's because not all melted rock beneath Earth's surface is the same.

For example, igneous rocks that form from melted rock containing a lot of silica will also have a lot of silica. One way it shows up in the rocks is as the mineral quartz. Igneous rocks that form from melted rock with little silica will have other kinds of minerals and will be different rocks.

Focus Skill CAUSE AND EFFECT

What causes igneous rocks to form?

Igneous Rocks

▲ *Basalt* (buh•SAWLT) is the most common type of igneous rock. It forms from melted rock that cools quickly. It has small mineral crystals.

▲ *Gabbro* is made of the same minerals as basalt, but it cooled slowly. It has big mineral crystals. Gabbro is sometimes used to make concrete.

▲ *Pumice* (PUHM•is) has a lot of air spaces and is very light. Some people use pumice stones to smooth their skin.

▲ *Obsidian* is also called volcanic glass. Surgeons once used blades made of obsidian because it breaks into sharp pieces.

Sedimentary Rocks

Picture a rock at the top of a hill. Every spring, rain falls on the rock, dissolving some of its minerals. In summer, the heat of the sun causes the rock to crack, and small pieces flake off. Fall arrives, and windblown dust slowly scratches the rock's surface. In winter, water seeps into cracks in the rock and freezes. The ice expands, breaking off more pieces of the rock. This rock is slowly being worn away.

What happens to all the little pieces of rock, called *sediment*, that have worn away? Sediment is carried off by water and wind. It is often set down, or *deposited*, in another place. This process in which sediment settles out of water or is dropped by the wind is called **deposition** (dep•uh•ZISH•uhn).

Over time, sediment piles up, one layer on top of another, pressing together tightly. Some minerals dissolved in water come out of solution, forming a kind of cement. This makes the sediment stick together. Cemented sediment forms a type of rock called **sedimentary rock** (sed•uh•MEN•tuh•ree).

Sedimentary rocks form from any rock that is worn down. Sediment of any size can be found in sedimentary rocks. Some sedimentary rocks have big pieces of sediment in them. Others contain grains of sand, or even smaller sediment pieces.

Sedimentary Rocks

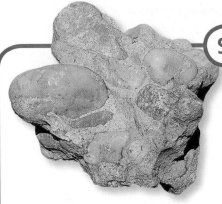

▲ A conglomerate (kuhn•GLAHM•er•it) is a sedimentary rock that is formed from sand, rounded pebbles, and larger pieces of rock.

▲ Shale is a sedimentary rock made up of tiny, dust-size pieces of sediment.

▲ Sandstone is a sedimentary rock made up of sediment pieces the size of sand grains.

▲ Limestone is a sedimentary rock that is usually formed in oceans from seashells, which are largely made of the mineral calcite. There is often more calcite between shells, cementing them together.

As water moves through Florida Caverns, it dissolves minerals from the rocks. As this mineral-rich water drips, some of it forms icicle-like *stalactites* (stuh•LAK•tytz). Drops pile up on the floor and harden to form *stalagmites* (stuh•LAG•mytz).

Some sedimentary rocks have the remains of living things, such as shells, within the sediment. Other sedimentary rocks form when mineral-rich water evaporates. Try placing a pan of salt water in a warm area. When the water dries up, you will have salt. When this happens in nature, the mineral formed is called *halite*. Large deposits of halite are rock salt, a sedimentary rock.

After a sedimentary rock forms, it might be worn away. Sediment from the rock may be deposited in a different location or in a different way, forming a completely different sedimentary rock. This is one way that rocks are constantly changing. In the next section and in Lesson 3, you'll learn about other ways that rocks change.

 CAUSE AND EFFECT

How do sedimentary rocks form?

Make a Sedimentary Rock

Mix small pebbles, sand, soil, and glue in a paper cup. When the glue hardens, tear the cup away. How is this similar to the formation of a sedimentary rock? Place your model rock in a jar of water. Gently shake the jar for two minutes. What happened to your rock?

Metamorphic Rocks

Have you ever seen a caterpillar change into a butterfly? This process is called *metamorphosis* (met•uh•MAWR•fuh•sis), from the Greek words *meta*, meaning "change," and *morphe*, meaning "form." Rocks, too, can change form under certain conditions. When rock is changed by heat and pressure, the new rock is called **metamorphic rock**. Metamorphic rocks can form from any rock.

Where is there enough pressure and heat to change rocks? Metamorphic rocks are found in every mountain range on Earth. Picture the processes working there. Suppose you have a ball of clay. You place a book on top of the clay, and then another and another book. Soon you have a dozen books piled on top of the clay. What happens to the clay? As you can imagine, it becomes flat and very, very thin!

Now suppose the ball of clay is a rock somewhere in northern New Mexico. Instead of a pile of books on top of it, there is a huge mountain with a mass of millions and millions of kilograms. The weight of the mountain squashes the rock. The rock also gets very hot, because as pressure increases, temperature rises. All this heat and pressure changes the old rock into a new rock—a metamorphic rock.

Metamorphic rocks also form in other places. Picture an ocean floor with new sediment layers constantly being added. These layers, stuck together by minerals that act as cement, become sedimentary rock.

These layers of metamorphic rock, called Vishnu Schist, were formed in the Grand Canyon when sandstone was changed by pressure and heat. ▼

▲ Schist (SHIST) may form from sandstone. As mountains build up, they put a huge amount of pressure on sedimentary rocks.

▲ Gneiss (NYS) can form when granite, an igneous rock, is subjected to a lot of pressure.

▲ Quartzite is formed from sandstone that is made almost entirely of the mineral quartz.

▲ Slate is formed from a small-grained sedimentary rock such as shale.

Marble forms from calcite-rich limestone, so it is often white. Small amounts of other minerals give marble its colors. ▶

In time, these rocks may be pushed under other rocks, causing them to change into metamorphic rocks.

Metamorphic rocks also form near some volcanoes. Volcanoes are places where melted rock rises above Earth's surface. The melted rock is extremely hot—not hot enough to melt nearby rocks, but hot enough to change them into metamorphic rocks. Even igneous rocks can become metamorphic rocks.

 CAUSE AND EFFECT

What causes metamorphic rocks to form?

How Rocks Are Used

Rocks have always been an important natural resource for people. Thousands of years ago, people used rocks called *flint* to make hand tools. Even today, rocks are used to make tools of many kinds—from sandpaper to surgical instruments.

People also use rocks such as sandstone, granite, limestone, and marble to build buildings and monuments. The Capitol building of the United States contains both sandstone and marble. The Great Pyramid of Giza in Egypt was made out of sandstone covered with limestone. In fact, everywhere in the world, you'll find important buildings and monuments made of rocks. Rocks are also used to make cement, glass, gravel, and other building materials.

Remember that rocks are made of minerals. Many minerals and the metals they contain are used in products such as cell phones, cars, and computers.

Rocks and minerals are natural resources, and so they must be conserved. People can conserve them by recycling metal products, such as cans, and by reusing rock from buildings. Recycling and reusing also protect the environment by reducing the need to dig into Earth for more resources.

Many things are made from granite, an igneous rock, including buildings, monuments, and kitchen countertops. ▼

▲ **This garden wall is made of limestone, a sedimentary rock. Pieces of the wall may have been used in an earlier wall or building.**

Focus Skill **CAUSE AND EFFECT** How does the durability of rocks affect the way people use them?

The Taj Mahal in India, like many grand buildings and monuments, is made of marble, a metamorphic rock. ▶

Essential Question

How Do Rocks Form?

In this lesson, you learned that there are three groups of rock: igneous, sedimentary, and metamorphic. You also learned that people use rocks in many different ways.

1. 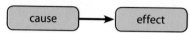 **CAUSE AND EFFECT** Draw and complete a graphic organizer that shows the causes of the way different rocks are formed.

cause ⟶ effect

2. **SUMMARIZE** Write a one-paragraph summary of the way sedimentary rock forms.

3. **DRAW CONCLUSIONS** You find an igneous rock with large crystals in it. Where do you think the rock formed? Explain your answer.

4. **VOCABULARY** Write three sentences that describe the three main types of rock. Give an example of each type.

Test Prep

5. **CRITICAL THINKING** How can different kinds of igneous rocks be classified?

6. What kind of rock is gneiss?
   - **A.** igneous
   - **B.** marble
   - **C.** metamorphic
   - **D.** sedimentary

Make Connections

 Math

Narrative Writing
Write a poem using as many adjectives as you can to **describe** how rocks form and change.

 Math

Use Mental Math
If it takes 150 years for a mountain to grow 2.5 cm, how many years will go by before the mountain is 10 cm taller?

 Art

Stone Sculptures
Over the centuries, sculptors have made many beautiful works of art from rock. Choose a sculpture. Make a fact sheet listing who made the sculpture and when, where, and why.

Investigate the ways that rocks change.

Read and learn about the rock cycle and how rocks move through this cycle.

Essential Question

How Are Rocks Changed?

Fast Fact

A Window on the World

North Window in Arches National Park, Utah, is a natural bridge—a hole worn through a rock. The hole was carved by water. In the Investigate, you'll see what it takes to change rocks!

Arches National Park, Utah

Vocabulary Preview

weathering [WETH•er•ing] The process of wearing away rocks by natural processes (p. 286)

erosion [uh•ROH•zhuhn] The process of moving sediment by wind, moving water, or ice (p. 287)

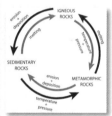

rock cycle [RAHK SY•kuhl] The continuous process in which one type of rock changes into another type (p. 288)

Molding Rocks

Start with Questions

Rocks change through different processes. They are shaped, folded, and molded by different forces.

- Can you see rocks change?

- How did water change the rocks in the picture below?

Investigate to find out. Then read and learn to find out more.

Prepare to Investigate

Inquiry Skill Tip

You can use a model to show how an object looks at a certain time. You can also use a model or a sequence of models to show how an object changes over time.

Materials

- small objects—gravel, sand, pieces of paper, several fake gems
- 2 aluminum pie pans
- 3 pieces of modeling clay, each a different color

Make an Observation Chart

Molding Rocks	
Type of Rock	Observations
igneous	
sedimentary	

Follow This Procedure

1 Suppose the small objects are minerals. Press two different kinds of "minerals" into each piece of clay. Now you have three different "igneous rocks."

2 What happens when wind and water wear down rocks? To model this process, break one of the rocks into pieces and drop the "sediment" into a pie pan filled with water.

3 On top of the sediment pile, drop pieces of the second rock. Then drop pieces of the third rock. Press the layers together by using the bottom of the empty pie pan. Now what kind of rock do you have?

4 Squeeze and mold the new rock between your hands to warm it up. What is making the rock change? Which kind of rock is it now?

Draw Conclusions

1. How did the igneous rocks change in this activity?

2. **Inquiry Skill** Scientists often use models to help them understand processes that occur in nature. What process did you model in Step 4 of this activity?

Step 1

Step 4

Independent Inquiry

Can any type of rock change into any other type? Make a model to explore this question.

VOCABULARY
weathering p. 286
erosion p. 287
rock cycle p. 288

SCIENCE CONCEPTS
▶ how rocks change over time
▶ how rocks move through the rock cycle

 **SEQUENCE**

Look for sequences in which rocks change.

Processes That Change Rocks

After a volcano erupts, molten rock hardens into igneous rock. But this isn't the end of the story for the newly formed rock. As you learned in Lesson 2, rocks are constantly being formed and worn away.

Igneous rocks, like all rock on Earth's surface, are exposed to wind, water, ice, sunlight, and more. All of these factors break down rocks into sediment. The process of wearing away rocks by natural processes is called **weathering**.

All rocks on Earth's surface are weathered. But not all rocks weather at the same rate. In Lesson 1, you discovered that minerals have different degrees of hardness. Some minerals, such as corundum and diamond, can't be easily scratched because they're hard. Others, such as talc, can be easily scratched because they're soft. Rocks that contain mostly hard minerals weather much more slowly than rocks that contain mostly soft minerals. So granite, which contains feldspar and quartz, weathers more slowly than limestone, which contains mostly calcite.

Weathering is only the beginning of a process that changes rocks on Earth.

After rock has been weathered, what remains may look unusual.

As soon as igneous rock cools, it begins to weather.

The Colorado River erodes sediment from one area and moves it downstream. Some of the sediment is deposited at the river's mouth, forming a delta.

The wind and water that weather rocks are part of another process. Wind and water move sediment from one place to another. The process of moving sediment by wind, water, or ice is called **erosion**.

After erosion, sediment can be deposited, pressed together, and cemented, forming sedimentary rock. As more layers of sediment are deposited, processes that cement the sediment speed up.

Processes using pressure and heat, which form metamorphic rock, can take place where mountain ranges have formed. Rock layers in mountain ranges are often folded, broken, and upturned, showing that the rocks have been through many changes.

Focus Skill SEQUENCE

What happens to sediment after weathering?

The rock layers exposed by this road cut were bent and folded as this mountain formed.

The Rock Cycle

Weathering, erosion, deposition, heat, and pressure can all change rocks. Together, these processes make up the rock cycle. The **rock cycle** is the continuous process in which one type of rock changes into another type. Study the Science Up Close feature to see how the rock cycle works.

Focus Skill **SEQUENCE** What sequence of events would have to take place to change a metamorphic rock into an igneous rock?

Insta-Lab

Squashing Stones

Use your metamorphic "rock" from the Investigate. Fold it in half and then in half again. Squeeze it tightly between your hands or under a board. Then cut through it with a plastic knife. How is this "rock" like the rock layers found in mountains?

Science Up Close

The Rock Cycle

Just as you recycle aluminum cans and waste paper, Earth recycles rocks through the rock cycle.

Igneous Rock

Granite, an igneous rock, can be changed into sandstone, a sedimentary rock, through weathering and erosion. Heat and pressure can change granite into a metamorphic rock. With enough heat, granite can melt and harden into a new igneous rock.

For more links and animations, go to **www.hspscience.com**

Sedimentary Rock

Heat and pressure can change sandstone, a sedimentary rock, into gneiss, a metamorphic rock. If sandstone is melted, it hardens into an igneous rock when it cools. If sandstone is weathered and eroded, it can form a new sedimentary rock.

Metamorphic Rock

Gneiss (NYS), a metamorphic rock, can be weathered, eroded, deposited, and cemented into a sedimentary rock. If a metamorphic rock is melted and then hardens again, it will become an igneous rock. With heat and pressure, a metamorphic rock can become a new metamorphic rock.

Soil Formation

The next time you're outside, take a close look at the soil under your feet. Soils around the world are very different from one another. They have many different colors and textures.

Some soils are good for farming. They contain the right amounts of both large and small particles. But some soils contain too much sand, which makes them dry out quickly. Other soils contain too much clay, which keeps them too wet. No matter how different soils are, though, they have one thing in common: they all come from weathered rock.

Soil can form from weathered rock right under it, or it can form from eroded sediment carried from far away. Because soils are made from rocks, they contain minerals. The kinds of minerals found in any soil depend on the kind of rock from which the soil formed. Certain minerals are needed for plant growth.

Most soil is made up of more than weathered rock. Rich farming soil also contains small pieces of decayed plant and animal matter, called *humus* (HYOO•muhs). Humus provides additional nutrients that plants need to grow. If these nutrients are missing, fertilizers must be added to the soil to meet the plants' needs.

SEQUENCE

What must happen first for soil to form?

Soil often forms layers, with the smallest particles and the most humus in the top layer, or topsoil. Layers below the topsoil have larger and larger pieces of weathered rock. ▶

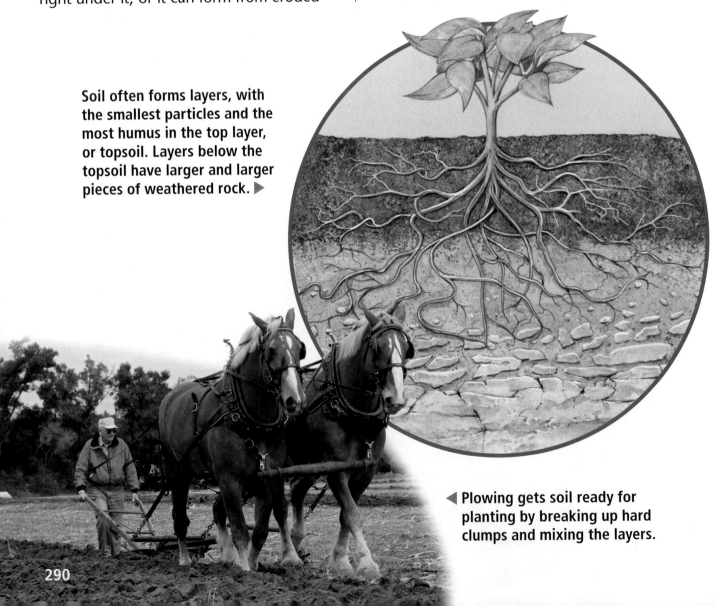

◀ **Plowing gets soil ready for planting by breaking up hard clumps and mixing the layers.**

Essential Question

How Are Rocks Changed?

In this lesson, you learned that rocks change and move through a continuous cycle. They change from one type of rock to another through weathering, erosion, deposition, pressure, heating, and cooling. You also learned that soil is formed from weathered rock.

1. **SEQUENCE** Draw and complete a graphic organizer showing one possible sequence through the rock cycle.

2. **SUMMARIZE** Write a one-paragraph summary of the processes that change rocks.

3. **DRAW CONCLUSIONS** How might a sedimentary rock change into another sedimentary rock?

4. **VOCABULARY** Write two or three sentences using terms from this lesson to explain how soil formation could be considered part of the rock cycle.

Test Prep

5. **CRITICAL THINKING** What determines how quickly a rock is weathered?

6. Which of the following processes can change a metamorphic rock into a sedimentary rock?
   A. adding pressure
   B. increasing temperature
   C. melting
   D. weathering

Make Connections

 Writing

Expository Writing
Write a newspaper article **describing** the erosion of a local valley or river bank.

 Math

Subtract Fractions
If $\frac{1}{4}$ of a granite rock is quartz, $\frac{5}{8}$ of the rock is feldspar, and the rest is mica, what fraction of the rock is mica?

Social Studies

Time Line
Research a famous landform. How old is it? How fast is it eroding? Make a time line showing the landform's changes.

Mack Gipson, Jr.

Mack Gipson grew up on a farm in South Carolina. He helped with farm work and was interested in nature. In junior high school, he read a book about Earth and began to wonder how rocks were formed and what caused Earth's layers.

Dr. Gipson finished college with a degree in natural sciences and became a high school teacher. He was drafted into the U.S. Army and decided to go back to school and study geology. So, he went back to college when he got out of the Army.

One of Dr. Gipson's jobs in college was to test core samples. A core sample shows layers of soil and rock from underground. To get a core sample, a long metal tube is drilled into the ground. Builders test core samples to make sure the ground can support the weight of a building or road.

After graduating from the University of Chicago, Dr. Gipson stayed on there to help study samples of rock and clay from the ocean floor. This study has helped scientists learn about how the oceans have changed over time.

▶ MACK GIPSON, JR.

▶ First African-American to earn a Ph.D. in geology
▶ Founding advisor for the National Association of Black Geologists and Geophysicists

Think and Write

1 How might studying a core sample show how much weight the ground could safely support?

2 What skills do you think are needed to study the ocean floor?

Florence Bascom

► FLORENCE BASCOM

► First woman to receive a Ph.D. from Johns Hopkins University
► First woman hired by the United States Geological Survey

Florence Bascom was one of the first women in the United States to enter the field of geology. Geology is the study of rocks, rock formations, and the structure of Earth.

In 1896, Bascom became the first woman hired by the United States Geological Survey (USGS). She studied how mountains formed, and she also became an expert in the study of crystals, minerals, rock composition, and landforms. She focused a lot of her attention on the Piedmont—or foothills—east of the Appalachian Mountains. The Appalachians are some of the oldest mountains in North America.

Bascom was also one of the first American geologists to use microscopes to study the composition of rocks and minerals.

Think and Write

❶ Why was it important for Bascom to join the USGS?

❷ Why do you think Bascom focused on the Piedmont area?

Career Geologist

Geologists study the makeup, changes, and history of Earth. They also work to understand how rocks were formed and what has happened to them since their formation. Many geologists work in preserving and cleaning up the environment.

Vocabulary Review

Use the terms below to complete the sentences. The page numbers tell you where to look in the chapter if you need help.

mineral p. 264

streak p. 265

luster p. 265

igneous rock p. 274

deposition p. 276

sedimentary rock p. 276

metamorphic rock p. 278

weathering p. 286

erosion p. 287

rock cycle p. 288

1. The way a mineral reflects light is its _____.

2. Rocks are broken down into sediment during _____.

3. Rock changed by heat and pressure is known as _____.

4. Rocks continually change into other types of rocks in the _____.

5. Pieces of sediment settle out of water or wind during _____.

6. You can rub a mineral against a white tile to see its _____.

7. A naturally occurring solid with a crystalline structure is a _____.

8. Pieces of sediment that have been pressed and cemented together form _____.

9. Melted rock cools to form _____.

10. Wind and water carry sediment from one place to another during _____.

Check Understanding

Write the letter of the best choice.

11. What property describes a mineral's ability to resist being scratched?
    A. erodibility   **C.** luster
    B. hardness   **D.** streak

12. Which of the following is a good definition of the word *rock*?
    F. A rock is any nonliving solid found in nature.
    G. A rock is anything found in the ground.
    H. A rock is a hard object.
    J. A rock is a mineral mixture.

13. You find an igneous rock with no visible mineral crystals. Where did this rock most likely form?
    A. deep underground
    B. in a cave
    C. on Earth's surface
    D. under a mountain

14. MAIN IDEA AND DETAILS Look at the picture below. What kind of rock is this an example of?

   F. basalt rock

   G. igneous rock

   H. metamorphic rock

   J. sedimentary rock

15. CAUSE AND EFFECT Which of the following lead to weathering?

   A. high temperatures

   B. mineral type and color

   C. pressure and light

   D. wind and rain

16. Which of the following are the main ingredients of soil?

   F. humus and weathered rock

   G. minerals and water

   H. sedimentary and igneous rocks

   J. soft minerals and cement

Inquiry Skills

17. Explain some ways in which minerals are **classified**.

18. What changes might you **observe** in a rock as it is weathered?

Critical Thinking

19. Monica found a clear mineral crystal. She wanted to identify its hardness. She tried to scratch it with her fingernail, a penny, and a steel nail. But none of these worked. Then she tried topaz, which did leave a scratch. The mineral was able to scratch glass. What mineral could Monica have found? Explain your answer.

20. Examine the pictures of the two rock samples. How did Rock A form? Where did Rock A form? How did Rock B form? Could Rock B have formed from Rock A? Explain your answers.

The Big Idea

ROCK A

ROCK B

Fossils of animal and plant remains help us understand Earth's history.

Essential Questions

Lesson 1

What Do Fossils Show About Earth's History?

Lesson 2

How Are Fossils Like Today's Living Things?

GO online

Student eBook
www.hspscience.com

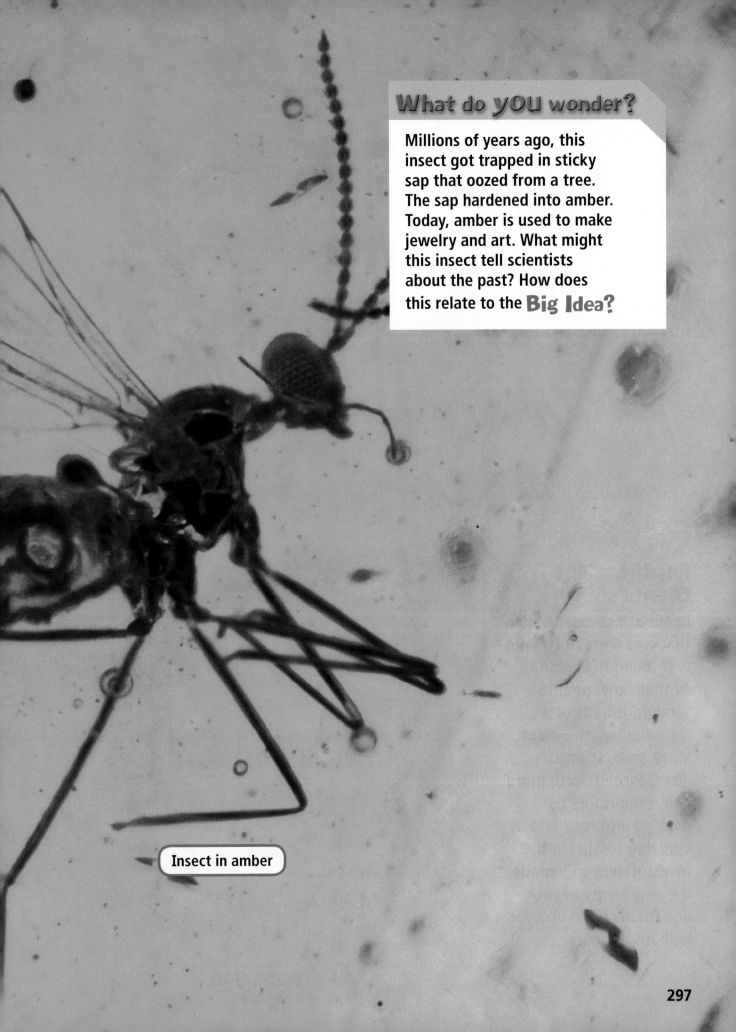

What do yOU wonder?

Millions of years ago, this insect got trapped in sticky sap that oozed from a tree. The sap hardened into amber. Today, amber is used to make jewelry and art. What might this insect tell scientists about the past? How does this relate to the **Big Idea?**

Insect in amber

Investigate how scientists use fossils to learn about the past.

Read and learn about Earth's geologic history and how fossils help us understand that history.

Essential Question

What Do Fossils Show About Earth's History?

Fast Fact

Reptiles, Not Giants

In 1685, a dinosaur bone that was 6 m (20 ft) long was found in England. At that time, people thought it had come from the leg of a giant. Since then, scientists have learned much more about dinosaurs by digging into rock and by studying fossils. In the Investigate, you'll model the way layers of rock and fossils build up over millions of years.

Fossils, like this one in Argentina, help us

fossil [FAHS•uhl] The remains or traces of past life, often found in sedimentary rock (p. 303)

mold [MOHLD] The hollow space that is left when sediment hardens around the remains of an organism and the remains then dissolve (p. 304)

cast [KAST] A fossil formed when dissolved minerals fill a mold and harden (p. 304)

index fossil [IN•deks FAHS•uhl] A fossil of an organism that lived in many places around the world for a short period of time; it can help scientists find the age of a rock layer (p. 306)

299

Reading Fossil Records

Start with Questions

Scientists can "read" rock layers. Using their knowledge of geology and the fossil record, they can infer what happened in the past.

- How is reading the fossil record like looking at the past?

- Do you think reading a fossil record is like reading a textbook?

Investigate to find out. Then read and learn to find out more.

Prepare to Investigate

Inquiry Skill Tip

Scientists make inferences based on things they observe. Be sure to make careful observations before you infer.

Materials

- 4 colors of modeling clay
- clear plastic cup
- 2 small seashells

Make an Observation Chart

Reading Fossil Records	
Layer	Observations
1	
2	
3	
4	
5	

Follow This Procedure

1. Place a layer of clay at the bottom of a cup.

2. Cover the first clay layer with a clay layer of a different color.

3. Press a shell into the clay, keeping the shell against the side of the cup. Using clay of a third color, add a layer on top of the shell and the clay already in the cup.

4. Add another layer made from clay of a fourth color. Then add the second shell as you did the first shell.

5. Make the top layer out of a color of clay that you already used once. Press the clay firmly on top of all the shells and clay in the cup.

Draw Conclusions

1. Which layer of the model can you **infer** represents the present time in Earth's history? How do you know?

2. Scientists often **make models** to understand processes that are difficult to **observe**. How does the model you made represent what happens on Earth?

3. **Inquiry Skill** Suppose each layer in your cup represents 100 years' worth of deposition of sediment. Which layer can you **infer** is oldest? How old is the older shell? Explain why.

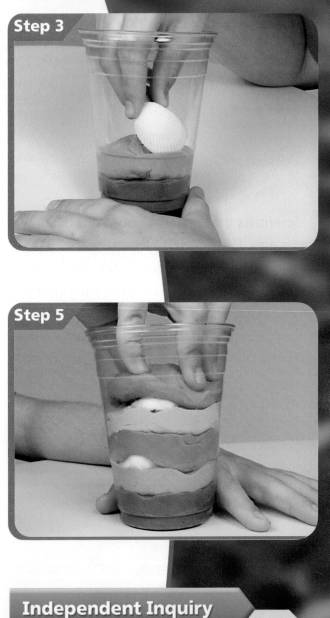

Step 3

Step 5

Independent Inquiry

Research the five eras of Earth's history. **Infer** which layer of clay could represent each era. Make a labeled drawing of the eras.

VOCABULARY

fossil p. 303
mold p. 304
cast p. 304
index fossil p. 306

SCIENCE CONCEPTS

▶ how fossils form
▶ what information fossils provide about Earth's history

 **SEQUENCE**

Look for the steps in the formation of a fossil.

Earth's History

Scientists theorize that about 4.5 billion years ago, Earth formed from a giant cloud of gas and dust. Over time, rocks from space pounded Earth's surface. The outer layer of Earth hardened, forming the crust. Volcanoes spewed lava, ash, and gases all over the planet. The atmosphere contained no oxygen. Oceans started to form.

Scientists also theorize that about 3.5 billion years ago, the first *organisms,* or living things, appeared. Each was one cell and reproduced by dividing. Over millions of years, other organisms developed. Many of these no longer exist, so how do we know about them?

Continental Drift

Pangea

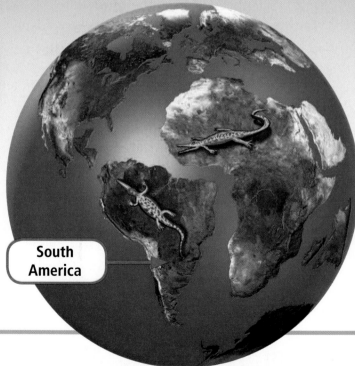

Fossils of *Mesosaurus*, an ancient reptile, have been found in Africa and in South America. Fossils that are of the same kind but are found in different places support the theory that the continents were once joined.

South America

The answer is that we get clues from fossils. A **fossil** is the preserved remains or traces of a living thing. Fossils show how organisms have changed over time.

Fossils also show us how Earth itself has changed. For example, similar fossils have been found on both sides of the Atlantic Ocean. Many of the organisms that left these fossils could not have crossed an ocean. The finding of these fossils in distant places supports the theory of *continental drift.* This is the theory that the continents have been slowly drifting apart for millions of years.

▲ **The rock layers found in this cliff along the coast of eastern South America match those found along the western coast of Africa.**

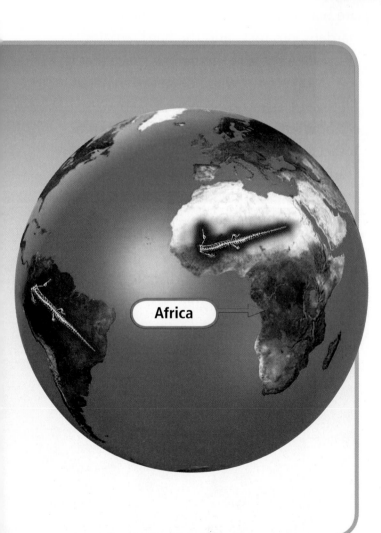

Africa

About 225 million years ago, all of Earth's landmasses were joined. This huge landmass is now called *Pangea* (pan•JEE•uh). It first broke into two pieces and then into smaller pieces—Earth's present continents. Then some continents drifted apart while others came together. If two continents that are now separated were once joined, the fossils and rocks at their edges should be the same. Scientists have found that this is true.

You'll learn later how fossils help scientists find the age of rocks. Most fossils form in sedimentary rock. Sedimentary rock forms when mud, sand, soil, small rocks, or a mixture of these build up in layers that are pressed together. Each layer may be millions or even billions of years old.

 **SEQUENCE** How did the continents form?

The ammonite (AM•uh•nyt) shown here died and sank to the bottom of the sea floor.

The ammonite was buried in layers of mud and sediment before other animals or the water could destroy it.

The soft parts of the ammonite decayed. The hard shell became a fossil. By examining the fossil, scientists can learn about ammonites and the time when they lived.

Fossil Formation

When organisms die, they usually are eaten or decay quickly. But some remains are buried in sediment, ice, or tree sap. These remains may become fossils. Fossils form in several ways.

Some fossils are the actual hard parts of organisms. Teeth, bones, and shells may be left behind after the soft parts decay.

Sometimes organisms or parts of organisms become *petrified*. Water with dissolved minerals in it seeps into the remains. The minerals replace the soft parts and harden into a rocklike fossil. Petrified wood forms this way.

Molds and casts preserve the shapes of organisms. Both begin when hard remains are buried in sediment. The sediment hardens into rock, and the hard remains dissolve. A **mold** is the hollow space that is left. A **cast** forms when dissolved minerals fill the space and harden.

Sometimes an entire animal is preserved. Insects, spiders, and even lizards have been trapped in tree sap. The tree sap hardened into amber. Scientists have found huge mammoths buried in ice and snow. The ice preserved their bodies.

These are mold (right) and cast (left) fossils of an ancient trilobite (TRY•luh•byt). ▼

◀ This young mammoth was found frozen in Siberia. The ice preserved it so well that even the contents of its stomach could be identified.

Trace fossils are evidence of an animal's activities. First, the animal makes tracks or burrows. Next, the tracks or burrows harden in mud. Finally, the mud becomes rock over millions of years. Scientists use trace fossils to estimate the size of an animal.

A *carbon film* is an extremely thin coating of carbon. All living things contain the element carbon. A carbon film forms when heat and pressure force out most of the remains of a buried organism. What is left is a thin film of carbon that shows the organism or some part of it in fine detail.

Almost all the different types of things that lived in the distant past are now extinct. You know that dinosaurs and mammoths no longer exist and will never live again. Many types of ferns, trees, insects, birds, and other organisms have also died out. Fossils tell scientists what these past organisms were like.

▲ This carbon film fossil formed when a plant was exposed to pressure.

Make a Mold Fossil Model

Press a leaf onto a flat slab of clay. Remove the leaf, and let the clay harden. How is this like a mold fossil? How could you use this model to make a model of a cast fossil?

(Focus Skill) **SEQUENCE** Choose one type of fossil, and describe the steps by which it formed.

Finding Clues in Rock Layers
This image shows layers of Earth and their ages in millions of years. About how old do you think the fossil is?

20 million

50 million

80 million

100 million

150 million

175 million

200 million

225 million

275 million

300 million

Fossils and Earth History

Suppose you want to wear your favorite shirt tomorrow. Then you remember that you threw it into the laundry hamper on Monday. Today is Friday. How far do you have to dig to find the shirt to wash it? You know it will be near the bottom, because you've thrown four days' worth of dirty clothes on top of it.

Scientists use a similar idea to figure out the ages of rocks. Remember that sedimentary rock forms in layers. The oldest layers are laid down first. Each layer is newer than the one below. Scientists use this fact to find the relative ages of rock layers. The *relative age* of a rock is its age compared with the ages of other rocks.

This method would work perfectly if rock layers were never disturbed. But earthquakes may upset the positions of the layers. Hot, melted rock from within Earth may push up through cracks in the layers. Wind and water wear away some layers and deposit new ones.

This is where fossils come into the picture. An **index fossil** helps scientists find the age of a rock layer. Index fossils come from organisms that lived in many places around the world during a brief period of time. Each type of index fossil formed at only one particular time. So index fossils provide a way to match rocks of the same age found in different places.

Relative dating does not tell the age of a rock in years. The age of a rock in years is its *absolute age*. Index fossils can help scientists determine the absolute age of a rock. Since each type of index fossil formed at only one time, the rock around such a fossil must have formed around that same time.

Scientists examine the elements found in different rocks and fossils. Some of these elements change in form or amount over a long period of time. By knowing how long these changes take, scientists can find the absolute age of a rock or fossil.

How old do scientists theorize Earth is? The oldest minerals scientists have found are about 4.3 billion years old. But because Earth's oldest rocks have been destroyed over time, scientists estimate that Earth may be more than 4.5 billion years old.

Earth has changed in many ways since it first formed. Continents have joined and split. Oceans once covered land that is now dry. Huge sheets of ice have often blanketed areas that are now forests or grasslands.

Fossils give scientists information about Earth's past environments. Fossils of ocean animals found on land suggest that seas once covered those areas. Fossils of ferns and reptiles have been found near the poles. This shows that the climate there was once much warmer than it is now.

Focus Skill SEQUENCE

How do scientists use index fossils to find the age of rocks?

The Grand Canyon is about 1.6 km (1 mi) deep. Its rock layers show nearly 2 billion years of geologic history. ▶

fish plate fossils
250 million years

footprints
260 million years

bryozoan
275 million years

trace fossil
400 million years

307

Fossils of the United States

Many states have honored Earth's ancient history by adopting state fossils. Fossils are found in almost every state. A state fossil provides information about the past life and environment of the state.

You can see examples of state fossils in the pictures below. Has your own state adopted a fossil? If so, what is it?

SEQUENCE

Which state's fossil probably formed under a sea—Ohio's or New Mexico's?

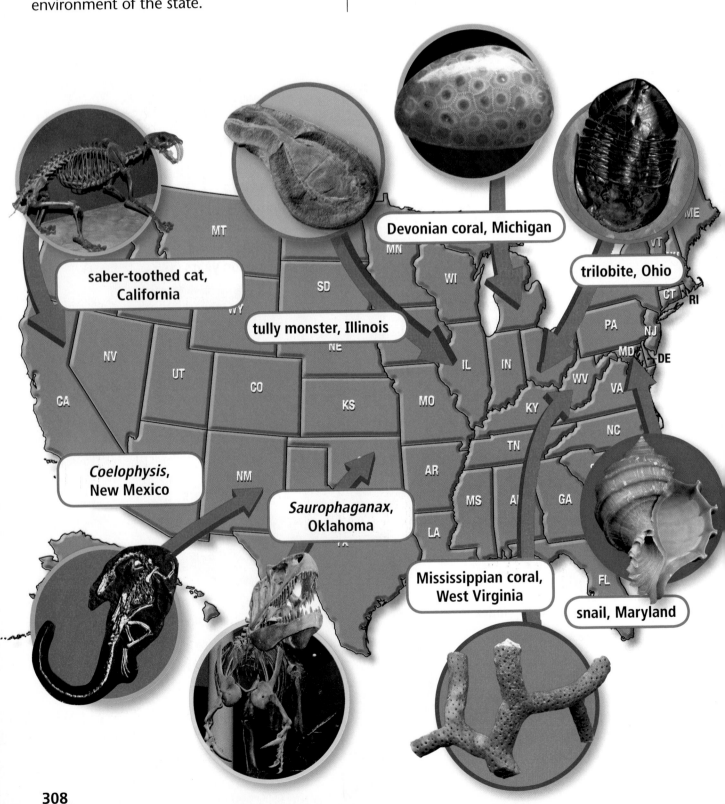

Devonian coral, Michigan

trilobite, Ohio

saber-toothed cat, California

tully monster, Illinois

Coelophysis, New Mexico

Saurophaganax, Oklahoma

Mississippian coral, West Virginia

snail, Maryland

Essential Question

What Do Fossils Show About Earth's History?

In this lesson, you learned that Earth's surface didn't always look like it does today and that many different organisms lived here then that don't exist here today. You also learned how fossils form.

1.  **SEQUENCE** Draw and complete a graphic organizer showing how the sequence of rock layers relates to Earth's history.

2. **SUMMARIZE** Write a summary that begins with the sentence *Fossils help us understand Earth's history.*

3. **DRAW CONCLUSIONS** Why are fossils of whole animals and plants rarely found?

4. **VOCABULARY** Write a sentence that explains why a trace fossil is a fossil.

Test Prep

5. **CRITICAL THINKING** Why are deep canyons important to scientists studying Earth's past?

6. Which **best** describes an index fossil?
   A. from a type of organism that lived over a long period of time
   B. the oldest fossil in a layer
   C. found in many places around the world
   D. found in most rock layers

Make Connections

 Writing

Expository Writing
Explain to a classmate how to use an index fossil to date a rock. Write a **how-to paragraph** that tells your classmate what to do.

 Math

Find Elapsed Time
Find out how scientists define different time periods in Earth's history. Make a chart with dates. Show the eras and periods, and find the length of each one.

 Language Arts

Dinosaur Names
Find out how scientists name dinosaurs. Write an explanation. Then use word roots to invent your own names for fictional dinosaurs. Share your words with the class.

Investigate different ways to classify fossils.

Read and learn about how organisms have changed over time.

Essential Question

How Are Fossils Like Today's Living Things?

Fast Fact

Terror of the Seas

This sea scorpion lived millions of years ago. Sea scorpions grew to be up to 2 m (7 ft) long. They may have been among the first animals to move from water to land. Does this scorpion look like any animal you've seen? In the Investigate, you'll compare living animals and fossils.

paleontology [pay•lee•uhn•TAHL•uh•jee] The study of fossils (p. 315)

Ancient sea scorpion

Classifying Fossils

Guided Inquiry

Start with Questions

Scientists classify fossils in the same way they classify living organisms. They use the classification system you learned about in Chapter 2.

- Do you think this helps you compare fossils to living plants and animals?

- Are there animals living today similar to this *T. rex*?

Investigate to find out. Then read and learn to find out more.

Prepare to Investigate

Inquiry Skill Tip

When you classify objects, you sort them into groups. You can start by dividing a large collection into two groups and then dividing those groups into smaller groups.

Materials

- hand lens
- 8 fossils

Make an Observation Chart

Fossil	Category 1: ___	Category 2: ___	Category 3: ___	Compare (living things)	Compare (specific features)
1					
2					
3					

Follow This Procedure

1. Scientists classify living things by their characteristics, such as whether they are plants or animals, where they live, and what they look like. Use a hand lens to **observe** characteristics of each fossil.

2. **Classify** the fossils. First, decide what categories you will use. Then, make a table with your categories.

3. In your table, include a section that **compares** each fossil with living things from today. Include another section that **compares** specific features of the fossils with features of modern organisms.

4. **Record** which fossils fit into each category. If necessary, use the information that came with the fossils.

Draw Conclusions

1. Based on what you **observed**, how do you think these fossils formed?

2. Which fossils are similar to plants or animals of today?

3. **Inquiry Skill** Scientists classify organisms to determine their similarities and differences. **Classify** the fossils by what you can infer about their structures. Explain your classification.

Step 1

Step 3

Independent Inquiry

Studying fossils requires careful observation. **Observe** one fossil especially closely. **Infer** as much as you can about it. Research the fossil to check your inferences.

313

VOCABULARY
paleontology p. 315

SCIENCE CONCEPTS
▶ how fossils show that organisms have changed
▶ how fossils and modern organisms are similar and different

COMPARE AND CONTRAST
(Focus Skill)

Look for ways in which fossils and modern organisms are similar and different.

alike ———— different

Fossils and Modern Animals

Look closely at the shells shown at the bottom of this page. Which one is a fossil? The top one is the fossilized shell of a scallop called *Chesapecten*. This kind of fossil is commonly found near the central east coast of the United States. The shell shown at the bottom is from a modern scallop, *Pecten*. The two shells look similar, even though *Chesapecten* lived millions of years ago.

Like scallops, some types of organisms haven't changed much through the years.

But many other organisms have become extinct. Fossils show what living things were like in the past and how they have changed through time.

For example, great white sharks can grow to be 6 m (20 ft) long. Suppose you traveled back in time about 14 million years. You might see a similar shark that was 16 m (52 ft) long. That's longer than a school bus!

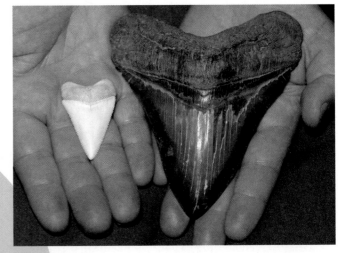

▲ A fossilized tooth of a megalodon, an ancient shark (right), can be as big as a person's hand—more than 17 cm (7 in.) long! Compare it to a tooth of a great white shark (left).

Today's scallop (right) is not much different from an ancient scallop (above). The ancient organism was suited to its environment, and the environment hasn't changed much.

▲ Scientists think that mastodons and mammoths were hunted to extinction by early humans about 10,000 years ago.

▲ There have been many different types of elephants. Two types—African elephants and Asian elephants—live today. Both resemble the mammoths.

How do we know how big the ancient shark would have been? Scientists called paleontologists compare fossils with similar organisms living today. **Paleontology** (pay•lee•uhn•TAHL•uh•jee) is the study of fossils. Paleontologists study ways living things have changed. They look for clues to a past organism's size and shape and try to learn what it ate and how it moved.

Paleontologists have compared the fossils of ancient sharks' teeth with the teeth of today's sharks. They have used what they know about modern sharks to infer the size of the ancient sharks.

Fossilized teeth of horselike animals tell a different story. Ancient horses ate foods similar to those eaten by today's horses. However, the ancient horses' teeth were very small, suggesting that the horses were also very small.

Changes in organisms often helped them survive. For example, ancestors of the elephant had no trunk or tusks. Over time, two teeth lengthened and became tusks. Tusks help elephants dig up food and strip bark off trees. The upper lip and nose combined and formed a trunk. The trunk helps elephants get water and grab food.

Mastodons, mammoths, and modern elephants may have had a common ancestor. Mastodons and mammoths lived during the Ice Ages. They had thick, shaggy hair that kept them warm. Elephants today live in warmer places. They are covered with thin, wiry hair.

 **COMPARE AND CONTRAST**

How were mammoths different from modern elephants?

Fossils and Modern Plants

For every organism that leaves a fossil, many more die without a trace. This is especially true of plants. They have no parts as hard as shells or bones, so they usually decay before they become fossils.

Most plant fossils that we do have are carbon films. These fossils show the details of roots, stems, and leaves. A few whole trees and parts of trees have been petrified. An object is *petrified* when dead cells are replaced by minerals. Like animal fossils, plant fossils show how living things have changed over time.

The first plants, like the first animals, lived in the sea. Scientists theorize that plants began to live on land about 430 million years ago. Most fossils of these older plants look different from modern plants.

However, fossils of many later plants look much the same as modern plants. For example, you'd probably recognize certain fossils as ferns. Ferns were the main type of plant for more than 175 million years. They were the first plants to have roots, stems, and leaves, which modern ferns also have. Most ancient ferns didn't have seeds. Neither do modern ferns.

Ancient ferns grew tall, up to 18 m (59 ft) high. Their fronds could be 3 m (10 ft) across. Some types of ferns today also grow very tall, up to about 24 m (79 ft) high.

Science Up Close

Petrified Wood

Petrified wood is a tree or tree part that has turned into a fossil.

Once the tree is buried, mineral-rich water seeps into its wood. As millions of years pass, silica and other minerals replace the wood fibers. ▼

▲ This ponderosa pine tree has died. Its remains may be buried by sediment.

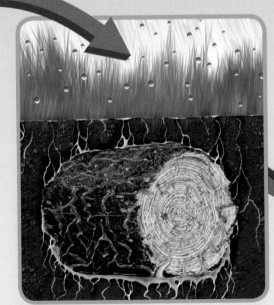

However, some past ferns didn't have the flat fronds that modern ferns have.

Plants with seeds appeared later than ferns—about 365 million years ago. Some of the earliest seed plants had cones. Ancient pine and ginkgo trees looked about the same as those trees do today. Flowering plants followed about 250 million years later. Many were similar to plants of today.

Plant fossils provide clues about past environments. Because plants have not changed as much as animals, scientists can infer the climates that existed on Earth millions of years ago.

Focus Skill COMPARE AND CONTRAST

How were some ancient ferns different from modern ferns?

▲ Ginkgoes haven't changed much in millions of years. Compare the fossil of the ginkgo leaf outlined in stone to the leaf from today.

The wood has become stone. The replacement by minerals may be so precise that you can see what the cells in the original wood looked like. ▼

For more links and animations, go to **www.hspscience.com**

Fossil Close-Up
Use a hand lens to look at a piece of petrified wood. Draw what you observe. How would this information help scientists understand changes to plants over time?

Unique Fossils

Some fossils look like nothing that lives on Earth today. These unusual fossils have led paleontologists to make some incorrect hypotheses. The truth can be stranger than what anyone expects!

Scientists first thought the fossils of *Anomalocaris* parts were different animals. They later learned that this large animal— 60 cm (2 ft) long—fell apart in pieces.

Fossil hunters first found a spine of *Wiwaxia* and decided the fossil represented the whole animal. However, the animal was actually round, with many spines.

COMPARE AND CONTRAST How did scientists' first ideas about *Anomalocaris* differ from what they later found out?

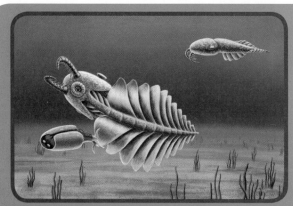

▲ *Anomalocaris* as it might have looked when alive

▲ *Anomalocaris* fossil

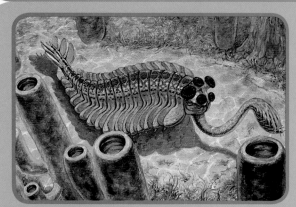

▲ *Opibinia* as it might have looked when alive

▲ *Opibinia* fossil

Wiwaxia as it might have looked when alive ▼

▲ *Wiwaxia* fossil

Essential Question

How Are Fossils Like Today's Living Things?

In this lesson, you learned that some organisms haven't changed much over time. We know this by studying fossils. You also learned that some fossils look like nothing alive on Earth today.

1.  Draw and complete a graphic organizer to compare and contrast these things: Fossil animals and modern animals; Fossil plants and modern plants.

   alike — different

2. **SUMMARIZE** Write a one-paragraph summary about what a paleontologist does.

3. **DRAW CONCLUSIONS** Suppose you find a fossil near your home that looks like a modern tropical plant. What can you conclude about the region in which you live?

4. **VOCABULARY** Define *paleontology* in a sentence.

Test Prep

5. **CRITICAL THINKING** Mammoths had heavy coats. How else might they have differed from today's elephants?

6. Which type of plants appeared **after** plants with cones?
   A. flowering plants
   B. ferns
   C. plants that lived in the sea
   D. plants with seeds

Make Connections

 Writing

Expository Writing
Suppose you could travel 50 million years into the future. Write two or three paragraphs telling what the animals you see look like. **Compare and contrast** them with animals of today.

 Math

Display Data
Make a bar graph that compares the average sizes of some dinosaurs and other ancient animals with the sizes of some modern animals.

 Social Studies

Dinosaur Map
Draw a map to show where scientists have found specific dinosaur fossils. Write a paragraph that explains what this shows about what Earth used to look like.

Attack of

Imagine a rodent that is bigger than an African lion. Researchers say they have found fossils of a 700-kilogram (1,543-pound) rodent in South America. The animal might have lived 6 to 8 million years ago.

"Imagine a weird guinea pig, but huge, with a long tail for balancing on its hind legs and continuously growing teeth," scientist Marcelo R. Sánchez-Villagra said. Researchers have nicknamed the creature "guinea-zilla" because it looked like a Godzilla-sized guinea pig.

Giant Rodent

The team dug up the skeleton of the giant rodent in the Urumaco fossil fields in Venezuela. Scientists believe that Urumaco, now a desert, was once lush with vegetation.

The prehistoric rodent was 2.7 meters (9 feet) long and more than 1.2 meters (4 feet) tall. Scientists think the animal lived near an ancient river, a thriving ecosystem. There it ate grasses and dodged predators.

Guinea-Zilla!

One of those predators was a truck-sized crocodile that weighed 12,000 kilograms (26,456 pounds) and grew to 12.1 meters (40 feet) long.

Smaller but More Abundant

Today, rodents come in much smaller sizes. Mice, rats, guinea pigs, and other rodents account for about 1,500 of the 4,000 living kinds of mammals. That's almost one-third of all mammals!

Why aren't giant-sized rodents roaming alleyways and subway tunnels today? Being big is no guarantee of survival, say scientists. "The question that really puzzles me is not how *Phoberomys* could have been so large but why [most] rodents are so small," biologist R. McNeill Alexander said.

Think About It

1 Why would scientists study the rocks in which a fossil is found?

2 Why is studying fossils of ancient animals important?

Fossil Facts

To figure out the age of fossils, scientists use different tools and methods. One way is to study the rocks in which a fossil is found. If scientists can tell the age of a rock that a fossil is in, they know how old the fossil is. Another method is to look for radioactive atoms, called isotopes, in a small sample of a fossil.

Find out more. Log on to
www.hspscience.com

Vocabulary Review

Use the terms below to complete the sentences. The page numbers tell you where to look in the chapter if you need help.

fossils p. 303   index fossil p. 306

mold p. 304   paleontology p. 315

1. The preserved remains or traces of living things are _____.

2. The study of fossils is _____.

3. The hollow space left when an animal's remains in hardened sediment dissolve is a _____.

4. The remains of something that lived during a short period of time and in many places around the world is an _____.

Check Understanding

Write the letter of the best choice.

5. **SEQUENCE** What is the first thing that happens during fossil formation?
   A. Rock layers form.
   B. An animal or a plant dies.
   C. A plant or an animal turns to stone.
   D. Sediments bury a plant or animal.

6. **COMPARE AND CONTRAST** How are frozen mammoths similar to insects encased in amber?
   F. Both are hardened by minerals.
   G. The organisms were buried in mud.
   H. The entire organisms are preserved.
   J. Heat forced out the soft parts.

7. If you were in a canyon with undisturbed rock layers, where would you find the oldest rocks?
   A. at the surface
   B. at the bottom rock layer
   C. in the top fossil layer
   D. in the canyon's stream

8. If fossils of the same land animal are on different continents, what do you infer?
   F. Fossils form in water.
   G. Animal fossils look alike.
   H. The animals swam across the ocean.
   J. The continents were once joined.

9. What have paleontologists learned from studying plant fossils?
   A. The first plants lived on land.
   B. Flowering plants developed before ferns.
   C. The oldest plants lacked roots, stems, and leaves.
   D. Older plants looked more like modern plants than newer plants did.

10. What was Pangea?
    F. the mass of earliest fossils
    G. Earth's ancient single ocean
    H. a mountain built by rock layers
    J. Earth's landmass millions of years ago

11. Which type of fossil is shown below?

A. carbon film   C. petrified

B. mold   D. trace

12. Where are fossils most often found?

F. in petrified wood

G. in ice

H. in sedimentary rock

J. in the bottom layer of rock

13. Which type of fossil is shown below?

A. amber   C. mold

B. cast   D. trace

14. Why are most plant fossils carbon films?

F. Plants lack hard parts that fossilize.

G. Most plants weren't buried in sediment.

H. Most plants are flat.

J. Only plants contain carbon.

15. How did elephants' ancestors change over time?

A. They became blind.

B. They formed interesting fossils.

C. They gained tusks and a trunk.

D. They became carnivores.

16. What is a cast?

F. a layer where fossils are found

G. a fossil formed when minerals fill in a mold

H. a fossil formed by ice

J. an imprint of a fossil

Inquiry Skills

17. What could you **infer** about the area where you find a *Pecten* (scallop) fossil?

18. How can you **classify** into two groups a *Pecten* fossil, a fern fossil, a petrified tree, and a dinosaur footprint trace?

Critical Thinking

19. Why do you think paleontologists find fossils of small water plants, but few other plants, in the deepest rock layers?

20. Suppose you're on a dig at a deep canyon. How could you use index fossils to help you tell the ancient history of the canyon? On your dig, you find the shell of an ancient type of turtle that no one has seen before. What are possible ways to determine its age?

The **Big** Idea

Changes to Earth's Surface

What's the Big Idea?

Earth's surface is constantly changing.

Essential Questions

Lesson 1

What Are Some of Earth's Landforms?

Lesson 2

What Causes Changes to Earth's Landforms?

Lesson 3

How Do Movements of the Crust Change Earth?

GO online   Student eBook
www.hspscience.com

In 1931, a young Navajo girl was exploring the countryside near her home in Arizona. She noticed a small slit in the ground. That small slit led to a canyon 40 m (130 ft) deep and more than 5 km (3 mi) long! Today, the canyon is called Antelope Canyon. What processes might have shaped this landform? How does this relate to the **Big Idea?**

Antelope Canyon

325

Investigate what some of Earth's landforms look like.

Read and learn about landforms that exist on Earth's surface and how they formed.

Essential Question

What Are Some of Earth's Landforms?

Fast Fact

Mitten of Rock
The landform shown here is called Right Mitten. Its unusual shape made it a popular location for car commercials. Vehicles were flown in by helicopter and placed on the top. How did Right Mitten form? Earth's surface seems to stay the same, but wind and water change landforms into interesting shapes. You can model some of these changes in the Investigate.

Right Mitten

landform (LAND•fawrm) A natural land shape or feature (p. 330)

topography (tuh•PAHG•ruh•fee) All the kinds of landforms in a certain place (p. 330)

glacier (GLAY•sher) A large, thick sheet of ice (p. 332)

sand dune (SAND DOON) A hill of sand, made and shaped by wind (p. 333)

Investigate

Modeling Earth's Landforms

Guided Inquiry

Start with Questions

Earth's landforms come in many shapes and sizes. They formed in different ways.

- How long does it take to shape a landform?

- What kind of landform is this skier going down?

Investigate to find out. Then read and learn to find out more.

Prepare to Investigate

Inquiry Skill Tip

You can use a model to see all the features of a large object at the same time or to enlarge the details of a small object.

Materials

- clay
- forceps
- plastic tray
- cup

Make an Observation Chart

Modeling Earth's Landforms	
Number of Clay Balls Removed	Observations of Landform
1	
2	
3	
4	
5	
6	
7	
8	
9	
10	

328

Follow This Procedure

1. With a partner, form clay into pea-size balls. Use the balls to **model** a landform, such as a mountain or a plain, in the tray.

2. One partner closes his or her eyes. Then the other partner changes the landform by removing one clay ball with forceps and putting the ball into a cup.

3. After the ball is removed, the partner whose eyes were closed **observes** the landform carefully. Can that person see any change? Switch roles and repeat Step 2.

4. Take turns removing clay balls and **observing** until one of you can describe a change in the landform.

5. Count the clay balls in the cup. If each ball represents a change that took place in 1000 years, how long did it take before a change was observed?

Draw Conclusions

1. Why might changes in hills and mountains be seen sooner than changes in plains?

2. **Inquiry Skill** Scientists often **use models** to help them understand natural processes. Why might a model be useful for understanding how landforms change?

Step 1

Step 3

Independent Inquiry

Build a **model** of a landform. Then show how the landform may look in 10,000 years.

329

VOCABULARY
landform p. 330
topography p. 330
glacier p. 332
sand dune p. 333

SCIENCE CONCEPTS
▶ what landforms are
▶ what makes each landform different from others

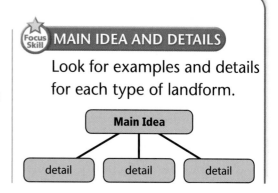

MAIN IDEA AND DETAILS

Look for examples and details for each type of landform.

```
          Main Idea
    ┌─────────┼─────────┐
  detail    detail    detail
```

Mountains, Hills, and Plains

What is the land around your town like? Is it wide and flat? Does it have rolling hills or steep mountains? Land has many different shapes. A natural land shape or feature is called a **landform**. When you describe the landforms around your town, you're describing the topography of the area. **Topography** is all the kinds of landforms in a certain area.

The jagged peaks of the Rocky Mountains are many thousands of feet higher than the surrounding land. ▼

Look at the pictures below. How would you describe the topography of the two areas? Both areas have mountains. A *mountain* is a landform that is much higher than the surrounding land. Often, mountains occur in groups called ranges. Mountain ranges can be very different from each other. The Rocky Mountains, for example, form tall, jagged peaks that rise thousands of feet above the surrounding land. The Appalachian Mountains are lower and more rounded. They are still thousands of feet high, but much lower than the Rocky Mountains.

The Appalachians are mountains, too, but their peaks are lower and more rounded than the peaks of the Rockies. ▼

▲ The Great Plains covers much of the middle of the United States. Because plains are flat, they are often good farming areas.

So, although these two areas have similar landforms—mountains—their topographies are very different.

The topography of volcanic areas differs in another way. Volcanoes usually occur as individual mountains, not in ranges. They may have steep sides or rounded slopes.

Hills are landforms that are like mountains, but not as high. Most have rounded slopes.

Not all landforms have slopes. A *plain* is a large, flat landform with little relief. *Relief* is the difference in elevation between high and low places. In the middle of the United States is a very large plain known as the Great Plains. Plains form in different ways, but all plains have the same topography. Right Mitten is flat on top, but the top is small and elevated, so it's not a plain.

Hills are lower than mountains and have gentle slopes. ▶

▲ Mount Etna, a volcano on the island of Sicily, is a single mountain.

Focus Skill **MAIN IDEA AND DETAILS** List details that describe mountains, hills, and plains.

Landforms from Ice

Look at the landforms shown below. They look different from each other, but they have one thing in common—they were both formed by glaciers. A **glacier** is a large, thick sheet of ice. As glaciers move, they change the land around and beneath them. For example, *moraines* (muh•RAYNZ) are long, low hills formed by materials carried by a glacier. As moving ice scrapes the land beneath it, rocks and other materials are picked up and carried along. This material is deposited when the glacier melts.

How can you tell a moraine from an ordinary hill? A moraine contains rocks, sand, and clay. If you dig into a moraine, you find these things deposited together. You do not find them together in most hills. There are many moraines in the northern part of the United States. Some are more than 200 km (120 mi) long!

Other landforms produced by glaciers are *glacial grooves*. These features form when a glacier scrapes and scratches the rock beneath it. As the glacier melts, grooves can be seen in the rock.

MAIN IDEA AND DETAILS

What detail tells you how a moraine is different from an ordinary hill?

▼ **In this glacier, you can see a moraine between ice flows.**

These glacial grooves on Kelley's Island, in Ohio, formed when ice scarred the rock. ▼

▲ Captiva is a barrier island on Florida's west coast. Because of currents, many shells wash up on the island's beaches in winter.

◄ Sand dunes form where the wind is strong and the sand deposits are plentiful. These sand dunes are in the Oregon Dunes Recreation Area.

Landforms of Sand

Some landforms are made of sand and small bits of rock. These landforms move and are shaped by both wind and water. Landforms of sand are more easily changed than landforms of rock.

A **sand dune** is a sand hill that is made and shaped by wind. As wind blows over a dune, the sand moves. This can change the dune's shape or even move the whole dune. Some dunes move as much as 30 m (100 ft) a year.

Like wind, water can also move sand. Water waves and currents reshape beaches, forming barrier islands and sand spits extending out into the water from the ends of many islands. *Sand spits* and *barrier islands* are long, narrow piles of sand that help protect the mainland from wave erosion. They are found all along the Atlantic coast and the Gulf of Mexico.

Rivers, too, can make sand landforms. Rivers carry sand from the land they flow through. When the flow of a river slows, the sand settles. This makes a landform called a *sandbar*. The Pacific coast has many sandbars where rivers flow into the ocean.

Focus Skill MAIN IDEA AND DETAILS

What details about sand dunes make them different from moraines?

Insta-Lab

Modeling Landforms

Use clay to make a model of a landform in your state. Ask your classmates to try to identify the landform.

This is the Grand Canyon, in Arizona. Canyons form wherever there is running water and land that is being uplifted.

Landforms from Water

The topography of the southwestern United States is beautiful and varied. There you will find landforms such as Mesa Verde ("green mesa"). A *mesa* is a tall, flat-topped rock feature. *Mesa* is a Spanish word meaning "table." A mesa forms as running water erodes the surrounding rock. The Southwest is home to many canyons and unusual rock formations.

Canyons are deep valleys with steep sides. They are found throughout the Southwest. The Grand Canyon, in Arizona, is the largest land canyon in the world. The rushing water of the Colorado River carved through many layers of rock to make this mile-deep canyon. Much of the topography of the Southwest resulted from erosion by the Colorado River and streams that flow into it.

Not all landforms made by water are as dramatic as those in the Southwest. However, landforms that water has made are found almost everywhere in the world.

(Focus Skill) **MAIN IDEA AND DETAILS**

What types of landforms in the Southwest were formed by running water?

▲ Monument Valley, along the Arizona-Utah border, was made by water and wind.

Essential Question

What Are Some of Earth's Landforms?

In this lesson, you learned about landforms such as mountains, hills, and plains. You also learned about some ways in which landforms are formed and shaped, such as by ice, water, and wind.

1. **MAIN IDEA AND DETAILS** Draw and complete a graphic organizer that has supporting details for this main idea: Landforms are features on Earth's surface.

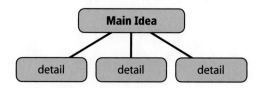

Main Idea

detail   detail   detail

2. **SUMMARIZE** Write a one-paragraph summary about how water helps shape landforms.

3. **DRAW CONCLUSIONS** How is the way a mesa forms similar to the way a canyon forms?

4. **VOCABULARY** Explain how the term *landform* is related to the term *topography*.

Test Prep

5. **CRITICAL THINKING** Suppose you find a hill containing a jumble of small and large rocks. What kind of landform might it be? Explain.

6. What makes sand dunes and moraines similar?
   A. Both are formed by ice.
   B. Both are formed by rivers.
   C. Both are found in the Southwest.
   D. Both are kinds of hills.

Make Connections

 Writing

Expository Writing
Research the geography of your state. Use the information to write a **narration** for a tour of landforms in your state.

 Math

Solve Problems
Suppose a sand dune travels 100 m in a year. At that rate, how long would it take for the dune to travel 1 km? How far would the dune travel in 15 years and 2 months?

 Social Studies

Topographic Maps
Find a topographic map of your area, and compare it to your area's landforms. Record your observations about how various landforms are shown on the map.

Investigate how one of Earth's landforms changes.

Read and learn about different ways that landforms change.

Essential Question

What Causes Changes to Earth's Landforms?

Fast Fact

Tons of Stuff

The Mississippi River carries millions of metric tons of sediment into the Gulf of Mexico every year. These deposits collect at the mouth of the river. There is enough sediment to extend the coastline of Louisiana by more than 90 m (300 ft) every year. You can make a model to help you understand how this happens.

The Mississippi River Delta

delta [DEL•tuh] An area of new land at the mouth of a river, formed from sediments carried by the river (p. 343)

sinkhole [SINGK•hohl] A large hole formed when the roof of a cave collapses (p. 344)

Rivers and Sand

Start with Questions

Water shapes many landforms. It weathers rock and erodes riverbanks.

- Where does the eroded sediment end up?

- Where might the river shown below end?

Investigate to find out. Then read and learn to find out more.

Prepare to Investigate

Inquiry Skill Tip

Observing means collecting information about events and their effects. You can observe by watching, listening, smelling, counting, and measuring.

Materials

- paint tray
- clay
- plastic cup
- clean sand
- water
- spoon
- kitchen baster

Make an Observation Chart

Rivers and Sand		
Trial	Speed of Flow	Observations
1		
2		
3		
4		
5		

Follow This Procedure

① Cover the slope of a paint tray with a thin layer of clay. Press and mold the clay to form a shoreline and a beach. Form a channel in the clay to model a riverbed.

② Add equal amounts of sand and water to a cup. Stir the mixture so the sand becomes suspended in the water. Then fill a kitchen baster with the mixture.

③ Place the baster at the top of the river channel. Squeeze the bulb to release a flow of the sand-and-water mixture.

④ Release the mixture several times, changing the speed of the flow. Observe the behavior of the sand and water as the mixture runs down the channel.

Draw Conclusions

1. What happened to the sand when it reached the mouth of the river in your model?

2. How was the speed of the mixture related to the deposition of the sand?

3. **Inquiry Skill** Scientists learn by observing. You observed how sand is deposited in water. What does this tell you about the way water changes land?

Step 1

Step 3

Independent Inquiry

How do continuing deposits of sediment affect a river? Plan and conduct a simple investigation that answers this question.

VOCABULARY
delta p. 343
sinkhole p. 344

SCIENCE CONCEPTS
▶ what causes weathering, erosion, and deposition
▶ how wind, water, ice, and plants cause Earth's landforms to change

Focus Skill CAUSE AND EFFECT

Look for the causes of change in Earth's landforms, and their effects.

| cause | ⟶ | effect |

Changes Caused by Wind

Imagine yourself standing on a beach with your face to the wind. Sand hits your skin so hard that it begins to sting.

Now imagine this blowing sand hitting a rock. Over time, the sand wears away the rock by breaking it into smaller pieces. Recall from an earlier chapter that the process of wearing away rocks by natural means is known as weathering.

The weathered pieces of rock, some as large as sand grains, are carried away by the wind. The pieces keep moving as long as the wind is blowing. But when the wind slows down, the large pieces fall to the ground.

Over a long time, the wind leaves small piles of sand in some areas. These piles grow as more and more sand is blown into the pile. Slowly, they become sand dunes.

Sand dunes are found in many places, such as in deserts, at beaches, and on lakeshores. Some desert dunes are as high as a 30-story building! Many beaches along the Atlantic coast have long lines of dunes. These dunes help protect the land during storms. But they can also damage nearby buildings and roads as they move inland, pushed by strong winds from the ocean.

Focus Skill CAUSE AND EFFECT

How can wind change landforms?

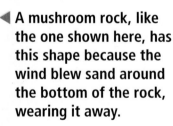

◀ A mushroom rock, like the one shown here, has this shape because the wind blew sand around the bottom of the rock, wearing it away.

Changes Caused by Moving Water

Suppose your hands are dirty after working in the garden. Rinsing your hands removes most of the soil. The water flows over your hands, picks up the soil, and carries it away. In a similar way, moving water can change Earth's surface by carrying soil and small pieces of rock away from landforms.

Water is an important cause of change for Earth's landforms. Moving water can dig a mile-deep canyon or change the path of a river.

For example, a rapidly flowing river erodes its banks and its bottom. Eroding the banks makes the river wider. Eroding the bottom makes the river deeper. The moving water then carries sediment downstream. When the flow of water slows down, sediment is deposited. Deposits on a river's banks make it narrower. Deposits on the bottom make the river shallower.

 **CAUSE AND EFFECT** How can water cause a river's banks to change?

Canyons along the Colorado River are examples of changes made by moving water. For millions of years, the river has been wearing away rocks and carrying sediment downstream. The river has carved deeper and deeper into the landforms of the Southwest. ▼

Erosion and Deposition

Moving wind or water has energy, which enables it to move sediment. The faster the wind or water moves, the more energy it has. Fast water, with a lot of energy, can erode a lot of sediment. Slow water, with little energy, can erode only a small amount of sediment. But all moving water, even a gentle rain, can erode some sediment.

Rain doesn't seem very powerful, but it can cause erosion. When rain falls on a bare hill or mountain, it splashes away soil. As it runs downhill, the water increases its speed and gains energy. The moving water carries away sediment. Over time, water erosion may leave gullies, or ditches, in the ground.

Ocean waves also cause erosion. Constant wave action can change sloping shorelines into cliffs. Waves crashing against the shore carry away broken bits of rock. Piece by piece, the cliffs get steeper. In many places, there is so much erosion that the top of a cliff overhangs the bottom. When this happens, the entire cliff can collapse into

▲ **The channels and gullies in this hillside were caused by rain.**

the ocean. Then waves begin eroding the collapsed rock and forming new cliffs.

Ocean waves change landforms in another way, too. If you stand on a beach and watch the waves, you see that each wave brings more sand onto the beach. Remember, the process by which sediment drops out of water is called deposition.

Why does deposition occur? You've read that sediment is carried in water as long as the water flows fast. Fast-flowing water has a lot of energy.

Crashing waves can change the face of a cliff.

Flooding

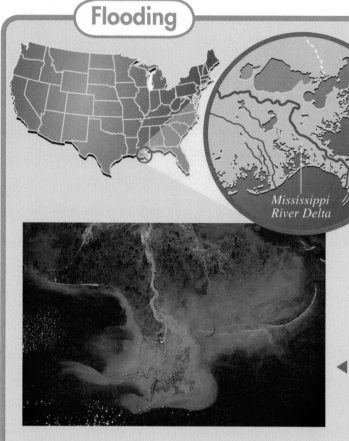

▲ Floods deposit nutrient-rich soil on the flood plain.

◀ When the Mississippi River enters the Gulf of Mexico, the water slows down. Sediment is deposited, and the delta grows.

Mississippi River Delta

When water slows down, it loses energy. Larger pieces of sediment drop out of the water first and settle to the bottom. As the water slows down more, smaller and smaller particles sink to the bottom.

A river often deposits sediment at its *mouth*, the place where it empties into the ocean. The flow of water slows as a river reaches the ocean. As a result, much of the sediment the river carries is deposited, forming a delta. A **delta** is an area of new land at the mouth of a river.

Flooding can deposit sediment near a river. During heavy rains, a flooding river sends water over its banks. When the rains end, the water slowly returns to the river, but the sediment it carried is deposited on the land. This sediment is rich in nutrients that plants need. As a result, *flood plains*, as these areas are called, are usually good for

farming. But living on a flood plain can be dangerous. Rapidly flowing water can move houses as well as sediment.

Focus Skill CAUSE AND EFFECT

What causes a delta to form?

Insta-Lab

Settle Down
You'll need a clear container, some water, and a mixture of soil and sand. Fill the container half full of water. Put the mixture in your hand, and slowly drop it into the container. How does the mixture settle out of the water?

343

Sinkholes and Landslides

Water can change not only landforms on Earth's surface but also features underground. For example, groundwater can weather and erode soft rocks. Underground erosion causes caves to form. Often, the roof of a cave collapses due to the weight of material above it. If the cave is near the surface, a large hole, called a **sinkhole**, may open suddenly. Most sinkholes are found where limestone is common, such as in Florida.

As you learned, water isn't the only factor that causes erosion and deposition. Gravity can also cause these land-changing processes to happen. Gravity can make soil, mud, and rocks move quickly down a slope. This form of erosion is called a *landslide*. Landslides can happen suddenly, especially after heavy rains or earthquakes.

CAUSE AND EFFECT

What causes a sinkhole to form?

This landslide in California was the result of heavy rains in the nearby hills. ▶

This sinkhole opened up suddenly in Winter Park, Florida, in 1981. It swallowed a city block. ▼

344

The Columbia ice field, in Canada, includes many glaciers.

▲ Glaciers carve deep U-shaped valleys as they flow slowly down a mountain.

Ice

Ice can change landforms in several ways. One way is by weathering rocks. The surfaces of most rocks have tiny cracks and holes that fill with water when it rains. If the weather is cold, the water turns to ice. As the water freezes, it expands, making the cracks bigger. The next time it rains, more water gets in, and the process continues. Over time, the rocks break into smaller and smaller pieces, until there is little more than a pile of sand.

Ice can change landforms in other ways, too. As you read in Lesson 1, glaciers can shape landforms by erosion and deposition. Glaciers often follow a river valley down a mountain. As they move, they change the V-shaped valley eroded by the river into a U-shaped valley.

Glaciers deposit their loads of sediment as they begin to melt. The result can be a huge moraine, such as Long Island in New York or Cape Cod in Massachusetts. Glacier deposits can also form small, round hills. Examples of these can be found in Wisconsin and Washington State.

Focus Skill CAUSE AND EFFECT

What changes to landforms can ice cause?

◀ Long Island, NY, and Cape Cod, MA, are huge moraines left by glaciers that once covered most of the northeastern United States.

Plants

Plants can also cause weathering and erosion. When a seed germinates on a rocky slope, it sends roots into tiny cracks or holes in the rock. The roots grow and may eventually become large enough to break the rock into smaller pieces. Some plants also release chemicals into the soil. These chemicals help weather rock by dissolving certain minerals.

Plants don't just weather rock. They also help preserve and protect Earth's landforms. Plant roots hold soil and sand in place. This helps prevent erosion by wind and water.

Farmers often plant clover or other *cover crops* in fields they aren't using to grow food crops. Cover crops help return nutrients to the soil and help prevent erosion. In some areas, farmers plant rows of trees to slow wind erosion of nearby fields.

This protection works naturally as well. Along many beaches, plants grow on dunes. The roots of these plants help hold the sand in place when the wind blows. That's why people should always use beach crossovers instead of walking across the dunes and damaging the plants.

CAUSE AND EFFECT

How do plants affect Earth's landforms?

Plant roots help hold sand in place. This preserves dunes that might otherwise blow away. ▼

The growth of plant roots can weather rock.

Essential Question

What Causes Changes to Earth's Landforms?

In this lesson, you learned how water and wind cause changes to many of Earth's landforms, both above and below the surface. You also learned how plants can cause weathering and erosion.

1. **CAUSE AND EFFECT** Draw and complete a graphic organizer showing the effects these causes have on landforms: wind; water; and glaciers.

2. **SUMMARIZE** Write a short paragraph summarizing two of the factors that change Earth's surface.

3. **DRAW CONCLUSIONS** How are wind erosion and water erosion alike?

4. **VOCABULARY** Describe the formation of deltas and of sinkholes.

Test Prep

5. **CRITICAL THINKING** Tell how snowdrifts and sand dunes are formed in similar ways. Then describe differences in how they are formed.

6. A 3-kg (7-lb) rock is placed on a hill. What do you hypothesize will happen to the rock in 100 years?
   A. will get heavier due to deposition
   B. will get lighter due to weathering
   C. will disappear completely
   D. will become a different rock

Make Connections

 Writing

Narrative Writing

Write a **description** of the events that made a landform look the way it does. You might tell about a mesa, a sand dune, or a moraine.

 Math

Use Mental Math

Suppose a weathered rock breaks into two pieces. Then each piece breaks in two. How many pieces will there be? How many pieces will there be if the process occurs five more times?

 Social Studies

Map Works

Draw a map showing places in the United States where you might find sand dunes, moraines, and deltas. On your map, color these places differently and include a key.

Investigate the way lava flows from a volcano.

Read and learn about Earth's layers and the movement of Earth's plates.

Essential Question

How Do Movements of the Crust Change Earth?

Fast Fact

No End in Sight
Since 1823, Kīlauea, a volcano on the island of Hawai`i, has erupted 59 times. On January 3, 1983, Kīlauea began erupting again and it hasn't stopped for long since then. That's more than 25 years of continual eruption! In the Investigate, you can make a model to help you understand volcanoes like Kīlauea.

Lava flow from Kīlauea volcano

Vocabulary Preview

plate [PLAYT] A section of Earth's crust and upper mantle that fits together with other sections, like puzzle pieces (p. 353)

earthquake [ERTH•kwayk] A shaking of the ground, caused by a sudden release of energy in Earth's crust (p. 354)

epicenter [EP•ih•sent•er] The point on Earth's surface directly above the focus of an earthquake (p. 354)

fault [FAWLT] A break in Earth's crust (p. 354)

magma [MAG•muh] Molten (melted) rock beneath Earth's surface (p. 356)

lava [LAH•vuh] Molten (melted) rock that reaches Earth's surface (p. 356)

volcano [vahl•KAY•noh] A mountain made of lava, ash, or other materials from eruptions that occur at an opening in Earth's crust (p. 356)

349

Modeling a Volcanic Eruption

Guided Inquiry

Start with Questions

An erupting volcano can be one of Earth's most violent events.

- What do you think causes a volcano to erupt?

- What forces might have affected how violent the eruption shown below was?

Investigate to find out. Then read and learn to find out more.

Prepare to Investigate

Inquiry Skill Tip

When you use a model to help predict events, think about which parts of the model are realistic and which are not. Your results depend on the differences between your model and the real thing.

Materials

- newspaper
- pie pan
- safety goggles
- plastic gloves
- film canister with lid
- effervescent antacid
- teaspoon
- potting soil
- red food coloring
- light corn syrup

Make an Observation Chart

Modeling a Volcanic Eruption	
	Observation
Before eruption	
During eruption	
After eruption	

Follow This Procedure

CAUTION: **Put on safety goggles and plastic gloves.**

1. Cover your workspace with newspaper, and place a pie pan on the paper.

2. Fill a film canister halfway with antacid.

3. Add some potting soil to the canister. Put on the lid, and shake the canister.

4. Open the canister, and add 10 drops of food coloring to the mixture.

5. Put the canister in the center of the pan. Add several handfuls of clean potting soil to the pan. Heap the soil against the canister to model the sides of a volcano.

6. Add some corn syrup to the canister. Observe what happens. It may take a few moments for the "lava" to start flowing.

Draw Conclusions

1. Did you observe clear paths in the lava flow? Explain.

2. **Inquiry Skill** Scientists use models to help them understand the dangers of certain natural processes. How might your model help communicate the potential danger of living near a volcano?

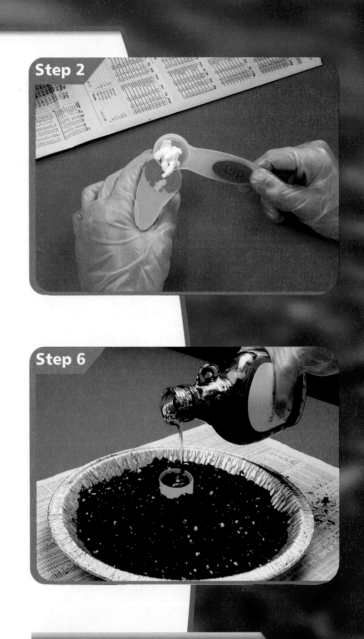
Step 2

Step 6

Independent Inquiry

To protect against lava flows, people often construct barriers. Hypothesize how a barrier might help protect a community.

Read and Learn

VOCABULARY

plate p. 353
earthquake p. 354
epicenter p. 354
fault p. 354
magma p. 356
lava p. 356
volcano p. 356

SCIENCE CONCEPTS

▶ how movements of Earth's crust change the surface

▶ how quickly Earth's landforms can change

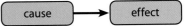 **CAUSE AND EFFECT**

Look for what causes earthquakes, volcanoes, and mountains.

cause ➔ effect

Earth's Structure

Imagine you're a miner digging for gold or gems. You dig deep into Earth, maybe 2 or 3 km (1 or 2 mi) down. But even at this depth, you've barely scratched Earth's surface. You'd need to dig down about 6000 km (4000 mi) to reach the center of Earth! What do you think you'd find at the center? Rock? The whole Earth seems to be rock, but it isn't.

Earth has three layers—the crust, the mantle, and the core, which is divided into the inner core and outer core. If you could dig a hole to the center of Earth, you'd find that the layers are different from one another. The thin *crust* is solid rock. So is the next layer, the *mantle*. But the rock within the mantle can flow.

As you continue toward Earth's center, the deeper you go, the hotter things become.

Earth's Layers

Crust 5–70 km (3–43 mi)
The crust is the surface layer of Earth.

Mantle 2885 km (1790 mi)
The mantle has two parts: the upper mantle and the lower mantle. The mantle is made up of solid rock, but it can flow.

Outer Core 2270 km (1410 mi)
The hot outer core is liquid iron.

Inner Core 1210 km (750 mi)
The inner core is iron and nickel. Even though the core is very hot, great pressure at the center of Earth keeps the inner core solid.

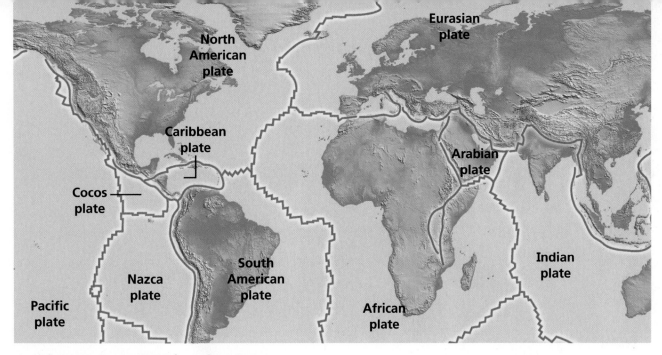

▲ This map shows Earth's major plates.

The *outer* core is liquid, but it's iron, not rock. The inner core is also metal, but it's solid due to intense pressure.

Earth's crust and uppermost mantle are divided into sections, called plates. **Plates** are blocks of crust and upper mantle rock that fit together like puzzle pieces.

Look at the map above. There are 10 major plates. Most of North America, Greenland, and part of the Atlantic Ocean are on the North American plate. Part of California and most of the Pacific Ocean are on the Pacific plate.

Plates "float" on the rock of the mantle. As this rock flows, plates move. Because plates fit together so closely, the movement of one plate affects other plates.

At different places, plates move toward each other, move away from each other, or slide past each other. These plate movements cause many changes in Earth's surface.

CAUSE AND EFFECT

What causes Earth's plates to move?

Thick continental crust and thin oceanic crust rest on the mantle. ▼

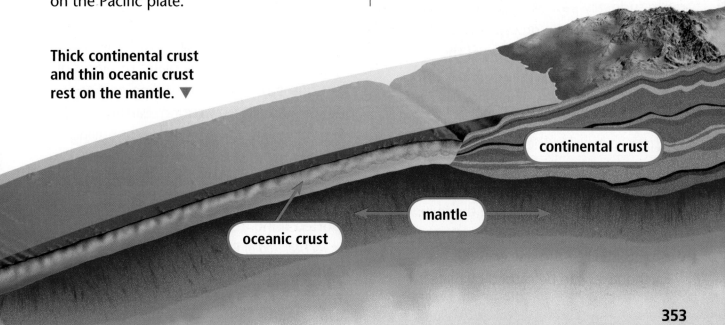

continental crust

mantle

oceanic crust

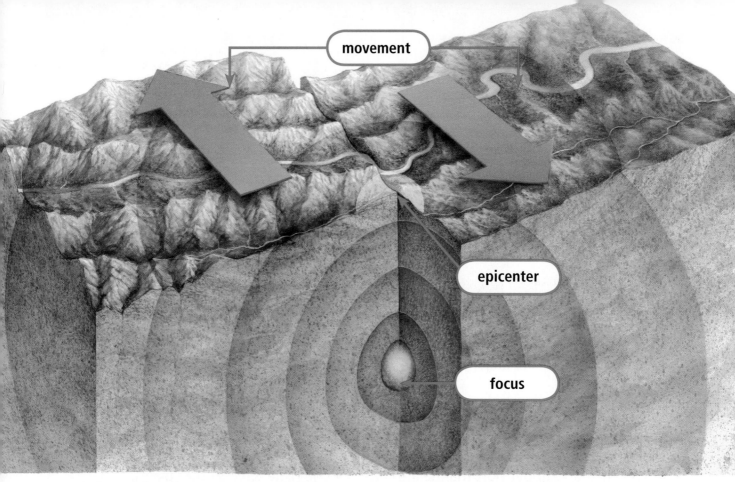

▲ An earthquake occurs when Earth's crust moves and releases energy. The energy of an earthquake spreads out like ripples on a pond. Places farther from the epicenter are likely to experience less damage than places near the epicenter.

Earthquakes

Suppose you press your palms together as hard as you can. If one hand slips, energy is released suddenly and your hands move past each other. When two of Earth's plates move suddenly past each other, energy is also released and the ground shakes.

An **earthquake** is a shaking of the ground caused by a sudden release of energy in Earth's crust. The place within the crust where energy is released during an earthquake is called the *focus*. The release of energy may hardly be noticed, or it may cause a lot of damage. The greatest damage is likely to occur directly above the focus. The point on Earth's surface directly above the focus is called the **epicenter**.

Earthquakes can be caused by plate movement. Plates pushing together, plates sliding past each other, and plates pulling apart all produce earthquakes.

Most earthquakes occur along a **fault**, or break in Earth's crust. Some faults occur in the middle of plates, but most are found near the edges of plates. Faults develop as plate movements bend and crack the crust.

Earthquakes caused by plates or pieces of crust pushing together or sliding past each other are usually very strong. Earthquakes caused by plates or pieces of crust pulling apart are usually weak. Scientists classify earthquakes by estimating their *magnitude*, or amount of energy released. This is reported using a scale of magnitude, such as the *Richter scale*. Earthquakes measuring 2.0 on the Richter scale are too small to be felt.

Major Earthquakes

Read the information in the table. Then, on a world map, mark the areas where these major earthquakes occurred. Using the information in the text below, estimate how many times stronger the 1964 Alaska earthquake was than the 1976 China earthquake.

Measurement on the Richter Scale	Year	Location
9.5	1960	Chile
9.2	1964	Alaska
9.0	2004	Indonesia
8.9	1933	Japan
8.2	1976	China
8.1	1979	Indonesia
8.1	1985	Mexico
7.9	2001	India
7.9	2002	Alaska

▲ An earthquake in Seattle in 2001 measured 6.8 on the Richter scale and caused a lot of damage.

The pattern of the rocks after an earthquake clearly show the San Andreas Fault. The map shows the location of this fault. ▶

There are millions of earthquakes like this every year.

An earthquake measuring 6.0 or higher on the Richter scale can cause a great deal of damage. This is because a 6.0 earthquake is not 3 times as strong as a 2.0 earthquake. It's more than 1,000,000 times as strong. Each increase of 1 on the Richter scale is an increase in strength of about 32 times. About 20 earthquakes of magnitude 6.0 or greater occur each year.

CAUSE AND EFFECT

What causes an earthquake?

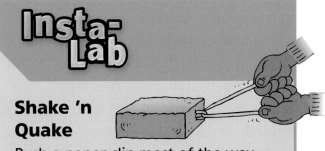

Insta-Lab

Shake 'n Quake

Push a paper clip most of the way into a block of clay. Tie a rubber band to the paper clip. Then use the rubber band to pull the clay across your desk. If the clay and the desk both represent plates, how does the clay's movement model an earthquake?

Volcanoes

There are places in Earth's mantle where solid rock melts. Melted, or *molten*, rock beneath Earth's surface is known as **magma**. Magma forms in places where plates push against each other or pull away from each other. Magma is less dense than solid rock, so it's pushed upward through the mantle and crust.

As magma travels upward, it sometimes reaches an opening, or *vent*, in the crust. Magma that has flowed out of a vent is called lava. **Lava** is molten rock that reaches Earth's surface. As more and more lava flows from a vent, a volcano begins to form. A **volcano** is a mountain made of lava, ash, or other materials from eruptions.

Lava may ooze slowly out of a vent. Or it may explode from a vent with tremendous force. The 1883 eruption of Krakatoa in Indonesia blew lava and ash 27 km (17 mi) into the air!

Some volcanoes form above an especially hot column of magma. This column is called a *hot spot*. A hot spot supplies a steady flow of magma that rises to the surface. As a plate moves slowly over a hot spot, volcanoes form in new locations. Eventually, a hot spot can produce a chain of volcanoes. This is how the Hawaiian Islands were formed. Hawai`i is the youngest island. Kure Atoll, about 2600 km (1620 mi) to the northwest, is the oldest.

Focus Skill CAUSE AND EFFECT

What causes a chain of volcanoes to form?

Science Up Close

Types of Volcanoes

Volcanoes have different shapes depending on the ways the volcanoes form. Some volcanoes are mostly hardened lava. Others are mostly ash, or they are a combination of lava and ash.

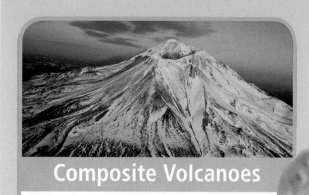

Composite Volcanoes

These volcanoes are wide with fairly steep slopes. They are made up of alternating layers of lava and ash. Mount St. Helens, in Washington State, is a composite volcano.

Conduit

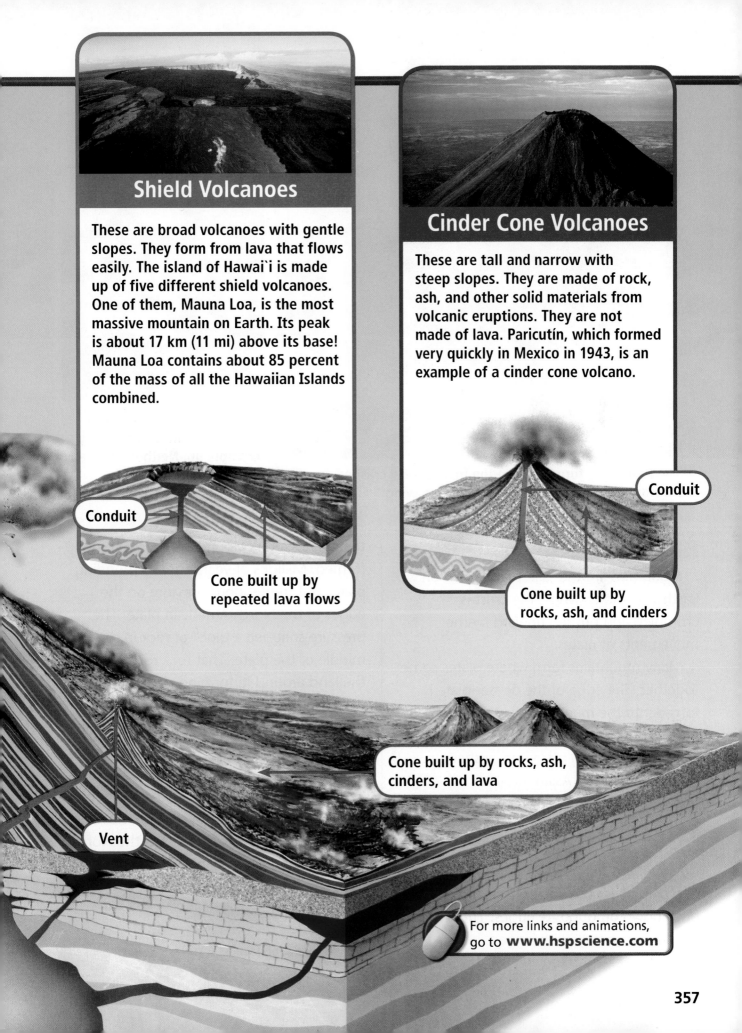

Shield Volcanoes

These are broad volcanoes with gentle slopes. They form from lava that flows easily. The island of Hawai`i is made up of five different shield volcanoes. One of them, Mauna Loa, is the most massive mountain on Earth. Its peak is about 17 km (11 mi) above its base! Mauna Loa contains about 85 percent of the mass of all the Hawaiian Islands combined.

Conduit

Cone built up by repeated lava flows

Cinder Cone Volcanoes

These are tall and narrow with steep slopes. They are made of rock, ash, and other solid materials from volcanic eruptions. They are not made of lava. Paricutín, which formed very quickly in Mexico in 1943, is an example of a cinder cone volcano.

Conduit

Cone built up by rocks, ash, and cinders

Cone built up by rocks, ash, cinders, and lava

Vent

For more links and animations, go to **www.hspscience.com**

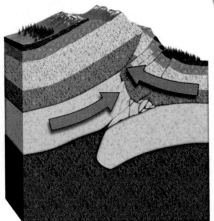

Because continental plates have the same density, they crumple up. Neither is forced into the mantle.

▲ The Himalayas formed when the Indian plate crashed into the Eurasian plate. They are still growing.

How Mountains Form

Mountains are the tallest landforms on Earth. They form where the crust is crumpled and pushed upward by the movements of plates.

Many mountains form where plates come together. The edge of the denser plate is forced into the mantle, while the less dense plate is pushed up. If the plates are the same density, both plates are pushed up. The Himalayas, an Asian mountain range that is the tallest on Earth, formed this way. Mountains in the Himalayas continue to rise about 2.5 cm (1 in.) each year.

Mountains may also form in the middle of a plate. Suppose you hold a cracker and push down on opposite edges. The cracker would soon break, with jagged, broken edges in the center moving up. This is how the Grand Teton Mountains, in Wyoming, formed. Millions of years ago, surrounding plates put tremendous pressure on the edges of the North American plate. The pressure snapped a block of rock in the middle of the plate. That rock rose up from the land around it, forming mountains.

Plates that move apart leave gaps between them. When this happens, mantle rock moves in to fill the gaps. Magma builds up along plate boundaries, forming a ridge. The mountains in this ridge are volcanoes, since they are made of lava that has cooled. The underwater ridge formed as the North American and Eurasian plates pulled apart is known as the Mid-Atlantic Ridge.

 CAUSE AND EFFECT

How do mountains form?

How Do Movements of the Crust Change Earth?

In this lesson, you learned that Earth is made of layers and that the crust is made of moving plates. The movement of these plates causes earthquakes. You also learned that this movement can form volcanoes and mountains.

1.  (Focus Skill) **CAUSE AND EFFECT** Draw and complete a graphic organizer that shows the causes of Earth's plate movements and their effects on Earth.

   > cause ⟶ effect

2. **SUMMARIZE** Write a one-paragraph summary of how plate movements cause changes to Earth's surface.

3. **DRAW CONCLUSIONS** How are earthquakes related to the formation of mountains?

4. **VOCABULARY** Explain how the terms in each pair are related: *faults* and *earthquakes*; *plates* and *mountains*; *volcanoes* and *magma*.

Test Prep

5. **CRITICAL THINKING** How might a volcanic eruption cause both slow changes and rapid changes to landforms?

6. Which is a cause of earthquakes and volcanic eruptions?

   A. weathering

   B. the outer core

   C. plate movement

   D. cinder cones

Make Connections

 Writing

Narrative Writing

Pompeii, an ancient Roman city, was destroyed in A.D. 79. Find out what happened to Pompeii. Write a **description** of the events as though you were there.

 Math

Organize Data

Mountain	Height in Meters
Mauna Kea	4600
Mount McKinley	6775
Mount Olympus	2428
Mount Rainier	4800

Make a bar graph of this data. How does the graph help you compare these mountains?

 Social Studies

Time Line

Use library references to make a time line showing the largest volcanic eruptions of the last 100 years.

Meltdown!

F ew plants or animals live on the icy mountaintops in southern Argentina and Chile. This South American region is cold, desolate, and snowy and is home to dozens of glaciers. These glaciers, many of which are nestled in the Andes Mountains, are in danger of melting away.

The glaciers in South America are some of the largest outside of the polar regions. Because of the region's rough terrain and harsh weather, scientists have trouble reaching the area by foot. To study the melting of the South American glaciers, scientists recently used satellite technology.

Slipping Away

Scientists used satellites to take pictures of the glaciers. Those pictures were compared with earlier information. What scientists found was that the glaciers in this area are rapidly wasting, or melting. In fact, they are melting twice as fast as they were just a few years ago. Erik Rignot, an expert who studied the glaciers, referred to the South American ice fields as the "fastest area of glacial retreat on Earth."

As the glaciers in South America, and in other parts of the world, retreat, their water flows into lakes or oceans. As a result, the meltdown is causing levels of Earth's oceans to rise. If ocean levels rise by even a foot, coastal cities around the world could be flooded.

The Heat Is On

What is causing the glaciers to pull a disappearing act? Warmer temperatures and less snowfall are to blame for the meltdown, say scientists. The warmer temperatures cause some glaciers to break off into the ocean as icebergs. That process, called calving, has increased in recent years. It's not just the South American glaciers that are on thin ice. Scientists warn that about 90 percent of the world's glaciers are melting from global warming.

 Think and Write

❶ How do you think a glacier might shape the Earth's surface?

❷ What other surface features of Earth could scientists use satellites to study?

FROSTY FACTS

Glaciers are large sheets of snow and ice that move slowly over land. Glaciers are found in the polar regions around the world and in mountain valleys.

 Find out more. Log on to
www.hspscience.com

Vocabulary Review

Use the terms below to complete the sentences. The page numbers tell you where to look in the chapter if you need help.

landform p. 330   **sinkhole** p. 344

topography p. 330   **earthquake** p. 354

glacier p. 332   **fault** p. 354

sand dune p. 333   **magma** p. 356

delta p. 343   **volcano** p. 356

1. A natural shape or feature of Earth's surface is a _____.

2. A _____ is a sheet of ice.

3. Molten rock beneath Earth's surface is _____.

4. The collapse of an underground cave may produce a _____.

5. A movement of the ground, caused by the sudden release of energy in Earth's crust, is an _____.

6. The landform of sand and other material deposited at the mouth of a river is called a _____.

7. A sand hill formed and shaped by wind is a _____.

8. A mountain made of lava and ash is a _____.

9. _____ is all the kinds of landforms in a certain place.

10. A break in Earth's crust is called a _____.

Check Understanding

Write the letter of the best choice.

11. In which order are the processes listed below most likely to occur?
    A. erosion—deposition—weathering
    B. deposition—erosion—weathering
    C. weathering—deposition—erosion
    D. weathering—erosion—deposition

12. **CAUSE AND EFFECT** Samantha made a display about changes on Earth. She made labels for a cause-and-effect table. Her brother tried placing the labels. These are his results.

Cause	Effect
Volcano	Sand Dune
Earthquake	Delta
Mountain	Deposition
Glacier	Moraine

Which of the causes is correctly paired with its effect?
    F. earthquake
    G. glacier
    H. mountain
    J. volcano

13. Which landform is most likely to be produced by windblown sand?
    A. canyon   C. mesa
    B. delta   D. sand dune

14. MAIN IDEA AND DETAILS Rita made this sketch of Echo Canyon. Which of the following most likely formed the canyon?

    F. lava   **H.** water erosion

    G. ice erosion   **J.** wind erosion

15. Look at the picture below. How were these landforms most likely produced?

    A. earthquake   **C.** water erosion

    B. ice erosion   **D.** wind erosion

16. If you wanted to make a model of how a delta forms, which of the following materials might be useful?

    F. a pile of cornflakes and a fan

    G. ice with dirt frozen inside

    H. mud and a bicycle pump

    J. water and fine sand in a bottle

Inquiry Skills

17. What can you **observe** about these pieces of rock that shows one was probably weathered by water?

18. How would you **make a model** of an earthquake?

Critical Thinking

19. Martin wants to put his pictures of landforms in order by how quickly the landforms were produced, from slowest to fastest. He has pictures of a fault after an earthquake, a cinder cone volcano, and a canyon. In what order should he put his pictures?

The Big Idea

20. Rocks that form from ash are very light and can almost float in water. Rocks that form from lava are heavy. Terry and her class take a trip to a volcano that no longer erupts. She wants to know what kind of volcano it is. She collects some rocks and finds a mixture of light rocks and heavy rocks. What kind of volcano has Terry visited? How can she use the rocks to support her conclusion in class?

Using Resources

What's the Big Idea?

People use resources to meet their needs in many ways, sometimes causing pollution.

Essential Questions

Lesson 1

How Do People Use Soil and Water Resources?

Lesson 2

How Can People Conserve Resources?

GO online

Student eBook
www.hspscience.com

What do yOU wonder?

Milk bottles, grocery bags, plastic toys—all these things can be recycled to make playground equipment like the things shown here. Why are many communities buying playground equipment made from recycled products? How does this relate to the **Big Idea?**

365

Investigate different ways pollution can be filtered out of water.

Read and learn about resources that humans use and how this use can lead to environmental problems.

Essential Question

How Do People Use Soil and Water Resources?

Fast Fact

The Big Fill

Glen Canyon Dam, on the Colorado River, was finished in 1963. Lake Powell was full 17 years later. Droughts cause the level of the lake to fall. This is a serious concern, as Lake Powell supplies water and hydroelectric energy to several western states. In the Investigate, you'll study another concern about water—how to keep it clean.

Lake Powell, Arizona

renewable resource
[rih•NOO•uh•buhl REE•sawrs] A resource that can be replaced in a reasonable amount of time (p. 370)

nonrenewable resource
nahn•rih•NOO•uh•buhl REE•sawrs] A resource that, once used, cannot be replaced in a reasonable amount of time (p. 371)

pollution [puh•LOO•shuhn] A waste product that harms living things and damages an ecosystem (p. 372)

367

Cleaning Water

Start with Questions

Water is a natural resource. Keeping it clean can sometimes be a problem.

- Do you think it is easy to clean water?

- In what ways can water be cleaned at home?

Investigate to find out. Then read and learn to find out more.

Prepare to Investigate

Inquiry Skill Tip

When you identify the variable that you will test in an investigation, decide which variables will remain unchanged and which variable will change. By changing only one variable, you can conclude that the changed variable is responsible for the results of the investigation.

Materials

- spoon
- water
- 2 funnels
- coffee filters
- pea-size gravel
- soil
- 3 clear plastic cups
- cotton balls
- charcoal

Make an Observation Chart

Cleaners Used	Results

Follow This Procedure

1. Stir one spoonful of soil into a cup of water until the water is cloudy.

2. Place a funnel in a clean cup. Think about how to clean the water with the materials you have. Then place two of the possible cleaners (cotton balls, coffee filters, charcoal, gravel) in layers in the funnel.

3. Pour the dirty water through the funnel. **Observe** the water after it has passed through the cleaners. **Record** your results.

4. Prepare a second cup of dirty water. **Control variables** by changing just one of the cleaners you used the first time.

5. Pour the dirty water through the funnel into a clean cup. **Observe** the water, and **record** your results.

6. **Compare** the cleaning systems.

Draw Conclusions

1. How do your water-cleaning systems compare with those used in community water treatment plants?

2. **Inquiry Skill** Identify the variable you tested with your two cleaning systems. Compare the effectiveness of the cleaners that varied.

Step 1

Step 3

Independent Inquiry

Plan and conduct an investigation in which you identify and control variables to find the best system to clean dirty water.

VOCABULARY
renewable resource p. 370
nonrenewable resource
   p. 371
pollution p. 372

SCIENCE CONCEPTS
▶ what natural resources are
▶ what pollution is

Focus Skill **MAIN IDEA AND DETAILS**

Look for details that support the main ideas.

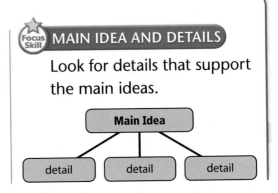

Natural Resources

You depend on natural resources every day. You breathe in air. You drink water found in nature and eat food grown in soil. The clothes you wear come from natural resources. Your bike, your CDs, your books, and your home were all made with natural resources. The light and heat in your home and the gasoline in your family car were produced using natural resources. Natural resources make life on Earth possible.

Some natural resources are reusable. One example is water, a resource that's essential for life. All the water people use is part of a natural water cycle. This cycle makes water usable again and again. Air is also reusable. Like water, it is a renewable resource.

A **renewable resource** is a resource that can be replaced within a human lifetime. A renewable resource is a reusable resource. Renewable resources can be used again and again—if we use them carefully.

How many renewable resources can you find in this photograph? ▽

Unfortunately, many resources can be used only once. They are nonrenewable. A **nonrenewable resource** is a resource that cannot be replaced within a human lifetime. Soil, for example, may take thousands of years to form. A large part of soil is weathered rock. The rock mixes with organic matter, water, and air. As the soil forms, it acquires nutrients that enable plants to grow. The richest soils are high in nutrients and are good for growing crops.

Many energy resources, such as coal and oil, are nonrenewable. It takes millions of years for coal to form from dead plants buried in Earth. Oil also takes millions of years to form.

Minerals, as well as metals, are nonrenewable, too. They occur in limited amounts in Earth's crust. Once these resources are used up, there will never be any more.

Even some plants are essentially nonrenewable resources. Trees such as fruit trees do grow quickly and may be replaced in a few years. But an old-growth forest contains trees that are hundreds of years old. Once these trees are cut down, they will not be replaced for hundreds of years to come.

Focus Skill **MAIN IDEA AND DETAILS**

What are three nonrenewable resources?

Wild animals are less important today as a resource, but 200 years ago, they were a primary food source for many people in North America. ▼

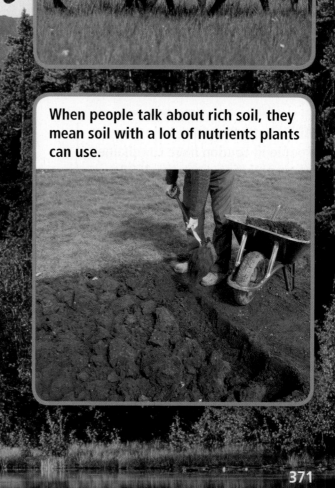

When people talk about rich soil, they mean soil with a lot of nutrients plants can use.

Air and Water Pollution

Some resources can be used again and again if people use them carefully. However, sometimes the use of resources leads to problems.

If you live near a city, you may have seen a hazy sky on what should have been a bright, sunny day. The haze may have been air pollution. **Pollution** is any change to the natural environment that can harm living organisms. Air pollution is one kind of pollution. Other kinds are water pollution and land pollution.

Most air pollution is caused by the burning of fuels such as coal and oil. Have you ever seen black smoke coming from a truck or bus? That's air pollution caused by burning diesel fuel. Like gasoline, diesel fuel comes from oil. When any fuel burns, it sends harmful substances into the air.

Air pollution can also appear as a yellow or brown haze called *smog*. Smog is a mixture of smoke, water vapor, and chemicals. It's usually produced by vehicles or factories.

Air pollution can cause acid rain. Vehicles and some energy stations release nitrous oxide, sulfur dioxide, and other chemicals into the air. These chemicals mix with water in the air and form acids. The acids fall to the ground as acid rain. Acid rain can kill fish when it falls into lakes, and it can damage trees and other plants. Acid rain can also damage buildings. The acid reacts with limestone and wears it away.

The biggest problems caused by air pollution are health related. Air pollution can irritate the eyes and cause breathing problems. Today, the United States has laws to control air pollution. The laws require vehicles and factories to release less of the substances that pollute the air.

Vehicles pollute less today than in the past, but the number of vehicles on the road today is greater than ever before. ▶

Air pollution in cities is not new. People in London have complained of air pollution since the 1600s.

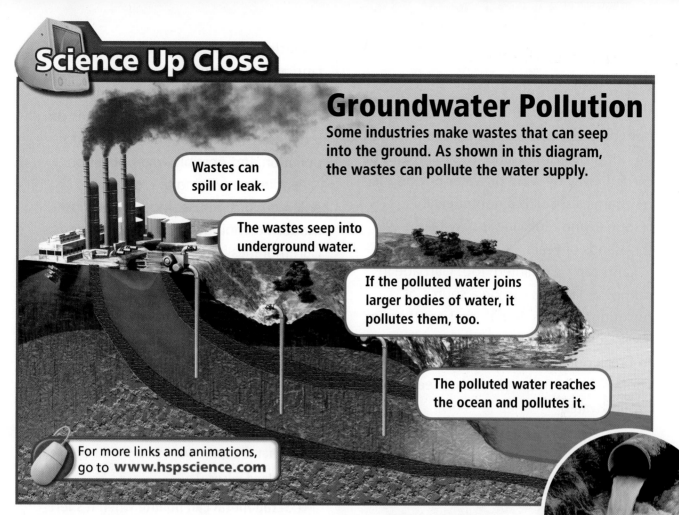

Groundwater Pollution

Some industries make wastes that can seep into the ground. As shown in this diagram, the wastes can pollute the water supply.

Wastes can spill or leak.

The wastes seep into underground water.

If the polluted water joins larger bodies of water, it pollutes them, too.

The polluted water reaches the ocean and pollutes it.

For more links and animations, go to www.hspscience.com

Water pollution comes from harmful substances that enter the water cycle. Some of these substances come from factories and mines that dump wastes into rivers and lakes. The wastes can get into groundwater, too. Fertilizers and pesticides used by farmers and homeowners can also pollute groundwater.

Another water pollution source is sewage. *Sewage* is human waste that is usually flushed away by water. If sewage gets into the water supply that people use, it can make people sick.

There are laws to control some sources of water pollution. The laws require industries and cities to clean surface water when they finish using it.

MAIN IDEA AND DETAILS

Where does most air pollution come from?

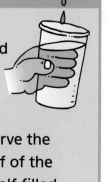

Underground water supplies can also be polluted by materials that soak into the ground. ▶

Traveling Pollution

Put three drops of red food coloring in half a glass of water. Observe the color of the water. Fill up the glass with water, and observe the color again. Then pour half of the water into another glass half filled with water. Observe the color. How does this process show how pollution spreads?

Land Pollution and Misuse

Some misuse of land comes from poor farming practices. For example, if farmers do not protect their land, the soil might be carried away by wind or water or poisoned by chemicals. Soil is a nonrenewable resource, and replacing it may take thousands of years.

Land can be polluted, too. Garbage in dumps or landfills can be a source of pollution. Many materials that are thrown away, such as plastics, take a long time to break down. Some garbage may contain harmful chemicals that seep into groundwater.

Wastes from industry can also harm the land and groundwater. Some poisonous wastes are buried in large containers or drums. If the drums leak, the poisons can seep into the ground. This causes land pollution and possibly water pollution.

People are working to stop land pollution and misuse. Most farmers use modern techniques to protect the land. Communities and companies can dispose of garbage, trash, and industrial wastes in ways that don't cause pollution. And governments spend millions of dollars removing poisons from the land. In the next lesson, you'll learn about other ways to prevent pollution and save natural resources.

Focus Skill **MAIN IDEA AND DETAILS**

What are some ways to solve the problem of land misuse?

◄ Scrap metal can pollute when it's left on the land. But some companies buy and reuse thousands of tons of scrap metal every year.

When land is left unplanted and unprotected like this, rainstorms can wash the soil away. ▼

Essential Question

How Do People Use Soil and Water Resources?

In this lesson, you learned about natural resources, both renewable and nonrenewable. You also learned that the use and misuse of these can lead to air, water, and land pollution.

1. 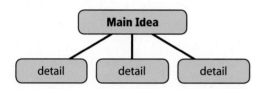 **MAIN IDEA AND DETAILS** Draw and complete a graphic organizer with supporting details for this main idea: Air, water, and land can all be affected by pollution.

   Main Idea

   detail   detail   detail

2. **SUMMARIZE** Write a one-paragraph summary of two nonrenewable resources and how humans use them.

3. **DRAW CONCLUSIONS** How can trees be both renewable and nonrenewable resources?

4. **VOCABULARY** Write a sentence that explains the meaning of the term *pollution*.

Test Prep

5. **CRITICAL THINKING** How can farming have both positive and negative effects on the environment?

6. Which is a major cause of air pollution?
   - **A.** soil loss
   - **B.** farming
   - **C.** landfills
   - **D.** driving cars

Make Connections

 Writing

Narrative Writing
Write a **story** about how people use natural resources and change the environment. Share your story with your class.

 Math

Solve a Problem
The Great Plains lost about 0.7 m of topsoil in the last 100 years. That left about 1.3 m of topsoil. How much will be left in another 100 years at this rate of loss?

 Social Studies

Oil Spills
When a ship that carries oil breaks up, the result can be an oil spill. Research an oil spill, and report on the damage it caused to the environment.

Essential Question

How Can People Conserve Resources?

Investigate one way plants are grown without soil.

Read and learn about ways that humans can help conserve resources.

Fast Fact

Water, Water

Growing plants in water—hydroponics—has a long history. Scientists think the ancient Babylonians sometimes grew plants this way, without soil. If people ever live on other planets, hydroponics will likely be the best way for them to grow vegetables. In the Investigate, you'll find out for yourself how to grow plants in water.

Hydroponic lettuce

conservation [kahn•ser•VAY•shuhn] The use of less of a resource to make the supply last longer (p. 381)

Growing Plants in Water

Guided Inquiry

Start with Questions

Soil is a nonrenewable resource. It is necessary for growing many kinds of plants.

- What resources are used to grow plants?

- How do plants grow without soil?

Investigate to find out. Then read and learn to find out more.

Prepare to Investigate

Inquiry Skill Tip

You may be able to draw a conclusion after you have experimented and collected data. Review your observations and measurements. Think about how they fit together. If you can't draw a conclusion, you may need to do more tests and make more observations.

Materials

- scissors
- plastic food container with lid
- soft, absorbent cloth
- dry plant food
- measuring spoon
- water
- liter bottle
- radish seeds

Make an Observation Chart

Growing Plants in Water	
Day	Observations
1	
3	
5	

Follow This Procedure

❶ Carefully use scissors to cut a slit in the lid of a food container. Then, in the lid, cut a hole large enough to pour water through.

❷ Cut a rectangle of cloth that will fit through the slit and touch the bottom of the container when the lid is in place. The cloth should be long enough to allow about 2 cm of it to lie on top of the lid.

❸ Push the cut cloth through the slit in the lid, leaving the end of the cloth on top.

❹ Follow the instructions on the package of plant food to make 1 L of plant-food solution. Half-fill the container with the solution. Snap the lid closed on the container.

❺ Place seeds on the cloth.

❻ Place the container in a sunny window. Add more plant food as necessary to keep the cloth moist.

Draw Conclusions

1. Why do you need to use plant food to grow seeds without soil?

2. **Inquiry Skill** Draw a conclusion about why this method of growing plants would be useful in desert areas.

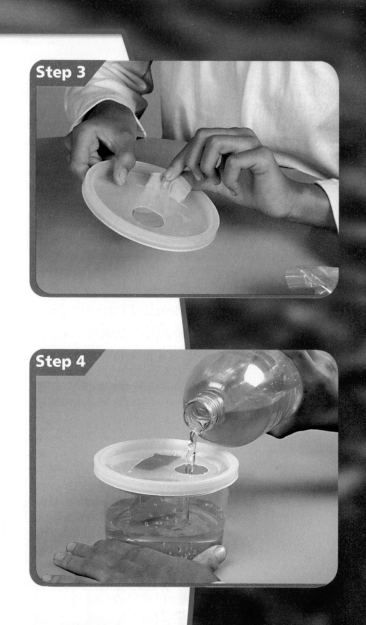

Step 3

Step 4

Independent Inquiry

Plan and conduct a simple investigation **for growing large plants without soil.**

Read and Learn

VOCABULARY
conservation p. 381

SCIENCE CONCEPTS
▶ what conservation is
▶ how people can help in conservation efforts

(Focus Skill) CAUSE AND EFFECT
Look for ways that conservation decreases pollution.

[cause] ⟶ [effect]

The Three R's: Reduce, Reuse, Recycle

When you leave a room and turn out the lights, you're saving natural resources. When you wash out a cottage cheese container and use it again, you're saving resources. Every time you throw a newspaper in the recycling bin, you're also saving resources. All these actions are examples of conservation.

Reuse
Think twice before you throw out that milk container! Could you use it for another purpose?

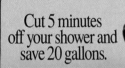

Cut 5 minutes off your shower and save 20 gallons.

Reduce
Communities with a shortage of water or energy may require people to use less water or energy.

Recycle
Recycling a ton of newspaper saves 17 trees from being cut down.

380

Conservation is preserving or protecting natural resources. The actions described in the photos are examples of the three *R*'s—reduce, reuse, and recycle. The three *R*'s are effective ways to conserve natural resources. When you *reduce,* you cut down on the amount of resources used. Appliances such as clothes dryers, water heaters, air conditioners, and lamps use a lot of electricity. When you use appliances less, the need for energy resources such as coal goes down. This also means less pollution caused by burning fuels.

When you *reuse,* you use items again that might have been thrown out. For example, if you reuse plastic food containers, fewer resources are needed to make new containers.

Reusing often means using items for new purposes. For example, you can wash out milk cartons and juice bottles and use them as planters or bird feeders. As a result, the cartons and bottles are saved from the landfill and you have items you can use. Sometimes you can't use items anymore. You might give those items, such as toys and clothes you've outgrown, to a resale shop. Then other people can reuse them. Reusing items saves resources, reduces pollution, and saves space in landfills.

When you *recycle,* items are changed into a form that can be used again. Many resources can be conserved by recycling. For example, aluminum, glass, and paper can be ground up or melted down and used to make new glass, aluminum, and paper products. When people recycle, energy is saved, too. And as with reducing and reusing, recycling saves resources and reduces pollution.

Focus Skill CAUSE AND EFFECT

What are some of the effects of reusing items instead of throwing them out?

Math in Science
Interpret Data

For which material could recycling be improved the most?

Recycling Rates for Some Materials

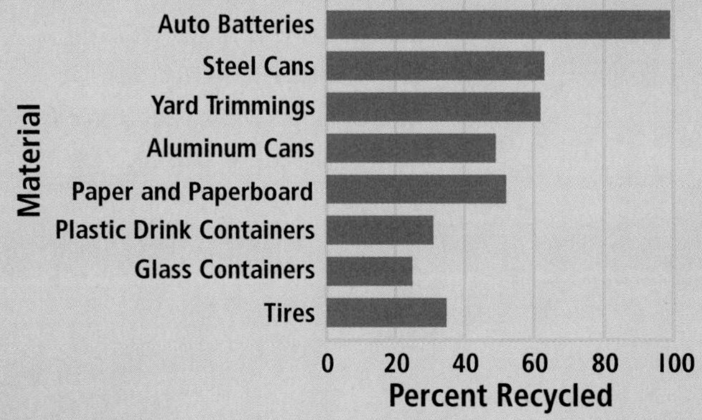
Auto Batteries
Steel Cans
Yard Trimmings
Aluminum Cans
Paper and Paperboard
Plastic Drink Containers
Glass Containers
Tires
Material
0
20
40
60
80
100
Percent Recycled

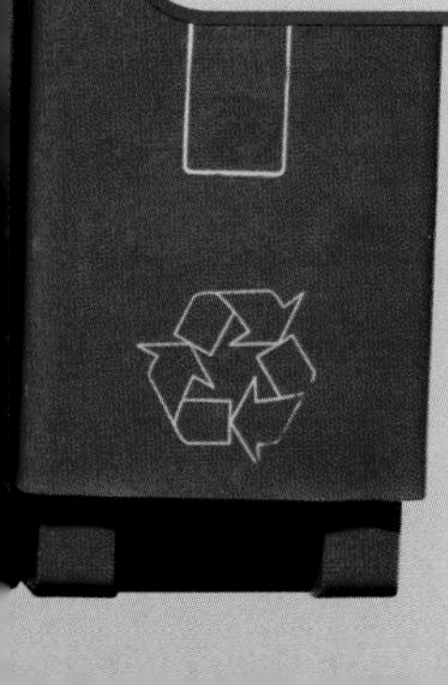

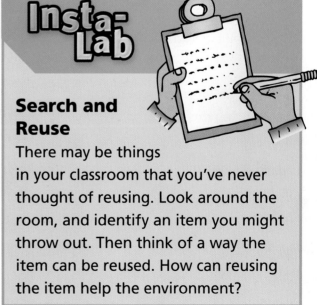

Insta-Lab

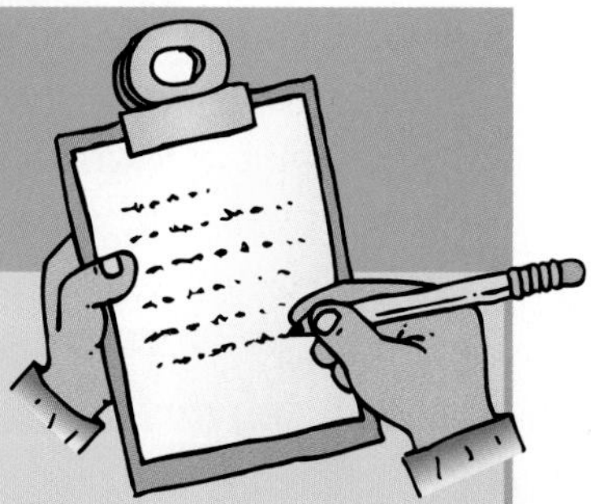

Search and Reuse

There may be things in your classroom that you've never thought of reusing. Look around the room, and identify an item you might throw out. Then think of a way the item can be reused. How can reusing the item help the environment?

Soil Conservation

A necessary resource for growing crops is soil. How can this resource be protected? Reducing, reusing, and recycling are general ways to conserve resources, but there are some specific methods of soil conservation.

When farmers of long ago cleared fields to plant crops, they pulled out trees and native plants that kept the soil in place. Sometimes wind and water carried away the unprotected soil and left the land unsuitable for farming.

As a result, farmers had to learn ways to protect the soil. Farmers in windy areas use windbreaks. These are rows of trees or fences that stop the wind from carrying away soil. Another method farmers use to keep soil in place is contour plowing. This is the planting of crops along the curves of sloping land, not down the slopes. With this type of plowing, water cannot flow quickly downhill and carry soil with it.

Strip cropping also helps keep soil in place. In strip cropping, farmers plant strips of grass or clover between strips of crops. The thick mat of plants between the crops holds the soil and helps hold water.

In areas where the land is very steep, farmers use terracing to help conserve soil.

◀ One practice, called intercropping, involves alternating different crops. A tall crop is planted next to a low crop that grows well in the shade.

Farmers lost millions of acres of soil in the 1930s. Government scientists then taught farmers contour plowing as a way to keep soil in place. ▼

They build up the soil to form level places. When terracing is finished, it can look like a series of steps going up a hill. Crops are then planted on the level areas. The result is that the soil is protected from being carried away by water running down the steep slopes.

Crop rotation is another way farmers conserve soil. Crop rotation is the changing of planted crops from year to year. When the same crop is planted year after year, the soil can lose important nutrients, such as nitrogen. These nutrients are often replaced by using chemical fertilizers. But by rotating crops, farmers can build up the soil's nutrients naturally. For example, corn takes nitrogen from the soil. Alfalfa, if grown after the corn, adds nitrogen to the soil. Avoiding chemicals in this way reduces the risk of land and water pollution.

A type of intercropping keeps soil healthy by reducing the need for pesticides. When farmers intercrop, they plant different crops near each other. This keeps some harmful insects from spreading, since many insects eat only one kind of crop.

What is an effect of contour planting?

Crop rotation helps control pests. The pests die when the plants they eat are not being grown. ▶

Water Conservation

If you're in the middle of a heavy rainstorm, the idea that water needs to be conserved may sound strange. For much of the country, though, fresh water is a precious resource.

The western United States has often been threatened by drought. And the population in many western states is growing. This means more water users. Several years of drought and the growing population have led many to believe that soon there will not be enough water for everyone.

As a result, governments, farmers, and others have begun to look for ways to conserve water. Some farmers have started growing crops that don't need much water. Others who once sprayed water onto their crops are now using drip irrigation. This method slowly drips water onto the ground. Less water is lost to evaporation.

Homeowners can conserve water by having a Xeriscape (ZIR•uh•skayp) instead of a lawn. Lawns require a huge amount of water, which isn't available in some areas. To conserve water, homeowners can plant native grasses, flowering plants, and shrubs that don't require as much water.

People can learn to conserve water in other ways, too. They can take shorter showers. They can remember not to leave faucets running. What else can you think of that would help conserve water?

Focus Skill **CAUSE AND EFFECT** What has caused farmers to use drip irrigation?

Drip irrigation uses hoses with tiny holes that slowly release water.

Landscapes that conserve water can include flowering plants and shrubs as well as native plants. ▼

Essential Question

How Can People Conserve Resources?

In this lesson, you learned about reducing, reusing, and recycling. You learned that these are ways to conserve. You also learned that farmers have different ways to conserve soil and water.

1. 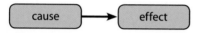 **CAUSE AND EFFECT** Draw and complete a graphic organizer that shows the effects of these three groups of causes: Reduce, Reuse, Recycle; Contour plowing, strip cropping, and windbreaks; Water shortage.

    | cause | → | effect |

2. **SUMMARIZE** Write a one-paragraph summary of three ways to conserve soil.

3. **DRAW CONCLUSIONS** Which of the three *R*'s—reduce, reuse, recycle—applies to landscapes that conserve water? Explain.

4. **VOCABULARY** Use the term *conservation* to explain how to save resources at home.

Test Prep

5. **CRITICAL THINKING** How can a farmer and a factory owner conserve water?

6. Which of the following can conserve energy?
    A. crop rotation
    B. intercropping
    C. drip irrigation
    D. recycling newspaper

Make Connections

 Writing

Persuasive Writing
Write a **letter** to local government officials to persuade them to find ways of conserving energy resources.

 Math

Display Data
Each day for a week, weigh the trash your class produces. At the end of the week, make a bar graph that shows the weight of the trash by day.

 Health

Air Quality
Reducing, reusing, and recycling mean less pollution. Research the health problems caused by air pollution, and find out what you can do to protect yourself from air pollution.

William Rathje

After 30 years of studying garbage, William Rathje's gotten used to the smell. He has been studying the garbage at landfills. Rathje has examined landfills by looking at different layers of garbage, the way an archeologist studies the site of an ancient civilization.

One important discovery by Rathje is that most garbage is not decomposing. He has found newspapers that look as good as the day they were delivered—in the 1950s!

Rathje wants to remind people that trash does not just disappear. Recycling bottles, cans, and cardboard can help conserve natural resources.

▶ **WILLIAM RATHJE**

▶ Anthropologist
▶ Founder and director of The Garbage Project

Think and Write

❶ Why is Rathje's work important?

❷ How would studying a landfill be like an archeological dig?

Dorothy McClendon

▶ **DOROTHY MCCLENDON**

▶ Microbiologist with the
U.S. Army Tank Automotive
Command (TACOM)

Dorothy McClendon worked for the U.S. Army Tank Automotive Command. She was not a soldier, however. She was a microbiologist. She studied living things too small to be seen without a microscope, such as fungi and bacteria.

Microorganisms are important. People have learned how to use microorganisms in making cheese and cleaning up oil spills. However, microorganisms can cause diseases or cause food to spoil and materials to decay.

Ms. McClendon was a specialist known as an industrial microbiologist. Her job was to develop ways to keep microorganisms from breaking down fuel oil and other materials that the army stores. She also worked on developing a new fungicide, a chemical that will kill fungi. It must do the job without being harmful to people.

Think and Write

❶ How are some microorganisms harmful to humans?

❷ Why might it be difficult to develop a chemical that kills fungi but doesn't harm humans?

Career Forest Worker

The forests in the United States are an important natural resource. Forest workers protect the forests by growing and planting new seedlings, fighting insects and diseases that attack trees, and helping to control soil erosion.

CHAPTER 10

Review and Test Preparation

Vocabulary Review

Use the terms below to complete the sentences. The page numbers tell you where to look in the chapter if you need help.

renewable resources p. 370

nonrenewable resources p. 371

pollution p. 372

conservation p. 381

1. Resources that can be replaced in a human lifetime are _____.

2. The preserving or protecting of resources is _____.

3. Resources that cannot be replaced in a human lifetime are _____.

4. Waste products that can change the environment are _____.

5. The exhaust that comes out of a car is a form of _____.

6. Sunlight and fresh water are examples of _____.

7. Turning off a light when you leave a room is one way to practice _____.

8. The gas used to make a car run comes from _____.

Check Understanding

Write the letter of the best choice.

9. **MAIN IDEA AND DETAILS** Which detail tells how acid rain forms?
   - **A.** Crop rotation causes pollution.
   - **B.** Polluted water reaches the sea.
   - **C.** Chemicals mix with water in the air.
   - **D.** Sewage reaches the water supply.

10. **CAUSE AND EFFECT** What is an effect of a Xeriscape yard?
    - **F.** Soil is preserved.
    - **G.** Lawns are greener.
    - **H.** Water is conserved.
    - **J.** Crops are planted in terraces.

11. Which is an example of recycling?
    - **A.** using less electricity
    - **B.** melting used aluminum to make new cans
    - **C.** burying newspaper deep underground
    - **D.** making a scoop from a milk container

12. Look at the picture. Which of the following resources will the person pollute first?
    - **F.** farms
    - **G.** land
    - **H.** surface water
    - **J.** groundwater

13. What does the illustration show?

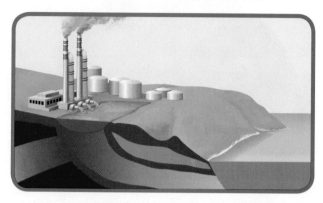

- **A.** the water cycle
- **B.** how water can become polluted
- **C.** how factories can be polluted
- **D.** the problems with landscaping

14. How would a glass jar be recycled?
- **F.** by using it again
- **G.** by not using it at all
- **H.** by melting it and making a new jar
- **J.** by making sure it is used efficiently

15. On which of the following would you be **most** likely to see this symbol?

- **A.** on a banana label
- **B.** on a juice container
- **C.** on a fertilizer spreader
- **D.** on a landscaped plot of ground

16. Which of these practices can homeowners use to conserve water?
- **F.** contour plowing
- **G.** Xeriscape landscaping
- **H.** strip cropping
- **J.** recycling

Inquiry Skills

17. **Draw a conclusion** about why manufacturing industries may have more problems controlling pollution than other kinds of businesses have.

18. How might you **control variables** in an experiment about landscaping techniques?

Critical Thinking

19. Explain how you can reduce, reuse, and recycle to avoid wasting plastic shopping bags.

20. Suppose you're a farmer who has just bought a farm. The land is in a drought area, and much of it is hilly. How can you use this land in ways that conserve both soil and water? How do farmers misuse land?

The **Big** Idea

Visual Summary

UNIT C EARTH SCIENCE

Tell how each picture shows the **Big Idea** for its chapter.

CHAPTER 7

Big Idea

Rocks and minerals are formed and changed through different Earth processes.

CHAPTER 8

Big Idea

Fossils of animal and plant remains help us understand Earth's history.

CHAPTER 9

Big Idea

Earth's surface is constantly changing.

CHAPTER 10

Big Idea

People use resources in many ways, sometimes causing pollution.

Cycles on Earth and in Space

CHAPTER 11
Weather and the Water Cycle. 392

CHAPTER 12
Earth's Oceans 430

CHAPTER 13
Earth, Moon, and Beyond. 466

Unit Inquiry

Beach Protection

Waves and currents at the beach are constant forces that can carry away large quantities of sand. How can humans build artificial structures to affect the action of waves? For example, can building jetties stop the loss of beach sand? Plan and conduct an experiment to find out.

Weather
and the
Water Cycle

What's the Big Idea?

Weather is a measurable and predictable part of the water cycle.

Essential Questions

Lesson 1

What Causes Weather?

Lesson 2

What Conditions Affect the Water Cycle?

Lesson 3

How Can Patterns in Weather Be Observed?

GO online

Student eBook
www.hspscience.com

In 2004, the state of Florida was hit by four hurricanes. Hurricanes are tropical storms with winds of at least 119 km/hr (74 mi/hr). More hurricanes hit Florida that year than had hit any single state for more than 100 years! Why do hurricanes form over tropical waters, and why do so many of them strike the East Coast of the United States? How does this relate to the **Big Idea?**

Hurricane Frances over the Atlantic Ocean

Investigate how the sun heats Earth unevenly, and how this affects temperatures of land and water.

Read and learn about characteristics of Earth's atmosphere and how the sun affects weather.

Essential Question

What Causes Weather?

Fast Fact

Each glass ball in this thermometer has a slightly different weight attached to it. As the temperature outside changes, the liquid inside the tube becomes less or more dense. The glass balls rise or fall to a certain level, depending on the temperature. You'll be using a more standard thermometer in the Investigate.

Galileo thermometer

atmosphere [AT•muhs•feer] The blanket of air surrounding Earth (p. 398)

troposphere [TROH•puh•sfeer] The layer of air closest to Earth's surface (p. 398)

air pressure [AIR PRESH•er] The weight of the atmosphere pressing down on Earth (p. 399)

local winds [LOH•kuhl WINDZ] Movements of air that result from local changes in temperature (p. 401)

prevailing winds [pree•VAYL•ing WINDZ] Global winds that blow constantly from the same direction (p. 402)

395

The Uneven Heating of Earth

Guided Inquiry

Start with Questions

Have you ever noticed that a paved parking lot gets really hot on a sunny day?

- Do water and land heat up and cool down at the same rates?

- Which is cooler on a sunny day at the beach, the sand or the water?

Investigate to find out. Then read and learn to find out more.

Prepare to Investigate

Inquiry Skill Tip

When you predict, you combine what you already know with what you have observed in the investigation. A prediction may turn out to be incorrect, but it can still guide your investigation. Even if the results show that your prediction was not correct, you have learned something new.

Materials

- 2 aluminum cans
- water
- dry soil
- spoon
- 2 thermometers

Make an Observation Chart

		Temperature (in °C)								
	Shade	Sunlight				Shade				
	10 min	0 min	10 min	20 min	30 min	0 min	10 min	20 min	30 min	
Water										
Soil										

Follow This Procedure

1. Fill one can about three-fourths full of water and the other can about three-fourths full of soil.

2. Place one thermometer in the can of water and the other in the can of soil. Put the cans in a shady place outside. Wait 10 minutes, and then **record** the temperature of the water and of the soil.

3. Put both cans in sunlight. **Predict** which can will heat faster. **Record** the temperature of each can every 10 minutes for 30 minutes.

4. Put the cans in the shade. **Predict** which can will show the faster temperature drop. Again, **record** the temperature of each can every 10 minutes for 30 minutes.

5. Make line graphs to show how the temperatures of both materials changed as they heated and cooled.

Draw Conclusions

1. How did your results match your predictions?

2. Which would you predict heats faster—oceans or land? Which would you predict cools faster? Explain.

3. **Inquiry Skill** Scientists learn by **predicting** and then experimenting to test their predictions. How did you test your predictions in this Investigate?

Step 1

Step 3

Independent Inquiry

Predict how fast moist soil, sand, and salt water heat up and cool down. Then **plan and conduct an investigation** to test your prediction.

Read and Learn

VOCABULARY
atmosphere p. 398
troposphere p. 398
air pressure p. 399
local wind p. 401
prevailing wind p. 402

SCIENCE CONCEPTS
▶ what the atmosphere is like
▶ how the sun affects weather conditions

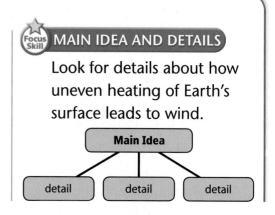

MAIN IDEA AND DETAILS

Look for details about how uneven heating of Earth's surface leads to wind.

The Atmosphere

You probably know that Earth is surrounded by a blanket of air called the **atmosphere**. The atmosphere is very thin compared to the size of Earth. In fact, if Earth were the size of a peach, the atmosphere would be thinner than the peach's fuzz!

The atmosphere is made up of several layers. Each layer has a different temperature. The layer closest to Earth's surface is called the **troposphere**. It's about 13 km (8 mi) thick, on average. Even the highest mountains on Earth are within it. The troposphere contains about 90 percent of the gases in the atmosphere. It also contains water, dust, and other tiny particles. Most of Earth's weather occurs there.

The stratosphere is the next higher layer. Most of Earth's ozone is in the stratosphere. Ozone is a gas that protects Earth's surface.

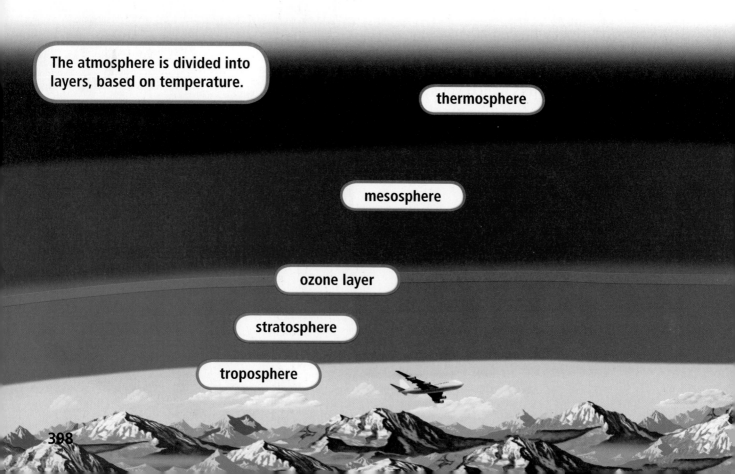

The atmosphere is divided into layers, based on temperature.

thermosphere

mesosphere

ozone layer

stratosphere

troposphere

Ozone blocks most of the sun's harmful ultraviolet rays. The air in the stratosphere is very dry, so clouds are rare. Above the stratosphere, the air is very thin—there is less air. The outermost layer of the atmosphere extends into space.

Gas molecules in the atmosphere are constantly moving. Gravity pulls them toward Earth's surface. As a result, air near the surface is dense and has considerable weight. **Air pressure** is the weight of the atmosphere pressing down on Earth.

Air pressure is greater at sea level than it is on a mountain. That's because there is more air closer to Earth's surface than away from the surface. Temperature also affects air pressure. Cold air is more dense than warm air, so it is heavier than warm air.

 **MAIN IDEA AND DETAILS**

What is the atmosphere made of?

The lower you are in the atmosphere, the greater the air pressure is, because air molecules higher up in the atmosphere press down on all the air molecules below them.

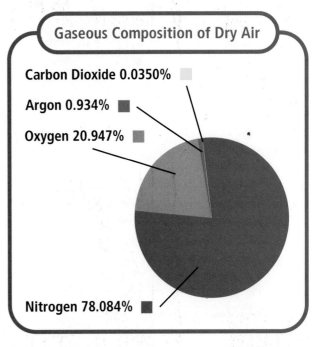

Gaseous Composition of Dry Air

Carbon Dioxide 0.0350%

Argon 0.934%

Oxygen 20.947%

Nitrogen 78.084%

▲ This circle graph shows the percentages of gases in dry air. However, most air in the troposphere is about 1 percent to 4 percent water vapor.

How Strong Is Air Pressure?
Put one end of a straw in a plastic bag. Use tape to seal the bag. Put the bag on a table, and lay a book on the bottom half of the bag. Blow through the straw. Observe what happens. In what ways might you use air pressure?

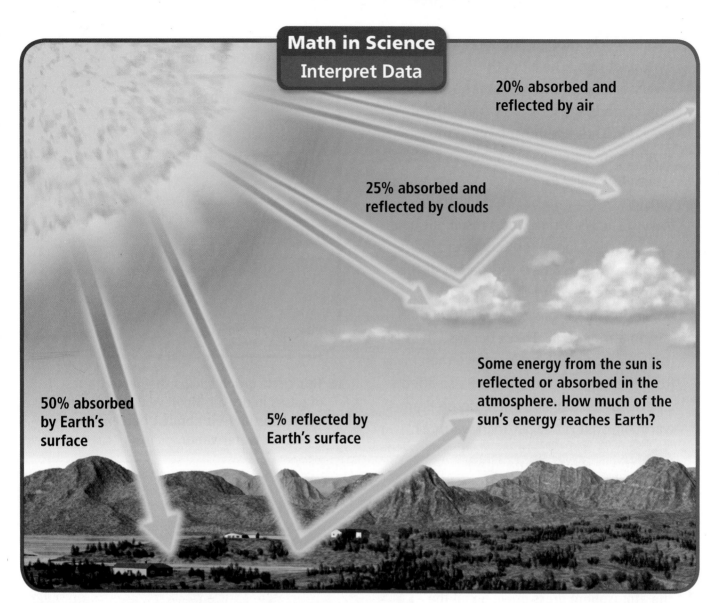

20% absorbed and reflected by air

25% absorbed and reflected by clouds

50% absorbed by Earth's surface

5% reflected by Earth's surface

Some energy from the sun is reflected or absorbed in the atmosphere. How much of the sun's energy reaches Earth?

Uneven Heating

When you left home this morning, how did the air feel? Was it hot or cold? Was it windy, or was it calm? If you were to go outside right now, would the air feel the same? It probably wouldn't. That's because the air around you is always moving and changing. Why is this so?

When the sun's energy reaches Earth, some of the energy bounces off objects such as clouds. Earth absorbs the rest of the energy. Different types of surfaces absorb different amounts of energy. For example, you learned in the Investigate that water can absorb more heat than an equal amount of

soil. That means if you're spending the day at the beach and you want to cool off, your best bet would be to take a swim. The sand is hotter than the water, so it gives off more heat. Because of this, the air over the beach will be hotter, too. The air over the water will be cooler.

Remember, cool air is denser than warm air. Dense air is heavy, so it sinks. Air that is warm—and less dense—is pushed up. This sinking and rising of air causes wind. In other words, wind is the result of uneven heating of the atmosphere.

 MAIN IDEA AND DETAILS

Why does air in the atmosphere move?

Local Winds

Air is always moving. Winds result from air moving from areas of high air pressure to areas of low air pressure. Because cool air has a higher pressure than warm air, wind blows from cooler places toward warmer places.

Sometimes, two places in the same area have slightly different temperatures. This produces a **local wind**, a wind that results from a local difference in temperature. Local winds often occur on lakeshores or seashores. During the day, the air over the land is warmer than the air over the water. Air over the water becomes more dense. The result is a wind that blows from the water toward the land. This wind is known as a sea breeze.

In the evening, the wind blows the opposite way. Remember, land cools off more quickly than water does. Once the land becomes cooler than the water, a wind blows from the land toward the water. This wind is called a land breeze.

 **MAIN IDEA AND DETAILS** What are the directions of a local wind along a shoreline?

During the day, the land heats up faster than the sea. Cooler sea air moves toward the land. This is called a *sea breeze*. ▼

At night, the land loses heat faster than the sea does. Cooler air over the land moves toward the sea. This is called a *land breeze*. ▼

Prevailing Winds

Local winds move short distances and can blow from any direction. But there are other, more constant winds. **Prevailing winds** are global winds that always blow from the same direction. Uneven heating of large areas of Earth's surface causes prevailing winds. Earth's rotation affects prevailing winds, too.

Earth's poles are covered with ice. Depending on the time of year, the poles receive indirect sunlight or no sunlight at all, so they're always cold. By contrast, Earth's equator gets direct sunlight all year long, so it's always warm. As a result, cold air above the poles sinks and moves toward the equator. At the same time, air at the equator moves up and goes toward the poles. But air doesn't just move in one big circle. As warm air at the equator moves up, it begins to cool. Some of the cooling air sinks before it reaches the poles. Air in the atmosphere travels in many circles as it continually warms and cools.

You might expect air moving within these circles to move straight north or south. Instead, air moves in curved paths. For example, over the United States, winds moving north curve to the east. Winds moving south curve to the west. The curving is due to Earth's rotation. This rotation causes the prevailing winds to blow mainly from the east or the west.

 **MAIN IDEA AND DETAILS**

What two factors cause prevailing winds?

The global winds that blow over most of the United States are called the prevailing westerlies. They blow from the west to the east. ▼

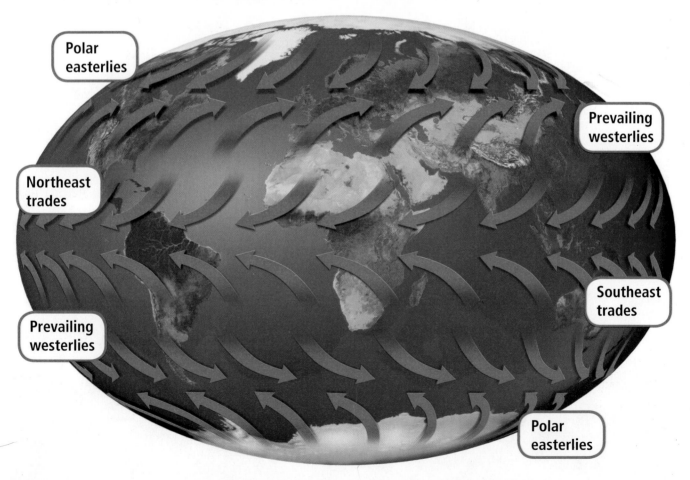

Polar easterlies

Prevailing westerlies

Northeast trades

Prevailing westerlies

Southeast trades

Polar easterlies

Essential Question

What Causes Weather?

You learned that an atmosphere made up of layers surrounds Earth. Not all energy from the sun reaches the Earth's surface. The energy is enough to cause different temperatures in different places, producing local and global winds.

1. **MAIN IDEA AND DETAILS** Draw and complete a graphic organizer with supporting details for this main idea: The atmosphere has several layers of air.

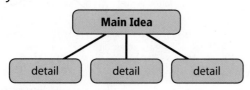

2. **SUMMARIZE** Write a paragraph describing how the sun influences winds on Earth.

3. **DRAW CONCLUSIONS** How does the troposphere affect everyday living?

4. **VOCABULARY** Choose three vocabulary terms from this lesson. Draw diagrams that illustrate the meanings of the three terms.

Test Prep

5. **CRITICAL THINKING** Suppose you're going fishing on a lake. Describe the winds that might occur along the lakeshore.

6. Which of the following is the most common gas in the troposphere?
   - **A.** carbon dioxide
   - **B.** nitrogen
   - **C.** oxygen
   - **D.** water vapor

Make Connections

Writing

Expository Writing

Suppose you're on vacation. Write a postcard **describing** the weather to a friend. Include temperature, wind speed, and wind direction.

Math

Solve Problems

Study the circle graph on page 399. Suppose the amount of carbon dioxide in the atmosphere doubled. Would you notice a large change in the circle graph? Explain why or why not.

Health

Sunscreen

Research how the sun affects human skin. Then make a brochure that explains how people can keep their skin healthy and why they should use sunscreen.

Investigate how energy from the sun moves water from one place to another.

Read and learn about the parts of the water cycle, the forms of precipitation, and some factors that affect the water cycle.

Essential Question

What Conditions Affect the Water Cycle?

Fast Fact

Blizzard!

The United States has an average of 105 snowstorms each year. A snowstorm can last from just a few hours to many days. During one snowstorm in Buffalo, New York, 96 cm of snow fell in 24 hours! In the Investigate, you'll see how water for rain or snow gets into the air.

Digging out after a blizzard

water cycle [WAW•ter SY•kuhl]
The process in which water
continuously moves from
Earth's surface into the
atmosphere and back again
(p. 408)

evaporation
[ee•vap•uh•RAY•shuhn] The
process of a liquid changing
into a gas (p. 409)

condensation
[kahn•duhn•SAY•shuhn] The
process of a gas changing into
a liquid (p. 409)

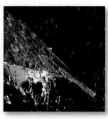

humidity [hyoo•MID•uh•tee]
A measurement of the amount
of water vapor in the air (p. 410)

precipitation
[pree•sip•uh•TAY•shuhn] Water
that falls from the air to Earth
(p. 410)

Water, Water Everywhere

Guided Inquiry

Start with Questions

When you leave for school in the morning, grass and plants outside might have drops of water on them. Sometimes, even the windows on cars and buses have water on them.

- Where does this water come from?

- Why does water collect on this leaf overnight?

Investigate to find out. Then read and learn to find out more.

Prepare to Investigate

Inquiry Skill Tip

You can think of **inferring** as solving a puzzle. If you put together several things that you know, what else is probably true?

Materials

- graduated cylinder
- water
- small plastic cup
- zip-top plastic bag

Make an Observation Chart

Day	Observations	Amount of Water (mL)
1		100
2		
3		
4		
	Difference in amount of water:	

Follow This Procedure

① Using a graduate, **measure** and pour 100 mL of water into a cup.

② Open a plastic bag and carefully put the cup inside. Then seal the bag. Be careful not to spill any water from the cup.

③ Place the sealed bag near a sunny window. **Predict** what will happen to the water in the cup.

④ Leave the bag near the window for 3 to 4 days. **Observe** the cup and the bag each day. **Record** what you see.

⑤ Remove the cup from the bag. **Measure** the water in the cup by pouring it back into the graduate. By **using the numbers** you recorded, find any difference in the amount of water poured into the cup and the amount of water removed from the cup.

Draw Conclusions

1. What did you observe during the time the cup was inside the bag?

2. What happened to the water in the cup?

3. **Inquiry Skill** Scientists often **infer** the cause of what they observe. What can you **infer** about where the water in the bag came from?

Step 1

Step 3

Independent Inquiry

Is the amount of water in the bag the same as the amount of water missing from the cup? Plan and conduct a simple investigation to find out.

Read and Learn

VOCABULARY
water cycle p. 408
evaporation p. 409
condensation p. 409
humidity p. 410
precipitation p. 410

SCIENCE CONCEPTS
▶ how water moves through the water cycle
▶ how the water cycle relates to weather

 **SEQUENCE**
Look for the order of steps in which water moves through the water cycle.

The Water Cycle

In Lesson 1, you learned that air always moves. Water is always moving, too. In fact, water continuously moves from Earth's surface to the atmosphere and back to Earth in a process called the **water cycle**.

The water cycle is important because people, plants, and animals need fresh water to live. Without rain and snow, we wouldn't have drinking water. We also wouldn't have water to grow crops.

Science Up Close

The Water Cycle

The water cycle is driven by heat energy from the sun. The sun's rays warm water on Earth's surface. The water evaporates, leaving behind the salt in sea water. The sun also heats the atmosphere unevenly. This causes the air, containing water vapor, to move from one place to another.

As moist air rises, it cools. If it cools enough, the water vapor in it condenses, forming clouds.

Water vapor mixes with dust and other particles in the air.

Every day, tons of water evaporate from Earth's oceans, lakes, rivers, and moist soil.

408

How does the water cycle work? You may remember that water on Earth exists in three states. Water is a liquid in oceans, lakes, and rivers and in rain. If water is heated, it turns into a gas—water vapor. If water is cooled enough, it changes to a solid—ice.

During part of the water cycle, liquid water changes to a gas by the process of **evaporation**. As a gas, water molecules are too spread out to be seen. You can observe the results of evaporation if, for example, you leave a glass of water uncovered for a long time. The water just seems to disappear. Water in the air remains a gas as long as the air is warm. If the air cools,

the water becomes a liquid. Water changes from a gas to a liquid in the process of **condensation**. When a large amount of water vapor condenses, a cloud forms. If the drops of water in the cloud become heavy enough, the water falls as rain.

When rain falls on the land, the water runs into streams, rivers, and lakes. Some of it soaks into the ground. Rivers carry the water back to the ocean. Water under the ground, called *groundwater,* also flows back to the ocean or into streams and rivers.

Focus Skill **SEQUENCE** What steps in the water cycle must occur before rain can fall?

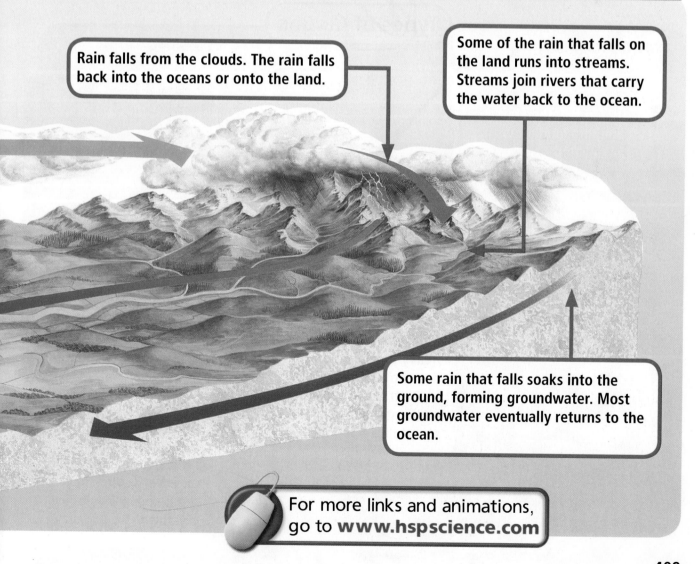

Rain falls from the clouds. The rain falls back into the oceans or onto the land.

Some of the rain that falls on the land runs into streams. Streams join rivers that carry the water back to the ocean.

Some rain that falls soaks into the ground, forming groundwater. Most groundwater eventually returns to the ocean.

For more links and animations, go to **www.hspscience.com**

Clouds and Precipitation

Much of what you may call weather is actually part of the water cycle. A large part of the water cycle occurs in the atmosphere. Water enters the atmosphere when it evaporates and becomes water vapor. Some areas of the atmosphere have more water vapor than other areas. The amount of water vapor in the air is **humidity**. The more water vapor in the air, the more humid the air is.

Humidity is partly limited by air temperature. Warm air can have more water vapor in it than cold air can have. Suppose you're on an island near the equator. The air over the island is warm, so it will contain a lot of water that has evaporated from the ocean. As warm air is forced up, it cools. Some of the water vapor begins to condense on dust and other particles in the air. As more and more water condenses, a cloud forms. A cloud is basically dust and condensed water.

Small water droplets inside the cloud join to form larger droplets. The larger droplets then join to make water drops. Water drops are too heavy to stay in the atmosphere. They fall from the clouds as precipitation. **Precipitation** (pree•sip•uh•TAY•shuhn) is water that falls from the atmosphere to Earth's surface. Rain is liquid precipitation.

Types of Clouds

CUMULUS CLOUDS
Cumulus (KYOO•myuh•luhs) clouds are puffy. They indicate fair weather, but as a cumulus cloud grows, rain can develop.

STRATUS CLOUDS
Stratus (STRAT•uhs) clouds form low in the atmosphere. They usually cover the sky. Heavy precipitation does not usually fall from stratus clouds, but moderate rainfall or snowfall is possible.

CIRRUS CLOUDS
Cirrus (SIR•uhs) clouds form high in the atmosphere, where the air is very cold. They are made mostly of ice crystals.

Several kinds of precipitation fall from cumulus clouds. This cloud is a cumulonimbus cloud. Cumulonimbus clouds can produce moderate to heavy rain, hail, or snow.

Rain

Snow

Sleet

Hail

The other forms of precipitation are solid. Solid precipitation is snow, hail, or sleet. Snow forms when water vapor turns directly into ice crystals. Sleet and hail form when liquid water passes through air that is cold enough to freeze water drops.

Water vapor doesn't always form precipitation as it condenses. Have you ever found dew on the ground after a cool night? Car windows and other objects may also be covered with dew. Why does dew form? The ground loses heat more quickly than the air does. When the ground becomes cold enough, water vapor in the air directly above the ground condenses. If the temperature is very cold, frost forms on the ground or on car windows. Frost is water vapor that turns directly into ice.

A similar weather condition can form fog. Fog is water vapor that has condensed into small water droplets near ground level.

 **SEQUENCE** What is the first step in the formation of a cloud?

Making Raindrops
Use a spray bottle to mist a piece of wax paper with water. This models a cloud. Move the wax paper around so that the small water droplets start to join into larger droplets. What process are you modeling? If this were a real cloud, what would happen?

Factors That Affect the Water Cycle

Many factors affect the water cycle. One factor is how close a place is to Earth's poles or the equator. Places close to the poles are always cold. Because of this, they're much more likely to get snow or sleet than places close to the equator.

Another factor that affects the water cycle is the shape of the land. Air must move around and over landforms such as mountain ranges. When air is pushed up the side of a mountain, it cools. Much of the water in the air condenses. This causes rain to fall, usually on one side of the mountain. If the mountain is high enough, snow may fall instead of rain. The snow stays on the mountain until spring. In spring, the snow melts, sending huge amounts of water flowing down the mountain in streams and rivers. This is called the spring melt.

Landforms such as coastlines also affect the water cycle. You've read about how sea breezes form along coastlines. A sea breeze usually carries humid air. As the air rises over the land, clouds form. If the drops of water in the clouds get large enough, rain falls.

Landforms and temperature affect the water cycle because they change the pressure of the air. Remember, warm air has lower pressure than cold air. And warm air can have more water in it than cold air can. Any factor that causes a change in air pressure can also cause a change in the water cycle.

 **SEQUENCE** What events on a mountain lead to the spring melt?

Fog is a stratus-like cloud that forms at ground level. Fog often forms on hills and mountains when humid air moves up a slope to the point where the water vapor in the air condenses and forms a cloud.

Essential Question

What Conditions Affect the Water Cycle?

In this lesson, you learned that the water cycle is responsible for the movement of water in Earth's atmosphere and on its surface. This cycle is vital for all living things. Water falls to Earth in many forms and is affected by different factors.

1. **(Focus Skill) SEQUENCE** Draw and complete a graphic organizer to show the sequence for the formation of these: rain, snow, groundwater.

2. **SUMMARIZE** Write a paragraph describing a sequence of events that happen to a water molecule during the water cycle.

3. **DRAW CONCLUSIONS** What would happen to the water cycle if the sun heated the atmosphere evenly?

4. **VOCABULARY** Compare and contrast the two terms within each pair: *evaporation* and *condensation*; *humidity* and *precipitation*.

Test Prep

5. **CRITICAL THINKING** You see cirrus clouds in the sky. Will it rain soon? Explain your answer.

6. You heat an ice cube, and it melts. What will happen to the water if you continue to apply heat?
   A. It will condense.
   B. It will evaporate.
   C. It will freeze.
   D. It will precipitate.

Make Connections

 Writing

Narrative Writing
Write a **description** of how the water cycle varies in your area during the year. Include the seasons in your description.

 Math

Draw Conclusions
Make a graph showing types and amounts of precipitation in 10 cities around the United States. What conclusions can you draw about snowfall amounts by comparing your graph to a map?

 Social Studies

Monsoons
Monsoons are weather systems that produce dry and wet seasons in some parts of the world. Research monsoons, and write a report about them.

Investigate how weather changes over a few days.

Read and learn about how weather conditions are measured and how these measurements can be used to predict weather.

Essential Question

How Can Patterns in Weather Be Observed?

Fast Fact

Blowing the Horn
During heavy fog, operators of the Golden Gate Bridge—in San Francisco—sound a horn. This helps ships avoid the bridge. From July through October, there's so much fog that the horn sounds for about five hours nearly every day! In the Investigate, you'll observe other predictable weather patterns.

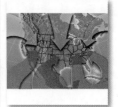

air mass [AIR MAS] A large body of air that has similar temperature and humidity throughout (p. 420)

front [FRUHNT] The border where two air masses meet (p. 421)

climate [KLY•muht] The pattern of weather an area experiences over a long period of time (p. 422)

The Golden Gate Bridge

Measuring Weather Conditions

Guided Inquiry

Start with Questions

When you look out a window, you can see if it is sunny or cloudy. If the wind is blowing, a wind vane like the one below would tell you the direction is it blowing. But none of these observations are measurements of weather.

- How do you think weather is measured?

- How do you think people measured and predicted weather 100 years ago?

Investigate to find out. Then read and learn to find out more.

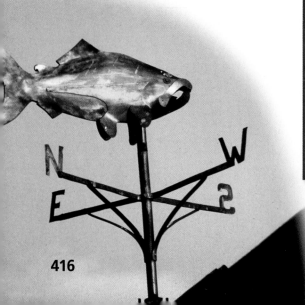

Prepare to Investigate

Inquiry Skill Tip

Data is the information that you obtain during an investigation. Gathering data often involves measuring, which can be done in many ways. In some cases, you gather data by observing. The most important part of gathering data is to be as accurate as possible.

Materials

- weather station

Make an Observation Chart

Weather Station Daily Record					
Date					
Time					
Temperature					
Rainfall or snowfall					
Wind direction and speed					
Cloud conditions					

Follow This Procedure

1 Copy the table titled Weather Station Daily Record. You'll use it to **record** the weather each day for five days. Try to **gather data** about weather conditions at the same time each day.

2 Place the weather station in a shady spot, about 1 m above the ground. Be sure the rain gauge will not collect runoff from buildings or trees. Put the wind vane where wind from any direction can reach it.

3 **Record** the amount of rain or snow, if any.

4 **Record** wind direction and speed. Identify wind by the direction from which it's blowing.

5 **Observe** and **record** the cloud conditions. Draw a circle, and shade part of it to show the fraction of the sky that is covered with clouds.

6 **Record** the temperature. Make a line graph showing how the temperature changes from day to day.

Draw Conclusions

1. **Compare** weather conditions you observed on two different days.

2. **Inquiry Skill** Scientists learn about the weather by **measuring** and **gathering data**. From the data you gathered, how might you **predict** the weather for tomorrow?

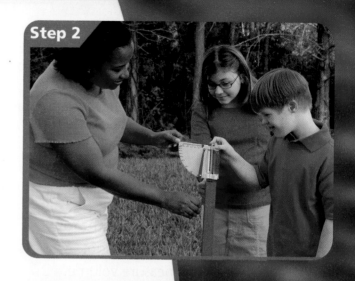

Step 2

Step 3

Independent Inquiry

Can clues about tomorrow's weather be found in today's weather data? Plan and conduct an investigation to find out if specific observations can help you predict upcoming weather.

417

VOCABULARY
air mass p. 420
front p. 421
climate p. 422

SCIENCE CONCEPTS
▶ how weather conditions
  are measured
▶ how weather can be
  predicted

(Focus Skill) **CAUSE AND EFFECT**
Look for what causes weather
to change.

[cause] ⟶ [effect]

Measuring Weather

You use a ruler to measure length. You use a spring scale to measure weight. And you use a graduate to measure volume. What do you use to measure weather? Because there are many different kinds of weather data, you need many different instruments.

You're probably familiar with one kind of weather instrument—a thermometer. A thermometer measures air temperature. A *hygrometer* measures humidity—the amount of water in the air. Another kind of weather instrument is the *barometer*. A barometer measures air pressure.

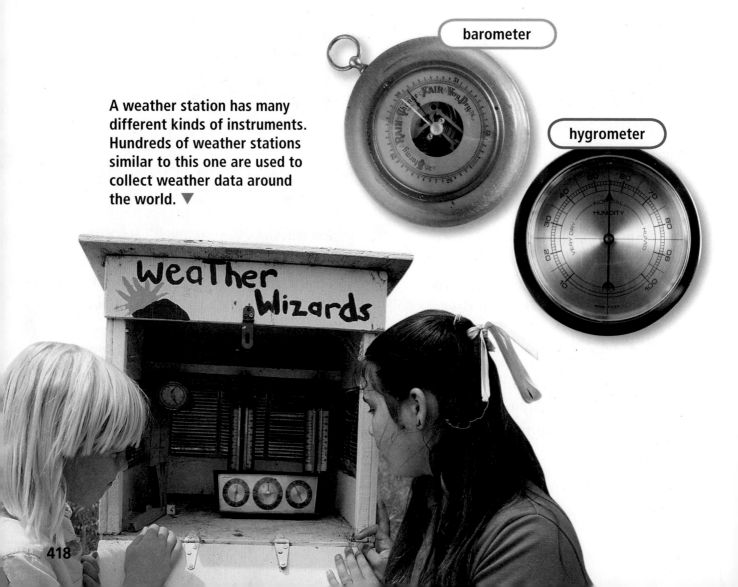

barometer

hygrometer

A weather station has many different kinds of instruments. Hundreds of weather stations similar to this one are used to collect weather data around the world. ▼

▲ In the past, people relied on simple observations to help them forecast the weather. Sayings such as "Red sky at night, sailors' delight" and "When the dew is on the grass, rain will never come to pass" helped people remember what their observations might predict about the weather.

Remember, air temperature and air pressure are related. A rising barometer, which shows increasing air pressure, often precedes the arrival of colder air. Since cold air has less water in it than warm air does, a rising barometer also means less humidity and less chance of rain.

There are several instruments that measure wind. An *anemometer* measures wind speed. *Windsocks* and *wind vanes* both show wind direction. It's important to measure wind because changes in wind often bring changes in the weather. Knowing from which direction the wind is blowing helps people predict the weather. For example, if it's winter and a wind starts blowing from the south, you can predict that the weather will soon be warmer. Any change in wind direction or speed usually means a change in the weather.

Weather changes can also be predicted, although less accurately, just by observing the sky. For example, observing the clouds can tell you a lot. There's a saying that goes "Red sky at night, sailors' delight. Red sky in the morning, sailors take warning." A red sky in the morning occurs when the rising sun reflects on storm clouds coming from the west. This often means it will rain later in the day. A red sunset means that no storms are approaching from the west, so the next day should be sunny. Also, as you learned, different cloud types are associated with different types of weather. Cumulus clouds can bring rain. Stratus clouds can also bring moderate precipitation.

 CAUSE AND EFFECT

How can rising air pressure lead to a prediction about temperature?

419

Air Masses and Fronts

You read in Lesson 1 that Earth's atmosphere heats unevenly. This causes the air in the atmosphere to move. Air doesn't move around Earth randomly in small amounts. Instead, air moves in regular ways in air masses. An **air mass** is a large body of air that has similar temperature and humidity throughout. In the United States, air masses often move from west to east, pushed along by the prevailing winds.

Air masses can be warm or cold. They can also be humid or dry. What determines an air mass's characteristics? An air mass takes on the characteristics of the region over which it forms. For example, an air mass that forms over the Caribbean Sea will be humid and warm. An air mass that forms over northern Canada will be dry and cold.

Look at the map. As you can see, there are four kinds of air masses that affect weather in the United States. Continental polar air masses (cP) bring cool, dry weather. Continental tropical air masses (cT) bring hot, dry weather. Maritime polar air masses (mP) bring cold, humid weather. Finally, maritime tropical air masses (mT) bring warm, humid weather.

When the weather changes in an area, it means that the air mass over the area is changing. That is, the current air mass is being replaced by a different air mass.

A continental air mass forms over land, so it is dry. A maritime air mass forms over water, so it is humid. A polar air mass forms over cold areas, so it is cold. A tropical air mass forms over warm areas, so it is warm. ▶

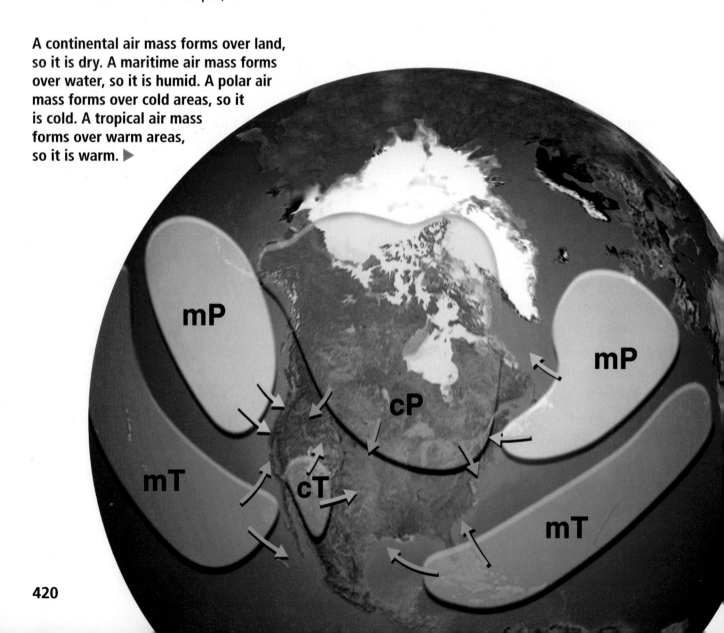

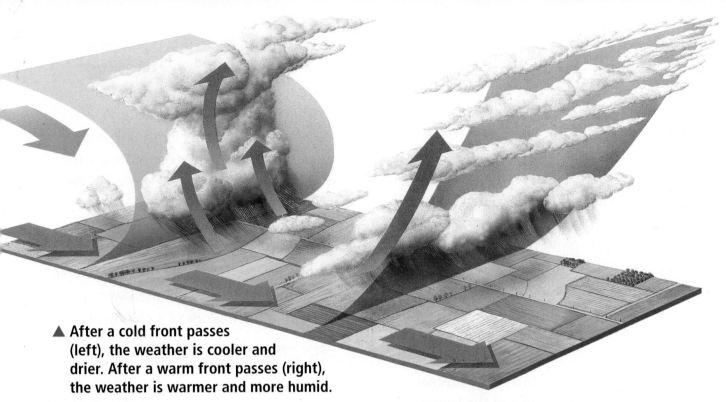

▲ After a cold front passes (left), the weather is cooler and drier. After a warm front passes (right), the weather is warmer and more humid.

The border where two air masses meet is called a **front**. Most weather changes occur along a front. For example, if a cold, dense air mass pushes into a warm, light air mass, the warm, light air begins to move up. As that air moves up, it cools. Water vapor in it condenses, and clouds form. There is usually precipitation along a front.

There are two main kinds of fronts: cold fronts and warm fronts. A *cold front* forms where a cold air mass moves under a warm air mass (left side of diagram above). The warm air mass is less dense, so it is pushed up. Cumulonimbus clouds form, producing heavy rain, thunderstorms, or snow near the front. Cold fronts usually move quickly, so the precipitation doesn't last long.

A *warm front* forms where a warm air mass moves over a cold air mass (right side of diagram above). As the warm air slides up and over the cold air, stratus clouds form ahead of the front. This causes rain or snow that can last for hours.

 **CAUSE AND EFFECT** What kind of air mass causes hot, humid weather?

On weather maps, cold fronts are shown by blue lines with triangles. Warm fronts are shown by red lines with half circles. ▶

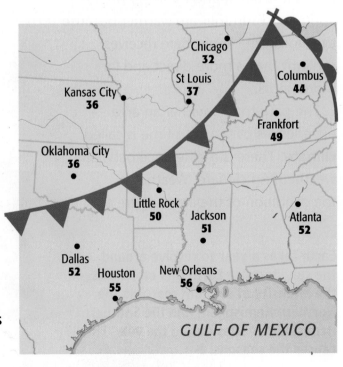

Chicago 32
St Louis 37
Columbus 44
Kansas City 36
Frankfort 49
Oklahoma City 36
Little Rock 50
Jackson 51
Atlanta 52
Dallas 52
Houston 55
New Orleans 56

GULF OF MEXICO

Weather Patterns and Climates

Weather in most locations occurs in regular patterns. You already know several factors that produce weather patterns. Local winds produce weather patterns in a small area. Prevailing winds produce weather patterns over large areas.

In addition to wind patterns, there are temperature patterns. For example, on most days, it's cool in the morning and warmer in the afternoon. The air warms up as the sun's energy heats Earth. When the sun sets, the air begins to cool off again.

Over a longer time, there are seasonal patterns. Every year, much of the United States has different weather during winter, spring, summer, and fall. The weather is coldest during winter and warmest during summer.

Like daily patterns, seasonal weather patterns are driven by the sun. Fall and winter are cool in the United States because the Northern Hemisphere receives sunlight that is less direct and for fewer hours. Spring and summer are warmer because the Northern Hemisphere receives sunlight that is more direct and for more hours.

The pattern of weather an area experiences over a long time is called **climate**. There is a difference between weather and climate. Weather is the condition of the atmosphere at a particular time. Climate is the average of weather conditions over many years. Average temperature and precipitation are the main characteristics of climate.

Because the sun heats Earth unevenly, areas close to the equator get more energy from the sun than areas closer to the poles do. As a result, the farther a place is from the equator, the colder its climate is. How wet or dry a climate is usually depends on how close a place is to large bodies of water. Therefore, coastal areas are often wetter than areas in the interior of a continent.

Focus Skill **CAUSE AND EFFECT** **What causes seasonal weather patterns?**

Earth takes a year to revolve around the sun. Because Earth tilts on its axis, the intensity of sunlight reaching the Northern Hemisphere and the Southern Hemisphere varies during the year. This causes the seasons. ▶

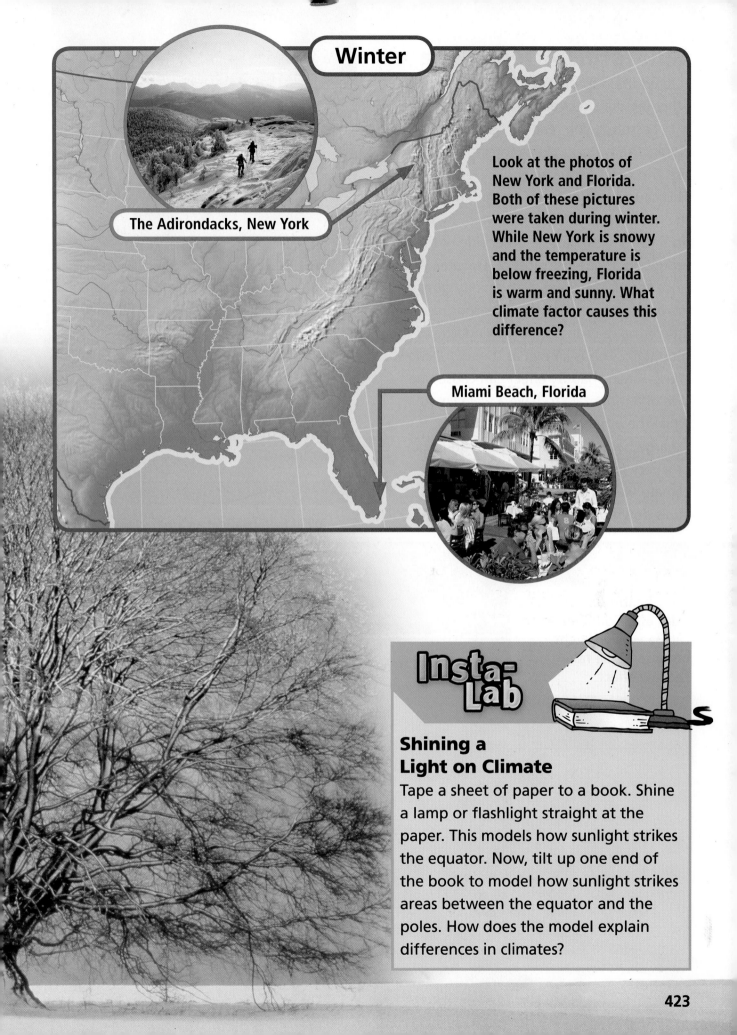

Winter

The Adirondacks, New York

Look at the photos of New York and Florida. Both of these pictures were taken during winter. While New York is snowy and the temperature is below freezing, Florida is warm and sunny. What climate factor causes this difference?

Miami Beach, Florida

Insta-Lab

Shining a Light on Climate

Tape a sheet of paper to a book. Shine a lamp or flashlight straight at the paper. This models how sunlight strikes the equator. Now, tilt up one end of the book to model how sunlight strikes areas between the equator and the poles. How does the model explain differences in climates?

Landforms Affect Climate

In addition to distance from the equator, other factors affect an area's climate.

In Lesson 2, you read that a mountain affects the water cycle by forcing air to rise and cool. As the air cools, clouds form. This causes rain or snow on the side of the mountain that faces the wind. By the time the air reaches the other side of the mountain, it has lost most of its water. And since the air is sinking, its humidity goes down even more. For these reasons, there is little or no rain on the downwind side of the mountain. This is known as the *rain shadow effect*. A rain shadow effect can cause one side of a mountain to have a wet climate while the other side has a dry climate.

Large bodies of water, such as an ocean or a very large lake, can affect an area's climate. Remember, water heats up and cools down more slowly than land does.

▲ Grapes grow more easily here because of the warming effect of the nearby lake.

So land near a large body of water tends to have a milder climate than other areas. This land is usually cooler in summer, warmer in winter, and more humid all year than areas farther inland.

CAUSE AND EFFECT

What factors affect an area's climate?

The climates on opposite sides of a mountain range can be very different because of the rain shadow effect.

Moist air blown from Pacific Ocean

Dry air moving toward desert

How Can Patterns in Weather Be Observed?

In this lesson, you learned how to gather data to predict weather. You also learned that weather forecasts depend on variables such as the properties of air masses, fronts, and landmasses.

1.  **CAUSE AND EFFECT** Draw and complete graphic organizers to show the effects of these: North Atlantic air mass; Warm Front; Climate of Houston, Texas.

cause ⟶ effect

2. **SUMMARIZE** Write a paragraph summarizing the two main types of fronts, how they form, and the type of weather they bring to an area.

3. **DRAW CONCLUSIONS** If Earth's oceans were much smaller, how would climates on Earth be affected?

4. **VOCABULARY** In your own words, write definitions for the following terms: *air mass*, *front*, and *climate*.

Test Prep

5. **CRITICAL THINKING** Suppose you feel strong winds, see dark clouds forming, and hear thunder. What could cause this weather?

6. Which of the following affects climate by causing air to move up?
   A. Earth's revolution
   B. large lakes
   C. mountains
   D. nearness to the poles

Make Connections

 Writing

Expository Writing
Write a **letter** that could be sent to a pen pal in another country to describe what the climate is like where you live.

 Math

Display Data
Find the average precipitation for your area for each month of the year. Also find the average temperature. Make bar graphs to display the data.

 Social Studies

Mountain Effects
Locate a mountain range with a rain shadow effect. Research the different kinds of plants and animals that live on the wet side and the dry side of the mountains.

On the Lookout

Weather forecasters have one of the toughest jobs around. Millions of people rely on weather forecasts to make their plans. But if a weather forecast is wrong, you can bet the weather experts hear about it.

Weather forecasting isn't easy, though. Forecasters can't use a crystal ball or flip a coin to predict the weather. They have to rely on data from different sources and use computers to be as accurate as possible in their predictions.

Pictures from Space

Satellites are some of the most important tools weather forecasters use. Satellites orbit about 35,000 kilometers (21,748 miles) above Earth. They give forecasters a bird's-eye view of clouds and how they are moving across land and water.

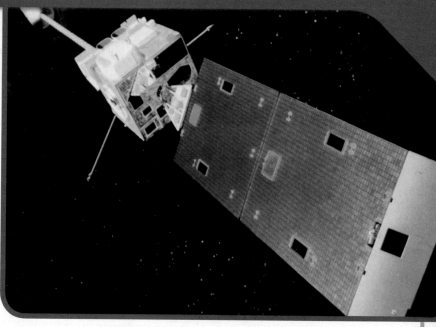

One pair of weather satellites, called GOES, is used by the National Weather Service. The satellites send weather data and pictures to forecasters on the ground. Using the images from the satellites, forecasters can track the movements of storm clouds.

Doppler Radar

Doppler radar also helps forecasters determine whether clouds hold snow, sleet, hail, or rain. The radar provides color-coded images that identify each type of precipitation. Precipitation is any form of water that falls to Earth from the clouds.

The various colors show the intensity of the precipitation. Light and dark blue colors usually indicate areas of light precipitation. Areas of red and pink colors usually indicate strong to severe thunderstorms. So if a radar image shows a broad band of pink moving toward a town, forecasters can warn people in the town of incoming severe weather.

Reliable Technology

Weather balloons have been used by forecasters for decades. The balloons show forecasters what is happening high in the atmosphere.

Think and Write

1 Why might the National Weather Service still use weather balloons?

2 Why are accurate weather forecasts important to people and to businesses?

Find out more. Log on to
www.hspscience.com

Up, Up, and Away

The National Weather Service releases weather balloons twice a day from 92 different locations around the world. The balloons can rise 32 kilometers (20 miles) high and have a transmitter, called a radiosonde, attached. The radiosonde sends temperature, humidity, wind, and air pressure data back to the scientists on the ground.

Vocabulary Review

Use the terms below to complete the sentences. The page numbers tell where to look in the chapter if you need help.

atmosphere p. 398

air pressure p. 399

local wind p. 401

prevailing winds p. 402

water cycle p. 408

evaporation p. 409

condensation p. 409

precipitation p. 410

air mass p. 420

climate p. 422

1. Water that falls from the air to Earth is _____.

2. Global winds that blow constantly in the same direction are _____.

3. The weight of the atmosphere pressing down on Earth is _____.

4. Water changes from a gas to a liquid in the process of _____.

5. The pattern of weather an area experiences over many years is _____.

6. The blanket of air surrounding Earth is the _____.

7. Water changes from a liquid to a gas in a process known as _____.

8. A large body of air is an _____.

9. A wind that results from local changes in temperature is a _____.

10. The movement of water between the atmosphere, the land, and the ocean is known as the _____.

Check Understanding

Write the letter of the best choice.

11. **MAIN IDEA AND DETAILS** In which layer of Earth's atmosphere does most weather occur?
    A. hydrosphere
    B. stratosphere
    C. thermosphere
    D. troposphere

12. **CAUSE AND EFFECT** Which of these is a common effect of a warm front?
    F. cold, clear weather
    G. many hours of rain
    H. strong, blowing winds
    J. violent thunderstorms

13. Of the following processes, which most likely left the moisture on the outside of the glass below?
    A. condensation
    B. evaporation
    C. humidification
    D. precipitation

14. Examine the diagram of a seashore. Why do sea breezes form?

    F. Air heats more slowly than land.
    G. Earth's surface is heated evenly.
    H. Land heats more slowly than water.
    J. Water heats more slowly than land.

15. What is shown in the picture below?

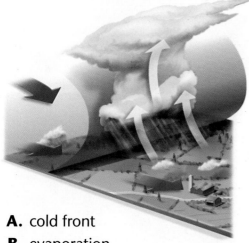

    A. cold front
    B. evaporation
    C. rain shadow
    D. warm front

16. Which of these is liquid precipitation?
    F. dew
    G. fog
    H. hail
    J. rain

Inquiry Skills

17. Which do you **predict** will heat up faster on a sunny day—a pond or a meadow? Explain your answer.

18. What two instruments are most important for the **measurements** of a region's climate? Explain your answer.

Critical Thinking

19. What type of weather should you expect when you see this type of cloud?

20. Suppose it is sunset on a warm, humid day. After dark, the temperature is predicted to drop. How does air temperature relate to the amount of water vapor in the air? What will happen to the water vapor in the air if the temperature drops as predicted?

The **Big Idea**

Earth's Oceans

What's the Big Idea?

Oceans are complex systems that interact with Earth's land, air, and living organisms.

Essential Questions

Lesson 1

What Are the Oceans Like?

Lesson 2

How Does Ocean Water Move?

Lesson 3

What Forces Shape Shorelines?

GO online

Student eBook
www.hspscience.com

Large brain coral in a coral reef

What do YOU wonder?

This diver is swimming over a bed of coral. Each coral formation is made up of the outer skeletons of hundreds of tiny animals called polyps. What are conditions like in ocean areas where corals live? How do corals interact with other organisms? How does this relate to the Big Idea?

431

Essential Question

What Are the Oceans Like?

Investigate whether salt water freezes at the same temperature as fresh water.

Read and learn about the characteristics of ocean water and the ocean floor.

Fast Fact

Ocean Ice

Some people believe that ocean water can't freeze because it's salt water. However, this ship is cutting through a layer of ice near Antarctica. Does ocean water freeze at the same temperature as fresh water? The Investigate will help you find out.

An icebreaker ship

salinity [suh•LIN•uh•tee] The amount of salt in water (p. 436)

water pressure [WAWT•er PRESH•er] The downward push of water on a given area (p. 437)

continental shelf [kahnt•uhn•ENT•uhl SHELF] The part of the ocean floor that drops gently near the land (p. 438)

continental slope [kahnt•uhn•ENT•uhl SLOHP] The part of the ocean floor that slopes steeply (p. 438)

abyssal plain [uh•BIS•uhl PLAYN] A large, flat area of the ocean floor (p. 438)

Investigate

Ice Water

Guided Inquiry

Start with Questions

Ocean water is different from drinking water or water in a lake, pond, or river. Ocean water is salty.

- Do ocean water and fresh water have other properties that are different?
- Will ocean water freeze if it is snowing like in the picture below?

Investigate to find out. Then read and learn to find out more.

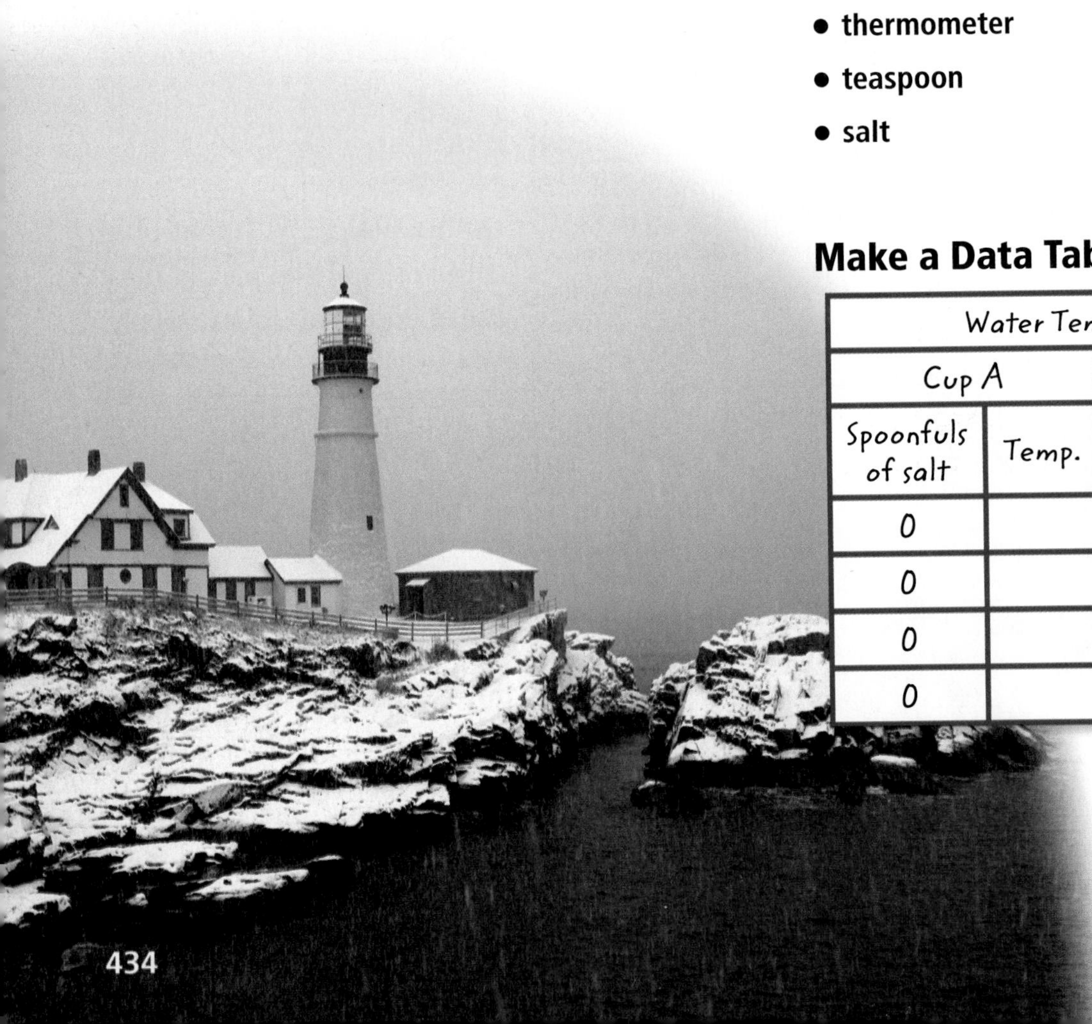

Prepare to Investigate

Inquiry Skill Tip

When you draw conclusions about the results of an investigation, consider the overall problem. Examine all your data, and think about what the results mean.

Materials

- 2 plastic measuring cups
- wax pencil
- ice cubes
- water
- thermometer
- teaspoon
- salt

Make a Data Table

Water Temperatures			
Cup A		Cup B	
Spoonfuls of salt	Temp.	Spoonfuls of salt	Temp.
0		0	
0		2	
0		4	
0		6	

Follow This Procedure

1 Copy the table.

2 Use a wax pencil to label the cups A and B. Fill each cup with ice cubes. Then add equal amounts of water to the cups.

3 Wait five minutes, and then use a thermometer to **measure** the temperature of the water in each cup. **Record** the data.

4 Stir 2 teaspoonfuls of salt into Cup B. Stir the water until the salt dissolves.

5 Wait two minutes, and then **measure** and **record** the temperature in each cup again.

6 Repeat Steps 4 and 5 two more times.

Draw Conclusions

1. What was the difference between the final temperatures?

2. What happened to the temperature of the salt water as more salt was added?

3. **Inquiry Skill** After reviewing the data, scientists **draw conclusions** about an experiment. What conclusion can you draw about the freezing temperature of salt water compared with that of fresh water?

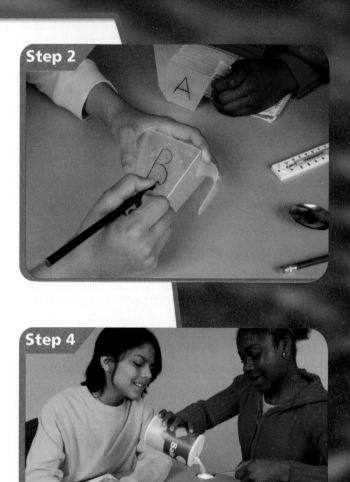

Step 2

Step 4

Independent Inquiry

Write a **hypothesis** and then **plan and conduct a simple investigation** about **how salt affects the boiling temperature of water.**

Read and Learn

VOCABULARY
salinity p. 436
water pressure p. 437
continental shelf p. 438
continental slope p. 438
abyssal plain p. 438

SCIENCE CONCEPTS
▶ what water is like in different parts of the ocean
▶ what the ocean floor looks like

MAIN IDEA AND DETAILS
Look for examples of features on the ocean floor.

Main Idea → detail, detail, detail

Ocean Water

If you've ever been swimming in the ocean, you know an important fact about it. Ocean water is salty.

The salt in the ocean comes from minerals that are washed out from the land. Water evaporates from the surface of the ocean, but the salt is left behind. Most of the salt is sodium chloride, table salt, but ocean water also has other salts.

The amount of salt in water is called **salinity** (suh•LIN•uh•tee). Oceans don't have the saltiest water on Earth. The salinity of the Dead Sea, a lake between Israel and Jordan, is ten times that of the oceans. Much less water flows into the Dead Sea than evaporates from it. This increases its salinity.

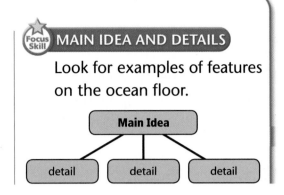

This diver wears a wet suit to keep warm when diving in deep, cold water. ▼

The area around the Dead Sea gets very little rain, so every year, the sea gets smaller and the water and shore get saltier. ▼

The submersible diving vehicle *Alvin* has thick walls so that it can dive about 4,000 m (13,000 ft) below the ocean surface. ▶

The pressure underwater can be very great. Water pressure crushed this foam cup.

The salinity of the ocean doesn't change much from place to place. But other conditions of the ocean depend on the water's depth. One of these conditions is temperature. At the surface, the water is warmed by the sun and by warm air above the surface. But most of the ocean is deep, and deep water is cold. About 90 percent of the ocean has a temperature between 0°C and 3°C (32°F and 37°F). That's cold!

The ocean also gets darker with depth. The water absorbs and scatters light, so the water gradually gets darker until there's no light at all. In some parts of the ocean, light reaches down as far as about 200 m (656 ft). In other places, light reaches down only about 30 m (100 ft).

Something else that depends on the ocean's depth is pressure. Imagine that you could dive 10 m (33 ft) into the ocean. There would be 10 m of water above you, pushing down. The downward push of water on a given area is called **water pressure**. Water pressure increases as you go deeper into the ocean, because more water pushes down. Water pressure at great depths can crush most objects.

To study the oceans, scientists use small submarines called *submersibles* (suhb•MER•suh•buhlz). The thick walls of a submersible don't collapse in water that would be deep enough to crush the hull of a regular submarine.

Focus Skill MAIN IDEA AND DETAILS

What are three details that describe conditions deep in the ocean?

Insta-Lab

Under Pressure
Use a pencil to carefully poke three small holes of exactly the same size in the side of a foam cup. One should be near the top, one near the middle, and one at the bottom. Hold the cup over a sink or a bucket. Quickly pour water into the cup, and observe what happens. How does the depth of the water affect pressure?

The Ocean Floor

In many ways, the ocean floor is like the land. Some parts of the ocean floor are flat. Some parts are sloped. The ocean floor has mountains, deep valleys, and even volcanoes.

As the ocean floor extends away from the land, it first drops gently and then slopes downward more steeply. The part of the ocean floor that slopes gently near the land is called the **continental shelf**.

The part of the ocean floor that slopes steeply is called the **continental slope**. Deep canyons can be found in some parts of the continental shelf and continental slope. These canyons were formed by large rivers flowing into the ocean.

Remember that rivers carry eroded rock called sediment. Sediment is carried out to sea and falls along the continental slope. It piles up at the base of the continental slope, forming the continental rise.

The largest, flattest areas in the ocean are the **abyssal plains** (uh•BIS•uhl PLAYNZ).

Science Up Close

Features of the Ocean Floor

The ocean floor slopes down from the edges of the continents. Then it becomes mostly flat, though it also has mountains and other surface features.

Continental Shelf
The continental shelf extends from the edge of the continent into the ocean. The depth of the shelf increases gradually. The average depth is about 140 m (460 ft). The width of the continental shelf ranges from about 1.6 km to 1200 km (1 mi to 750 mi).

Continental Slope
The continental slope drops steeply to about 3000 m (10,000 ft) below the surface of the ocean.

Continental Rise
The continental rise drops down to about 4000 m (13,000 ft) below the surface of the ocean.

For more links and animations, go to www.hspscience.com

These deep, mostly flat areas are covered by a thick layer of sediment. However, abyssal plains aren't completely flat. In some places, they are cut by deep trenches. The Mariana Trench, in the Pacific Ocean, is the deepest trench. At its greatest depth, it is about 11,000 m (36,000 ft) below the surface of the ocean.

Abyssal plains also have mountains rising from their underwater surface. Some underwater mountains were formed by volcanic eruptions. Underwater mountains sometimes build up enough rock to extend above the water. Some islands in the ocean are the tops of mountains. The Hawaiian Islands formed from volcanic eruptions that took place over millions of years.

In the middle of the ocean, the sea floor rises to form ridges of underwater mountains. Mid-ocean ridges, as they are known, extend about 60,000 km (37,500 mi) through the Pacific, Atlantic, Arctic, and Indian Oceans.

Focus Skill MAIN IDEA AND DETAILS What are three features found on abyssal plains?

Note: Diagram not to scale.

Abyssal Plains
The average depth of the abyssal plains is about 4500 m (15,000 ft). An abyssal plain can have mountain ridges, volcanoes, and deep trenches.

Changes to the Ocean Floor

The ocean floor is always changing. Almost every day, somewhere under the ocean, a volcano is erupting. Over time, an island may form.

In 1963, an underwater volcano near Iceland began to erupt, building up layers of lava. Six months later, the volcano reached the surface of the water, forming the island of Surtsey. The volcano continued to erupt for four more years and then finally stopped. Now Surtsey is getting smaller. The island has sunk slightly, and ocean waves are wearing away the rock.

Islands in the ocean can disappear completely. Bora-Bora, an island in the Pacific Ocean, formed from a volcano. Coral reefs then grew in a ring around the island. Over time, the main island has been sinking and the ocean has worn away much of the rock. In the future, Bora-Bora will be gone. The ring of coral will still be there, forming an island called an *atoll* (A•tawl).

(Focus Skill) MAIN IDEA AND DETAILS

What are three main ways islands in the ocean can change?

▲ The main island of Bora-Bora is slowly being eroded away.

The island of Surtsey formed from a volcanic eruption. The steam and ash from the eruption shot up as high as 305 m (1000 ft) in the air.

Lesson Review

Essential Question
What Are the Oceans Like?

In this lesson, you learned that the ocean has many properties that other bodies of water don't have. You also learned about the features of the ocean floor and how they are constantly changing.

1. **MAIN IDEA AND DETAILS** Draw and complete a graphic organizer with details for this main idea: The ocean floor has several features.

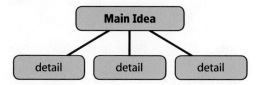

2. **SUMMARIZE** Write a one-paragraph summary of how the characteristics of the ocean change with depth.

3. **DRAW CONCLUSIONS** Coral is made of the outer skeletons of animals. How does this allow a coral reef to last longer than the island around which it grew?

4. **VOCABULARY** Make a crossword puzzle that uses the terms from this lesson.

Test Prep

5. **CRITICAL THINKING** What might happen to a hollow rubber ball if a submersible took it 300 m (1000 ft) below the ocean surface? Explain.

6. What could cause the salinity of a sea to increase?
   - **A.** an increase in rainfall
   - **B.** an increase in fresh water flowing into it
   - **C.** an increase in salt water flowing out of it
   - **D.** an increase in evaporation

Make Connections

 Writing

Narrative Writing
Suppose you are an explorer making an underwater voyage across the floor of the Atlantic Ocean. Write a **story** about your voyage.

 Math

Make a Bar Graph
Make a bar graph to compare the deepest points in the oceans. Use these numbers:
Atlantic Ocean—8648 m
Arctic Ocean—5450 m
Indian Ocean—7725 m
Pacific Ocean—11,033 m

 Health

Don't Drink the Water
Research the reason for not drinking ocean water. Then write a paragraph that tells what you learned.

Investigate one way in which waves form.

Read and learn the different ways that waves form and how the sun and moon cause ocean water to move.

Essential Question

How Does Ocean Water Move?

Fast Fact

Wave Sets

When waves approach the shore, they seem to move in sets. In each set, the waves get bigger and bigger and then smaller again. Then another set begins. In the Investigate, you will make and observe your own waves.

California coast

wave [WAYV] A disturbance that carries energy through matter or space (p. 446)

current [KER•uhnt] A stream of water that flows like a river through the ocean (p. 448)

tide [TYD] The repeated rise and fall of the water level of the ocean (p. 450)

Making Waves

Start with Questions

The waters of the world's oceans are continuously moving. At the beach, the tide moves in and out at the same time that waves crash near the shore.

- How do you think waves form?

- How is the movement of these sailboats similar to the formation of waves?

Investigate to find out. Then read and learn to find out more.

Prepare to Investigate

Inquiry Skill Tip
Use your own knowledge and experience when you make inferences in an investigation. An inference is a statement about what you believe is true, based on your observations.

Materials

- rectangular pan
- water
- straw

Make an Observation Chart

Trial	Observations
1	
2	
3	

Follow This Procedure

1. Fill a pan halfway with water. The pan of water represents an ocean.

2. Hold a straw near one side of the pan, and gently blow across the surface of the water. What happens? Remember to blow across the water, not downward into the water.

3. **Observe** the height of the waves and how fast they move. **Record** your observations.

4. Repeat Step 2 several times, blowing a little harder each time. What do you **observe** about the waves? **Record** your observations about the height and speed of each set of waves.

Draw Conclusions

1. What can you conclude about the relationship between how hard you blew and the height of the waves?

2. What can you conclude about the relationship between how hard you blew and the speed of the waves?

3. **Inquiry Skill** Scientists often make inferences from their observations. From your observations, what can you **infer** about the cause of ocean waves?

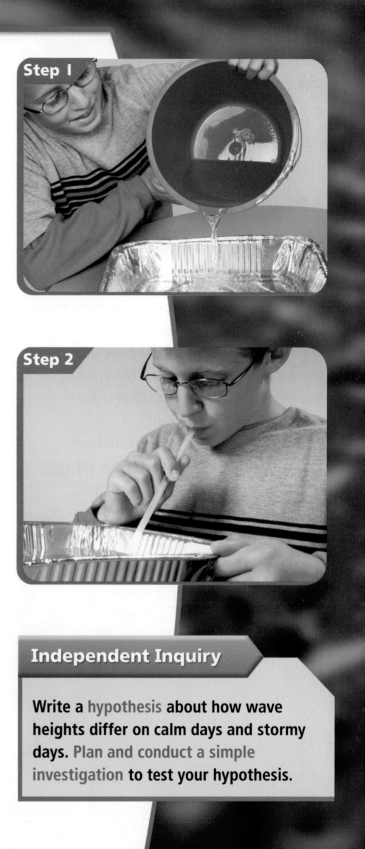

Step 1

Step 2

Independent Inquiry

Write a **hypothesis** about how wave heights differ on calm days and stormy days. **Plan and conduct a simple investigation** to test your hypothesis.

VOCABULARY
wave p. 446
current p. 448
tide p. 450

SCIENCE CONCEPTS
▶ how waves form
▶ what causes currents and tides

COMPARE AND CONTRAST
Look for ways waves and currents are alike and different

| alike | — | different |

Waves

Have you ever stood on a beach and watched the waves? From a distance, waves look like traveling ridges of water. But the water in waves doesn't move across the ocean. The water actually moves up and down. A **wave** is the up-and-down movement of surface water.

In the Investigate, you saw that air blowing across water makes waves. Energy from the moving air moves the water. When wind blows across the ocean, it pushes the water up, forming ripples. When wind blows on the ripples, more water moves up. Soon, the ripples form waves.

A wave carries energy, not water, across the ocean. Inside the wave, water turns in small ovals. After the water moves around the ovals, it returns to about the place where it started. The energy, however, travels forward.

Water moves up and down and energy moves forward until it approachs the shore.

Modern surfing began in Hawai`i in the 1800s. ▼

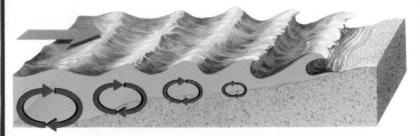

Wave Movement

As a wave approaches the shore, the bottom of the wave slows down and the top falls forward.

A tsunami, like the one that caused this damage in Sri Lanka in 2004, is the most destructive of all ocean waves. ▶

As the water becomes shallow, the waves slow down. They also become higher and closer together.

The bottom of the wave slows the most, so the top moves ahead of the bottom. When the top gets far enough ahead, the wave falls over, or *breaks*. It's like tripping over something. Your foot stops moving, but the rest of you keeps going, causing you to fall forward. Breaking waves are what people see crashing onto the shore at the beach.

Some waves are caused by more than ordinary winds. A hurricane or other strong storm moving over the ocean pushes water forward. This adds to the usual height of the waves. The mound of water that pushes onto shore in a hurricane is called a *storm surge.* Storm surges are highest in places where the continental shelf is nearly flat.

The biggest waves are not caused by winds. The great energy of an earthquake or a volcanic eruption can produce a wave called a *tsunami* (tsoo•NAH•mee). In the open ocean, a tsunami isn't a high wave, but it is long and moves very fast. When a tsunami approaches the shore, it slows down. This makes it become much higher. In 1958, an earthquake near Alaska produced a tsunami that was 524 m (1719 ft) high!

 **COMPARE AND CONTRAST** How is a tsunami different from other waves?

Math in Science
Interpret Data

Waves Around the World

Scientists use the movement of buoys offshore to calculate how high waves will be and how fast the wind is moving. These are the predictions for one week. Why do you think the waves were predicted to be higher near Australia than near Florida?

Waves Around the World		
Location	Open-Ocean Wave Heights (m)	Wind Speeds (km/hr)
Capetown, South Africa	2–7	11–45
Long Beach, California	1–2	3–21
Port Orange, Florida	0–1	3–11
Hilo, Hawai`i	2–4	6–27
Gold Coast, Australia	1–8	5–39

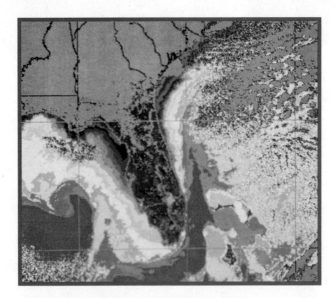

▲ On this satellite image, the warm water of the Gulf Stream is shown in orange. Cooler water is yellow, green, and blue.

Currents

Would you be surprised to learn that the sun causes ocean water to move? Air around the equator is heated by the sun. This air moves north, toward the poles. As it moves, the air pushes ocean water forward. The result is a **current**, a stream of water that flows like a river through the ocean.

Large currents in the open ocean are known as surface currents. These carry water great distances across the surface.

The Gulf Stream is a surface current that flows all the way across the Atlantic Ocean. The current begins in the Gulf of Mexico and flows north along the eastern coast of the United States. Then it turns east and flows across the Atlantic Ocean to Europe.

Oceans also have smaller currents that stay near coasts. These currents erode and deposit sand, helping shape beaches.

Sometimes people coming out of the ocean after a swim have trouble finding their beach towels. A current, called a longshore current, sometimes flows along the shore. It carries swimmers away from the place where they entered the water.

Another kind of current along some shores is a rip current. Rip currents carry water away from the beach. This makes them dangerous for swimmers. A rip current can flow faster than 2.4 m/sec (7.9 ft/sec). That's faster than even an Olympic swimmer can swim back to shore.

The gaps in these waves are caused by rip currents. The water on either side of them flows toward shore. If you get caught in a rip current, don't swim against it. Swim parallel to the shore until you leave the rip current.

The huge red-and-white areas in the Pacific show warmer waters caused by an El Niño. The purple area shows water kept cool by the El Niño. ▼

▲ Rain from an El Niño has caused many landslides along the California coast.

Some currents flow deep in the ocean. Off the west coast of South America, for example, winds blow warm surface water away from the land. Deep-ocean currents then carry cooler water up toward the surface near the coast.

Changing winds can affect these currents. If the winds don't blow toward the west, the warm surface water stays near the coast. The deep, cold currents don't reach the surface, and the coastal water stays very warm. This warm water causes an *El Niño* (EL NEEN•yoh), a change in the weather patterns over the Pacific Ocean.

How does the warm water affect the weather? Warm water evaporates faster than cool water does. Where the ocean is warm, clouds form and bring rain. In most years, the wind pattern pushes the warm water to the west. As a result, Australia gets rain, and South America and the west coast of North America have dry weather.

During an El Niño, however, the weather pattern reverses. Australia has very dry

weather, and the west coasts of South America and North America get storms and huge amounts of rain. This can cause flooding in some areas that aren't used to such heavy rains.

Focus Skill **COMPARE AND CONTRAST**

How is a surface current different from a current near a coast?

A Kitchen El Niño

Fill a large container with very warm water. Fill a small cup with very cold water, and add a few drops of food coloring. Use tongs to gently lower the cup straight down into the warm water, below the surface. Observe what happens. How is this similar to what happens during an El Niño?

Tides

Imagine walking along the shore and seeing a boat resting in the mud. You might wonder why someone would leave a boat in such a place. But if you walked by later, you might see the boat floating in water, even though it's in the same place.

Each day, the water level at an ocean shore rises and falls. This rise and fall in the water level of the ocean is called a **tide**. At certain times, the water is high enough to float a boat at the shore. At other times, there isn't enough water to float the boat.

Tides are caused by the "pull" of the sun and moon on Earth's oceans. Although the sun is larger, the moon affects tides more because it is closer to Earth.

The moon pulls on all of Earth. The land doesn't move much, but the water does. As a result, two bulges of water form. One bulge is on the side of Earth facing the moon. The second bulge is on the opposite side of Earth, where the pull of the moon is slightly less. The level of the ocean is higher in the bulges, producing a *high tide*. In the

parts of the ocean between the bulges, the water level is lower. At those places, a *low tide* occurs.

There are usually two high tides and two low tides every day. Earth turns on its axis once every 24 hours. This means that the beach with the boat is closest to the moon once a day and farthest from the moon once a day. At these two times, the beach has high tides. The beach has low tides between the two high tides.

Focus Skill COMPARE AND CONTRAST

How is high tide different from low tide?

When the moon and the sun align, their effects combine to produce large tidal changes, called *spring tides*. Smaller changes occur during neap tides.

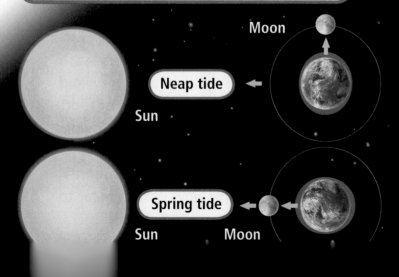

As high tide approaches, the water level can rise by several meters.

At low tide, the water level is low and more of the land can be seen.

Essential Question

How Does Ocean Water Move?

In this lesson, you learned that a wave carries energy, not water, across the ocean. You also learned about the influences the sun has on ocean currents, as well as the influence of both the sun and the moon on ocean tides.

1.  **COMPARE AND CONTRAST** Draw and complete a graphic organizer that compares and contrasts these things: waves, currents, storm surges, tsunami.

```
( alike ) —— ( different )
```

2. **SUMMARIZE** Write a one-sentence summary, using a real-life example, for each of the vocabulary terms in this lesson: *wave, current, tide*.

3. **DRAW CONCLUSIONS** Why is it helpful for ships going from North America to Europe to travel in the Gulf Stream?

4. **VOCABULARY** Write a sentence for each vocabulary term to show that you understand it.

Test Prep

5. **CRITICAL THINKING** Scientists study satellite images that show the temperatures of different areas of the Pacific Ocean. Why is this information important?

6. Which can cause tsunamis?
   A. currents
   B. earthquakes
   C. tides
   D. winds

Make Connections

 Writing

Narrative Writing
What would it be like to ride a wave that was traveling across the ocean? Write a **story** that tells what would happen on such a journey.

 Math

Describe Patterns
Find tide tables in an almanac or a newspaper. Study the four tides listed for one day. At what times do the high tides occur? At what times do the low tides occur? How much time is there between the two high tides?

 Language Arts

Editing
After writing the first draft of your wave story, exchange stories with a classmate for comments and corrections. Check your classmate's spelling, grammar, and story construction.

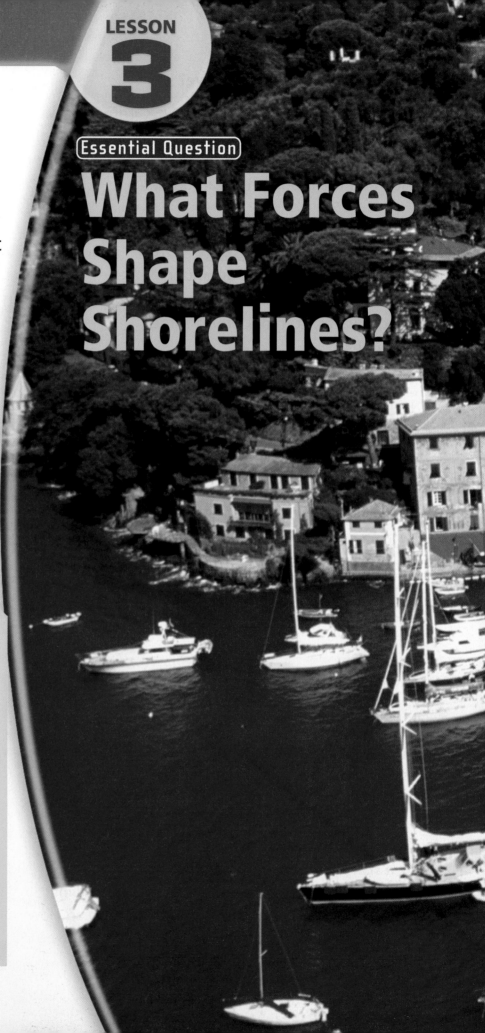

Investigate one of the forces that shapes shorelines.

Read and learn about the different features on a shoreline and how they can change.

Essential Question

What Forces Shape Shorelines?

Fast Fact

Ocean View

These houses were built in Portofino, Italy, along the edge of the Mediterranean Sea. Houses along the shore and on nearby cliffs have changed the natural patterns of coastal erosion. In the Investigate, you can make a model to see how waves change a beach.

Portofino, Italy

shore [SHAWR] The area where the ocean and the land meet and interact (p. 456)

headland [HED•luhnd] A point of land at the shore where hard rock is left behind and other materials are washed away (p. 456)

tide pool [TYD POOL] A temporary pool of ocean water that gets trapped between rocks when the tide goes out (p. 457)

jetty [JET•ee] A wall-like structure that sticks out into the ocean to prevent sand from being carried away (p. 459)

The Effect of Waves on a Beach

Start with Questions

Have you ever built a sandcastle at the beach? What happened when the waves crashed on shore?

- What factors influence the amount of erosion a wave causes?

- Does a wave cause more erosion on a steep beach than on a gently sloping beach?

Investigate to find out. Then read and learn to find out more.

Prepare to Investigate

Inquiry Skill Tip

When you observe things that happen during an investigation, pay attention to details. Think about how changing a variable affects what you see.

Materials

- sand
- large flat, shallow pan
- water

Make an Observation Chart

Height of Beach	Observations
2 cm	1st trial: 2nd trial: 3rd trial:
4 cm	1st trial: 2nd trial: 3rd trial:
6 cm	1st trial: 2nd trial: 3rd trial:

Follow This Procedure

1 Use sand to **make a model** of a beach at one end of a pan. The beach should have a gentle slope down toward the other end.

2 Add water until the pan is about half full. Add the water slowly so that you do not disturb the beach.

3 Lift the sand end of the pan about 2 cm above the tabletop. Then quickly but gently put it down to make a wave. What do you **observe** about the beach and the water?

4 Repeat Step 3 several times. **Record** your observations.

5 Repeat Steps 1–4, but this time, build a beach that is much steeper than the first one. **Record** your observations.

Draw Conclusions

1. Use your observations to explain how waves affect a beach.

2. Does the slope of a beach make a difference in the effect of waves on it? Explain your answer.

3. **Inquiry Skill** When scientists study something carefully, they make observations. What could you not **observe** about wave action by using your model?

Step 1

Step 5

Independent Inquiry

Make a model of a coast by using different materials. Make a prediction about how waves affect different kinds of coastlines. **Plan and conduct a simple investigation** to test your prediction.

VOCABULARY
shore p. 456
headland p. 456
tide pool p. 457
jetty p. 459

SCIENCE CONCEPTS
▶ what features are found along a shore
▶ how a shore can be changed

Focus Skill **MAIN IDEA AND DETAILS**
Look for examples of ways a shore can be changed.

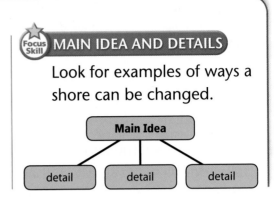

Shores

Have you ever been to the coast along an ocean? Was there a sandy beach, or were there rocky cliffs? The area where the ocean and the land meet and interact is called a **shore**. Shores have many different features.

At some places, the shore is a flat beach covered with sand or pebbles. This kind of shore is like the first beach in the Investigate. As you observed, waves can carry the sand away. At other places along a shore, there may be a steep cliff, like the second beach in the Investigate.

In the Investigate, the sand was the same all along the shore. But the materials of a shore may vary. At some places, there may be sand or soft rock that waves easily wear away. At other places, there may be hard rock that does not wear away as easily. Soft rock and hard rock may also be together. When the soft rock is worn away, the hard rock left behind may form a point of land called a **headland**.

At low tide, a tide pool keeps many small ocean animals from drying out. Sea stars, such as those seen here, can often be found in tide pools. ▼

The sand on this beach in the Indian Ocean consists of weathered pieces of rock from the land around it.

Waves carved this sea arch from rock in the Mediterranean Sea. ▼

◀ The area where a river meets the ocean is an estuary. The depth and salinity of an estuary change with the tides. Plants and animals that live in estuaries must survive these changes.

After a headland forms, waves wear away its rock slowly, sometimes forming caves in the rock. Over time, the waves can make these caves deeper and deeper. Eventually, the waves may cut all the way through the rock, making a hole called a *sea arch*.

All beaches have an area that is underwater at high tide and exposed at low tide. On rocky beaches, small pools of water can be trapped between rocks when the tide goes out. A temporary pool of ocean water is called a **tide pool**.

At high tide, water fills in the area around the pools. Some animals are then free to leave or enter the pools. At low tide, these animals are trapped until the water rises again. Some plants and animals live their entire lives in the same tide pool.

Where a river flows into the ocean, an *estuary* (ES•tyoo•air•ee) forms. Estuaries are rich in plant and animal life. Many kinds of fish breed in estuaries.

MAIN IDEA AND DETAILS What are two features that can be seen along a shore?

457

Human Activities Affect Shores

Waves erode sand from beaches every day. This erosion is a natural process. The sand that is washed away by waves is deposited either at other places along the shore or on the floor of the ocean.

Currents also cause erosion from beaches. Longshore currents that carry swimmers along a beach also carry sand. Sand that is eroded by a current is deposited at another place when the current slows. Often, the sand is deposited in a channel at the mouth of a river.

The movement of sand causes two problems for humans. First, it makes some beaches smaller and others larger. Second, it fills in channels, which then become too shallow for boats to pass through.

People sometimes solve these two problems at the same time. Sand is dredged, or scooped out, from a channel and then dumped on a beach. Workers use bulldozers to spread out the sand, making sure the beach has the correct slope.

This process of replacing sand is called *beach restoration*. It can cost millions of dollars, but many people think saving beaches is worth the cost. Beach restoration is not permanent, however. Natural processes take over as soon as the work is finished. After several years, people must do the work again.

▲ People build jetties, like this one at Coos Bay, Oregon, to stop the loss of sand from beaches.

People need huge machines to move sand in a beach restoration project.

458

◀ Artificial reefs are made of many kinds of objects.

▲ Hundreds of old subway cars from New York City have been dropped into the ocean. They now form artificial reefs off the coasts of New Jersey, Virginia, Delaware, South Carolina, and Georgia.

Replacing sand is very expensive, so it's better to keep the sand from being lost in the first place. People have tried many ways to prevent the loss of sand, including building structures that block currents. This prevents the currents from carrying away sand and eroding the beach.

One structure that can do this is a **jetty**, a wall-like structure that sticks out into the ocean. Jetties are usually built of large rocks. As a longshore current moves along the coast, the jetty traps sand and small rocks. This protects the beach above the jetty. But because the current is blocked, beaches below the jetty don't get the sand they normally would. As a result, one beach benefits and the others don't.

In some parts of the world, huge coral reefs near the coast absorb the energy of waves before they hit the shore. In this way, the reefs protect the coast from damage. People have suggested building artificial reefs to protect beaches. In Australia, a long reef of huge containers of sand was built offshore. When a storm approaches, the waves hit the reef. By the time the waves reach shore, they are smaller and weaker.

Artificial reefs are being built in places all around the world. Most of these, however, are not meant to protect beaches. Instead, they provide homes for fish and other sea life. Mussels, barnacles, corals, and sponges grow on the reefs. Many kinds of fish hide within the shelter of the reefs. These reefs form their own communities.

Focus Skill MAIN IDEA AND DETAILS

How do people restore beaches?

459

Mysteries of the Oceans

People have always been curious about the oceans. Since the oceans are huge and deep, people can't just swim down and take a look.

However, scientists have found ways to travel deep into the oceans, where water pressure is high. Diving bells, diving suits, and submarines have made deep-sea exploration possible. Scientists also send down remote-controlled vehicles equipped with cameras.

Deep-sea exploration has led to the discovery of some interesting things, such as *hydrothermal* (hy•droh•THER•muhl) *vents*. These are cracks in the ocean floor that release hot water and minerals into the ocean. Worms that live near these vents can be up to 3 m (10 ft) long! Further exploration may help us understand such mysteries of the oceans.

▲ Sir Edmond Halley invented a diving bell in the 1690s. It was lowered into the ocean with barrels of air to let the diver breathe.

▲ Hard suits like this one make it possible for divers to work at great depths.

Focus Skill **MAIN IDEA AND DETAILS**

How have explorers been able to travel deep into the oceans?

Insta-Lab

A Diving Bell
Crumple a piece of paper, and push it into the bottom of a small plastic cup. Turn the cup upside down, and lower it straight down into a container of water. Remove the cup, and take the paper out. What do you observe about the paper? Explain what you see.

Water heated by molten rock beneath the ocean floor rushes out through hydrothermal vents like these "black smokers."

What Forces Shape Shorelines?

In this lesson, you learned some different characteristics of shores and how these characteristics are influenced by nature and human activities. You also learned about some ways people have explored the deep ocean.

1. 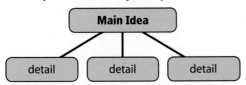 **MAIN IDEA AND DETAILS** Draw and complete a graphic organizer with supporting details for this main idea: Coastal formations and features are shaped in many ways.

2. **SUMMARIZE** Write a one-paragraph summary about ways that humans help slow down beach erosion.

3. **DRAW CONCLUSIONS** If you're in an airplane flying over a beach, you might see that sand is piled up on one side of a jetty but not on the other side. Explain why.

4. **VOCABULARY** Write a paragraph that uses all the vocabulary terms from this lesson.

Test Prep

5. **CRITICAL THINKING** Why is a tide pool considered a temporary feature of a beach?

6. What does a beach restoration project try to replace?
   A. coral reefs
   B. headlands
   C. sand
   D. sea animals

Make Connections

 Writing

Persuasive Writing
Suppose you live near a beach that is wearing away. Write a **letter** to local government officials, urging them to protect the beach.

 Math

Solve a Problem
A diver using a hard diving suit can go down to 600 m below the surface in 20 minutes. How far down can the diver go in 1 minute?

 Social Studies

The Color of Sand
The sand on many beaches is white. But it's black on some beaches in Hawai`i and Iceland and pink on Bermuda beaches. Do research to find out why beach sand is different colors.

Wen-lu Zhu

Most people look at rocks and see only their color or shape. Wen-lu Zhu looks at rocks and unlocks the secrets found deep down on the ocean floor.

Zhu is an associate scientist at the Woods Hole Oceanographic Institution. She studies rocks found at hydrothermal vents. Hydrothermal vents are geysers in the ocean floor. Ocean water seeps into the cracks and is heated by magma deep within Earth. The heated water rises and flows back out of the vents. As the heated water reacts with cold seawater, hydrothermal vent deposits form. These are the materials that Zhu examines. She wants to know their structure and composition and how the heated water flows inside the vent deposits. It's an important question because hydrothermal vents are home to some of the most unusual life forms on Earth. The chemistry of the heated water affects the organisms around hydrothermal vents.

Zhu X-rays the vent deposits. With the X-ray scan, Zhu can find out how porous a rock is. Porous rocks have tiny openings. The more openings a rock has, the more chances for the hydrothermal water to move through it. This procedure helps Wen-lu Zhu compare different vent deposits to the fluids moving through them.

▶ **WEN-LU ZHU**

▶ Associate scientist, Dept. of Geology and Geophysics, at the Woods Hole Oceanographic Institution

 Think and Write

❶ Why is Zhu's research important?

❷ Scientists recreate the processes that take place at hydrothermal vents. Why don't they study the processes directly?

Hugo Loaiciga

▶ **DR. HUGO LOAICIGA**

▶ Professor in the Geography Dept. at UC, Santa Barbara
▶ Water scientist
▶ Leading researcher in water conservation

Homeowners who use wells know that if they pump too much groundwater, their wells will run dry. But just how much water can they pump without using up all the water in an aquifer? Until recently, homeowners had no way of knowing. That bothered Dr. Hugo Loaiciga of the University of California. If people didn't know how much water they could safely pump from their wells, they might not conserve enough groundwater.

Loaiciga came up with an equation that models how quickly groundwater can be replaced. Loaiciga then made computer software based on his model. Homeowners and business owners can use the software to calculate the amount of water they can take from an aquifer without having it dry up.

Think and Write

1 How might Loaiciga's software be used to help people conserve water?

2 Why is it important to not overuse an aquifer?

Career Hydrologist

Hydrologists test drinking water, issue flood warnings, check underground water supplies, and protect water in other ways. Many work in government agencies, city or state offices, consulting firms, and waste-treatment plants.

Vocabulary Review

Match the terms to the definitions. The page numbers tell you where to look in the chapter if you need help.

continental shelf p. 438

continental slope p. 438

abyssal plain p. 438

wave p. 446

current p. 448

tide p. 450

headland p. 456

tide pool p. 457

1. the up-and-down movement of surface water

2. the part of the ocean floor that slopes gently away from the land

3. a stream of water that flows through the ocean

4. a sharp point of rock that extends from the coast

5. the part of the ocean floor that drops steeply

6. a large, flat area on the ocean floor

7. an area in which ocean water collects during low tide

8. the rise and fall of the ocean level

Check Understanding

Write the letter of the best choice.

9. **MAIN IDEA AND DETAILS** What is the main purpose of this structure?

Focus Skill

  A. to protect beaches
  B. to increase wave action
  C. to form estuaries
  D. to form an artificial reef

10. **COMPARE AND CONTRAST** How are waves and currents alike?

Focus Skill

  F. Both decrease during an El Niño.
  G. Both result from earthquakes.
  H. Both strengthen coastal areas.
  J. Both form shoreline features.

11. Which increases as you go deeper into the ocean?
  A. salinity
  B. amount of light
  C. water pressure
  D. water temperature

12. Marie wades into the ocean. On what structure is she standing?

   F. continental rise

   G. continental shelf

   H. abyssal plain

   J. mid-ocean ridge

13. What caused this structure to form?

   A. Waves wore away some of the rock.

   B. Currents washed sand away from the rock.

   C. Waves piled up rocks near the coast.

   D. People piled rocks to protect the shore.

14. Henry and his dad floated in the ocean for a half hour. When they came out onto the beach, they couldn't see the rest of the family. What kind of current had carried them away from their family?

   F. deep-ocean   **H.** rip

   G. longshore   **J.** surface

15. What is beach restoration?

   A. rebuilding houses near the shore

   B. building new roads to a beach

   C. replanting trees along a beach

   D. putting sand back on a beach

16. What causes tides?

   F. an earthquake under the ocean

   G. winds blowing across the ocean

   H. the pull of the moon

   J. currents lifting water to the surface

Inquiry Skills

17. You put a cup of fresh water and a cup of salt water into a freezer at the same time. **Predict** which will freeze first.

18. You visit a beach you haven't seen in five years. The shore looks very different. What can you **infer**?

Critical Thinking

19. You are at the beach, and you notice that the sand above the water level is wet. Is the tide rising or falling? Explain your answer.

20. An El Niño is forming, and a friend wants to know what that means. How will you explain the cause of the El Niño? What might be some of the effects of the El Niño?

The **Big** Idea

Earth, Moon and Beyond

What's the Big Idea?

Earth is part of a solar system, which is made up of many different objects orbiting a sun.

Essential Questions

Lesson 1

How Does Earth's Orbit Affect the Seasons?

Lesson 2

How Do Earth and the Moon Compare?

Lesson 3

What Makes Up Our Solar System?

GO online
Student eBook
www.hspscience.com

The world's largest single-dish radio telescope is in Arecibo, Puerto Rico. Scientists use the telescope—whose dish is 305 m (1000 ft) wide—to study deep space. In what ways do scientists study objects in our solar system and how does this relate to the

Big Idea?

Radio telscope in Arecibo, Puerto Rico

Investigate how Earth, the moon, and the sun interact with one another.

Read and learn why we have day and night and what causes Earth's changing seasons.

Essential Question

How Does Earth's Orbit Affect the Seasons?

Fast Fact

Sunrise from Space

Astronauts in space may see 16 sunrises and 16 sunsets every day as they travel around the Earth. In the Investigate, you'll learn about movements of Earth and the moon and why, here on Earth, we see only 1 sunrise and 1 sunset each day.

International Space Station

Vocabulary Preview

sun [SUHN] The star at the center of our solar system (p. 472)

---

rotate [ROH•tayt] To spin on an axis (p. 472)

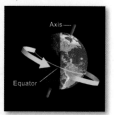

axis [AK•sis] An imaginary line that passes through Earth's center and its North and South Poles (p. 472)

---

revolve [rih•VAHLV] To travel in a closed path (p. 474)

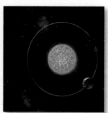

orbit [AWR•bit] The path one body takes in space as it revolves around another (p. 474)

---

equator [ee•KWAYT•er] An imaginary line around Earth equally distant from the North and South Poles (p. 474)

469

Investigate

Moving Through Space

Guided Inquiry

Start With Questions

As you sit in class, Earth is moving through space. Many other objects are also moving through space.

- How does Earth move in our solar system?
- How does our moon move in space?

Investigate to find out. Then read and learn to find out more.

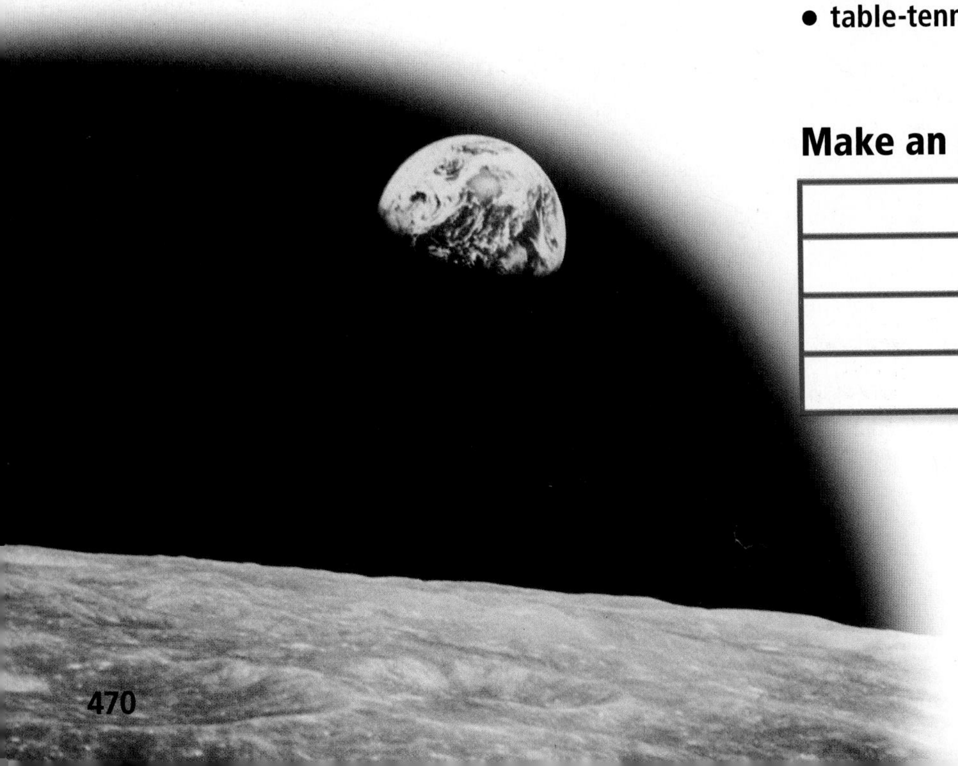

Prepare to Investigate

Inquiry Skill Tip

You have to think about time and space relationships to understand the movement of objects in space. Consider the positions of objects at one time, and then consider their positions at some later time. In this investigation, your model sun doesn't move. But the real sun spins on its axis and moves with other stars.

Materials

- beach ball
- baseball
- table-tennis ball

Make an Observation Chart

Observations

Follow This Procedure

➊ Work in a group of four. You will **use a model** to show the **time and space relationships** among Earth, the moon, and the sun. One person should hold the beach ball (the sun). Another should stand far away and hold the baseball (Earth). A third person should hold the table-tennis ball (the moon) near the baseball. The fourth person should **record** the movements.

➋ For the **model**, Earth should move around the sun in a circle and spin at the same time. The real Earth spins about 365 times during each complete path around the sun.

➌ While the model Earth moves, the model moon should move around Earth in a nearly circular path. The real moon spins once during each complete path around Earth. Earth spins about $29\frac{1}{2}$ times from one new moon to the next.

Draw Conclusions

1. One movement in the model represented a year. Which movement was that?

2. **Inquiry Skill** Use your understanding of **time and space relationships** to compare the moon's and Earth's movements. How are they alike? How are they different?

Step 1

Step 3

Independent Inquiry

Make a **model** to show how you think the amount of sunlight reaching different parts of Earth changes during the year.

VOCABULARY

sun p. 472
rotate p. 472
axis p. 472
revolve p. 474
orbit p. 474
equator p. 474

SCIENCE CONCEPTS

▶ how the movements of Earth and the sun result in day and night and the seasons

▶ why we have time zones

(Focus Skill) MAIN IDEA AND DETAILS

Look for the details about Earth's movements.

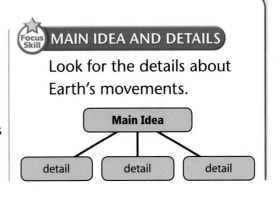

Day and Night

Every day the **sun**, the star at the center of our solar system, appears to rise in the east. It appears to reach its highest point around noon, and to set in the west. After a period of darkness, this process repeats.

This cycle of day and night occurs because Earth **rotates**, or spins on its axis. Earth's **axis** is an imaginary line that passes through the North and South Poles. When a place on Earth faces the sun, it is day in that place. When that place faces away from the sun, it is night.

Our system of time is based on Earth's 24-hour cycle of daylight and darkness. Because of Earth's rotation, sunrise and sunset occur at different times in different places. Long ago, people didn't need to know the exact time. And each place used local time—time based on sunrise and sunset in that place. This changed in the late 1800s. Trains were starting to travel long distances. If each train station had kept its own time, there would have been confusion. People needed to develop standard times.

The sun appears to rise and set. Of course it actually doesn't. Earth's rotation causes what appear to be a sunrise and a sunset.

Time Zones

▲ It's 7 A.M. in Seattle, on the west coast.

▲ Much of the United States is within one of four time zones. Time zone lines aren't perfectly straight, partly because of state boundaries.

▲ In New York City, on the east coast, it's 10 A.M.

In 1884, standard times were set up in 24 time zones around the world. Each time zone represents one of the hours in the day. All the places within a time zone have the same time. If you travel east from one time zone to the next, the time becomes one hour later. If you travel west from one time zone to the next, the time becomes one hour earlier. In the middle of the Pacific Ocean is the International Date Line. If you go west across that line, you travel into the next day. Crossing the line eastward, you travel into the previous day. For example, if it's 3 A.M. Tuesday and you cross the International Date Line while going west, the time becomes 2 A.M. Wednesday, not Tuesday.

The United States has seven time zones, from Puerto Rico in the east to Hawai`i in the west. If you're just about to have dinner at 6 P.M. in Florida and you call a friend in Oregon, it will be 3 P.M. there. Your friend may be just getting home from school.

MAIN IDEA AND DETAILS

Explain why officials needed to set up time zones in the late 1800s.

Insta-Lab

Sunrise, Sunset
Use a flashlight and a ball to model day and night. Where on the ball are sunrise and sunset represented?

Earth's Seasons

You probably know that most places on Earth have seasons. During the summer, there are more hours of daylight than hours of darkness. The temperature is usually higher, too. During the winter, there are fewer hours of daylight and the temperature is lower. These seasonal changes are a result of the tilt of Earth's axis.

In addition to rotating on its axis, Earth **revolves**, or travels in a path around the sun. The path Earth takes as it revolves is its **orbit**. One orbit takes about 365 days, or one year.

Some people think we have seasons because Earth is closer to the sun in the summer than in the winter. This isn't so. (Earth is actually closer to the sun during our winter.) The shape of Earth's orbit is only slightly elliptical; that is, it's nearly circular. It's the tilt of Earth's axis that produces seasons.

Earth's axis is not straight up and down in relation to its orbit. If it were, the angle of the sun's rays when they hit Earth would be the same all year long. There would be no seasons. But Earth's axis is tilted about 23.5°. During part of the year, half of Earth is tilted toward the sun. On that part of Earth, it is summer. On the part tilted away from the sun, it is winter.

Earth is divided into Northern and Southern Hemispheres by the equator. The **equator** is an imaginary line going all the way around Earth halfway between the North and South Poles. When the Northern Hemisphere is tilted toward the sun, the Southern Hemisphere is tilted away.

To see this process, follow the seasons shown in the diagram. When the Northern Hemisphere is tilted toward the sun, it is summer. The number of hours of daylight is greater than the number of hours of darkness. The sun's rays strike part of the hemisphere directly, so the weather is warm.

When it is summer in the Northern Hemisphere, . . .

. . . it is winter in the Southern Hemisphere.

A

D

B

C

▲ The position of Earth in relation to the sun changes, depending on where the Earth is in its orbit. During summer in the Northern Hemisphere (C), that hemisphere is tilted toward the sun. During spring (B) and fall (D), neither hemisphere is tilted toward the sun.

Even in Alaska, summer temperatures can reach 30°C (86°F).

As Earth continues in its orbit, the Northern Hemisphere is tilted away from the sun. There are fewer hours of daylight and more hours of darkness in that hemisphere. The rays of the sun strike the Northern Hemisphere at more of an angle. The weather is much cooler, even in Florida.

The day when the amount of daylight is the greatest is called the *summer solstice* (SAHL•stis). In the Northern Hemisphere, it's June 20 or 21, depending on the year. The winter solstice, the day with the least amount of daylight is December 21 or 22.

Halfway between the solstices, neither hemisphere is tilted toward the sun. The hours of daylight and darkness are about

▲ During the Northern Hemisphere's summer, the number of hours of daylight is at its highest. During summer also, the sun's rays hit the Northern Hemisphere more directly, not at as great an angle as in winter. This causes more heating because the sun's rays don't spread out as much.

equal. These days are called the *equinoxes* (EE•kwih•nahks•uhz). In the Northern Hemisphere, the autumn equinox is September 22 or 23. The spring equinox is March 20 or 21.

Focus Skill MAIN IDEA AND DETAILS

What are the days called that have the most and the fewest hours of daylight?

475

Highs and Lows

Seasons at the North and South Poles are very different from seasons everywhere else. In the summer, the poles get six months of daylight and no darkness. Winter brings six months of darkness, with no daylight.

Even though the South Pole has a summer of nonstop daylight, it's never very warm. Sunlight that reaches Antarctica, even in the summer, is at a low angle and more spread out. This results in low temperatures all year.

At the equator, halfway between the poles, days and nights are about 12 hours each all year. Temperatures stay about the same all year, too. The warmest places in the world are just south and north of the equator. Rain at the equator keeps temperatures from reaching highs like those in deserts such as the Sahara. Kenya, Indonesia, and Brazil are all on the equator.

 **MAIN IDEA AND DETAILS** In Antarctica, why is it cold even in the summer?

The lowest temperature ever recorded on Earth, −89°C (−129°F), was at Russia's Vostok Station, in Antarctica in 1983.

The highest temperature ever recorded on Earth, 58°C (136°F), was in Al Aziziyah, Libya, in the Sahara in 1922.

Essential Question

How Does Earth's Orbit Affect the Seasons?

In this lesson you learned that Earth rotates on its axis, which is tilted at an angle. At the same time, Earth orbits the sun. This causes changes on Earth throughout the year.

1. **MAIN IDEA AND DETAILS** Draw and complete a graphic organizer with supporting details for this main idea: Earth moves in two ways.

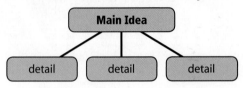

```
        Main Idea
    ┌───────┼───────┐
  detail   detail   detail
```

2. **SUMMARIZE** Write a summary by answering the question in the lesson title.

3. **DRAW CONCLUSIONS** If Earth were not tilted on its axis, how would life be different?

4. **VOCABULARY** Use the words *revolve* and *rotate* to explain Earth's movements in space.

Test Prep

5. **CRITICAL THINKING** A friend lives where there are 12 hours of daylight every day. Where does this person live, and how do you know?

6. What season is it in the Northern Hemisphere when the Southern Hemisphere points toward the sun?
   A. fall
   B. spring
   C. summer
   D. winter

Make Connections

 Writing

Narrative Writing

Living at a research station in Antarctica would be an unusual experience for most of us. Write a **story** telling what a week of your summer vacation there would be like.

 Math

Solve Problems

Use the highest and lowest temperatures ever recorded on Earth (see previous page) to determine the range of temperatures on Earth.

 Social Studies

Maya Calendar

Research the Maya calendar. Write a paragraph comparing that calendar with the calendar we use today. Draw a picture of the calendar to go with your paragraph.

Investigate the formation of a crater.

Read and learn about the similarities and differences between Earth and the moon, the phases of the moon, and how an eclipse happens.

Essential Question

How Do Earth and the Moon Compare?

Fast Fact

The Moon Rocket

The Saturn V launch vehicle shown here is 36 stories high. Powered by the Saturn launch vehicle, six Apollo missions landed on the moon. In 1969, Neil Armstrong was the first person to walk on the moon's cratered surface. In the Investigate, you'll make a model of craters being formed.

Saturn V

Vocabulary Preview

moon [MOON] Any natural body that revolves around a planet (p. 482)

crater [KRAYT•er] A low, bowl-shaped area on the surface of a planet or moon (p. 482)

moon phase [MOON FAYZ] One of the shapes the moon seems to have as it orbits Earth (p. 485)

eclipse [ih•KLIPS] An event that occurs when one object in space passes through the shadow of another object in space (p. 486)

refraction [rih•FRAK•shuhn] The bending of light as it moves from one material to another (p. 486)

Making Craters

Guided Inquiry

Start With Questions

The moon and Earth have many craters on their surfaces. Some have been created by erupting volcanoes. Some were created another way.

- How did these craters form?

- What do you think formed the crater shown below?

Investigate to find out. Then read and learn to find out more.

Prepare to Investigate

Inquiry Skill Tip

When you use models, remember that your results depend on the similarities between your model and the real thing. You should always try to make a realistic model.

Materials

- safety goggles
- aluminum pan
- large spoon
- 1 cup flour
- meterstick
- newspaper
- apron
- $\frac{1}{2}$ cup water
- marble

Make an Observation Chart

Trial	Height	Width of Crater
1	20 cm	
2	20 cm	
3	20 cm	
1	40 cm	
2	40 cm	
3	40 cm	
1	80 cm	
2	80 cm	
3	80 cm	
1	100 cm	

Follow This Procedure

1. Copy the table.

2. Spread the newspaper on the floor. Place the pan in the center of the newspaper.

3. Put on the apron. Use the spoon to mix the water and most of the flour in the pan. Spread out the mixture. Lightly cover the surface of the mixture with dry flour to **make a model** of the moon's surface.

4. **CAUTION: Put on the safety goggles to protect your eyes from flour dust.**

   Drop the marble into the pan from a height of 20 cm. Carefully remove the marble.

5. **Measure** the width of the crater, and **record** it in the table. Repeat Step 4 two more times. Measure and record each time.

6. Now drop the marble three times from each of the heights 40 cm, 80 cm, and 100 cm. **Measure** and **record** the crater's width after each drop. Compare your results with those of your classmates.

Draw Conclusions

1. How did height affect crater size?

2. **Inquiry Skill** Scientists use models to study space. By making a model, what did you learn about how the moon's craters may have been formed?

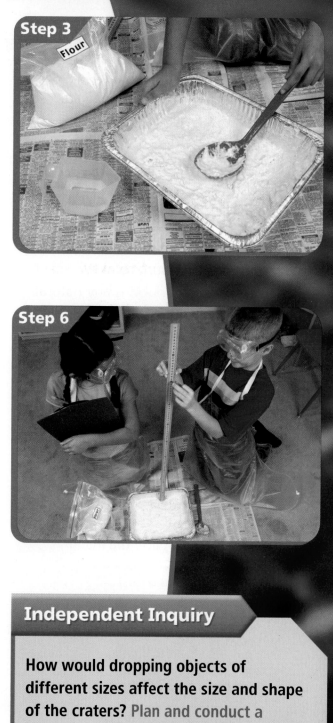

Step 3

Step 6

Independent Inquiry

How would dropping objects of different sizes affect the size and shape of the craters? Plan and conduct a simple investigation to find out.

VOCABULARY
moon p. 482
crater p. 482
moon phase p. 485
eclipse p. 486
refraction p. 486

SCIENCE CONCEPTS
▶ how the moon and Earth are alike and different
▶ how the phases of the moon and solar and lunar eclipses happen

(Focus Skill) COMPARE AND CONTRAST

Look for ways the phases of the moon are alike and different.

[alike]———[different]

The Moon and Earth

If you stare at the moon at night, you may wonder what the surface of this silent, round object is like. A **moon** is any natural body that revolves around a planet. Earth and its moon are similar in several ways. Both are rocky and fairly dense. Both are made of many of the same elements, including aluminum, oxygen, calcium, silicon, and iron. Both the moon and Earth have craters. A **crater** is a low, bowl-shaped area on the surface of a planet or moon.

However, there are also important differences between the moon and Earth. One clear difference is size. The moon's diameter is about 3476 km (2160 mi), only about one-fourth of Earth's diameter.

The moon's pull of gravity is only about one-sixth that of Earth. A person who weighs 800 newtons (180 lb) on Earth would only weigh 133 newtons (30 lb) on the moon. The moon, unlike Earth, has almost no atmosphere and no liquid water. Temperatures on the moon can vary.

From space, the moon looks gray because of its rocks and dust. ▼

From space, Earth looks blue because of its oceans. There is no liquid water on the moon.

▲ Astronauts need spacesuits on the moon to provide air to breathe and to protect them from the extreme temperatures. The heavy suits and other equipment feel much lighter on the moon than on Earth because of the weaker gravitational pull of the moon.

Temperatures can be more than 100°C (212°F) during the day to –155°C (–247°F) at night. Earth's temperatures are less extreme.

The moon's surface is covered with craters, many more than on Earth. The craters were made by objects falling from space, like the marbles in the Investigate.

Most objects that fall from space toward Earth burn up in the atmosphere before they reach the ground. The craters that do form on Earth are usually worn down by weathering. Objects that fall to the moon, though, do not burn up, because there is hardly any atmosphere. And there is no erosion, because of the lack of atmosphere and lack of water. As a result, craters on the moon last indefinitely.

 **COMPARE AND CONTRAST** How is the moon's surface different from that of Earth?

A footprint on Earth doesn't last long, but a footprint on the moon could last millions of years due to lack of erosion.

Insta-Lab

Astronaut Moves

To work on the moon or in space, astronauts need to wear spacesuits to protect themselves. Try to thread a nut on a bolt while wearing heavy gloves. How difficult do you think it would be to work on the moon or in space?

Phases of the Moon

On some nights, you may notice that the moon seems to have disappeared. On other nights, you see a large, white moon shining brightly. The moon, though, has not changed at all. Instead, the moon and Earth have moved.

In the Investigate in Lesson 1, you learned how Earth travels around the sun and how the moon travels around Earth at the same time. Earth orbits the sun in a slight ellipse. The moon's orbit around Earth is a slight ellipse, too. When the moon is closest to Earth, it is about 356,400 km (221,000 mi) away.

Both Earth and the moon rotate as they revolve, though at different speeds. The moon rotates more slowly. It completes a rotation every $29\frac{1}{2}$ Earth days. So a day on the moon is $29\frac{1}{2}$ Earth days long.

The moon rotates as it orbits Earth, but the same side of the moon always faces Earth. That's because one lunar cycle, from new moon to new moon, takes $29\frac{1}{2}$ days, the same amount of time the moon takes to complete one rotation.

The side of the moon we can't see from Earth was once called the dark side of the moon. A better name is the far side of the moon. Although we can't see the far side of the moon, the sun shines on that side as often as on the side we see.

The moon is often bright at night, but it doesn't give off its own light. As the moon orbits Earth, its position in the sky changes. The part of the moon that is exposed to the sun reflects the sun's light.

The Apollo 8 mission, in 1968, was the first mission to carry people in orbit around the moon. While in orbit, the crew took pictures like this one of the moon's far side.

Phases of the Moon

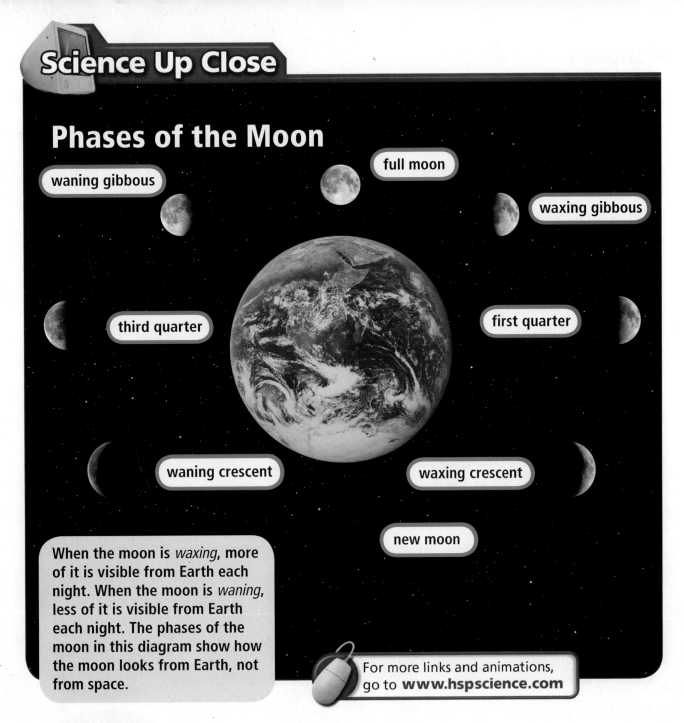

waning gibbous

full moon

waxing gibbous

third quarter

first quarter

waning crescent

waxing crescent

new moon

When the moon is *waxing*, **more of it is visible from Earth each night. When the moon is** *waning*, **less of it is visible from Earth each night. The phases of the moon in this diagram show how the moon looks from Earth, not from space.**

For more links and animations, go to **www.hspscience.com**

The way the moon looks from Earth changes daily. At any time, half of the moon is lit by the sun. But how much you see depends on the moon's phase. A **moon phase** is one of the shapes the moon seems to have as it orbits Earth. When Earth is between the moon and the sun, you see a full moon. When the moon is between Earth and the sun, you can't see the moon at all. This is called a new moon.

The cycle of phases of the moon takes $29\frac{1}{2}$ days. During the cycle, the visible portion of the moon changes gradually. Starting with a new moon, you see more and more of the moon each day until the full moon. Then you see less and less each day until the next new moon.

Focus Skill COMPARE AND CONTRAST

Contrast the appearance of the moon during a full moon and a new moon.

Eclipses

Objects in space block some of the sun's light, producing shadows. An **eclipse** occurs when one body in space blocks light from reaching another body in space.

Eclipses we see on Earth are solar eclipses and lunar eclipses. They are alike because both occur when Earth, the sun, and the moon line up. However, solar and lunar eclipses also differ.

A solar eclipse occurs when the moon—always a new moon—casts a shadow on Earth. In some places the moon seems to cover the sun, and the sky gets dark. Only the outer atmosphere of the sun is visible, as a bright glow around the moon. At other places, only part of the sun is covered.

A lunar eclipse occurs when the moon—always a full moon—passes through the shadow of Earth. Earth blocks the sun's light from reaching the moon, but the moon does not look black. Instead, it looks red. This is because Earth's atmosphere bends red light, which then reflects off the moon. Scientists call this bending of light **refraction**.

You might think that eclipses happen with every new or full moon. But the moon and Earth are not always in the proper alignment. Sometimes only a partial eclipse occurs. Partial solar and lunar eclipses each occur two to four times a year.

COMPARE AND CONTRAST

How do solar and lunar eclipses differ?

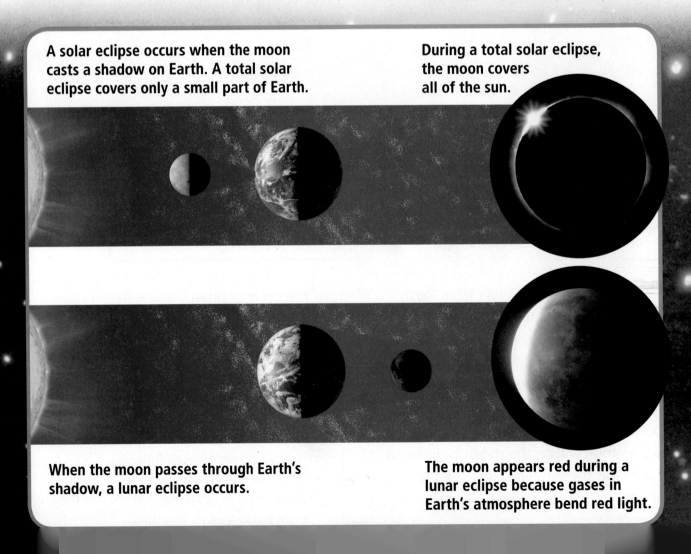

A solar eclipse occurs when the moon casts a shadow on Earth. A total solar eclipse covers only a small part of Earth.

During a total solar eclipse, the moon covers all of the sun.

When the moon passes through Earth's shadow, a lunar eclipse occurs.

The moon appears red during a lunar eclipse because gases in Earth's atmosphere bend red light.

Essential Question

How Do Earth and the Moon Compare?

In this lesson, you learned about the relationship between the moon and Earth. You also learned about the phases of the moon and what happens during an eclipse.

1. 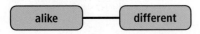 **COMPARE AND CONTRAST** Draw and complete a graphic organizer that compares and contrasts Earth's and the moon's atmosphere, temperatures, and craters.

   alike ———— different

2. **SUMMARIZE** Write a one-paragraph summary of the phases of the moon.

3. **DRAW CONCLUSIONS** How would the moon be different if it had liquid water?

4. **VOCABULARY** Explain in a sentence what an eclipse is.

Test Prep

5. **CRITICAL THINKING** On a night when you see a full moon, where are the moon, sun, and Earth relative to each other in space?

6. Which of these are on the surfaces of both the moon and Earth?
   A. craters
   B. liquid water
   C. oxygen
   D. windstorms

Make Connections

 Writing

Narrative Writing
Think about the differences between the moon and Earth. Then write a **story** that describes the differences. Use as many descriptive words as you can.

 Math

Use Fractions
During a full moon, you can see half of the moon's surface. During a first quarter, what fraction of the moon's surface can you see on a clear night?

 Physical Education

Running to the Moon
The moon is about 221,000 mi from Earth at its closest point. To get an idea of how far that is, run or walk 221 steps. Each step represents 1000 miles.

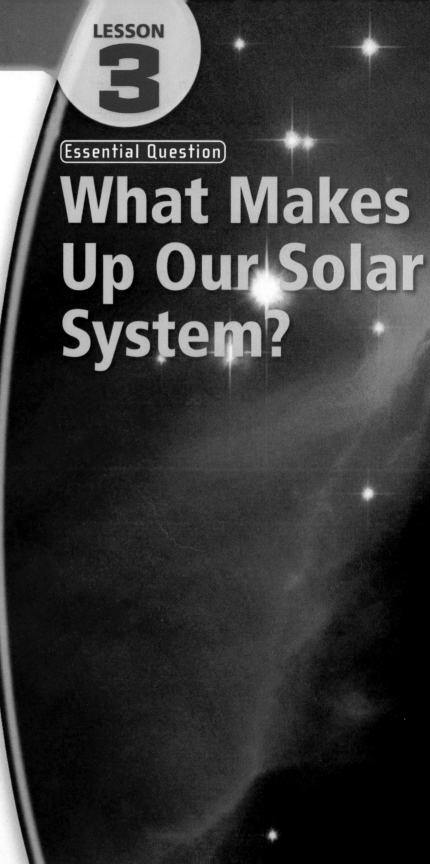

Investigate how to make a telescope.

Read and learn about the objects that make up our solar system, as well as other objects in the universe.

Essential Question

What Makes Up Our Solar System?

Fast Fact

Deep Space Close-Up

Since the launch of the Hubble Space Telescope in 1990, people have studied and enjoyed many of the Hubble's amazing images, like this one of the Cone Nebula. Some of the objects shown in Hubble images are at a distance greater than 10 billion light-years (60 billion trillion mi). In the Investigate, you'll make your own telescope—though you won't see as far as with a telescope like the Hubble.

star [STAR] A huge ball of very hot gases in space (p. 492)

solar system [SOH•ler SIS•tuhm] A star and all the planets and other objects that revolve around it (p. 492)

constellation [kahn•stuh•LAY•shuhn] A pattern of stars, named after a mythological or religious figure, an object, or an animal (p. 493)

planet [PLAN•it] A body that revolves around a star (p. 495)

universe [YOO•nuh•vers] Everything that exists, including such things as stars, planets, gas, dust, and energy (p. 498)

galaxy [GAL•uhk•see] A grouping of gas, dust, and many stars, plus any objects that orbit those stars (p. 498)

The Cone Nebula

489

Make a Telescope

Start With Questions

At night, you can see bright points of light in the sky. A few of these are the planets that are closest to Earth. From Earth, they look tiny.

- What is one way you can see things that are far away?

- How can you make your own telescope?

Investigate to find out. Then read and learn to find out more.

Prepare to Investigate

Inquiry Skill Tip

Observing means more than just recording results. When you observe, you should look for details and changes. Think about what characteristics or events are important to your investigation.

Materials

- 2 sheets of construction paper
- tape
- 2 convex lenses
- modeling clay

Make an Observation Chart

Objects	With the Telescope	Without the Telescope

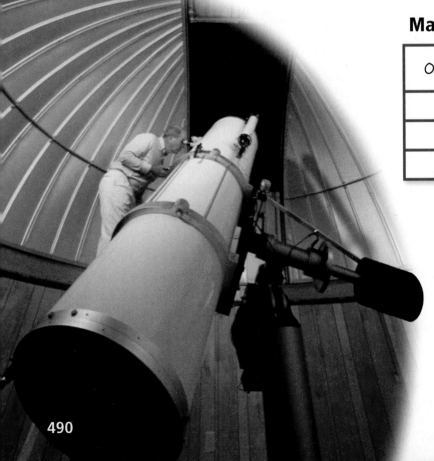

Follow This Procedure

1. Roll and tape a sheet of construction paper to form a tube slightly larger in diameter than the lenses. Make a second tube just large enough for the first tube to fit inside it.

2. Slide most of the smaller tube into the larger tube.

3. Use some of the clay to hold one of the lenses in one end of the smaller tube. This will be the telescope's eyepiece.

4. Use clay to hold the other lens in the far end of the larger tube. This will be the lens closer to the object you are viewing.

5. Choose three distant objects to view.
   CAUTION: **Do not look at the sun.**
   Slide the smaller tube to focus on each object.

6. **Observe** each object twice, once without the telescope and once with it. **Record** each observation in a drawing.

Draw Conclusions

1. Compare the drawings made with and without the telescope. Why do they differ?

2. **Inquiry Skill** How was your observing similar to using a space telescope?

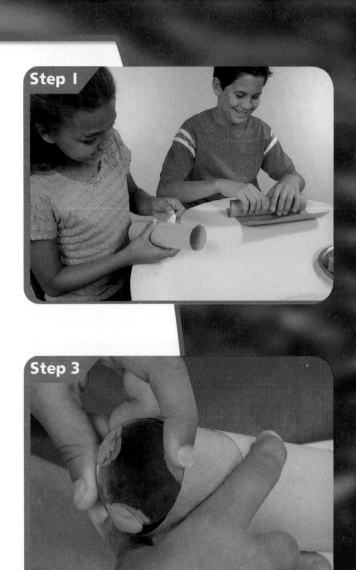

Step I

Step 3

Independent Inquiry

Use your telescope to observe the brightest object in the eastern night sky. List details you can see with the telescope but not without it.

Read and Learn

VOCABULARY

star p. 492
solar system p. 492
constellation p. 493
planet p. 495
universe p. 498
galaxy p. 498

SCIENCE CONCEPTS

▶ what objects make up our solar system
▶ what other objects are in the universe

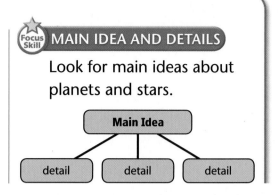

MAIN IDEA AND DETAILS

Look for main ideas about planets and stars.

```
            Main Idea
         /      |      \
     detail   detail   detail
```

The Sun and Other Stars

One object that you can see in the sky without a telescope is the sun. But you should NEVER look directly at the sun. The sun is a **star**, a huge ball of very hot gases in space. The sun is at the center of our solar system. A **solar system** is made up of a star and all the planets and other objects that revolve around that star.

The sun is the source of much of the energy on Earth. Plants use energy from the sun to make food and store energy. Animals eat plants to use that food energy. When plants and animals die, they decay, or rot. Some that died long ago became fossil fuels, such as oil, that people use today.

The sun's features make it different from everything else in our solar system. The sun is huge: a million Earths could fit inside it.

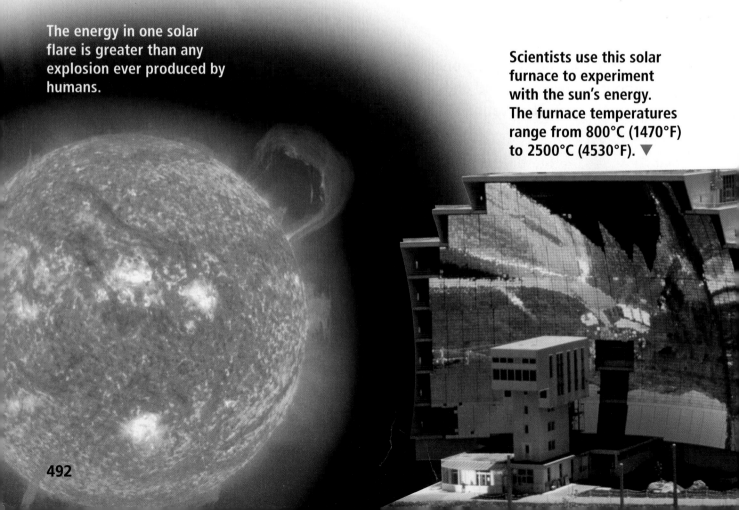

The energy in one solar flare is greater than any explosion ever produced by humans.

Scientists use this solar furnace to experiment with the sun's energy. The furnace temperatures range from 800°C (1470°F) to 2500°C (4530°F). ▼

492

▲ There are many ways to classify stars. A star can be classified according to its size, its brightness, its temperature, and its color.

The constellation Ursa Major, or the Great Bear, was named by the ancient Greeks. It contains a more familiar star pattern—the Big Dipper.

The glowing surface of the sun is what we see from Earth. On the sun's surface are sunspots visible from Earth. Sunspots are darker, cooler areas of the sun. They can produce brief bursts of energy called solar flares. Above the sun's surface is the corona. This area of hot gases extends about 1 million km (600,000 mi) from the surface of the sun.

The sun is important to us because of its energy. But the sun is just one of billions of stars in the universe. Among all those stars, the sun is average. It's a yellow star of medium size, medium brightness, and medium heat.

One way scientists classify stars is by color. Star colors range from blue, white, and yellow to orange and red. The color of a star is a clue to its surface temperature. Blue stars are the hottest, and red stars are the coolest.

Another way scientists classify stars is by brightness. How bright a star appears depends on two factors. One is how far it is from Earth. The other is how bright it actually is.

Since ancient times, people have grouped stars into constellations. A **constellation** is a pattern of stars that is named after a religious or mythical object or animal. One set of constellations is visible from the Northern Hemisphere. Another set is visible from the Southern Hemisphere.

 MAIN IDEA AND DETAILS

What are two ways scientists classify stars?

Mercury
diameter: 4900 km
(about 3040 mi)
distance from sun:
58,000,000 km
(about 36,000,000 mi)
length of year:
88 Earth days

Venus
diameter: 12,100 km
(about 7500 mi)
distance from sun:
108,000,000 km
(about 67,000,000 mi)
length of year:
225 Earth days

Earth
diameter: 12,700 km
(about 7900 mi)
distance from sun:
150,000,000 km
(about 93,000,000 mi)
length of year:
365.25 Earth days

Math in Science
Interpret Data

Weight on Different Planets

The pull of gravity at a planet's surface depends on
the planet's diameter and on how much mass the
planet has. The greater the planet's pull of gravity,
the more you would weigh on its surface. Here are
the weights on different planets for a person who
weighs 100 pounds on Earth.

Note: Diagrams not to scale.

Planet	Weight (lb)
Mercury	37.8
Earth	100.0
Venus	90.7
Mars	37.7

Does Venus have a stronger or weaker
pull of gravity than Earth?

The Inner Planets

Our solar system includes eight planets. A **planet** is a body that revolves around a star. A planet is held in its orbit by the gravitational force between the planet and the star.

Scientists divide the planets that revolve around the sun into four inner planets and four outer planets. These groups are separated by the huge asteroid belt between Mars and Jupiter. The *asteroid belt* is a ring-shaped area where many small, rocky bodies, or asteroids, are located.

The four inner planets are rocky and dense. Mercury, which is closest to the sun, is about the size of Earth's moon. Like the moon, Mercury has almost no atmosphere and a surface covered with craters and dust. The side of Mercury facing the sun is hot—about 430°C (810°F). The side not facing the sun can become very cold, however—about −180°C (−290°F).

Venus is the brightest object in the night sky, after the moon. This planet is about the same size as Earth, and it is rocky. The similarities end there. Venus can become very hot, reaching about 460°C (860°F). It is even hotter than Mercury because Venus's thick atmosphere keeps heat from escaping.

Earth is the only planet to support life, because of its liquid water and atmosphere. Earth's atmosphere maintains temperatures in which living things can survive.

Mars is called the red planet because of its reddish soil. Its atmosphere is mostly carbon dioxide. Its valleys are evidence that Mars once had liquid water. Mars has the largest volcano in the solar system, and it has dust storms that can last for months.

 **MAIN IDEA AND DETAILS** What separates the inner planets from the outer planets?

Mars
diameter: 6800 km
(about 4200 mi)
distance from sun:
228,000,000 km
(about 142,000,000 mi)
length of year:
687 Earth days

The Outer Planets and Pluto

Beyond the asteroid belt are the outer planets. These are called gas giants, because they are composed mostly of hydrogen and helium.

Jupiter is the largest planet in the solar system. It has rings and dozens of moons. There is a huge storm on Jupiter that has lasted for about 400 years. The storm, like a hurricane, has a name—the Great Red Spot.

Saturn is best known for its rings, made of ice, dust, boulders, and frozen gas. The rings stretch about 136,200 km (84,650 mi) from the center of the planet. Like Jupiter, Saturn has dozens of moons.

Uranus also has many moons and rings. This planet rotates on an axis that is tilted much more than those of other planets. Compared with the other planets, Uranus looks like a top that has fallen over but is still spinning.

Neptune has many rings and moons and the fastest winds in the solar system. The winds can reach 2000 km/hr (1200 mi/hr)!

For almost 80 years Pluto was listed as the ninth planet. In 2006, scientists met to form a new definition of a planet. They decided that a planet is a large round object in a clear orbit around a star. Because Pluto is not in a clear orbit, scientists removed it from the list of planets. They classified it as a "dwarf planet." The large asteroid Ceres, and Eris, which orbits beyond Pluto, are also classified as "dwarf planets."

Focus Skill **MAIN IDEA AND DETAILS**

What are some characteristics of the gas giants?

Jupiter
diameter: 143,000 km
(about 89,000 mi)
distance from sun:
778,000,000 km
(about 483,000,000 mi)
length of year:
11.9 Earth years

Note: Diagrams not to scale.

asteroid Ida

Saturn
diameter: 120,000 km
(about 74,000 mi)
distance from sun:
1,427,000,000 km
(about 886,000,000
mi)
length of year:
29.5 Earth years

Uranus
diameter: 51,000 km
(about 32,000 mi)
distance from sun:
2,869,000,000 km
(about 1,783,000,000 mi)
length of year:
84 Earth years

Neptune
diameter: 49,000 km
(about 30,000 mi)
distance from sun:
4,505,000,000 km
(about 2,799,000,000 mi)
length of year:
165 Earth years

Asteroids and Comets

Both asteroids and comets orbit the
sun. Asteroids are chunks of rock less
than 1000 km (621 mi) in diameter.
Comets have a small, solid, frozen
core. As a comet nears the sun,
however, its core begins to melt,
forming a cloud of gas that is pushed
into a long tail by energy from the
sun. A comet's tail can be tens of
millions of kilometers long.

comet Hale-Bopp

Beyond the Solar System

Look up on a clear night, and you may think you can see the universe. But what you see is only a small fraction of it. The **universe** is everything that exists—all the stars, the planets, dust, gases, and energy.

If it's dark enough where you live, you may see what look like ribbons of stars overhead. These ribbons are part of the Milky Way Galaxy, the galaxy that includes our solar system. A **galaxy** is gas, dust, and a group of stars, including any objects orbiting the stars. The Milky Way Galaxy has more than 100 billion stars and is one of the largest galaxies in the universe. Scientists estimate that the universe contains more than 100 billion galaxies.

Galaxies are classified by shape. There are four basic types: spiral, barred spiral, elliptical, and irregular. A spiral galaxy has a bulge of stars in the center and rotating arms around a disk. A barred spiral galaxy is similar to a spiral galaxy, but the spiral arms extend from a bar of stars that stretches across the center.

For a long time, scientists thought the Milky Way was a spiral galaxy. New research suggests that it may actually be a barred

A spiral galaxy can look like a giant pinwheel spinning through space. The arms wind around the center as the galaxy turns. ▼

The Hubble Space Telescope produced this image. Each bright spot is a galaxy containing countless stars. But even this image shows just one relatively small region of space. There are billions of galaxies in the universe.

spiral galaxy. The sun is in one of the Milky Way Galaxy's spiral arms. The sun makes one complete turn around the center of the galaxy in about 200 to 250 million years.

Elliptical galaxies make up about half of all galaxies. Their shapes range from almost a sphere to a flattened football shape. They do not seem to rotate. Irregular galaxies are groups of stars with no obvious shape.

Galaxies form groups known as clusters. The Milky Way Galaxy is one of about 30 galaxies in a cluster called the Local Group. There are thousands of galactic clusters in the universe.

Astronomers hypothesize that stars form in a nebula. A nebula is a huge cloud of hydrogen, helium, and tiny particles of dust. The matter of a nebula may clump together to form a *protostar*, a collection of gas clouds that starts reacting chemically. When a protostar is hot enough, it forms a star and begins to release energy in the form of heat and light.

Black holes are other, less understood parts of the universe. A black hole is an object of extremely intense gravity. Black holes are so dense that even light gets pulled into them. Scientists have concluded that a black hole forms when a large star collapses.

Focus Skill **MAIN IDEA AND DETAILS**

Describe the sun's position and movement in the Milky Way Galaxy.

A nebula may be composed of matter shed by an aging star. ▶

Rolling in Space
With supervision, sit in a desk chair that has wheels, lift up your feet, and try to move to another part of the room without touching the floor. How is the feeling you get the same as how you'd feel in space?

The Hubble Space Telescope took this image in 1994 of a huge spiral of dust being pulled into a black hole.

Space Exploration

In ancient times, people observed the sky and asked questions about what they saw. With the invention of the telescope in 1609, people first got a closer look into space. Early telescopes allowed astronomers to see details of the moon's surface, as well as moons around Jupiter. It was not until the mid-twentieth century, though, that people could launch vehicles into space.

The Russian satellite *Sputnik 1* was launched into Earth's upper atmosphere in 1957. A *satellite* is any body that orbits another. In the 1960s, Russian and United States spacecraft carried the first humans into space. In 1969, U.S. astronaut Neil Armstrong became the first person to walk on the moon.

Since the Apollo missions that flew astronauts to the moon from 1969 to 1972, much of space exploration has focused on other parts of the universe. In 1977, the United States launched the *Voyager 1* and *Voyager 2* space probes to study deep space. These robot vehicles have traveled to the edge of the solar system, past all the planets, and are still sending back information to Earth.

In 2004, the *Cassini* spacecraft reached Saturn. From its orbit around Saturn, *Cassini* has given scientists a wealth of information about the planet's famous rings.

Today's scientists use telescopes, satellites, and space probes to continue to explore space. All these devices are helping scientists understand more about our universe.

Focus Skill MAIN IDEA AND DETAILS

How has space exploration changed since the Apollo missions?

Two *Mars Rovers* landed on Mars in 2003. The six-wheeled rovers traveled over the surface of Mars collecting data, taking photographs, and analyzing Martian rocks and soil. ▶

In 1976, *Viking 1* and *Viking 2* became the first space probes to successfully land on Mars.

Essential Question

What Makes Up Our Solar System?

In this lesson, you learned that our sun is a star and that it is the center of our solar system, which is made up of many planets and other objects. Our solar system is part of a galaxy, which has billions of stars. The universe contains billions of galaxies.

1. **Focus Skill MAIN IDEA AND DETAILS** Draw and complete a graphic organizer with details for this main idea: The solar system is made up of the sun and the many objects that orbit it.

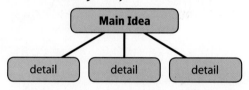

Main Idea

detail   detail   detail

2. **SUMMARIZE** Write a one-paragraph summary about two different ways that scientists explore space.

3. **DRAW CONCLUSIONS** Why is Earth a unique planet in our solar system?

4. **VOCABULARY** How are *star, solar system,* and *galaxy* related?

Test Prep

5. **CRITICAL THINKING** Why haven't scientists found life on other planets in the solar system?

6. Where is the asteroid belt?
   - **A.** in the nebula
   - **B.** in Saturn's rings
   - **C.** between Jupiter and Mars
   - **D.** between Earth and Venus

Make Connections

 Writing

Persuasive Writing
Should the United States increase the money spent for space exploration? Write a **letter** that tells your point of view. Include reasons that support your position.

 Math

Multiply Numbers
An astronomical unit (AU) is about 149,600,000 km, the distance between Earth and the sun. If an object is 4 AU from Earth, how far away is it?

 Literature

Space Poetry
Myra Cohn Livingston writes poetry about space. Read a book of her poetry, and write a paragraph about the poem you liked best.

Beyond the Shuttle

An elevator to space? A spaceship with engines so powerful that the vehicle can take off like an airplane and fly— not blast off—into orbit? Those might sound like the basis of an episode of Star Trek, but the ideas are currently under development by the National Aeronautics and Space Administration (NASA).

Taxi! Taxi!

On the top of NASA's list is a space taxi. The vehicle would ferry ten astronauts at a time to and from the International Space Station (ISS) beginning in 2010. NASA is spending $882 million to design a craft called the Orbital Space Plane.

The space plane would be a shuttlelike craft on top of a rocket. The rocket would blast the plane into Earth orbit. "It would not be a space shuttle replacement."

Barry Davidson of Syracuse University said of the space plane, "It would be the next-generation vehicle out there."

Within the next 15 years or so, scientists say, NASA will have to replace the three space shuttles—*Discovery, Atlantis,* and *Endeavour*—which were all built in the 1970s and early 1980s.

NASA might also replace the shuttles with a spacecraft that would be attached to the back of a large aircraft. Once both vehicles are airborne, the spacecraft would release itself and speed into orbit using a super-powerful jet engine called a ramjet or a scramjet. The ramjet or scramjet engine would propel the craft into orbit at ten times the speed of sound.

Sound Byte

Sound travels through air at about 340 meters (1100 feet) per second.

Next Stop, Space

Some scientists say the easiest way to get into space might just be by elevator. NASA scientists are currently working on a plan that would put a large satellite in orbit about 35,000 kilometers (21,748 miles) above the equator. The satellite would be programmed to constantly hover over the same spot on Earth's surface.

Scientists would attach to the satellite a very long cable and an elevator that could then be used to transport people and equipment into space. "We think we can have it up and operational in about 15 years," said scientist Bradley C. Edwards.

Think and Write

1. Why is it a good idea to have a space plane that is easy to reuse?

2. Do you think it's important for people to keep exploring outer space? Why or why not?

Find out more. Log on to
www.hspscience.com

Vocabulary Review

Use the terms below to complete the sentences. The page numbers tell you where to look in the chapter if you need help.

revolve p. 474   **eclipse** p. 486

orbit p. 474   **solar system** p. 492

equator p. 474   **constellation** p. 493

moon p. 482   **universe** p. 498

crater p. 482   **galaxy** p. 498

1. The path that Earth takes as it moves around the sun is its _____.

2. The sun is the center of our _____.

3. Everything that exists, including planets, stars, dust, and gases, is the _____.

4. Stars, gas, and dust make up our _____.

5. To travel in a path around another object is to _____.

6. Earth is divided into Northern and Southern Hemispheres by the _____.

7. When one body in space blocks light from reaching another body, there is an _____.

8. A bowl-shaped low place on a surface is a _____.

9. A natural body that revolves around a planet is a _____.

10. A pattern of stars is a _____.

Check Understanding

Write the letter of the best choice.

11. **MAIN IDEA AND DETAILS** Which detail explains why summers at the North Pole are cold?

    A. Winters are long at the poles.

    B. The North Pole is covered with ice.

    C. Earth's orbit around the sun is elliptical.

    D. The sun's rays are indirect at the North Pole.

12. **COMPARE AND CONTRAST** Which is a correct comparison of the moon and Earth?

    F. They have similar gravitational force.

    G. They both undergo weathering.

    H. They both are rocky and dense.

    J. They have similar atmospheres.

13. What does this illustration show?

    A. a full moon

    B. a new moon

    C. a waning moon

    D. a waxing moon

14. Which is a correct statement about what happens during summers in the Northern Hemisphere?

   F. Earth has its winter equinox.

   G. The Southern Hemisphere is tilted away from the sun.

   H. The Northern Hemisphere is not tilted toward the sun.

   J. Rays of the sun hit the equator more intensely than during the winter.

15. Which planet is labeled X?

   A. Earth

   B. Mars

   C. Mercury

   D. Venus

16. What determines the seasons on Earth?

   F. Earth's orbit and tilt

   G. the sun's speed and the orbit of the sun

   H. changing directions of Earth's orbit

   J. the position of the moon in relation to Earth

Inquiry Skills

17. How could you **use a model** to learn more about eclipses?

18. What tools do scientists use to **observe** deep space?

Critical Thinking

19. Explain how Saturn and Jupiter differ from Mercury.

20. The moon is Earth's only natural satellite. We know now about many of the moon's characteristics. Think about the differences between Earth and the moon. Then make a plan for a settlement on the moon. Explain what settlers will need to take to the moon or change on the moon to make it suitable for life.

The **Big Idea**

Visual Summary

Tell how each picture shows the **Big Idea** for its chapter.

Big Idea

11

Weather is a measurable and predictable part of the water cycle.

Big Idea

12

Oceans are complex systems that interact with Earth's land, air, and living organisms.

Big Idea

13

Earth is part of a solar system, which is made up of many different objects orbiting a sun.

PHYSICAL SCIENCE

Science on Location and Projects for Home or School

Advanced Animatronics 508
The Circus Center 510
U.S. Olympic Training Center . . 512
What Floats Your Boat? 514

UNIT E

Matter and Energy **515**

CHAPTER 14
Properties of Matter 516
CHAPTER 15
Energy 554
CHAPTER 16
Electricity 602
CHAPTER 17
Sound and Light 638

UNIT F

Forces and Motion **669**
CHAPTER 18
Forces 670
CHAPTER 19
Motion 706

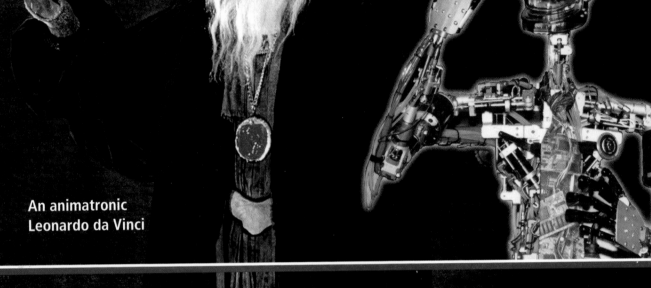

An animatronic
Leonardo da Vinci

Advanced Animations

Have you ever seen a life-size moving dinosaur? How about a two-story-tall talking warrior? These are real things. They are not special effects in a movie. They're animatronic, or animated, figures made by Advanced Animations in Stockbridge, Vermont. Fluids and complex electronics make each figure move. Pumps move the fluids through valves and cylinders. The fluids are kept under high pressure. The fluid pressure moves the figure's arms, legs, and body faster and more smoothly than ordinary mechanical parts would. It helps the figure move more naturally.

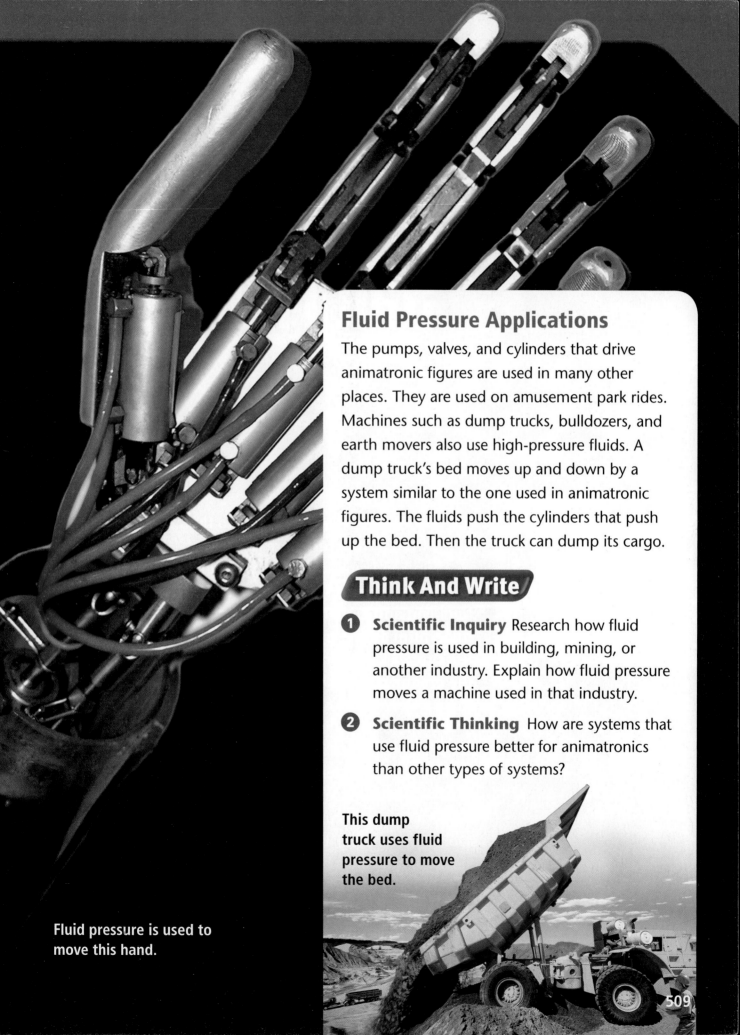

Fluid Pressure Applications

The pumps, valves, and cylinders that drive animatronic figures are used in many other places. They are used on amusement park rides. Machines such as dump trucks, bulldozers, and earth movers also use high-pressure fluids. A dump truck's bed moves up and down by a system similar to the one used in animatronic figures. The fluids push the cylinders that push up the bed. Then the truck can dump its cargo.

Think And Write

1. **Scientific Inquiry** Research how fluid pressure is used in building, mining, or another industry. Explain how fluid pressure moves a machine used in that industry.

2. **Scientific Thinking** How are systems that use fluid pressure better for animatronics than other types of systems?

This dump truck uses fluid pressure to move the bed.

Fluid pressure is used to move this hand.

Circus Center, San Francisco

Would you like to learn how to fly from a trapeze? There is a school in San Francisco where you can learn to be a circus star. It has classes in tumbling and juggling. You can learn to perform on the trapeze. You can learn to walk on thin wires high above the ground. Do you want to learn how to be a clown? You can do that, too.

The Circus Center is one of the few schools in the United States that teach students how to perform in a circus. The school was founded in 1984 as part of the Pickle Family Circus. Feats such as acrobatics, tumbling, balancing, juggling, and aerial work are a big part of the circus. All of these things use knowledge of forces, such as gravity or friction, and motion, such as position and momentum.

Circus Skills

For trapeze work, you need balance, strength, and flexibility. You also need to know about forces that act on a body. Speed, velocity, acceleration, and momentum are all things that need to be considered when swinging and flying high above the ground. Students must first take classes to get in good physical shape. Then they move on to classes in trapeze skills. These skills are taught on equipment that is very close to the ground. The low equipment lets students learn complicated skills safely. Once all the skills are mastered, it's on to the flying trapeze, high above the ground. Safety nets are always below the students and other performers, but knowing that doesn't make the flying trapeze any less scary for first-timers!

Think And Write

1. **Scientific Inquiry** What physical science skills are important for a trapeze artist? Why?

2. **Scientific Thinking** Why do you think work on the trapeze is called an art and not a sport?

U.S. Olympic Training Center

Just fractions of a second can separate first place from last place in the 50-meter freestyle swim. At the U.S. Olympic Training Center in Colorado Springs, Colorado, swimmers train to win. Runners can train on a treadmill. Now swimmers have their own "treadmill"—a flume. In the flume, they swim against a current. The current can be any speed from 0 to 3 meters per second. The force of the swimmers' strokes is balanced against the force of the current. As a result, the swimmers' positions don't change even though they are swimming. This is an example of balanced forces.

The flume is in a room that can imitate the effects of different altitudes. It can copy conditions from sea level to 2400 meters (8000 ft) above sea level. This allows the effects of altitude on a swimmer to be tested. At higher altitudes, the air is thinner because air pressure is lower. So, a swimmer gets less oxygen in each breath at higher altitudes. A swimmer may need to adjust his or her style when competing at higher altitudes. Training in this type of facility helps swimmers make those adjustments.

This swimmer is using science to train for the Summer Olympics.

Science Helps Swimmers

Underwater cameras in the flume allow coaches to study and correct an athlete's strokes. Computers record a swimmer's arm and leg motions. The swimmer can then adjust his or her style and stroke after reviewing the computer data. This training helps make a swimmer's stroke as efficient as possible. With a better stroke, the swimmer may reach the finish faster than ever before. A swimmer's speed, velocity, and acceleration can improve with this technology. When fractions of a second count, science could help win the gold medal.

Think and Write

1 **Scientific Thinking** Why doesn't a swimmer's position change inside the flume?

2 **Scientific Inquiry** Why would height above sea level affect a swimmer?

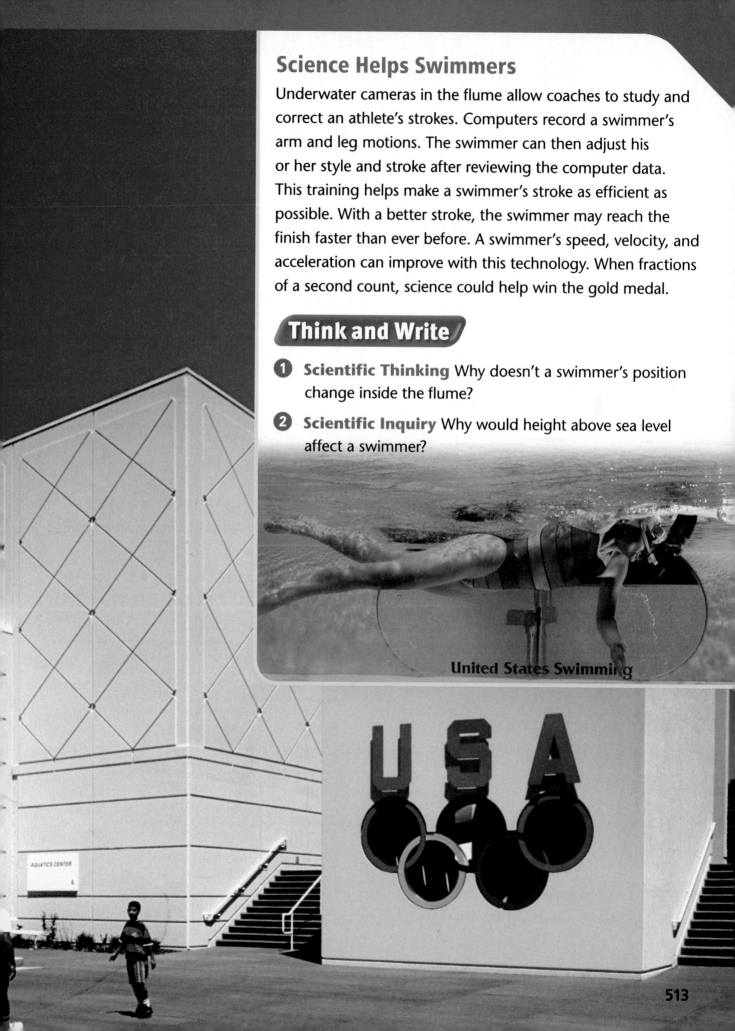

United States Swimming

AQUATICS CENTER
6

Project | What Floats Your Boat?

Materials

- a bucket of water, about half-full
- small objects, such as metal washers, rocks, or lead sinkers
- a small container, such as a small bowl or jar

Procedure

❶ Drop the objects, one at a time, into the water. Record your observations.

❷ Take the objects out of the water, and put the small container in the water. Record your observations.

❸ Begin putting the objects into the small container. Observe what happens to the small container as you add the weighted objects one by one. Continue until you have added all objects. Record your observations.

Draw Conclusions

❶ How can you explain what you observed when you dropped the weighted objects into the water?

❷ Describe what you observed about the small container as you filled it with weighted objects. Explain why you think this happened.

❸ Look up the words *density* and *buoyancy*. What can you conclude about the relationship between buoyancy and density?

Design Your Own Investigation

What About the Shape of Things?

Do you think the shape of an object will affect whether it floats or sinks? Write a hypothesis, and design an experiment to test your hypothesis.

Matter and Energy

UNIT
E
PHYSICAL SCIENCE

CHAPTER 14
Properties of Matter 516

CHAPTER 15
Energy 554

CHAPTER 16
Electricity 602

CHAPTER 17
Sound and Light 638

Unit Inquiry

Make Your Own Paper

Many people throw away old papers that are no longer needed. Instead of throwing away paper, it is possible to recycle the paper. When paper is recycled, it goes through several changes before it is ready to be used again. Find out about how to recycle paper. What ingredients do you need to make a sheet of recycled paper? What ingredients can you add to change how the paper looks? Plan and conduct an experiment to find out.

What's the Big Idea?

All matter has properties that can be observed, described, and measured.

Essential Questions

Lesson 1

What Is the Structure of Matter?

Lesson 2

What Are Physical Properties and Changes?

Lesson 3

What Are Chemical Properties and Changes?

GO online

Student eBook
www.hspscience.com

What do yOU wonder?

Scuba divers often search for sunken ships or lost treasure. It looks as if this diver has found something interesting! All three states of matter are shown in this photo. Can you find a solid, a liquid, and a gas? How does this relate to the **Big Idea?**

Investigate how observations and measurements can lead to accurate predictions.

Read and learn about matter, what it is made of, and its different states.

Essential Question

What Is the Structure of Matter?

Fast Fact

Water Shapes and Sounds

Water leaps into the air from the fountain at Centennial Park in Atlanta, Georgia. The fountain is the largest of its kind in the world, with 251 jets of water. It even plays music and lights up at night. In the Investigate, you will explore different ways to learn about matter—even matter you can't see.

Water fountain in Atlanta, Georgia

volume (VAHL•yoom] The amount of space an object takes up (p. 523)

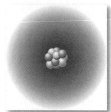

atom [AT•uhm] The smallest particle that still behaves like the original matter it came from (p. 524)

molecule [MAHL•ih•kyool] Two or more atoms joined together (p. 524)

nucleus [NOO•klee•uhs] A dense area in the center of an atom that contains protons and neutrons (p. 525)

element [EL•uh•muhnt] Matter made up of only one kind of atom (p. 526)

periodic table [pir•ee•AHD•ik TAY•buhl] A chart that scientists use to organize the elements (p. 526)

519

Mystery Boxes

Guided Inquiry

Start with Questions

It's usually easy to tell what something is by looking at it. But what if it's not easy?

- How could you find out what is in a sealed box?

- Can you tell what is in a gift-wrapped present just by holding the package?

Investigate to find out. Then read and learn to find out more.

Prepare to Investigate

Inquiry Skill Tip

Recording measurements and observations in a table makes comparing easier. You can easily see which properties are the same and which are different when you place them side by side.

Materials

- sealed box provided by your teacher
- ruler
- balance
- magnet

Make an Observation Chart

Box	Height (cm)	Length (cm)	Width (cm)	Mass (g)
Sealed				
Empty				

Follow This Procedure

1. Look carefully at the box. Move it around and listen. Is there one object inside, or are there several? **Record** what you hear.

2. Use the ruler to **measure** the height, length, and width of your box. **Record** your data.

3. Use the balance to **measure** the mass of the box. **Record** your data.

4. Put the magnet on the box, and tilt the box. Does the magnet attract any objects? Repeat, with the magnet in different positions. **Record** your findings.

5. **Predict** what the number, size, and nature of the objects inside the box will prove to be. Open your box. Were your predictions correct?

6. Remove the objects from the box. Repeat Steps 2 and 3. **Record** your data.

Draw Conclusions

1. Which observations and measurements led you to correct predictions? Which led you to incorrect predictions? Why?

2. **Inquiry Skill** Compare the masses and volumes of the box with and without the objects inside. How were these measurements affected by the objects?

Step 2

Step 4

Independent Inquiry

Predict what will prove to be inside a mystery box that a classmate makes for you. **Observe** and **measure** to test your prediction.

Read and Learn

VOCABULARY	SCIENCE CONCEPTS	MAIN IDEA AND DETAILS

VOCABULARY

volume p. 523
atom p. 524
molecule p. 524
nucleus p. 525
element p. 526
periodic table p. 526

SCIENCE CONCEPTS

▶ that matter has mass and takes up space

▶ what matter is made of

MAIN IDEA AND DETAILS

Look for what matter is and what it is made of.

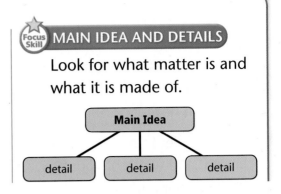

Matter

Think about the mystery box in the Investigate. How are the box, the objects inside it, the ruler, air, and people all alike? They are all made of matter. *Matter* is anything that has mass and takes up space. You used a balance to measure the mass of the box. You used a ruler to measure how much space the box takes up.

When you measure the amount of matter in an object, you're measuring the object's *mass*. Although mass and weight are not the same, they are related. Weight is a measure of how much the mass is pulled by gravity.

The mystery box would weigh less on the moon than on Earth, because the moon's gravitational pull is less than Earth's. The box's mass, however, is the same both on Earth and on the moon.

An object's mass doesn't change if you cut up the object or change its shape. Look at the apples on the balance below. On the left, you see a whole apple. On the right, you see an apple of the same mass that has been cut up. Notice that the apple contains as much matter after it was cut as it did before. Scientists say that its mass is *conserved*, or kept the same.

How can you tell that the whole apple and the apple slices have the same mass? ▼

This balloon and the air inside it have mass and take up space. ▼

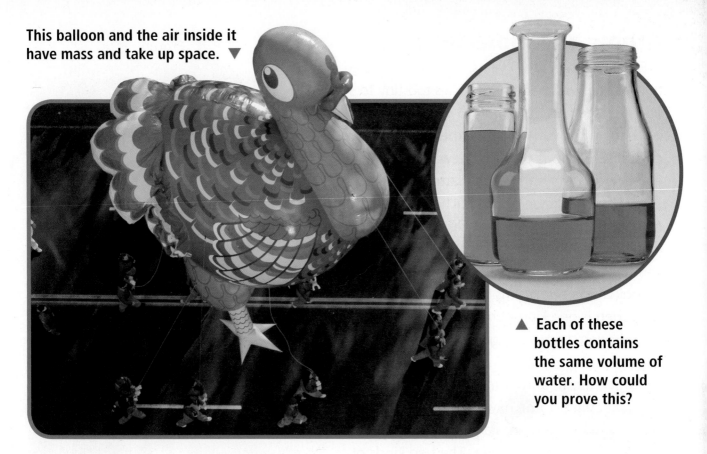

▲ Each of these bottles contains the same volume of water. How could you prove this?

In the Investigate, you changed the total mass of the mystery box when you removed objects from it. The mass changed because the box contained less matter.

Did the size of the box change when you took objects out of it? As your measurements showed, the box took up the same amount of space when it was empty as it did with objects in it. The amount of space an object takes up is its **volume**.

It's easy to find the volume of a solid object with a regular shape, such as a box. You can use a ruler to measure the object's length, width, and height. Then you can multiply the three numbers to find the volume. How do you measure the volume of a liquid, such as water? You can use a measuring cup or a graduated cylinder that marks the level of the liquid.

Scientists say the volume, like mass, is conserved. The amount of space a measured volume takes up doesn't change if we move

it, divide it, or change its shape. Pour the same amount of water into containers of different shapes. The volume may look different, but it isn't. Try it for yourself!

Focus Skill MAIN IDEA AND DETAILS

What are two properties of all matter?

Matter Up Close

Look closely at a small sample of sugar or salt. Draw a picture to record your observations. Then use a hand lens to study the sample more closely. Draw another picture. How did the hand lens change your observations?

Atoms and Molecules

For more than 2000 years, scientists guessed that matter was made of particles too tiny to see. The idea seemed right, but no one could test it. Then, in the early 1800s, experiments with chemical reactions provided new clues. They helped scientists learn what matter is made of.

All matter is made of tiny particles called atoms. An **atom** is the smallest particle that can still be identified as the matter it came from. Atoms are so small that they're invisible to the naked eye.

Look at the two atoms shown to the right. Hydrogen is one kind of matter. It is made of hydrogen atoms. Oxygen is another kind of matter. Oxygen atoms are different from hydrogen atoms and from every other kind of atom. People breathe oxygen gas to survive. Like oxygen, hydrogen is a gas, but people can't breathe it instead of oxygen. The two kinds of matter have very different properties.

Water is another kind of matter. It can form when two atoms of hydrogen join with one atom of oxygen. Each tiny, invisible particle of water is made of three atoms. The water particle is called a *molecule* (MAHL•ih•kyool). A **molecule** is made up of two or more atoms joined together. This water molecule looks and acts differently from the hydrogen and oxygen it's made up of. Oxygen and hyrdrogen are gases at room temperature.

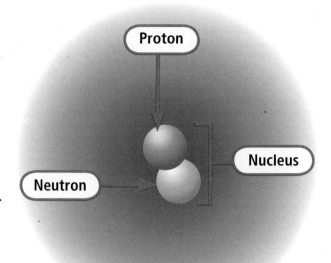

▲ This hydrogen atom has one proton in its nucleus.

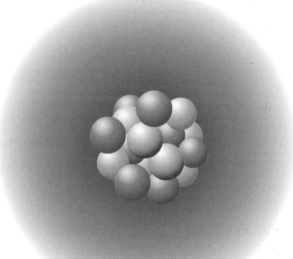

▲ This oxygen atom has eight protons in its nucleus.

This water molecule is made up of two hydrogen atoms and one oxygen atom. This waterfall has millions and millions of water molecules in it.

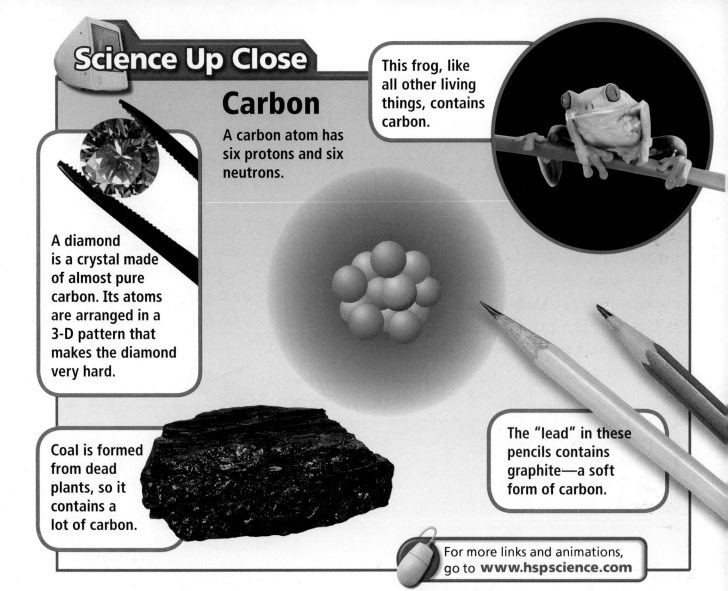

Carbon

A carbon atom has six protons and six neutrons.

This frog, like all other living things, contains carbon.

A diamond is a crystal made of almost pure carbon. Its atoms are arranged in a 3-D pattern that makes the diamond very hard.

Coal is formed from dead plants, so it contains a lot of carbon.

The "lead" in these pencils contains graphite—a soft form of carbon.

For more links and animations, go to **www.hspscience.com**

Water, however, is a liquid at room temperature.

People used to think that an atom was the smallest possible particle of matter. Today, we know that's not true. Atoms can be broken down into even smaller particles.

Look again at the hydrogen and oxygen atoms. Each of these has a dense area in the center, called the **nucleus** (NOO•klee•uhs). Inside the nucleus are smaller particles. One kind of particle is called a *proton* (PROH•tahn). It has a positive (+) electrical charge. Another kind of particle in the nucleus is a *neutron* (NOO•trahn). It has no electrical charge. Another way to say this is that it has a neutral charge.

One or more *electrons* (ee•LEK•trahnz) circle the nucleus of an atom. Electrons have a negative (–) electrical charge. Usually, the number of electrons in an atom is the same as the number of protons.

Different atoms contain different numbers of particles. The number of protons is especially important. A hydrogen atom has one proton. All atoms that contain one proton are hydrogen atoms. In the same way, all oxygen atoms contain eight protons. What can you say about carbon atoms, such as the one shown above?

Focus Skill MAIN IDEA AND DETAILS

What is an atom, and what are its parts?

Elements

Diamonds and graphite are made mostly of carbon atoms. Carbon is one kind of matter, and its atoms contain six protons. Matter that's made of only one kind of atom is an **element**. Carbon, then, is an element. So are hydrogen and oxygen. Water is not an element, because it's made of two kinds of matter.

Scientists have identified 116 elements. Some of them are familiar to you. For example, iron is an element. Useful items such as horseshoes can be made from iron. Gold is another element. People make jewelry from gold. Another familiar element is neon. When people trap neon gas inside a glass tube and send an electric current through it, the neon glows red.

To organize the elements, scientists use a chart called the **periodic table**. Each element has its place in the table. Each box within the table has a symbol that stands for the name of an element. Some symbols are obvious. Hydrogen's symbol is H. Oxygen's is O. Carbon's is C. Other symbols aren't so obvious, because they come from Latin or Greek words. Iron's symbol, for example, is Fe. Gold's is Au.

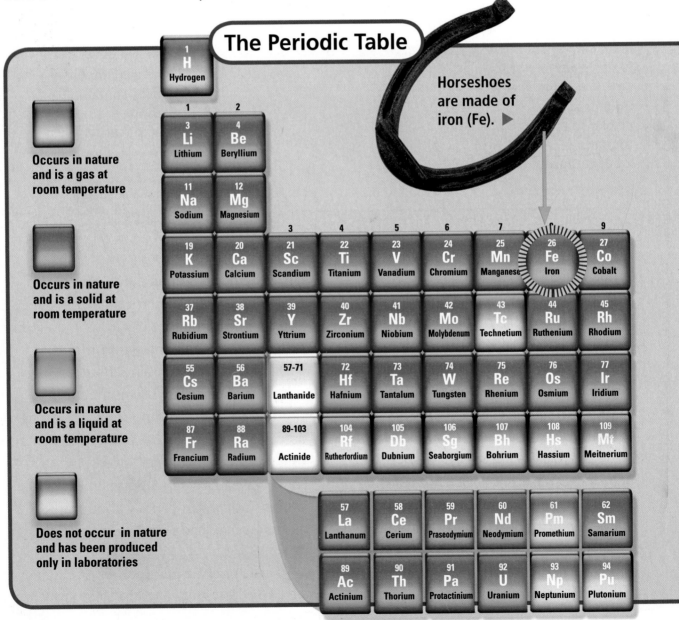

The Periodic Table

Horseshoes are made of iron (Fe). ▶

Occurs in nature and is a gas at room temperature

Occurs in nature and is a solid at room temperature

Occurs in nature and is a liquid at room temperature

Does not occur in nature and has been produced only in laboratories

In the periodic table, the elements are arranged in order by the number of protons in the nucleus. An element's number of protons is called its *atomic number*. A hydrogen atom has one proton, so its atomic number is 1. Oxygen has eight protons, so its atomic number is 8. Find iron (Fe) in the periodic table below. What is its atomic number? How many protons does it have? What element has an atomic number of 79? How many protons does it have?

The periodic table tells us a lot about each element. All the elements on the left side of the periodic table, except hydrogen, are metals. Metals are mostly shiny solids. Aluminum (Al) is a metal. Find aluminum in its place at atomic number 13. Tin (Sn) is also a metal. Its atomic number is 50. Find it in the table.

The elements to the far right of the periodic table are nonmetals. Carbon (C), hydrogen (H), and oxygen (O) are nonmetals. So is neon (Ne). Find neon in the table. What is its atomic number?

Focus Skill **MAIN IDEA AND DETAILS** How are elements arranged in the periodic table?

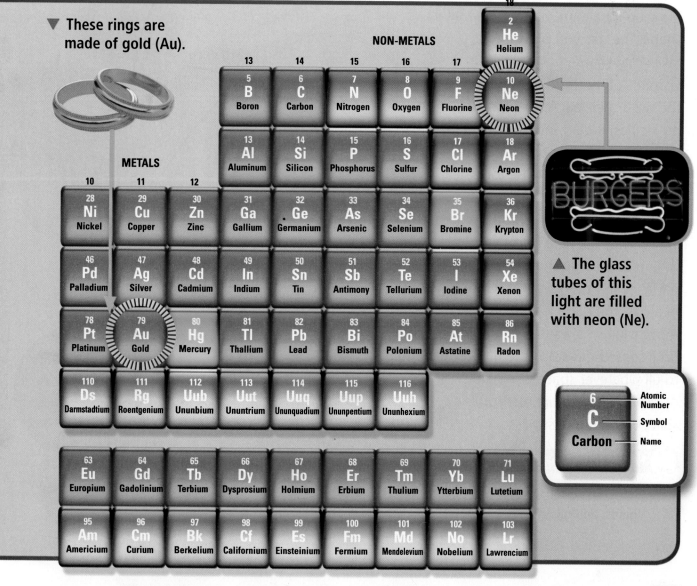

These rings are made of gold (Au).

NON-METALS

METALS

The glass tubes of this light are filled with neon (Ne).

The glass tubes of this light are filled with neon (Ne).

	6	Atomic Number
	C	Symbol
	Carbon	Name

Solids, Liquids, and Gases

The periodic table uses a color code to show the *state of matter* of each natural element at ordinary temperatures. We usually talk about three states of matter: solid, liquid, and gas. A solid has its own shape and volume. A liquid has its own volume, but it takes the shape of its container. A liquid can be poured from one container into another. Whatever shape the container is, the liquid fills that shape, from the bottom up. A gas doesn't have a definite shape or volume. It expands to take up whatever space is available. Think about balloons. When you blow up a balloon, no matter what its shape, the gas you blow into it takes that shape.

States of matter differ due to the ways their particles (atoms or molecules) are arranged and the ways they move. In a solid, the particles are packed close together and vibrate in place. As a result, a solid is rigid. In a liquid, the particles are farther apart. They are able to move a little, so liquids change shape and flow. The particles will stay relatively close together. In a gas, the particles are far apart. They move rapidly, always getting farther apart until something stops them. They expand to fill whatever space is available. At room temperature, carbon is a solid. Neon is a gas.

Focus Skill MAIN IDEA AND DETAILS

How are particles arranged in solids, liquids, and gases?

This toy truck is made of solid pieces that keep their own shapes and volumes. ▼

These paints are liquids that take the shapes of their cans. ▼

Air is a mixture of gases that expand to fill the balloons. ▼

Essential Question

What Is the Structure of Matter?

In this lesson, you learned that matter has mass and takes up space. You learned that matter is made up of atoms, and you also learned about the elements that make up all matter.

1. 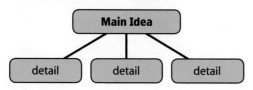 **MAIN IDEA AND DETAILS** Draw and complete a graphic organizer that shows supporting details for the states and structures of matter.

Main Idea
detail   detail   detail

2. **SUMMARIZE** Write a one-paragraph summary about the organization of the periodic table of elements.

3. **DRAW CONCLUSIONS** What is the difference between an atom and an element?

4. **VOCABULARY** Define *molecule*, and give an example.

Test Prep

5. **CRITICAL THINKING** Tell why the periodic table is useful.

6. Aaron looks at four elements in the periodic table—aluminum, silicon, phosphorus, and sulfur (atomic numbers 13–16). What can he correctly say about them?
   A. Aluminum has the fewest protons.
   B. They are all nonmetals.
   C. Their symbols are Al, Si, Ph, and Su.
   D. They are all gases at room temperature.

Make Connections

 Writing

Expository Writing

Write a conversation between an oxygen atom and a carbon atom. Have them discuss ways they are alike and ways they are different. Write your conversation in **play** form, and have actors perform it.

 Math

Draw a Diagram

Find magnesium and sulfur on the periodic table. Draw a diagram of each atom. How many more protons are in the nucleus of sulfur than magnesium?

 Health

Essential Minerals

Study the nutritional labels on cereal boxes. Find the names of some elements that are needed for good health. How much of each of these elements does a serving of one kind of cereal provide?

Essential Question

What Are Physical Properties and Changes?

Investigate the different physical states of water.

Read and learn different physical characteristics and properties of matter.

Fast Fact

3, 2, 1, Blastoff!
Even on a cold day, this geyser blasts a cloud of hot water and steam into the air. It erupts because water from rain and snow trickles underground, where hot rocks turn it to steam. Then it expands—and explodes! The steam melts the snow and starts all over again. In the Investigate, you'll explore how other changes in water are caused by changes in temperature.

physical change [FIZ•ih•kuhl CHAYNJ] A change in which the form of a substance changes, but the substance still has the same chemical makeup (p. 534)

density [DEN•suh•tee] The measure of how closely packed an object's atoms are (p. 537)

mixture [MIKS•chuhr] A combination of two or more different substances (p. 538)

solution [suh•LOO•shuhn] A mixture in which all the parts are mixed evenly (p. 539)

Geyser at Yellowstone National Park in Wyoming

Changing States of Matter

Start with Questions

At different temperatures, water can be either a liquid, a solid, or a gas.

- How can you tell if water is a solid, a liquid, or a gas?

- Why is this ice melting?

Investigate to find out. Then read and learn to find out more.

Prepare to Investigate

Inquiry Skill Tip

When you compare measurements that you made during an investigation, don't expect the masses and temperatures that you record to be exact. Differences occur because of the way you make a measurement or because the balance isn't precise. If you think a measurement is wrong, repeat it several times.

Materials

- 2 ice cubes
- measuring cup
- plastic spoon
- balance
- zip-top plastic bag
- hot plate
- glass beaker
- cold water
- thermometer
- safety goggles

Make an Observation Chart

	Temperature (°C)	Mass (g)	Inference
Bag of ice cubes			
Bag of melted water			
Boiling water			

Follow This Procedure

1. Place the ice cubes in the beaker. Add 1 cup of cold water.

2. Stir with the plastic spoon. Use the thermometer to **measure** and **record** the temperature.

3. Pour the contents of the beaker into the zip-top bag. Seal the bag.

4. Use the balance to **measure** the mass of the bag and its contents. **Record the data.**

5. Set the bag in a warm place. Leave it there until the cubes disappear. **Infer** what happened to the cubes. **Record** your inference.

6. Repeat Step 4.

7. Pour the contents of the bag back into the beaker. Repeat Step 2.

8. CAUTION: **Put on safety goggles.**

   Your teacher will boil the water and measure its temperature. **Record data** and **inferences**.

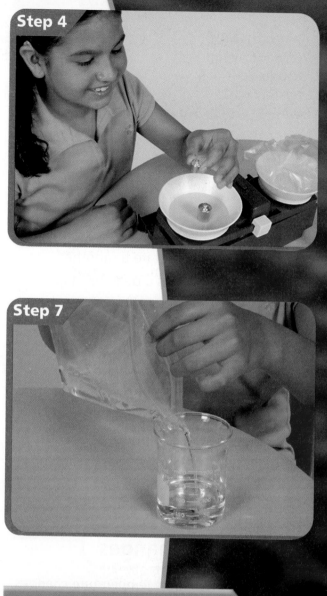
Step 4

Step 7

Draw Conclusions

1. Water can exist in three states: solid, liquid, and gas. Use your data to tell the temperatures at which water changes state.

2. **Inquiry Skill** Use your data to **compare** the mass of the bag and its contents before and after the ice melted.

Independent Inquiry

Pour 1 cup of water into each of two different containers. Leave them out until the water disappears. Where did the water go? Hypothesize why the water disappeared from one sooner than it did from the other.

VOCABULARY
physical change p. 534
density p. 537
mixture p. 538
solution p. 539

SCIENCE CONCEPTS
▶ how matter changes state
▶ how mixtures and solutions differ

COMPARE AND CONTRAST

Look for physical changes in matter.

| alike | | different |

Changing States of Matter

In the Investigate, you showed that water can change from one state to another. Solid water is ice. It has a definite shape and volume. Liquid water flows and takes the shape of its container, but it still has a definite volume. Water as a gas is called *water vapor*. In this state, water disappears into the air. You caused the changes in state by changing the temperature.

A change in state is a **physical change**, a change in which the substance itself is still the same substance. Its form changes, but its chemical makeup doesn't. Follow the arrows to see the *processes* that cause physical changes:

- At 0°C (32°F), ice *melts*. It changes from a solid to a liquid.
- At 100°C (212°F), liquid water *boils*. It changes from a liquid to a gas.

Now look at the processes in the other direction:

- At 100°C (212°F), water vapor *condenses* to form liquid water.
- At 0°C (32°F), liquid water *freezes* to form a solid.

Water Changes

When its temperature changes, water can change from a solid to a liquid to a gas and back again.

melting

freezing

534

Infer how solid carbon dioxide, or "dry ice," can be made from carbon dioxide gas.

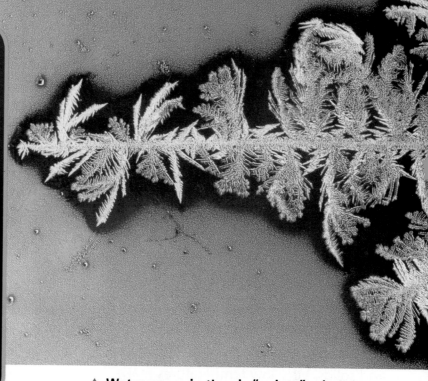

▲ Water vapor in the air "paints" windows in winter, but no liquid is needed.

The pictures show that 0°C is both the *melting point* and the *freezing point* of water. Whether the temperature is a melting point or a freezing point depends on which state the water is changing to. The pictures also show that 100°C is both the *boiling point* and the *condensing point* of water. Again, the temperature is a boiling point if the water is changing from liquid to gas, but it's the condensing point if the water is changing from gas to liquid.

Some solids and gases can change state without forming liquids. On a cold window, water vapor from the air *deposits* onto the glass as a solid—frost.

The solid form of carbon dioxide, called "dry ice," *sublimes* (suh•BLYMZ). To *sublime* means "to change from a solid to a gas without becoming a liquid." Carbon dioxide and water are two substances that can sublime.

boiling

condensing

 COMPARE AND CONTRAST

How are melting and freezing alike?

How are condensing and boiling different?

Melting and Boiling Points

Hold an aluminum soft-drink can in your hand. Look at it and feel it. What is its state of matter? Run some water through your fingers. What is its state of matter? Take a deep breath. Feel your chest expand. What state of matter did you pull into your lungs?

It's hard to think about some solids, such as aluminum, becoming liquid or gas. But aluminum can change states. At very high temperatures, aluminum melts.

Also, substances that are gases at room temperature can be changed into liquids and solids. Very low temperatures make these things happen.

You have learned that water's melting point is 0°C and its boiling point is 100°C. Melting point and boiling point are *physical properties* that describe matter. State of matter is also a physical property.

Some substances, such as salt and aluminum, have high melting and boiling points. It takes high temperatures to turn salt or aluminum into a liquid or a gas. It also takes extreme conditions to turn nitrogen gas into a liquid or a solid. Nitrogen has low melting and boiling points.

Melting points are always lower than boiling points, but be careful not to think of one as "cold" and the other as "hot." For nitrogen, for example, both numbers are well below 0°C. The difference between them isn't always large, either. For nitrogen, the difference is only 14°C (57°F).

COMPARE AND CONTRAST

How are melting and boiling points alike? How are they different?

Which substance has the greatest difference between melting and boiling points?

At very high temperatures, aluminum melts. ▼

Math in Science
Interpret Data

Melting and Boiling Points

■ melting point
■ boiling point

Water   Table Salt   Aluminum

Nitrogen boils at very low temperatures. ▼

536

Copper is denser than aluminum. Aluminum is denser than wood. These cubes all have the same volume. Which has the greatest mass? ▼

wood

copper

aluminum

Density

Think about going to the grocery store. You see lettuce on sale for one dollar a head. All the heads of lettuce are about the same size. They have the same volume. Which head should you choose? Put the lettuce heads on the grocer's scale. Some have more weight and mass than others, even though their volumes are the same.

Density is a measure of how closely packed an object's atoms are. It shows the relationship between mass and volume. To find density, divide the mass by the volume. The larger the volume for the same mass, the less dense an object is. So, the greater the mass for the same volume, the greater the density.

Like melting point, boiling point, and physical state, density is a physical property of matter. Density is a useful idea in science, because most substances, unlike lettuce, have densities that don't change. A solid cube of copper that measures 1 cm (0.4 in.)

corn oil

water

shampoo

dish soap

anti-freeze

maple syrup

▲ Less-dense liquids float on denser ones.

on each side has a mass of about 9 g (0.3 oz). A block of twice that volume has a mass of 18 g (0.6 oz). A block of three times that volume has a mass of 27 g (1.0 oz). Do you see the pattern? For solid copper, the mass is always 9 times the volume. Or, looking at it the other way, the volume is always $\frac{1}{9}$ of the mass.

Every substance has its own density. In fact, if you know that a substance is an element, you can figure out which element it is just by knowing its density.

COMPARE AND CONTRAST How is density different from mass and volume?

Mixtures and Solutions

If you put a teaspoon of sugar in some water and stir, what happens? What happens if you use sand instead of sugar?

In both cases, you mixed two substances together. A **mixture** is a combination of two or more substances. The substances in a mixture aren't permanently combined and their properties don't change. The substances can be separated from the mixture and be the same as they were before they were mixed.

For example, you can separate the sugar and water by boiling. The water passes into the air as water vapor. The sugar remains in the pot. How can you separate the sand and water?

Most materials found in nature are mixtures. Sand at the beach is a mixture of rocks, broken shells, and other materials. You can separate the materials on the beach by sifting or by other methods. The individual pieces keep their original properties.

Think back to the sand-and-water mixture. Is the sand evenly distributed throughout the water, or is it concentrated in certain areas? The substances in a mixture aren't always evenly distributed. You can see that sand and water form a mixture. The parts look different. You can see the sand sink to the bottom.

Some mixtures, however, blend so well that it is hard to see all the different parts.

Mixing solids such as cement, gravel, and sand with water forms concrete. ▼

▲ A solid and a liquid can make a solution that's good enough to drink.

▲ Salad dressing is a mixture of oil, vinegar, and herbs.

The sugar-and-water mixture looks as if it's only water. The sugar seems to disappear. A mixture in which all parts are mixed evenly is called a **solution**. Solutions can be combinations of gases, liquids, and solids.

Focus Skill COMPARE AND CONTRAST

How is a solution different from a mixture?

◀ Two or more liquids can make a mixture.

Insta-Lab

Is It a Solution?
Half-fill two small jars with water. Add a teaspoon of raw, unrefined sugar to each. Let one jar sit. Stir the other jar with a plastic spoon for one minute. What do you observe? How can you explain what you see?

Gases in Air

Oxygen 21%

Other gases 1%

Nitrogen 78%

A scuba diver's tank contains air—a solution of gases. Use the graph to tell what they are. ▼

This solution is a mixture of a liquid and a gas. ▼

539

Other Physical Changes

Suppose you cut down a tree, remove the bark, and make a baseball bat. This change is physical. The wood is still wood. Only its form has changed.

What other physical changes do you encounter every day? If you break a glass bottle, it's still glass. If you knit a sweater, the wool is still wool. If you paint a plastic model, the paint is still paint and the plastic is still plastic.

Physical changes are all around us: breaking, crushing, cutting, bending, melting, freezing, and boiling. Some physical changes happen naturally. Water evaporates from puddles. Rain falls and causes puddles to form again. Some physical changes are caused by people. We use physical changes to do helpful things. At a paper-recycling plant, for example, used paper is shredded, mashed with water to make a pulp, and pressed to make new paper. The paper is still paper. Only its form is different. At a metal-recycling plant, used aluminum cans are crushed and melted and the liquid is poured into molds to make new cans. The aluminum is still the same metal, but a physical change makes it useful again.

Focus Skill COMPARE AND CONTRAST

How are all physical changes alike?

▲ **What physical change has happened to these aluminum cans?**

Cutting paper is a physical change. ▼

What Are Physical Properties and Changes?

In this lesson, you learned that matter can change states at different temperatures. You also learned about solutions, mixtures, density, and some other ways that matter can change physically, such as breaking, crushing, and bending.

1.  Draw and complete a graphic organizer comparing and contrasting the different states of matter.

alike ——— different

2. SUMMARIZE Write a one-paragraph summary of the differences between a mixture and a solution.

3. DRAW CONCLUSIONS If two pure substances have the same density, are they the same substance? Explain.

4. VOCABULARY Define *physical change*, and give an example.

Test Prep

5. CRITICAL THINKING All solutions are mixtures, but not all mixtures are solutions. Explain why.

6. You find that the density of solid silver is 10.5 g/cm³. How would its density as a liquid and a gas compare?

   A. less as a liquid, more as a gas

   B. less as a liquid, less as a gas

   C. more as a liquid, less as a gas

   D. more as a liquid, more as a gas

Make Connections

 Writing

Expository Writing
Find out about the density of the Dead Sea. Then write a one-paragraph **explanation** of why swimmers don't sink in it.

 Math

Make a Bar Graph
Gold's melting point is 1064°C, and its boiling point is 2808°C. Use this data to make a bar graph for gold like the graph on page 536. What does your graph tell you?

 Social Studies

Recycling
Visit a recycling plant, or invite someone from a recycling center to visit your class and answer your questions. Find out why some materials are easier to recycle than others.

LESSON
3

Essential Question

What Are Chemical Properties and Changes?

Investigate the chemical properties of different household items.

Read and learn what a chemical change is and how matter is conserved in this process.

Fast Fact

Match-Making

When it comes to chemistry, matches can't be matched! It takes more than 30 ingredients to make a match flammable, or able to burn. Some matches are made with the elements phosphorus, potassium, chlorine, and oxygen. Burning is one sign of a chemical reaction. In the Investigate, you will look for other signs of chemical reactions.

542

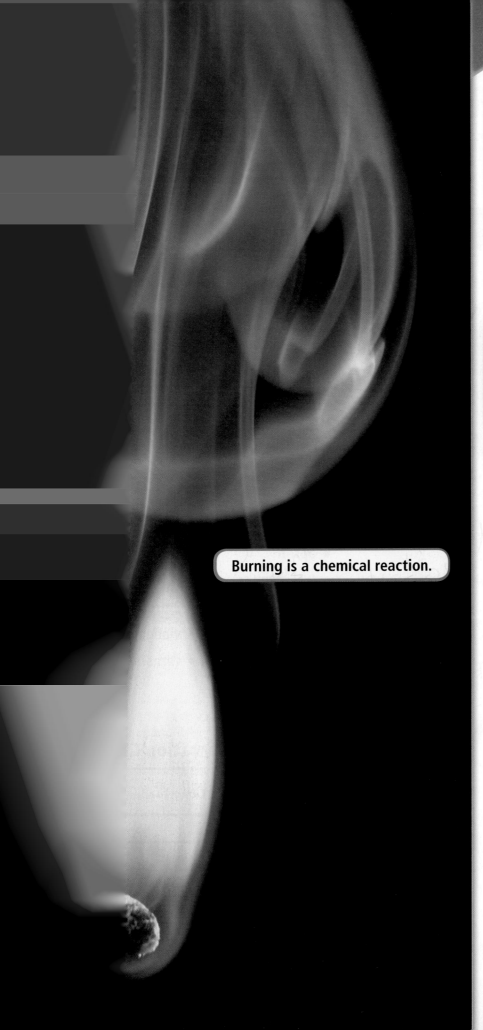

Burning is a chemical reaction.

combustibility [kuhm•buhs•tuh•BIL•uh•tee] A measure of how easily a substance will burn (p. 546)

reactivity [ree•ak•TIV•uh•tee] The ability of a substance to go through a chemical change (p. 547)

543

Chemical Properties

Start with Questions

Household chemicals have properties, just like chemicals that scientists use.

- What is the difference between a chemical change and a physical change?

- Is the rust on this car caused by a physical change or a chemical change?

Investigate to find out. Then read and learn to find out more.

Prepare to Investigate

Inquiry Skill Tip

Think about causes and effects when you infer why something happens in an investigation. Make a list of causes. These may be things that you change or procedures that occur during the investigation. Next to each cause, write the effect, or what happens because of the cause.

Materials

- apron
- 9 test tubes
- baking soda
- water
- iodine solution
- baby powder
- safety goggles
- 3 plastic spoons
- 3 droppers
- vinegar
- cornstarch

Make an Observation Chart

	Baking Soda	Cornstarch	Baby Powder
Water			
Vinegar			
Iodine			

Follow This Procedure

① **CAUTION: Wear an apron and safety goggles for the entire investigation.**

② Label one test tube *water*, a second *vinegar*, and a third *iodine*. Use a plastic spoon to put a *tiny* bit of baking soda in each of these test tubes.

③ To the first test tube, add 3 drops of water. Record your observations.

④ To the second test tube, add 3 drops of vinegar. Record your observations.

⑤ To the third test tube, add 3 drops of iodine solution. Record your observations.

⑥ Using a clean spoon, put a tiny bit of cornstarch in each of 3 test tubes. Repeat Steps 3–5.

⑦ Using a clean spoon, put a tiny bit of baby powder in each of 3 test tubes. Repeat Steps 3–5.

Draw Conclusions

1. What effect did vinegar have on the baking soda? Did any other combination show the same effect?

2. **Inquiry Skill** In which combinations of a solid with a liquid can you infer that a chemical change took place? Explain.

Step 2

Step 3

Independent Inquiry

Get a "mystery powder" from your teacher. Test with liquids, and use your observations to infer what the powder actually is.

VOCABULARY
combustibility p. 546
reactivity p. 547

SCIENCE CONCEPTS
▶ what a chemical change is
▶ how matter is conserved when it changes chemically

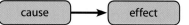
CAUSE AND EFFECT

Look for what a chemical change is and what causes one.

cause ⟶ effect

Chemical Changes

A match burns. A solution bubbles. Two substances mixed together turn a color different from either of them. These events are evidence that a chemical change may have taken place. Chemical changes are different from physical changes. They change the chemical nature and properties of substances to form new substances.

Toasting marshmallows is a good example. If you warm a marshmallow only enough to melt it, you cause a physical change. The marshmallow changes its form but not its chemical makeup. If you burn the marshmallow, however, you change

it into another substance. This change is a *chemical reaction*. Oxygen from the air combines with carbon in the marshmallow to form carbon dioxide gas and water vapor. The black, burned area on the marshmallow is carbon. Such a change is burning, or *combustion*. The **combustibility** (kuhm•buhs•tuh•BIL•uh•tee) of a substance is a measure of how easily it will burn, or combine rapidly with oxygen.

Another kind of chemical change is the corrosion (kuh•ROH•zhuhn) of metal. When iron combines with oxygen in the air, rust forms. The rust is a brand new substance.

▲ Is the melting of chocolate a chemical change?

These burned marshmallows have gone through a chemical change. ▶

It's a combination of iron and oxygen with properties different from either of them. A chemical change has taken place.

Corrosion is chemical change in a metal. The Statue of Liberty is made of iron and copper. For a century, it corroded in the damp environment of New York Harbor. It had to be closed to the public from 1984 to 1986 so that it could be repaired and restored.

Sometimes, gas bubbles show that a chemical change has taken place. Have you ever poured hydrogen peroxide on a cut? If you have, you may have noticed the wound bubbling. The peroxide reacts with blood and releases oxygen gas. The ability of a substance to go through a chemical change is its **reactivity**. Peroxide is very reactive.

A change in color may also tell you that a chemical change has occurred. Fireworks are a good example. When substances with copper in them burn, they release blue light. Substances with aluminum make white light. Strontium makes red light, and barium makes green light.

The Statue of Liberty stood for nearly 100 years before corrosion forced the landmark to be closed for repairs. ▶

▲ Hydrogen peroxide reacts with raw meat, forming bubbles.

Some chemical changes produce explosions and colored light. ▼

Focus Skill **CAUSE AND EFFECT**

What is the effect of a chemical change?

Insta-Lab

Shining Pennies
Put a dull, brown penny in a dish. Pour some white vinegar on it. Watch closely for several minutes. What do you observe? Rinse the penny with water, and dry it with a soft cloth. What happened? Why?

Conservation of Matter

Chemical changes don't make new matter. They only make new products from the substances that react. For example, when you dropped vinegar onto baking soda, you saw bubbles. They were bubbles of carbon dioxide gas. A chemical reaction between the vinegar and the baking soda caused them.

Suppose you calculated the mass of the vinegar and the baking soda before you combined them. Suppose also that after the reaction, you found the mass of the liquid in the jar, *plus* the mass of the carbon dioxide gas. (It takes some work to find the mass of a gas, but it can be done!) You would get the same number for the two masses. The total mass of the products that form equals the total mass of the substances that react. This is the *law of conservation of matter.*

When iron corrodes, it gains mass, so it might appear that the chemical change made more mass. But you must take into account the mass of the oxygen in the air that combined with the iron to form the rust. When you do, you find that the two amounts are the same. Matter is conserved.

A marshmallow has less mass after it is burned than it did before. Was matter destroyed? No. It went into the air as water vapor and carbon dioxide gas. The mass of the burned marshmallow plus the mass that became a gas is the same as the mass of the marshmallow before it was burned.

CAUSE AND EFFECT

What is the effect of a chemical change on the mass of matter?

What happens to the mass of a glow stick when a chemical reaction causes it to light? ▼

Essential Question

What Are Chemical Properties and Changes?

In this lesson, you learned that chemical changes are different from physical changes. A chemical change forms a new substance. You also learned about chemical properties such as combustibility and reactivity.

1. 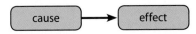 **CAUSE AND EFFECT** Draw and complete a graphic organizer that shows the effects of different chemical properties.

cause → effect

2. **SUMMARIZE** Write a one-paragraph summary about the conservation of matter.

3. **DRAW CONCLUSIONS** Is a highly combustible substance also a highly reactive substance? Explain.

4. **VOCABULARY** Write a dictionary entry for each vocabulary term.

Test Prep

5. **CRITICAL THINKING** Explain why burning paper is a chemical change but cutting it isn't.

6. Which is the **best** statement of the law of conservation of matter?

   A. The law requires citizens to recycle aluminum and paper.

   B. The volume of an apple doesn't change if you cut it into pieces.

   C. A chemical change doesn't change the amount of matter.

   D. Masses and volumes of two samples of a pure substance are the same.

Make Connections

 Writing

Expository Writing
Write an **explanation** of why burning a candle is a chemical change.

 Math

Solve a Problem
If 56 g of iron reacts with oxygen to produce 80 g of rusted iron, what is the mass of the oxygen that reacts?

 Social Studies

History
Find out about the life and work of the scientist Antoine Lavoisier. Report what you learn to your class.

Claudia Benitez-Nelson

▶ **CLAUDIA BENITEZ-NELSON**

▶ Associate Professor of Chemical Oceanography at the University of South Carolina

Global warming has the potential to affect how and where people will live in the future. Claudia Benitez-Nelson is one of the scientists leading the effort to understand this complex phenomenon.

Benitez-Nelson, a chemist at the University of South Carolina, researches how carbon moves through oceans. This element is analyzed and is used to predict changes in Earth's climate. For example, increases in atmospheric carbon dioxide are linked to the increase in Earth's temperatures commonly known as global warming. Oceans absorb some carbon dioxide from the atmosphere when tiny marine organisms make their own food through photosynthesis. Thus, oceans play a role in keeping Earth's temperatures stable.

Benitez-Nelson wants to know how much carbon is used during photosynthesis and where the carbon goes. She measures the changes in the amount of carbon found in oceans. Like all true scientists, Benitez-Nelson has found that her questions lead to still more questions. Her research has expanded her knowledge, so that this chemist now works comfortably as a physicist, biologist, meteorologist, and oceanographer.

 Think and Write

1. How do oceans help keep Earth's temperatures stable? Why is this important?

2. Why would it be helpful for a scientist such as Benitez-Nelson to know several fields of study?

Yuan Tseh Lee

► **YUAN TSEH LEE**

► Former researcher at Lawrence Berkeley Lab
► Won Nobel Prize for work on chemical reactions

As a student in Taiwan, Yuan T. Lee was a serious reader. He was very inspired by a biography of Marie Curie. Her dedication to science and her belief that science could make the world better convinced Lee to be a scientist.

In 1986, Lee and two other scientists won the Nobel Prize for their study of chemical reactions. After winning the prize, Lee returned to Taiwan to help that country develop. He thinks scientists and researchers at universities should be concerned about the future of humankind. "We need to become good citizens in the global village instead of competing," he said. He thinks we should be researching things that will make people's lives better and help the world become safer.

 ## Think and Write

1 How do you think Marie Curie's ideas affected Yuan Lee?

2 What kinds of things do chemical researchers study the most?

Career Chemical Manufacturer

A chemical manufacturer produces chemicals that are used by other manufacturers to make products. Making chemicals can be a risky business. Some chemicals can be dangerous if they are mixed with other chemicals or are not stored correctly.

Vocabulary Review

Use the terms below to complete the sentences. The page numbers tell you where to look in the chapter if you need help.

atom p. 524

molecule p. 524

nucleus p. 525

periodic table p. 526

element p. 526

density p. 537

solution p. 539

combustibility p. 546

1. How easily and quickly a substance burns is its _____.

2. Two or more atoms joined together make up a _____.

3. The relationship of the mass of a substance to its volume is its _____.

4. A chart of the elements is the _____.

5. The dense center of an atom is its _____.

6. Matter made of only one kind of atom is an _____.

7. A mixture in which all the parts are mixed evenly is a _____.

8. The smallest particle that still behaves like the matter it came from is an _____.

Check Understanding

Write the letter of the best choice.

9. **MAIN IDEA AND DETAILS** The element zinc is atomic number 30 in the periodic table. Of which kind of particle does zinc have 30?
   A. atoms
   B. electrons
   C. neutrons
   D. protons

10. **CAUSE AND EFFECT** How do the melting point and the freezing point of a substance compare?
   F. They are the same.
   G. The melting point is hot, and the freezing point is cold.
   H. The freezing point is higher than the melting point.
   J. They occur only at high temperatures.

11. A substance has less mass after a chemical change than it had before. What is the most likely cause?
   A. The chemical change destroyed matter.
   B. The matter was cut into pieces, and some of the pieces were removed.
   C. Some matter went into the air as a gas.
   D. The matter rusted.

12. Which of the following is a **true** statement about matter?

    F. All substances are pure elements.

    G. Liquids have more atoms than gases have.

    H. All matter is made up of tiny, invisible particles.

    J. Physical changes and chemical changes are the same thing.

13. How many elements does a mixture of iron, copper, and zinc contain?

    A. 1   **C.** 3

    B. 2   **D.** 4

14. What kind of change is grinding chalk into a powder?

    F. chemical   **H.** physical

    G. combustion   **J.** reaction

15. If you take a water molecule apart, what do you get?

    A. atoms   **C.** mixtures

    B. molecules   **D.** solutions

16. More matter can be added easily to a container full of matter in which state?

    F. liquid   **H.** solid

    G. gas   **J.** solution

Inquiry Skills

17. Use a model (a drawing) to show how a molecule can contain two atoms but only one element.

18. Two scientists claim that they can use a chemical reaction to make matter. How would you **communicate** the reason they're wrong?

Critical Thinking

19. Which is denser, a cup of feathers or a cup of pennies? Why?

20. You have two substances. The atoms of both substances have the same number of protons in the nucleus. Are the substances the same element? Explain. The atoms of one substance have a different atomic number from the atoms of the other substance. Are the substances the same element? Explain.

The **Big** Idea

CHAPTER 15 Energy

What's the Big Idea?

Energy exists in many forms and can be changed from one form to another.

Essential Questions

Lesson 1

What Are Kinetic and Potential Energy?

Lesson 2

What Are Some Forms of Energy?

Lesson 3

How Is Heat Transferred?

Lesson 4

How Do People Use Energy Resources?

GO online Student eBook www.hspscience.com

554

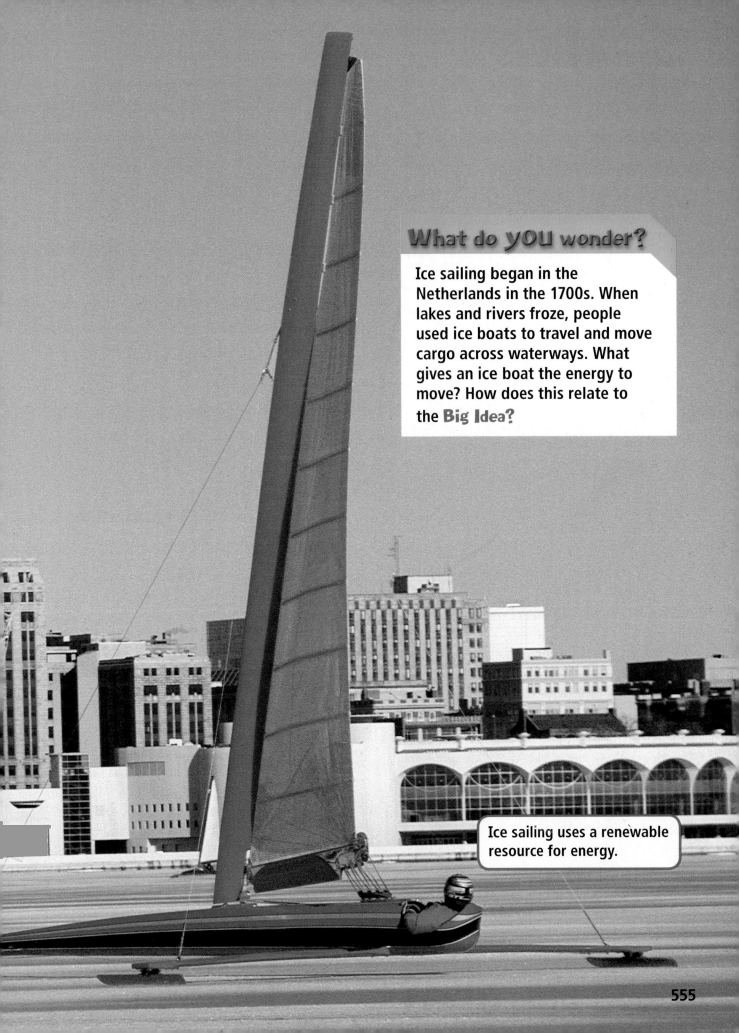

Ice sailing began in the Netherlands in the 1700s. When lakes and rivers froze, people used ice boats to travel and move cargo across waterways. What gives an ice boat the energy to move? How does this relate to the **Big Idea**?

Ice sailing uses a renewable resource for energy.

Investigate the relationship between potential and kinetic energy.

Read and learn about energy, kinetic energy, and potential energy.

Essential Question

What Are Kinetic and Potential Energy?

Fast Fact

Bull's-eye!

The farther back an archer pulls the bow, the more energy the arrow has when it's released. Some Olympic archers can score a bull's-eye from 90 m (295 ft) away. The arrow must hit the target before it falls too far. In the Investigate, you'll explore factors that affect how objects fall.

This arrow has potential energy.

energy [EN•er•jee] The ability to cause changes in matter (p. 560)

kinetic energy [kih•NET•ik EN•er•jee] The energy of motion (p. 562)

potential energy [poh•TEN•shuhl EN•er•jee] The energy an object has because of its condition or position (p. 562)

energy transfer [EN•er•jee TRANS•fer] Movement of energy from one place or object to another (p. 564)

Going Up!

Start with Questions

A skier standing still at the top of a hill has a lot of potential energy, but no kinetic energy.

- What is the difference between these two kinds of energy?

- Does this golfer have kinetic energy or potential energy?

Investigate to find out. Then read to find out more.

Prepare to Investigate

Inquiry Skill Tip

When you draw conclusions, first review the record you made of your observations, and then consider what the observations mean. If you have difficulty drawing conclusions, discuss your results with other students.

Materials

- paper strip, 100 cm long
- tape measure
- tape
- colored pencils
- rubber ball

Make an Observation Chart

Drop Height	Trial	Height of Bounce (cm)
50 cm	1	
	2	
	3	
100 cm	1	
	2	
	3	

Follow This Procedure

1 Work with a partner. Tape the paper to the wall as shown. Using the tape measure, mark the paper strip at 10-cm intervals. Start with 0 cm at the floor, and end with 100 cm at the top.

2 Have your partner hold the ball next to the 50-cm mark. You should sit facing the paper, with your eyes at the level of the 50-cm mark.

3 Have your partner drop the ball while you **observe** how high it bounces. **Record** the height with a colored mark on the paper.

4 Repeat Steps 2 and 3 two more times. **Record** each height in a different color.

5 Switch roles with your partner. This time, drop the ball from the 100-cm mark and **record** the height. Repeat twice.

Draw Conclusions

1. How did your results change when you dropped the ball from 100 cm?

2. **Inquiry Skill** For this experiment, you dropped the ball from 50 cm and 100 cm. **Draw conclusions** about what was different when you dropped the ball from 100 cm.

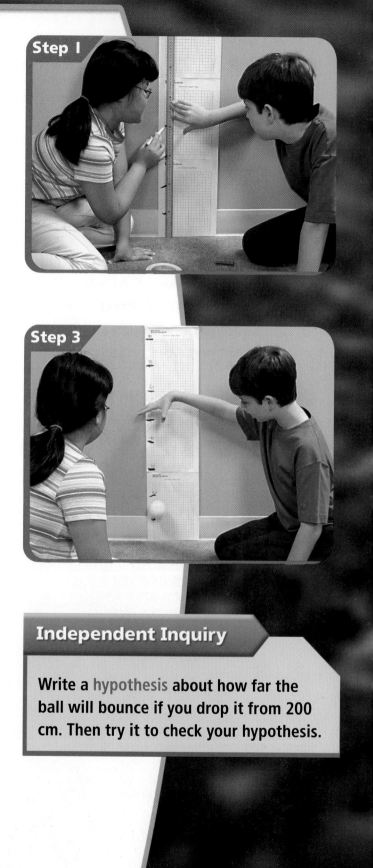

Step 1

Step 3

Independent Inquiry

Write a **hypothesis** about how far the ball will bounce if you drop it from 200 cm. Then try it to check your hypothesis.

VOCABULARY
energy p. 560
kinetic energy p. 562
potential energy p. 562
energy transfer p. 564

SCIENCE CONCEPTS
▶ how kinetic energy differs from potential energy

COMPARE AND CONTRAST

Look for similarities and differences between potential energy and kinetic energy.

alike ━━━ different

Energy

Sometimes a simple word can be hard to define. For example, how would you define the word *show*? You've probably used it often but haven't thought much about its meaning. A common word is often used in different ways.

Defining common words can be especially difficult in science. Some words are so ordinary that people use them without thinking. And the words used in science may have several everyday meanings. But scientists need specific definitions.

For example, think about the word *energy*. You might say after school that you don't have enough energy to do your chores. This personal feeling about energy is not based on the scientific definition. Scientists define **energy** as the ability to cause a change in matter.

The energy from this falling ice produces a big splash, a movement of the water.

One kind of change is movement, or a change in position. Does the glacier in the photograph have energy? Since part of it is moving, a scientist would say it has energy.

The race car in the photo is also moving, so it has energy. But where does its energy come from? A car can't just make the energy it needs. This is part of the *law of conservation of energy.* The law states that energy can never be made or destroyed, but it can change forms.

The race car's engine changes the energy stored in gasoline into movement. The car moves, or changes position, because one form of energy changes into another. This happens with many machines.

The vollyeball player below is giving energy to the ball, making it move. Where does the volleyball player get this energy? It comes from inside his body, from the food he eats. During a hard game, he may feel that he lacks energy because he is tired. In the scientific sense, though, he has energy.

People use the energy stored in food to move, to talk, and even to sleep. Energy stored in food is used in the body for all life processes and also for making the body and objects move.

(Focus Skill) COMPARE AND CONTRAST How is the everyday use of the word *energy* different from the way a scientist uses the word?

The volleyball player's muscles provide the energy for the ball to move. ▼

▲ **The car's engine provides the energy to move the car forward on the track.**

Kinetic and Potential Energy

There are many forms of energy and many ways to classify them. One way divides all forms into two groups: kinetic energy and potential energy.

Kinetic energy is the energy of motion. If something is moving, it has kinetic energy. The faster an object is moving, the more kinetic energy it has. An airplane flying through the air has more kinetic energy than a person riding a bicycle.

Potential energy is the energy an object has because of its condition or position. For example, the higher an object is, the more potential energy it has. So, a ball on the roof of a building has more potential energy than a ball on your desk, because it can fall farther.

Think about a book on a shelf. It has the potential to move down if it falls off the shelf, so it has potential energy. If it did fall and hit the floor, it would no longer have the same amount of potential energy.

An object can have potential and kinetic energy at the same time. As the book falls from the shelf, it loses potential energy and gains kinetic energy.

As the roller coaster car in the photo moves to the top of a hill, it gains potential energy. The higher the car rises, the more potential energy it has. When the car moves down, it has kinetic energy. As it falls, its kinetic energy increases and its potential energy decreases.

The other photo shows a boy jumping up and down on a pogo stick. When he first jumps onto the pogo stick, he is moving down, so he has kinetic energy. Other things also happen when he moves down.

Is the roller coaster car gaining potential energy or using kinetic energy?

As he moves down, the spring in the pogo stick compresses. This adds potential energy to the spring.

At the bottom of the jump, the boy is not moving, so he has no kinetic energy. But the spring's potential energy transfers to him. It moves him up, so he has kinetic energy.

At the top of the jump, the boy stops moving. He has no kinetic energy, but he has potential energy. As he moves down the potential energy changes back to kinetic energy.

Focus Skill COMPARE AND CONTRAST

How is kinetic energy different from potential energy?

◀ As the boy goes up and down, sometimes he has potential energy, sometimes he has kinetic energy, and sometimes he has both.

Insta-Lab

Energy Release

Balance a ruler on top of a pencil. Place a small wad of paper on one end. Push the other end down quickly. When did you add potential energy? When did you see the effect of kinetic energy?

563

Energy Transfer

Energy can move between places or objects, as shown in this picture. In the picture, an acrobat is standing still on a teeterboard. He has no kinetic energy, and he doesn't have potential energy.

There is also a man flying through the air. He's moving, so now he has kinetic energy. What will happen when he lands on the teeterboard? His kinetic energy will be transferred to the other acrobat. When he drops, he will push his end of the teeterboard down. This will give potential energy to the first acrobat as the teeterboard raises up. He will also gain kinetic energy and be launched off the teeterboard.

Energy transfer is the movement of energy from one place or object to another. In the circus act, energy moved from the first acrobat to the second. Remember the boy on the pogo stick? His kinetic energy was transferred to the spring, where it changed into potential energy. As the spring expanded, that potential energy was transferred to the boy as kinetic energy, bouncing him into the air.

 COMPARE AND CONTRAST

How is the circus teeterboard like the spring in the pogo stick?

What would happen if the acrobat dropped onto the side of the teeterboard that was on the ground? Would the teeterboard transfer any of the energy? ▼

Essential Question

What Are Kinetic and Potential Energy?

In this lesson, you learned that energy is the ability to cause change in matter. You also learned that all energy can be classified into two categories: potential and kinetic. Energy can also be transferred between places or objects.

1. **COMPARE AND CONTRAST** Draw and complete a graphic organizer comparing and contrasting potential and kinetic energy.

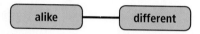

alike —— different

2. **SUMMARIZE** Write a one-paragraph summary about energy transfers.

3. **DRAW CONCLUSIONS** If you throw a baseball, where does the ball's kinetic energy come from?

4. **VOCABULARY** Write a dictionary entry for each vocabulary word.

Test Prep

5. **CRITICAL THINKING** Why does a book on a high shelf have more potential energy than a book on a low shelf?

6. Which has potential energy?
   A. a bike lying on a driveway
   B. a rock at the top of a cliff
   C. a chair sitting on the floor
   D. a baseball lost in the weeds

Make Connections

 Writing

Expository Writing
Your class is making a science video about energy. One part will show a girl playing with a yo-yo. Write the **narration** for this scene, describing the potential and kinetic energy in the yo-yo at any time.

 Math

Compare Numbers
When compressed fully and then released, Spring A sent a 10-kg mass 2 m into the air. Under the same conditions, Spring B sent the mass 8 m into the air. Which spring had more potential energy?

 Language Arts

Definitions
Look up an everyday meaning of the word *potential*. Write a paragraph explaining that meaning and how it relates to potential energy.

Investigate one form of energy.

Read and learn about different forms of energy and changing energy forms.

Essential Question

What Are Some Forms of Energy?

Fast Fact

Cool Lights!

Neon tubes give off light in bright colors, but unlike some light bulbs, they don't get hot. The reaction that takes place in these tubes releases light energy but not much heat. In the Investigate, you'll test another reaction to see if it releases heat.

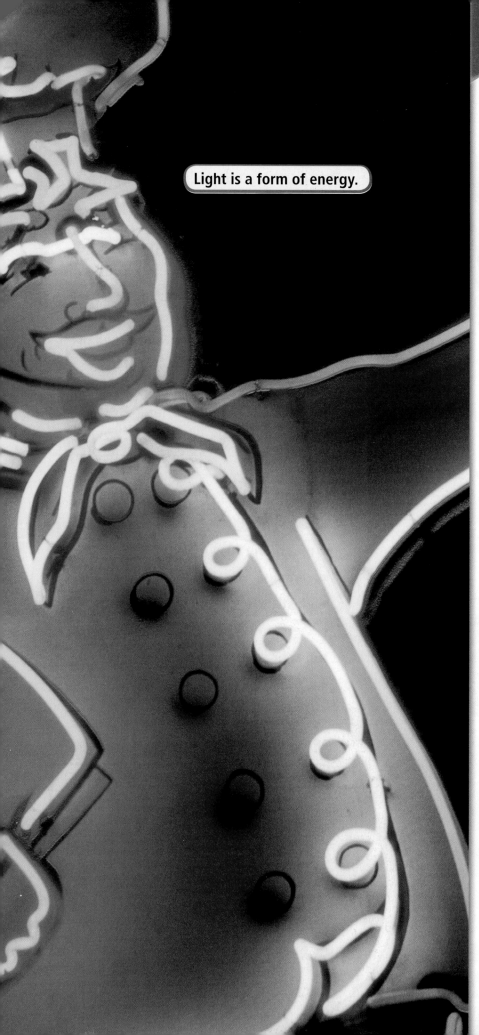

Light is a form of energy.

solar energy [SOH•ler EN•er•jee] Energy that comes from the sun (p. 570)

light [LYT] Radiation that we can see (p. 570)

chemical energy [KEM•ih•kuhl EN•er•jee] Energy that can be released by a chemical reaction (p. 572)

mechanical energy [muh•KAN•ih•kuhl EN•er•jee] The combination of all the kinetic and potential energy that something has (p. 572)

electric energy [ee•LEK•trik EN•er•jee] Energy that comes from an electric current (p. 574)

567

Warmer or Cooler?

Start with Questions

When the sun shines, you can feel it. When a car drives by, you know it is using fuel. Can you see the effects of different kinds of energy?

- What kinds of energy do you use every day?

- What kind of energy does this greenhouse use?

Investigate to find out. Then read and learn to find out more.

Prepare to Investigate

Inquiry Skill Tip

When you make inferences about things that happen during an investigation, consider the causes and effects of changes in variables. Changes in dependent variables are the *effects*, or the results. Changes that you make to the independent variable *cause* the changes in the dependent variable.

Materials

- safety goggles
- measuring cup
- water
- plastic cup
- thermometer
- plastic spoon
- calcium chloride

Make an Observation Chart

Time	Temperature (°C)
Before dissolving calcium chloride	
30 seconds after dissolving	
1 minute after dissolving	
2 minutes after dissolving	

Follow This Procedure

❶ Make a table like the one shown.

CAUTION: Put on safety goggles. Do not touch the calcium chloride.

❷ Measure 50 mL of water, and pour it into the plastic cup.

❸ Using the thermometer, measure the temperature of the water. Then record the temperature in your table.

❹ Add 2 spoonfuls of calcium chloride to the water, and stir until the calcium chloride is dissolved. Wait 30 seconds.

❺ Measure the temperature of the water, and record it in your table.

❻ Repeat Step 5 one minute and two minutes after the calcium chloride has dissolved.

Draw Conclusions

1. How did the temperature of the water change after you added the calcium chloride?

2. **Inquiry Skill** What energy change can you infer takes place when calcium chloride dissolves in water?

Step 4

Step 6

Independent Inquiry

Write a hypothesis about what would happen if you used 100 mL of water. Then plan and conduct a simple investigation to test your hypothesis.

VOCABULARY
solar energy p. 570
light p. 570
chemical energy p. 572
mechanical energy p. 572
electric energy p. 574

SCIENCE CONCEPTS
▶ how to identify and describe different forms of energy
▶ how energy can be changed from one form to another

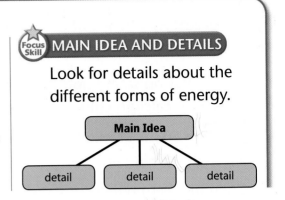

MAIN IDEA AND DETAILS

Look for details about the different forms of energy.

Solar Energy

You have read that all energy can be classified as potential energy or kinetic energy. Scientists also classify energy in other forms. However, the classification of energy you'll read about here isn't as simple as the main division into potential energy and kinetic energy. Sometimes two or more forms of energy overlap.

One form of energy is around you every day. Energy that comes from the sun is called **solar energy**. The word *solar* means "of the sun." People use solar energy in many ways. Do you have a calculator that doesn't need batteries? Many calculators have solar cells that change light energy from the sun into electricity. You'll learn more about electricity, or electric energy, later on.

Other forms of energy come from the sun directly. Energy from the sun travels as *radiation*. The sun produces several kinds of radiation. **Light** is radiation we see, and heat is radiation we feel. X rays and ultraviolet rays also come from the sun. The sun even produces radio waves, which we hear as static on radios.

On a warm, dry day you can feel radiation from the sun. You can also see the effects of radiation changing the temperature of the air.

◀ Most of the heat and hot water for this home comes from the sun's energy, collected by the solar panels on the roof.

Without solar energy, Earth would be just a ball of frozen rock with no life. Heat from the sun allows Earth to support life forms. Light from the sun helps plants make food and oxygen. In fact, the sun is the source of almost all energy on Earth. Its energy is stored in fossil fuels—the coal, oil, and natural gas that come from long-dead plants and animals. The sun's energy is also the source of weather. Uneven heating of the Earth's surface produces winds and the water cycle.

Solar energy is useful in other ways, too. You know that light from the sun can provide electricity for tools such as calculators. Solar cells can also provide electricity for places that are hard to reach with standard power lines. Solar collector panels are used to absorb the sun's energy to heat water. The heated water can then be used to heat swimming pools or to provide hot water for home use.

However, although solar energy is free, solar cells and collectors can be expensive. Another problem is that many places don't have enough sunny days to make solar energy practical.

 **MAIN IDEA AND DETAILS** What forms of energy come directly from solar energy?

Solar Chips
Put a handful of chocolate chips on each of two plates. Place both plates in the sun. Then use a hand lens to focus sunlight on the chips on one of the plates. What happens? What do you think causes this?

Chemical energy in fuel is used to keep this remote-controlled model helicopter flying.

Chemical and Mechanical Energy

It takes a lot of energy to move something as heavy as a car. Where does that energy come from? In most cars, an engine burns gasoline, a fuel. Burning a fuel releases the energy stored in it.

The energy stored in fuel is **chemical energy**. This is energy that can be released by a chemical reaction, such as burning. When it is not being used, chemical energy is potential energy. A chemical reaction is needed to change this potential energy into kinetic energy.

Earlier, you read that your muscles get energy from the food you eat. The potential energy stored in food is chemical energy. When it's released, it gives you kinetic energy to move.

Have you ever used a heat pack to warm your hands or feet? The pack contains substances that have potential chemical energy. When you squeeze the pack, the substances mix, and a chemical reaction occurs. The heat from the reaction is what warms you up.

Many substances release energy in chemical reactions. For example, wood releases heat when it is burned. A glow stick releases light when a chemical reaction occurs. In the Investigate, you observed the release of chemical energy stored in a substance called calcium chloride.

Another form of energy that includes both potential energy and kinetic energy is mechanical energy. **Mechanical energy** is the combination of all the potential and kinetic energy which something contains.

The windup toy in the photo has a key attached to a spring. When you turn the key, you wind up, or tighten, the spring, giving the toy potential energy. The tighter the spring is wound, the more potential energy the toy has.

When the toy is moving, it has kinetic energy. Since the spring is still partly wound up, the toy also has some potential energy. The toy's mechanical energy is the combination of its potential energy and its kinetic energy. When the toy stops, it doesn't have potential or kinetic energy.

The remote-control helicopter is moving, so you know that it has kinetic energy. The fuel in its tank has chemical energy, which is potential energy. The helicopter's mechanical energy is the combination of its kinetic and its potential energy.

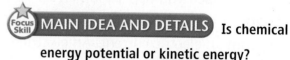

MAIN IDEA AND DETAILS Is chemical energy potential or kinetic energy?

Chemical energy is stored in fireworks. ▶

▲ A windup toy is operated by mechanical energy. Where does this toy get its kinetic energy?

Electricity and Sound

Have you ever experienced a blackout? Candles can help you see during a blackout, but they don't provide enough light to read easily. Televisions and computers don't work. Kitchen appliances don't either, so cooking is difficult. In a blackout, you realize how much you depend on electricity. Electricity, or **electric energy**, is energy that comes from an electric current. An electric current results from the movement of electrons. Electrons are particles in atoms.

You can see some effects of electric energy when you use appliances. You may have even felt electric energy. Have you ever walked across a rug on a dry day and then touched a doorknob? You probably felt electric energy in the form of a small shock.

People have invented a great many devices that use electric energy to make life better. These include all the basic things you'd miss in a blackout. They also include modern, battery-operated devices such as portable games, cell phones, and music players.

Another useful form of energy is sound. *Sound* is energy in the form of vibrations that travel through matter.

Sound vibrations pass through the particles of matter in a kind of domino effect. When a vibration reaches a particle of matter, that particle starts to vibrate, too. That particle may be close to other particles.

This band uses a lot of electric energy and produces a lot of sound energy. ▼

A megaphone focuses sound in one direction. Without the megaphone, the energy would spread out in all directions.

▲ Electric energy makes sound louder with this bull horn.

Those other particles may also start to vibrate. In this way, sound vibrations can spread out in all directions.

Like light energy, sound energy can travel through many objects. Sound vibrations travel easily through air, so people can hear sounds—even quiet ones—at a distance.

Deep inside the ear is a thin membrane called the eardrum. Hearing begins with the vibration of the eardrum. When sound vibrations in the air reach the eardrum, it vibrates. These vibrations are transmitted deeper into the ear, where they are changed into nerve messages that travel to the brain. If the sound you are listening to is too loud, its vibrations can damage your ears and affect your hearing.

People can also experience sound energy in other ways. If you place your hands on the radio or television, you can feel the sound vibrations. Some people with hearing disabilities have been able to become dancers by feeling the vibrations of the music through their feet.

Another time you might be able to feel sound is at a fireworks show. Many fireworks produce not only bright colors, but also loud whistles, pops, and bangs. You can often feel the energy of these sounds on your body.

Focus Skill MAIN IDEA AND DETAILS

List three things in your classroom that use electric energy.

This emergency radio uses mechanical energy from a person to produce electric energy. News is available even if batteries are not.

▲ The batteries in a flashlight contain chemical energy. What happens to the chemical energy when you turn on the flashlight?

Changing Energy Forms

In this lesson, you've examined different energy forms and some of their uses. Often, one form of energy changes into another form.

The batteries in a flashlight contain chemical energy, but the flashlight bulb gives off light. Where does the light come from? The batteries' chemical energy changes into electric energy. Then the bulb in the flashlight changes the electric energy into light energy.

When you turn the crank of an emergency radio, you add potential energy to the radio. When you turn on the radio, sound energy is produced. The potential energy you added was changed into electric energy. Then the electric energy was changed into sound energy.

Look again at the photo of the concert stage. The microphones change sound energy into electric energy, which is amplified, or increased. Then the speakers change the electric energy back into sound. In this situation and many others, energy is constantly being changed from one form to another in order to make it more useful to us.

 **MAIN IDEA AND DETAILS**

Why do people change energy from one form to another?

Lesson Review

Essential Question

What Are Some Forms of Energy?

In this lesson, you learned that energy takes many forms, such as solar, chemical, mechanical, electrical, and sound. You also learned that these forms of energy can be changed into other forms of energy.

1. **(Focus Skill) MAIN IDEA AND DETAILS** Draw and complete a graphic organizer that shows the supporting details for this main idea: Energy takes many forms.

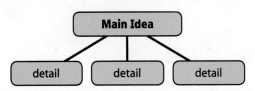

Main Idea — detail, detail, detail

2. **SUMMARIZE** Write a one-paragraph summary of the relationship of mechanical, potential, and kinetic energy.

3. **DRAW CONCLUSIONS** A light bulb changes electric energy into two other forms of energy. What are they?

4. **VOCABULARY** Make a crossword puzzle, including clues, that contains all of this lesson's vocabulary words.

Test Prep

5. **CRITICAL THINKING** Bess says that thunder produces sound energy. Her friend says kinetic energy comes from thunder. Who is correct? Explain.

6. Which of the following changes chemical energy directly into light energy?
   A. a candle
   B. a car key
   C. a flashlight
   D. a light switch

Make Connections

 Writing

Narrative Writing
Many forms of energy are around us and within us. Write two or three paragraphs **describing** some ways you use energy in a typical day.

 Math

Compare Fractions
Battery A contains a full charge of chemical energy. Battery B has $\frac{3}{8}$ of a full charge, and Battery C has $\frac{2}{5}$ as much energy as Battery A. Which battery contains the least chemical energy?

 Music

Ecosystems and People
Write a one-minute song about energy. Include lyrics and, if possible, a melody.

How Is Heat Transferred?

Investigate the transfer of heat from one place to another.

Read and learn about the movement of heat.

Fast Fact

Where's the Heat?

A thermogram shows the heat patterns in a person's body. The colors show the different levels of heat that the body gives off. Red and yellow show the warmest areas, and green and blue show the coolest. In the Investigate, you'll observe some other heat patterns.

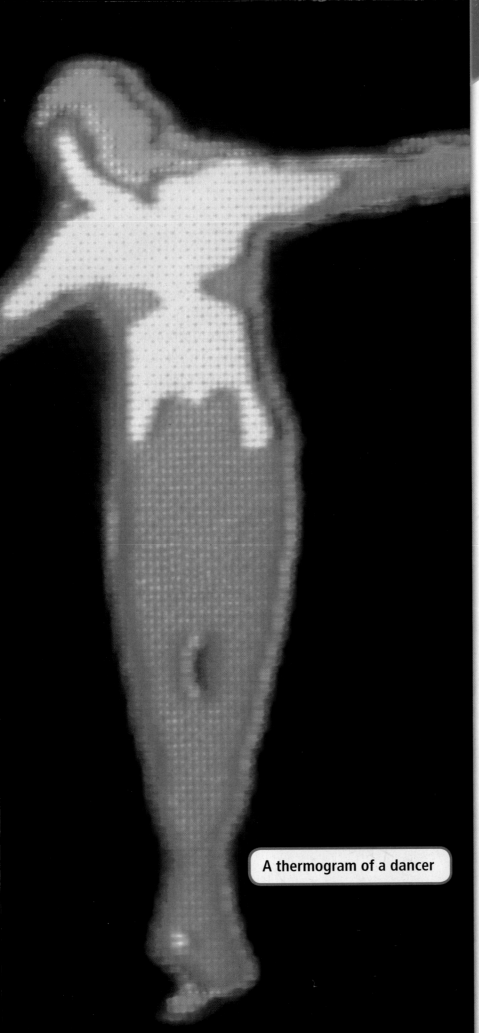

A thermogram of a dancer

Vocabulary Preview

heat [HEET] The transfer of thermal energy between objects with different temperatures (p. 582)

system [SIS•tuhm] A group of separate elements that work together to accomplish something (p. 583)

conduction [kuhn•DUHK•shuhn] The transfer of heat from one object directly to another (p. 584)

convection [kuhn•VEK•shuhn] The transfer of heat through the movement of a gas or a liquid (p. 584)

radiation [ray•dee•AY•shuhn] The transfer of energy by means of waves that move through matter and space (p. 585)

reflection [rih•FLEK•shuhn] The bouncing of heat or light off an object (p. 585)

Hot Buttered Knives

Start with Questions

Pots heat on the stove, and cakes bake in the oven.

- How is heat transferred from the burner on the stove or from the coils in the oven?

- How does sitting beside a campfire help you keep warm on a cold night?

Investigate to find out. Then read and learn to find out more.

Prepare to Investigate

Inquiry Skill Tip

For this investigation, you can draw a conclusion based on a comparison of observations. Think about how your observations for the two events are alike and how they are different. Then think about what caused the differences.

Materials

- cold butter
- metal knife
- large plastic foam cup
- hot water
- plastic knife

Make an Observation Chart

Type of Knife	Observations
Plastic	
Metal	

Follow This Procedure

1 Place two pats of butter on the blade of the metal knife—one in the middle and one near the tip. Place the knife, handle first, in the cup to check that both pats are above the rim. Remove the knife.

CAUTION: Be careful when pouring the hot water.

2 Fill the cup with hot water. Carefully place the knife, handle first, back in the cup.

3 **Observe** the knife and the pats of butter for 10 minutes. **Record** your observations.

4 Repeat Steps 1–3, substituting the plastic knife for the metal one. **Record** your observations.

Draw Conclusions

1. On which knife did the butter melt faster? On that knife, which pat of butter melted faster?

2. **Inquiry Skill** Draw a conclusion about which material—metal or plastic—transfers heat faster.

Step 1

Step 4

Independent Inquiry

Write a **hypothesis about which knife would *lose* heat faster. Then plan and conduct a simple investigation to check.**

VOCABULARY
heat p. 582
system p. 583
conduction p. 584
convection p. 584
radiation p. 585
reflection p. 585

SCIENCE CONCEPTS
▶ how heat moves by means of conduction, convection, and radiation

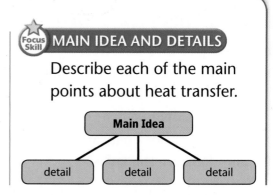

MAIN IDEA AND DETAILS

Describe each of the main points about heat transfer.

Heat and Temperature

You probably know that the terms *heat* and *temperature* are related, but you may not know how. You also know that objects with a high temperature give off heat, but what exactly is heat?

Remember that all matter is made up of tiny particles that are always moving. Since they move, they have kinetic energy that can also be called *thermal energy*. The faster the particles move, the more thermal energy the matter has.

When particles of one substance come in contact with particles of another substance that are moving at a different rate, thermal energy is transferred. **Heat** is the transfer of thermal energy between objects with different temperatures.

Thermal energy travels from a warmer object to a cooler object. Energy from the stove burner flows through the pot and into the water, causing it to get hot. Energy doesn't travel from the low-temperature water to the high-temperature burner.

But what is temperature? *Temperature* is the measurement of the average kinetic energy of all the particles in a substance. Use a thermometer to measure temperature.

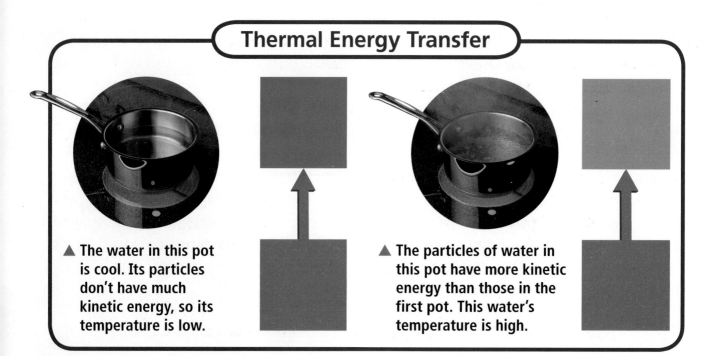

Thermal Energy Transfer

▲ The water in this pot is cool. Its particles don't have much kinetic energy, so its temperature is low.

▲ The particles of water in this pot have more kinetic energy than those in the first pot. This water's temperature is high.

Is the melting point of lead closer to the melting point of chocolate or the melting point of iron?

Substance	Melting Point
Ice	0°C
Chocolate	42°C
Lead	327°C
Iron	1535°C

◀ The particles of iron have so much heat energy that the iron has melted and become a liquid.

The number shown on a thermometer is related to the amount of kinetic energy.

Some systems are very efficient at transferring thermal energy. A **system** is a set of parts acting together as a whole object. A burner, a pot, and water are a system through which thermal energy moves. The burner transfers thermal energy to the pot. The pot transfers thermal energy to the water. As the water receives more and more thermal energy, its particles move faster and faster.

The movement of particles helps explain changes in state. In ice, water particles are held together in a rigid pattern. They don't move around, but they vibrate in place. As thermal energy is added, they vibrate faster and faster. At a certain point, the particles

have so much energy that they break out of the rigid pattern and flow easily around each other. The ice melts.

If you keep adding thermal energy, the water particles keep moving faster and faster. Finally, they have so much thermal energy they separate from each other and rise into the air. The water boils.

Some systems need more thermal energy than others to cause a change of state. For example, more energy is needed to make iron melt than to make chocolate melt. This is because it takes more energy to separate the particles in iron from each other than to separate the particles in chocolate.

MAIN IDEA AND DETAILS

How is temperature related to heat?

583

Thermal Energy Transfer

There are three ways heat can move through a system. The first is by **conduction**, or the transfer of thermal energy from one object directly into another. In other words, if an object is touching a hotter object, thermal energy will flow from the hotter object directly into the cooler object.

The pot in the burner-pot-water system is heated by conduction. The pot is in contact with the burner, so thermal energy from the burner flows directly into the pot. The water is in contact with the pot, so thermal energy from the pot flows into the water.

Of course, only the water at the bottom and the sides is actually in contact with the pot. The water in the middle is heated by a process called convection. **Convection** is the transfer of thermal energy through the movement of a gas or a liquid. As a gas or a liquid is heated, the heat causes it to move upward, carrying heat to the area above the heat source.

That's how the water in the middle gets warm. Thermal energy from the pot flows into the water at the bottom by conduction. Then the heated water moves upward by convection, bringing thermal energy to the water above it.

▲ **Heat from the iron moves directly into the clothing by conduction.**

Inside the balloon, heated air moves up, carrying thermal energy to the air above it by convection. ▶

The meerkat is warming itself under the lamp. Radiation carries thermal energy from the lamp to the meerkat.

The third way thermal energy can be transferred is by radiation. **Radiation** is the transfer of energy by waves that move through matter and space. Remember that solar energy travels as light, X-ray, radio, and ultraviolet waves. It also travels as infrared waves. Infrared waves carry thermal energy from the sun and from heat sources such as campfires and toasters.

Unlike conduction and convection, radiation doesn't need matter for the heat to travel through. Conduction requires that two objects be in contact. Convection requires a gas or a liquid. Radiation can transfer thermal energy from the sun across 150 million km (93 million mi) of space to Earth.

Not all of this radiation from the sun reaches Earth's surface. Some of it is reflected back into space by the atmosphere. **Reflection** occurs when heat or light bounces off an object.

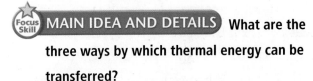 **MAIN IDEA AND DETAILS** What are the three ways by which thermal energy can be transferred?

Distance and Heat

Hold a thermometer 40 cm from a light bulb. (Don't use a fluorescent light.) After two minutes, record the temperature. Repeat the procedure, holding the thermometer 30, 20, and 10 cm from the bulb. How does distance affect the transfer of thermal energy?

Insulators and Conductors

On a hot beach, the drinks inside an ice chest stay cold. It seems as if heat doesn't move from the air into the drinks. In fact, the heat does move, but it moves very slowly because the cooler is an insulator. Anything that slows the movement of thermal energy is an *insulator*.

Heat always moves from something warmer to something cooler. However, certain factors affect the rate at which heat moves from one object to another.

Not all insulators keep things cool. Thick coats keep us warm by trapping heat close to our bodies on winter days. Coats prevent warm air from escaping.

There are also things that allow heat to move through them very easily. If you use a metal spoon to eat hot soup, the handle may get very hot, even though it never touches the soup. Heat moves from the soup to and through the spoon by conduction. Anything that allows thermal energy to move through it easily is called a *conductor*. Have you ever seen a pan with a copper bottom? Copper is a good conductor of heat, so food in the pan cooks quickly and evenly. Many metals are good conductors of heat. Silver, gold, and aluminum are also good conductors of thermal energy.

 **MAIN IDEA AND DETAILS**

What are insulators and conductors?

◄ **The lunch bag prevents heat in the air from moving into the bag. This keeps the food in the bag cool.**

The cookie sheet is a conductor. The oven mitts are insulators.

Essential Question

How Is Heat Transferred?

In this lesson, you learned that heat and temperature are related but different. You learned that heat can be transferred in three ways: by conduction, by convection, and by radiation. Certain materials slow or speed up the movement of heat.

1. **MAIN IDEA AND DETAILS** Draw and complete a graphic organizer that shows supporting details for this main idea: Heat can be transferred in three ways.

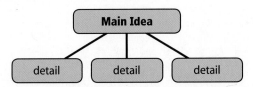

```
        Main Idea

  detail   detail   detail
```

2. **SUMMARIZE** Write a one-paragraph summary of a system by using these terms: *heat*, *temperature*, and *system*.

3. **DRAW CONCLUSIONS** When you face a campfire, why does your front feel warmer than your back?

4. **VOCABULARY** Use each lesson vocabulary term in a sentence.

Test Prep

5. **CRITICAL THINKING** If you put one thermometer 10 cm (4 in.) above a flame and another one 10 cm to the side of the flame, which would show the higher temperature? Explain.

6. If you want heat to move from a light bulb to an object by conduction, where should you place the object?
   A. above the light bulb
   B. next to the light bulb
   C. below the light bulb
   D. touching the light bulb

Make Connections

 Writing

Expository Writing
Suppose you're tutoring a younger student in science. Write an **explanation** of how heat can be transferred within a system. Be sure to keep your explanation as simple as possible.

 Math

Solve Problems
A substance in a beaker has a temperature of 22°C. At 1:00, you begin to heat it. After 14 minutes, its temperature reaches 48°C, and you stop heating it. By 2:03, it has cooled back down to 22°C. How long did it take to cool?

 Language Arts

Word Usage
Use a dictionary to find as many words as you can that are related to the word *conduction*. List and define the words.

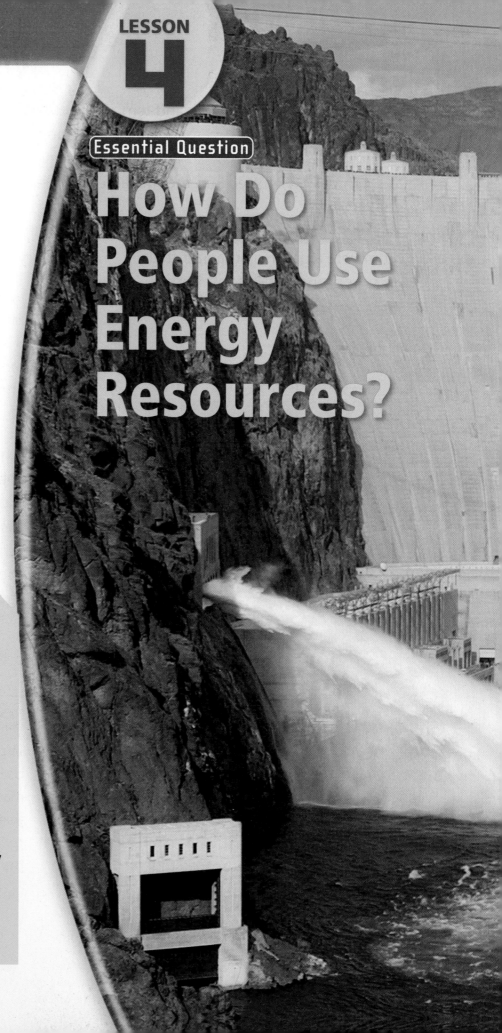

Investigate a model of a water-powered turbine.

Read and learn how we use energy resources, how some resources can be replaced, and which resources cannot be replaced.

Essential Question

How Do People Use Energy Resources?

Fast Fact

Power Up

The energy station at Hoover Dam, on the border between Arizona and Nevada, has 17 turbines that produce electricity. All the turbines are turned by the energy of falling water. In the Investigate, you will experiment to discover the effect distance has on the energy of falling water.

Hoover Dam

fossil [FAHS•uhl] The remains or traces of past life, found in sedimentary rock (p. 592)

resource [REE•sawrs] Any material that can be used to satisfy a need (p. 593)

nonrenewable resource [nahn•rih•NOO•uh•buhl REE•sawrs] A resource that, once used, cannot be replaced in a reasonable amount of time (p. 593)

conservation [kahn•ser•VAY•shuhn] The use of less of a resource to make the supply last longer (p. 593)

renewable resource [rih•NOO•uh•buhl REE•sawrs] A resource that can be replaced within a reasonable amount of time (p. 594)

pollution [puh•LOO•shuhn] A waste product that harms living things and damages an ecosystem (p. 596)

589

Water Power

Guided Inquiry

Start with Questions

Water is necessary for life. It is also useful to people in other ways.

- What are some ways that people use water?

- How does a water mill use water?

Investigate to find out. Then read and learn to find out more.

Prepare to Investigate

Inquiry Skill Tip

Before you draw conclusions, make a list of changes that occurred during the investigation. Beside each one, list differences that might have caused the change.

Materials

- 2 plastic disks
- stapler
- scissors
- pencil
- string, 100 cm
- masking tape
- 10-g mass (paper clip, weight)
- 2 washers
- bottle of water
- basin
- meterstick
- stopwatch

Make a Data Table

Height (cm)	Time (s)
10	
15	
20	

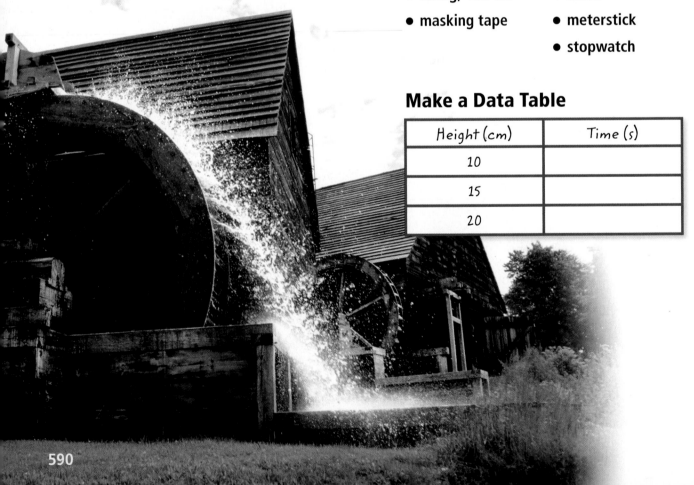

Follow This Procedure

CAUTION: **Be careful with the scissors.**

1. Staple the disks together at their centers. Cut four 3-cm slits as shown. On the right side of each slit, fold the disks in opposite directions to form a vane.

2. Carefully pierce a small slit through the center of both disks. Insert the pencil.

3. Tape one end of the string to the pencil. Tie or tape the mass to the string.

4. Slide a washer onto each end of the pencil. Hold your water wheel by the washers so it can turn freely. Hold it horizontally over the basin, with the closed ends of the vanes away from you.

5. Have a partner slowly pour water from a height of 10 cm onto the vanes. **Measure** and **record** the time it takes for the mass to be wound up to the pencil. Repeat, pouring water from 15 cm and 20 cm.

Draw Conclusions

1. What **variable** did you **control**? What variable did you change?

2. **Inquiry Skill** What can you **conclude** about the effect of the distance the water fell on the speed at which the water wheel turned?

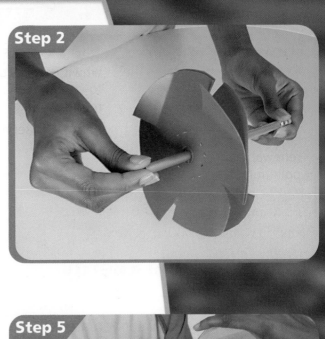

Step 2

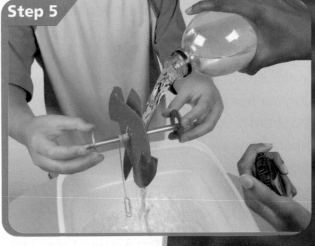

Step 5

Independent Inquiry

Write a **hypothesis** about how the rate of the water's flow affects the speed of the water wheel. Then plan and conduct an experiment to check it.

VOCABULARY

fossil p. 592
resource p. 593
nonrenewable resource
      p. 593
conservation p. 593
renewable resource p. 594
pollution p. 596

SCIENCE CONCEPTS

▶ why it is important
  to conserve energy
  resources
▶ how to conserve energy
  resources

Focus Skill COMPARE AND CONTRAST

Look for similarities and
differences between
renewable energy sources
and nonrenewable energy
sources.

(alike)————(different)

Nonrenewable Energy Resources

Think about the hot water you use at home. Where does the energy that heats the water in your home come from? If your water heater is electric, it gets its energy, as your home's other electric appliances do, from an electric energy station. Some energy stations, such as the one at Hoover Dam, produce electricity by using the energy of falling water. Electricity made in this way is known as *hydroelectric energy*.

Most energy stations burn coal, oil, or natural gas as sources of energy to produce electricity. Burning these fuels changes their chemical energy to thermal energy, which is used to change water to steam. The steam, like the falling water in dams, powers the machines that produce electricity.

Coal, oil, and natural gas are *fossil fuels*. A **fossil** is the remains or traces of past life, often found in sedimentary rock. Fossil fuels are fuels that formed from the remains of once-living things.

This energy station in Australia burns coal to produce electricity. The coal comes from the remains of plants that lived and died millions of years ago. ▼

It takes millions of years for coal, oil, and natural gas to form. When supplies are used up, there will be no more. This is why coal, oil, and natural gas are called nonrenewable resources. A **resource** is any material that can be used to satisfy a need. A **nonrenewable resource** is a resource that, once used up, cannot be replaced within a reasonable amount of time.

Does this mean that we will use up our nonrenewable resources? This will happen in time, but there are things we can do to keep from using them up before we find other resources to use in their place.

One thing people can do is use less of these fuels. Using less of something to make the supply last longer is called **conservation**. For example, if everyone uses less hot water, less fossil fuel will be burned to make electricity to heat the water. That will help make the world's supply of fossil fuel last longer.

Another thing people can do to conserve nonrenewable resources is switch to using resources that won't run out. Scientists are working to develop new ways to do this.

 **COMPARE AND CONTRAST** What do coal, oil, and natural gas have in common?

Since there is a limited supply of oil, the more gasoline we use now, the less we will have in the future for driving and manufacturing.

As oil resources are used up, it takes more work to get the oil that is left. This drilling platform pumps oil from under the ocean floor.

Renewable Energy Resources

Some resources are renewable. A **renewable resource** is a resource that can be replaced within a reasonable amount of time.

You may be wondering how an *energy* resource can be renewable. After all, once you burn a fuel, isn't it gone?

The key is that not all energy resources need to be burned in order to release energy. As you read at the beginning of this chapter, there are many different forms of energy.

One form of energy is solar energy, which can be changed directly into electric energy by solar cells. Some highway signs use solar cells in the daytime to produce the electricity they need to light them at night. Since Earth gets sunlight every day, solar energy is a renewable energy resource.

Science Up Close

For more links and animations, go to **www.hspscience.com**

A Hybrid Car

A hybrid car runs on electricity at slow speeds and on gasoline at high speeds.

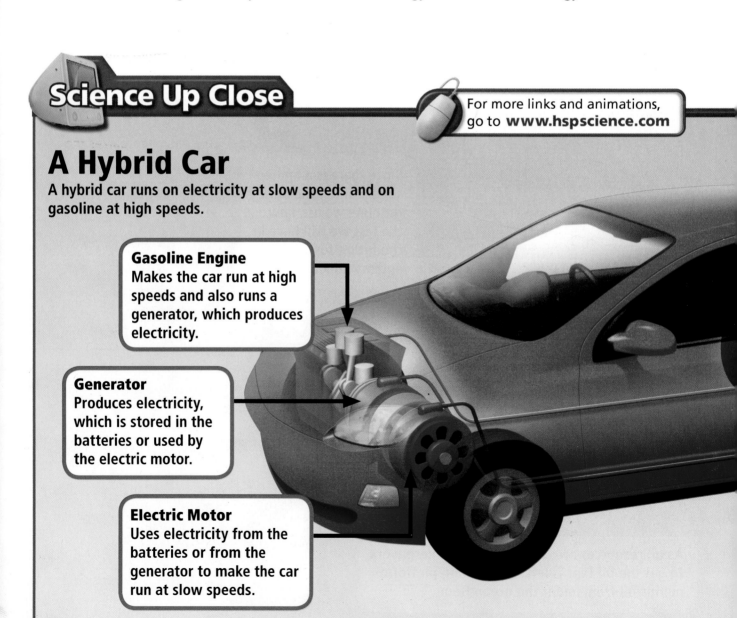

Gasoline Engine
Makes the car run at high speeds and also runs a generator, which produces electricity.

Generator
Produces electricity, which is stored in the batteries or used by the electric motor.

Electric Motor
Uses electricity from the batteries or from the generator to make the car run at slow speeds.

◀ One windmill can produce only a small amount of electricity. That's why energy companies build "wind farms" that have hundreds of windmills.

You have just read about energy stations that use the energy of falling water to produce electricity. Falling water is a renewable energy resource, too. Water is constantly recycled and is not used up as fossil fuels are.

Wind is another renewable energy resource. Moving air can power windmill turbines that produce electricity, just as falling water powers turbines in dams.

Today, we still need nonrenewable resources. We don't yet have the technology to get enough energy from renewable resources at a reasonable cost. However, scientists are working to find lower-cost ways of using renewable energy resources in the future. An example is the research being done on windmills. Research also continues on ways to conserve nonrenewable resources, such as by using hybrid cars.

Focus Skill **COMPARE AND CONTRAST**

How are renewable energy resources the same as nonrenewable energy resources? How are they different?

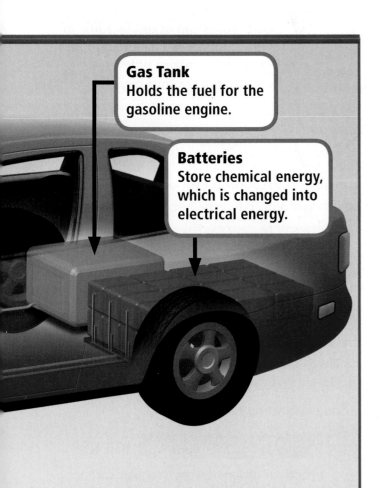

Gas Tank
Holds the fuel for the gasoline engine.

Batteries
Store chemical energy, which is changed into electrical energy.

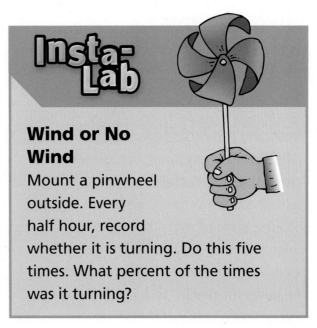

Insta-Lab

Wind or No Wind
Mount a pinwheel outside. Every half hour, record whether it is turning. Do this five times. What percent of the times was it turning?

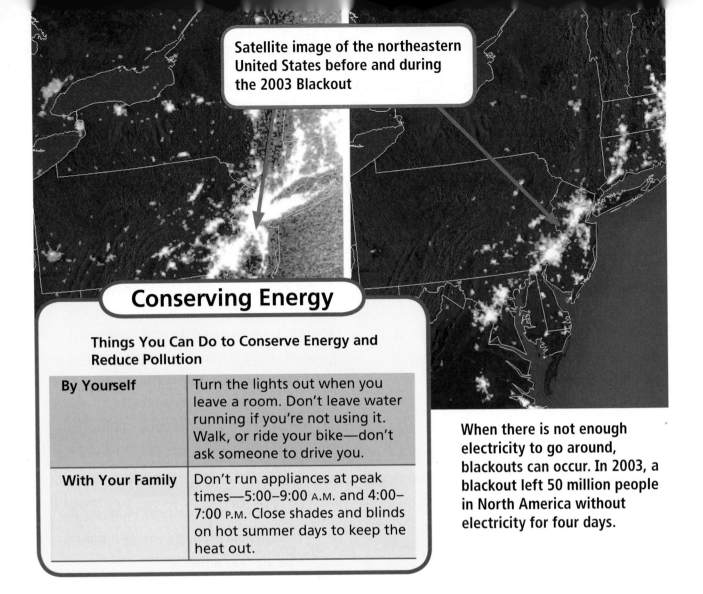

Satellite image of the northeastern United States before and during the 2003 Blackout

Conserving Energy

Things You Can Do to Conserve Energy and Reduce Pollution

By Yourself	Turn the lights out when you leave a room. Don't leave water running if you're not using it. Walk, or ride your bike—don't ask someone to drive you.
With Your Family	Don't run appliances at peak times—5:00–9:00 A.M. and 4:00–7:00 P.M. Close shades and blinds on hot summer days to keep the heat out.

When there is not enough electricity to go around, blackouts can occur. In 2003, a blackout left 50 million people in North America without electricity for four days.

Conservation and the Environment

An advantage of conserving energy resources is that it reduces harm to the environment. The burning of coal, oil, and natural gas to release the energy stored in them also produces pollution.

Pollution is anything that dirties or harms the environment. When coal, oil, and natural gas are burned, gases are released into the atmosphere. These gases are forms of *air pollution*. Some of these gases are poisonous. Others combine with water in the air to form acid, which harms plants and animals.

The conservation methods and the inventions you have read about not only save energy resources, they also reduce pollution. For example, a hybrid car runs on gasoline just part of the time. This means that when it travels the same distance as a regular car, it burns less fossil fuel. Driving a hybrid car can help conserve fossil fuel.

There are many other things people can do to conserve energy resources. The table above lists some of them.

 **COMPARE AND CONTRAST** How is a hybrid car different from a regular car?

Essential Question

How Do People Use Energy Resources?

In this lesson, you learned that some resources can't be reused or replaced easily. You also learned that renewable resources can be just as effective as fossil fuels but may cost more.

1. 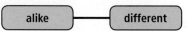 **COMPARE AND CONTRAST** Draw and complete a graphic organizer to compare and contrast renewable and nonrenewable resources.

```
alike ———— different
```

2. **SUMMARIZE** Write a one-paragraph summary about the need for conservation. Include an example about one resource.

3. **DRAW CONCLUSIONS** Solar panels on roofs can produce electricity for homes. Why don't all homes have solar panels?

4. **VOCABULARY** Write a paragraph using all of the lesson vocabulary terms.

Test Prep

5. **CRITICAL THINKING** Suppose someone invented an inexpensive solar cell for producing electricity from sunlight. What drawback would the solar cell still have?

6. Which of the following is a renewable energy resource?
   A. coal
   B. gasoline
   C. oil
   D. wind

Make Connections

 Writing

Expository Writing
"Reduce, reuse, recycle" is a motto about protecting the environment. Find out what each of these words means. Then write a brief **definition** of each one.

 Math

Find Area
An array of solar cells covers a rectangle that measures 450 m on two sides and 200 m on the other two sides. What is the area of the array?

 Social Studies

Hydropower
Find out how long people have been using water power and what technologies they have used to capture it. Summarize your findings in a brief report with diagrams.

Dream Machines

Welcome to the car showroom of the future. Step right up and take a look at some of our new models. If going fast is your thing, climb into this superfast car that can zip along at 405 km (252 miles) per hour! Say goodbye to smog with these other cars. The AUTOnomy runs on clean-burning hydrogen instead of gasoline. The Hypercar runs on gasoline and hydrogen.

Zoom, Zoom, Zoom

In 2005, a European car maker unveiled its 1001-horsepower, ultrafast supercar, which can reach a top speed of 405 km (252 miles) per hour. The car is made of lightweight materials. It also has specially made tires that won't melt when the car hits high speeds.

Engineers also designed the bottom of the car to create the venturi effect. The venturi effect is a downward pull that helps keep the car on the road.

H Is for Hydrogen Power

Can engineers design a car that doesn't cause pollution and doesn't rely on oil?

An American carmaker thinks it can. The carmaker is working to build cars that operate on hydrogen-powered fuel cells.

Fuel cells, like batteries, store energy. But unlike batteries, fuel cells never lose power or need to be recharged as long as there is enough hydrogen fuel. Fuel cells create energy through the combination of hydrogen and oxygen. That energy can power an electric car motor.

The new AUTOnomy car runs on a series of hydrogen fuel cells. Instead of producing pollution, the AUTOnomy produces water vapor. Scientists expect AUTOnomy's hydrogen-powered system to get the equivalent of 161 km (100 miles) per gallon of gasoline.

Another type of hydrogen-powered car is the Hypercar, which will run on a gasoline- and hydrogen-powered fuel system. Scientists say the vehicle will be able to travel 482 km (300 miles) on a gallon of gas.

The design of the Hypercar is environmentally friendly, too. The vehicle is made from lightweight materials called composites—two or more substances that strengthen the individual properties of each material. The Hypercar is not as heavy as a typical vehicle, so it needs less energy to accelerate.

Drive, He Said

The cars of the future are already here as prototypes and might be available by the time you get your driver's license.

Think and Write

1. How might cars powered by fuel cells help prevent pollution?

2. How might using lighter materials to build a car help with fuel efficiency?

Find out more. Log on to
www.hspscience.com

Vocabulary Review

Use the terms below to complete the sentences. The page numbers tell you where to look in the chapter if you need help.

energy p. 560

kinetic energy p. 562

potential energy p. 562

solar energy p. 570

chemical energy p. 572

conduction p. 584

convection p. 584

radiation p. 585

conservation p. 593

renewable resource p. 594

1. Saving something so it doesn't get used up is _____.

2. Energy that comes from the sun as heat and light is _____.

3. The transfer of thermal energy between touching objects is _____.

4. The transfer of thermal energy within a hot-air balloon is _____.

5. Hydroelectric energy is an example of using a _____.

6. Energy released through a chemical reaction is _____.

7. The ability to cause changes in matter is _____.

8. The energy of an object because of its condition or position is _____.

9. The energy of motion is _____.

10. The transfer of energy in waves through matter and space is _____.

Check Understanding

Write the letter of the best choice.

11. MAIN IDEA AND DETAILS Which is a nonrenewable resource?

A. natural gas   **C.** water

B. sunlight   **D.** wind

Use the diagram to answer questions 12 and 13.

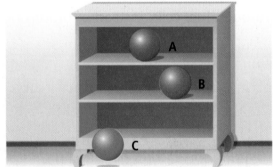

12. COMPARE AND CONTRAST Which statement is correct?

F. Ball A has more potential energy than Ball B or C.

G. Ball B has more potential energy than Ball A or C.

H. Ball C has more potential energy than Ball A or B.

J. All the balls have the same amount of potential energy.

13. Which ball has the most kinetic energy?

A. Ball A

B. Ball B

C. Ball C

D. They all have the same amount.

14. Which type of heat transfer does an oven mitt reduce?

F. conduction

G. convection

H. radiation

J. all of the above

15. Which kind of energy is stored in a battery?

A. kinetic energy

B. solar energy

C. chemical energy

D. light energy

16. Which change in form of energy occurs in a stereo speaker?

F. sound energy to electrical energy

G. chemical energy to sound energy

H. potential energy to kinetic energy

J. electrical energy to sound energy

Inquiry Skills

17. The Jenkinses' car can go 19 km on a gallon of gasoline. The Guerreros' car can go 23 km on a gallon of gasoline. The Watanabes' car can go 90 km on a gallon of gasoline. What can you **infer** about the Watanabes' car?

18. If you leave a solar-powered flashlight in the sun for 8 hours, it will be able to stay lit for 3 hours. **Hypothesize** what would happen if you placed the flashlight under a bright light bulb for 8 hours.

Critical Thinking

19. A car is rolling down a hill. What determines how much potential energy and how much kinetic energy it has?

20. Energy changes form in many modern devices. In a movie projector, how does energy change, and what forms of energy result? Do the same changes happen in a TV set? Explain.

The **Big Idea**

CHAPTER

16 Electricity

What's the Big Idea?

Electricity is a form of energy that plays an important role in our lives.

Essential Questions

Lesson 1

How Are Electricity and Magnetism Related?

Lesson 2

What Are Static and Current Electricity?

Lesson 3

What Are Electric Circuits?

GO online ▸ Student eBook
www.hspscience.com

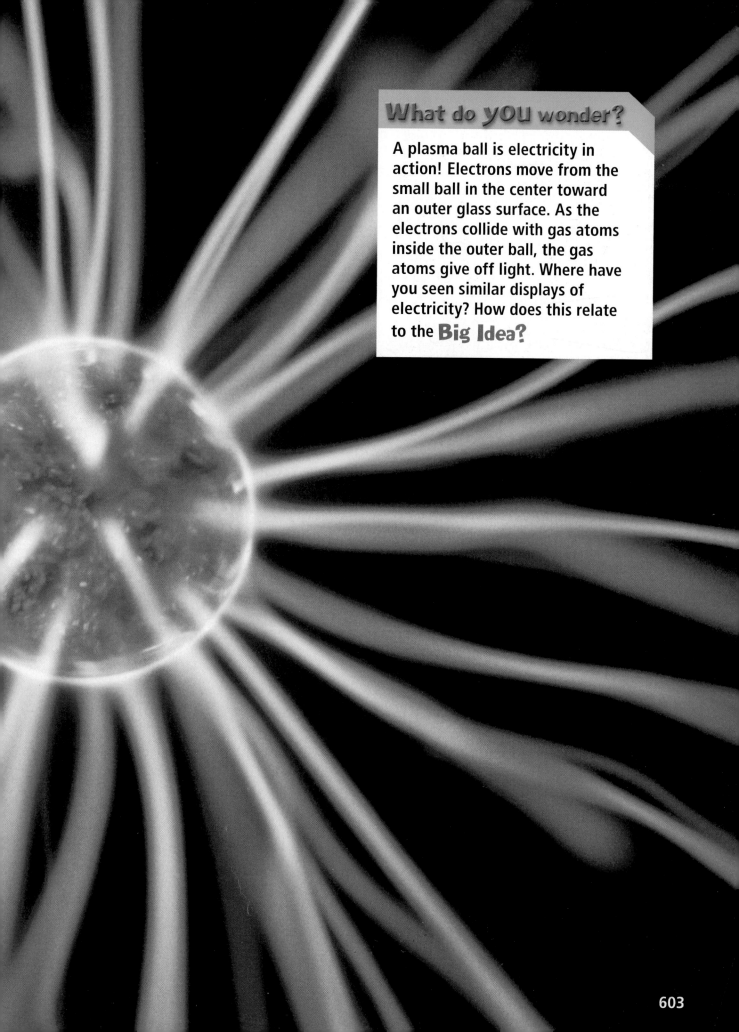

What do YOU wonder?

A plasma ball is electricity in action! Electrons move from the small ball in the center toward an outer glass surface. As the electrons collide with gas atoms inside the outer ball, the gas atoms give off light. Where have you seen similar displays of electricity? How does this relate to the **Big Idea?**

Investigate the relationship between electricity and magnetism.

Read and learn about electricity and ways it can be changed into other forms of energy.

Essential Question

How Are Electricity and Magnetism Related?

Fast Fact

The Northern Lights

Electrically charged particles from the sun follow Earth's magnetic field as they travel toward the North Pole. As they speed through the atmosphere, the particles collide with gas atoms, causing the atoms to give off light. This produces the aurora borealis, or northern lights, often seen in parts of Alaska and Canada. In the Investigate, you'll discover another way in which electricity and magnetism are related.

electricity [ee•lek•TRIS•ih•tee] A form of energy produced by moving electrons (p. 609)

electromagnet [ee•lek•troh•MAG•nit] A magnet made by coiling a wire around a piece of iron and running electric current through the wire (p. 610)

The northern lights

Build an Electromagnet

Guided Inquiry

Start with Questions

You use electricity every day. Do you use magnets every day? This electric guitar uses devices called electromagnets to convert electric energy into sound.

- What makes a magnet?

- How does an electromagnet work?

Investigate to find out. Then read to find out more.

Prepare to Investigate

Inquiry Skill Tip

To compare things is to tell how they are alike and different. When you compare a model with a real object, identify how any parts of the model differ from parts of the real thing.

Materials

- 3 m of insulated copper wire
- iron nail, 15 cm long
- battery holder for D-cell battery
- paper clips
- D-cell battery
- sheet of paper

Make an Observation Chart

	Paper Clips Picked Up	Other Observations
Without battery		
With battery		

Follow This Procedure

1. Wrap the wire in a tight coil around the nail. Leave about 20 cm of wire free at each end.

2. Connect the ends of the wire to the battery holder.

3. Put a small pile of paper clips on your desk. Hold the nail above the pile, and lower it toward the clips. **Observe** what happens.

4. Turn on your electromagnet by putting the D-cell into the battery holder.

5. Hold the nail above the pile of paper clips, and lower it slowly. **Observe** what happens.

6. While you hold the nail and paper clips above a sheet of paper, have your partner remove the cell from the battery holder. **Observe** what happens. Count and **record** the number of paper clips your electromagnet picked up.

Step 1

Step 5

Draw Conclusions

1. How did the nail change when the D-cell was connected?

2. **Inquiry Skill** Electromagnets are used on construction cranes to pick up steel. **Compare** a construction crane's electromagnet with yours.

Independent Inquiry

What would happen if you added another D-cell to your electromagnet? Plan and conduct a simple experiment to find out.

VOCABULARY
electricity p. 609
electromagnet p. 610

SCIENCE CONCEPTS
▶ how electricity produces magnetism
▶ that electricity can be changed to other forms of energy

Focus Skill **MAIN IDEA AND DETAILS**

Look for examples of how electricity and magnetism are related.

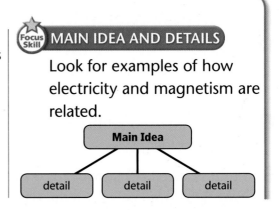

Electricity

Have you used electricity in the past hour? Did you turn on a lamp? Did you watch TV? Did you get something cold to drink from the refrigerator? If you did any of these things, you used electricity.

You use electricity every day, but do you know what it is? To understand electricity, you have to think about atoms. Recall that atoms contain charged particles. A proton has a positive charge. An electron has a negative charge.

An atom can have more electrons than protons. This gives the atom a negative charge. An atom with more protons than electrons has a positive charge. Atoms with opposite charges attract each other.

In an atom, electrons move around outside the nucleus. In some elements, electrons can also move from one atom to another. Protons don't move in this way.

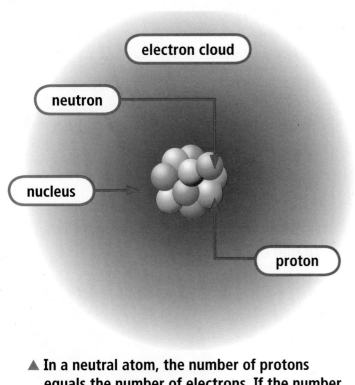

▲ In a neutral atom, the number of protons equals the number of electrons. If the number of protons and the number of electrons are not equal, the atom has a charge.

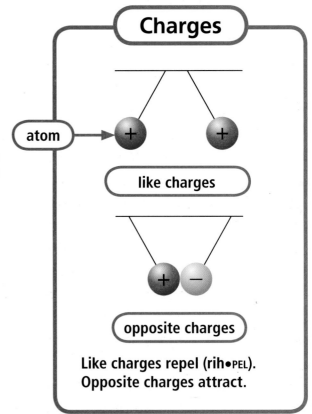

Charges

like charges

opposite charges

Like charges repel (rih•PEL). Opposite charges attract.

The lights on this fountain and in the buildings around it all use electricity. Electricity is changed to motion as water is pumped through the fountain, and it is changed to light in the buildings.

Electron movement produces electricity. **Electricity**, or electric energy, is a form of energy produced by moving electrons.

Electricity can be changed to other forms of energy. People use electricity to run lights in homes, schools, and offices. Electricity also runs street lights and traffic lights. Lamps change electricity into light energy.

Look at the fountain shown on this page. The lights use electricity. The fountain also uses electricity in another way. Electric motors pump the water through the fountain and push it up into the air. Here, electricity changes to motion, or mechanical energy.

Electric motors can be small enough to power a model train. They can be large enough to drive a huge freight train or a ship loaded with cargo. Electric motors even run some cars.

Electricity can also change to heat energy. Toasters and electric ovens produce heat

▲ Electricity can also be changed to heat. For example, people can use a small electric heater to warm a room.

from electricity. So do hair dryers. Many homes are heated by electricity.

What do a doorbell and a radio have in common? They both use electricity to produce sound energy. Radios use the electricity from batteries or outlets to produce sound.

 MAIN IDEA AND DETAILS

What are four kinds of energy that electricity can be changed into?

Electricity and Magnetism

In the Investigate, you used electricity to make a magnet. But your magnet worked only when the wire was connected to the battery. The battery was a source of electricity.

You wrapped the wire around a nail. When electricity flowed through the wire, the nail became a kind of magnet. An **electromagnet** is a magnet made by coiling a wire around a piece of iron and running electricity through the wire.

While electricity was flowing through the wire, the wire had a magnetic field around it. A single wire doesn't have a very strong magnetic field. Winding the wire into a coil makes the magnetic field stronger. Each extra turn of the wire makes the field even stronger.

Electromagnets are useful because they can be turned on and off. In some buildings, they are used to hold heavy fire doors open. In an emergency, the electricity can be turned off. Because the magnet no longer works, the doors close, blocking the spread of a fire.

Electromagnets are used on cranes in steel recycling centers. The magnets can lift heavy iron or steel objects, such as old cars. Electromagnets can also be used to lift metal objects on and off ships.

Electromagnets are used in recycling centers and junkyards to move cars and other iron or steel objects. ▶

electromagnet

An electromagnet causes a cone inside the speaker to vibrate, producing sound. ▼

cone

Inside a Doorbell

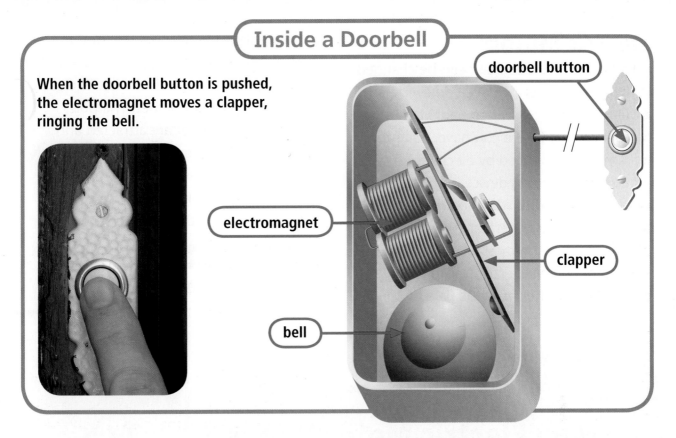

When the doorbell button is pushed, the electromagnet moves a clapper, ringing the bell.

doorbell button

electromagnet

clapper

bell

Scientists and engineers are working to develop a shipping dock that uses electromagnets. Today, a tugboat must pull a ship to a dock. The new magnetic dock will pull the steel ship toward it. The magnets will be strong enough to hold the ship in place without any ropes.

A much smaller electromagnet is used in a doorbell. When you press the button, electricity flows through the electromagnet, which pulls a steel spring toward it. The spring moves a clapper that hits the bell.

A speaker in a stereo system is similar to a doorbell. An electromagnet makes parts inside the speaker vibrate. You hear the vibrations as sound.

You have seen that electricity can produce magnetism. This also works the other way around—a magnet can produce electricity. That's how an energy station works.

In an energy station, a coil of wire turns inside the magnetic field of a huge magnet. When the wires cut across the magnetic field, electricity flows through the wires. Electricity travels from the station over a series of wires to schools, homes, and offices. Magnets produce the electricity we use every day.

Focus Skill **MAIN IDEA AND DETAILS**

What are some ways in which electromagnets are used?

Insta-Lab

Is It Magnetic?
Hold a compass near some metal objects. Observe the direction in which the needle points. Now hold the compass next to an electric fan. Turn on the fan. What happens to the needle?

Electric Motors

You know that electricity can be changed to mechanical energy. Have you ever made a fruit drink in a blender or cooled off with an electric fan? If you have, you have seen motion produced by electricity. The motion of an electric device is produced by an electric motor. The electric motor is the opposite of a generator that produces electricity in an energy station.

A motor contains a coil of wire that can spin inside the magnetic field of a permanent magnet. When the motor is switched on, electricity produces a magnetic field in the coil of wire. The coil becomes an electromagnet. The poles of this electromagnet are attracted and repelled by the poles of the permanent magnet. This causes the electromagnet to spin. The motion of the spinning coil can turn the blades of the blender or the fan.

MAIN IDEA AND DETAILS

What are the two main parts of a motor?

Science Up Close

How an Electric Motor Works

The electric motor inside a fan contains a coil of wire and a permanent magnet. When the fan is turned on, the coil becomes an electromagnet. The poles of the electromagnet are attracted to the opposite poles of the permanent magnet, so the coil turns. To keep the coil moving, the direction of the electricity keeps changing. This causes the coil and the permanent magnet to alternately attract and repel

Inside the Motor

The wires are a part of the turning coil.

The curved gray object is the permanent magnet.

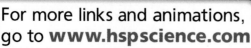

For more links and animations, go to **www.hspscience.com**

Essential Question

How Are Electricity and Magnetism Related?

In this lesson, you learned that electricity is a form of energy that can be used to do many things, from lighting your school to running the refrigerator at home. You also learned about electromagnets and the uses they have in many kinds of devices.

1. (Focus Skill) **MAIN IDEA AND DETAILS** Draw and complete a graphic organizer that shows supporting details for this main idea: Electricity can be used in many different ways.

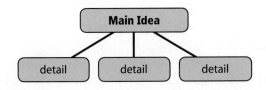

Main Idea

detail   detail   detail

2. **SUMMARIZE** Write a one-paragraph summary about how an electric motor functions.

3. **DRAW CONCLUSIONS** Why is electricity sometimes described as a flow of electrons?

4. **VOCABULARY** Show how the vocabulary words are related by using them together in a sentence.

Test Prep

5. **CRITICAL THINKING** How do neutrons affect electric charge?

6. How can you make an electromagnet stronger?

   A. Keep it turned on longer.

   B. Add more turns of wire to the nail.

   C. Use a smaller nail.

   D. Shorten the wire.

Make Connections

 Writing

Expository Writing

Many household devices, such as TVs, radios, speakers, and refrigerators, use electromagnets. Research one of these devices, and write a **description** explaining how it works.

 Math

Solve Problems

An iron nail electromagnet with 10 coils of wire picks up 6 paper clips. With 20 coils of wire, it picks up 12 paper clips. How many paper clips would it pick up with 30 coils of wire?

 Health

Pacemakers

Some people wear pacemakers, devices that use electricity to keep the heart beating regularly. Research pacemakers. Draw and label a diagram that shows how they work.

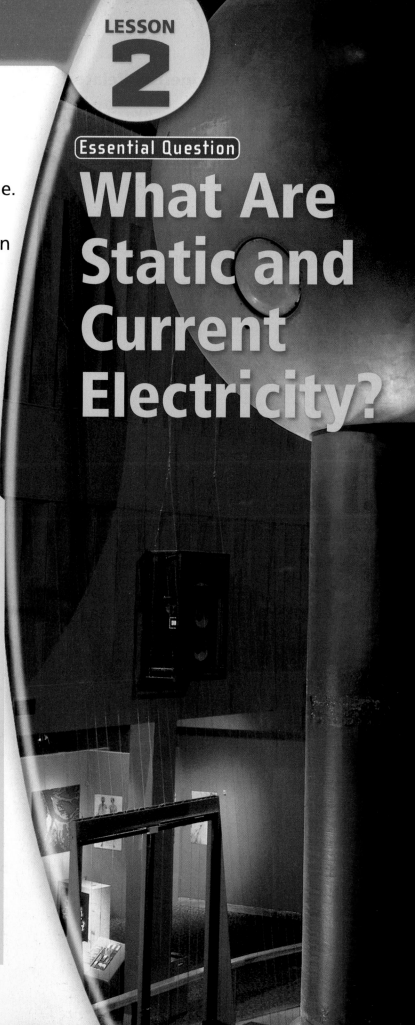

Investigate how to detect an electric charge.

Read and learn about the differences between static electricity and current electricity.

What Are Static and Current Electricity?

Fast Fact

Super-Size Sparks!

The Van de Graaff generator was invented in 1929 by the physicist Robert Van de Graaff. This machine produces huge electrical charges that jump between objects the way lightning does. Machines such as this can produce electrical discharges of millions of volts of electricity. In the Investigate, you'll see how charges that are much smaller affect matter.

Van de Graaff generator

static electricity [STAT•ik ee•lek•TRIS•ih•tee] The buildup of charges on an object (p. 618)

electric current [ee•LEK•trik KER•uhnt] The flow of electrons (p. 620)

current electricity [KER•uhnt ee•lek•TRIS•ih•tee] A kind of kinetic energy that flows as an electric current (p. 620)

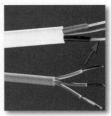

conductor [kuhn•DUHK•ter] A material that carries electricity well (p. 622)

insulator [IN•suh•layt•er] A material that does not conduct electricity well (p. 622)

615

Make an Electroscope

Start with Questions

We are surrounded by electric energy. Many things you encounter every day—from your TV to the lights in your classroom to the instruments your favorite band plays—use electricity.

- Are there different types of electricity?

- Why is this girl's hair standing up?

Investigate to find out. Then read and learn to find out more.

Prepare to Investigate

Inquiry Skill Tip

The best predictions are based on data you already have. Analyze what you know from the investigation in order to predict what will happen next.

Materials

- steel paper clip
- cardboard, 10 cm by 10 cm
- aluminum foil
- wide-mouth glass jar
- tape
- plastic comb
- wool cloth

Make an Observation Chart

	Observations
Comb not rubbed with cloth	
Comb rubbed with the cloth	

Follow This Procedure

1. Straighten one end of the paper clip to form a J-shaped hook.

2. Push the paper clip's straight end through the middle of the piece of cardboard. Tape it in place so that 2 or 3 cm of the straight end extend above the cardboard.

3. Cut two strips of foil, 1 cm wide and 4 cm long. Push the hook through one end of the foil strips so that they hang together from it.

4. Set the cardboard on the jar, with the hook inside, and tape it in place. You have completed your electroscope.

5. Hold the comb near the end of the paper clip. **Observe** what happens.

6. Rub the comb with the cloth. Repeat Step 5. Observe what happens as you move the comb away from and toward the paper clip.

Draw Conclusions

1. What happened as you moved the rubbed comb toward or away from the electroscope?

2. **Inquiry Skill** Scientists often predict what they think will happen in a certain situation. **Predict** what you think will happen to the foil if you rub the comb with the cloth and hold the cloth near the electroscope. Explain your prediction. Then test it. Was it correct?

Step 3

Step 4

Independent Inquiry

What do you think will happen if you touch the comb, the cloth, or your finger to the paper clip? Plan and conduct a simple experiment to test your ideas.

Read and Learn

VOCABULARY
static electricity p. 618
electric current p. 620
current electricity p. 620
conductor p. 622
insulator p. 622

SCIENCE CONCEPTS
▶ what causes static electricity
▶ what causes electricity to flow

Focus Skill CAUSE AND EFFECT
Look for conditions that cause electricity to build up or flow.

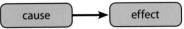

Static Electricity

Have you ever heard crackling noises or felt small shocks when you pulled a sweater over your head? If the room was dark, you might have seen tiny flashes of light. These effects are caused by electricity.

Most objects have no charge. The atoms making up the matter are neutral. They have equal numbers of protons and electrons. But when one object rubs against another, electrons move from atoms of one object to atoms of the other object. The numbers of protons and electrons in the atoms are no longer equal. The objects become either positively or negatively charged. The buildup of charges on an object is called **static electricity**.

When you took off your sweater, it rubbed against your other clothing, your skin, and your hair. Then, what happened?

A large buildup of static electricity can cause spectacular lightning bolts.

Static electricity on the wires of this device, called a Tesla coil, is discharged in a spark.

All the cat's hairs are charged alike, so they repel one another. The balloon carries the opposite charge, so the hairs are attracted to it.

You and the sweater both became electrically charged. After you pulled the sweater over your head, did your hair stand out from your head? If it did, the strands of hair all had the same charge, so they repelled one another.

Opposite charges attract each other. Charged objects can also attract neutral objects. When items of clothing rub together in a dryer, they can pick up a static charge. Because some items are positive and some are negative, they stick together.

When objects with opposite charges get close, electrons sometimes jump from the negative object to the positive object. This evens out the charges, and the objects become neutral. The shocks you felt when you pulled off the sweater were sparks caused by electrons moving to balance the charges. These sparks are called *static discharge.* The crackling noises you heard were the sounds of the sparks.

Lightning is also a static discharge. Where does the charge come from? Scientists hypothesize that collisions between water droplets in a cloud cause the drops to become charged. Negative charges collect at the bottom of the cloud. Positive charges collect at the top of the cloud. When electrons jump from one cloud to another, or from a cloud to the ground, you see lightning. The lightning heats the air, causing it to expand. As cooler air rushes in to fill the empty space, you hear thunder.

Earth can absorb lightning's powerful stream of electrons without being damaged. But lightning that strikes a tree or a house can start a fire. If lightning strikes a beach, it can melt grains of sand into pieces of glass!

Focus Skill **CAUSE AND EFFECT** What causes an object to build up a static charge?

Insta-Lab

Static Cereal
Place some puffed rice cereal on a sheet of paper. Hold a plastic comb above the cereal, and observe what happens. Rub the comb with a piece of wool cloth. Hold the comb over the cereal again. What happens?

Current Electricity

Static electricity is a kind of potential energy. Energy is stored when electrons move from one object to another and a static charge builds up. The potential energy can change to kinetic energy. This is what happens when electrons move in a static discharge.

The kinetic energy of a static discharge can change to other forms of energy. For example, the electrical energy of lightning changes into heat, light, and sound.

Because a static discharge is a short burst of kinetic energy, it isn't very useful as an energy source. For electricity to be a useful source of energy, it must be a steady flow of charges. If electrons have a path to follow, the charges will move in a steady flow, instead of building up a static charge. This flow of charges is called an **electric current**. Electricity that flows in this way is a kind of kinetic energy called **current electricity**.

To keep the charges flowing, a constant supply of electrons is needed. Cells supply the flow of charges to flashlights and other small devices. Energy stations produce a much larger flow of charges to supply electric current to whole cities. An energy station's electrical system can include homes, businesses, and factories. When you plug in a lamp, you are connecting to such an electrical system.

You can compare using current electricity to watering a garden or washing a car.

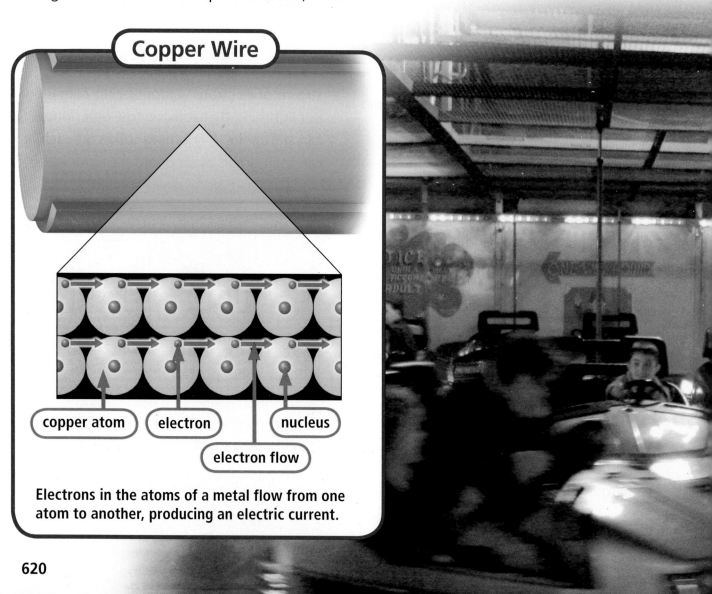

Copper Wire

copper atom electron nucleus

electron flow

Electrons in the atoms of a metal flow from one atom to another, producing an electric current.

When you use a hose, you connect it to a pipe and turn on the water. Water pressure pushes water through the hose.

To use current electricity to light a lamp, you connect the lamp to the wires in your home. Then you switch on the lamp. Electrical pressure forces charges through the wires, giving the electrons energy. This electrical pressure is measured in *volts.* Batteries have labels that show the number of volts they supply. One lightning strike can have more than 1 billion volts of electricity!

The rate at which electric charges flow is measured in *amps.* There are many more amps in power lines than you need to operate the appliances in your home.

The combination of volts and amps can be dangerous, which is why many objects that use electricity have warning labels.

The electrical devices you use all change electricity into some other form of energy. But not all of them use the same amount of electricity. The amount of electrical energy a device uses each second is measured in *watts.* A label on a hair dryer, light bulb, or clock shows how many watts it uses.

Electric energy companies bill people for the amount of electricity they use. A watt is a very small unit, so electrical use is measured in kilowatts. One kilowatt is equal to 1,000 watts.

 **CAUSE AND EFFECT** What causes an electric current to keep moving?

The current electricity that powers a bumper car flows from the ceiling, down the pole, and into the motor that makes the car move.

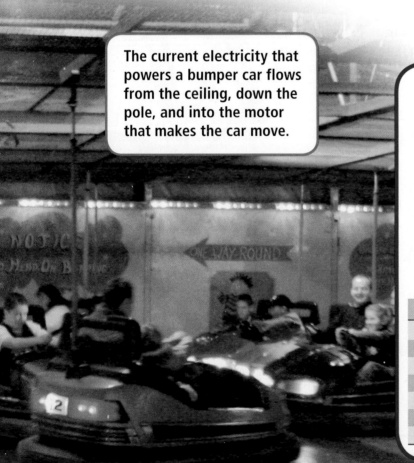

Math in Science
Interpret Data

Using Electricity
Some devices use more electrical energy than others. For example, a 100-watt light bulb uses four times the amount of energy that a 25-watt bulb uses. How many 100-watt light bulbs use the same amount of energy as a toaster?

Device	Energy Use
Hair dryer	1600 watts
Microwave oven	1000 watts
Computer and monitor	270 watts
Clothes washer	400 watts
DVD player	25 watts
TV	110 watts
Toaster	900 watts

Conductors and Insulators

Electricity moves more easily through some kinds of matter than others. A material through which electricity moves well is a **conductor**. Most metals are conductors. The electrons of metals are held loosely by the atoms. This makes it easy for the electrons to move between atoms, causing current to flow.

Copper is a very good conductor. It's used for most electrical wiring in homes. The inside of the cord you use to plug in a lamp is made of copper wire.

If you look at a lamp cord, you won't see the copper wire. The copper is covered with a layer of plastic. Plastic doesn't conduct electricity well. Its electrons are not free to move between atoms. A material that conducts electricity poorly is an **insulator**. Wood, glass, and rubber are also insulators.

Insulators are important because they protect you from the electric current in the wire. If the layer of plastic on a wire peels off or cracks, the wire should be replaced. If you touch a bare wire that is conducting current, the charges will flow through you and could hurt you. Also, wires get warm when they carry electricity. A bare wire that touches paper or cloth could start a fire.

Focus Skill **CAUSE AND EFFECT**

What causes a metal to be a good conductor?

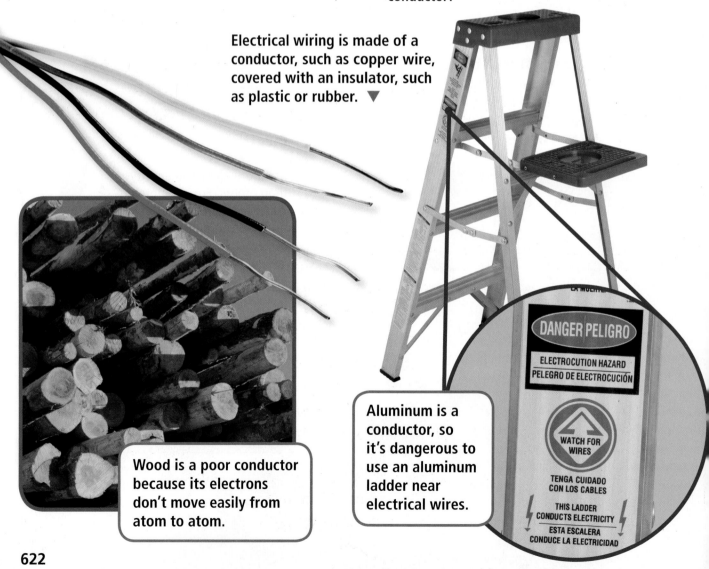

Electrical wiring is made of a conductor, such as copper wire, covered with an insulator, such as plastic or rubber. ▼

Wood is a poor conductor because its electrons don't move easily from atom to atom.

Aluminum is a conductor, so it's dangerous to use an aluminum ladder near electrical wires.

DANGER PELIGRO

ELECTROCUTION HAZARD
PELEGRO DE ELECTROCUCIÓN

WATCH FOR WIRES

TENGA CUIDADO CON LOS CABLES

THIS LADDER CONDUCTS ELECTRICITY
ESTA ESCALERA CONDUCE LA ELECTRICIDAD

Essential Question

What Are Static and Current Electricity?

In this lesson, you learned that static electricity is a buildup of charges on an object and that it can be discharged in a short burst of kinetic energy. You learned that current electricity is a more useful form of electricity because it is constant and because it can be turned on and off.

1. 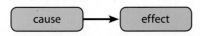 **CAUSE AND EFFECT** Draw and complete a graphic organizer that shows some of the causes of static electricity.

   cause → effect

2. **SUMMARIZE** Write a one-paragraph summary about electric conductors and insulators.

3. **DRAW CONCLUSIONS** What kind of electricity does a TV use? What kinds of energy does the TV produce from this electricity?

4. **VOCABULARY** Use the vocabulary terms to make a crossword puzzle.

Test Prep

5. **CRITICAL THINKING** Some air filters have metal plates that build up a static charge. How can this clean the air?

6. What is the volt used to measure?
   A. electrical pressure
   B. speed of an electric current
   C. amount of electrical energy used
   D. how well an insulator works

Make Connections

 Writing

Expository Writing
Write a **business letter** to your local power company, asking for information on how the company generates electricity.

 Math

Compare Numbers
A 100-watt light bulb costs $1. It lasts about 1000 hours. A 15-watt fluorescent bulb provides the same amount of light. It costs $6 and lasts about 10,000 hours. Which bulb is the better buy? Why?

 Social Studies

Scientists in History
Scientific units are often named after early scientists in the field. Research and report on Alessandro Volta, James Watt, or André-Marie Ampère.

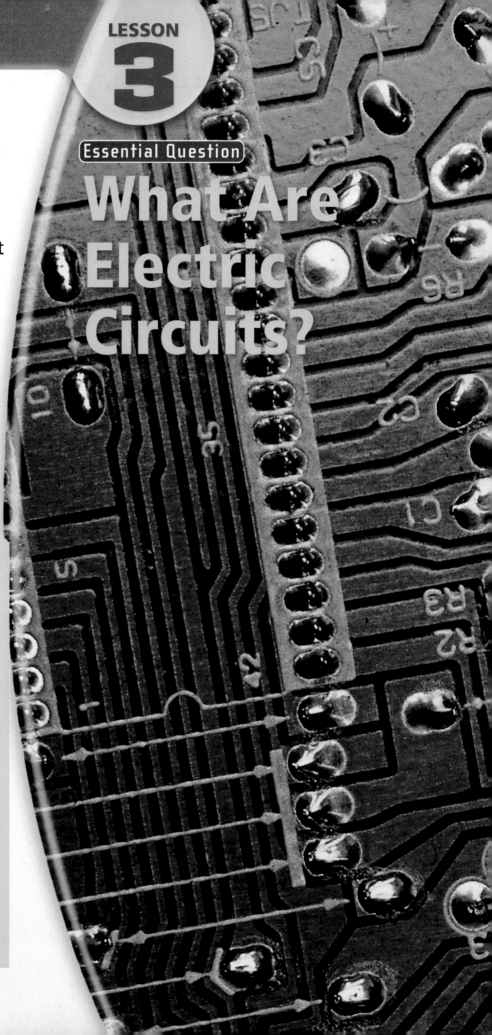

Investigate the path electricity takes in a circuit.

Read and learn about the different types of electric circuits.

Essential Question

What Are Electric Circuits?

Fast Fact

Printed Circuits

The circuits in many electronic devices, such as computers and MP3 players, are printed on boards like this one. The lines on the board are tiny metal wires that conduct electricity. The wires are printed onto the board in a process similar to printing a photograph. In the Investigate, you will connect larger wires and see how they conduct electricity.

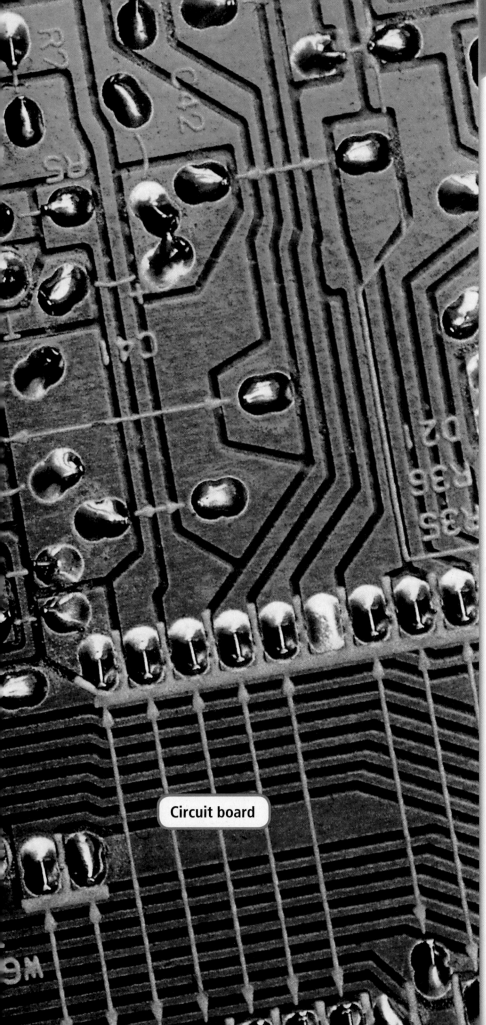

Circuit board

electric circuit [ee•LEK•trik SER•kit] The path an electric current follows (p. 628)

series circuit [SIR•eez SER•kit] An electric circuit in which the current has only one path to follow (p. 629)

parallel circuit [PAIR•uh•lel SER•kit] An electric circuit that has more than one path for the current to follow (p. 630)

Build an Electric Circuit

Guided Inquiry

Start with Questions

For electricity to be useful, it needs a path to follow. Electricity needs to move from its source to a place where it's needed. But it can't do this without some control.

- How do circuits control electricity?

- How does this switch turn on this light?

Investigate to find out. Then read to find out more.

Prepare to Investigate

Inquiry Skill Tip

Even though you may understand how something works, if you make a model, you may be surprised to discover things you didn't know before. In the process of making a model, you have to think about each part of an object and how the parts interact.

Materials

- 3 lengths of insulated wire with bare ends
- 2 light-bulb holders
- battery holder
- 2 light bulbs
- batteries

Make an Observation Chart

	Observations
With batteries	
Without batteries	

Follow This Procedure

1 Use the wire to connect the light-bulb holders and the battery holder as shown in the diagram. Have your teacher check to make sure you have assembled the parts correctly.

2 Screw the light bulbs firmly into the holders.

3 Insert the batteries into the battery holder. **Observe** and **record** what happens.

4 Remove the batteries from the battery holder. **Observe** and **record** what happens.

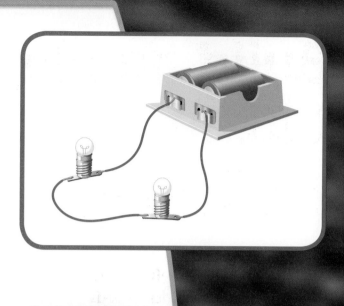

Draw Conclusions

1. What happened when you put the cells into the battery holder?

2. What happened when you took the cells out of the battery holder?

3. Think about the path you made for the electric current. How did putting the cells into the holder affect this path?

4. **Inquiry Skill** Draw a diagram of the path you made for the electric current. **Make a model** of how the current in one room of your home might move through various appliances, such as lamps or the TV. Draw a diagram of your model.

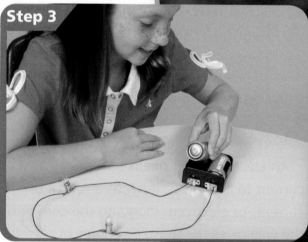
Step 3

Independent Inquiry

Is there another way to connect two light bulbs and a battery of cells? Plan and conduct a simple experiment **to find out.**

VOCABULARY
electric circuit p. 628
series circuit p. 629
parallel circuit p. 630

SCIENCE CONCEPTS
▶ what parts make up an electric circuit
▶ how series and parallel circuits compare

Focus Skill **MAIN IDEA AND DETAILS**

Look for details about the difference between series and parallel circuits.

Main Idea

detail   detail   detail

Series Circuits

If the toaster doesn't toast your bread, the first thing you do is check to see that it's plugged in. You know that the toaster won't work unless it's connected to the wires in your home. The wires give the electricity a path to follow. The path an electric current follows is called an **electric circuit**.

An electric circuit needs two things for current to flow. First, it needs a source of current, or electrons. Plugging the cord into the wall gives the toaster a source of current. Second, the circuit has to be complete. If there is a break in the circuit, the current won't flow. In the Investigate, the battery of

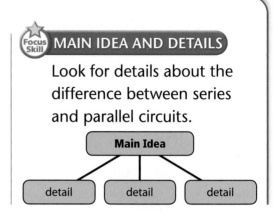

Old signs like this one were wired with series circuits.

cells was the source of current. The battery, wires, and light bulbs formed a complete circuit.

A switch controls the flow of current by opening and closing the circuit. When the switch is on, the circuit is complete. The light comes on. When you turn the switch off, a piece of metal inside the switch moves. This breaks the flow of current, and the light goes out.

Lights Out!

Use the circuit you built in the Investigate. Insert the batteries, and make sure the lights come on. Remove one of the lights from its socket. What do you observe? Explain your observations.

The kind of circuit that you built in the Lesson Investigate is called a series circuit. In a **series circuit**, the current has only one path to follow. The parts are connected one after the other in a single loop. Removing any part of the circuit breaks the circuit, and current stops flowing.

Series circuits aren't used for most wiring in buildings. The only way for current to flow in a series circuit is to have everything connected at the same time. What would that be like in a home? All electric devices would have to be switched on all the time. If you unplugged a radio, all the lights in your home would go out!

Series circuits were once used in lighted signs and scoreboards that had only a few lights. If one light burned out, the whole sign went out. Series circuits were also used in strings of decorative lights. If one light didn't work, none of the others worked, either. People didn't know which bulb had burned out, so they had to check them all. It was easy to check and replace a small number of lights. But for anything with a lot of bulbs, keeping a series circuit working took a lot of time.

Focus Skill MAIN IDEA AND DETAILS

What two things are needed in order for current to flow in a circuit?

Strings of decorative lights used to be wired in series. If one light burned out, they all went out. Imagine having to climb a tree to find and replace the burned-out bulb!

Series Circuit

In a series circuit, all the parts are connected in a loop. The circuit must be unbroken to work.

A parallel circuit has more than one path that current can follow. Use your finger to trace the different paths shown here.

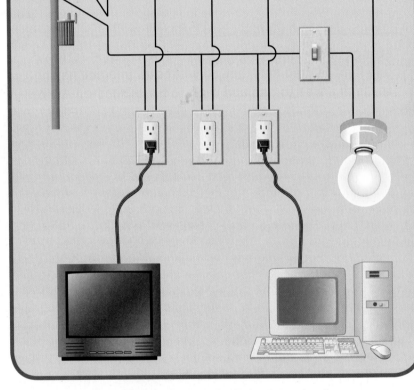

This circuit diagram shows how several devices can be connected in a parallel circuit.

Parallel Circuits

You have seen why a series circuit isn't very convenient to use. Luckily, there's a better way to connect the parts of a circuit. Instead of giving the current only one path, you can make a path for each device in the circuit. A circuit that has more than one path for current to follow is called a **parallel circuit**.

Let's say you wanted to change your circuit from the Investigate to a parallel circuit. You would use extra wire to give each bulb its own loop branching off from the battery. The current for each bulb would have a separate path. If one path was broken, current could still flow through another path. The second bulb would stay lit.

In a parallel circuit, if one device is turned off or removed, current stops flowing along the loop for that device. But current continues to flow through the rest of

the circuit. The other devices don't stop working. This makes a parallel circuit more practical to use than a series circuit.

Think of a parallel circuit as a path that branches and comes together again. Suppose you are walking in the woods with a friend, and the path splits into two paths. You know that each path has a bridge across a nearby river. You take one of the paths.

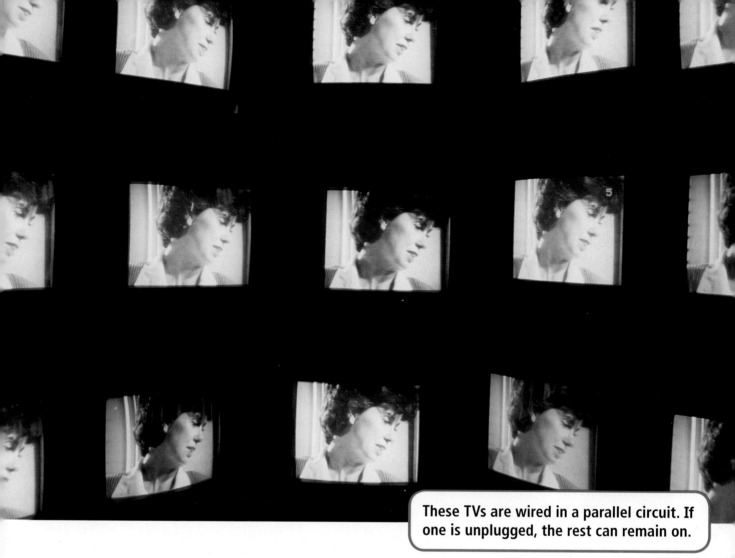

These TVs are wired in a parallel circuit. If one is unplugged, the rest can remain on.

Your friend takes the other. After you each cross a different bridge, you meet where the paths join.

What happens if you get to the river and see that the bridge on your path has washed away? You can go back and take the other path. This time, you use the same bridge that your friend used.

Homes, schools, and businesses are wired with parallel circuits. Each loop of a parallel circuit may have a switch in it. The switch controls only that one loop. For example, a ceiling light is usually controlled by a switch in the wall, so you don't have to reach the ceiling. But the switch doesn't affect other loops of the circuit. If you turn off a ceiling light, the clock, the TV, and other devices in the room stay turned on.

Remember the sign with light bulbs connected in a series circuit? If the bulbs were connected in a parallel circuit, one bulb could burn out and the other lights would remain on.

A parallel circuit has another advantage over a series circuit. You can connect more devices in a parallel circuit. If you connect too many light bulbs in a series circuit, they all become dimmer. That's why old signs wired in series circuits didn't have many bulbs. But in a parallel circuit, adding more bulbs doesn't change how bright they are.

Focus Skill MAIN IDEA AND DETAILS

What are two advantages that parallel circuits have over series circuits?

Drawing Circuits

You have learned that devices that use electricity have circuits inside them. Engineers design these circuits. Some circuits, such as those in a blender or a lamp, are simple. Some, such as those in a car or an airplane, are more complicated.

When engineers work on a new design, they don't begin by connecting a lot of wires. Instead, they draw diagrams of the circuits they will use. Circuit diagrams use symbols to show the parts of a circuit. Each part of a circuit has a different symbol.

A diagram of the series circuit you built in the Investigate would have symbols for the battery, the wires, and the two lights. These symbols would be connected in a single loop.

A circuit diagram of a washing machine includes symbols for wires, switches, a motor, and a pump. A parallel circuit

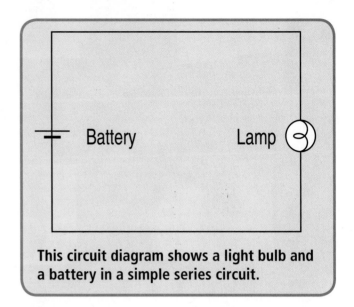

This circuit diagram shows a light bulb and a battery in a simple series circuit.

diagram of the washer and a dryer would have many different loops.

A jet airliner has more than 56 km (35 mi) of wire in it. Just imagine how complicated that circuit diagram would be!

MAIN IDEA AND DETAILS

What do you see on a circuit diagram?

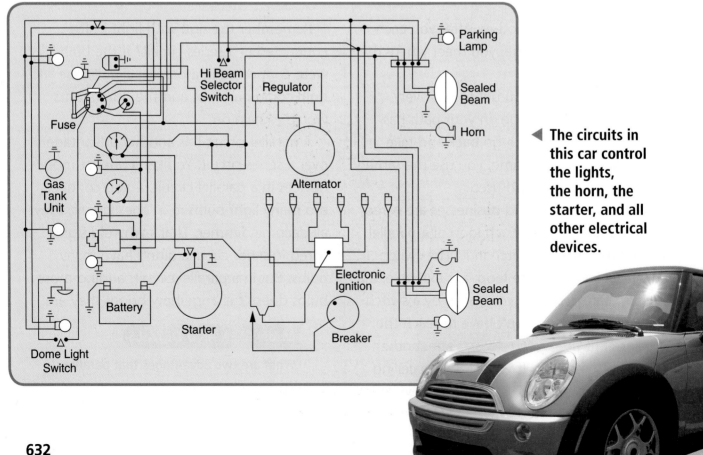

◄ The circuits in this car control the lights, the horn, the starter, and all other electrical devices.

Essential Question

What Are Electric Circuits?

In this lesson, you learned the difference between a series circuit and a parallel circuit. You also learned how engineers design and draw circuits.

1. **Focus Skill MAIN IDEA AND DETAILS** Draw and complete a graphic organizer that shows supporting details for this main idea: There are two types of basic circuits.

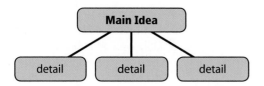

2. **SUMMARIZE** Summarize the lesson by writing a paragraph that compares and contrasts series and parallel circuits.

3. **DRAW CONCLUSIONS** Why do many appliances include circuit diagrams in their instructions?

4. **VOCABULARY** Look up *series*, and tell why this word is a good choice to name a type of circuit.

Test Prep

5. **CRITICAL THINKING** If you want a switch to turn a light on and off, should you connect them in series or in parallel? Explain.

6. What two things are needed for current to flow in a circuit?
   A. wires and a switch
   B. a current source and a light bulb
   C. a current source and a path
   D. extra paths for the current

Make Connections

 Writing

Narrative Writing
Write a **short story** that tells about the journey of an electron as it flows through the circuit you built in the Investigate.

 Math

Make a Bar Graph
Keep a log of the ways you use electricity at school. For example, keep track of the number of hours a day the lights are on and the number of hours you use the TV. Make a bar graph to show your use of each device.

 Art

Wire Art
Draw a circuit diagram for a recreation room you would like to have. Attach pictures cut from magazines to show the devices in the circuit.

Hertha Marks Ayrton

At a time when women were not allowed to vote, Hertha Marks Ayrton worked to break down the barriers for women in other ways.

Ayrton was born and raised in England in the late 1800s. She marched in the streets for the right of women to vote. She trained as a mathematician and had a deep interest in electricity. She was the first woman invited to join the Institution of Electrical Engineers. She received the Royal Society of London's Hughes Medal for her work with electricity. The Hughes Medal is awarded to a person who has made an original discovery in physical science. She is the only woman ever to have been awarded this medal.

Today, Ayrton is remembered as a pioneer in the study of electricity. She wrote a book about electric arcs. An electric arc is an electric current that flows through a gas that is normally not a conductor, such as the air we breathe. Electric arc lamps were used to light streets in England in the late 1800s. They were much brighter than other types of electric lamps, but they hissed loudly and were not stable. Ayrton found that parts of the lamps needed to be redesigned to conduct electricity better.

▶ **HERTHA MARKS** ▲

▶ First woman to join the Institution of Electrica
▶ Only woman in histor awarded the Hughes the Royal Society of L

 Think and Write

❶ What barriers did Ayrton face as a scientist?

❷ How did her work with electric arc lamps help people on the streets of London?

Meredith Gourdine

▶ **MEREDITH GOURDINE**

▶ Physicist, engineer, and inventor
▶ Won the Silver Medal in the long jump at the 1952 Summer Olympics

As an undergraduate at Cornell University, Meredith Gourdine majored in engineering physics and served as captain of the track team. He went on to earn a doctorate at the California Institute of Technology.

Dr. Gourdine invented many things, such as a system for removing smoke from burning buildings and a method for removing fog from airport runways. Both of these inventions work by giving particles in the air a negative charge. The charged particles are then attracted to the ground by electromagnets.

Dr. Gourdine also worked to perfect a generator that converts low-voltage electricity to high-voltage electricity. His generator may provide a much-needed new source of energy in the future.

Think and Write

1 Why is it important to give airborne particles such as smoke and fog a negative charge?

2 Why do you think Dr. Gourdine's generator might be important in the future?

Career Electric Line Installer

An installer's job is to run long lengths of cable from energy sources to customers. Installers may also check connections for proper voltage readings and install circuit breakers, switches, fuses, and other equipment to control and direct the electric current.

Vocabulary Review

Use the terms below to complete the sentences. The page numbers tell you where to look in the chapter if you need help.

electricity p. 609   conductor p. 622

electromagnet p. 610   insulator p. 622

static electricity p. 618   series circuit p. 629

current electricity   parallel circuit
    p. 620   p. 630

1. The buildup of charges on an object is _____.

2. Electricity that flows along a path is _____.

3. An electric circuit in which current has only one path to follow is a _____.

4. A material that doesn't allow electricity to flow easily through it is an _____.

5. The form of energy produced by moving electrons is _____.

6. A material that allows electricity to flow easily through it is a _____.

7. An electric circuit in which current has more than one path to follow is a _____.

8. A device that acts as a magnet when electricity is flowing through it is an _____.

Check Understanding

Write the letter of the best choice.

9. Which of these is a conductor?
   A. copper
   B. glass
   C. plastic
   D. wood

10. **CAUSE AND EFFECT** What causes the behavior of the balloons in this picture?
    F. Neither balloon has a charge.
    G. The red balloon is positive, and the blue balloon is negative.
    H. The red balloon is positive, and the blue balloon is neutral.
    J. Both balloons have the same charge.

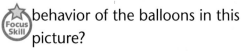

11. What is the path that electric current follows?
    A. an insulator
    B. an electric circuit
    C. potential energy
    D. kinetic energy

12. Tai walked across a carpet and felt a shock when she touched a doorknob. What caused the shock?

    F. The knob was an electromagnet.

    G. The knob was an insulator.

    H. Tai developed a static charge.

    J. The carpet was a conductor.

13. What device is used to start and stop the flow of electric current in a circuit?

    A. a battery

    B. an electromagnet

    C. a motor

    D. a switch

14. **MAIN IDEA AND DETAILS** Jamal built the circuit shown here. Use the diagram to infer what happens when he takes the bulb out of holder 2.

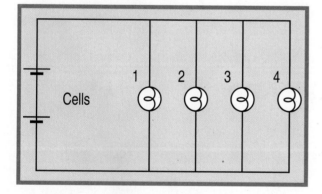

    F. Only bulbs 1 and 2 go out.

    G. Only bulbs 3 and 4 go out.

    H. All the other bulbs go out.

    J. All the other bulbs stay on.

15. When a microwave oven's timer beeps, to what kind of energy is electricity being changed?

    A. heat

    B. light

    C. motion

    D. sound

16. Which appliance costs the most to use for a half hour?

    F. a 1200-watt hair dryer

    G. a 110-watt TV

    H. a 1000-watt vacuum cleaner

    J. a 75-watt window fan

Inquiry Skills

17. **Predict** what will happen to the brightness of the bulbs if you add two more bulbs to the circuit shown here.

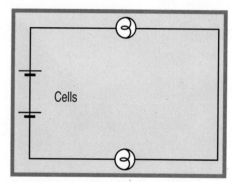

18. How would you **plan an experiment** to test whether a substance is a conductor?

Critical Thinking

19. Why is the electron the part of the atom that moves when an electric current flows?

20. For a party, you are about to hang a string of tiny lights wired in a parallel circuit. You test the string, and the bulbs all light. Your friend is worried because you have no spare bulbs to replace any that burn out. What will happen if a bulb burns out? How can you explain your answer to your friend?

The **Big** Idea

Sound and Light

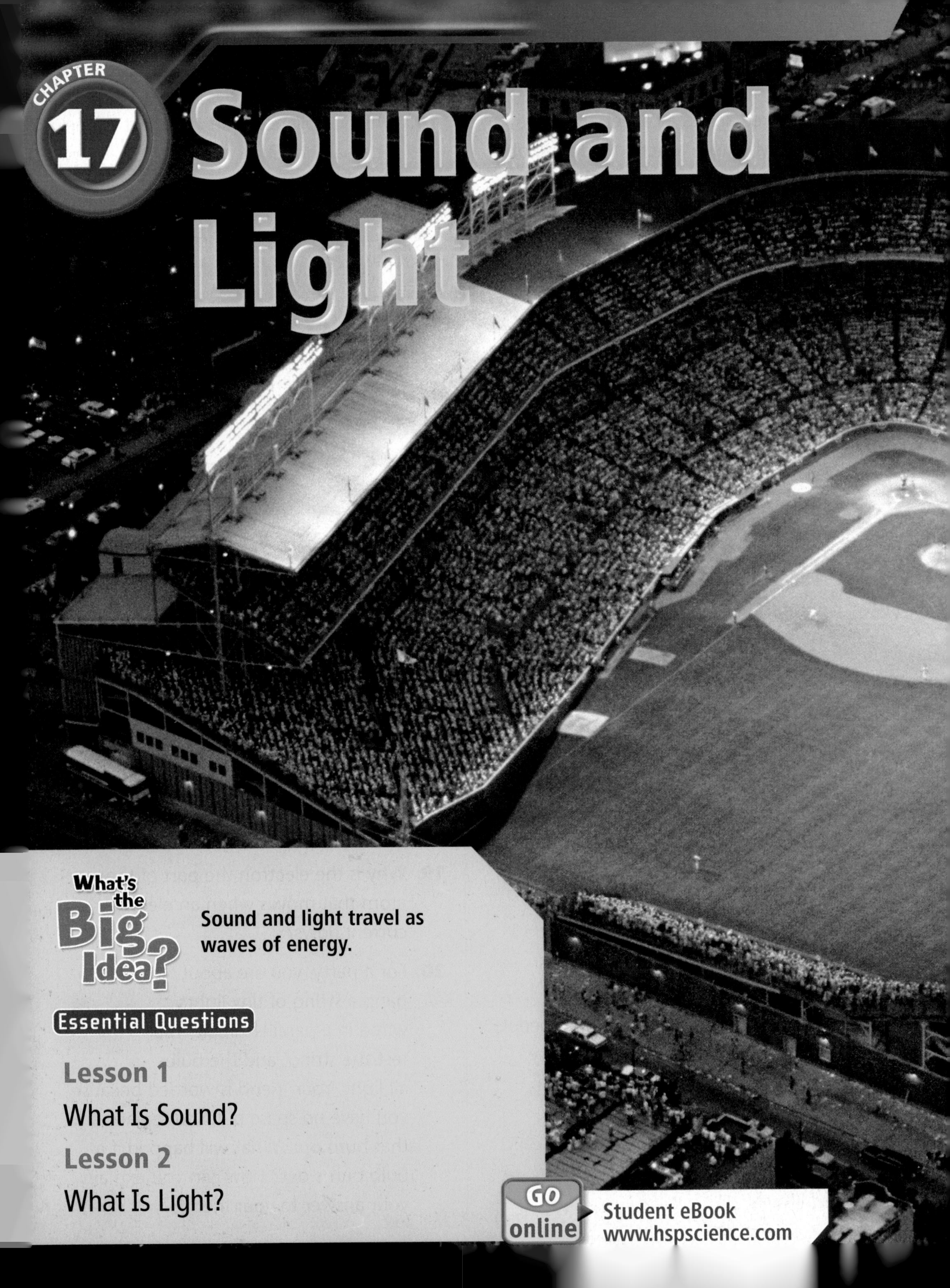

What's the Big Idea?

Sound and light travel as waves of energy.

Essential Questions

Lesson 1

What Is Sound?

Lesson 2

What Is Light?

GO online
Student eBook
www.hspscience.com

Wrigley Field, in Chicago, Illinois, is right in the middle of a crowded neighborhood. The people who live nearby can hear the roar of the crowd. At night, the stadium lights up the sky. How does sound and light travel from the baseball stadium to the area that surrounds it? How does this relate to the Big Idea?

Wrigley Field, Chicago

What Is Sound?

Investigate how sound is affected by the distance it travels.

Read and learn how sound travels in waves through matter.

Fast Fact

Pipe Organ

A pipe organ makes sounds by blowing air through pipes. This large organ in Salt Lake City, Utah, has 11,623 pipes. The longest pipe is about 10 m (32 ft) high. The smallest pipe is about the size of a drinking straw. In the Investigate, you'll find out how the length of part of a musical instrument can affect the sound that's made.

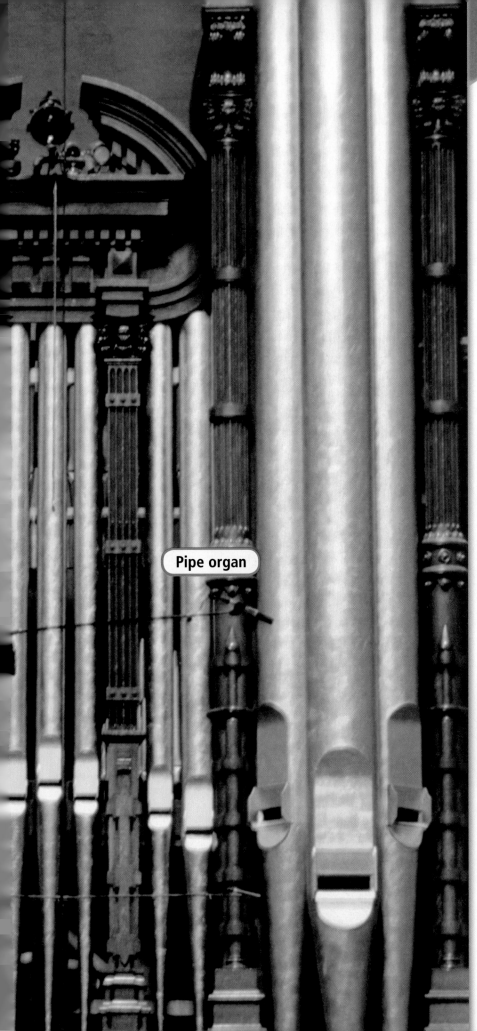

Pipe organ

Vocabulary Preview

vibration [vy•BRAY•shuhn] A back-and-forth movement of matter (p. 644)

volume [VAHL•yoom] The loudness of a sound (p. 645)

pitch [PICH] How high or low a sound is (p. 646)

frequency [FREE•kwuhn•see] The number of vibrations per second (p. 646)

Making Sound

Guided Inquiry

Start with Questions

You can hear sounds from outside as you sit inside. The sounds move through the walls.

- Can sound move through string?

- How does a piano produce sounds?

Investigate to find out. Then read to find out more.

Prepare to Investigate

Inquiry Skill Tip

When you identify variables in an investigation, you think about all the properties you could observe and all the measurements you could make. You then test one of these variables by changing it and observing the results. You keep all the other variables the same.

Materials

- 2 pieces of string, 100 cm each
- 2 metal spoons
- meterstick

Make an Observation Chart

Length of String	Observations
75 cm	
50 cm	
25 cm	

Follow This Procedure

1. Tie one end of each piece of string to one of the spoons.

2. Wrap the other end of each piece of string around one of your index fingers. One finger on each hand should be wrapped with a string. Gently place the wrapped fingers in your ears.

3. Let the spoons hang freely. Have a partner **measure** the string lengths between your fingers and the spoons. Wrap more string around your fingers until the lengths are 75 cm each.

4. Have your partner gently tap the spoon with the other spoon. **Record** your observations.

5. Repeat Steps 2, 3, and 4, but shorten the string lengths to 50 cm.

6. Repeat Steps 2, 3, and 4, but shorten the string lengths to 25 cm.

Draw Conclusions

1. What did you hear in Step 4 of the activity?

2. Did the sound change when you shortened the strings? If so, how?

3. **Inquiry Skill** Before scientists conduct experiments, they must **identify the variables** to be tested. What variable did you test in this activity?

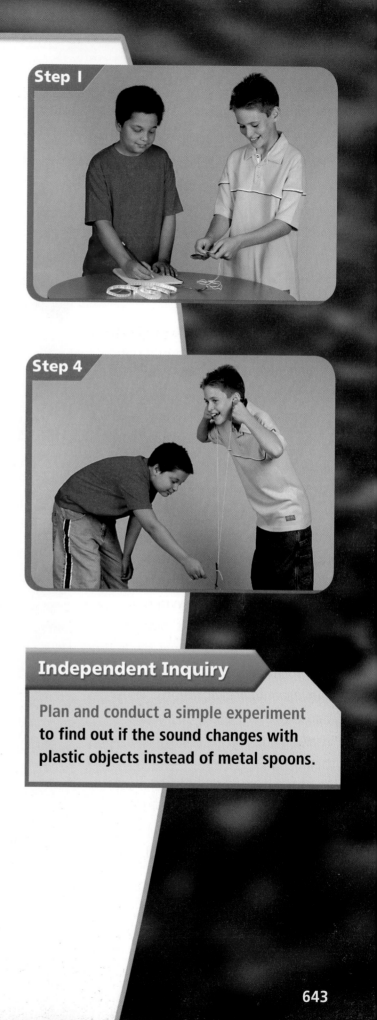

Step 1

Step 4

Independent Inquiry

Plan and conduct a simple experiment **to find out if the sound changes with plastic objects instead of metal spoons.**

VOCABULARY
vibration p. 644
volume p. 645
pitch p. 646
frequency p. 646

SCIENCE CONCEPTS
▶ what makes sounds vary
▶ how sounds travel

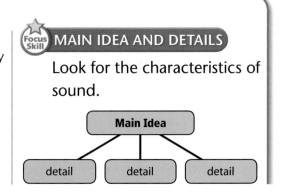

MAIN IDEA AND DETAILS
Look for the characteristics of sound.

Sound Energy

Have you ever been to a Native American powwow? People dance and celebrate to the rhythm of a drum. The drum may be big—about 1 m (3 ft) in diameter. Eight or more people play the drum and sing. The sound gets very loud and can be heard far away.

Sound is a form of energy that travels through the air. Sound is made when something vibrates. A **vibration** is a back-and-forth movement of matter. When a drummer hits a drum's head, or covering, the head moves back and forth very quickly. These movements are vibrations. They cause the air nearby to vibrate, making the sound energy that you hear.

Musical instruments make sounds in various ways. A woodwind instrument, like a clarinet, has a thin wooden reed attached to it.

The head of a drum—a thin covering—is flexible and tight, so it vibrates when it is hit. ▲

Math in Science
Interpret Data

How Loud Are Some Sounds?

Sound	Decibel Level
Whisper	20 dB
Quiet radio	40 dB
Conversation	60 dB
Dishwasher	80 dB
Jackhammer	100 dB
Thunderclap	120 dB

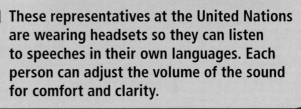

Why do factory workers and jack-hammer operators wear ear protection?

◀ These representatives at the United Nations are wearing headsets so they can listen to speeches in their own languages. Each person can adjust the volume of the sound for comfort and clarity.

When the player blows into the instrument, the reed vibrates. Some instruments, like drums, vibrate when they're hit. A stringed instrument, like a violin, vibrates when the player plucks the strings or draws a bow across them.

Some sounds are louder than others. If the drummers at the powwow hit the drum gently, the sound is soft. If they hit the drum harder, the sound gets stronger and louder. The loudness of a sound is called the **volume**. Can you think of a sound with a low volume and a sound with a high volume?

When a drummer hits a drum harder, more energy is transferred to the drum and to the sound. The more energy a sound has, the greater its volume is.

The volume of a sound is measured in units called *decibels* (DES•uh•buhlz), abbreviated *dB*. The softest sound a human can hear is 0 dB. A high-decibel sound is loud and has a lot of energy. Have you ever heard a sound that made your ears ring? Sounds above 100 dB can cause pain and can damage a person's ears. That's why people who work around loud sounds wear ear plugs or other ear protection.

MAIN IDEA AND DETAILS

Describe the ways in which three types of musical instruments make sound.

645

Sound Waves

Sound travels through the air as waves. When a jackhammer strikes the sidewalk, the sidewalk vibrates and pushes on the air directly above it. Molecules of air are *compressed,* or squeezed together. The compressed air pushes on the air next to it. This passes the compression along, like a wave at the beach.

You already know that some sounds are higher than others. If you've ever listened to a brass band, for example, you know that a trumpet makes a higher sound than a tuba does. The **pitch** of a sound is how high or how low it is. In the Investigate, you found that changing the length of the strings altered the pitch of the sound you heard. That's because the length of the strings affected how fast they vibrated. A shorter string vibrates faster. There are more vibrations per second. The number of vibrations per second is the **frequency** of a sound.

A sound with a high frequency has a high pitch. A sound with a low frequency has a low pitch. Small objects often vibrate at higher frequencies than large objects do. In the Investigate, shortening the strings made them vibrate at a higher frequency. A trumpet is smaller than a tuba, so the trumpet makes sound waves with higher frequencies.

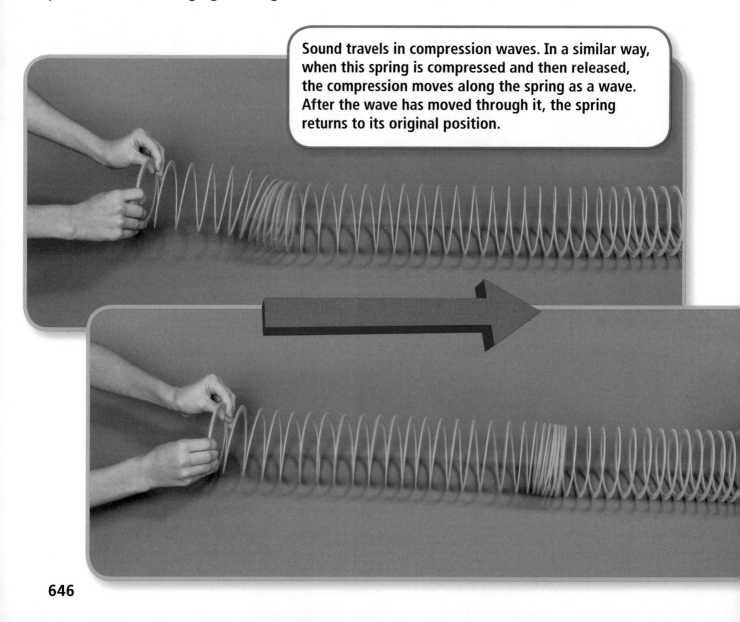

Sound travels in compression waves. In a similar way, when this spring is compressed and then released, the compression moves along the spring as a wave. After the wave has moved through it, the spring returns to its original position.

▲ If you shout toward a hard surface, such as a cliff, you may hear an echo of your voice. The echo isn't as loud as the original sound because the surface absorbs some of the energy.

Sound waves move out in all directions from an object that makes a sound. When a sound wave hits something, some or all of the energy is absorbed. Soft surfaces absorb more sound energy than hard surfaces. A sound that hits a hard surface bounces back—not much of it is absorbed. A sound that bounces off a surface is called an *echo*. If you stand at the foot of a cliff and shout, you may hear an echo of your voice. Some caves and canyons are famous for the echoes they produce.

MAIN IDEA AND DETAILS

How do sounds travel?

Playing the Glasses

You can make a sound by tapping on a drinking glass. If you put water in the glass, the pitch of the sound changes. Use water and several glasses to make different notes. How does adding water to the glasses affect the pitch of the sounds you make?

Sound Transmission

Have you ever set up a line of dominoes and then knocked them down? The first domino pushes over the second and so on. The wave of energy moves down the line, but the individual dominoes do not. Sound has energy just like the dominoes. Waves can carry energy a long distance. The energy travels from place to place, but the matter that carries the energy stays where it is.

In a similar way, sound waves move through air because particles in the air vibrate right where they are.

When you talk to a friend, vibrations move from you to your friend through the air. But the air doesn't have to move to your friend. If it did, a breeze blowing in your face would prevent your friend from hearing your words because they'd be blown back to you!

Science Up Close

For more links and animations, go to www.hspscience.com

How Sound Reaches You

Molecules of air carry sound waves from the source to the listeners.

When the performer sings, she produces vibrations that compress the air.

The sound moves through the air as compression waves.

Air is not the only matter that can carry sound waves. Any kind of matter can be made to vibrate and carry sound. Matter that carries sound waves is called a *medium.* Sound waves can't travel without a medium. That's why there's no sound in space, which has no air or other suitable medium.

The speed of sound depends on the medium through which it's moving. The speed doesn't depend on how loud or soft the volume is or how high or low the pitch is. All sounds travel through a certain kind of medium at the same speed.

If the medium changes, the speed of sound changes. Sound moves faster in warm air than in cold air. It travels faster in solids and liquids than it does in gases.

 **MAIN IDEA AND DETAILS** In reference to sound traveling, what is a medium?

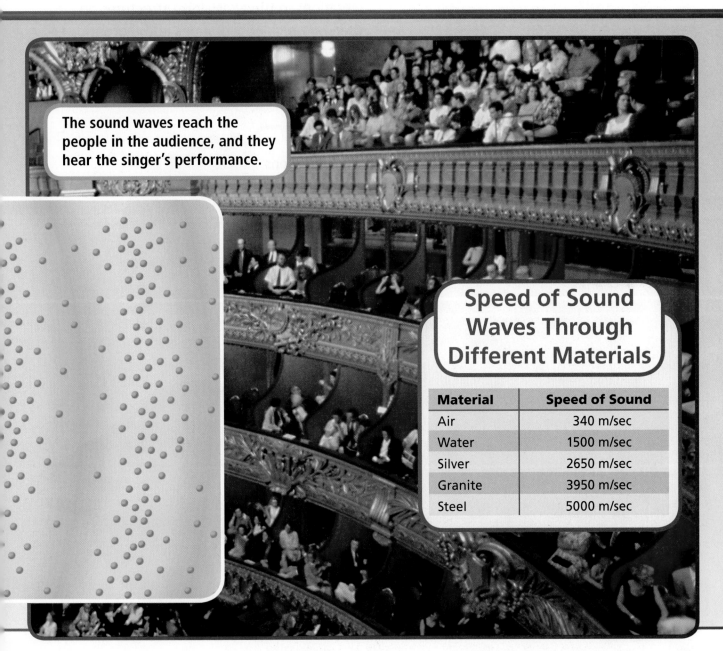

The sound waves reach the people in the audience, and they hear the singer's performance.

Speed of Sound Waves Through Different Materials

Material	Speed of Sound
Air	340 m/sec
Water	1500 m/sec
Silver	2650 m/sec
Granite	3950 m/sec
Steel	5000 m/sec

Animals and Sound

People can hear sounds over a wide range of frequencies. The highest sounds that people can hear have frequencies of about 20,000 vibrations per second.

Many animals can hear sounds that are outside the range of human hearing. Dogs can hear sounds with higher frequencies than people can hear—frequencies of 25,000 vibrations per second.

Bats have better hearing than most other animals. They can hear sounds with frequencies as high as 100,000 vibrations per second. Bats can also produce sounds with that frequency.

As a bat flies, it produces many short, high-frequency sounds. These bounce off objects in the bat's path, and the bat hears the echoes. The echoes help the bat fly at night by giving it information about its surroundings. They also help the bat hunt. Echoes that bounce from insects give information to the bat about where to find its next meal.

People, dogs, and bats have parts of their ears on the outside of their bodies. But this isn't true for all animals. Snakes and birds have no outside ear parts.

Grasshoppers pick up vibrations in several ways. A membrane near the leg picks up vibrations in the air. Hairlike structures on the body pick up vibrations in the ground.

 **MAIN IDEA AND DETAILS** What are two ways animals sense vibrations?

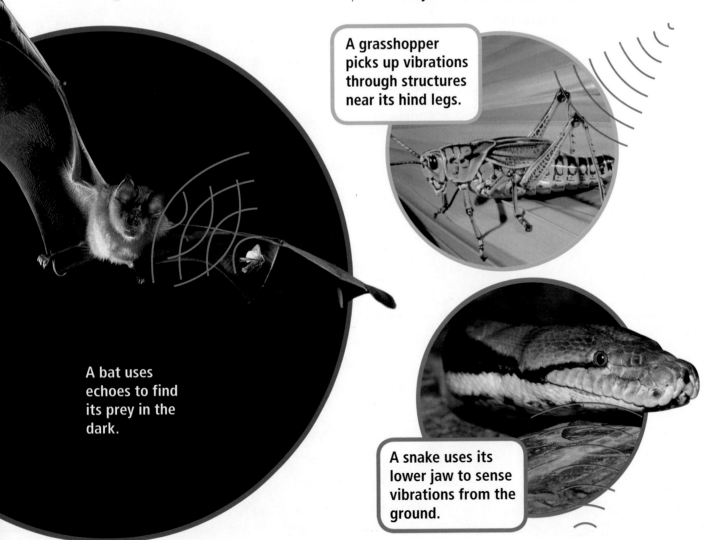

A bat uses echoes to find its prey in the dark.

A grasshopper picks up vibrations through structures near its hind legs.

A snake uses its lower jaw to sense vibrations from the ground.

Essential Question

What Is Sound?

In this lesson, you learned that sound is a form of energy that is produced when something vibrates. Sound travels in waves and needs to be carried by some form of matter.

1. **Focus Skill** **MAIN IDEA AND DETAILS** Draw and complete a graphic organizer that lists supporting details for this main idea: Frequency and volume are two characteristics of sound.

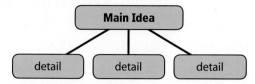

Main Idea

detail   detail   detail

2. **SUMMARIZE** Write a one-paragraph summary about sound waves.

3. **DRAW CONCLUSIONS** To change the length of the vibrating part of a string, a guitar player holds the string down against a fret, a ridge on the guitar. What does changing the length in this way do to the sound?

4. **VOCABULARY** Write a paragraph that uses this lesson's vocabulary terms.

Test Prep

5. **CRITICAL THINKING** Why does carpet make a room seem quiet?

6. What happens to a sound if the frequency of the vibrations increases?
   - **A.** The volume decreases.
   - **B.** The pitch increases.
   - **C.** The sound echoes.
   - **D.** The sound gets louder.

Make Connections

 Writing

Narrative Writing
Write a **story** about how a bat hunts for insects. Write your story from the bat's point of view.

 Math

Construct a Graph
Research the speed sound travels through different materials. Make a bar graph to show your data. Be sure to include the materials listed in Science Up Close.

 Social Studies

The Sound Barrier
A vehicle that travels faster than the speed of sound is said to break the sound barrier. Find out what kinds of vehicles have broken the sound barrier. Make a time line to show your findings.

Investigate how light is reflected.

Read and learn about light energy, light waves, and ways to control light.

Essential Question

What Is Light?

Fast Fact

Laser Shows

Dozens of lasers are used to make a display like this. The color of each laser beam depends on the kind of material contained in the laser. Each laser also contains a pair of mirrors that reflect energy from the material inside.

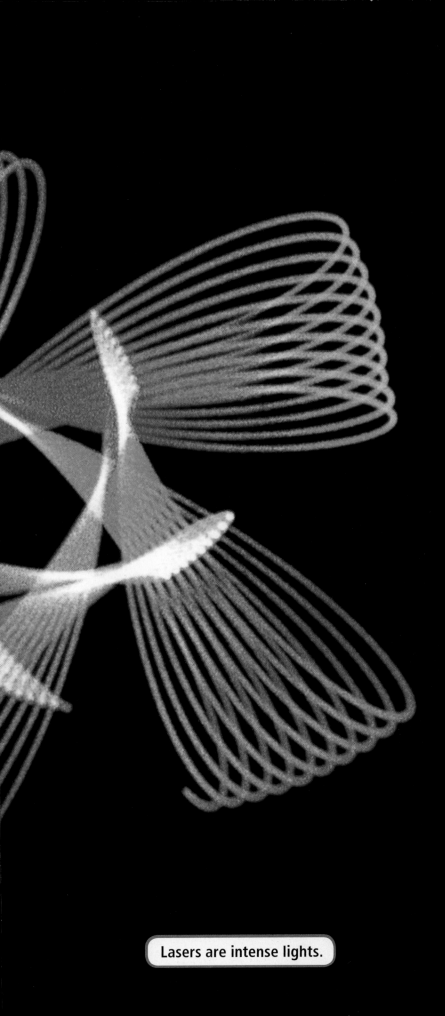

Lasers are intense lights.

reflection [rih•FLEK•shuhn] The bouncing of heat or light off an object (p. 660)

opaque [oh•PAYK] Not allowing light to pass through (p. 660)

translucent [trans•LOO•suhnt] Allowing only some light to pass through (p. 661)

transparent [tranz•PAIR•uhnt] Allowing light to pass through (p. 661)

refraction [rih•FRAK•shuhn] The bending of light as it moves from one material to another (p. 661)

concave lens [kahn•KAYV LENZ] A lens that is thicker at the edges than it is at the center (p. 662)

convex lens [kahn•VEKS LENZ] A lens that is thicker at the center than it is at the edges (p. 662)

653

The Path of Reflected Light

Guided Inquiry

Start with Questions

Light usually moves in a straight line until it hits an object. When you turn on a lamp, the light goes from the light bulb to your eyes. What if you look at the lamp in a mirror?

- Can light be bent?

- How does this ball change the path of light?

Investigate to find out. Then read and learn to find out more.

Prepare to Investigate

Inquiry Skill Tip

When you predict what might happen in an investigation, don't just guess. Using your observations and facts you already know, decide what is the most reasonable thing that might happen.

Materials

- piece of corrugated cardboard, 10 cm by 10 cm
- masking tape
- small, flat mirror
- 3 pushpins of different colors
- ruler
- protractor

Make a Data Table

	From 1st pin to 3rd pin	From 2nd pin to 3rd pin
Angle to Mirror		

Follow This Procedure

❶ Lay the cardboard flat, and use tape to stand the mirror vertically at one end of the cardboard. Push two of the pins into the cardboard, about 5 cm in front of the mirror.

❷ Position yourself so your eyes are level with the pins. Align yourself so that your view of one pin lines up with the reflection of the other pin. Push a third pin into the cardboard, at the edge of the mirror, right in front of where you see the reflection. The first pin, the third pin, and the reflection of the second pin should appear to be in a straight line.

❸ Draw lines on the cardboard to connect the third pin with the others. These lines show how the light from the second pin traveled to your eye.

❹ Draw a line along the front of the mirror, and remove the mirror from the cardboard. Using the protractor, measure the angle between each line and the edge of the mirror. Record your results.

Draw Conclusions

1. Compare the two angles you measured.

2. **Inquiry Skill** Suppose you know the angle at which light hits a mirror. Predict the angle at which the light will reflect.

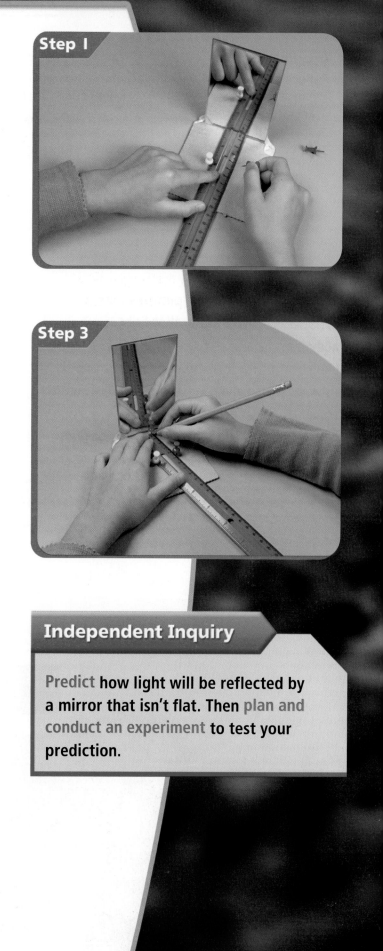

Step 1

Step 3

Independent Inquiry

Predict how light will be reflected by a mirror that isn't flat. Then plan and conduct an experiment to test your prediction.

VOCABULARY
reflection p. 660
opaque p. 660
translucent p. 661
transparent p. 661
refraction p. 661
concave lens p. 662
convex lens p. 662

SCIENCE CONCEPTS
▶ what kinds of light waves there are
▶ how matter affects light

Focus Skill **MAIN IDEA AND DETAILS**
Look for ways that light can be changed.

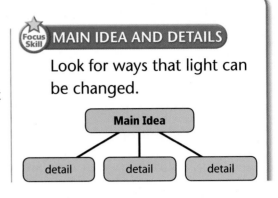

Light Energy

Have you ever taken pictures with a camera? Did you know that light is what allows an image to form on the film? Light, like sound, is a form of energy that travels in waves. However, unlike sound, light can travel through empty space. All waves carry energy. When the waves reach an object, some of the energy can be absorbed by that object. You often see the results. For example, light energy that strikes film in a camera causes a chemical change, enabling a picture to be made.

Light is a small part of a range of energy known as the *electromagnetic spectrum*. The waves that make it up differ in frequency.

Electromagnetic Spectrum

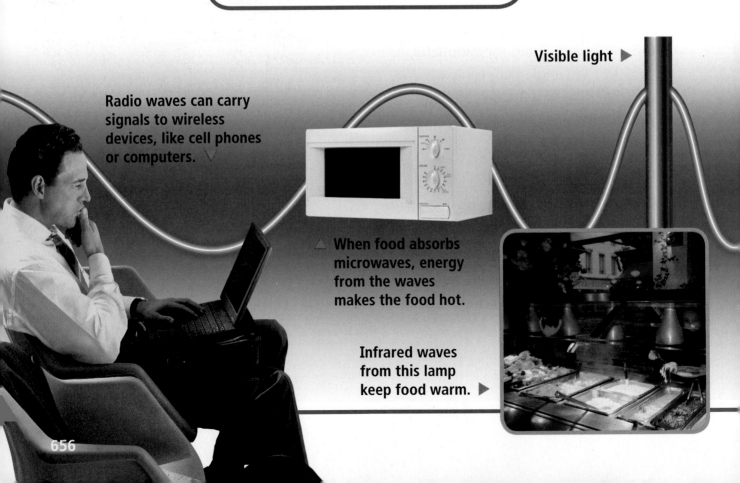

Radio waves can carry signals to wireless devices, like cell phones or computers. ▽

△ When food absorbs microwaves, energy from the waves makes the food hot.

Infrared waves from this lamp keep food warm. ▶

Visible light ▶

656

The part of the spectrum that humans can see is called *visible light*. Radio waves have lower frequencies than visible light waves. X rays have higher frequencies.

Waves with high frequencies carry more energy than waves with lower frequencies. High-energy waves pass through matter more easily. You know that light doesn't pass through your body. But other forms of waves, such as X rays, do, at least partially. Has a dentist ever taken an X-ray image of your teeth? You hold a piece of film in your mouth, and the dentist points an X-ray machine at your jaw. X rays go from the machine, through your jaw, and to the film.

Did you notice that your teeth are white on the X ray, but everything else is dark? When X rays pass through your jaw, your teeth absorb more of the X-ray energy than the rest of your mouth does. The result is that different amounts of energy reach the film in different places.

On the film, the X-ray energy causes changes that can be seen. The different amounts of energy in different places make a picture of your teeth on the film.

Focus Skill **MAIN IDEA AND DETAILS**

What types of waves are found in the electromagnetic spectrum?

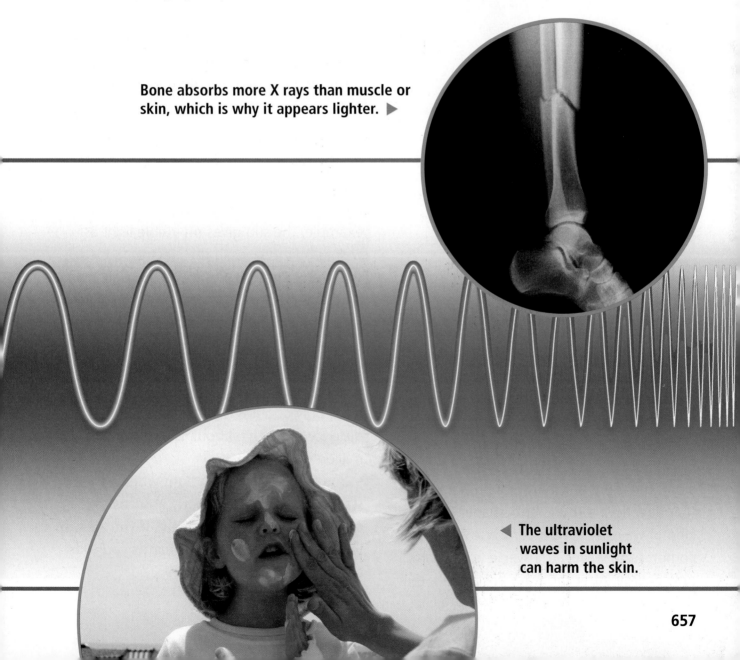

Bone absorbs more X rays than muscle or skin, which is why it appears lighter. ▶

◀ The ultraviolet waves in sunlight can harm the skin.

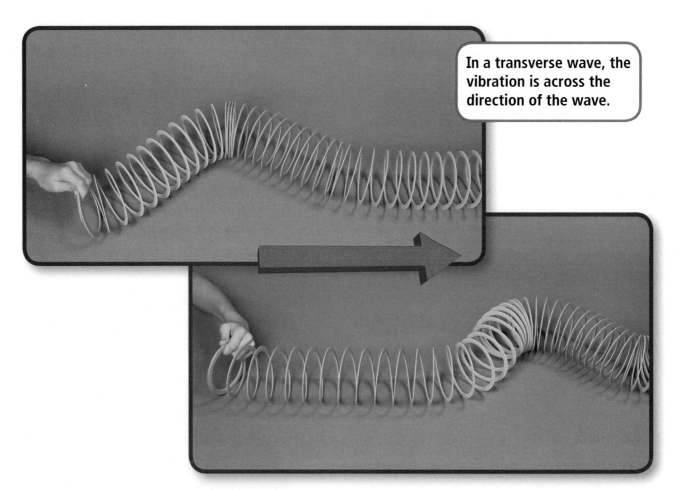

In a transverse wave, the vibration is across the direction of the wave.

Light Waves

Light is unlike anything else in the universe! Scientists have been studying light for centuries, but there is a great deal yet to be discovered about it. Many scientists theorize that light travels in waves.

Light waves are different from sound waves. Sound waves travel as compressions in matter. Light does not compress matter.

Have you watched waves at the ocean or on a lake? While the water moves up and down, it does not move forward or backward. Light moves like ocean waves.

If you hold one end of a rope and shake it up and down, you make a wave that moves along the rope. But the vibration is across that direction, forming an S shape. This kind of wave is called a *transverse* wave. Like compression waves, transverse waves carry only energy. After the wave has passed, the rope is still in your hand, even though the energy has traveled away from you.

Since light waves do not need matter, light can travel through empty space. For example, the sun gives off visible light as well as other waves in the electromagnetic spectrum. These waves travel through space and reach Earth.

Light travels very fast. Scientists have not found anything faster. Even the slowest light waves move thousands of times faster than sound waves. Light is so fast that sunlight takes only about 8 minutes to travel the distance to Earth—about 150 million km (93 million mi).

You feel the energy in light when you stand in sunlight. Your body absorbs the energy, and you feel it as heat. If you absorb too much of that energy, it harms your skin and you get a sunburn.

The light from a light bulb doesn't have as much energy as sunlight. You can't get a sunburn from standing under an ordinary lamp. A light bulb gives off heat because an electric current heats up the filament, or wire, inside the bulb. This makes the filament give off light.

The sun and a light bulb give off light in all directions. A laser, though, gives off light in a narrow beam. Inside a laser, light waves line up, like the members of a band marching in step in one direction. When the waves come out of the laser, they stay together and don't spread out. The concentrated light is very powerful. It is also dangerous. You should never look into a source of laser light.

Focus Skill MAIN IDEA AND DETAILS

What characteristics do light waves have?

Laser

The light energy from lasers is so concentrated that factories use lasers to cut steel. ▶

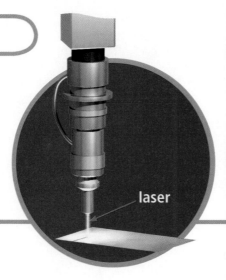

laser

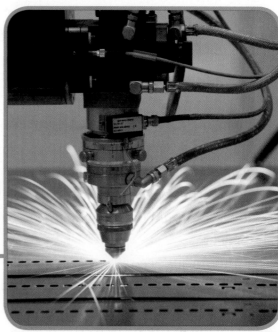

Light Bulb

The light from an ordinary light bulb spreads out in all directions. The energy you get from the bulb decreases as you move away. ▶

Absorption, Reflection, and Refraction

Have you ever seen frosted glass? Its surface is rough, not smooth. Some light passes through, but you can't see objects clearly through the glass.

When light hits an object, the object affects the path of the light. An object can absorb light, make it bounce back, or let it pass through.

Some of the light energy that hits an object is absorbed. Objects of different colors absorb different amounts of light. Dark-colored objects absorb the most light.

Objects don't absorb all the light that hits them. Some of the light bounces off. **Reflection** is the bouncing of light from a surface. Usually, light scatters as it is reflected. The reflected light that reaches your eyes from an object enables you to see the object.

A smooth surface reflects light in a predictable way. The light isn't scattered. Instead, it reflects in a pattern that you see as an image in the surface. This is what happens when you see the sky reflected by the smooth windows of a building or when you see yourself in a mirror.

Whether the surfaces are smooth or rough, most objects absorb some light and reflect the rest. They don't allow light to pass through them. Materials that do not allow light to pass through are **opaque** (oh•PAYK). Most of the objects around you—books, chairs, walls, floors—are opaque. You can't see through them.

The glass used in this building is coated with chemicals that reflect light like a giant mirror. ▶

▲ A prism refracts white light into a rainbow of colors. Refraction of light as it leaves the water makes the pelican's belly and legs look separated from its body.

Materials that allow only some amount of light to pass through are **translucent** (trans•LOO•suhnt). Wax paper and bubble wrap are translucent. So are some kinds of window shades.

With the shades up, though, you can look through glass windows to see what's outside. You can see through glass because light passes through it. A material that allows light to pass through is **transparent**. Most glass, water, and plastic wrap are transparent. Transparent objects don't scatter light like translucent objects can.

You may think that light doesn't change as it passes through transparent materials. But when light moves into a different material, it bends. This bending of light as it moves from one material to another is called **refraction**. Refraction changes the angle at which you see things. When you look at an object through two different materials, the bent light can make a solid object look as if it's in two parts.

(Focus Skill) MAIN IDEA AND DETAILS

Give one example each of transparent, translucent, and opaque materials.

Dark objects absorb more light energy than light-colored objects do. That's why it's good to wear light colors on a bright summer day. ▶

661

Lenses

Use a hand lens to look at this page. A hand lens magnifies objects, or makes them look larger. Most hand lenses contain one glass or plastic lens. A lens is a curved transparent object that bends light. The shape of the curve affects how the light bends.

There are two basic kinds of lenses. A **concave lens** is thicker at the edges than it is at the center. It spreads light waves apart. The viewfinder of a camera has a concave lens. The lens makes objects look smaller. That way, you can look in the viewfinder and see what the whole picture will look like.

A **convex lens** is thicker at the center than it is at the edges. It bends light waves to make them come together. A convex lens can be used as a magnifier or to make an image on a screen. The lens of a camera is a convex lens, too. It brings light waves together on the film, producing an image.

MAIN IDEA AND DETAILS

What are the two basic types of lenses?

Water Lens

Fill a test tube completely with water. Hold the test tube over a sink or pan to catch spills as you close the test tube with a stopper. Make sure the stopper is tight. Then hold the test tube over some writing, and look through it. How does your water lens change what you see? What kind of lens is it?

Camera Lenses

A concave lens spreads light waves apart. ▶

What kinds of lenses are in this camera? ▼

LENS

1:2.8 5.5mm

▲ A convex lens brings light waves together.

Essential Question

What Is Light?

In this lesson, you learned that light is part of the electromagnetic spectrum. It travels as waves. You also learned that light can be absorbed, reflected, and refracted.

1. **Focus Skill** **MAIN IDEA AND DETAILS** Draw and complete a graphic organizer that shows details for this main idea: Light waves change when they hit objects.

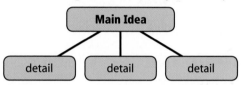

Main Idea

detail detail detail

2. **SUMMARIZE** Write a one-paragraph summary about the parts of the electromagnetic spectrum.

3. **DRAW CONCLUSIONS** Is the glass in a stained-glass window transparent, translucent, or opaque? Explain.

4. **VOCABULARY** Use the vocabulary terms in this lesson to make a crossword puzzle.

Test Prep

5. **CRITICAL THINKING** Which have more energy—microwaves or X rays? Explain your answer.

6. Which is true of a concave lens?
   A. Its center is thicker than its edges.
   B. It projects an image on a screen.
   C. It spreads light rays apart.
   D. It is used in a camera lens.

Make Connections

 Writing

Expository Writing
Suppose you are standing at the rim of a canyon, holding a telescope and a camera. Write a **paragraph** describing what you see through each device.

 Math

Estimating
Light travels at about 300 million m/sec through empty space or through air. Sound travels at about 340 m/sec through air. About how many times faster does light travel than sound?

 Health

Sunscreens
Find out how sunscreens work and what the SPF ratings mean. Summarize your findings in a brief report.

A SOUND IDEA

For six years, Joanne Peterson lived in a silent world. Because she was deaf, Peterson could see her son play the piano, but she could not hear him. Thanks to a recently developed bionic ear, Peterson can hear again.

Electrical Impulses

Peterson was one of the first Americans to use the device. Unlike traditional hearing aids, which amplify sounds, the bionic ear changes sounds into electrical impulses. The bionic ear is also called a *cochlear implant*.

The first step is to surgically implant part of the bionic ear into the back of a patient's head. The doctors actually use tiny wires to attach an electrode to nerves. Those nerves are connected to the part of the brain that controls hearing.

The user wears a microphone that captures speech and sounds. The microphone is attached to a computer processor. The processor converts the sound into electrical impulses. Those impulses are sent to the surgical implant inside the user's head.

The implant then delivers the electrical impulses, through the tiny wires, to the

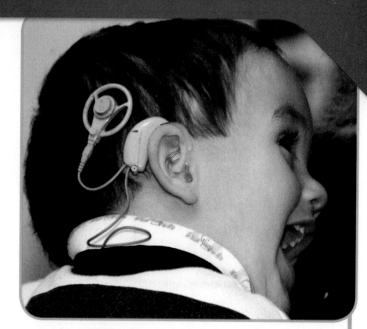

A young child with a cochlear implant.

nerves that are connected to the part of the brain that controls hearing. The brain is able to translate the impulses into sounds, allowing the user to hear.

Hearing Again

Doctors say the people who benefit the most from the bionic ear are those whose hearing is so bad that they cannot hear a telephone ring.

"I adore [the bionic ear]. At first it was a major shock to the system, to my head," said Cassie Bunker, who also regained hearing with the bionic ear. She thought, "I'm hearing things."

She Longed to Hear Music

"He played Beethoven," Peterson said after listening to her son play the piano. "I thought that was so pretty to sit and listen to."

✎ Think and Write

1 Other than helping people hear, what else do nerves do in the body?

2 How is the bionic ear different from traditional hearing aids?

Find out more. Log on to
www.hspscience.com

Vocabulary Review

Use the terms below to complete the sentences. The page numbers tell you where to look in the chapter if you need help.

volume p. 645	**transparent** p. 661
pitch p. 646	**refraction** p. 661
opaque p. 660	**concave lens** p. 662
translucent p. 661	**convex lens** p. 662

1. A sound with a high frequency has a high _____.

2. A material that does not allow any light to pass through is _____.

3. Light rays are bent and brought together by a _____.

4. The loudness of a sound is also known as _____.

5. Water and plastic wrap are materials that are _____.

6. A lens that is thicker at the edges than at the middle is a _____.

7. The bending of light as it moves from one material to another is _____.

8. Wax paper is _____.

Check Understanding

Write the letter of the best choice.

9. **MAIN IDEA AND DETAILS** *(Focus Skill)* Which of the following is a characteristic of sound waves?
   - **A.** A medium is necessary for the waves to travel.
   - **B.** The waves are transverse.
   - **C.** Different types can be compared on the electromagnetic spectrum.
   - **D.** They travel faster than other waves.

10. In the picture, Tod is using a microscope to examine a slide.

Which type of lens makes it possible for Tod to identify what is on the slide?
   - **F.** concave
   - **G.** convex
   - **H.** opaque
   - **J.** transparent

11. **MAIN IDEA AND DETAILS** *(Focus Skill)* What must happen for a sound wave to form?
   - **A.** An electric current must flow.
   - **B.** A certain frequency must be reached.
   - **C.** Matter must vibrate.
   - **D.** Volume must be absorbed.

12. Which of the following surfaces would bounce back almost all the light waves that hit it?

    F. a white wall

    G. a piece of plastic wrap

    H. a stained-glass window

    J. a mirror

13. Which of these musical instruments makes sounds with the lowest frequencies?

    A.

    B.

    Note: instruments not to scale

    C.

    D.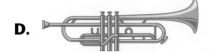

14. When we see a colored object, what are we really seeing?

    F. light that has been absorbed

    G. light that has not been absorbed

    H. light that has been refracted

    J. light that has not been refracted

15. What is the result when someone hits a drum harder than before?

    A. The number of decibels increases.

    B. Pitch decreases.

    C. Frequency increases.

    D. The number of vibrations decreases.

16. What kind of image does this lens produce?

    F. a distorted image

    G. a larger image

    H. a reflected image

    J. a smaller image

Inquiry Skills

17. Stephen is making sound waves by using strings of 12 different lengths. **Identify the variable** in Stephen's experiment.

18. **Predict** whether light and sound would be observed by somebody watching an explosion that occurs in space. Explain.

Critical Thinking

19. Elephants can detect underground sources of water by using their feet. Use what you know about sound waves to explain how this is possible.

20. Shakira is watching an approaching thunderstorm from her house. She can see and hear the lightning and thunder in the distance. Does Shakira see the lightning first or hear the thunder first? Explain. How will Shakira's observations of the lightning and thunder change as the thunderstorm gets closer?

The **Big** Idea

Visual Summary

Tell how each picture shows the **Big Idea** for its chapter.

 CHAPTER **14**

Big Idea

All matter has properties that can be observed, described, and measured.

CHAPTER **15**

Big Idea

Energy exists in many forms and can be changed from one form to another.

 CHAPTER **16**

Big Idea

Electricity is a form of energy that plays an important role in our lives.

CHAPTER **17**

Big Idea

Sound and light travel as waves of energy.

Forces and Motion

CHAPTER 18
Forces 670

CHAPTER 19
Motion 706

Unit Inquiry

Modern Rocket Stages

Scientists study the universe from Earth and from space. Studying the universe from space requires rockets that can send heavy payloads deep into space. What rocket design will carry heavy payloads the farthest? For example, is one large rocket more powerful than several smaller rockets? Plan and conduct an experiment to find out.

Forces, such as magnetism and gravity, interact with objects, such as you and Earth, to produce motion.

Essential Questions

Lesson 1

What Forces Affect Objects on Earth Every Day?

Lesson 2

What Are Balanced and Unbalanced Forces?

Lesson 3

What Is Work, and How Is It Measured?

GO online

Student eBook
www.hspscience.com

What do YOU wonder?

For 800 years, the Leaning Tower of Pisa has been tilted. Officials in Pisa, Italy, worried that it would fall over. In 1999, scientists were able to remove soil from one side of the building to stabilize the tower. What forces are acting on the Leaning Tower of Pisa? How does this relate to the **Big Idea?**

The Leaning Tower of Pisa

Investigate one force that acts on surfaces.

Read and learn about different forces and how forces affect motion.

Essential Question

What Forces Affect Objects on Earth Every Day?

Fast Fact

Get a Grip

The grooves in a car's tires help the tires grip the road and drain water on a rainy day. This means that more force is needed to move the car. Drag-race cars have no grooves in their tires so that they can move off the starting line faster. In the Investigate, you will explore how forces work with and against one another.

A drag-racing car at the starting line

force [FAWRS] A push or pull that may cause an object to move, stop, or change direction (p. 676)

friction [FRIK•shuhn] A force that opposes motion (p. 677)

gravity [GRAV•ih•tee] The force of attraction between objects (p. 678)

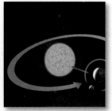

gravitational force [grav•ih•TAY•shuhn•uhl FAWRS] The pull of all objects in the universe on one another (p. 678)

magnetic [mag•NET•ik] Having the property of attracting iron objects (p. 680)

magnetic force [mag•NET•ik FAWRS] The force produced by a magnet (p. 680)

On A Roll

Start with Questions

Have you ever pulled a wagon? Was it easy or hard?

- Would it be easier or harder to pull the wagon with someone in it?

- Why does the trailer in the photo have wheels?

Investigate to find out. Then read and learn to find out more.

Prepare to Investigate

Inquiry Skill Tip

Scientists rely on good communication to share ideas and to learn from the experiences of others. When you communicate the results of an investigation, you should describe your results and explain what you think the results mean.

Materials

- shoe box without lid
- 20-cm piece of string
- blocks or other heavy objects
- unsharpened pencils
- spring scale

Make an Observation Chart

Setup	Force (N)
Box sliding directly on the table	
Box sliding on the pencils	

674

Follow This Procedure

1. Punch a small hole in one end of a shoe box, near the center.

2. Thread string through the hole. Tie the string to itself. You should be able to pull the box by the string.

3. Place some blocks, weights, or other heavy objects in the box.

4. Line up pencils on a tabletop. The pencils should be close to one another but not touching. Keep the pencils parallel.

5. Place the box on a smooth, flat surface. Attach the string to a spring scale, and use the scale to pull the box. **Observe** the amount of force you use to move the box.

6. Place the box on the array of pencils. Pull the box with the scale again. **Observe** the amount of force you use this time.

Draw Conclusions

1. Is the box easier to move with the pencils or without them? Why?

2. **Inquiry Skill** Scientists **communicate** to share ideas. Why does putting wheels on heavy objects make them easier to move?

Step 5

Step 6

Independent Inquiry

Investigate to **compare** the amounts of force needed to move the box on different surfaces. What kind of surface makes the box easiest to pull?

VOCABULARY
force p. 676
friction p. 677
gravity p. 678
gravitational force p. 678
magnetic p. 680
magnetic force p. 680

SCIENCE CONCEPTS
▶ what the different kinds of forces are
▶ how motion is affected by weak and strong forces

Focus Skill CAUSE AND EFFECT

Find out how different forces affect the objects around you.

cause ➝ effect

Forces

What pushes you up in the air when you jump and then pulls you back down to Earth? What pulls magnets together or pushes them apart? What makes a skateboard roll, and what makes it stop? Forces do all these things.

A **force** is a push or a pull that may cause changes in motion. A force speeds things up, slows things down, or makes them change direction.

Nothing changes its position, speed, or direction unless a force acts on it. For example, a book doesn't fall off a table by itself. Something has to push it. Can your backpack jump onto your back by itself? Of course not! You have to pull on it to lift it up. Without a force, the backpack can't move.

There are different kinds of forces. You will learn about some of them in this chapter. You are already familiar with the force from your muscles as you push or pull things. Other forces are just as important and just as easy to observe.

Focus Skill CAUSE AND EFFECT

What are two forces that could cause a ball to roll down a hill?

▲ The dominoes stand still until the boy applies a force.

The boy's push is the force that sets the first domino in motion. The first domino applies a force to the second, and so on down the line. ▶

Friction

When a soccer ball rolls across the grass, it slows down. Why? The ball slows mainly because of a force called friction. **Friction** is a force that works against motion. Friction can make things slow down or stop, or it can keep things from moving at all.

Friction is present whenever surfaces touch. When you erase a pencil mark, there is friction between the eraser and the paper.

Friction is greater between rough surfaces than between smooth ones. Have you ever walked on a newly waxed floor? It's not easy. There isn't much friction between your feet and the floor because the floor is smooth.

The speed skater in the picture glides across the ice because there is little friction between the skate blades and the ice. However, when she forces the blades of the skates against the ice, friction increases. The speed skater constantly changes the amount of friction between the skate blades and ice to control her direction and speed.

Friction has another important effect. It can make heat. Rub your hands together. Can you feel them getting warmer? Friction changes energy of motion to heat as objects rub together.

Focus Skill **CAUSE AND EFFECT**

How do you know there is friction when a saw cuts through wood?

When the speed skater's skates dig into the ice, friction increases, so the skater can stop. ▶

A speed skater must learn how to control the amount of friction between the skates and the ice.

Gravity

Gravity is the attraction between you and Earth. Gravity pulls you to the floor if you fall off your chair. When you drop a ball, gravity pulls the ball to the ground.

Did you know that gravity causes falling objects to speed up as they fall? In the picture, the feather and the apple are falling in a vacuum, where there is no air. Photographs were taken at equal time intervals. At first, the objects fell a shorter distance per interval. Later, they fell a larger distance. This shows that objects move faster, or *accelerate*, as they fall.

The speed of any falling object is about 10 m/sec (33 ft/sec) after the first second. After another second, the object falls at a speed of about 20 m/sec (66 ft/sec). After the third second, it falls at about 30 m/sec (98 ft/sec). Can you see the pattern?

All objects in the universe pull on one another. That is, they exert a **gravitational force**. The gravitational force can be strong or weak, depending on the masses of the objects and the distances between them. The closer the objects are and the greater their mass, the greater the gravitational force between them is.

Earth has a lot of mass, so it pulls all objects toward its center with a lot of force.

▲ Gravity pulls the apple and the feather downward. Their speeds increase as they fall. Both fall at the same rate in a vacuum because there is no air to slow down the feather.

Earth's gravity attracts objects near its surface, pulling them toward its center. ▶

The moon has less mass than Earth, so the moon pulls objects toward its center with less gravitational force.

There is a simple way to measure the gravitational force acting on an object. Find the object's weight. Weight is the measurement of gravitational force acting on an object.

Objects weigh more on Earth than they do on the moon. Earth has more mass and, therefore, more gravitational force than the moon. In other words, Earth pulls things harder, so they weigh more. Mass doesn't change, though, so an astronaut has the same mass on the moon as on Earth.

CAUSE AND EFFECT

Why don't you need to apply a force to your bike to make it go downhill?

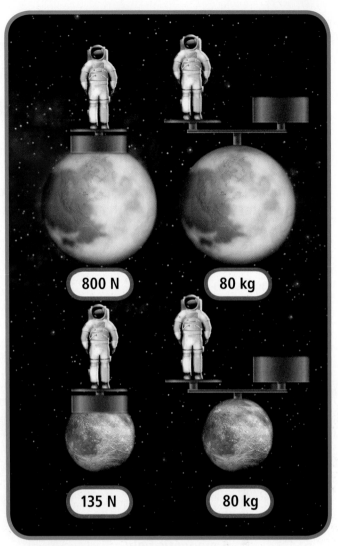

800 N   80 kg

135 N   80 kg

▲ The moon has less mass than Earth, so it has less gravitational force. On the moon, objects weigh about one-sixth of what they weigh on Earth.

All Fall Together?
See if objects really fall at the same rate. Drop a pencil and an eraser from the same height. Do they land at the same time?

Magnets and Compasses

For hundreds of years, people have used magnets to find direction. The first magnets used were made of a heavy natural mineral called *lodestone*. Today, scientists also call this mineral *magnetite*.

A compass needle points along an imaginary line connecting the North and South Poles. This is because Earth is like a giant magnet.

A compass needle is a magnet. Its north-seeking pole points toward Earth's magnetic North Pole.

This compass may have guided sailors across the ocean hundreds of years ago.

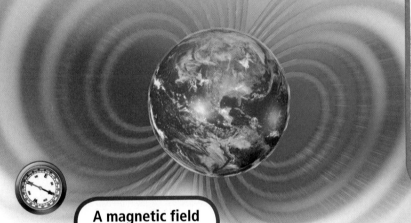

A magnetic field fills the space around Earth.

Magnetic Force

Hold a magnet near some metal paper clips. What happens? The magnet pulls the paper clips, and they stick to the magnet. An object that attracts iron is **magnetic**.

The force of a magnet is called **magnetic force**. The magnet is surrounded by a force field called a *magnetic field*. A magnet has two ends, called *poles*. The pulling force of the magnet is strongest at the poles. If a bar magnet can move freely, its *north-seeking pole* always points north, and its *south-seeking pole* points south. A magnet's poles are often marked *N* and *S*.

You may have observed that magnets both attract each other and repel, or push away, each other. These forces get stronger as the poles get closer together.

If two magnets are held with their two *N* or two *S* poles near each other, they push away from each other. If the *N* pole of one magnet and the *S* pole of another are held near each other, they pull the magnets together. Unlike poles attract. Like poles repel.

Focus Skill CAUSE AND EFFECT How can you make two magnets repel each other?

What Forces Affect Objects on Earth Every Day?

In this lesson, you learned that a force is a push or a pull that causes changes in motion. Forces speed up things, slow down things, or make things change direction. Some forces are friction, gravity, and magnetism.

1. 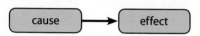 **CAUSE AND EFFECT** Draw and complete a graphic organizer that shows the effects of these forces: friction; gravity; magnetic force.

```
cause ——→ effect
```

2. **SUMMARIZE** Write a one-paragraph summary about gravitational force.

3. **DRAW CONCLUSIONS** What forces act on a meteor as it falls toward Earth?

4. **VOCABULARY** Write a comic strip that uses each vocabulary term in this lesson.

Test Prep

5. **CRITICAL THINKING** How is the force of gravity different from the force you apply when you push or pull something?

6. The gravitational force between two objects depends on their
   A. colors.
   B. masses.
   C. shapes.
   D. temperatures.

Make Connections

 Writing

Write to Describe
Describe the force of gravity. What factors affect the force of gravity? Is the force of gravity the same everywhere in the solar system?

 Math

Use an Equation
The speed of an object can be written as:
speed = distance ÷ time.
What is the speed of an object that travels 12 meters in 4 seconds?

 Social Studies

History
Use library references to find out what Sir Isaac Newton contributed to our knowledge of gravity.

Investigate balanced and unbalanced forces.

Read and learn how forces combine and interact.

Essential Question

What Are Balanced and Unbalanced Forces?

Fast Fact

A Delicate Balance

What keeps these cards from falling? A house of cards is an example of forces in balance. The forces working to pull the cards down are balanced by the forces working to hold them up. If the forces change, the cards will fall. In the Investigate, you will explore how forces work with one another and against one another.

balanced forces [BAL•uhnst FAWRS•iz] Forces that act on an object but cancel out each other (p. 686)

unbalanced forces [uhn•BAL•uhnst FAWRS•iz] Forces that act on an object and don't cancel out each other; unbalanced forces cause a change in motion (p. 686)

net force [NET FAWRS] The combination of all the forces acting on an object (p. 688)

buoyant force [BOY•uhnt FAWRS] The upward force exerted on an object by water (p. 690)

Predict the Force

Start with Questions

It is possible for more than one force to act on an object.

- What happens when a force acts on a moving object?

- What forces are acting on this seesaw?

Investigate to find out. Then read and learn to find out more.

Prepare to Investigate

Inquiry Skill Tip

Think carefully about the results of an investigation before you infer an explanation. Ask yourself, "What caused this to happen?" "What does this mean?" and "Why did I get these results instead of other results?"

Materials

- medium-size cardboard box
- 2 books
- 2 spring scales

Make an Observation Chart

Balanced and Unbalanced Forces			
	1st spring scale	Prediction	2nd spring scale
Empty box			
Box with 1 book			
Box with 2 books			

Follow This Procedure

1. Place the cardboard box on a flat surface such as a table or on the floor.

2. Hook the first spring scale to one side of the empty box. Gently pull the spring scale until the box begins to move. **Record** the force as the box begins to move.

3. Repeat Step 2 with one book placed inside the box. **Record** the force. Repeat Step 2 with both books placed inside the box. **Record** the force. Remove the books from the box.

4. Attach the second spring scale to the opposite side of the empty box. Gently pull the box, using the first spring scale. **Predict** the amount of force needed to stop the movement of the box.

5. Have a partner pull in the opposite direction with the second spring scale. **Record** the force shown on the second spring scale as the box stops moving.

6. Repeat steps 4 and 5 with one book and then two books inside the box.

Draw Conclusions

1. What was the amount of force needed to move the box? What was the amount of force needed to stop the box?

2. **Inquiry Skill** Scientists **infer** to explain events. What can you infer about the amount of force needed to stop the box's movement?

Step 2

Step 4

Independent Inquiry

Plan and conduct a simple experiment to see what would happen if you used two spring scales on one side and one spring scale on the opposite side.

VOCABULARY
balanced forces p. 686
unbalanced forces p. 686
net force p. 688
buoyant force p. 690

SCIENCE CONCEPTS
▶ how balanced and unbalanced forces affect motion
▶ what buoyant force is

 COMPARE AND CONTRAST

Look for the effects of balanced and unbalanced forces.

(alike)———(different)

Balanced and Unbalanced Forces

There is usually more than one force acting on an object. When you go down a slide, you apply a force to push yourself forward. Then gravity's pull takes over. At the same time, friction acts in the opposite direction. If friction is equal to your push, what happens? You don't move at all. The forces on you cancel one another. They are equally strong, but they act in opposite directions. Forces that act on an object but cancel each other are called **balanced forces**.

Suppose you are sitting at the top of the slide. The forces are balanced. Then you push forward with a force greater than

the surface's friction. Now the forces are unbalanced. The forces in one direction are stronger, so they don't cancel each other.

When **unbalanced forces** act on an object, motion changes. The object may start, speed up, slow down, stop, or change its direction.

What force is acting on the dresser and is equal and opposite to the girls' pushes? ▼

The two teams' forces are balanced, so they cancel one another. ▶

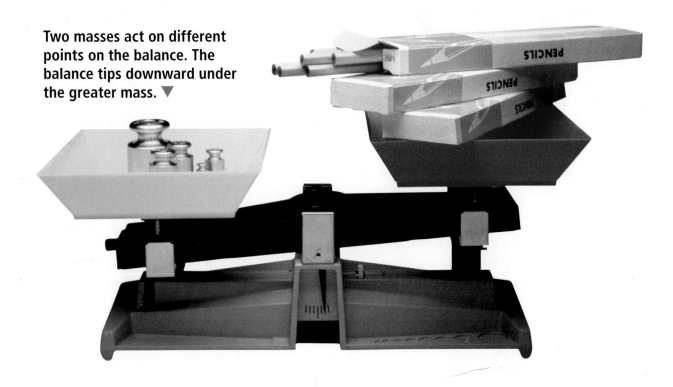

Two masses act on different points on the balance. The balance tips downward under the greater mass. ▼

When a tug of war starts and both teams pull the rope with the same force, the rope does not move one way or the other. The forces are balanced. When one team pulls harder, though, the rope and the other team move toward them.

A seesaw can show balanced and unbalanced forces. If the weight on one end of the seesaw is greater than the weight on the other end, the heavier end of the seesaw moves down. If the weights on both ends of the seesaw are the same, the forces are balanced, and the seesaw doesn't move.

Focus Skill **COMPARE AND CONTRAST**

Two people are arm wrestling, but neither one is winning. How do the forces acting on them compare?

Build an Instant Balance

Build a balance. Center a ruler on top of a pencil. Test coins or classroom objects to see how they compare on your balance. Can two nickels balance five dimes? What balances a quarter?

Net Force

The combination of all the forces acting on an object is called the **net force**. Net force affects an object's motion. To know how an object will move, you don't need to know the details of all the forces that are acting on the object. You just need to know the net force. When forces are balanced, the net force is zero.

In the picture, one elk is pushing to the right and the other to the left. Another force—friction—is pushing one elk to the right and the other to the left. The result is a net force of zero, so there is no change in the motion of either elk.

Have you ever watched two children trying to pull a toy in opposite directions? This is another example of a zero net force. If both children pull with equal strength, their forces are balanced. The net force on the toy is zero, so its motion doesn't change. The net force on each child is also zero, so they stay where they are.

Sometimes the net force on an object isn't zero. This happens when forces are unbalanced, or when motion changes.

Forces are acting, but no change in motion results. ▼

When wrestlers push in opposite directions with unequal strengths, a change in motion results. ▶

Think about the children pulling on the toy. What will the net force on the toy be if one child pulls harder?

To calculate net force, assign a plus (+) to the forces acting in one direction. Forces acting in the opposite direction get a minus (–). Add the strengths of the forces to get the net force. Usually, forces pushing or pulling to the right are given positive values. Forces pushing or pulling to the left are given negative values.

Suppose one child pulls the toy to the right with a force of 100 N. If the other child pulls to the left with a force of 50 N, the net force on the toy is 100 N + (–50 N) = 50 N. Since the net force is positive, the answer is that the net force on the toy is 50 N to the right.

If all the forces on an object push or pull in the same direction, the net force is easy to calculate. Simply add the forces together. In the picture below, both horses are pulling in the same direction, so their forces are added to calculate the net force. If one horse pulls with a force of 3000 N and the other horse pulls with a force of 4000 N, the net force on the sleigh is 7000 N.

Focus Skill COMPARE AND CONTRAST

Compare the forces if one child pulls a chair to the left with a force of 100 N and another child pulls it in the opposite direction with a force of 200 N.

The net force is the sum of all the forces. When forces act in the same direction, find the net force by adding the individual forces. ▶

Buoyant Force

Why is lifting a heavy object in water easier than lifting the same object on land? The reason is that water pushes up on the object. This upward force is called a **buoyant force**. Because it pushes up on objects, they seem to weigh less.

The buoyant force isn't always equal to the *weight of an object*. It equals the *weight of the fluid* that the object displaces, or pushes aside. Large objects have a greater buoyant force acting on them, since they displace more water than smaller objects.

Buoyant force acts in the opposite direction from weight. As a result, buoyant force helps objects float. If the buoyant force on an object is equal to or greater than the object's weight, the object floats.

If the object's weight is greater than the buoyant force, the object sinks.

Ships are made of steel and are very heavy, yet they float. How is this possible? Ships are large, but they are not solid; they are filled with air. A ship's overall weight is the weight of its steel walls plus the air inside the ship. This total weight is less than the weight of the water the ship displaces. The buoyant force is greater than the ship's weight, so it floats.

(Focus Skill) COMPARE AND CONTRAST

Is the buoyant force greater on a cherry tomato or on a regular tomato? Why?

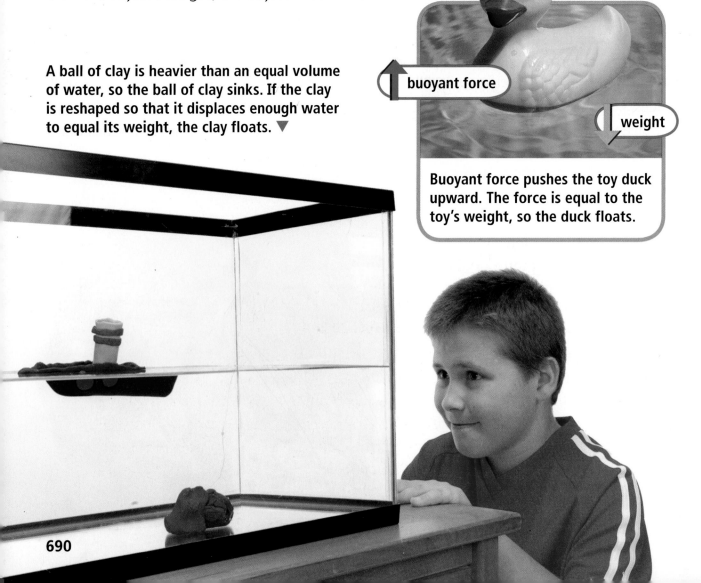

A ball of clay is heavier than an equal volume of water, so the ball of clay sinks. If the clay is reshaped so that it displaces enough water to equal its weight, the clay floats. ▼

buoyant force

weight

Buoyant force pushes the toy duck upward. The force is equal to the toy's weight, so the duck floats.

Essential Question

What Are Balanced and Unbalanced Forces?

In this lesson, you learned that if an object's motion doesn't change, the forces acting on it are balanced. An object's motion does change when one force on it is stronger than any others. Unbalanced forces cause motion changes.

1.  **COMPARE AND CONTRAST** Draw and complete a graphic organizer that compares and contrasts balanced forces and unbalanced forces.

   alike ——— different

2. **SUMMARIZE** Write a one-paragraph summary of net force.

3. **DRAW CONCLUSIONS** Two balls of the same size are put in water. One floats and one doesn't. How is this possible?

4. **VOCABULARY** For each vocabulary term in this lesson, write a sentence that gives an everyday example of it.

Test Prep

5. **CRITICAL THINKING** The forces on a parked car are balanced. If the car starts moving, what has happened to the forces?

6. The buoyant force works against the force of
   A. gravity.
   B. magnetism.
   C. pulling.
   D. pushing.

Make Connections

 Writing

Expository Writing
Write two paragraphs **describing** the balanced forces at work on a floating object.

 Math

Solve a Problem
A girl pushes a crate along the floor with a force of 100 N. The force of friction on the crate is 1 N. What is the net force on the crate?

 Physical Education

Design Exercises
Design exercises that use balanced forces. Include some exercises that stretch your muscles and some that raise your heart rate.

Investigate a way to make lifting things easier.

Read and learn about work and how simple machines affect work.

Essential Question

What Is Work, and How Is It Measured?

Fast Fact

Machines for Play

Machines help people do things as different as assemble cars, plow soil, design clothing, and animate cartoons! Long ago, catapults like this one were made for war. They were used to fling heavy stones at an enemy. This one was made to chuck pumpkins at a fall festival. In the Investigate, you will use a machine to lift a load.

A catapult

work [WERK] The use of a force to move an object through a distance (p. 696)

simple machine [SIM•puhl muh•SHEEN] A device that makes a task easier by changing the size or direction of a force or the distance over which the force acts (p. 698)

lever [LEV•er] A bar that makes it easier to move things (p. 698)

fulcrum [FUHL•kruhm] The balance point on a lever that supports the arm but does not move (p. 698)

wheel-and-axle [weel•and•AK•suhl] A wheel with a rod, or axle, in the center (p. 698)

pulley [PUL•ee] A wheel with a rope that lets you change the direction in which you move an object (p. 699)

inclined plane [in•KLYND PLAYN] A ramp or another sloping surface (p. 699)

Lifting Things the Easy Way

Guided Inquiry

Start with Questions

Every time you use a doorknob, you are using a simple machine. Simple machines are everywhere.

- Can you name some simple machines?

- How does this hammer make taking out the nail easier?

Investigate to find out. Then read and learn to find out more.

Prepare to Investigate

Inquiry Skill Tip

When you **predict** what will happen in an investigation, you should do more than just guess. Look for patterns and causes that will help you decide what is most likely to happen.

Materials

- several small books
- ruler
- 2 unsharpened pencils

Make an Observation Chart

Method of Lifting	Height Books Were Lifted
With finger only	
With pencil lever	

Follow This Procedure

1 Stack several small books at one edge of your desk.

2 Slide your little finger under the stack.

3 Keep your hand palm up, and move just your little finger to lift the stack of books as far as you can.

4 Add more books, and repeat until you can barely lift the stack with your little finger. **Observe** and **measure** how far you can raise the stack of books.

5 Now make a lever. To do this, put an unsharpened pencil under your stack. Put another unsharpened pencil under and at right angles to the first pencil.

6 Lift the books by pressing down on the outer end of the top pencil with your little finger. **Observe** and **measure** how high you can lift the books.

Draw Conclusions

1. Did you use more force when you lifted the books with only your finger or when you used your pencil lever?

2. **Inquiry Skill** Scientists **predict** to understand what might happen in a situation, based on observations. What do you **predict** would happen if you lifted the books with a meterstick?

Step 2

Step 3

Independent Inquiry

Explore how levers work by **comparing** distances between the load end and the other end of levers of different lengths.

VOCABULARY
work p. 696
simple machine p. 698
lever p. 698
fulcrum p. 698
wheel-and-axle p. 698
pulley p. 699
inclined plane p. 699

SCIENCE CONCEPTS
▶ the scientific meaning of *work*
▶ simple machines make work easier

⭐ **MAIN IDEA AND DETAILS**
Look for things that make work easier to do.

```
        Main Idea
      /     |      \
detail    detail    detail
```

Work

Some science terms are familiar words. However, their scientific definitions are more precise than their everyday meanings. *Work* is an example.

You might think you're doing work when you spend a couple of hours reading a book for a report. Scientifically speaking, however, you haven't done any work. In science, the only way to do work is to make something move. Unless something moves, no work is done.

In science, **work** is using a force to move an object through a distance. This equation shows that definition:

Work = Force × Distance

Notice that work is a product of two things. The force applied to an object is multiplied by the distance it is moved.

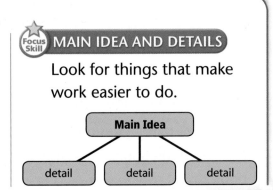

Math in Science
Interpret Data

Work Needed to Lift Pails			
Object to Be Moved	Force Needed (Weight of Object)	Distance	Work Done (Force × Distance)
Empty pail	5 N	3 m	5 N × 3 m = 15 J
Pail of water	40 N	3 m	40 N × 3 m = 120 J
Pail of nails	180 N	3 m	180 N × 3 m = 540 J

How much more work is done lifting the nails than lifting the water?

▲ The boy has done work. He applied a force to the ball as he lifted it up.

Which is more work—rowing a boat 1 km (0.6 mi) or 10 km (6 mi)? Rowing 10 km (6 mi) is more work, since work depends on distance.

But force matters, too. It takes more force to lift a heavy object than it does to lift a light object. Lifting a brick is more work than lifting a feather.

Work is measured in units called *joules*. How much work is one joule (1 J)? A medium-size apple weighs about 1 N. If you lift that apple 1 m, you do 1 J of work.

 MAIN IDEA AND DETAILS What two things determine how much work is needed to lift your backpack onto your back?

Work and Weight
Weigh an object by using a spring scale. Record the weight in newtons. Measure the vertical height of a flight of stairs with a meterstick, and record it. Then carry the object up the stairs. Calculate how much work you did on the object.

Machines and Work

Moving a heavy object a long distance is a lot of work. One way to make work easier is to use a machine.

Machines don't actually reduce the amount of work. Remember, work is the product of force and distance. Machines make work easier by reducing the amount of force people must use to do the work. Most machines allow you to use less force, but you apply it over a greater distance. The product of force and distance remains the same.

Many machines are collections of several simple machines. A **simple machine** is a tool that makes a task easier by changing the strength or direction of a force or the distance over which the force acts.

A **lever** is a bar that makes it easier to move things. Levers have two parts. One part, the *lever arm*, moves. The other part is the balance point, or **fulcrum**. The fulcrum supports the arm but doesn't move. A rake is an example of a lever. This simple machine reduces the force needed to lift or move an object.

A **wheel-and-axle** helps you open a door. This simple machine is a wheel with a rod, or axle, in the center. When you turn the wheel (the doorknob), the axle inside the knob turns and pulls back the latch. Opening a door would be much harder if you had to turn just the axle.

Building a playhouse involves using many simple machines. Wedges, levers, a screw, and an inclined plane are some of the simple machines used here. ▶

▲ **Which simple machine do you think this potter's wheel uses?**

698

A **pulley** is a wheel with a groove for a rope. It works by changing the direction of a force. Pulleys allow you to lift things by pulling down on the rope rather than by pushing up on the object. Think back to the boy lifting the pail in the Interpret Data.

An example of an **inclined plane** is a ramp. It allows you to use less force over a distance to make work easier.

The *wedge* is made up of two inclined planes that form a cutting edge. A knife and a chisel are both wedges. An ax is a wedge that is used to chop wood.

What are the parts of a lever?

▲ A dumbwaiter uses a pulley. You pull a load up by pulling down on a rope.

Compound Machines

Compound machines are made up of two or more simple machines. Like simple machines, compound machines make work easier. Most of them reduce the force you need to apply. Remember, machines don't reduce the work done. You usually push with less force through a greater distance when you use a machine.

A push lawn mower is a compound machine. It uses a wedge—the blade—to cut grass. The blades are attached to a wheel-and-axle, which turns them as the mower is pushed through the grass. The handle of the mower is a lever.

A hand-operated can opener is another compound machine. When cans were first invented, in the early 1800s, they had to be opened with a hammer and a chisel. That method was difficult and dangerous. A can opener uses two simple machines, a wedge and a wheel-and-axle, to change a small input force into an output force great enough to cut through the lid.

Sailors and movers often use a compound machine called a *block and tackle*. A block and tackle is made up of a series of pulleys. Heavy loads such as pianos and car engines can be lifted by one person using a block and tackle. That's because the combined pulleys reduce the force you need to lift the object.

(Focus Skill) MAIN IDEA AND DETAILS

Name a compound machine that you use and the simple machines it is made up of.

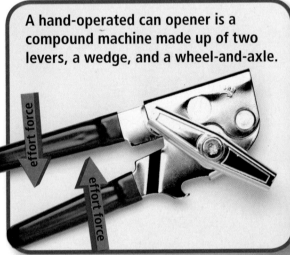

A hand-operated can opener is a compound machine made up of two levers, a wedge, and a wheel-and-axle.

effort force

effort force

A block and tackle is a system of pulleys used to lift heavy loads. Each pulley in the system makes the work a little easier. ▷

700

Essential Question

What Is Work, and How Is It Measured?

In this lesson, you learned that work is using a force to move an object through a distance. Simple machines make work easier but don't reduce the amount of work. Many machines are made up of two or more simple machines.

1. **Focus Skill** **MAIN IDEA AND DETAILS** Draw and complete a graphic organizer with details for this main idea: Simple machines make work easier.

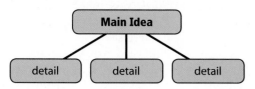

2. **SUMMARIZE** Write a one-paragraph summary of work. Use a chore you do around the house, such as vacuuming or mowing the lawn, as a starting point.

3. **DRAW CONCLUSIONS** Name two simple machines that make up a pencil sharpener.

4. **VOCABULARY** Make a crossword puzzle that uses the vocabulary terms for this lesson. Provide an answer key.

Test Prep

5. **CRITICAL THINKING** How do machines make work easier?

6. Which of these is a simple machine that allows you to lift things by pulling down on a rope?
   A. inclined plane
   B. lever
   C. pulley
   D. wedge

Make Connections

 Writing

Write to Describe
Write a paragraph that **compares** three simple machines. Describe how they are similar and how they are different.

 Math

Calculate Work
How much work does it take to move a cat weighing 20 N from the kitchen to the bedroom upstairs 12 m away? Does moving a 10-N cat 10 m take less or more work?

 Social Studies

Research
Use library resources to research the Greek scientist Archimedes, who lived about 2,200 years ago. Write a few paragraphs about Archimedes and the ideas for which he is known.

Ephraim Fischbach

▶ **EPHRAIM FISCHBACH**

▶ Professor of Physics at Purdue University

Among the most important ideas of modern science are the laws of motion. Although Isaac Newton described these laws in the 1600s, they are still used to calculate orbits for satellites and flight paths for space probes. His law of gravitation essentially states that all objects attract all other objects over any distance.

Physics professor Ephraim Fischbach and a group of researchers tried to find if this law is always true. The scientists studied the idea that a force other than gravity might be at work in certain situations. Predictions based on the law of gravitation may not be accurate over all distances. So far, the group has not found what other force besides gravitation could be acting on objects, but they have discovered some exceptions to the law.

Dr. Fischbach has also been working on nanotechnology. Nanotechnology controls matter on a microscopic scale. Tiny machines as small as atoms and molecules may be possible with nanotechnology. Dr. Fischbach and a group of scientists have been working to solve some of the problems that may arise when working with such tiny machines and the forces that will act on them.

Think and Write

1. How might nanotechnology be useful in the future?

2. Why is it important for scientists to continue testing ideas that are considered to be "laws" of science?

Patricia Cowings

▶ PATRICIA COWINGS

▶ Research psychologist
▶ Professor of psychiatry at UCLA
▶ Principal investigator of the Psychophysiological Research Laboratory at NASA's Ames Research Center

Astronauts in space often experience physical problems, such as nausea and swelling of the legs and feet. The nausea is similar to the motion sickness some people feel on boats or a roller coaster. Patricia Cowings is trying to cut down on these problems or prevent them.

In order to study the problems that astronauts experience, Dr. Cowings produces conditions on Earth that are similar to conditions in space. Dr. Cowings teaches astronauts to control certain body functions, such as heart rate, blood pressure, and breathing rate. If, for example, an astronaut's breathing rate increases just before the feeling of nausea, he or she can learn to slow the rate and, perhaps, prevent the nausea.

Think and Write

1 Why is it important to overcome physical problems in space?

2 Why do you think astronauts experience nausea in space?

Career Aeronautical Engineer

Aeronautical engineers design the engines and wings that power and lift aircraft. They also design and build aircraft that are as light as possible so that they can carry a lot of passengers or cargo without using too much fuel.

Vocabulary Review

Use the terms below to complete the sentences. The page numbers tell you where to look in the chapter if you need help.

friction p. 677

gravity p. 678

balanced forces p. 686

net force p. 688

work p. 696

simple machine p. 698

lever p. 698

fulcrum p. 698

pulley p. 699

inclined plane p. 699

1. Using a force to move an object through a distance is called _____.

2. The balance point of a lever is the _____.

3. A machine that allows you to lift things by pulling down on a rope is a _____.

4. The combination of all the forces acting on an object is the _____.

5. Forces acting on an object that are equal and opposite are _____.

6. A force that works against motion is _____.

7. A bar that moves against a fulcrum is a _____.

8. A ramp is an example of a simple machine called an _____.

9. The force that Earth applies to objects near its surface is _____.

10. A machine that makes work easier is a _____.

Check Understanding

Write the letter of the best choice.

11. **MAIN IDEA AND DETAILS** A can opener is made up of several simple machines. One is a wedge. What is another one?
   A. fulcrum   **C.** ramp
   B. pulley   **D.** wheel-and-axle

12. **CAUSE AND EFFECT** Which force causes a ship to float in water?
   F. air resistance
   G. buoyant force
   H. friction
   J. magnetism

13. Which simple machine is part of a screw?

   A. fulcrum   **C.** pulley

   B. inclined plane **D.** wheel-and-axle

14. Which force makes a compass work?

   F. buoyant force   **H.** gravity

   G. friction   **J.** magnetic force

15. Which of these machines is a wheel-and-axle?

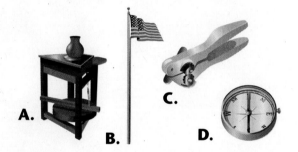

16. Which of these machines can be used to lift a piano into a second-story window?

   F. block-and-tackle **H.** screw

   G. lever   **J.** wedge

Inquiry Skills

17. You use a shovel to dig. Identify and **communicate** the simple machines that make up a shovel.

18. As you go down a slide, your movement is not smooth. What can you **infer** about the forces acting on you?

Critical Thinking

19. You want to move a large, heavy box of toys up into your treehouse. The box is too heavy and awkward to carry up the rope ladder. How can you move the box with a simple machine?

20. Think about the forces acting on the weight lifter and the weights. Are the forces acting on the weight lifter and the weights balanced or unbalanced? Explain. Identify the forces acting on the weight lifter and the weights.

The **Big Idea**

What's the Big Idea?

Motion can be observed, measured, and described.

Essential Questions

Lesson 1

What Factors Affect Motion?

Lesson 2

What Are the Laws of Motion?

Student eBook
www.hspscience.com

Cyclists in motion

What do YOU wonder?

These cyclists are racing around a track known as a velodrome. The sides of the velodrome are angled, which changes the forces acting on the cyclists. The angled sides allow them to go faster than 50 km/hr (30 mi/hr)! What other factors affect the cyclists' motion? How does this relate to the **Big Idea?**

Investigate how a change in motion affects objects.

Read and learn how motion is described and measured.

Essential Question

What Factors Affect Motion?

Fast Fact

Giant Tops

This spinning-ring ride seems to defy gravity when it's moving. Carnival rides like this one are based on NASA training equipment. An astronaut trainee can turn in all directions: up and down, left and right, and sideways. In the Investigate, you will observe the way an air bubble moves when you apply force from different directions.

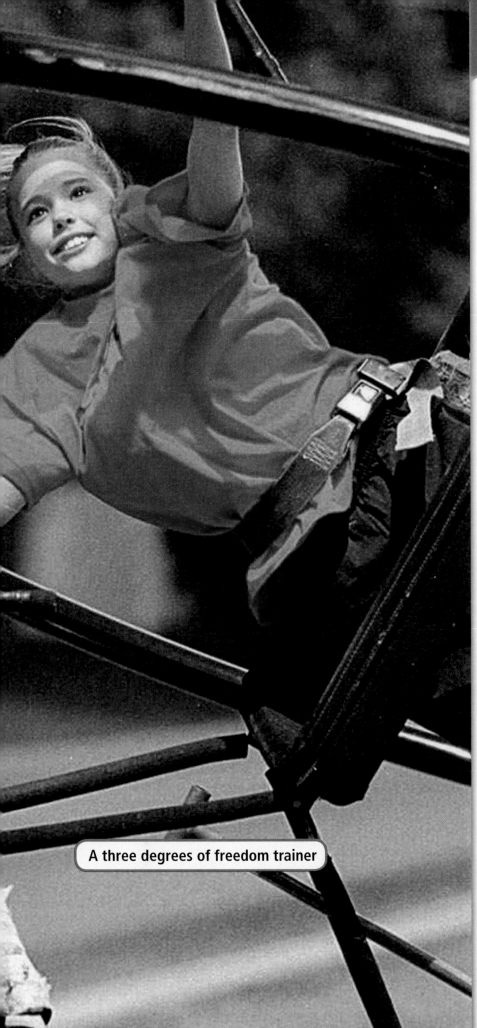

A three degrees of freedom trainer

position [puh•ZISH•uhn] The location of an object in space (p. 712)

speed [SPEED] The distance an object travels in a certain amount of time (p. 714)

velocity [vuh•LAHS•uh•tee] A measure of an object's speed in a particular direction (p. 714)

acceleration [ak•sel•er•AY•shuhn] The rate at which velocity changes (p. 716)

Changes in Motion

Start with Questions

Different factors affect an object's motion. When you ride a bike, friction keeps it from rolling forever after you stop pedaling.

- What other forces affect motion?

- What affects these ice skaters' motions?

Investigate to find out. Then read and learn to find out more.

Prepare to Investigate

Inquiry Skill Tip

To make it easier to infer why something happens, write a description of the conditions before and after the action occurs.

Materials

- clear, 1-L plastic bottle with cap
- water
- small piece of soap

Make an Observation Chart

Action	Prediction	Observation
Turn the bottle		
Move the bottle at a steady speed		
Move the bottle at an increased speed		

Follow This Procedure

1. Fill a bottle with water, but leave just enough space for a small air bubble. Add a small piece of soap. Cap the bottle tightly.

2. Lay the bottle on its side on a flat surface. You should see one small bubble in the bottle. Hold the bottle steady until the bubble moves to the center of the bottle and stays there.

3. **Predict** what will happen to the air bubble if you turn the bottle to the left or right. Turn the bottle, and **observe** what happens. **Record** your observations.

4. Repeat Step 3, but this time, move the bottle forward at a steady speed.

5. Repeat Step 4, but this time, increase the speed.

Draw Conclusions

1. Compare the results of all these types of movement with one another. Were they similar to or different from one another?

2. **Inquiry Skill** Scientists often form inferences to explain why something happened. **Infer** why the bubble moved the way it did.

Step 2

Step 4

Independent Inquiry

Hypothesize **what will happen to the air bubble if the bottle is moving at a steady speed and its direction changes.** Plan and conduct a simple investigation **to test your hypothesis.**

VOCABULARY
position p. 712
speed p. 714
velocity p. 714
acceleration p. 716

SCIENCE CONCEPTS
▶ how different kinds of force affect motion
▶ how motion is measured

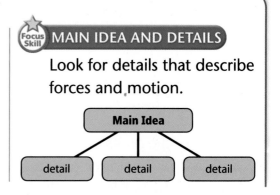

MAIN IDEA AND DETAILS

Look for details that describe forces and motion.

```
          Main Idea
      ┌──────┼──────┐
   detail  detail  detail
```

Forces and Motion

Have you ever been sitting in an unmoving car when the car next to you started to move? Did you feel as if you were moving forward or backward? When you looked at the street you realized you weren't moving at all! In order to determine if an object is moving, you must have a *frame of reference.* Your frame of reference is the moving object and a background that isn't moving. If you were at the park watching the girls on the swings, the trees and ground would help you determine that the girls were changing their position.

You can tell the difference between a moving object and one that's still. But how would you *define* motion? An object is in motion when its position changes. **Position** is the location of an object in space, and it is always relative to a frame of reference. We use many words to express position, such as *east, west, above, below,* and *beside.*

Forces can make objects change their position. All forces—from gravity to magnetism to friction to a kick of your foot—are pushes and pulls. What force is making the girls on the swings move?

You know these girls are moving, because their positions are changing.

712

Gravitational force attracts two objects. Gravitational force increases as the objects' masses increase. Mass is the amount of matter in an object. If you get out of a chair and walk around the room, your chair stays where it is, because Earth is very large—its gravitational pull is strong. Your chair doesn't move to stay near you because your mass is much smaller than Earth's.

Friction is a force that opposes motion. It either prevents motion or slows it down. Friction acts between two surfaces. The smoother the surfaces of two objects, the less friction there usually is between them. This is why you slip on ice. The smooth ice and the soles of your shoes don't produce much friction when they slide past each other.

Often, several forces act together on an object. Think about an airplane in flight. *Drag* from the air slows the plane. Thrust works against drag. *Thrust* is the forward force produced by the plane's engine. Gravity opposes lift. For the plane to fly, the forces of lift and thrust must equal or be greater than the opposing forces of gravity and drag.

Gravity pulls the girls down the slide. Friction slows their motion.

MAIN IDEA AND DETAILS

Why does a skydiver fall to the ground when she jumps out of a plane?

A maglev train doesn't have wheels. It uses magnetic force— the pull between magnetic objects—to float above the track.

Speed and Velocity

What makes a roller coaster so much fun? Many people think that it's the roller coaster's speed. **Speed** is the distance an object travels in a certain amount of time. Speed tells you how quickly or slowly something is moving.

An object's speed is an important property of its motion. Suppose you read that a certain roller coaster zooms along 853 m (2800 ft) of track. Does that make you want to ride it? Maybe. You read on and learn that the top speed of the roller coaster is 193 km/hr (120 mi/hr). It's the fastest roller coaster in the world. Now, *that* sounds like fun!

You can calculate speed by using this formula.

$$\text{speed} = \frac{\text{distance}}{\text{time}}$$

If you walk 5 km (3.1 mi) in 1 hour, your speed is 5 km/hr. What is your speed if you walk 10 km in 2 hours?

Sometimes you need to know the *direction* of an object as well as its speed. Suppose some friends are meeting you at the park at 3:00. Will they be there on time? Yes—*if* they're moving fast enough *and* in the right direction. In other words, your friends must travel at the correct velocity. **Velocity** is the measure of an object's speed in a particular direction.

Suppose your friends are walking southeast at a speed of 5 km/hr. Their velocity is 5 km/hr, southeast. Now suppose they pass another group of people walking 5 km/hr in the opposite direction. The two groups are moving at the same speed but at different velocities.

Math in Science

Interpret Data

Vehicles and Record Speeds

The table shows world-record speeds for cars, planes, and boats. About how many times as fast as the car is the plane? About how many times as fast as the boat is the plane?

World's fastest car	*Thrust SSC*, 1228 km/hr (763 mi/hr)
World's fastest plane	*X-43A*, more than 10,800 km/hr (6700 mi/hr)
World's fastest boat	*Spirit of Australia*, 511 km/hr (317.6 mi/hr)

The *Thrust SSC* is the world's fastest car. It set the world speed record for a car by traveling at a speed of 1228 km/hr (763 mi/hr).

Speed = 110 km/hr (68.4 mi/hr)
Velocity = 110 km/hr (68.4 mi/hr), east

Velocity is a more complete way to describe an object's motion. It includes the object's speed and its direction.

A car traveling down a straight highway at a constant speed has *constant velocity.* This means that the car is moving steadily in the same direction. It doesn't speed up or slow down. It doesn't turn. It only moves in a straight line.

We can also describe velocity as *changing.* In this case, the object's speed is changing *or* its direction is changing—or both. A car driving at a steady speed in a circle has a changing velocity. The car's speed is constant, but its direction changes every moment as it turns along the circle. When anything speeds up, slows down, stops, starts, or turns, its velocity changes.

★ Focus Skill **MAIN IDEA AND DETAILS**

What are four ways the friends walking to the park can change their velocity?

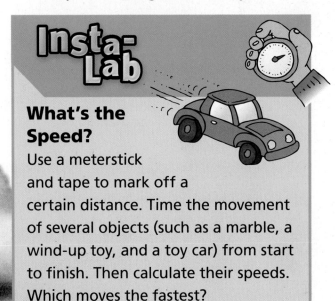

Insta-Lab

What's the Speed?

Use a meterstick and tape to mark off a certain distance. Time the movement of several objects (such as a marble, a wind-up toy, and a toy car) from start to finish. Then calculate their speeds. Which moves the fastest?

Acceleration

A car's velocity changes slowly as it backs out of a parking spot. But its velocity changes quickly if the driver slams on the brakes. Motion can be described by how quickly an object changes velocity, or *accelerates*. **Acceleration** is the rate at which velocity changes.

You can calculate acceleration by using this formula.

$$\text{acceleration} = \frac{\text{change in velocity}}{\text{time}}$$

Suppose you see an ad for a sports car that accelerates to 100 km/hr (62 mi/hr) in 5 seconds. What is its acceleration? Subtract the starting speed from the final speed to find the change in speed. Divide the change in speed by the time it takes for the speed to change. Use *a* for *acceleration*.

$$a = \frac{100 \text{ km/hr} - 0 \text{ km/hr}}{5 \text{ s}} = 20 \text{ km/hr/s}$$

The car is constantly accelerating by 20 km/hr during each second. At the end of one second, the car's speed is 20 km/hr (12.4 mi/hr). After two seconds?

▲ The whale thrusts the performer into the air with great force. As a result, the performer's velocity changes—he accelerates.

The car is going faster. Now its speed is 40 km/hr (24.9 mi/hr). What is the car's speed after three seconds?

The sports car also accelerates when it slows down or stops. Remember that acceleration is the rate of *change* in velocity over time. Velocity involves speed and direction. So, acceleration can happen through a change in either speed or direction—or both.

Several parts of a car control its acceleration. The gas pedal causes the car to gain speed. The brake slows down the car or stops it. The steering wheel changes the car's direction.

An object has a large acceleration when it changes its velocity quickly. For example, a motorcycle can have a lesser acceleration than a child's tricycle. Suppose the motorcycle is zipping down a highway in a straight line at a constant speed. Its acceleration is zero. But a tricycle in a driveway is accelerating as the rider slows down, speeds up, or turns.

⭐ Focus Skill **MAIN IDEA AND DETAILS**

What two properties of an object's motion can change when it accelerates?

A roller coaster car is almost always accelerating during a ride because its speed and its direction are almost always changing. ▼

A jet plane has limited runway space to land on the deck of an aircraft carrier. The plane must come to a stop very quickly. So, the acceleration of the plane is large. ▼

Momentum

A truck and a car are cruising down a highway. They have the same speed, the same velocity, and the same acceleration. Are the motions of the two vehicles the same?

The motion of the car differs from that of the truck in one important way—momentum. *Momentum* is a property of motion that describes how hard it is to slow down or stop an object. Momentum also describes how an object will affect something that it bumps into. Momentum depends on mass and velocity. You can calculate momentum by using this formula.

momentum = mass × velocity

In the example, the truck has a far greater mass than the car. So, the momentum of the truck is much greater than the momentum of the car. The truck will be harder to stop or slow down. If the truck bumps into something, it will cause more damage than the car would.

However, objects with different masses can have the same momentum if the object with less mass has more velocity. Momentum increases if either mass or velocity increases.

Consider two football players. One is big and heavy, and the other is small and light. Suppose the large player runs slowly and the smaller player runs quickly. They could each have the same momentum. Each player could be equally hard to stop. And each player could have an equally crushing effect on the other team!

 **MAIN IDEA AND DETAILS** What two factors determine an object's momentum?

A big truck moving at a fast speed has a lot of momentum. How much momentum does this small car have?

Essential Question

What Factors Affect Motion?

In this lesson, you learned that motion happens when an object changes position and that different forces might affect an object's position. You also learned terms that can be used to describe motion and position: *speed*, *velocity*, *acceleration*, and *momentum*.

1. 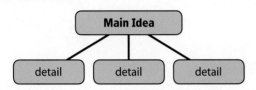 **MAIN IDEA AND DETAILS** Draw and complete a graphic organizer that shows supporting details for this main idea: Motion is studied by analyzing its features.

2. **SUMMARIZE** Write a one-paragraph summary of motion using the terms *speed* and *velocity*.

3. **DRAW CONCLUSIONS** A car is moving in a straight line at a constant speed of 40 km/hr. Is it accelerating?

4. **VOCABULARY** Use the vocabulary terms in this lesson to create a crossword puzzle with answers.

Test Prep

5. **Critical Thinking** The speed of a ball falling from a high shelf to the floor is 9.8 m/sec. What is its velocity?

6. A motorcycle is accelerating at a rate of 1 km/hr/sec. If its speed is 20 km/hr after 5 seconds, what is its speed after 6 seconds?
   - **A.** 20 km/hr
   - **B.** 21 km/hr
   - **C.** 100 km/hr
   - **D.** 120 km/hr

Make Connections

 Writing

Narrative Writing

Write a **short story** that features world records for fast movers. You might choose animals, human runners, or vehicles. Use the vocabulary you have learned in this chapter.

 Math

Solve a Problem

Find the speed of a motorcycle that travels 32 km in 16 minutes. Show the formula you used as well as your work.

 Social Studies

Multicultural Studies

Compare the numbers of bicycles and cars in other countries with the numbers of these vehicles in the United States. Write a report explaining your findings.

Investigate how mass affects acceleration.

Read and learn about Isaac Newton's three laws of motion as well as about motion in space.

Essential Question

What Are the Laws of Motion?

Fast Fact

Crash Test Dummies

Car manufacturers use crash tests to ensure that new vehicles are safe to drive. Traveling at 48 km/hr (30 mi/hr), a car that hits a concrete wall will cave in about 0.6 m (2.0 ft). Even though the car stops, the crash test dummies keep moving forward. In the Investigate, you will model a crash test.

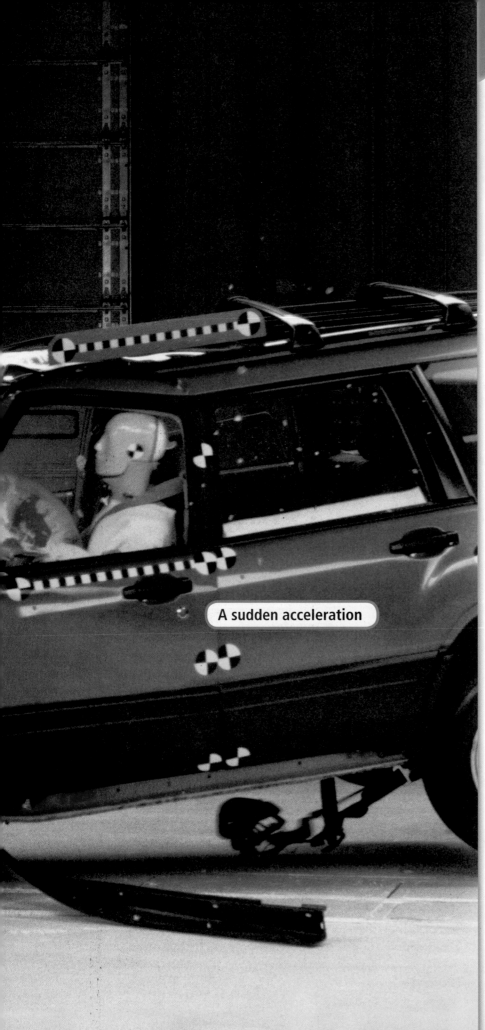

A sudden acceleration

inertia [in•ER•shuh] The property of matter that keeps it at rest or moving in a straight line (p. 725)

Momentum Crash Test

Start with Questions

When you ride a bike, it does not move on its own. Newton's first law explains this.

- What happens to a baseball when a batter hits it?

- What happens when the skater goes down one side of the half-pipe?

Investigate to find out. Then read and learn to find out more.

Prepare to Investigate

Inquiry Skill Tip

When you do an investigation, you need to identify and control variables. Check your setup to make sure that everything stays the same except the variable you are testing.

Materials

- game board
- several books
- meterstick
- small toy car
- dime
- quarter

Make an Observation Chart

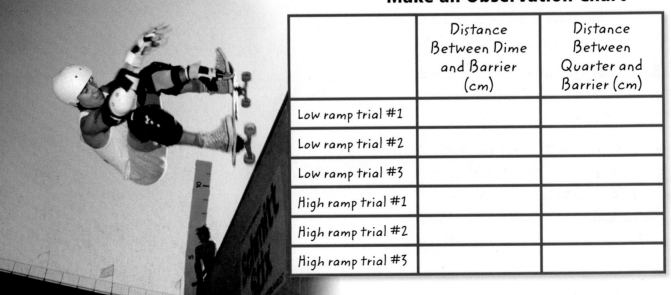

	Distance Between Dime and Barrier (cm)	Distance Between Quarter and Barrier (cm)
Low ramp trial #1		
Low ramp trial #2		
Low ramp trial #3		
High ramp trial #1		
High ramp trial #2		
High ramp trial #3		

Follow This Procedure

1. Make a ramp by setting one end of a game board on a stack of books about 15 cm high. Place another book as a barrier about 10 to 15 cm from the bottom of the ramp. Be sure the barrier is lower than the front end of the car.

2. Put the car at the top of the ramp. Put a dime on the front end of the car. Let the car roll down the ramp and hit the barrier. **Observe** what happens to the dime. **Measure** and **record** the dime's distance from the barrier. Repeat several times.

3. Repeat Step 2, but use a quarter. Repeat several times.

4. **Predict** how the results will differ if you make the ramp higher. Add another book to the stack under the ramp. Repeat Steps 2 and 3 several times. Was your prediction correct?

Draw Conclusions

1. Put your data in a table. Compare data for the dime with data for the quarter. How does a coin's mass relate to the distance it travels?

2. What happened when you made the ramp higher? Infer why this happened.

3. **Inquiry Skill** What was the **controlled variable** in Steps 2 and 3? What was the tested variable?

Step 1

Step 3

Independent Inquiry

Experiment with several methods of keeping the coin on the car when the car strikes the barrier. Conduct several trials for each method.

723

VOCABULARY
inertia p. 725

SCIENCE CONCEPTS
▶ how inertia affects motion
▶ how force, mass, and acceleration are related

Focus Skill 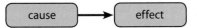 **CAUSE AND EFFECT**
Find out how forces affect motion.

cause ⟶ effect

Newton's First Law of Motion

A soccer ball doesn't roll across a field on its own. It takes a force, such as a kick from you, to get it moving. But once it's moving, the ball doesn't go on forever. Sooner or later, it stops.

You might think that the natural state of an object is to be still. You might also think that once it's moving, it stops only because the force that pushed it stops, too. In other words, the ball stops because you aren't kicking it anymore.

However, objects stop because a force acts on them. On Earth, gravity and friction stop moving objects. The force of gravity pulls objects toward Earth. If you throw a ball, it eventually curves and hits the ground. Suppose gravity didn't exist. The ball would keep moving through the air until drag stopped it.

Friction acts in the direction opposite to motion. The less friction between the ground and a rolling ball, the farther the ball will move. When pushed with the same force, the ball will roll farther down a paved street than down a grassy field.

◀ Isaac Newton (1642–1727) is a giant in the history of science. He is most famous for his three laws of motion, his law of gravitation, and his experiments with light and prisms.

▲ The ball doesn't move until a force hits it. Once the ball has been hit, will the ball keep moving forever? Why not?

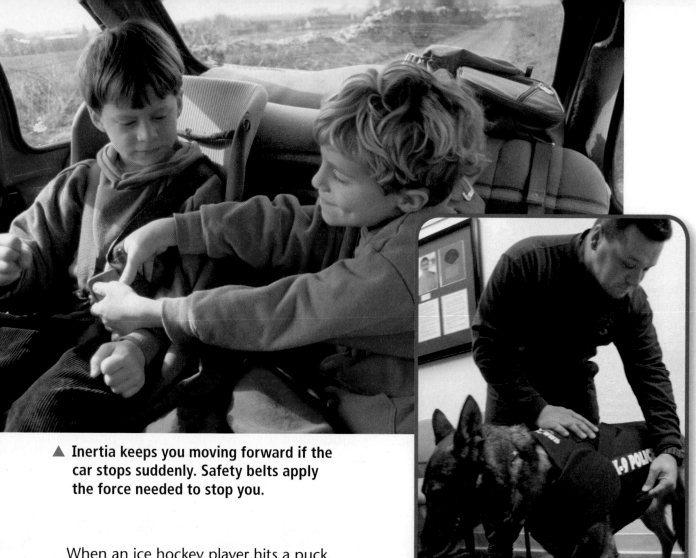

▲ Inertia keeps you moving forward if the car stops suddenly. Safety belts apply the force needed to stop you.

When an ice hockey player hits a puck, the puck slides a long way because ice is very slippery. If the friction between the puck and the ice disappeared, the puck would slide forever. It would move in the same direction and at a constant speed.

Isaac Newton described the effects of forces in three laws of motion. Newton's first law of motion describes inertia. **Inertia** is the tendency of objects to resist a change in motion. Objects at rest don't move unless a force moves them. Objects in motion don't slow down, stop, or turn unless a force makes them do so. A simple way to state the first law of motion is *No acceleration can happen without a force.*

Have you ever seen a performer pull a tablecloth from under the dishes and silverware on a table? The dishes and

▲ The bulletproof vest is made of strong material that can absorb the force of a bullet, slowing it down.

silverware remain in place, amazing the audience. This trick works because of Newton's first law of motion. The inertia keeps the dishes and silverware in place. Only a small force is applied by snapping away the tablecloth. This force isn't large enough or long enough to move the table setting very far.

Focus Skill **CAUSE AND EFFECT**

Why are safety belts such an important safety feature in cars?

725

Newton's Second Law of Motion

Newton's first law tells you that when you kick a ball, the ball will move. Newton's second law tells you that if you kick the ball harder, it will move faster. It also tells you that a heavy ball is harder to move than a lighter ball.

The long row of empty shopping carts requires more force to accelerate than one empty cart requires. ▼

Newton's second law says that when a force acts on an object, the object accelerates. The law also tells you how much the object accelerates. Recall that acceleration is the rate at which velocity changes. In other words, the second law says *An object's acceleration depends on the object's mass and the force applied to it.*

Let's look at how force and mass affect acceleration. The larger the force is, the greater the acceleration is. Suppose you push a scooter gently. The scooter speeds up slowly. If you use more strength to push, the scooter's speed changes quickly. In both cases, the scooter moves in the direction in which it is pushed.

Let's take another example. A car will stop suddenly if the driver slams on the brakes. But if the driver applies the brakes gently, the car gradually slows down.

The ribbon requires only a little bit of force to accelerate because it has a small mass.

For more links and animations, go to **www.hspscience.com**

Impact Between a Baseball and a Bat

When a bat and a baseball strike each other, acceleration results.

1 The baseball moves toward the bat as the bat moves toward the baseball.

2 The baseball applies a force to the bat as the bat applies a force to the baseball. The force from the bat gives different accelerations to individual particles of the baseball. This causes the baseball to change shape.

3 Both the baseball and the bat accelerate. The push of the bat on the baseball changes the baseball's speed and direction. The push of the baseball on the bat slows the bat.

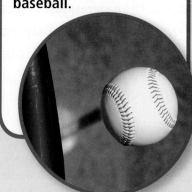

The less an object's mass is, the less force is needed to move it. It's much easier to push an empty shopping cart than a full one. Light cars are used in drag racing because a car with less mass accelerates faster than a car with more mass.

For a force to move an object, the force must overcome other forces. Suppose you want to pick up a box of books. The force you use to lift the box is your muscles. Gravity acts against your muscles.

Recall that weight is the measure of the force of gravity on an object. If the weight of the books is greater than your muscle strength, you can't move the box. However, you could take out some of the books to decrease the mass of the box. Or you could get someone to help you, increasing the force applied to the box. To hold or lift an object, the lifting force must be equal to or greater than the weight of the object.

You can write the second law of motion as an equation.

$$\text{acceleration} = \frac{\text{force}}{\text{mass}}$$

The standard unit of force is the newton.

Focus Skill CAUSE AND EFFECT

What is the effect on a car's acceleration if six people ride in the car instead of one?

Newton's Third Law of Motion

Suppose you're running without watching where you're going. You run into a wall. Ouch!

Are you hurt because you hit the wall? No—you can't feel the force on the wall. You can feel forces only on your body. You're hurt because the wall hit you.

The wall didn't reach out and hit you, of course. But it did push you with the same amount of force with which you pushed it. If it hadn't, you would have moved the wall.

The third law of motion states: *Whenever one object applies a force to a second object,* *the second object applies an equal and opposite force to the first object.*

A simple way to state this law is that forces always occur in pairs. For every action force, there is an equal and opposite reaction force. When your feet touch the ground, the ground touches your feet. When a hammer hits a nail, the nail hits the hammer. When Earth pulls on the moon, the moon pulls back on Earth—all with equal, but opposite, force.

Here's a way to make Newton's third law of motion easier to understand. Just remember that when one object pushes on another, the other object pushes back on the first.

As the boy pushes off the boat, the boat pushes back on him in the opposite direction. ▼

action force   reaction force

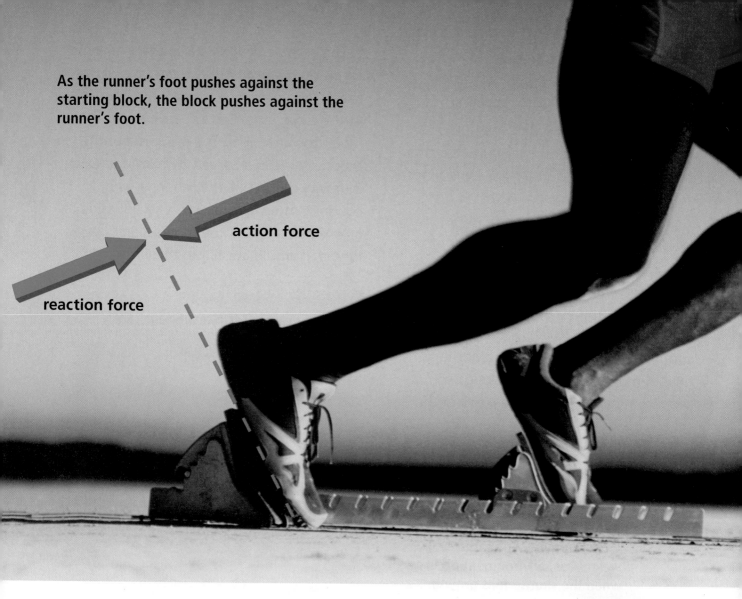

As the runner's foot pushes against the starting block, the block pushes against the runner's foot.

action force

reaction force

A horse pulls a cart. Can you name the opposing forces? Just think of the rule. The horse pulls on the cart. So, Newton's third law tells you that the cart pulls on the horse.

Newton's third law shows that forces always happen in pairs. An action force can't occur without an equal and opposite reaction force. The forces push with the same strength, but in opposite directions, at exactly the same time.

Focus Skill CAUSE AND EFFECT

You push a broom. What pushes on you, and in what direction?

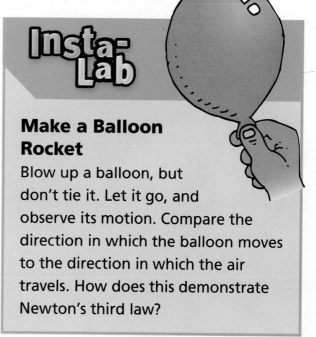

Insta-Lab

Make a Balloon Rocket

Blow up a balloon, but don't tie it. Let it go, and observe its motion. Compare the direction in which the balloon moves to the direction in which the air travels. How does this demonstrate Newton's third law?

Motion in Space

Astronauts inside the space shuttle float as if no gravity were acting on them. However, Earth's gravity at the shuttle isn't zero or even near zero. The shuttle's orbit is close enough to Earth that gravity is almost as strong there as it is on Earth.

Why do the astronauts seem to be weightless? After the shuttle reaches orbit, its engines shut down. Inertia carries the shuttle forward. Space near Earth has only a little drag to slow down objects. Gravity causes the shuttle to fall. The shuttle falls continuously toward Earth. But at the same time, it moves forward fast enough to keep from hitting Earth. The curve of the shuttle's path as it moves is the same as the curve of Earth, so the shuttle doesn't get any closer to Earth's surface.

This same principle explains why planets and moons stay in orbit. Earth's moon, for example, moves forward because of inertia. At the same time, Earth's gravity pulls the moon toward Earth. The result is that the moon moves in a curved path around Earth. If gravity didn't pull the moon, it would continue moving forever in a straight line at a constant speed. If the moon didn't have inertia, it would crash into the Earth.

Focus Skill CAUSE AND EFFECT

What causes Earth to orbit the sun?

A microgravity, or nearly weightless, environment occurs when the shuttle falls around Earth at a constant speed. The astronauts don't feel the effects of Earth's gravity. ▼

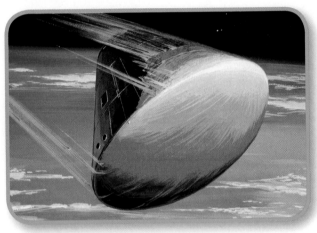

▲ Drag acts on this space capsule as it reenters Earth's atmosphere.

▲ The satellite orbits Earth. It's pulled toward Earth by Earth's gravity.

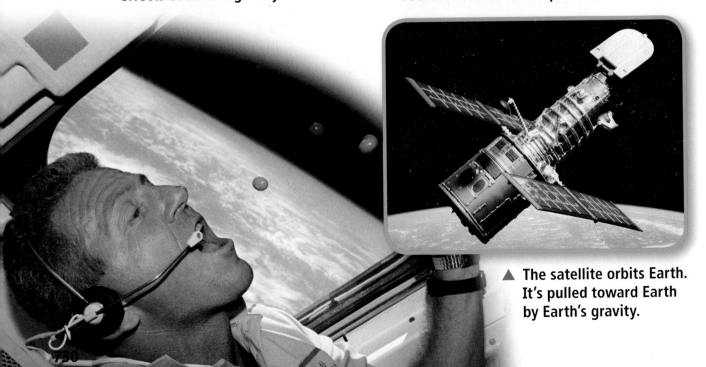

Essential Question

What Are the Laws of Motion?

In this lesson, you learned that Isaac Newton described the effects of forces in three laws of motion. You also learned about the motion of a spacecraft in orbit around Earth as well as the motion of planets around the sun.

1. 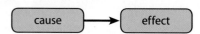 **CAUSE AND EFFECT** Draw and complete a graphic organizer that shows the effects of the three laws of motion.

cause → effect

2. **SUMMARIZE** Write a one-paragraph summary of the motion of objects around Earth and the sun.

3. **DRAW CONCLUSIONS** The first law of motion states that you don't have to apply a force to maintain motion. Why, then, do you have to keep pedaling your bike to keep moving?

4. **VOCABULARY** Make up a riddle or a quiz question about inertia. Provide the answer.

Test Prep

5. **CRITICAL THINKING** Give an example from your everyday life of the third law of motion.

6. A girl throws a ball. If the ball's acceleration is 12 m/sec/sec and its mass is 0.5 kg, how much force did the girl apply to the ball?

   A. 0.04 newtons   C. 6 newtons

   B. 0.6 newtons   D. 12.5 newtons

Make Connections

 Writing

Narrative Writing
Find out how microgravity affects the daily activities of astronauts. Write a **skit** that describes a typical day in an astronaut's life.

 Math

Solve Problems
Forces that act in the same direction add like regular numbers. A girl and a boy pull a wagon to the right. The girl applies 10 newtons. The boy applies 8 newtons. What's the total force on the wagon?

 Social Studies

History of Science
Use library resources to research the life of Isaac Newton. Write a story for younger students that tells how he came up with the three laws of motion.

Building a Safer Race Car

Fasten your seat belt. The world's most dangerous sport just got safer. The car-racing world was shocked in 2001 when stock-car champion Dale Earnhardt died in a crash at the Daytona 500. Earnhardt died when his car struck the track's retaining wall during the last lap of the race.

The accident, which followed three other fatal accidents that year, showed just how dangerous car racing is. Now new equipment for both cars and drivers has made stock-car racing safer.

Strapped In

The most important safety change has been to improve the way drivers are strapped into their seats. NASCAR (National Association for Stock Car Auto Racing) now requires that all drivers wear head-and-neck restraints. These restraints help keep a driver's head from violently slamming about during a crash. Other new restraints are designed to help keep a driver's head and arms inside the car during an accident.

Racing teams are also now experimenting with new seat materials and designs to help keep a driver safe. For example, some new seats are being made from a carbon fiber material. This material is superstrong but is also lightweight.

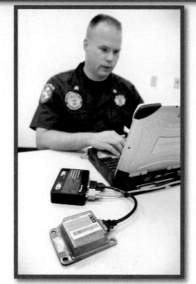

The Black Box

After Dale Earnhardt's accident, NASCAR officials began installing "black boxes" on cars. A black box monitors a vehicle's motion throughout a race and records information on what goes on inside the car during a crash. Investigators use similar recorders to help determine the causes of airplane accidents.

Other safety developments include these:

- NASCAR engineers have recommended that new kinds of fire extinguishers be built into cars.
- Since race car doors do not open, some race cars have been equipped with rooftop escape hatches to let a driver out quickly.
- Engineers have developed a superstrong strap to help keep a car's wheels from flying off during a crash.

- Mechanics have installed special air filters that keep deadly gases, such as carbon monoxide, from seeping into the cockpit of a race car.

Safety has not been limited to race cars. At many racetracks, engineers have begun installing "soft walls." These barriers are made of steel-and-foam cushioning. The soft walls help absorb energy when struck at high speeds by a 3,400-pound race car.

✎ Think and Write

1 Why does a race driver need so much safety equipment?

2 How would "soft walls" at a race track absorb a car's energy?

Speeds in NASCAR races can exceed 200 mph. ▼

Find out more. Log on to
www.hspscience.com

Vocabulary Review

Use the terms below to complete the sentences. The page numbers tell you where to look in the chapter if you need help.

speed p. 714

velocity p. 714

acceleration p. 716

inertia p. 725

1. The speed and direction of a moving object is its _____.

2. The distance an object travels in a certain amount of time is its _____.

3. The rate of change of velocity is _____.

4. The tendency of an object to maintain its state of motion is _____.

Check Understanding

Write the letter of the best choice.

5. When a boy lands on a trampoline, he pushes down on the trampoline. What is the reaction force?
   A. gravity pulling the boy down
   B. the boy pushing down
   C. the friction between the boy and the trampoline
   D. the trampoline pushing upward

6. The picture shows a force acting on an object. What is the direction of the object's acceleration?

   F. opposite to the force
   G. the same direction as the force
   H. at right angles to the force
   J. in any direction

7. What force helps you stop when you're skateboarding?
   A. friction   C. inertia
   B. gravity   D. magnetism

8. A worm crawls 2 meters in 2 hours. What is the worm's speed?
   F. 1 m/hr   H. 4 m/hr
   G. 2 m/hr   J. 10 m/hr

9. Which of the following is not part of Newton's second law?
   A. mass   C. acceleration
   B. position   D. force

10. A girl ice-skates in a circle at a constant speed of 10 km/hr. What part of her motion is changing?
    F. acceleration   H. speed
    G. friction   J. velocity

11. Which of the following does not cause a car to accelerate?
    A. steering wheel   C. tires
    B. gas pedal   D. brakes

12. If you were a bicycle racer, what feature would you look for in a bike?

  F. large tires

  G. tires with high friction

  H. low mass

  J. high mass

13. A balloon rises at a rate of 2 km/hr. What is its velocity?

  A. 2 mph, upward   **C.** 2 km/sec^2

  B. 2 km/hr, upward   **D.** 2 km/hr

14. **CAUSE AND EFFECT** If you walk on a log that's floating in water, the log moves backward. Which of the following explains this?

  F. Newton's first law

  G. Newton's second law

  H. Newton's third law

  J. friction

15. A truck, a car, a motorcycle, and a train are all moving at the same speed. Which has the most momentum?

  A. car   **C.** train

  B. motorcycle   **D.** truck

16. **MAIN IDEA AND DETAILS** Which two factors make up momentum?

  F. mass and velocity

  G. force and mass

  H. mass and acceleration

  J. velocity and gravity

Inquiry Skills

17. Mercury is the smallest planet in the solar system. **Infer** whether you would feel lighter or heavier on Mercury than on Earth. Explain why.

18. How can a race-car driver keep the same engine (the force) but increase the acceleration of the car? **Identify** the control **variable** and the test variable.

Critical Thinking

19. Look at the diagrams. For each one, state the reaction force.

A.

B.

C.

D.

20. A cyclist travels at 40 km/hr going north. Another cyclist travels at 40 km/hr going south. Are the cyclists traveling at the same speed? The same velocity? Explain. In what ways can the cyclists change their velocities? Name as many as you can.

The **Big Idea**

735

Tell how each picture shows the **Big Idea** for its chapter.

CHAPTER 18

Big Idea

Forces, such as magnetism and gravitation, interact with objects, such as you and Earth, to produce motion.

CHAPTER 19

Big Idea

Motion can be observed, measured, and described.

Visit the Multimedia Science Glossary to see illustrations of these words and to hear them pronounced.
www.hspscience.com

Every entry in the glossary begins with a term and a *phonetic respelling.* A phonetic respelling writes the word the way it sounds, which can help you pronounce new or unfamiliar words. The definition of the term follows the respelling. An example of how to use the term in a sentence follows the definition.

The page number in ( ) at the end of the entry tells you where to find the term in your textbook. These terms are highlighted in yellow in the lessons of your textbook. Each entry has an illustration to help you understand the term. The Pronunciation Key below will help you understand the respellings. Syllables are separated by a bullet (•). Small, uppercase letters show stressed syllables.

Pronunciation Key

Sound	As in	Phonetic Respelling	Sound	As in	Phonetic Respelling
ah	lock	(lahk)	oo	pool	(pool)
ar	argue	(ar•gyoo)	oy	foil	(foyl)
aw	law	(law)	s	cell	(sel)
ay	face	(fays)		sit	(sit)
e	test	(test)	th	that	(that)
ee	eat	(eet)	u	pull	(pul)
	ski	(skee)		talent	(tal•uhnt)
	fern	(fern)		onion	(uhn•yuhn)
i	bit	(bit)		dull	(duhl)
k	card	(kard)		ripe	(ryp)
ngk	bank	(bangk)	zh	treasure	(trezh•er)

Multimedia Science Glossary: www.hspscience.com

A

abyssal plain
[uh•BIS•uhl PLAYN] **A large, flat area of the ocean floor:** The *abyssal plain* covers almost half of Earth's surface. (438)

acceleration
[ak•sel•er•AY•shuhn] **The rate at which velocity changes over time:** This boat's *acceleration* changes depending on the force applied to the sail. (716)

acid rain
[AS•id RAYN] **A mixture of rain and acids from air pollution that falls to Earth:** *Acid rain* can damage natural resources and human-made objects. (238)

adaptation
[ad•uhp•TAY•shuhn] **A trait or characteristic that helps an organism survive:** The dolphin's flippers are an *adaptation* that helps it swim. (219)

air mass
[AIR MAS] **A large body of air that has similar temperature and humidity throughout:** The blue arrows represent cool *air masses*. (420)

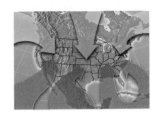

air pressure
[AIR PRESH•er] **The weight of the atmosphere pressing down on Earth:** *Air pressure* changes with altitude. (399)

angiosperm
[AN•jee•oh•sperm] **A flowering vascular plant whose seeds are surrounded by fruit:** Strawberry plants are *angiosperms*. (133)

atmosphere
[AT•muhs•feer] **The blanket of air surrounding Earth:** Earth's *atmosphere* has several layers. (398)

atom [AT•uhm] The smallest particle that still behaves like the original matter it came from: Nearly all *atoms* have neutrons. (524)

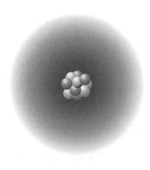

axis [AK•sis] An imaginary line that passes through Earth's center and its North and South Poles: Earth spins on its *axis* while orbiting the sun. (472)

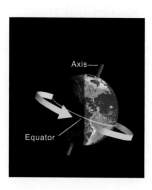

Axis

Equator

 B

balance [BAL•uhns] A tool that measures the amount of matter in an object (the object's mass): The *balance* shows that the masses of these objects are equal. (11)

balanced forces [BAL•uhnst FAWRS•iz] Forces that act on an object but cancel each other out: *Balanced forces* occur when there is no motion. (686)

buoyant force [BOY•uhnt FAWRS] The upward force exerted on an object by water: *Buoyant force* keeps the rubber duck and the ball afloat. (690)

C

carnivore [KAHR•nuh•vawr] An animal that eats other animals; also called a second-level consumer: *Carnivores* have sharp teeth to help them tear and eat meat. (200)

cast [KAST] A fossil formed when dissolved minerals fill a mold and harden: This *cast* is of an organism that lived long ago. (304)

cell [SEL] The basic unit of structure and function in all living things: Plant *cells* have a cell wall. (54)

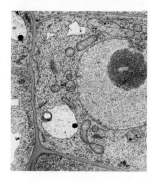

cell membrane

[SEL MEM•brayn] **The thin covering that surrounds every cell:** Animal cells have only a *cell membrane* to protect everything within the cell. (56)

chemical energy

[KEM•ih•kuhl EN•er•jee] **Energy that can be released by a chemical reaction:** *Chemical energy* is stored in fireworks and released when they explode. (572)

chlorophyll

[KLAWR•uh•fihl] **A green pigment in plants that allows a plant cell to use light to make food:** *Chlorophyll* is what makes leaves green. (192)

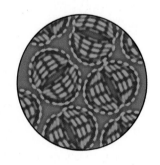

chromosome

[KROH•muh•sohm] **A threadlike structure in the nucleus, made up of DNA:** Humans have 23 pairs of *chromosomes*. (150)

circulatory system

[SER•kyoo•luh•tawr•ee SIS•tuhm] **The organ system—made up of the heart, blood vessels, and blood—that transports materials throughout the body:** The *circulatory system* moves blood throughout the body. (74)

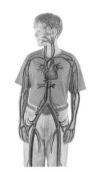

classification

[klas•uh•fih•KAY•shuhn] **The process of grouping similar things together:** A *classification* chart would help this student categorize the different objects. (94)

climate

[KLY•muht] **The pattern of weather an area experiences over a long period of time:** Glaciers exist in cold *climates*. (422)

combustibility
[kuhm•buhs•tuh•BIL•uh•tee] **A measure of how easily a substance will burn:** Many chemicals have warnings of high *combustibility*. (546)

community
[kuh•MYOO•nuh•tee] **A group of populations that live together:** A *community* has many kinds of organisms. (218)

competition
[kahm•puh•TISH•uhn] **A kind of contest among populations that need to get a certain amount of food, water, and shelter to survive:** A dry desert increases *competition* for food. (219)

concave lens
[kahn•KAYV LENZ] **A lens that is thicker at the edges than it is at the center:** Objects seen through a *concave lens* will appear smaller. (662)

condensation [kahn•duhn•SAY•shuhn] **The process by which a gas changes into a liquid:** Rain results from *condensation*. (409)

conduction
[kuhn•DUHK•shuhn] **The transfer of heat from one object directly to another:** The hot liquid is heating the metal through *conduction*. (584)

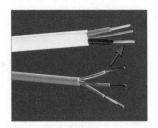

conductor
[kuhn•DUHK•ter] **A material that carries electricity well:** Metal, such as these copper wires, is a good *conductor*. (622)

conservation
[kahn•ser•VAY•shuhn] **The preserving and protecting of a resource:** Protecting water resources is a part of *conservation*. (240, 381, 593)

constellation

[kahn•stuh•LAY•shuhn]
A pattern of stars, named after a mythological or religious figure, an object, or an animal: Ursa Major is a *constellation* that many people think looks like a bear. (493)

consumer

[kuhn•SOOM•er]
An animal that eats plants, other animals, or both: Animals are *consumers*. (194)

continental shelf

[kahnt•uhn•ENT•uhl SHELF] **The part of the ocean floor that drops gently near the land:** You may see some of the *continental shelf* during low tide. (438)

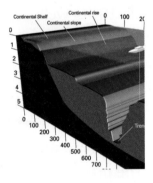

continental slope

[kahnt•uhn•ENT•uhl SLOHP] **The part of the ocean floor that slopes steeply:** The *continental slope* is very steep in places. (438)

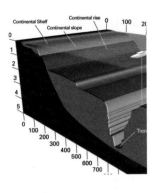

convection

[kuhn•VEK•shuhn]
The transfer of heat through the movement of a gas or a liquid: *Convection* in the atmosphere produces rain clouds. (584)

convex lens

[kahn•VEKS LENZ] **A lens that is thicker at the center than it is at the edges:** *Convex lenses* are used in making eyeglasses to help people see faraway objects. (662)

crater

[KRAYT•er] **A low, bowl-shaped area on the surface of a planet or moon:** *Craters* in volcanoes are caused by eruptions. (482)

current [KER•uhnt] **A stream of water that flows like a river through the ocean:** Ocean *currents* flow in only one direction. (448)

current electricity [KER•uhnt ee•lek•TRIS•ih•tee] **A kind of kinetic energy that flows as an electric current:** *Current electricity* provides the energy to light the bulb. (620)

cytoplasm [SYT•oh•plaz•uhm] **The jellylike substance between a cell membrane and the nucleus, containing most organelles:** *Cytoplasm* helps protect organelles. (56)

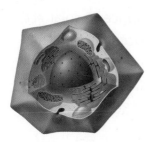

D

decomposer [dee•kuhm•POHZ•er] **A consumer that obtains food energy by breaking down the remains of dead plants and animals:** These *decomposers* are breaking down a tree. (201)

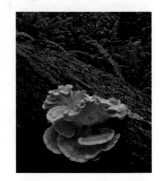

delta [DEL•tuh] **An area of new land at the mouth of a river, formed from sediments carried by the river:** Some *deltas* look like triangles when viewed from space. (343)

density [DEN•suh•tee] **The measure of how closely packed an object's atoms are:** The rock has a higher *density* than the cork. (537)

deposition

[dep•uh•ZISH•uhn] **The process in which sediment settles out of water or is dropped by wind:** These rocks were part of the *deposition* process. (276)

digestive system

[dih•JES•tiv SIS•tuhm] **The organ system that turns food into nutrients that body cells need for energy, growth, and repair:** The *digestive system* includes the stomach and the intestines. (66)

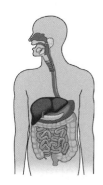

dominant trait

[DAHM•uh•nuhnt TRAYT] **A trait that appears even if an organism has only one factor for the trait:** A *dominant trait* can determine hair or eye color in a child. (160)

 E

earthquake

[ERTH•kwayk] **A shaking of the ground, caused by a sudden release of energy in Earth's crust:** Seismographs can measure the magnitude of an *earthquake*. (354)

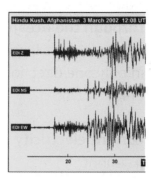

eclipse

[ih•KLIPS] **An event that occurs when one object in space passes through the shadow of another object in space:** A solar *eclipse* occurs when the moon blocks sunlight from reaching Earth. (486)

ecosystem

[EE•koh•sis•tuhm] **A community of organisms and the environment in which they live:** This *ecosystem* includes water, fish, grass, flowers, and air. (200)

electric circuit
[ee•LEK•trik SER•kit]
The path an electric current follows: The lights in your home are on an *electric circuit*. (628)

electric current
[ee•LEK•trik KER•uhnt]
The flow of electrons: *Electric current* flows through a circuit. (620)

electric energy
[ee•LEK•trik EN•er•jee]
Energy that comes from an electric current: *Electric energy* is flowing from the socket to the light bulb. (574)

electricity
[ee•lek•TRIS•ih•tee]
A form of energy produced by moving electrons: Many things in your home run on *electricity*. (609)

electromagnet
[ee•lek•troh•MAG•nit]
A magnet made by coiling a wire around a piece of iron and running electric current through the wire: You can make an *electromagnet* with a nail, some wire, and a battery. (610)

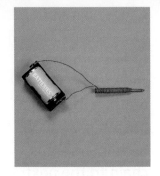

element
[EL•uh•muhnt] **Matter made up of only one kind of atom:** Gold is an *element* because it is made of only gold atoms. (526)

energy [EN•er•jee]
The ability to cause changes in matter: Fire produces light and heat *energy*. (560)

energy pyramid

[EN•er•jee PIR•uh•mid]
A diagram that shows how much food energy is passed from each level in a food chain to the next: *Energy pyramids* have producers at the bottom and third-level consumers at the top. (205)

energy transfer

[EN•er•jee TRANS•fer]
Movement of energy from one place or object to another: Often *energy transfer* happens through waves. (564)

environment

[en•VY•ruhn•muhnt]
All the living and nonliving things that surround and affect an organism: Many kinds of living things can share the same *environment*. (176)

epicenter

[EP•ih•sent•er] The point on Earth's surface directly above the focus of an earthquake: The greatest damage occurs around the *epicenter* of an earthquake. (354)

equator [ee•KWAYT•er]
An imaginary line around Earth, equally distant from the North and South Poles: The *equator* separates the Northern and Southern Hemispheres. (474)

erosion

[uh•ROH•zhuhn] The process of moving sediment by wind, moving water, or ice: This gully was formed by *erosion*. (287)

evaporation

[ee•vap•uh•RAY•shuhn]
The process of a liquid changing into a gas: *Evaporation* is one part of the water cycle. (409)

evidence
[EV•uh•duhns]
Information, collected during an investigation, to support a hypothesis: A scientist gathers *evidence* from an experiment. (32)

excretory system
[EKS•kruh•tawr•ee SIS•tuhm] **The organ system, including the kidneys and bladder, that removes waste materials from the blood:** Cellular wastes leave the body through the *excretory system.* (82)

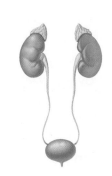

experiment
[ek•SPEHR•uh•muhnt]
A procedure carried out under controlled conditions to test a hypothesis: An *experiment* is an important part of the scientific method. (21)

extinction
[ek•STINGK•shuhn]
The death of all the organisms of a species: Scientists do not know the reason for the *extinction* of the dinosaurs. (232)

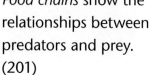

fault [FAWLT] **A break in Earth's crust:** The San Andreas *fault* is more than 1,300 kilometers (800 mi) long. (354)

food chain [FOOD CHAYN] **The transfer of food energy between organisms in an ecosystem:** *Food chains* show the relationships between predators and prey. (201)

food web [FOOD WEB] **A diagram that shows the relationships between different food chains in an ecosystem:** A *food web* shows how organisms in an ecosystem are connected. (202)

force [FAWRS] **A push or pull that may cause an object to move, stop, or change direction:** *Forces* affect the movement of objects. (676)

fossil [FAHS•uhl] **The remains or traces of past life, often found in sedimentary rock:** Scientists use *fossils* to learn about extinct organisms. (303, 592)

frequency [FREE•kwuhn•see] **The number of vibrations per second:** The *frequency* of a sound wave determines the sound's pitch. (646)

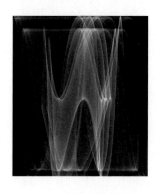

friction [FRIK•shuhn] **A force that opposes motion:** *Friction* causes heat. (677)

front [FRUHNT] **The border where two air masses meet:** Sometimes you will be able to locate a *front* by just watching the clouds. (421)

fulcrum [FUHL•kruhm] **The balance point on a lever that supports the arm but does not move:** The *fulcrum* is the pivot point on the lever. (698)

G

galaxy [GAL•uhk•see] **A grouping of gas, dust, and many stars, plus any objects that orbit those stars:** Earth is part of the Milky Way *Galaxy.* (498)

gene [JEEN] **The part of a chromosome that contains the DNA code for an inherited trait:** *Genes* are passed down from parents to offspring. (166)

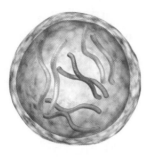

germinate [JER•muh•nayt] **To sprout:** Plants *germinate* as part of their life cycle. (136)

glacier [GLAY•sher] **A large, thick sheet of ice:** Very high mountains often have *glaciers*. (332)

gravitational force [grav•ih•TAY•shuhn•uhl FAWRS] **The pull of all objects in the universe on one another:** The *gravitational force* of the sun keeps Earth in orbit. (678)

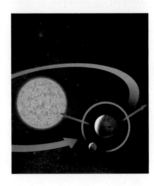

gravity [GRAV•ih•tee] **The attraction between objects and Earth:** On a roller coaster, you experience the effects of *gravity*. (678)

gymnosperm [JIM•noh•sperm] **A plant that produces naked seeds:** Pine trees are *gymnosperms*; their seeds are in pinecones. (132)

H

habitat [HAB•i•tat] **An area where an organism can find everything it needs to survive:** A gopher tortoise's *habitat* includes its burrow. (239)

hardness [HARD•nis] **A mineral's ability to resist being scratched:** Minerals that can be scratched with a fingernail have a low *hardness*. (266)

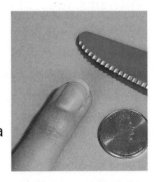

headland [HED•luhnd]
A point of land at the shore where hard rock is left behind and other materials are washed away: *Headlands* make dramatic landscapes. (456)

heat [HEET] **The transfer of thermal energy between objects with different temperatures:** These steel bars have been exposed to a lot of *heat*. (582)

herbivore [HER•buh•vawr] **An animal that eats only producers:** *Herbivores* have flat teeth to help them eat plants. (200)

humidity [hyoo•MID•uh•tee] **A measurement of the amount of water vapor in the air:** When the *humidity* is high, sweat evaporates slowly. (410)

hypothesis [hy•PAHTH•uh•sis] **A statement that provides a testable possible answer to a scientific question:** These students are testing a *hypothesis* with their experiment. (29)

I

igneous rock [IG•nee•uhs RAHK] **Rock that forms when melted rock cools and hardens:** Granite is one kind of *igneous rock*. (274)

inclined plane [in•KLYND PLAYN] **A ramp or other sloping surface:** An *inclined plane* can make moving heavy objects easier. (699)

index fossil [IN•deks FAHS•uhl] **A fossil of an organism that lived in many places around the world for a short period of time; helps scientists find the age of a rock layer:** Trilobite remains help scientists find the age of Earth's layers because they are *index fossils*. (306)

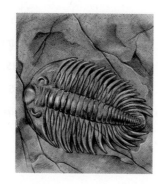

inertia [in•ER•shuh] **The property of matter that keeps it at rest or moving in a straight line:** It takes more force to start something moving due to *inertia*. (725)

inherited trait [in•HAIR•it•ed TRAYT] **A characteristic passed from parents to their offspring:** Fur color is an *inherited trait* in mice. (158)

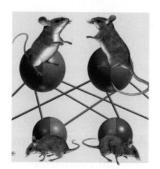

inquiry [IN•kwer•ee] **An organized way to gather information and answer questions:** Observe carefully when you perform a scientific *inquiry*. (18)

instinct [IN•stinkt] **A behavior that an organism inherits:** Birds have an *instinct* to build nests. (172)

insulator [IN•suh•layt•er] **A material that does not conduct electricity well:** *Insulators* are important because they protect you from the electric current in wires. (622)

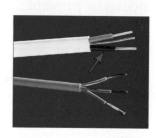

invertebrate [in•VER•tuh•brit] **An animal without a backbone:** Earthworms are *invertebrates* you can find living in soil. (106)

investigation
[in•ves•tuh•GAY•shuhn]
A procedure carried out to gather data about an object or event: The student is conducting an *investigation* and recording the results. (18)

J

jetty [JET•ee] **A wall-like structure that sticks out into the ocean to prevent sand from being carried away:** A *jetty* can be long or short. (459)

K

kinetic energy
[kih•NET•ik EN•er•jee]
The energy of motion: The balls that are swinging have *kinetic energy.* (562)

kingdom [KING•duhm]
A major, large group of similar organisms: All species of animals are part of the animal *kingdom.* (95)

L

landform
[LAND•fawrm] **A natural land shape or feature:** This mountain valley is a *landform.* (330)

lava [LAH•vuh] **Molten (melted) rock that reaches Earth's surface:** *Lava* erupts from volcanoes. (356)

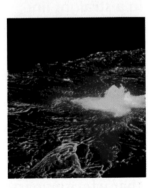

learned behavior
[LERND bee•HAYV•yer]
A behavior that an animal acquires through experience: Following their mother to find food is a *learned behavior* for these ducklings. (174)

lever [LEV•er] **A bar that makes it easier to move things:** A *lever* helps you do work. (698)

life cycle [LYF SY•kuhl] **The stages that a living thing passes through as it grows and changes:** Tadpoles and adult frogs are part of the same *life cycle*. (149)

light [LYT] **Radiation that we can see:** The sun produces *light* energy. (570)

local wind [LOH•kuhl WIND] **Movement of air that results from local changes in temperature:** A land breeze is a *local wind* that comes from the land. (401)

luster [LUS•ter] **The way a mineral's surface reflects light:** Minerals with a metallic *luster* look shiny. (265)

M

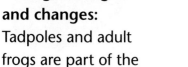

magma [MAG•muh] **Molten (melted) rock beneath Earth's surface:** When molten rock is inside a volcano, it is called *magma*. (356)

magnetic [mag•NET•ik] **Having the property of attracting iron objects:** A magnet is surrounded by a *magnetic* field. (680)

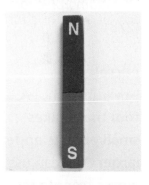

magnetic force [mag•NET•ik FAWRS] **The force produced by a magnet:** The *magnetic force* of this object is shown by the pattern of the metal filings. (680)

mechanical energy [muh•KAN•ih•kuhl EN•er•jee] **The combination of all the kinetic and potential energy that something has:** This helicopter has a lot of *mechanical energy*. (572)

metamorphic rock [met•uh•MAWR•fik RAHK] **Rock formed when high heat and great pressure change an existing rock into a new form:** Gneiss is one kind of *metamorphic rock*. (278)

microscope [MY•kruh•skohp] **A tool that makes small objects appear larger:** You can use a *microscope* to see things that you can't see with your eyes alone. (8)

microscopic [my•kruh•SKAHP•ik] **Too small to be seen without using a microscope:** Objects that can be seen only with a microscope are *microscopic*. (54)

mineral [MIN•er•uhl] **A naturally occurring, nonliving solid that has a specific chemical makeup and a repeating structure:** Most gemstones are *minerals*. (264)

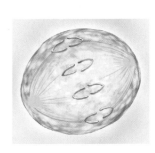

mitosis [my•TOH•sis] **The process by which most cells divide:** Copies of chromosomes separate during the middle stage of *mitosis*. (150)

mixture [MIKS•chuhr] **A combination of two or more different substances:** Fruit salad is a *mixture*. (538)

mold [MOHLD] **The hollow space that is left when sediment hardens around the remains of an organism and the remains then dissolve:** Some kinds of fossils are made in a *mold*. (304)

molecule [MAHL•ih•kyool] **Two or more atoms joined together:** This *molecule* has two different kinds of atoms. (524)

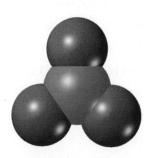

moon [MOON] **Any natural body that revolves around a planet:** Earth's *moon* causes ocean tides on Earth. (482)

moon phase [MOON FAYZ] **One of the shapes the moon seems to have as it orbits Earth:** The *moon phase* that occurs after a new moon is a waxing crescent moon. (485)

muscular system [MUHS•kyoo•ler SIS•tuhm] **The organ system that includes the muscles and allows the body to move:** Your *muscular system* and skeletal system work together to help you move. (78)

N

nervous system [NER•vuhs SIS•tuhm] **The organ system—including the brain, spinal cord, and nerves—that senses your surroundings and controls other organs:** The *nervous system* connects all the tissues and organs in the body to the brain. (80)

net force [NET FAWRS] **The combination of all the forces acting on an object:** As she leaps, this dancer has a positive *net force*. (688)

nonrenewable resource [nahn•rih•NOO•uh•buhl REE•sawrs] A resource that, once used, cannot be replaced in a reasonable amount of time: Coal and other fossil fuels are *nonrenewable resources*. (371, 593)

nucleus (of a cell) [NOO•klee•uhs] The part of a cell that directs all of the cell's activities: The *nucleus* controls all cell activities. (56)

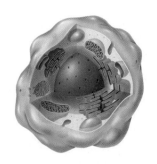

nucleus (of an atom) [NOO•klee•uhs] A dense area in the center of an atom that contains protons and neutrons: All atoms have a *nucleus*. (525)

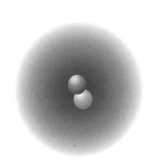

O

opaque [oh•PAYK] Not allowing any light to pass through: This *opaque* umbrella blocks the sunlight. (660)

orbit [AWR•bit] The path that one body takes in space as it revolves around another body: Earth takes 365.25 days to complete its *orbit* around the sun. (474)

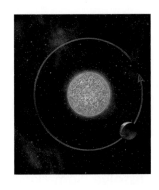

organ [AWR•guhn] A group of tissues that work together to perform a certain function: The heart is one of your *organs*. (65)

organ system [AWR•guhn SIS•tuhm] A group of organs that work together to do a job for the body: The circulatory system is one kind of *organ system*. (66)

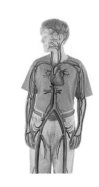

organism [AWR•guhn•izm] Any living thing that maintains vital life processes: Plants and animals are *organisms*. (54)

P

paleontology [pay•lee•uhn•TAHL•uh•jee]
The study of fossils: A scientist who studies *paleontology* is a paleontologist. (315)

parallel circuit
[PAIR•uh•lel SER•kit] **An electric circuit that has more than one path for the current to follow:** If one bulb in a *parallel circuit* goes out, the others stay on. (630)

periodic table
[pir•ee•AHD•ik TAY•buhl] **A chart that scientists use to organize the elements:** This picture shows one part of the *periodic table.* (526)

phloem [FLOH•em]
Vascular tissue that carries food from leaves to all plant cells: *Phloem* helps transport food throughout a plant. (121)

photosynthesis
[foht•oh•SIHN•thuh•sis]
The process in which plants make food by using water from the soil, carbon dioxide from the air, and energy from sunlight: Plants need light and water for *photosynthesis.* (124, 192)

physical change
[FIZ•ih•kuhl CHAYNJ] **A change in which the form of a substance changes but the substance still has the same chemical makeup:** Melting is one kind of *physical change.* (534)

pitch [PICH] **How high or low a sound is:** Sounds with a very high *pitch* can hurt your ears. (646)

planet [PLAN•it] **A body that revolves around a star:** Our solar system has eight *planets.* (495)

plate [PLAYT] **A section of Earth's crust and upper mantle that fits together with other sections like puzzle pieces:** There are 10 major *plates*. (353)

pollution [puh•LOO•shuhn] **A waste product that harms living things and damages an ecosystem:** Factory smoke is a source of air *pollution*. (238, 372, 596)

population [pahp•yuh•LAY•shuhn] **A group of organisms of one kind that live in one location:** *Populations* must share resources in an ecosystem. (218)

position [puh•ZISH•uhn] **The location of an object in space:** This pencil's *position* is not changing. (712)

potential energy [poh•TEN•shuhl EN•er•jee] **The energy an object has because of its condition or position:** Being on top of a hill increases *potential energy*. (562)

precipitation [pree•sip•uh•TAY•shuhn] **Water that falls from the air to Earth:** Rain is *precipitation*. (410)

predator [PRED•uh•ter] **An animal that kills and eats other animals:** A bobcat hunts living animals, so it is a *predator*. (222)

prevailing wind [pree•VAYL•ing WIND] **Global wind that blows constantly from the same direction:** The picture shows Earth's *prevailing winds*. (402)

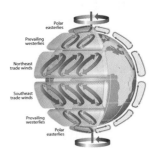

prey [PRAY] An animal that is eaten by a predator: Rabbits are one kind of *prey*. (222)

producer [pruh•DOOS•er] A living thing, such as a plant, that makes its own food: Plants are *producers* because they make food through photosynthesis. (194)

protist [PROHT•ist] A simple, single-celled or multi-celled organism with a nucleus and organelles: This *protist* performs photosynthesis and swims. (58)

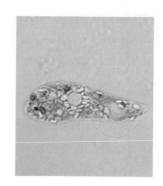

pulley [PUL•ee] A wheel with a rope that lets you change the direction in which you move an object: A *pulley* makes lifting heavy objects easier. (699)

R

radiation [ray•dee•AY•shuhn] The transfer of energy by means of waves that move through matter and space: Some hot objects heat through *radiation*. (585)

reactivity [ree•ak•TIV•uh•tee] The ability of a substance to go through a chemical change: These candles have a higher *reactivity* than some other substances. (547)

recessive trait [rih•SES•iv TRAYT] A trait that appears only if an organism has two factors for the trait: If both a dominant and a recessive factor are present for a trait, the *recessive trait* does not appear. (160)

reclamation [rek•luh•MAY•shuhn] **The process of cleaning and restoring a damaged ecosystem:** *Reclamation* is necessary when an ecosystem is damaged by humans or nature. (242)

reflection [rih•FLEK•shuhn] **The bouncing of heat or light off an object:** You will see the *reflection* of anything in front of a mirror. (585, 660)

refraction [rih•FRAK•shuhn] **The bending of light as it moves from one material to another:** *Refraction* causes the straw to appear broken. (486, 661)

renewable resource [rih•NOO•uh•buhl REE•sawrs] **A resource that can be replaced within a reasonable amount of time:** Wind is a *renewable resource*. (370, 594)

resource [REE•sawrs] **Any material that can be used to satisfy a need:** This beaver uses *resources* to build shelter. (593)

respiratory system [RES•per•uh•tawr•ee SIS•tuhm] **The organ system, including the lungs, that exchanges oxygen and carbon dioxide between the body and the environment:** Your lungs are a part of your *respiratory system*. (77)

revolve [rih•VAHLV] **To travel in a closed path around another object:** The planets in the solar system *revolve* around the sun. (474)

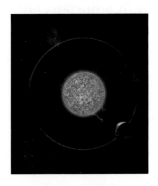

rock [RAHK] **A natural substance made of one or more minerals:** *Rocks* come in all colors, shapes, and sizes. (274)

rock cycle [RAHK SY•kuhl] **The continuous process in which one type of rock changes into another type:** In the *rock cycle*, the same minerals may become different rocks. (288)

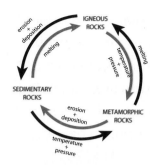

rotate [ROH•tayt] **To spin on an axis:** The earth *rotates* on its axis once every day. (472)

S

salinity [suh•LIN•uh•tee] **The amount of salt in water:** Ocean water has a higher *salinity* than fresh water. (436)

sand dune [SAND DOON] **A hill of sand, made and shaped by wind:** Some *sand dunes* move as much as 30 m (100 ft) a year. (333)

scientific method [sy•uhn•TIF•ik METH•uhd] **A series of steps that scientists use when performing an experiment:** You can use the *scientific method* to answer your science questions. (28)

sedimentary rock [sed•uh•MEN•tuh•ree RAHK] **Rock formed when sediments are cemented together:** *Sedimentary rocks* often form beneath lakes or rivers. (276)

series circuit [SIR•eez SER•kit] **An electric circuit in which the current has only one path to follow:** If one bulb in a *series circuit* goes out, the others also go out. (629)

shore [SHAWR] **The area where the ocean and the land meet and interact:** The *shore* is what many people call the beach. (456)

simple machine
[SIM•puhl muh•SHEEN]
A device that makes a task easier by changing the size or direction of a force or the distance over which the force acts: This wheelbarrow uses a *simple machine*: a lever. (698)

sinkhole [SINGK•hohl]
A large hole formed when the roof of a cave collapses: Water underground is usually the cause of *sinkholes*. (344)

skeletal system
[SKEL•uh•tuhl SIS•tuhm]
The organ system, including the bones, that protects the body and gives it structure: Your *skeletal system* includes all of the bones in your body. (78)

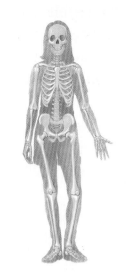

solar energy [SOH•ler EN•er•jee] **Energy that comes from the sun:** Many people are starting to use *solar energy* to heat their houses. (570)

solar system [SOH•ler SIS•tuhm] **A star and all the planets and other objects that revolve around it:** The center of our *solar system* is the sun. (492)

solution
[suh•LOO•shuhn] **A mixture in which all the parts are mixed evenly:** These liquids are *solutions*. (539)

species [SPEE•sheez] **A unique kind of organism:** Wildebeests are one *species* living in Africa. (96)

speed [SPEED] **The distance an object travels in a certain amount of time:** The *speed* of the race car is found by measuring how far and how fast the race car traveled. (714)

spore [SPAWR] **A single reproductive cell that can grow into a new plant:** A *spore* is part of the fern's reproductive cycle. (130)

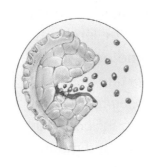

star [STAR] **A huge ball of very hot gases in space:** *Stars* look small from Earth's surface. (492)

static electricity [STAT•ik ee•lek•TRIS•uh•tee] **The buildup of charges on an object:** *Static electricity* might make your clothes stick together. (618)

streak [STREEK] **The color of the powder left behind when you rub a mineral against a rough white tile or a streak plate:** This mineral leaves a brown *streak* on the tile. (265)

succession [suhk•SESH•uhn] **A gradual change in the kinds of organisms living in an ecosystem:** You can see *succession* after a volcanic eruption. (228)

sun [SUHN] **The star at the center of our solar system:** The *sun* provides light and heat energy to our solar system. (472)

symbiosis [sim•by•OH•sis] **A relationship between different kinds of organisms:** There are three kinds of *symbiosis*. (220)

system [SIS•tuhm] **A group of separate elements that work together to accomplish something:** The burner, pot, and water are a *system* through which thermal energy moves. (583)

tide [TYD] **The rise and fall of the water level of the ocean:** The moon's gravitational force is responsible for the *tides* on Earth. (450)

tide pool [TYD POOL] **A temporary pool of ocean water that gets trapped between rocks when the tide goes out:** *Tide pools* are more common on rocky beaches. (457)

tissue [TISH•OO] **A group of cells that work together to perform a certain function:** The lining of the stomach is one kind of *tissue*. (64)

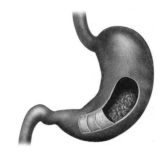

topography [tuh•PAHG•ruh•fee] **All the kinds of landforms in a certain place:** The *topography* of this area includes hills, a river, and mountains. (330)

translucent [trans•LOO•suhnt] **Allowing only some light to pass through:** You can see light through *translucent* objects, but you cannot see clearly through them. (661)

transparent [trans•PAIR•uhnt] **Allowing light to pass through:** The glass in these containers is *transparent*. (661)

transpiration
[tran•spuh•RAY•shuhn]
The loss of water from a leaf through the stomata: These leaves are playing a role in the *transpiration* process. (191)

troposphere
[TROH•puh•sfeer] **The layer of air closest to Earth's surface:** Planes travel in the *troposphere*. (398)

U

unbalanced forces
[uhn•BAL•uhnst FAWRS•iz] **Forces that act on an object and don't cancel each other out; unbalanced forces cause a change in motion:** This beam balance moves because the *unbalanced forces* do not cancel each other out. (686)

universe
[YOO•nuh•vers]
Everything that exists, including stars, planets, and energy: Billions of galaxies make up the *universe*. (498)

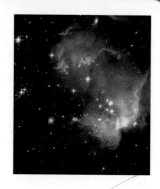

V

vascular tissue
[VAS•kyuh•ler TISH•oo]
Tissue that supports plants and carries water and food: You can find *vascular tissue* in tree trunks. (121)

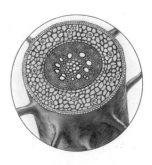

velocity
[vuh•LAHS•uh•tee]
A measure of an object's speed in a particular direction: *Velocity* describes the direction of motion as well as the speed. (714)

vertebrate
[VER•tuh•brit] **An animal with a backbone:** This golden retriever is a *vertebrate*. (104)

vibration

[vy•BRAY•shuhn] **A back-and-forth movement of matter:** *Vibration* of certain materials can create sound. (644)

volcano

[vahl•KAY•noh] **A mountain made of lava, ash, or other materials from eruptions that occur at an opening in Earth's crust:** *Volcanoes* form over vents in Earth's crust. (356)

volume [VAHL•yoom]

The amount of space something takes up: You can measure *volume* with science tools. (523)

volume [VAHL•yoom]

The loudness of a sound: This television's *volume* can be low or high. (645)

water cycle [WAW•ter SY•kuhl]

The process in which water continuously moves from Earth's surface into the atmosphere and back again: The *water cycle* includes evaporation and precipitation. (408)

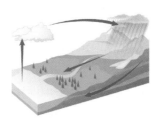

water pressure

[WAWT•er PRESH•er] **The downward push of water:** *Water pressure* increases as you go deeper into the ocean. (437)

wave [WAYV] **The up-and-down movement of surface water:** *Waves* carry energy to the shore. (446)

weathering
[WETH•er•ing] **The process of wearing away rocks by natural processes:** Rocks can be affected by mechanical and chemical *weathering.* (286)

wheel-and-axle
[weel•and•AK•suhl] **A wheel with a rod, or axle, in the center:** A doorknob is a *wheel-and-axle* that you use every day. (698)

work [WERK] **The use of a force to move an object through a distance:** Pushing is a kind of *work.* (696)

xylem [ZY•luhm] **Vascular tissue that carries water and nutrients from roots to every part of a plant:** *Xylem* moves water from the roots up to the leaves. (121)

Index

A

Absolute age of rocks, 306–307
Absorption
    of light, 660
    of sound, 647
Abyssal plains, 439
Acceleration, 716–717
    force for, 725–727
Acid rain, 238, 372
Action forces, 728–729
Adaptations
    biological, 162–163
    for competition, 219
    for survival, 164–165
Adjustment knob
    (microscopes), 9
Africa, 303
African plate, 353
Age
    of Earth, 307
    of rocks, 306–307
Agouti, 105
Air
    composition of, 399
    gases in, 539
    as mixture, 528
    movement of, 401
    reusable resources, 370
    sound travel through, 646
    wind energy from, 595
Air masses, 420–421
Airplanes, designing, 17
Air pollution, 238, 372, 596
Air pressure, 399
    measuring, 418, 419
Al Aziziyah, Libya, 476

Alexander, R. McNeill, 321
Algae, 58
Aluminum, 527
    changes in state of, 536
    chemical changes with, 547
    density of, 537
    as insulator, 622
    recycling, 241
Alveoli, 76, 77
Alvin submersible, 437
Amber, 296–297
Amethyst quartz, 264
Ammann, Karl, 111
Ammonia, 82
Ammonite fossils, 304
Amoebas, 55
Amphibians, 104, 105
Amps, 621
Andes Mountains, 360
Anemometers, 419
Anemones, 106
Angiosperms, 133
Animal kingdom, 95
    invertebrates, 106–107
    vertebrates, 104–105
Animals
    with backbones, 104–105
    without backbones, 106–
        107
    cell division in, 150
    cells of, 55–57
    classifying, 95–97, 104–107
    as decomposers, 201
    in ecosystems, 218
    in energy pyramid, 204–
        205
    extinction of, 232
    food for, 194

    in food webs, 202–203
    fossil and modern, 314–315
    growth and development
        of, 148–149
    inherited behaviors of,
        172–173
    inherited traits in, 158
    instincts of, 172–173
    learned behaviors in, 174–
        175
    natural cycles and, 206
    needs of, 176
    service, 175
    sharing habitats with, 239
    sound and, 650
Anomalocaris fossils, 318
Antarctica, seasons in, 476
Anteater, 163
Antelope Canyon, Arizona,
    324–325
Anthers, 134, 135
Ants, 173, 220
Apatite, hardness of, 266
Aphids, 173, 220
Apollo missions, 478, 484
Appalachian Mountains, 330
Arabian plate, 353
Arachnids, 107
Archery, 556
Arches National Park, Utah,
    282
Arctic fox, 162, 164–165
Arecibo, Puerto Rico, radio
    telescope, 466–467
Argentina, 360
Argon, 399
Armadillo, 164
Armstrong, Neil, 478, 500

Arp, Allissa J., 245
Arteries, 74, 75
Arthropods, 107
Artificial reefs, 459
Asexual reproduction, 151
Asian plate, 358
Asking questions, 28, 34
Asteroid belt, 495
Asteroids, 232, 497
Astronauts, 468, 483, 730
Atlantic Ocean
    Gulf Stream in, 448
    mid-ocean ridges in, 439
Atmosphere, 398–399
    air masses and fronts,
      420–421
    on inner planets, 495
    local winds, 401
    on moon, 482, 483
    prevailing winds, 402
    reflection of radiation by,
      585
    uneven heating of, 400
    water cycle and, 408–409
Atolls, 440
Atomic number, 527
Atoms, 524–525
    charges in, 608
    density of matter and, 537
    states of matter and, 528
Aurora borealis, 604
AUTOnomy, 598, 599
Autumn equinox, 475
Axis (Earth's), 472
    seasons and, 474
Ayrton, Hertha Marks, 634
Azaleas, 114–115

Backbones
    animals with, 104–105

animals without, 106–107
    building model of, 103
Bacteria, 58
    classifying, 95
    commensalism and, 220
    division of, 144
    nitrogen changed by, 206
    as parasites, 221
    reproduction of, 149
Bacteria kingdom, 95
Balance (instrument), 11,
    687
Balanced forces, 686–687
Barium, 547
Barometers, 418, 419
Barred spiral galaxies, 499
Barrier islands, 333
Basalt, 275
Bascom, Florence, 293
Base (microscopes), 9
Baseballs, 727
Bats, hearing of, 650
Batteries, 576
    in hybrid cars, 595
    pollution from, 241
    voltages of, 621
Beaches, 455–457
Beach restoration, 458
Bears, 196
Bees, 107
    pollination by, 135
Beetles, 107
Behaviors
    environmental influences
      on, 176
    inherited, 158, 171
    instinctive, 172–173
    learned, 171, 174–175
Benitez-Nelson, Claudia, 550
Bionic ears, 664–665

Birds, 104, 105
    instincts of, 172, 174
    learned behaviors of, 174
    seed-eating, 135
Bison, 194
Black bear, 165
Black boxes (race cars),
    732–733
Black holes, 499
Bladder, 82
Block and tackle, 700
Blood, 60
    ammonia in, 82
    in circulatory system, 74–75
    as connective tissue, 65
    in digestive system, 67
    in lungs, 77
Blood cells, 74
    production of, 78
    red, 60, 65, 74
    white, 65, 74
Blood vessels, 74, 75
Boiling point, 535, 536
Bones
    as connective tissue, 64
    in skeletal system, 78
Bora-Bora, 440
Bouncing, 559
Brain
    in central nervous system,
      80
    messages from, 80–81
    nerve cells in, 70
    nervous tissue in, 64
Brightness of stars, 493
Bronchi, 77
Bulletproof vests, 725
Bunker, Cassie, 665
Buoyant force, 690
Burning, 542, 546, 572

Burrs, 135
Butterflies
 as arthropods, 107
 classification of, 97
 life cycle of, 149
 metamorphosis in, 149

C

Cacti, 121, 123
Calcite
 crystal structure of, 268
 hardness of, 266
Calving (icebergs), 361
Camouflage, color as, 217
Canada geese, 172, 174
Can openers, 700
Canyons, 334, 341
Cape Cod, Massachusetts,
 345
Capillaries
 in circulatory system, 74, 75
 in lungs, 77
Capitol Building,
 Washington, D.C., 280
Captiva Island, Florida, 333
Capuchin monkeys, 175
Carbohydrates, digestion of,
 67
Carbon, 526
Carbon atom, 525
Carbon cycle, 206
Carbon dioxide
 in air, 399
 in dry ice, 535
 elimination of, 82
 in photosynthesis, 192
 in plant food production,
 191
 in respiratory system, 76,
 77
 using, 189

Carbon film, 305
Cardiac muscle, 79
Cardinals, 105
Caribbean plate, 353
Caribou, 200
Carnival rides, 708
Carnivores, 200, 202, 203
Cars
 energy-efficient, 598–599
 grooves in tires for, 672
 hybrid, 594–596
 safer race cars, 732–733
Cartilage, 64, 78
Cassini spacecraft, 500
Casts, 304
Cats
 classification of, 96–97
 instincts of, 173
Caves, along shores, 457
Cell division, 144, 148, 150–
 151
Cell membrane, 56–57
 in mitosis, 150
Cells, 54–55
 animal, 56–57
 in asexual reproduction,
 151
 blood, 60, 65, 74, 78
 definition of, 54
 gametes, 130
 in growth and
 development, 148–149
 in human body, 64, 65, 148
 nerve, 70
 observing, 53
 plant, 56–57
 reproduction of, 147
 secretory, 48–49
 in sexual reproduction, 152
Cell walls, 56–58
Celsius, Anders, 10

Celsius thermometers, 10
Centennial Park, Atlanta,
 Georgia, 518
Central nervous system, 80,
 81
Centrioles, 151
Chameleons, 214
Charges, electric, 608
 static electricity and, 618–
 619
Charts, 34
Cheetahs, 174, 222
Chemical changes, 546–547
 conservation of matter and,
 548
Chemical energy, 572, 573
 in batteries, 576
Chemical properties, 545
Chemical reactions, 546
 with matches, 542
 to release energy, 572
Chesapecten, 314
Chile, 360
Chlorophyll, 124, 192, 193
Chloroplasts, 56–57
 chlorophyll in, 192
 photosynthesis and, 124
 of single-celled organisms,
 58
Chromosomes, 56, 150
 genes on, 166
 in mitosis, 150, 151
 in sexual reproduction, 152
 of single-celled organisms,
 58
Cinder cone volcanoes, 357
Circuit diagrams, 632
Circuits
 drawing, 632
 electric (See Electric circuits)
 electronic, 624

Circulatory system, 74–75
  nutrients moved by, 67
Cirrus clouds, 410
Clams, 106
Classes (of living things), 96
Classification, 94
  of animals, 104–107
  of consumers, 199
  definition of, 19
  of fossils, 313
  invertebrates, 106–107
  of living things, 94–98
  of minerals, 263
  of rocks, 273
  of shoes, 93
  of stars, 493
  structure and function in,
    108
  vertebrates, 104–105
Clear quartz, 264
Climates, 422–423
  landforms' effect on, 424
  mass extinctions and, 232
  succession and changes in,
    228
Climax communities, 229
Clouds, 410–411
  formation of, 424
  types of weather and, 419
Coal, 592–593
  formation of, 525
  as nonrenewable resource,
    371
  pollution from, 372
Cochlear implants, 665
Coconuts, 135
Cocos plate, 353
Coelophysis fossils, 308
Cold fronts, 421
**Colorado River, 287, 334,
  341**

Colors
  as camouflage, 217
  of minerals, 264, 265
  of stars, 493
Combustibility, 546
Combustion, 546
Comets, 497
Commensalism, 220
Communicating results
  definition of, 21
  how backbone works, 103
  in scientific method, 33
  wheels on objects, 675
Communities, 218
  climax, 229
Comparison
  definition of, 19
  electromagnets, 607
  mass and volume of boxes,
    521
  states of matter, 533
Compasses, 680
Competition, 218, 219
Composite materials, 599
Composite volcanoes, 356
Compound machines, 700
**Compression, by sound
  waves, 646**
Computers, 34
Concave lenses, 662
Condensation, 409
Condensing point, 535
Condition, energy of. *See*
  Potential energy
Conducting an investigation
  definition of, 20
  in scientific method, 31
Conduction, 584, 585
Conductors
  of electricity, 622
  of heat, 586

Cone Nebula, 488
Cones, 132
Conglomerate rock, 276
Coniferous plants, 98
Connective tissues, 64, 65
  blood, 74
  cartilage, 78
  ligaments, 78
**Conservation (in general),
  240–241**
  of energy, 596
  environment and, 596
  of natural resources,
    240–241
  of nonrenewable fuels, 593
  of rocks and minerals, 280
  of soil, 382–383
  three R's of, 380–381
  of water, 384
Conservation, laws of
  energy, 561
  mass, 522
  matter, 548
Constellations
  definition of, 493
  Ursa Major, 493
Consumers, 194
  carnivores, 200
  in energy pyramid,
    204–205
  herbivores, 200
  omnivores, 201
  ordering, 199
  in pond ecosystem, 203
  in prairie ecosystem, 202
Continental air masses, 420
Continental crust, 353
Continental drift, 302–303
Continental rise, 438
Continental shelf, 438
Continental slope, 438

Continents, 303
Contour plowing, 382
Controlling variables
definition of, 21
effects of fertilizer, 237
momentum crash tests, 723
in scientific method, 30
Convection, 584, 585
Convex lenses, 662
Coos Bay, Oregon, 458
Copper
chemical changes with, 547
as conductor, 622
density of, 537
in Statue of Liberty, 547
Copper wire, 620
Coral, 106, 430–431
Coral fossils, 308
Coral reefs, 440, 459
Core (Earth), 352
Cork, 54
Corn, 123
Corona (sun), 493
Corrosion, 546–547
Corundum, 267
Cotyledons, 136
Cover crops, 346
Cowings, Patricia, 703
Crabs, 107
Crash test dummies, 720
Crash tests, 723
Craters
definition of, 482
making, 481
on moon, 482, 483
Crescent moons, 485
Crocodiles, 321
Crop rotation, 383
Crown Jewels of Great
Britain, 260

Crust (Earth), 352, 353
earthquakes in, 354–355
volcanoes in, 356–357
Crustaceans, 107
Crystalline structure, 264
of igneous rocks, 274–275
Cumulonimbus clouds, 411,
421
Cumulus clouds, 410, 411
Current electricity, 620–621
in parallel circuits, 630–631
in series circuits, 629
Currents, ocean, 448–449
blocking, 459
erosion from, 458
Cuttlefish, 107
Cytoplasm, 56–58

D

Davidson, Barry, 502–503
Day, 472–473
Daylight
at poles, 476
seasonal changes in, 474,
475
dB (decibels), 645
Dead Sea, 436
Decibels (dB), 645
Decomposers, 201
Deltas, 343
Density, 537
Deposition, 276, 277
by glaciers, 345
landforms and, 342–343
by Mississippi River, 336
by rivers, 341
in rock cycle, 288–289
Devonian coral fossils, 308
Diamond, 260
carbon in, 525
hardness of, 266, 267

Diatoms, 50, 58
Diesel fuel, pollution from,
372
Digestive cells, 55
Digestive system, 66–68,
84–85
Dinosaurs, 232
fossils of, 298
Diseases, from parasites, 221
Displaying data
definition of, 18
in scientific method, 33
Distance, work and, 696
Diving bells, 460
Diving suits, 460
DNA, 150
in genes, 166
information in, 154
in mitosis, 150
Dogs
hearing of, 650
instincts of, 173
learned behaviors of, 175
service, 175
Dolphins, 175
Dominant traits, 160–161
genes for, 166
Doorbells, 611
Doppler radar, 427
Douglas, Marjorie
Stoneman, 110
Drag, 713, 730
Dragonflies, 108
Drawing conclusions
definition of, 21
dropping balls, 559
growing plants in water,
379
icy water, 435
in scientific method, 32

transfer of heat, 581
water power, 591
Dredging, 458
Drip irrigation, 384
Droppers, 6
Droughts, 384
Dry ice, 535
Duckweed, 121
Dumbwaiters, 699

Eardrum, 575
Earlobes, 161
Earnhardt, Dale, 732
Ears, bionic, 664–665
Earth, 494, 495
  age of, 307
  atmosphere of, 398–399
  day and night on, 472
  eclipses and, 486
  gravity of, 678–679
  history of, 302–303
  layers of, 352
  moon of, 482–483
  moon phases and, 484
  prevailing winds on, 402
  seasons on, 474–475
  structure of, 352–353
  uneven heating of, 397, 400
Earthquakes, 354–355
  tsunamis from, 447
Earthworms, 106
Echinoderms, 107
Echoes, 647, 650
Eclipses, 486
Ecosystems
  damaging, 238–239
  definition of, 200
  extinction in, 232
  food webs in, 202–203

interactions in, 218–219
natural cycles in, 206
pond, 203
prairie, 202, 239
primary succession in, 228–229
producers in, 200
protecting, 240–241
restoring, 242
salt marshes, 224
secondary succession in, 230–231
shared, 212–213
symbiosis in, 220–221
Edwards, Bradley C., 503
Eggs (reproduction), 131, 134, 149, 152
Electric charge, of electrons, 525
Electric circuits
  building, 627
  definition of, 628
  drawing, 632
  parallel, 630–631
  series, 628–629
Electric current, 620
  measurement of, 621
  See also Current electricity
Electricity (electric energy), 574, 608–609
  current, 620–621
  hydroelectric, 592
  magnetism and, 610–611
  safety with, 12
  from solar cells, 571
  static, 618–619
Electric motors, 609, 612
Electromagnetic spectrum, 656–657
Electromagnets, 610–612
  building, 607

Electrons, 525, 608–609
  in current electricity, 620
Electroscopes, 617
Elements, 526–527
Elephants, 315
Elk, 212–213, 688
Elliptical galaxies, 499
El Niño, 449
Embryo (plant), 135, 136
Energy, 560–561
  changing forms of, 576
  chemical, 572, 573
  conservation of, 561, 596
  definition of, 560
  electric, 608–609
  from food, 194, 200–201, 561, 572
  from fossil fuels, 592–593
  hydroelectric, 592, 595
  kinetic, 562–564
  light, 656–657
  mechanical, 572–573
  in moving wind or water, 342
  as nonrenewable resource, 371
  nonrenewable sources of, 592–593
  in ocean waves, 446–447
  for plant embryos, 136
  potential, 562–564
  radiation, 570
  renewable sources of, 594–595
  solar (from sun), 492, 493, 570–571, 594
  in solar flares, 492
  sound, 574–576, 644–645
  thermal, 582, 584–585

transfer of, 200–201, 564, 582, 584–585
from water, 591
Energy, electric, 574
Energy pyramid, 204–205
Energy stations, 592
magnetic production of electricity in, 611
Engines
energy and movement caused by, 561
in hybrid cars, 594
Environment
definition of, 176
in ecosystems, 218
energy conservation and, 596
as influence on behavior, 176
pollution of, 372
Epicenter, 354
Epidermis, of plant leaves, 124, 191
Epithelial tissue, 64, 65
Equator, 474
Equinoxes, 475
Erosion, 287
of beach sand, 458
of landforms, 342
landslides from, 344
on moon, 483
by plants, 346
prevention of, 382–383
by rivers, 341
in rock cycle, 288–289
sinkholes and, 344
Esophagus, 67
Estuaries, 457
Eurasian plate, 353, 358
Evaporation, 408, 409

Evidence, 32, 33
Excretory system, 82
Excursion activities, 46, 256, 514
Experiments, 21
definition of, 20
without scientific method, 34
Extinction, 165, 232
fossil evidence of, 305, 314
Eyepiece (microscopes), 9

F

Factors (inheritance), 159
Fahrenheit, Daniel, 10
Fahrenheit thermometers, 10
Fall, weather patterns during, 422
Families (of living things), 96
Farming
hydroponic, 138–139
soil conservation in, 382–383
soils for, 290
Faults, 354, 355
Fences, 239
Ferns, 98, 131
fossils of, 316–317
reproduction of, 130
Fertilization (reproduction), 131, 132
Fertilizers
observing effects of, 237
reducing use of, 383
water pollution from, 373
Fibrous roots, 122–123
Fireworks, 575
First-quarter moon, 485
Fischbach, Ephraim, 702

Fish, 90, 104, 105
koi, 142–143
in reefs, 459
Flint, 280
Floating, 690
Flooding, deposition by, 343
Flood plains, 343
Florida, hurricanes in, 392–393
Florida Caverns, 277
Flowering plants, 98
origin of, 317
pollination of, 133
seeds from, 134–135
Flowers
parts of, 134
Fluorite
hardness of, 266
unique properties of, 268
Focus (earthquakes), 354
Food
competition for, 219
in digestive system, 66–67
energy from, 194, 200–201, 561, 572
in energy pyramid, 204–205
from photosynthesis, 192–193
produced by plants, 190–194
Food chains, 201
in food webs, 202
levels of, 205
Food webs, 202–203
Forceps, 6, 7
Forces, 676
acceleration and, 726–727
balanced, 686–687

buoyant, 690

with compound machines, 700

friction, 677

gravity, 678–679

in houses of cards, 682

magnetic, 680

motion and, 712–713

net force, 688–689

pairs of, 728–729

picturing, 685

in stopping, 724

unbalanced, 686–689

work and, 696, 697

Forest fires, 230–231

Forests

destroying, 239

old-growth, as nonrenewable resource, 371

secondary succession in, 230–231

Fort DeSoto Park, Florida, 242

Fossil fuels, 592–593

air pollution from, 238

Fossil records, reading, 301

Fossils

classifying, 313

clues of Earth's history from, 303, 306–307

definition of, 303, 592

determining age of, 321

of dinosaurs, 298

formation of, 304–305

index, 306

in La Brea tar pits, 232

modern animals and, 314–315

modern plants and, 316–317

of rodents, 320–321

of states in United States, 308

trace, 305

unique, 318

Frame of reference, 712

Freezing, of ocean water, 432

Freezing point, 535

Frequency (sounds), 646

Friction, 677, 713

stopping by, 724

Frogs

as amphibians, 105

carbon in, 525

legs of, 108

metamorphosis in, 149

Fronds (fern), 131

Fronts, 421

Frost, 535

Fruits

seed dispersal by, 135

seeds in, 132

Fruit trees, 133

Fuel cells, 598–599

Fuels

chemical energy from, 572

for energy stations, 592

fossil, 238, 592–593

pollution from, 372

Fulcrum, 698

Full moon, 485

Function (in classification), 108

Fungi kingdom, 95

classifying, 95

as decomposers, 201

as parasites, 221

G

g (grams), 11

Gabbro, 275

Galaxies, 498

Galilei, Galileo, 10, 394

Gametes, 130, 152

Gametophyte generation, 130

Gametophytes, 131

Gases, 528

in air, 539

air pollution and, 596

changes in state for, 535

in chemical changes, 547

ozone, 398–399

of sun, 493

water as, 534

Gasoline, pollution from, 372

Gathering data, 18

Generators

in hybrid cars, 594

Van de Graaff, 614

Genes, 166

Genus, 96

Germination of seeds, 136

Geysers, 530

Giant squid, 106

Gibbous moons, 485

Gills, 105

Ginkgoes, 317

Gipson, Mack, 292

Giraffes, 104

Glacial grooves, 332

Glaciers, 332

in South America, 360–361

valleys carved by, 345

Glass, as insulator, 622

Glen Canyon Dam, Colorado River, 366
Global winds, 402
Gneiss
formation of, 279
in rock cycle, 289
GOES weather satellites, 427
Gold, 526
Golden Gate Bridge, San Francisco, California, 414
Gourdine, Meredith, 635
Grams (g), 11
Grand Canyon, Arizona, 278, 307, 334
Grand Teton Mountains, Wyoming, 358
Granite
formation of, 274
in rock cycle, 288
uses of, 280
weathering of, 286
Graphite, 525
Grasses
in energy pyramid, 204
roots of, 123
Grasshoppers, 108, 650
Gravitational force, 678–679
Gravity, 678–679, 713
erosion and deposition by, 344
on moon vs. Earth, 482
in space, 730
stopping by, 724
weight and, 522
Great Bear constellation, 493
Great Plains, 331
Great Pyramid of Giza, Egypt, 280
Great Red Spot, 496
Great white sharks, 314

Groundwater
pollution of, 373
in water cycle, 409
Grouping. See Classification
Guide dogs, 175
Gulf Stream, 448
Gymnosperms, 132
Gypsum, 265, 266

Habitats, 239
Hail, 411
Hale-Bopp comet, 497
Halite, 277
Halley, Sir Edmond, 460
Hand lenses, 6, 7, 662
Hardness (minerals), 266–267
Hawai`i, 356, 357
Hawaiian Islands, 356, 357
Headlands, 456–457
Hearing, 575
of animals, 650
with cochlear implants, 665
Hearing dogs, 175
Heart
cardiac muscle of, 79
in circulatory system, 74, 75
tissues in, 65
Heartwood, 123
Heat, 570
conductors of, 586
definition of, 582
from electricity, 609
from friction, 677
insulators for, 586
movement of, 584–585
in rock cycle, 288–289
from sun, 571
temperature and, 582–583

thermograms, 578
transfer of, 581
Hematite, 265
Herbivores, 200
in energy pyramid, 204
in food webs, 202
High tides, 450
Hills, 331
moraines vs., 332
sand dunes, 333
Himalayas, 358
Hooke, Robert, 8, 54
Hoover Dam, 588, 592
Hot-air balloons, 584
Hot spots, 356
Hubble Space Telescope, 488, 498
Human activities
extinctions caused by, 232
physical changes from, 540
pollution from, 176
Human body
cells in, 48–49, 64, 65
circulatory system, 74–75
digestive system, 66–68
excretory system, 82
muscular system, 78–79
nerve cells in brain, 70
nervous system, 80–81
number of cells in, 148
organization of, 68
organs in, 65
respiratory system, 76–77
skeletal system, 78–79
tissues in, 64–65
Humans
inherited traits in, 158, 159
instincts of, 174
learned behaviors of, 174
recessive traits in, 161

Humidity, 410, 418, 419
Hummingbirds, 108
Humus, 290
Hurricanes, 392–393
Hybrid cars, 594–596
Hydras, 58
Hydroelectric energy, 592, 595
Hydrogen, 526
Hydrogen atom, 524
Hydrogen fuel cells, 598–599
Hydrogen peroxide, 547
Hydroponics, 138–139, 376
Hydrothermal vents, 460
Hygrometers, 418
Hypercar, 598, 599
Hypothesis
   definition of, 29
   forming, 29
   not supported, 32
   testing, 21, 30–31
Hypothesizing
   airplane design, 17
   definition of, 20

Ice
   landforms from, 332, 345
   in oceans, 432
Icebergs, 361
Ice sailing, 554–555
Ida (asteroid), 497
Identifying variables
   cleaning water, 369
   effects of fertilizer, 237
   making sound, 643
   measurements, 5
Igneous rocks, 274–275
   in rock cycle, 288
   weathering of, 286

Inclined planes, 699
Index fossils, 306
Indian Ocean
   beaches along, 456
   mid-ocean ridges in, 439
Indian plate, 353, 358
Inertia, 725
Inference
   amounts of water, 407
   changes in motion, 711
   chemical changes, 545
   definition of, 19
   energy change, 569
   forces on springs, 685
   fossil record, 301
   functions of plant parts, 119
   inherited characteristics, 157
   learned and inherited behaviors, 171
   ocean waves, 445
   reaction time, 73
Infrared waves, 585
Inherited behaviors, 171
   instincts as, 172–173
Inherited traits, 157–159
   genes for, 166
   predicting, 160
Inner core (Earth), 352, 353
Inner planets, 494–495
Inquiry, 18–19
   definition of, 18
   tools for (See Science inquiry tools)
Inquiry skills, 18–22
   in investigations, 18–19
   models, time, and space, 22
   in scientific method, 28
   using, 20–21
Insects, 107
   as pollinators, 126

Instincts, 172–173
Insulators
   for electricity, 622
   for heat, 586
Intercropping, 382
International Date Line, 473
International Space Station (ISS), 502
Interpreting data
   definition of, 19
   tables and charts for, 34
Intestines, 66, 67, 85
Intestine transplant, 85
Invertebrates, 106–107
Investigations
   definition of, 18
   scientific method for, 28–33
   without scientific method, 34
Involuntary muscles, 79
Iron, 526
   atomic number of, 527
   in Statue of Liberty, 547
Irrigation, 384
Islands
   barrier, 333
   volcanic, 440
Isotopes, 321
ISS (International Space Station), 502

Jellyfish, 106
Jetties, 459
Joshua Tree National Park, California, 258–259
Joules, 697
Jupiter, 496

K

Kelley's Island, Ohio, 332
Kelp "forest," 90
kg (kilograms), 11
Kidneys, 82
Kīlauea volcano, Hawai`i, 348
Kilograms (kg), 11
Kinetic energy, 562–564
    in chemical and mechanical energy, 572–573
    of static discharge, 620
    thermal, 582
Kingdoms, 95
Kite, 2
Koi, 142–143
Kooyman, Shirley Mah, 244
Krakatoa volcano, Indonesia, 356
Kudzu, 229
Kure Atoll, 356

L

La Brea tar pits, California, 232
Lake Powell, Arizona, 366
Land breezes, 401
Landfills, 234, 241
Landforms
    changed by ice, 332, 345
    changed by plants, 346
    changed by water, 334, 341
    changed by wind, 340
    climate affected by, 424
    definition of, 330
    deposition and, 342–343
    erosion of, 342
    hills, 331
    landslides, 344
    modeling, 329

    mountains, 330–331
    plains, 331
    of sand, 333
    sand dunes, 340
    sinkholes, 344
    water cycle and shapes of, 412
Landslides, 344
Lasers, 652, 659
Lava, 356
Lawns, 384
Laws of conservation
    of energy, 561
    of mass, 522
    of matter, 548
Leaning Tower of Pisa, 670–671
Learned behaviors, 171, 174–175
Leaves, 124
    color changes in, 192
    of embryo plants, 136
    of ferns, 131
    in plant food production, 191
    vascular tissue in, 121
Lee, Yuan Tseh, 551
Leeuwenhoek, Anton van, 8
Legs, artificial, 292–293
Lenses, 8, 662
Lever arm, 698
Levers, 698
Lichens, 200, 229
Life cycles, 149
    of butterflies, 149
    of ferns, 131
    of moss, 130
Lift, 695, 713
Ligaments, 64
Light, 656–657
    absorption of, 660

    angle of reflection, 655
    from chemical changes, 547
    during eclipses, 486
    lasers, 652
    from moon, 484
    from neon, 566
    in ocean depths, 437
    radiation of, 570
    reflection of, 660–661
    refraction of, 486, 661
    from sun, 571
Light bulbs, 659
Lightning, 206, 620
    as static discharge, 619
Light waves, 656, 658–659
Limestone
    acid rain damage to, 372
    formation of, 276
    uses of, 280
    weathering of, 286
Limiting factors, 219
Liquids, 528
    density of, 537
    mixtures of, 538–539
    physical changes in, 540
    solutions of, 538
    water as, 534
Living things. *See* Organisms
Loaiciga, Hugo, 463
Lobsters, 107
Local Group (galaxies), 499
Local winds, 401, 422
Locusts, 204
Lodestone, 268, 680
Long Island, New York, 345
Longshore currents, 448, 458
Low tides, 450
Lunar cycle, 484
Lunar eclipses, 486

Lungs
in respiratory system, 76, 77
tissues in, 65
Luster of minerals, 265

M

Machines, 692
compound, 700
simple, 698–699
work and, 698–699
Maglev trains, 713
Magma, 356, 358
Magnetic field, 680
Magnetic force, 680
Magnetism, electricity and, 610–612
Magnetite, 268, 680
Magnets
compasses and, 680
electromagnets, 607
Magnification, 8
Magnifying boxes, 6, 7
Magnitude (earthquakes), 354, 355
Making models, 22
of craters, 481
of electric circuits, 627
of landforms, 329
of rocks, 285
of volcanic eruptions, 351
Mammals, 104, 105
growth and development of, 149
Mammoths, 304, 305, 315
Mangroves, 116, 123
Mantle (Earth), 352, 353
Marble
formation of, 279
uses of, 280
Mariana Trench, 439

Maritime air masses, 420
Mars, 495, 500
Marshes, 224
Mars Rovers, **500**
Mass, 522–523, 713
conservation of, 522
conservation of matter and, 548
on Earth vs. moon, 679
measurement of, 522
measuring, 11
momentum and, 718
Mass extinctions, 232
Mastodons, 315
Matches, 542
Matter, 522–523
atoms, 524–525
changes caused in, 560–561
chemical changes in, 546–547
conservation of, 548
definition of, 522–523
density of, 537
elements, 526–527
as medium, 649
melting and boiling points of, 536
molecules, 524–525
physical changes in, 534, 538–540
states of, 528 (*See also* States of matter)
Mauna Loa, 357
McClendon, Dorothy, 387
Measurement, 5
definition of, 18
of electric current, 621
of gravitational force, 679
of mass, 11, 522
temperature, 10

tools for, 6–7
of volume, 523
of weather, 417–419
of weight, 11, 522
Measuring cups, 6, 7
Mechanical energy, 572–573
in emergency radios, 576
Medium, 649
Megabite kite, 2
Megalodons, 314
Meiosis, 152
Melting point, 535, 536
Mendel, Gregor, 158–160, 179
Mercury (planet), 494, 495
Mesas, 334
Mesosphere, 398
Metallic luster, 265
Metal ores, 264
Metals, 527
as conductors of heat, 586
melting temperatures for, 10
as nonrenewable resource, 371
Metamorphic rocks, 278–279
in rock cycle, 289
Metamorphosis, 149, 278
Mice, fur color in, 160
Microgravity, 730
Microscopes, 8–9
cell observation with, 54
parts of, 9
research, 9
Microscopic cells, 54
Mid-Atlantic Ridge, 358
Mid-ocean ridges, 439
Migration, 163
Milky Way Galaxy, 498

Minerals
colors of, 264, 265
definition of, 264
hardness of, 266–267
luster of, 265
as nonrenewable resource, 371
properties of, 263–268
in soils, 290
streak, 265
unique properties of, 268
weathering of rocks and, 286
Mississippian coral fossils, 308
Mississippi River, 336
deposition by, 343
pollution of, 209
Mistletoe, 220
Mites, 107
Mitochondria, 56–57
Mitosis, 150–151
Mixtures, 538–539
Mobility-assist dogs, 175
Models, 22, 304. *See also* **Making models**
Mohs, Friedrich, 266
Mohs' hardness scale, 266–267
Molding rocks, 285
Molecules, 524–525
states of matter and, 528
Mollusks, 100, 106, 107
Momentum, 718
Monument Valley, Utah, 334
Moon (of Earth), 482–483
eclipses of, 486
first person on, 478
phases of, 484–485
tides and, 450
Moon phases, 484–485

Moons
definition of, 482
of planets, 496
Moraines, 332, 345
Mosquitoes, 107
Mosses, 98, 229
as nonvascular plants, 120
reproduction of, 130, 131
Motion
acceleration, 716–717
changes in, 711
forces and, 712–713
momentum, 718
Newton's first law of, 724–725
Newton's second law of, 726–727
Newton's third law of, 728–729
in space, 730
speed and velocity, 714–715
with unbalanced forces, 686–687
See also Movement
Motors
electric, 609, 612
in hybrid cars, 594
Mountains, 330–331
formation of, 358
precipitation on, 412
underwater in oceans, 439
Mount Etna, 331
Mount St. Helens, 230, 356
Mouth (human), digestion in, 67
Mouth (rivers), 343
Movement
of electrons, 609
energy of, 561 (*See also* Kinetic energy)

of heat, 584–585
of light, 656
of sound waves, 648–649
with wheels, 675
See also Motion
Mudflows, 344
Muscles
cardiac, 79
involuntary, 79
skeletal, 79
smooth, 79
voluntary, 79
Muscle tissue, 64, 65
Muscular system, 78–79
Mushroom rock, 340
Musical instruments
pitches of, 646
sound from, 644, 645
Mutualism, 220

Naked seeds, 132
NASA (National Aeronautics and Space Administration), 502–503
NASCAR racing, 732–733
National Aeronautics and Space Administration (NASA), 502–503
National Weather Service, 427
National Zoological Park, Front Royal, Virginia, 42–43
Natural bridges, 282
Natural cycles, 206
Natural gas, 592–593
Natural resources, 370–371
conservation of (*See* Conservation)

nonrenewable, 371, 592–593

renewable, 370, 594–595

rocks as, 280

Nazca plate, 353

Neap tides, 450

Nebula, 499

Nectar, 134, 135

Negative charges, 608

Neon, 526

atomic number of, 527

light from, 566

Neptune, 496, 497

Nerve cells, in brain, 70

Nerves, 80, 81

nervous tissue in, 64

Nervous system, 80–81

Nervous tissue, 64, 65

Net force, 688–689

Neutrons, 524, 525

New moon, 484

Newspapers, in landfills, 241

Newton, Isaac, 724, 725

Newton's laws of motion

first, 724–725

second, 726–727

third, 728–729

Night, 472–473

Nitrogen cycle, 206, 399, 539

Nonflowering plants, 98

Nonmetallic luster, 265

Nonmetals, 527

Nonrenewable resources, 371, 592–593

Nonvascular plants, 98, 120

reproduction of, 130

North American plate, 353, 358

Northeast trades, 402

Northern Hemisphere, seasons in, 474–475

Northern lights, 604

North Pole, seasons at, 476

North-seeking pole, 680

North Window, Arches National Park, Utah, 282

Nosepiece (microscopes), 9

Nucleus (atoms), 524, 525

Nucleus (cells), 56–57

chromosomes in, 150

of single-celled organisms, 58

Nutrients

digestive system and, 66–67

in human circulatory system, 74

from humus, 290

in hydroponic farming, 138–139

movement through plant, 122, 123

for nonvascular plants, 120

from photosynthesis, 124

for plants, 124

Observation

cell reproduction, 147

of cells, 53

of changes in pond, 227

definition of, 18

function of an apple, 129

of sand deposition, 339

in scientific method, 28, 32

using telescopes, 491

wave action on beaches, 455

Obsidian, 275

Ocean floor, 438–439

changes to, 440

hydrothermal vents in, 460

Oceanic crust, 353

Oceans

currents on, 448–449

freezing of, 432

mysteries of, 460

shores of, 456–457

tides in, 450

water in, 436–437

Ocean waves, erosion from, 342

Octopods, 100, 106

Octopus, 100, 106

Oil, 592–593

as nonrenewable resource, 371

pollution from, 372

Omnivores, 201, 202

One-celled organisms. *See* **Single-celled organisms**

Opaque materials, 660

Orbital Space Plane, 502–503

Orbits

of Earth, 474, 475

forces on, 730

of moon, 484

of outer planets, 496

of planets, 495

Orchids, 121

Orders (of living things), 96

Oregon Dunes Recreation Area, 333

Organelles, 55, 56

Organisms (living things), 54–55

carbon in, 525

classifying, 94–97

damage to ecosystems by, 239

definition of, 54

environmental influences on, 176

extinction of, 232

first appearance of, 302–303

genes of, 166

growth and development of, 148–149

interactions among, 218

kingdoms of, 95

life cycles of, 149

predator-prey relationships among, 222

primary succession of, 228–229

reproduction of (*See* Reproduction)

secondary succession of, 230–231

single-celled, 58

structure and function of, 108

succession caused by, 228–229

symbiosis, 220–221

Organizing data, 32

Organs, in human body, 65

Organ systems, 68

circulatory, 74–75

digestive, 66–68

excretory, 82

muscular, 78–79

nervous, 80–81

respiratory, 76–77

skeletal, 78–79

Orthoclase, 267

Ospreys, 172, 174

Outer core (Earth), 352, 353

Outer planets, 496–497

Ovaries (flowers), 134

Ovules (plants), 132, 134, 135

Owls, 204

Oxygen

in air, 399, 539

atomic number of, 527

as element, 526

in photosynthesis, 124, 192, 193

in respiratory system, 76, 77

Oxygen atom, 524

Oxygen cycle, 206

Oysters, 106

Ozone, 398–399

Ozone layer, 398

P

Pacific Ocean

El Niños and, 449

International Date Line, 473

Mariana Trench, 439

mid-ocean ridges in, 439

Pacific plate, 353

Paleontologists, 315

Paleontology, 315

Pangea, 302, 303

Parallel circuits, 630–631

Paramecia, 58

Parasitism, 220–221

Paricutín volcano, Mexico, 357

Partial eclipses, 486

Pea plants, 160

Pecten, **314**

People in Science

Ammann, Karl, 111

Arp, Allissa J., 245

Ayrton, Hertha Marks, 634

Bascom, Florence, 293

Benitez-Nelson, Claudia, 550

Cowings, Patricia, 703

Douglas, Marjorie Stoneman, 110

Fischbach, Ephraim, 702

Gipson, Mack, 292

Gourdine, Meredith, 635

Kooyman, Shirley Mah, 244

Lee, Yuan Tseh, 551

Loaiciga, Hugo, 463

McClendon, Dorothy, 387

Mendel, Gregor, 179

Rathje, William, 386

Shi, Wei, 178

Zhu, Wen-Lu, 462

Periodic table, 526–527

Peripheral nervous system, 80

Peristalsis, 67

Peroxide, 547

Pesticides, water pollution from, 373

Petals (flowers), 134

Peterson, Joanne, 664–665

Petrified organisms, 304

Petrified wood, 316–317

Phloem, 121

food carried by, 190

in leaves, 124

Photosynthesis, 124, 192–193

Phyla, 96, 98

of invertebrates, 106, 107

of vertebrates, 104, 105

Physical changes in matter, 534, 538–540

Physical properties of matter, 536

density, 537

melting and boiling points, 536

Pigments in plant leaves, 192

Pine trees, 132

Pioneer plants, 229

Pipe organs, 640

Pitch (sounds), 646

Plains, 331

Planets
definition of, 495
inner, 494–495
outer, 496–497

Planning an investigation
definition of, 20
in scientific method, 30

Plant kingdom, 95

Plants
cells of, 55–57
classifying, 95, 98
in ecosystems, 218
erosion caused/prevented by, 346
extinction of, 232
food produced by, 190–194
fossil and modern, 316–317
growth and development of, 148–149
hydroponic farming of, 138–139, 376, 379
inherited traits in, 159, 160
leaves, 124
natural cycles and, 206
needs of, 176
nitrogen for, 206
as nonrenewable resource, 371
nonvascular, 120
photosynthesis in, 192–193
pioneer, 229

primary succession of, 228–229
as producers, 194
reproduction of, 130–136
roots, 122–123
stems, 123
structures of, 190–191
vascular, 119, 121

Plasma (blood), 65, 74

Plasma balls, 602–603

Plate boundaries, 358

Platelets, 65, 74

Plates, 353
earthquakes and movement of, 354
mountain formation and, 358

Pluto, 496, 497

Polar air masses, 420

Polar easterlies, 402

Poles
magnetic, 680
water cycle and closeness to, 412

Pollen, 132

Pollen tube, 134

Pollination, 133, 134

Pollinators, 126

Pollution, 596
air, 372
from decaying organic matter, 238
definition of, 238, 372
effect on living things, 176
groundwater, 373
laws against, 240
reclamation after, 242
of rivers, 209
water, 209, 238, 373

Pond food web, 203

Pond water, single-celled organisms in, 58

Populations (of organisms), 218
competition among, 219
extinction of, 232

Porcupine, 164

Portifino, Italy, 452

Position, energy of, 712. *See also* **Potential energy**

Positive charges, 608

Potential energy, 562–564
in chemical and mechanical energy, 572–573
in emergency radios, 576
static electricity as, 620

Prairie ecosystems
damage to, 239
fencing of, 239
food webs in, 202

Prairie food web, 202

Praying mantis, 107

Precipitation, 410–411

Predators, 222

Prediction
angle of reflected light, 655
building rockets, 27
carbon dioxide in water, 189
definition of, 19
electroscopes, 617
lifting, 695
uneven heating of Earth, 397
using color to hide, 217

Pregracke, Chad, 208–209

Pressure
air, 399, 418, 419
in oceans, 437
in rock cycle, 288–289

Prevailing westerlies, 402

Prevailing winds, 402, 422
Prey, 222
Primary succession, 228–229
  with secondary succession, 231
Printed circuits, 624
Prisms, 661
Producers, 200
  in energy pyramid, 204–205
  plants as, 194
  in pond ecosystem, 203
  in prairie ecosystem, 202
Prop roots, 116, 123
Protist kingdom, 95
Protists, 58
  classifying, 95
  as parasites, 221
  reproduction of, 149
Protons, 524, 525, 608
  atomic number and, 527
Protostars, 499
Protozoa, 58
Pulleys, 699, 700
Pumice, 275
Pyrite, 265

Q

Quartz
  colors of, 264, 265
  hardness of, 267
  unique properties of, 268
Quartzite, 279
Queen conch, 107
Questions, 34
  in scientific method, 28

R

Rabbits, 165
Race cars, 732–733

Radar, Doppler, 427
Radiation
  of energy, 570
  of heat, 585
Radio telescopes, 466–467
Radio waves, 570, 657
Rain, 410
  acid, 238, 372
  erosion from, 342
  water cycle and, 409
Rain shadow effect, 424
Rathje, William, 386
Rattlesnakes, 163, 164
Reaction forces, 728–729
Reaction time, 73
Reactivity, 547
Recessive traits, 160–161
  genes for, 166
Reclamation, 242
Recording data
  definition of, 18
  in scientific method, 31
Recycled products, 364–365
Recycling, 241, 380–381
Red blood cells, 60, 65, 74
Reducing use of resources, 240, 380–381
Redwood trees, 121
Reefs
  artificial, 459
  coral, 440, 459
Reflection
  of light, 655, 660–661
  of radiation by atmosphere, 585
  of sunlight, 400
Reflexes, 81
Refraction (of light), 486, 661
Regeneration, 150
Reindeer moss, 200

Relative age of rocks, 306
Relief (elevation), 331
Remora, 220
Renewable resources, 370, 594–595
Reproduction, 130–136, 147
  asexual, 151
  genes, 166
  meiosis, 152
  mitosis, 150–151
  seed-bearing plants, 132–136
  sexual, 152
  simple plants, 130–131
  survival and, 164–165
Reptiles, 104, 105
Research microscopes, 9
Resources, 593. *See also* Natural resources
Respiratory system, 76–77
Restoring ecosystems, 242
Reusable resources, 370
Reusing resources, 240–241, 380–381
Revolution (of Earth), 474
Rhyolite, 274
Richter scale, 355
Ridges, underwater, 439
Right-handedness, 161
Right Mitten, 326
Rignot, Erik, 360
Rip currents, 448
Rivers
  cleaning, 209
  deposition by, 341
  erosion by, 341
  sand deposited by, 339
  sand landforms from, 333
Roaches, 107
Rock cycle, 288–289
Rockets, building, 27

Rocks
definition of, 274
identifying, 273
igneous, 274–275
layers of, 306–307
metamorphic, 278–279
molding, 285
processes that change, 286–297
relative age of, 306
sedimentary, 276–277
on shores, 456–457
in soils, 290
uses of, 280
weathering of, 286–287, 340
Rocky Mountains, 330
Rodents
fossils of, 320–321
modern, 321
Roots, 122–123
erosion prevented by, 346
fibrous, 122–123
in plant food production, 190
prop, 116, 123
vascular tissue in, 121
Rose quartz, 264
Rotation
of Earth, 472, 484
of moon, 484
Roundworms, 106, 221
Rubber, as insulator, 622
Rulers, 6, 7
Runners, 123
Runoff, river pollution from, 209

S

Saber-toothed cat fossils, 308

Saber-toothed cats, 232
Safety
of race cars, 732–733
in science, 38
in science lab, 12
Safety belts, 725
Safety goggles, 12
Salamanders, 55
Salinity, 436, 437
Saliva, 67
Salt marshes, 224
Salt water, 436
freezing of, 432
in oceans, 436–437
San Andreas Fault, 355
Sánchez-Villagra, Marcelo R., 320
Sand
deposited by rivers, 339
erosion of, 458
landforms of, 333
weathering of rock by, 340
Sand dollars, 107
Sand dunes, 333, 340
Sand spits, 333
Sandstone
formation of, 276
in rock cycle, 288, 289
uses of, 280
Satellites
for space travel, 503
weather, 427
Saturn, 496, 497, 500
Saturn V launch vehicle, 478
Saurophaganax fossils, 308
Scallops, 314
Schist, 279
Science inquiry tools, 6–12
balances, 11
droppers, 6

forceps, 6, 7
hand lenses, 6, 7
magnifying boxes, 6, 7
measuring cups, 6, 7
for measuring temperature, 10
microscopes, 8–9
rulers, 6, 7
safety in working with, 12
spring scales, 6, 7, 11
tape measures, 6
thermometers, 6
Science Up Close
carbon, 525
comparing plant and animal cells, 56–57
features of ocean floor, 438–439
form and function, 108
groundwater pollution, 373
how electric motor works, 612
how sound reaches you, 648–649
hybrid car, 594–595
impact between baseball and bat, 727
inside a flower, 134
magnets and compasses, 680
mitosis, 150–151
petrified wood, 316–317
phases of the moon, 485
photosynthesis, 192–193
rock cycle, 288–289
secondary succession, 230–231
types of volcanoes, 356–357
water cycle, 408–409

Scientific method, 28–34
  conducting an investigation in, 31
  drawing conclusions in, 32
  forming hypothesis in, 29
  observing/asking questions in, 28
  planning an investigation in, 30
  steps in, 28
  writing a report in, 33
Scorpions, 107
Scuba diving, 516–517, 539
Sea arches, 457
Sea breezes, 401, 412
Sea lampreys, 221
Sea scorpions, 310
Seasons, 474–475
  cause of, 422
  at North and South Poles, 476
  weather patterns during, 422–423
Sea stars, 107
Sea urchins, 107
Secondary succession, 230–231
Secretory cells, 48–49
Sediment, 276, 277
  in continental rise, 438
  deposition of, 342–343
Sedimentary rocks, 276–277
  fossils in, 303
  layers of, 306
  in rock cycle, 289
Seed coat, 132, 135, 136
Seeds
  in angiosperms, 133
  germination of, 136
  in gymnosperms, 132
  origin of plants with, 317

in plant reproduction, 132–136
  spores vs., 129
Sensory receptors, 81
Sepals, 134
Series circuits, 628–629
Service animals, 175
Sewage, water pollution from, 373
Sexual reproduction, 152
Shale, 276
Sharks, 220
  fossils of, 314, 315
  whale, 184–185
Shi, Wei, 178
Shield volcanoes, 357
Ships, 690
Shoes, classifying, 93
Shores, 456–457
  effect of human activities on, 458–459
Shrimp, 107
Simple machines, 698–699
  in compound machines, 700
Singh, Stephanie, 84–85
Single-celled organisms, 58
  classifying, 95
  as decomposers, 201
  division of, 144
  as parasites, 221
Sinkholes, 344
Skeletal muscles, 79
Skeletal system, 78–79
Skeleton, muscle tissue and movement of, 64
Skin
  epithelial tissue in, 64
  as organ, 65
Slate, 279
Sleet, 411

Small intestine, 66, 67
Smog, 372
Smoky quartz, 264
Smooth muscle, 79
Snail fossils, 308
Snails, 106
Snakes, 104, 650
  in energy pyramid, 204
Snowstorms, 404, 411
Sodium chloride, 436
Soils, 290
  conservation of, 382–383
  formation of, 290
  as nonrenewable resource, 371
Solar cells, 570, 571
Solar eclipses, 486
Solar energy, 570–571, 594
Solar flares, 492, 493
Solar panels, 571
Solar system
  definition of, 492
  inner planets, 494–495
  outer planets, 496–497
  sun, 492–493
Solids, 528
  changes in state for, 535
  density of, 537
  mixtures of, 538
  physical changes in, 540
  water as, 534
Solstices, 475
Solutions, 538, 539
Sori, 131
Sound, 574–576, 644–645
  animals and, 650
  from electricity, 609
  making, 643
  speed of, 503
  transmission of, 648–649

Sound waves, 646–647
transmission of, 648–649
South America, 302
glaciers in, 360–361
South American plate, 353
Southeast trades, 402
Southern Hemisphere,
seasons in, 474
South Pole, seasons at, 476
South-seeking pole, 680
Space
motion in, 730
moving through, 471
Space exploration, 500
Space relationships, 22
moon and Earth
movements, 471
SpaceShipOne, **24**
Space shuttles, 503, 730
Spacesuits, 483
Space taxi, 502–503
Species, 96
extinction of, 232
inherited behaviors of, 173
Speed, 714–715
of falling objects, 678
Speed skating, 677
Sperm, 130, 132
Spiders, 107
Spiderwebs, 168
Spinal cord
in central nervous system,
80
nervous tissue in, 64
Spindles, 151
Spiral galaxies, 498, 499
Sponges, 106
Spores, 98
in plant reproduction, 130,
131

seeds vs., 129
Sporophyte generation, 130
Sporophytes, 131
Spring, weather patterns
during, 422
Spring equinox, 475
Spring melt, 412
Spring scales, 6, 7, 11
Spring tides, 450
Sputnik 1, **500**
Squid, 106
Squirrels, 173
Sri Lanka, 447
Stage (microscopes), 9
Stalactites, 277
Stalagmites, 277
Stars, 107, 498–499
classifying, 493
constellations, 493
definition of, 492
in galaxies, 498
in nebula, 499
sun as, 493
State fossils, 308
States of matter, 528
changing, 533–535
thermal energy and
changes in, 583
Static discharge, 619, 620
Static electricity, 618–619
Statue of Liberty, 547
Stems, 123
in plant food production,
190–191
vascular tissue in, 121
Stentors, 58
Stereo systems, 611
Stigma, 134, 135
Stomach, 67, 68
Stomata, 124, 191

Storms
on Jupiter, 496
ocean waves during, 447
Storm surges, 447
Stratosphere, 398–399
Stratus clouds, 410, 421
Strawberry plants, 123
Streak (minerals), 265
Strip cropping, 382
Strip mines, 238, 242
Strontium, 547
Structure
in classification, 108
crystalline, 264
Sublimes, 535
Submarines, 460
Submersibles, 437
Succession
definition of, 228
primary, 228–229
secondary, 230–231
Summer, weather patterns
during, 422
Summer solstice, 475
Sun, 492–493
day/night and, 472
eclipses, 486
energy from, 400, 492,
570–571
light from, 658
observing, 492
radiation from, 585
tides and, 450
water cycle and, 408–409
Sunlight, 571, 658
food energy from, 194
in photosynthesis, 124, 192
reflected, 400
Sunrise, 468, 472
Sunsets, 468, 472

Sunspots, 493
Surface currents, 448
Surtsey, 440
Switches, electric, 628
Symbiosis, 220–221
Synapses, 80
Systems
    in human body (*See* Organ
        systems)
    movement of heat through,
        584–585
    transfer of thermal energy
        in, 583

T

Tables, 34
Taj Mahal, India, 280
Talc, 265, 266
Tanzanite, 260
Tape measures, 6
Tapeworms, 221
Taproots, 122
Technology
    alternative fuel cars, 598–
        599
    bionic ears, 664–665
    glacier melting, 360–361
    hydroponic farming, 138–
        139
    intestine transplants, 84–85
    prehistoric rodents, 320–
        321
    safer race cars, 732–733
    space travel, 502–503
    trash, 208–209
    weather forecasting, 426–
        427
Telescopes
    Hubble Space Telescope,
        488
    making, 491

    radio, 467
    in space exploration, 500
Temperature
    air pressure and, 399
    changes in, 569
    definition of, 582
    heat and, 582–583
    highest and lowest on
        Earth, 476
    on inner planets, 495
    melting and boiling points,
        536
    on moon, 482, 483
    of ocean water, 437
    seasonal changes in, 474,
        475
    tools for measuring, 10
    water cycle and, 412
Tendons, 64, 78, 79
Terracing, 383
Tesla coil, 618
Thermal energy, 582
    transfer of, 584–585
Thermograms, 578
Thermometers, 6, 583
    Galileo's, 394
    measuring air temperature
        with, 418
Thermosphere, 398
Third-quarter moon, 485
Thrust, 713
Ticks, 107
Tide pools, 88–89, 457
Tides, 450
    tide pools and, 457
Tigers, 219
Time
    day and night, 472–473
    on Earth, 472
Time relationships, 22
    time zones, 473

Time zones, 473, 527
Tissues
    in human body, 64–65
    regeneration of, 150
    in stomach, 68
    vascular, 121
Tongues
    of chameleons, 214
    rolling, 161
Tools. *See* Science inquiry
    tools
Topaz, 265, 267
Topography, 330
Topsoil, 290
Trace fossils, 305
Trachea, 77
Traits
    dominant, 160–161, 166
    genes for, 166
    inherited, 157–159
    recessive, 160–161, 166
Translucent materials, 661
Transparent materials, 661
Transpiration, 191
Transplant operations, 85
Transport tubes, 98
Transverse waves, 658
Trash, 234, 239
Trebuchets, 692
Trees
    stems of, 123
    as vascular plants, 121
Trenches, ocean, 439
Trilobite fossils, 308
Tropical air masses, 420
Troposphere, 398
Tsunamis, 447
Tully monster fossils, 308
Tundra, consumers in, 200

Turbines
at Hoover Dam, 588
for wind farms, 595
Turtles, 219

Ultraviolet rays, 570
Unbalanced forces, 686–689
Underwater ridges, 358
Universe, 498
Uranus, 496, 497
Urea, 82
Ureters, 82
Urine, 82
Ursa Major, 493
Urumaco fossil fields,
Venezuela, 320–321
Using numbers, 18

Vacuoles, 56–57
Valleys carved by glaciers,
345
Van de Graaff generator,
614
Variables, 21
definition of, 21
in investigations, 30
Vascular plants, 121
parts of, 119
reproduction of, 130–136
Vascular tissue, 98, 121
Vehicles, pollution from, 372
Veins
in circulatory system, 74, 75
in plant leaves, 191
pulmonary, 77
Velocity, 714–715
acceleration and, 716
momentum and, 718

Velodrome, 706–707
Venom, 163
Venus' flytrap, 191
Vermilion Cliffs, Arizona,
270
Vertebrates, 104–105
Vibrations (sound), 644, 645
definition of, 644
as energy, 574–575
in hearing, 575
Viking **space probes, 500**
Villi, 66, 67, 85
Viruses, 221
Visceral myopathy, 84–85
Vishnu Schist, 278
Visible light, 657
Volcanic eruptions
modeling, 351
succession after, 230–231
tsunamis from, 447
Volcanic glass, 275
Volcanoes, 331, 356–357
cinder cone, 357
composite, 356
definition of, 356
on Mars, 495
metamorphic rocks near,
279
in ridges, 358
shield, 357
underwater, 440
Volts, 621
Volume, 523
measurement of, 523
of sound, 645
Voluntary muscles, 79
Vostok Station, Antarctica,
476
Voyager **space probes, 500**

Waning crescent moon, 485
Waning gibbous moon, 485
Warm fronts, 421
Water
acidic, 238
buoyant force in, 690
changing states of, 534–
535
cleaning, 369
climate of area and, 424
conservation of, 384
energy from, 342, 591, 592,
595
erosion from, 342–343
in geysers, 530
growing plants in, 138–139,
376, 379
hydroponic farming, 138–
139
landforms changed by, 333,
334, 341
landslides and, 344
measuring, 407
melting and boiling points
of, 535, 536
on moon, 482
movement through plants,
122, 123
for nonvascular plants, 120
in oceans, 436–437
physical changes in, 540
in plant leaves, 124
reusable resources, 370
sinkholes and, 344
in transpiration, 191
weathering
Water cy
412

Water fountains, 518

Water molecule, 524

Water pollution, 209, 238, 373

Water pressure, 437, 460

Water vapor, 534, 535

   precipitation formed from, 411

   water cycle and, 408–409

Watts, 621

Waves

   light, 656, 658–659

   ocean, 442, 445–447, 455

   radio, 657

   sound, 646–647

   transverse, 658

Waxing crescent moon, 485

Waxing gibbous moon, 485

Weather

   air masses, 420–421

   clouds and precipitation, 410–411

   forecasting, 419

   fronts, 421

   measuring, 417–419

   patterns of, 422–423

   at poles, 476

   seasonal changes in, 474, 475

   solar energy as source of, 571

   warm ocean currents and, 449

   water cycle and, 408–409

Weather forecasters, 426–427

Weathering

   by ice, 345

   by plants, 346

   rock cycle, 288–289

   rocks, 286–287

   soils formed from, 290

   by wind, 340

Weather maps, 421

Weather satellites, 427

Weather stations, 418

Wedges, 699, 700

Weight

   buoyant force and, 690

   on Earth vs. moon, 679

   on inner planets, 494

   measurement of, 11, 522

   on moon vs. Earth, 482

   in space, 730

Wetlands

   destroying, 239

   reclaiming/restoring, 242

Whale sharks, 184–185

Wheel-and-axle, 698, 700

White blood cells, 65, 74

Wind(s)

   energy in, 342

   landforms changed by, 340

   local, 401

   on Neptune, 496

   ocean currents and, 449

   patterns of, 422

   prevailing, 402

   weathering by, 287

Windbreaks, 382

Wind farms, 595

Windmills, 595

Windpipe, 77

Windsocks, 419

Wind vanes, 419

Wings, 108

Winter, weather patterns during, 422, 423

Winter Park, Florida, 344

Winter solstice, 475

Wiwaxia fossils, 318

Wood

   density of, 537

   as insulator, 622

   petrified, 304, 316–317

Work, 696–697

   definition of, 696

   with machines, 698–699

Worms, 106

   near ocean vents, 460

Wright, Orville and Wilbur, 14

Wrigley Field, Chicago, Illinois, 638–639

Writing reports, 33. *See also* Communicating results

X — Y — Z

Xeriscapes, 384

X rays, 570, 657

Xylem, 121

   in heartwood, 123

   in leaves, 124

   movement of water and nutrients through, 122, 190

Years

   on inner planets, 494–495

   on outer planets, 496–497

Yeast, 151

Yellowstone National Park, 239

Zhu, Wen-Lu, 462

Zygotes, 131, 152

Photo Credits

Page Placement Key: (t) top, (b) bottom, (l) left, (c) center, (bg) background, (fg) foreground; (i) inset.

Cover: (frontcover) Frans Lanting; (spine) Frans Lanting.

Title Page: (c) Frans Lanting. Copyright Page: (cl) Frans Lanting.

Introduction
2 Roy Morsch/Corbis; 3 (tr) Tetra Images/Alamy; 4 Getty Images for Ameriquest; 8 (tr) SSPL/The Image Works; 9 (br) Andrew Douglas/Masterfile; 12 (tl) Jeff Sherman/Getty Images; 12 (b) Purestock/Alamy; 18 (b) Patrick Ward/Corbis; 22 (b) David Young-Wolff/Photo Edit; 22 (cr) NASA; 24 Robert Galbraith/Reuters/Corbis; 25 (br) Peter West/National Science Foundation; 34 (cr) Tom Grill/Corbis; 38 Purestock/Alamy.

Unit A
39 Naturfoto Honal/Corbis; 46 (tl) C Squared Studios/Photodisc/Getty Images; 46 (bcr) George Diebold/Corbis; 46 (cl) Lester Lefkowitz/Getty Images; 46 (tcl) Photodisc/Getty Images; 46 (bl) Photodisc/Getty Images; 46 (br) Photodisc/Getty Images; 48 (bg) VVG/Photo Researchers, Inc.; 50 (c) Alfred Pasieka/Photo Researchers, Inc.; 51 (tr) Biophoto Associates/Photo Researchers; 52 (bl) Foodcollection/Getty Images; 54 (bc) Omikron/Photo Researchers, Inc.; 54 (l) SSPL/Getty Images; 55 (bl) Clouds Hill Imaging Ltd./Corbis; 55 (cl) Clouds Hill Imaging Ltd./Corbis; 55 (tl) David Tomlinson/Lonely Planet Images/Getty Images; 55 (cr) Dwight Kuhn; 55 (tr) Dwight Kuhn; 55 (tr) M. I. Walker/Photo Researchers, Inc.; 58 (tr) Science VU/Visuals Unlimited.; 58 (tr) Tierbild Okapia/ Photo Researchers, Inc.; 60 (c) P. Motta & S. Correr/Photo Researchers, Inc.; 61 (cr) SIU/Visuals Unlimited; 64 (cr) Adrian Peacock/Imagestate/Photolibrary; 64 (br) ImageState-Pictor/Photolibrary; 68 (br) Dean Berry/Photolibrary; 70 (c) Dr. Torsten Wittmann/Photo Researchers; 72 (bl) Roy McMahon/Corbis; 74 Dr. Richard Kessel & Dr. Gene Shih/Visuals Unlimited/Corbis; 75 Dr. Fred Hossler/Visuals Unlimited/Corbis; 80 (l) Francois Paquet-Durand/Photo Researchers, Inc.; 87 (cr) Phototake Inc./Alamy; 88 (bg) Brandon D. Cole/Corbis; 90 Chuck Davis/Stone/Getty Images; 91 (br) Kennan Ward/Corbis; 92 (bl) Dale C. Spartas/Corbis; 94 (c) Ralph Hopkins/Getty Images; 94 (br) Timothy Laman/National Geographic/Getty Images; 95 (b) TonyP_Images/Alamy; 95 (tr) BSIP/Photo Researchers, Inc.; 95 (tl) Digital Vision/Getty Images; 95 (tl) Jeremy Woodhouse/Getty Images; 95 (cr) M.Markiw/BCI USA/Photoshot; 98 (inset) Isabelle Rozenbaum/Photoalto/Photolibrary; 98 (tr) James Randklev/Corbis; 98 (l) Robert Glusic/Getty Images; 100 Paul Whitehead/Alamy; 101 (br) CMCD/Photodisc/Getty Images; 101 (tr) PhotoDisc/Getty Images; 102 (bl) Macduff Everton/Corbis; 104 (r) Andreas Feininger/Getty Images; 104 (bl) Werner Bollmann/Photolibrary/Getty Images; 105 (tl) imagebroker/Alamy; 105 (tr) WaterFrame/Alamy; 105 (cl) David B Fleetham/Photolibrary/Getty Images; 105 (cr) Jeremy Woodhouse/Getty Images; 105 (bl) Morales Morales/Photolibrary; 106 (br) Karen Moskowitz/Getty Images; 106 (bl) Tsuneo Nakamura/Photolibrary; 107 (br) blickwinkel/Alamy; 107 (tr) Bruce Coleman/BCI USA/Photoshot; 107 (cr) Gary Bell/Photolibrary; 108 (tl) altrendo nature/Getty Images; 108 (cl) Tom Walker/Photographer's Choice/Getty Images; 110 (bg) Jeff Greenberg/PhotoEdit, Inc.; 110 (inset) Morton Beebe/Corbis; 111 (bg) Digital Vision/Getty Images; 112 (c) John Foxx/Stockbyte/Getty Images; 112 (r) Davies & Starr/Getty Images; 114 (bg) Freeman Patterson/Masterfile; 116 (c) Danita Delimont/Alamy; 118 (bl) Philippe Psaila/Photo Researchers, Inc.; 120 (br) philipus/Alamy; 120 (b) Ron Fehling/Masterfile; 121 (r) Sherman Hines/Masterfile; 122 (t) Chuck Brown/Photo Researchers, Inc.; 122 (tr) Nigel Cattlin/Photo Researchers, Inc.; 122 (tl) Keate/Masterfile; 123 (br) Biophoto Associates/Photo Researchers, Inc.; 123 (r) J.A. Kraulis/Masterfile; 124 (l) Adam Hart-Davis/Science Photo Library/Photo Researchers, Inc.; 124 (bc) M. I. Walker/Photo Researchers, Inc.; 126 (c) Clive Nichols/GAP Photos/Getty Images; 127 (br) Arco Images GmbH/Alamy; 128 (bl) AgStock Images/Corbis; 130 (b) Tony Wharton/Corbis; 131 (bc) Biophoto Associates/Photo Researchers, Inc.; 131 (br) David M Dennis/Photolibrary; 132 (bl) Michael P. Gadomski/Photo Researchers, Inc.; 132 (br) James Richardson/Visuals Unlimited; 133 (t) Lloyd Sutton/Masterfile; 135 (br) Royalty-Free/Corbis; 135 (bl) Tim Fitzharris/Masterfile; 136 (bl) Dwight Kuhn; 136 (bc) Dwight Kuhn; 136 (bc) Dwight Kuhn; 136 (br) Dwight Kuhn; 138 (b) AP Photo/Bill Kaczor; 139 (r) AP Photo/The Emporia Gazette, David Doemland; 139 (l) AP Photo/The Emporia Gazette, David Doemland; 140 (br) Biophoto Associates/Photo Researchers, Inc.; 141 (tr) Stan Osolinski/Photolibrary/Getty Images; 142 Akira Kaede/White/Photolibrary; 144 (c) Prof.G.Schatten/Photo Researchers, Inc.; 145 (tr) John M. Burnley/Photo Researchers; 146 (bl) Michael Newman/PhotoEdit, Inc.; 148 (r) Photo Researchers, Inc.; 149 (tr) JohnAnderson/Alamy; 149 (cr) Naturfoto Honal/Corbis; 149 (cl) Ralph A. Clevenger/Corbis; 149 (tl) Robert Pickett/Corbis; 150 (br) Dr. Alexey Khodjakov/Photo Researchers, Inc.; 152 Biodisc/Visuals Unlimited/Corbis; 152 (c) Carolina Biological Supply Company/Phototake; 154 (c) Don W. Fawcett/Photo Researchers, Inc.; 156 (b) David Young-Wolff/PhotoEdit, Inc; 158 John Daniels/Ardea.com; 159 (t) Alan and Linda Detrick/Photo Researchers, Inc., Inc.; 159 (br) Alan Powdrill/Taxi/Getty Images; 161 (bl) Yann Arthus-Bertrand/Corbis; 162 (inset) Steven J. Kazlowski/Alamy; 162 (b) Tom Murphy/Getty Images; 163 (bl) Kenneth W. Fink/Ardea.com; 163 (r) Mark Boulton/Photo Researchers, Inc., Inc.; 164 (cr) Nigel J. Dennis; Gallo Images/Corbis; 164 (b) Rolf Nussbaumer/Alamy; 164 (l) Joel Sartore/Getty Images; 165 (t) AP Photo; 166 (tl) Andrew Syred/Photo Researchers, Inc.; 166 (bc) Veronique Burger/Photo Researchers, Inc.; 168 (c) Peter Skinner/Photo Researchers, Inc.; 169 (br) Jeremy Woodhouse/Corbis; 169 (cr) PhotoLink/Photodisc/Getty Images; 169 (tr) William Leaman/Alamy; 170 (bl) Gregory G. Dimijian, M.D./Photo Researchers, Inc.; 172 (b) Nik Wheeler/Corbis; 173 (t) George D. Lepp/Corbis; 174 Tom Brakefield/Corbis; 175 (t) Jacques Pavlovsky/Sygma/Corbis; 176 (bg) D. Greco/The Image Works; 176 (cl) Dwight Kuhn; 178 (bg) OJ Staats/Custom Medical Stock Photo; 178 (t) Courtesy of Dr. Wei Shi; 179 (bg) Alan and Linda Detrick/Photo Researchers, Inc., Inc.; 181 Tom Brakefield/Corbis; 182 (cl) David B Fleetham/Photolibrary/Getty Images; 182 (cr) Lloyd Sutton/Masterfile; 182 (b) Nik Wheeler/Corbis.

Unit B:
Getty Images; 188 (bl) Adam Jones/Photo Researchers, Inc.; 190 (bc) Andreas Kuehn/Getty Images; 191 (tr) Andrew Syred/Science Photo Library/Photo Researchers, Inc.; 194 Mike Grandmaison/Corbis; 196 Mark Newman/Photo Researchers, Inc.; 198 Andrew Howe/iStock Exclusive/Getty Images; 200 (br) Paul A. Souders/Corbis; 200 (bl) Raymond Gehman/Corbis; 200 (bg) Charles Mauzy/Corbis; 201 (br) Eye of Science/Photo Researchers, Inc.; 201 (bl) Peter Lilja/Getty Images; 204 (tc) Dwight Kuhn/Dwight Kuhn Photography; 204 (bc) Natalie Behring-Chisolm/Getty Images; 204 (b) W.Cody/Corbis; 204 (t) W.Perry Conway/Corbis; 206 (br) Dr. Jeremy Burgess/Photo Researchers, Inc.; 208 Greg Ball/Quad City Times; 209 Greg Ball/Quad City Times; 211 (tc) Dwight Kuhn/Dwight Kuhn Photography; 211 (bc) Natalie Behring-Chisolm/Getty Images; 211 (b) W.Cody/Corbis; 211 (t) W.Perry Conway/Corbis; 212 (bg) Paul A. Souders/Corbis; 214 Frans Lanting/Corbis; 215 (tr) Gregory G. Dimijian/Photo Researchers, Inc.; 216 (b) Jeff Lepore/Photo Researchers, Inc.; 218 (b) Corinne Humphrey/Visuals Unlimited; 218 (inset) Franco Banfi/Getty Images; 219 (bl) Bruce Coleman, Inc./Photoshot; 219 (t) IKAN/Photolibrary; 219 (cr) Rights Free Reuters/China Photo; 220 (c) Darlyne A. Murawski/National Geographic Images; 220 (tl) James Watt/Visuals Unlimited; 221 (tr) Chris Johns/Getty Images; 222 (b) Chris Johns/National Geographic Images; 224 Eastcott-Momatiuk/The Image Works; 225 (tr) USGS/CVO; 226 PHOTO 24/Getty Images; 230 (inset) M.Philip Kahl/Kahlm/Bruce Coleman, Inc./Photoshot; 231 (tr) M.Timothy O'Keefe/Bruce Coleman, Inc./Photoshot; 231 (tr) Raymond Gehman/National Geographic Images; 232 (b) Kenneth W. Fink/Bruce Coleman, inc./Photoshot; 234 (c) David Overcash/Bruce Coleman, Inc./Photoshot; 235 (br) Colin Young-Wolff/Photo Edit; 235 (tr) D. Falconer/PhotoLink/Photodisc/Getty Images; 235 (cr) William H. Mullins/Photo Researchers, Inc.; 236 (bl) Tony Freeman/PhotoEdit, Inc.; 238 (bl) Adam Jones/Visuals Unlimited; 238 (b) Jenny Hager/The Image Works; 239 (t) Mark Newman/Bruce Coleman, Inc./Photoshot; 239 (tr) Martin Harvey; Gallo Images/Corbis; 240 (t) Myrleen Ferguson Cate/Photo Edit, Inc.; 241 (tr) IPS Agency/Photolibrary; 241 (br) Jose Luis Pelaez, Inc./Corbis; 241 (cr) Nancy Richmond/The Image Works; 242 Earl Neikirk/AP Photo; 244 (bg) Abode/Beateworks/Corbis; 245 (bg) wolfgang Herath/Photolibrary; 247 (cr) Pat O'Hara/Corbis; 247 (cl) Peter Johnson/Corbis; 248 (b) AP Photo/Earl Neikirk.

Unit C:
249 Paul A. Souders/Corbis; 256 (tl) C Squared Studios/Photodisc/Getty Images; 256 (bcr) George Diebold/Corbis; 256 (cl) Lester Lefkowitz/Getty Images; 256 (tcl) Photodisc/Getty Images; 256 (bl) Photodisc/Getty Images; 256 (br) Photodisc/Getty Images; 258 (bl) Arnold Fisher/Photo Researchers, Inc.; 258 Dennis Flaherty/The Image Bank; 260 (c) Bob Burch/Photolibrary; 261 (cr) Jose Manuel Sanchis Calvete/Corbis; 262 (bl) Shaffer Smith/Photolibrary; 264 (Smoky Quartz) GC Minerals/Alamy; 264 (clear quarz) Siede Preis/Getty Images; 264 (Amethyst quartz) Siede Preis/Getty Images; 265 (Pyrite) Editorial Image, LLC/Alamy; 265 (Gypsum) Bureau of Mines/U.S. Geological Survey; 265 (tl) Paul Silverman/Fundamental Photographs; 265 (cr) Roberto de Gugliemo/Photo Researchers, Inc.; 266 (Fluorite) Editorial Image, LLC/Alamy; 266 (gypsum) Bureau of Mines/U.S. Geological Survey; 266 (Calcite) Charles D. Winters/Photo Researchers, Inc.; 266 (Apatite) Joel Arem/Photo Researchers, Inc.; 266 (talc) Mark A. Schneider/Photo Researchers, Inc; 267 (corundum) ephotocorp/Alamy; 267 (quartz) GC Minerals/Alamy; 267 (bc) Aaron Haupt/Photo Researchers, Inc.; 267 (bl) Bill Aron/Photo Edit; 267 (tl) Biophoto Associates/Photo Researchers, Inc.; 267 (tr) Biophoto Associates/Photo Researchers, Inc.; 267 (cr) David Young-Wolff/PhotoEdit; 267 (br) Richard Megna/Fundamental Photographs; 267 (tc) Roberto de Gugliemo/Photo Researchers, Inc.; 268 (cr) Colin Keates/Dorling Kindersley/Getty Images; 268 (b) DEA/A. RIZZI/De Agostini Picture Library/Getty Images; 268 (cl) Mark A. Schneider/Photo Researchers, Inc.; 270 (c) Joseph Sohm;ChromoSohm Inc./Corbis; 271 (br) Jon Sparks/Alamy; 271 (cr) Visuals Unlimited; 272 (bl) Alan Oddie/PhotoEdit, Inc.; 274 (c) Dr. Albert Copley/Visuals Unlimited/Alamy; 274 (b) Michael S. Yamashita/Corbis; 274 (bl) Joyce Photographics/Photo Researchers, Inc.; 275 (pumice) Tony Lilley/Alamy; 275 (cl) Doug Martin/Photo Researchers, Inc.; 275 (obsidian) Doug Martin/Photo Researchers, Inc.; 275 (gabbro) Joel Arem/Photo Researchers, Inc.; 276 (tr) The Natural History Museum/Alamy; 276 (br) Charles D. Winters/Photo Researchers, Inc.; 276 (bl) Joel Arem/Photo Researchers, Inc.; 276 (cl) John R. Foster/Photo Researchers, Inc.; 277 (tl) M. H. Sharp/Photo Researchers, Inc.; 277 (tr) M H Sharp/Millard H. Sharp Wildlife and Nature Photography; 277 (l) Millard H. Sharp/Photo Researchers, Inc.; 278 (inset) Bruce Coleman/Photoshot; 278 (b) Jani Radebaugh/Univeristy of Arizona; 279 (cl) Andrew J. Martinez/Photo Researchers, Inc.; 279 (tr) Andrew J. Martinez/Photo Researchers, Inc.; 279 (br) Andy Christiansen/HRW; 279 (cr) Joyce Photo/Photo Researchers, Inc., Inc.; 279 (tl) Joyce Photographics/Photo Researchers, Inc.; 280 (bg) Getty Images; 280 (bl) Bob Croxford/Alamy Images; 280 (tc) PhotoLink/Photodisc/Getty Images; 280 (inset) Photolocate/Alamy Images; 280 (cr) PhotosIndia.com LLC/Alamy; 280 (cl) Rodney Hyett; Elizabeth Whiting & Associates/Corbis; 282 Robert Cable/Getty Images; 283 (tr) David Hoffman Photo Library/Alamy; 283 (cr) Greg Probst; 284 (bl) Lon C. Diehl/Photoedit, Inc.; 286 (bc) Stephen Coll/Alamy Images; 286 (b) Westend61 GmbH Alamy; 287 (bc) Marc C. Burnett/Photo Rearcher, Inc.; 287 (tl) Jim Wark/Airphoto; 287 (t) Marc C. Burnett/Photo Researchers, Inc.; 288 (cr) Joyce Photographics/Photo Researchers, Inc.; 289 (b) Andrew J. Martinez/Photo Researchers, Inc.; 289 (tr) The Natural History Museum/Alamy; 290 (bl) Pat Canova/Alamy; 292 (bg) Nadia Isakova/Alamy; 293 (bg) Pat & Chuck Blackley/Alamy; 293 (inset) U.S. Geological Survey; 295 (t) Andrew J. Martinez/Photo Researchers, Inc.; 295 (bc) Joyce Photographics/Photo Researchers, Inc.; 295 (br) The Natural History Museum/Alamy; 296 Scenics & Science/Alamy; 298 (c) Carlos Goldin/Science Photo Library/Photo Researchers, Inc.; 299 (tr) S. Meltzer/PhotoLink/Photodisc/Getty Images; 300 (bl) IPS Co., Ltd./Beateworks/Corbis; 303 (tr) Francesc Muntada/Corbis; 305 (cr) AGE Fotostock; 305 (tl) Tkachev Andrei/ITAR-TASS/Corbis; 307 (tc) Bob Ribokas; 307 (t) Demetrio Carrasco/DK Images; 307 (bc) Demetrio Carrasco/Dorling Kindersley/DK Images; 307 (r) Michael Dalton/Fundamental Photographs; 307 (bc) William H. Mullins/Photo Researchers, Inc.; 308 (tl) Albert Copley/Visuals Unlimited; 308 (tcr) Charles D. Winters/Photo Researchers, Inc; 308 (br) Dale Shelton/Maryland Geological Survey; 308 (tcl) John Weinstein/The Field Museum, #GEO86371_01d; 308 (tr) Kevin Schafer/Corbis; 308 (bcr) Mark Schneider/Visuals Unlimited; 308 (bcl) Sam Noble Museum of Natural History; 308 (bl) Sinclair Stammers/SPL/Photo Researchers, Inc.; 310 (c) Kaj R. Svensson/Science Photo Library/Photo Researchers, Inc.; 312 David R. Frazier/Photo Researchers, Inc.; 314 (cl) Colin Keates/DK Images; 314 (bc) Dr. Don W. Fawcett/Visuals Unlimited; 314 (cr) Jeff Rotman/Alamy; 315 (tr) Alamy Images; 315 (tl) Jonathan Blair/Corbis; 316 (l) David Jensen; 317 (tr) DK Limited/Corbis; 317 (c) Bernhard Edmaier/Photo Researchers, Inc.; 318 (cr) A.J. Copley/Visuals Unlimited; 318 (br) Albert Copley/Visuals Unlimited; 318 (cl) David W. Miller; 318 (bl) John Maisano; 318 (tr) Kevin Schafer/Alamy; 318 (tl) Richard Bizley/Photo Researchers, Inc.; 324 Digital Vision/Getty Images; 326 Mark Vaughn/Masterfile; 327 (tr) Digital Vision/Getty Images; 327 (br) Dusty Pixel photography/Flickr/Getty Images; 327 (bcr) Harvey Lloyd/Getty Images; 327 (tcr) Robert Glusic/PhotoDisc/Getty Images; 328 (bl) Lee Cohen/Corbis; 330 (bl) David Jensen; 330 (b) Jenny Hager/The Image Works; 331 (cl) Doug Wilson/USDA; 331 (t) Jake Rajs/Getty Images; 331 (br) Jim Wark/AirPhotona; 331 (cr) Owen Franken/Corbis; 332 (cl) Beth Davidow/Visuals Unlimited; 332 (b) Glacial Grooves/Kelleys Island; 333 (tl) Bill Brooks/Masterfile; 333 (t) Alex Gore/Alamy; 334 (l) Daryl Benson/Masterfile; 334 (br) Jim Wark/Air Photona; 336 (c) Jim Wark/AirPhotona; 338 (bl) Rudi Von Briel/PhotoEdit, Inc.; 340 (l) Craig Ruaux/Alamy; 341 Erik Isakson/Getty Images; 342 (b) Adalberto Rios Szalay/Sexto Sol/Getty Images; 342 (tr) Bruce Coleman/Bruce Coleman, Inc./Photoshot; 343 (tl) Corbis; 343 (tr) Jim Wark/AirPhotona; 344 (b) AP Images; 344 (c) Paul Sakuma/AP Photo; 345 (t) Danny Lehman/Corbis; 345 (bl) George Banks/NASA Visible Earth; 345 (tr) Michael T. Sedam/Corbis; 346 (bg) Radius Images/Alamy; 348 Douglas Peebles/Corbis; 349 (br) Photodisc/Getty Images; 350 Tammy Peluso/Photolibrary/Getty Images; 355 (tc) AFP/Getty Images; 355 (c) David Parker/Photo Researchers, Inc.; 356 (tr) Royalty-Free/Corbis; 357 (tr) De Agostini/Getty Images; 357 (tl) Michael T. Sedam/Corbis; 358 (t) Tim Hauf/Visuals Unlimited; 360 2009 by Daniel Rivademar and Odyssey Productions, Inc.; 361 (r) Hubert Stadler/Corbis; 361 (l) Robert Glusic/Photodisc/Getty Images; 363 Joseph Sohm;ChromoSohm Inc./Corbis; 363 (tc) Joyce Photographics/Photo Researchers, Inc.; 364 (bg) Tony Freeman/PhotoEdit; 366 Raymond Forbes/Photolibrary; 367 (tr) Corbis; 367 (br) D. Falconer/PhotoLink/Photodisc/Getty Images; 370 (bg) Daryl Benson/Masterfile; 371 (cr) Kevin R. Morris/Corbis; 371 (br) Peter Anderson/DK Images; 372 (inset) INSADCO Photography/Alamy; 372 (bg) Michael Newman/Photo Edit; 373 (cr) Chris Howes/Getty Images; 374 (b) David Wasserman/Alamy Images; 374 (cl) Lester Lefkowitz/Corbis; 376 (c) Joseph H. Bailey/Getty Images; 377 (tr) D Falconer/PhotoLink/Getty Images (Royalty-free); 378 (bl) Jose Carillo/PhotoEdit, Inc.; 380 (cl) David Young-Wolff/PhotoEdit; 380 (br) Emma Lee/Life File/Getty Images; 380 (cr) Myrleen Ferguson Cate/Photo Edit; 382 (bg) Donovan Reese/Panoramic Images/NGSImages.com; 382 (cl) Nigel Cattlin/Photo Researchers, Inc.; 383 (cr) Holly Kuper/Index Stock Imagery/Photolibrary; 384 (fg) Bob Rowan; Progressive Image/Corbis; 386 (bg) Rachel Epstein/PhotoEdit, Inc.; 387 (bg) CDC/Janice Carr; 388 Spencer Grant/PhotoEdit; 390 (cr) Adalberto Rios Szalay/Sexto Sol/Getty Images; 390 (tr) Joseph Sohm;ChromoSohm Inc./Corbis; 390 (b) Nigel Cattlin/Photo Researchers, Inc.

Unit D:
392 NASA/Science Photo Library/Photo Researchers, Inc.; 394 SSPL/Getty Images; 396 Purestock/Getty Images; 401 (t) Joseph Sohm/ChromoSohm Media/Photo Researchers, Inc.; 401 (b) Thomas Wiewandt/ChromoSohm Media/Photo Researchers, Inc.; 404 Syracuse Newspapers/Buffalo News/The Image Works; 405 (bl) Andrew Hetherington/Gettyimages; 406 Gustoimages/Photo Researchers, Inc.; 410 (br) John Eastcott and Yva Momatiuk/National Geographic Image Collection; 410 (bg) K.H. Hanel/Panoramic Images/National Geographic Image Collection; 410 (bc) Paul Nicklen/National Geographic Image Collection; 411 (t) George Post/Photo Researchers, Inc.; 412 Gretchen Graham/Alamy; 414 J.A. Kraulis/Masterfile; 415 (br) Corbis; 415 (cr) Eastcott/Momatiuk/The Image Works; 416 (bl) Jeff Greenberg/PhotoEdit, Inc.; 418 (c) ANA/The Image Works; 418 (bl) Frank S. Balthis; 418 (cr) Mark Antman/The Image Works; 419 DAJ/Getty Images; 422 (bg) Matheisl/Getty Images; 423 (tl) Alden Pellett/The Image Works; 423 (cr) Jeff Greenberg/Age Fotostock; 424 (tr) Digital Vision/Getty Images; 426 Getty Images/PhotoDisc/Stocktrek; 428 David Bishop/Getty Images; 429 (tl) Joseph Sohm/ChromoSohm Media/Photo Researchers, Inc.; 429 (cr) K.H. Hanel/Panoramic Images/National Geographic Image Collection; 430 Chris A Crumley/Alamy; 432 (c) Kim Westerskov/Getty Images; 434 (bl) Altrendo Travel/Getty Images, Inc.; 436 (b) Richard T. Nowitz/Corbis; 436 (cr) Roberto Rinaldi/Tips Italia/Photolibrary; 437 (r) AP Images/Sonya Senkowsky; 437 (l) Dr. Ken MacDonald/Photo Researchers, Inc.; 440 (cl) Chad Ehlers/Photographer's Choice/Getty Images; 440 (b) Pierre Vauthey/Corbis SYGMA; 442 Dennis Hallinan/Alamy Images; 443 (br) Georg Gerster/Photo Researchers, Inc.; 443 (tr) SambaPhoto/Eduardo Queiroga - Lumiar/SambaPhoto/Getty Images; 445 (bl) Onne Van der Wal/Corbis; 446 (b) Royalty-Free/Corbis; 447 Yves Herman/Reuters/Corbis; 448 (tl) NOAA/Science Photo Library/Photo Researchers, Inc.; 448 (b) Stephen Wilkes/Getty Images; 449 (r) Kim Kulish/Corbis; 449 (tl) NASA/APWW; 450 (cr) Andrew J. Martinez/Photo Researchers, Inc.; 450 (br) Andrew J. Martinez/Photo Researchers, Inc.; 452 (c) Lonnie Duka/Index Stock Imagery/Photolibrary; 453 (cr) Peter Lewis/Photolibrary/Getty Images; 453 (br) Ron Chapple Stock/Photolibrary; 454 (bl) David Frazier/Photo Researchers, Inc.; 456 (b) Mark A. Johnson/Corbis; 456 (fg) Pat O'Hara/Corbis; 457 (t) Hubert Stadler/Corbis; 457 (cl) Michael Pole/Corbis; 458 (b) AP Photo/Luis M. Alvarez; 458 (fg) Marli Miller/Visuals Unlimited; 459 (t) AP Photo/Roberto Borea; 459 (cl) WaterFram/Alamy; 460 (tr) Amos Nachoum/Corbis; 460 (r) Science VU/Visuals Unlimited; 460 (tl) The Granger Collection, New York; 462 (bg) Ralph White/Corbis; 462 (inset) Michael Neelon/Alamy; 463 (tl) Geography Department/UC Santa Barbara; 463 (bg) VEER Cheryl North Coughlan/Getty Images; 464 (tr) Marli Miller/Visuals Unlimited; 465 (tl) Hubert Stadler/Corbis; 466 (bg) Stephanie Maze/Corbis; 468 (c) NASA; 470 (bl) Library of Congress/Corbis; 472 (b) International Stock Photography/Getty Images; 473 (r) Corbis Royalty Free; 473 (tl) Wolfgang Kaehler/Corbis; 474 (br) image100/Corbis; 474 (bl) Paul Edmonson/Getty Images; 476 (bg) Craig Aurness/Corbis; 476 (bl) Kim Heacox/Getty Images; 478 (c) NASA; 479 (br) StockTrek/Photodisc/Getty Images; 479 (tr) USGS/Cascades Volcano Observatory; 480 StockTrek/Photodisc/Getty Images; 482 (br) NASA; 482 (bg) Photodisc/Getty Images; 483 (cl) Brand X Pictures/Getty Images; 483 (tr) NASA; 483 (t) NASA; 484 (bc) NASA; 485 (t) John Sanford/Science Photo Library/Photo Researchers, Inc.; 486 (cr) David Nunuk/Photo Researchers, Inc.; 486 (br) Mike Hewitt/Getty Images; 488 (c) NASA Marshall Space Flight Center; 489 (br) Celestial Image Co./Photo Researchers, Inc.; 490 (bl) Ed Young/Photo Researchers, Inc; 492 (bl) SOHO/EIT Consortium/NASA; 492 (br) Tony Craddock/Photo Researchers, Inc.; 493 (t) Don Figer/STScI/NASA; 493 (tr) Roger Harris/Science Photo Library/Photo Researchers, Inc.; 496 (br) NASA Jet Propulsion Laboratory/NASA; 497 (br) NASA Kennedy Space Center/NASA; 498 (b) STScI/NASA; 498 (cr) STScI/NASA/Science Photo Library/Photo Researchers, Inc.; 499 (b) NASA Marshall Space Flight Center; 499 (cr) Roeland P. van der Marel, Frank C. van den Bosch/NASA; 500 (b) NASA/Photo Researchers, Inc.; 500 (cr) SPL/Photo Researchers, Inc.; 506 (cl) Mark A. Johnson/Corbis; 506 (tr) Syracuse Newspapers/Buffalo News/The Image Works.

Unit E:
507 (bg) Royalty Free/Corbis; 514 (tl) C Squared Studios/Photodisc/Getty Images; 514 (bcr) George Diebold/Corbis; 514 (cl) Lester Lefkowitz/Getty Images; 514 (tcl) Photodisc/Getty Images; 514 (bl) Photodisc/Getty Images; 514 (br) Photodisc/Getty Images; 516 (bg) M.S. Guijarro/Cover/The Image Works; 518 Jeff Greenberg/The Image Works; 520 (bl) Royalty Free/Corbis; 523 (tl) Bernd Obermann/Corbis; 524 (bl) Goodshoot/Alamy Images; 525 (cl) Andrew J. Martinez/Photo Researchers, Inc.; 525 (tl) PhotoLink/Getty Images; 525 (tr) Tetra Images/Getty Images; 526 (cr) Corbis RF/PictureQuest; 527 (cr) Klaus Hackenberg/zefa/Corbis; 528 (tr) Brand X Pictures/JupiterImages; 528 (cr) C Squared Studios/Photodisc/Getty Images; 528 (br) PhotoDisc/Getty Images; 530 (c) Jeff Vanuga/Corbis; 531 (br) Royalty-Free/Corbis; 531 (tr) Visual Cuisines/Foodpix/Getty Images; 532 Pete Turner/Stone/Getty Images; 534 (br) Image Source/Jupiterimages; 534 (bl) Topham/The Image Works; 535 (tl) Charles D. Winters/Photo Researchers, Inc.; 535 (tr) Pekka Parviainen/Science Photo Library/Photo Researchers, Inc.; 535 (bl) Tony Freeman/Photo Edit; 536 (br) Andrew McClenaghan/Science Photo Library/Photo Researchers, Inc.; 536 (bl) Syracuse Newspapers/John Berry/The Image Works; 537 (r) Richard Megna/Fundamental Photographs; 538 (bl) Manfred Idem/zefa/Corbis; 539 (tl) David Bishop/FoodPix/JupiterImages; 539 (br) Kurt Amsler/Ardea.com; 539 (bl) Larry Latimer/Getty Images; 540 (tr) Ken Sherman/Phototake; 542 (c) Mark Sykes/Science Photo Library/Photo Researchers, Inc.; 543 (cr) Corbis; 544 (bl) Jeff Greenberg/PhotoEdit, Inc.; 546 (br) Augustus Butera/Getty Images; 546 (bl) Visual Cuisines/Foodpix/Getty Images; 547 (tr) Joel Sartore/National Geographic Image Collection; 547 (cr) Richard Megna/Fundamental Photographs; 550 (bg) Biophoto Associates/Photo Researchers, Inc.; 550 (inset) Courtesy of Claudia Benitez-Nelson; 551 (inset) Adek Berry/AFP/Getty Images; 551 (bg) Alfred Pasieka/Science Photo Library; 554 Craig M. Wilson/Kite Aerial Photography; 556 (c) Randy Faris/Corbis; 557 (br) Alison Wright/Corbis; 557 (tr) Corbis; 557 (cr) Martin F. Chillmaid/Science Photo Library/Photo Researchers, Inc.; 558 Table Mesa Productions/Index Stock Imagery, Inc./Photolibrary; 560 (b) Paul Souders/IPN; 561 (r) Meeke/Corbis; 561 (cl) Peter Walton/Photolibrary; 562 Haruyoshi Yamaguchi/Corbis; 564 Neal Preston/Corbis; 566 (c) John and Lisa Merrill/Corbis; 567 (tr) K-P Wolf/Getty Images; 567 (cr) Otto Rogge/Corbis; 568 Sheila Terry/Photo Researchers, Inc.; 570 David Hancock/Alamy; 571 Robert Harding World Imagery/Alamy Images; 572 (t) Martin G. Kleinsorge; 573 (r) Otto Rogge/Corbis; 574 Visions of America, LLC/Alamy; 575 (l) Comstock Images/Alamy Images; 575 (r) Jeff Gross/Getty Images; 576 (l) David Young-Wolff/Photo Edit; 578 Dan McCoy/Rainbow; 579 (cr) Charles D. Winters/Science Photo Library/ Photo Researchers, Inc.; 580 Richard T. Nowitz/Photo Researchers, Inc.; 583 David Pollack/Corbis; 584 (b) Ron Crabtree/Photographer's Choice RF/Getty Images; 584 (t) Tom Prettyman/Photo Edit; 585 Reuters/Corbis; 586 (r) Royalty Free/Corbis; 586 (l) Spencer Grant/Photo Edit; 588 Joe Cavaretta/AP Photo; 589 (br) Corbis; 590 Nancy Sheehan/PhotoEdit, Inc.; 592 (b) Bill Bachman/Alamy; 592 (inset) Corbis Royalty Free; 593 (inset) AP Images/Tyler Morning Telegraph, D.J. Peters; 593 (b) Royalty-Free/Corbis; 594 (t) Lloyd Sutton/Masterfile; 596 Reuters/Corbis; 598 Reuters/Newscom; 599 (b) KRT/Newscom; 599 (t) Stephen Hird/Reuters/Corbis; 602 Steve Cole/Getty Images; 604 (c) Chris Madeley/Photo Researchers, Inc., Inc.; 606 Royalty-Free/Corbis; 609 (t) Kim Karpeles/Alamy; 609 (cr) Grace Davies Photography; 610 (l) Jeremy Walker/Photo Researchers, Inc.; 610 (r) Judith Collins/Alamy Images; 611 Sergio Piumatti; 612 Science Museum, London/Topham-HIP/The Image Works; 614 Theater of Electricity/Museum of Science/Boston; 615 (br) Andrew Lambert Photography/Photo Researchers, Inc.; 615 (cr) Andrew Lambert Photography/Photo Researchers, Inc.; 616 Michael Newman/PhotoEdit; 618 (bg) Nigel Blythe/Alamy Images; 618 (fg) Photodisc/Getty Images; 620 (bg) Russ Merne/Alamy Images; 621 (cr) Photodisc/Getty Images; 622 (cl) Dennis MacDonald/Photo Edit; 622 (bl) Tom Tracy/Getty Images; 624 Royalty-Free/Corbis; 628 DigiStock/Alamy Images; 629 (bg) Kelly-Mooney Photography/Corbis; 631 Bob Rowan; Progressive Image/Corbis; 632 Sergio Piumatti; 634 (bg) Ingo Boddenberg/zefa/Corbis; 634 (inset) Institute of Electrical Engineers (IEE) Archives; 635 (bg) Kirsty Wigglesworth/AP Wide World Photos; 638 Bettmann/Corbis; 640 Chris Rogers/Index Stock Imagery/Photolibrary; 641 (br) Alfred Pasieka/Photo Researchers, Inc.; 642 Myrleen Ferguson Cate/PhotoEdit, Inc.; 644 AFP/Getty Images; 645 (l) Brooks Kraft/Corbis; 645 (r) Gary Braasch/Getty Images; 648 Erik Butler/Getty Images; 649 Macduff Everton/Corbis; 650 (br) Alistair Dove/Alamy; 650 (cr) Corbis Royalty Free; 650 (l) Stephen Dalton/Photo Researchers, Inc.; 652 Jay Heck/LFI International; 654 DesignPics Inc./Photolibrary; 656 (c) Getty Images Royalty Free; 656 (r) Jeff Greenberg/Alamy; 656 (l) Royalty-Free/Corbis; 657 (b) Gary Roebuck/Alamy; 657 (t) Science Photo Library/Photo Researchers, Inc.; 659 (b) Juan Carlos Munoz/age fotostock; 660 (inset) Richard Megna/Fundamental Photographs; 660 (bg) Sergio Piumatti/Sergio Piumatti, Inc.; 661 (tl) David Parker/Photo Researchers, Inc., Inc.; 661 (tr) R. Ian Lloyd/Masterfile; 662 David Young-Wolff/Photo Edit; 664 AP Photo/Naashon Zalk; 665 Reuters/Will Burgess; 667 SSPL/The Image Works; 668 (b) AFP/Getty Images; 668 (cr) Kelly-Mooney Photography/Corbis; 668 (cl) Otto Rogge/Corbis; 668 (t) Topham/The Image Works.

Unit F:
670 Franco Origlia/Getty Images; 672 (c) Philip Baily/Corbis; 673 (br) Werner H. Muller/Corbis; 674 Royalty Free/Corbis; 677 (bg) John Kelly/Getty Images; 677 (fg) John Kelly/Getty Images; 678 (l) Erich Schrempp/Photo Researchers, Inc.; 678 Jim Sugar/Corbis; 680 Owaki-Kulla/Corbis; 682 Picture Quest/Corbis; 683 (tr) David J Slater/Alamy; 683 (br) Thomas Barwick/Digital Vision/Getty Images; 683 (br) Thomas Barwick/Digital Vision/Getty Images; 684 AP Photo; 686 (cr) Bob Daemmrich/The Image Works; 686 (b) Pete Stone/Corbis; 687 (t) Ken Karp/Omni-Photo Communications; 688 David J Slater/Alamy; 689 (b) David Madison/Getty Images; 689 (t) Dimitri Iundt/Corbis; 690 (cr) Murry Wilson/Omni-Photo.com; 692 Kevin Fleming/Corbis; 694 Royalty Free/Corbis; 696 Gary Rhijnsburger/Masterfile; 697 (t) Michael Newman/Photo Edit; 698 Pawel Kumelowski/Omni-Photo Communications; 699 Marc Garanger/Corbis; 700 (l) Brian Hagiwara/JupiterImages; 700 (r) Paul Almasy/Corbis; 702 (bg) Corbis; 702 (t) Ephraim Fishback; 703 (bg) Gary I. Rothstein/epa/Corbis; 705 Mike Powell/Allsport/Getty Images; 706 Duomo/Corbis; 708 David Grubbs/Billings Gazette/AP Photo; 709 (cr) Peter Walton/Index Stock Imagery/Photolibrary; 709 (tr) Yo/Getty Images; 709 (tr) Yo/Getty Images; 710 AP Photo; 712 Mika/Corbis; 712 Mika/Corbis; 713 (br) HASHIMOTO NOBORU/Corbis; 713 (bg) Jeff Greenberg/Age Fotostock; 714 (b) David Taylor/Getty Images; 715 (t) Andy Rouse/Getty Images; 715 (inset) Andy Rouse/Getty Images; 716 (l) Kelly-Mooney Photography/Corbis; 716 (bg) Mark Segal/Index Stock Imagery/Photolibrary; 717 (r) Yogi, Inc./Corbis; 718 (r) Martyn Goddard/Corbis; 718 (l) Reed Kaestner/Corbis; 720 Tim Wright/Corbis; 721 (tr) Brand X Pictures/Getty Images; 722 Mark Richards/PhotoEdit, Inc.; 724 (c) Bettmann/Corbis; 724 (r) Scott Halleran/Getty Images; 725 (t) Jennie Woodcock/Reflections Photolibrary/Corbis; 725 (cr) Reuters/Corbis; 726 (b) Dimitri Iundt/Corbis; 726 (inset) Justin Sullivan/Getty Images; 727 (l) Tony Freeman/PhotoEdit; 727 (c) Tony Freeman/PhotoEdit; 727 (r) Tony Freeman/PhotoEdit; 729 Patrick Giardino/Corbis; 730 (br) Denis Scott/Corbis; 730 (cr) NASA; 730 (bl) NASA/JSC; 732 Tom Raymond/Stone/Getty Images; 733 (t) AP Photo/Robert F. Bukaty; 733 (b) George Tiedemann/GT Images/Corbis; 736 (b) Mark Segal/Index Stock Imagery/Photolibrary; 736 (t) Michael Newman/Photo Edit.

Glossary:
R2 (br) Arco Images GmbH/Alamy; R2 (bl) Jupiterimages.com/Creatas/Alamy; R2 (tc) Rob and Ann Simpson/Visuals Unlimited; R2 (tcl) Sharon Green/Corbis; R3 (bl) David J Slater/Alamy; R3 (br) Biophoto Associates/Photo Researchers; R3 (cr) Corbis; R4 (br) Corbis; R4 (tcl) Otto Rogge/Corbis; R5 (bcr) Andrew Lambert Photography/Photo Researchers, Inc.; R5 (tcr) Charles D. Winters/Science Photo Library/ Photo Researchers, Inc.; R5 (br) D Falconer/PhotoLink/Getty Images (Royalty-free); R5 (tcl) Jeremy Woodhouse/Photodisc/Getty Images; R6 (tcr) Ryan McGinnis/Getty Images; R6 (cr) Ryan McGinnis/Getty Images; R6 (br) USGS/Cascades Volcano Observatory; R7 (tr) Inga Spence/Visuals Unlimited; R8 (br) Bruce Heinemann/Photodisc/Getty Images; R8 (tl) Corbis; R8 (tr) James King-Holmes/Science Photo Library/Photo Researchers, Inc.; R8 (cr) StockTrek/Photodisc/Getty Images; R9 (br) Corbis; R9 (cr) Corbis RF; R10 (cl) Comstock/Getty Images; R10 (bcr) Greg Probst; R10 (bl) Jeremy Woodhouse/Corbis; R11 (cr) Francois Gohier/Photo Researchers, Inc.; R11 (tl) Peter West/National Science Foundation; R12 (bl) Alfred Pasieka/Photo Researchers, Inc.; R12 (br) Celestial Image Co./Photo Researchers, Inc.; R12 (tcr) Eastcott/Momatiuk/The Image Works; R12 (bcl) S. Meltzer/PhotoLink/Photodisc/Getty Images; R13 (tr) Bill Bachmann/PhotoEdit; R13 (bcl) Harvey Lloyd/Getty Images; R13 William H. Mullins/Photo Researchers, Inc.; R14 (bl) Andrew Hetherington/Gettyimages; R14 (tcl) C. P. George/Visuals Unlimited; R14 (cl) PhotoLink/Photodisc/Getty Images; R15 (bcr) Andrew Lambert Photography/Photo Researchers, Inc.; R15 (cl) Brand X Pictures/Getty Images; R15 (br) CMCD/Photodisc/Getty Images; R15 (tcr) William Leaman/Alamy; R16 (tcr) Digital Vision/Getty Images; R16 (bl) Martin F. Chlilmaid/Science Photo Library/Photo Researchers, Inc.; R16 (bcr) Photodisc/Getty Images; R16 (br) PhotoLink/Photodisc/Getty Images; R16 (cl) Ron Chapple Stock/Photolibrary; R17 (tcr) INTERFOTO/Alamy; R17 (tcl) John M. Burnley/Photo Researchers; R17 (tr) Jose Manuel Sanchis Calvete/Corbis; R17 (bcl) K-P Wolf/Getty Images; R17 (br) Werner H. Muller/Corbis; R18 (br) Royalty-Free/Corbis; R18 (tl) Andy Selinger/Alamy; R18 (cl) Jon Sparks/Alamy; R18 (tcr) Siede Preis/PhotoDisc/Getty Images; R18 (bl) Tetra Images/Alamy; R20 (tcr) SIU/Visuals Unlimited; R20 (br) MedioImages/Corbis; R21 (br) USGS/Photo Researchers, Inc.; R21 (tcr) Visual Cuisines/Foodpix/Getty Images; R22 (tr) Alison Wright/Corbis; R22 (tl) Corbis; R22 (tcl) D. Falconer/PhotoLink/Photodisc/Getty Images; R22 (bcl) Gregory G. Dimijian/Photo Researchers, Inc.; R22 (bcr) Joe McDonald/Corbis; R22 (tcr) Peter Cade/Getty Images; R23 (bcl) Michael Abbey/Visuals Unlimited; R23 (cr) Corbis; R23 (tr) D. Hurst/Alamy; R23 (tcr) D. Normark/PhotoLink/Photodisc/Getty Images; R24 (tl) Colin Young-Wolff/Photo Edit; R24 (bl) Corbis; R24 (br) Joyce Photographics/Photo Researchers, Inc.; R24 (br) Stan Celestian/Glendale Community College, Arizona; R24 (tr) W. Perry Conway/Corbis; R25 (bl) Dusty Pixel photography/Flickr/Getty Images; R25 (br) James Randklev/Photographer's Choice RF/Getty Images; R25 (bcl) PhotoDisc/Getty Images; R25 (tcr) Visuals Unlimited; R26 (br) Kennan Ward/Corbis; R27 (bcr) Jupiterimages; R27 (bcl) Lucas Janin/Flickr/Getty Images; R27 (tl) Peter Walton/Index Stock Imagery/Photolibrary; R27 (tcr) USGS/CVO; R28 (tl) David Chasey/Getty Images; R28 (cl) Georg Gerster/Photo Researchers, Inc.; R28 (bl) Peter Lewis/Photolibrary/Getty Images; R28 (cr) Robert Glusic/PhotoDisc/Getty Images; R28 (br) Tomi/PhotoLink/Photodisc/Getty Images; R29 (tl) Ken Karp/GGS Design/HMH; R29 (br) PhotoDisc/Getty Images; R30 (tcr) Corbis; R30 (cr) Peter Pinnock/Photographer's Choice; R30 (bcl) Siede Preis/Photodisc/Getty Images; R31 (t) David Hoffman Photo Library/Alamy.

All other photos © Houghton Mifflin Harcourt Publishing Company. Houghton Mifflin Harcourt Photos provided by Houghton Mifflin Harcourt photographers; Weronica Ankarorn, Victoria Bowen, Eric Camden, Doug Dukane, Ken Kinzie, April Riehm, and Steve Williams.